FO
IB

MW01259302

English Language & Literature

Neo Esmé- Eclipse

FOR THE
IB DIPLOMA

English Language & Literature

Lindsay Tandy
Alice Gibbons
Joseph Koszary
Series editor: Carolyn P. Henly

Author acknowledgements

From Carolyn Henly: Many thanks to Lindsay, Alice, and Joseph for their excellent work on and their commitment to this project.

Orders: please contact Bookpoint Ltd, 130 Park Drive, Milton Park, Abingdon, Oxon OX14 4SE. Telephone: +44 (0)1235 827827. Fax: +44 (0)1235 400401. Email education@bookpoint.co.uk Lines are open from 9 a.m. to 5 p.m., Monday to Saturday, with a 24-hour message answering service. You can also order through our website: www.hoddereducation.com

First published in 2019 by
Hodder Education,
An Hachette UK Company
Carmelite House
50 Victoria Embankment
London EC4Y 0DZ

www.hoddereducation.co.uk

Impression number 10 9 8 7 6 5 4 3 2 1

Year 2023 2022 2021 2020 2019

Typeset in Integra Software Services Pvt. Ltd., Pondicherry, India

Printed in Italy

A catalogue record for this title is available from the British Library.

ISBN: 978 1 5104 6322 6

Contents

Introduction

OBJECTIVES OF CHAPTER

- To understand the role of this coursebook in the English Language and Literature for the IB Diploma course.
- To introduce the three areas of exploration and define them.
- To introduce the seven course concepts and define them.
- To introduce the concept of global issues and to give examples.
- To define inquiry-based learning.

English Language and Literature for the IB Diploma

Technology in the twenty-first century has made communication easier than ever before. If you have access to the internet, you can connect with a wide range of media, such as cartoons, photos, paintings, blogs, tweets, newspaper articles, online encyclopedias, opinion essays, and much more – right at your fingertips. We call these kinds of media, as a group, non-literary texts. We also have access to literary works, such as novels, short stories, plays and poems. There are also many non-fiction literary works, such as memoirs, biographies, travel writing, and literary essays. We may find fewer of these works online, but we have ready access to them through libraries and bookstores.

You probably find it reasonably easy to understand and differentiate all of these different types to some degree, but reading is a skill that can be developed to a high level of sophistication, enabling you to understand all of the works you encounter in a complex way. Your English Language and Literature for the IB Diploma course will help you to develop your skills so that you will have access to the nuances and complexities of literary works, as you have been accustomed to studying in other English classes, but it will also help you to develop your skills as a reader of non-literary texts with the same attention to the sophisticated ways in which those texts have been created.

Reading literary works

Throughout the course, you will learn what features to look for in order to develop sophisticated interpretations. With literary works, you will learn about a variety of literary strategies such as metaphors, symbols, and allusions, as well as structural features such as rhyme, sentence structure, and the overall organization of a work. Many literary strategies can appear in all the different literary forms, but each form will also have characteristic features of its own.

By applying your toolkit of literary features to any new text, you will be able to discover ideas which are not obvious on first reading. This will be true of texts which seem simple at first, such as the poem on page 3 by Robert Frost.

The language of the poem is not very difficult – perhaps the word 'subside' may be unfamiliar (it means 'to sink back') – but all the rest of the words are likely to be known to most fluent speakers of English. The poem is only eight lines long and the lines are short. The last line seems quite straightforward, and it seems to suggest that the poem is about the sad loss of precious things.

If we know what kinds of literary features to look for, however, we can begin to find more subtle ideas in the poem. The table on page 3 shows some of the literary elements we can find in this poem if we know to look for them:

Nothing Gold Can Stay

Nature's first green is gold,
Her hardest hue to hold.

Her early leaf's a flower;
But only so an hour.

Then leaf subsides to leaf.
So Eden sank to grief,

So dawn goes down to day.
Nothing gold can stay.

(Robert Frost)

Line no.	Literary element
1	Paradox: 'green is gold'
1	Imagery: nature's first green is literally gold. If you observe a plant when it just breaches the surface of the ground, it is yellow. It has not been exposed to sunlight, and sunlight is what is needed for photosynthesis to take place (and turn the leaves green).
1	Metaphor: we often use the word 'gold' to indicate something of great value. In this case, valuable because it is very rare.
1–2	Rhyme
3	Paradox: 'leaf's a flower'
3	Metaphor: the leaf (which will be green after photosynthesis takes hold) is gold, like a flower is.
4	Description: 'only so an hour'. This is likely also literally true; it probably takes an hour or less for the sunlight to do its work and the pale golden plant to turn green.
3–4	Rhyme
5	Paradox: 'leaf subsides to leaf'. If it's already a leaf, how can it sink back into being a leaf? The answer, of course, is that it's a leaf when it's gold, and then, when it turns green, it sinks back into being a regular leaf. The implication of 'subside' is a sinking back, so that the green is not as special as the gold.
6	Religious allusion to the Garden of Eden; this gives us something to think about, because we don't necessarily think of Eden lasting only an hour, and we don't think of Eden sinking into grief because of sunlight. The comparison, however, is really interesting: you can argue that what put an end to Adam and Eve's life in Eden was the gaining of knowledge, which is very often symbolized by light.
5–6	Rhyme
7	Comparison: the turning of the leaf from gold to green is now compared to the dawn turning into morning.
8	Extrapolation: the poet draws a conclusion here, based on the three things he has now compared to each other. His conclusion is that we must always lose that which is gold. We might see this as a rather depressing conclusion, or we might see it as an observation that one of the reasons that we see things as golden – special – is that they are rare and fleeting.
7–8	Rhyme

Taking all these observations together, we can start to think more deeply about the poem. The poem takes a very close observation of nature – the transition of golden budding plants to green leaves when sunlight hits them for the very first time – as a metaphor for the idea that a very particular kind of golden innocence, the innocence that occurs before any experience begins to lead us to knowledge, is fleeting. The poem suggests that such innocence of the world is a treasure, but that inevitably it cannot last. Perhaps there is even a faint suggestion that once the process of experiencing the world is underway, there is already a hint of our mortality. If we know what to look for, then, we can read this poem in a completely different way than we can if we do not really know what to look for and are only able to understand the words and their surface meaning.

That is not to say that a simple reading is a bad experience or a wrong one, but that there are many riches waiting for a reader capable of engaging on a deeper level.

In your Language and Literature class, you will also develop the skills necessary to allow you to interpret a much harder text. Let's look at a poem which is likely to make many readers a little nervous on first reading! You might already recognize it as one of William Shakespeare's sonnets and, because it is a much older poem, it uses a style of language that is not familiar to us today.

Sonnet 44

If the dull substance of my flesh were thought,
Injurious distance should not stop my way;
For then despite of space I would be brought,
From limits far remote where thou dost stay.

No matter then although my foot did stand
Upon the farthest earth removed from thee;
For nimble thought can jump both sea and land
As soon as think the place where he would be.

But ah! thought kills me that I am not thought,
To leap large lengths of miles when thou art gone,
But that so much of earth and water wrought
I must attend time's leisure with my moan,

Receiving nought by elements so slow
But heavy tears, badges of either's woe.

(William Shakespeare)

Obviously, this poem is much harder to read and understand than Robert Frost's. The sentence structure is unfamiliar, as is some of the vocabulary. Some of the words will be completely new to most readers; others will be familiar but used in unfamiliar ways. The content too is difficult, because it deals with sophisticated ideas. Like the first text, however, it has stayed with us for a very long time and is still read and appreciated today.

Some of the skills that are needed to understand this poem in a sophisticated way are the same as those we needed for Frost's poem. One important element of much literature, especially prose fiction and certain poems, is the speaker or narrator. In this instance, if we understand the perspective of the narrator, we can see that he is deeply in love and wishes to be close to his loved one. Once we can understand that perspective, we can begin to explore the idea that he is using in order to express that wish.

This poem is William Shakespeare's 'Sonnet 44', the first half of a pair of sonnets that explore an idea about how the speaker's physical body is a barrier to his ability to be with the woman he loves. In these two sonnets, the content is actually quite intriguing. In this sonnet, as in 'Nothing Gold Can Stay', there is an allusion – though it is historical, rather than religious. It is a reference to an older way of thinking about the substance of the universe. It was once believed that all matter consisted of earth, air, fire, and water. That idea is referred to in lines 11 and 13. Shakespeare takes that belief and posits the imaginative alternative that thought is a fifth type of substance, which we can see in line 1. The speaker wishes he were made of the same substance from which thoughts are made, because thoughts can be wherever they want instantaneously, thus allowing him to be with his love whenever he wants.

The idea that we might be able to transport through time and space as if we had no body appeals to anyone who would like to travel all around the world without needing time or transport. That idea is a staple of science fiction from *Star Trek* to the 2017 novel *The Punch Escrow*, by Tal M Klein.

We can see from the analysis of this sonnet that knowledge of sonnets, knowledge of the context in which a poem is written, and knowledge of historical attitudes (which is part of the context) can be quite helpful in creating an effective interpretation.

Don't worry if you're not able, at this point, to understand these two poems on your own. The purpose of the discussion here is to illustrate the kinds of reading and thinking you will learn to do in your course. This coursebook will take you through a wide range of literary strategies and give you many examples of how to apply them so that you can develop your own skills and independent reading.

Reading non-literary texts

Interpreting non-literary texts requires a different set of skills, though you will also find that there is some overlap. Many non-literary texts are **multimodal**, that is, they include multiple types of information such as language, images, charts, statistics, and so on. You will also focus on the author's purpose and the intended audience. When you are dealing with language, you may find that there are some features which you recognize from literary analysis, but often you will be analysing other features of language. Let's take a look at two examples of non-literary texts.

The first text is not a multimodal text; it is an imaginative cartoon. On the surface, it might seem fairly obvious what the cartoon is about: we see a person sleeping, and a night sky, and a fish. Perhaps the cartoon is about a dream of a flying fish.

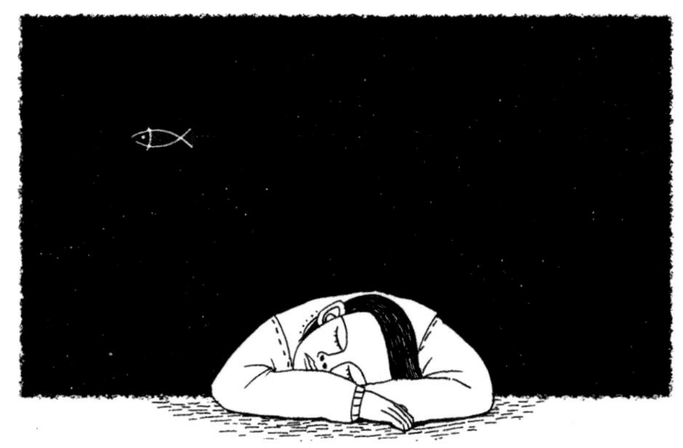

Since this cartoon is not a multimodal text, we only have to focus on what the graphical (visual) elements might mean. Among the things you will consider when analysing cartoons and other images are the use of color and the structure of the elements in the image – where they are placed in relation to each other and to the frame of the image. We must also consider what the images are, and what they might signify.

Colour

- This particular image is all in black and white.
- Those colors provide us with a sharp contrast appropriate to the content: the person appears to be sleeping, because their eyes are closed and their head is resting on their arms – a position familiar to us from having seen others sleep.
- Another effect of the use of black and white is to make it seem as if the sleeping person is in the light, in contrast to the darkness of the night sky. Light often signifies truth or knowledge – perhaps we are meant to think that their dreams provide a kind of truth.
- A third effect of the two-tone image is that the white spots in the night sky – stars, we assume – and the black lines in the white surface at the bottom complement each other. Maybe the stars

have risen into the night sky from the solid world of the surface at the bottom, and maybe the black lines in the bottom fourth of the panel have slipped down there from the night sky. These reciprocal images blur the lines between light and dark/day and night/earth and sky so that they appear to be two parts of one thing, with the sleeping figure as the bridge between them. That seems a very effective way to visualize the experience of sleeping and dreaming.

Structure of the image

- The image is divided into two distinct parts: the black sky and the white surface upon which the person is lying.
- The line which follows the fish, indicating its progress through the night sky, divides the black part of the image into two parts.
- The person sleeping, extending well into the night sky, also further divides the black portion of the panel.
- Overall, the cartoon can be seen as being divided into four fairly equal parts:
  - the night sky at the top, above the fish
  - the night sky between the fish and the person
  - the night sky from the top of the person down
  - and the white surface at the bottom.

  This emphasizes the fish and underlines the effect of the sleeping person being the bridge between the two different parts of the panel – the night outside and the surface indoors.
- One further interesting feature of the structure is that there is no frame drawn for the bottom quarter of the picture, so the impression given is that the indoor world extends all down below the cartoon on the white page, as well as surrounding the night sky. The fact that white encompasses all the black without boundary implies that the night sky is contained, as a dream.
- The person is centered precisely in the side-to-side orientation of the cartoon, though not from top-to-bottom. Because the white extends down, however, it is easy to see them as the center of the image, so we must consider the person is intended to be the center of our attention.

Nature of the images themselves

- The images of physical objects in the cartoon contrast each other.
- The sleeping person is fairly realistic. We can easily recognize they are sleeping and, perhaps, dreaming.
- The fish, on the other hand, although easily recognizable as a fish, is doing something entirely unexpected: it appears to be flying through the night sky.
- Because the fish appears in the picture above the head of the sleeping person, we are inclined to think of the fish as the dream of that person; however, that assumption is naturally a conflict with another assumption we are accustomed to making: fish swim in water. It's not hard to see the black space in the drawing as water – light does not filter down into the deep sea, and so the oceans are, below a certain depth, very dark.

All of these elements taken together create a more complicated and ambiguous effect than the initial, more obvious, idea that the cartoon simply depicts a sleeping person having a dream of the impossible, a not uncommon experience! Once we discover the ambiguities between the fish swimming and flying, and between the night sky and the deep ocean, and the melting together of the ocean/sky and the surface on which the person is sleeping, we can see the whole image as being dual in nature. However, it can also be seen as a depiction of a fish swimming in dark water with a sleeping person who has just emerged, partway from the deep ocean, and is now lying on a beach with the sand extending far away in all directions. That interpretation is hardly more realistic than the idea of a fish flying through the night with the stars shining on it. The overall cartoon, then, might be seen as being about a depiction of the way in which dreams can take us to places where things happen which cannot possibly happen in the real world. Part of the impossibility of dreams – and of this image – is that in dreams we can be in two places at once – in the heavens above us or in the deep sea below.

Just by looking closely at three significant features of images – the use of color, the structure of the space, and the implications of the features of the objects in the image – we discovered many ideas that were not obvious at first look. These three features, then, are some of the ones you will learn to look for as a basis for your analysis. The rest of this coursebook will return to these as well as many other tools for interpreting non-literary texts.

Now let's look at a multimodal text.

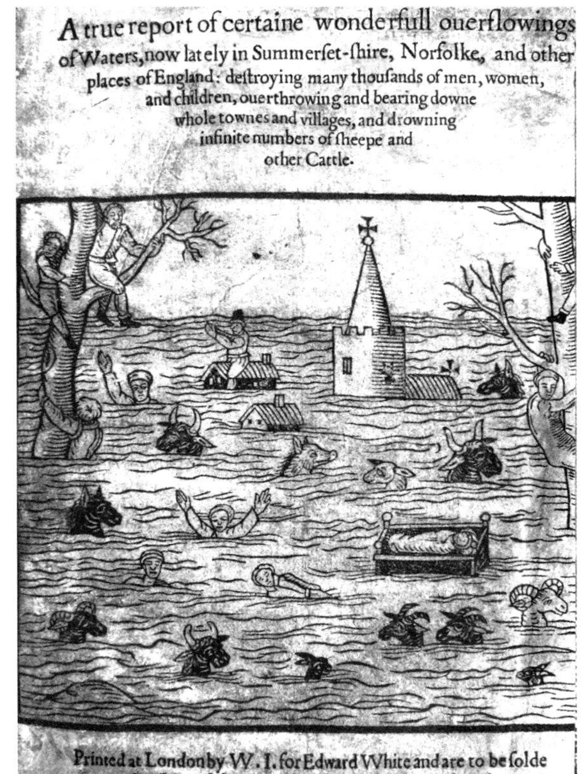

A true report of certaine wonderfull ouerflowings of Waters, now lately in Summerſet-ſhire, Norfolke, and other places of England: deſtroying many thouſands of men, women, and children, ouerthrowing and bearing downe whole townes and villages, and drowning infinite numbers of ſheepe and other Cattle.

Printed at London by W. I. for Edward White and are to be ſolde at the ſigne of the Gunne at the North doore of Paules

A multimodal text contains both words and images, so we must consider the significance of both. This image is a frontspiece from a book or brochure, which we can tell from the fact that it includes printing information at the bottom. One of our first jobs is to work out what the words are, since the spelling is unfamiliar to us. The symbol that looks like this: ſ is called a long S and dates back to Roman days. It was used in early printed materials anywhere that there was a single 's' at the beginning or middle of a word, such as in the word 'ſigne' at the bottom of the page. It was not used at the ends of words, as you can see in the word 'Paules', also at the bottom of the page. ſ was also used as the first 's' anywhere there was a double-S, such as in the word 'uſeleſs' (useless), but no such words appear in this image. You will also notice that the character 'u' appears where we would expect to see a 'v', such as in the word 'ouerflowings' at the top of the page. Our recognition of the use of those symbols tells us right away that we are looking at a document from before the mid-nineteenth century, which is helpful, as there is no date in the image itself. We know that we will have to consider the beliefs and values of the times in which this document was created – something you will learn much more about in the second section of this course book (Time and space), which focuses on the ways in which time and place affect the meaning of a text or work.

We know from the text at the bottom that the brochure was printed in London by a printer named Edward White, and we know that the subject of the brochure is a flood in Somersetshire (which is the modern spelling) and Norfolk, as well as elsewhere. Now we can do some research to find out a bit more about what this document is about. A short search on Google takes us to a Wikipedia page which reveals that there was a flood in this area in 1607. (There was an earlier flood, in 1287, but that was before the invention of the printing press in 1493.) Note that we always have to be careful with information found on Wikipedia, as anyone who registers can make changes to Wikipedia entries. In this particular case, if you click on the entry for the 1607 flood, which you can do by using the QR code, the image we are investigating comes up as the source! Thus, our research has provided us with the information that the brochure was created in 1607.

The text at the top of the page tells us, as well, that the flood was a terrible one. It tells us that thousands of people were killed, as were 'infinite numbers' of livestock. We can see from this

interesting juxtaposition that in the mind of the author, the deaths of all the cattle and sheep were as significant as the deaths of the people. This idea makes sense, if we consider that the floods were out in the countryside, where most people would have made their living from the livestock. The loss of the animals along with the people means that there is nothing left to start over with.

One other important religious reading is suggested by the focus on both people and animals: the author could be alluding to Noah's flood in the Christian Bible – an event in which all the people and animals of the earth, except those on Noah's ark who were preserved so that the world might be repopulated, were destroyed in a huge flood lasting 40 days and 40 nights. We could theorize that the author is alluding to the idea that just as God sent Noah's flood, He also sent this flood as a punishment for sins committed by the people living in this area. The purpose of the document in that sense might be to function as a religious warning.

The structure of the elements of the text on the page suggests a hierarchy of importance: the words about the flood and its resulting deaths come first, usually the spot of greatest importance. They are then followed by the image, which, although secondary in importance in that way, also takes up most of the page. Both, we might think, are equally important.

The elements of the image reveal that the image perfectly supports the words of the text and the purpose that we have hypothesized: there are more animals than people – 11 people and 13 animals – though not as many more as the text suggests. The drawing has captured a moment before the creatures have drowned – all the heads are above water – and, although some people are in trees or on roofs, there is no indication that any rescue will be possible. We are seeing both people and animals up to their necks in water, possibly at the last moment before they will drown. If the readers of this text have enough imagination, they can understand the terror that the creatures in the water must feel. The fact that one of the people is a baby in a cradle makes the tragedy more poignant still.

Rising above the water, at the center of the frame, and in the back, at the highest position of the drawing, is a church. The placement of that image might suggest one of two things: the sin in this town was an abandonment of the church, which too will be submerged by the waters, or that the church rises above all sin, and God is in some way watching these people receive their punishment.

Together, the words and ideas combine to suggest that the purpose of the drawing and the brochure was to warn other sinners of the punishment that will come down upon them if they do not change their ways. We cannot be certain about this, but it is a good hypothesis, which accounts for all of the features of the multimodal text.

In fact, if you wished to do a little more research, you could find that this is, indeed, the frontspiece of a brochure published in 1607 as a warning to others about the consequences of sin. You can use the QR code to read the full text of the brochure if you are interested. The introduction reads:

> Reader I haue to these late accidents (whereby some parts of this our kingdom haue bin punnished) ad|ded some other, that hap|ned in the yeare 1570. to the intent that by compa|ring the one with the o|ther, Gods Iustice and mercy may both be seene: If those Waters of his wrathe (powred downe then,) we are more cruell then these. It is a signe (and a comfort let it bee vnto vs) that he doth but stil threaten and shake the rod, for no doubt but our faults at this time are as great as in those daies: If this affliction laide vppon our Countrey now, bee sharper than that before, make vse of it: tremble, before warned, Amend least a more feareful punishment, and a longer whip of correction draw blood of vs. Farewell.
>
> *('1607. A true report ...')*

Our work on the image led us to the right idea. To interpret this text, then, we analysed the words both in terms of what they could tell us about the historical time period and an important religious allusion. We also examined the image, using the same techniques we used in assessing the meaning of the cartoon above. We had to take the additional step of combining the information from both parts in order to see how they complemented and supported each other. One final thing that this example illustrates is the fact that sometimes a little careful research will be necessary in order to develop a thorough interpretation of some texts.

As with the two literary examples: don't worry if you are unable, at this point, to understand these two non-literary texts very well on your own. They are examples of the kinds of things you will be looking at and the kinds of ideas you will be engaging with. This coursebook will give you many examples with models of how to analyse them in order to help you learn how to read a wide array of non-literary texts, so the analyses you have been reading here are examples of what you will be able to do for yourself by the end of your English Language and Literature for the IB Diploma course.

The course will take you on a journey through how to engage with each text as an independent text by using your own skills as a reader of both literary and non-literary texts. It will also teach you to explore the relationship of texts to the time and place in which they were created, so that you can understand how the culture of a writer and the historical development of texts in that culture contribute to the **style** and **form** and **content** of future texts. Finally, the English Language and Literature for the IB Diploma course will help you to explore the relationships among texts and of individual non-literary texts as part of bodies of work by the same creator so that you can recognize the ways in which texts build off the ideas in other texts and how texts from different times and places deal with similar themes.

The more skilled you become as a reader, the more you will get out of any given text, and the more fun your reading will be.

Several elements of the course curriculum identify and guide you through the complexities both of Language and Literature and of your learning to interpret it. These elements are:

- **areas of exploration**
- **concepts**
- **global issues.**

This introductory chapter will take you through each of these to define them and explain their role in the course.

Before you begin your studies, you will need to understand the nature and terminology of all the required elements of the course. We will begin with the areas of exploration.

Areas of exploration

The areas of exploration are broad topics, each one of which helps you to consider how to interpret literature from a different perspective. The three areas of exploration for the English Language and Literature for the IB Diploma course are:

- **Readers, writers and texts**
- **Time and space**
- **Intertextuality: connecting texts.**

A good way to think of the aims of the three areas of exploration is that you will consider your reading from the **perspective** of the **immanent**, the **contextual**, and the **comparative**.

Readers, writers and texts → **Immanent perspective**

You study the text solely as a work of art, entire of itself. You engage with the text personally as a reader, and in trying to construct its meaning, you consider only its literary features or the conventions of its text type, without concerning yourself with the time or place in which the text was written or how it might be like or different from other texts.

Time and space → **Contextual perspective**

You take into account the background information of **where** and **when** the text was written, shaping your understanding of the meaning of the work in the context of its historical time and place. You will also try to consider whether your understanding of the background against which a work was written influences your interpretation in a meaningful way.

Intertextuality: connecting texts → **Comparative perspective**

You consider the work in light of other works - both from the same and/or different time and place. You will consider how they are alike and how they are different in their meaning.

This book is organized around the three areas of exploration. There is one section on each, and each one will be explored in detail. Within each area of exploration, we will make connections to the other two important structural elements of the course: the concepts and the global issues.

Concepts

This section is intended as a reference to which you can return to as needed, throughout your course. You may wish to read it through now to familiarize yourself with the ideas, but there is no need to try to learn everything right now. Each chapter in the coursebook has features called 'concept connections' which identify examples of how you might see each of the concepts at work in the exploration of literature. Bookmark this page, and then you can return here whenever you find a concept connection and need a refresher about what that concept means in detail.

CONCEPT CONNECTION

Concepts will be inside these feature boxes, so look out for this colour.

You will find the detailed concept definitions on the following pages:

- Identity: page 11
- Culture: page 12
- Creativity: page 15
- Communication: page 17
- Perspective: page 18
- Transformation: page 20
- Representation: page 23

The word **concept** comes from the study of cognition and how people come to understand the world. There is some disagreement amongst psychologists about the proper way to define 'concept', but for our purposes, we can accept the version from those researchers who suggest that a concept is an idea which gets formed by generalizing from experience, and people form concepts all the time to help them organize that experience (Spitzer 36). The concepts included in your Language and Literature course are ideas that help to describe important aspects of the way in which readers make meanings from literary works and non-literary texts. The seven concepts you are required to investigate during your IB Language and Literature course are:

Identity

One of the great joys of reading literature is the discovery of the mind behind it. When you read a book and experience those moments of great insight about the world, or the realization that someone – the author – shares a world view with you, or feels passionately about something that you feel passionately about, or thinks the way you do about the way the world ought to be, you experience great satisfaction and even excitement. These are the books you are most likely to love and remember and reread. That connection to books comes from the connection to the author.

In order to experience that kind of connection to an author, you must, of course, build a conception of the author's **identity**, an understanding of what the author is like, at least as represented by that particular literary work or text. The concept of identity, then, is about the ways in which a reader develops an understanding of an author's identity through reading the text; it serves as the evidence available to the reader for learning about that author.

The process of discovering the author's identity through the text, however, is tricky. It is tempting to think that we can tell what the author thinks just by reading the work and accepting at face value the idea that the text directly represents what the author thinks, feels and believes; however, this is seldom – if ever – the case. Authors create not just characters and situations, but also narrators (the voices which tell the story in a **narrative**) or speakers (the voices which speak poems, some of which are also narrative).

Because all of these 'people' are inventions, we have to be open to the fact that authors can represent people with very different ideas and values from their own. Authors can create characters ranging from the virtuous and exemplary to the immoral and the downright wicked. They can create characters who do represent people who are, in the author's view, exemplary human beings, or they can create characters who, in the author's view, are perfect examples of how not to live and behave. You cannot read a text with a character who exhibits bad behaviour and values, and attribute those values to the author. The author expects you to understand that the character deserves none of our admiration. Conversely, if you come across an admirable character or narrator, you don't assume that the character or narrator is the author; however, you can assume that a good character or narrator represents the author's idea of a good person. The process of interpretation, although complex, does still give us insight into the author's identity.

In the novel *The Book Thief*, for example, Markus Zusak gives us Death as a narrator. Clearly Death, the narrator, is a creation. Death does not exist as a person walking around in the world, and Zusak himself is an award-winning writer from Australia. We know, therefore, that we cannot figure out anything about Zusak's identity by assuming that Death, the narrator, somehow **personifies** Zusak. Instead, we will have to see what we can work out indirectly. As you read *The Book Thief*, you will discover that this Death has been presented as a fairly sympathetic character who cares about the people he has to collect at the ends of their lives, and who feels empathy for them. We can get a glimmer from that fact of the kind of person Zusak might be, since he has chosen this version of Death rather than a scary, vengeful hunter.

Zusak, then, might be someone who sees death as inevitable, but not inevitably cruel or meaningless. Of course, this is one tiny idea out of the whole complex vision of the world and human experience that will reflect for us Zusak's identity when we read his novel.

Your understanding of the author's identity, then, is indirect. You will consider the characters and infer the author's ideas and attitudes. It will always be important for you to realize that whatever understanding you generate of who 'the author' is from your reading of a text is a **construct**, and not the actual author. You create the identity from your interpretation, and your understanding will inevitably fail to match the real person for many reasons – for one thing, what you can understand from one text will necessarily be limited. You might come closer to reality if you read everything that a particular author creates, but, just as your backyard looks different when looked at through a frosted window, your vision of the author will be different to the vision you could get if you knew him or her personally for many years.

Even when you are reading a non-literary text such as a travelogue or a memoir, you must recognize that the understanding you develop of the identity of the author is a construct. In such texts, authors often serve as their own narrators, but the communication is still indirect and no one text can provide you with a fully realized portrait of the complex person that the author is in real life.

The primary reason that your understanding of the author must be understood as a construct is that *you* constructed it. One of the most important facts about trying to create meaning from any literary text is that every individual reader approaches the text through the filter of his or her own identity. Consider *The Book Thief*, for example: if you were a person who could not, because of whatever experiences you had in your life, bring yourself to see Death as a sympathetic, and even, at times, humorous, character, you would not interpret either his role as the narrator or what that role suggests about the author's identity in the same way that a different reader, who could easily accept Death as a fine character, could. This kind of understanding is what we mean by interpretation. You would not be wrong, nor would the other reader be wrong. You would be interpreting the text differently.

You can see, therefore, that the identity of the reader is also extremely important in the construction of an interpretation of the text, and in terms of the kind of connection that it is possible to make with the identity of the author. Chapter 1.3 provides an in-depth look at the role that the reader's knowledge, background, and perspective influence how that reader generates meaning from a literary work or a non-literary text. The discussion of the political cartoon in the next section on culture as a main course concept will give you an example of how the outlook of the reader can colour his or her interpretation of a text.

Culture

All texts, literary or non-literary, are written in a **cultural context**. The values and beliefs of that culture will have influenced the author in terms of how that author sees the world, what she or he wants to write, and the words, images, metaphors and symbols that she or he will use to express the ideas. The more you learn about the culture in which the literary work was created, the better you will understand some of the nuances of that work.

This political cartoon, by a German artist, who goes by the name Rudie, depicts a struggle which has very particular relevance in time and place. The cartoon is a multimodal non-literary text, so we need to consider both the words and the images if we are to interpret it well. The image is in some ways easy to understand. We can tell that there are two groups struggling against each other in a tug-of-war, because we see that the people are dressed differently depending on which side they are on. At this point in the struggle, the center of the rope has not been advanced more toward one side or the other, so, at this moment, it would appear that the battle is evenly matched. If we look more closely, however, we can see that even though there are six people on the right compared to five on the left, the team on the right is beginning to fail. Three of the six people are not holding the rope, and one has even fallen down. The members of the team on the right, however, are all holding onto the rope as a team, so the image suggests they might be on the verge of gaining the upper hand.

We need a good bit of cultural knowledge, however, in order to understand the nuances of the cartoon. We need to recognize that the choice of clothing that the artist put on the people in the tug-of-war is not arbitrary. The people on the right are wearing clothing in the pattern of the Union Jack while the people on the left are wearing clothing in the pattern of the flag of the European Union. If we don't know that, we likely can't see the drawing as having a political dimension as a struggle between two different governments.

There is only one word in the cartoon: 'deal'. It is at the center of the tug-of-war but has started to split right down the middle. We could deduce that the struggle between these two groups is about to destroy the 'deal', but if we don't have the cultural knowledge of what the deal/no deal struggle in Brexit is, we can't fully appreciate the message in the cartoon.

The cartoon offers a comment on the process of Britain's effort to leave the European Union – a process known as Brexit. In June 2016, there was a referendum in the United Kingdom which resulted in a vote to leave the EU. Former Prime Minister Teresa May brought a deal agreement to the British Parliament setting out the terms of Britain's exit; however, it was voted down three times. The European Union declined to re-negotiate beyond what they had already agreed to. An extension to the deadline was agreed and May stepped down, and Boris Johnson became Prime Minister. Johnson is comfortable with the idea of a no-deal Brexit, and he was not expected to make any effort to try to negotiate a new deal with the EU (at the time of this coursebook going to press).

There was great concern that if Britain left the European Union without a formal deal, then the UK would have to begin trading with the EU as a foreign entity immediately, without any transition period. This possibility would bring with it a number of consequences for the people of Britain. You can use the QR code to read about 10 consequences that would affect Britons in their everyday lives. Those consequences range from what kind of food people could buy, to the problems they might have crossing borders of countries (especially between Ireland and Northern Ireland), to falling house prices.

This political situation is, as we can see, very complicated. The more we understand the details of the problem, the better we can understand the implications of a political cartoon which strongly suggests that, in the opinion of the cartoonist, the European Union is winning the Brexit battle, and that the chances of a deal being made are coming apart. This particular cartoon was, of course, drawn by a German artist who may well be living in the European Union. Given that perspective, we might consider that the depiction of the British tug-of-war team in disarray implies that the artist thinks they are heading towards defeat due to an inability to work together effectively. If readers of this text do not have sufficient knowledge of the cultural political situation involved in Brexit, they will not be able to understand the point the artist is making.

Another aspect of the concept of culture as it relates to studying literature is the fact that all works of literature are written at a particular moment in the long tradition of literature produced in that geographical place. Knowing the literary tradition of a particular time and place can help you, as the reader, to understand the ways in which a particular work of literature continues a tradition or breaks with a tradition. Students frequently want to know why Shakespeare wrote his plays in iambic pentameter and why he used such apparently convoluted sentence structures and strange vocabulary. Most English teachers have been asked whether people in Shakespeare's day talked the way so many characters in his plays talk, but of course they did not. Shakespeare was both adhering to and breaking the **conventions** of his day.

Shakespeare was writing plays mostly in blank verse – which means that the predominant meter was **iambic pentameter**, lines of ten syllables with a stress on every other syllable, but without a set rhyming pattern. The use of blank verse and of verse in general pre-dated Shakespeare by a long way, even back to the ancient Greeks. Here, for instance, are the opening lines of *Oedipus Rex*, by Sophocles, written in the fifth century BCE:

My children, latest born to Cadmus old,
Why sit ye here as suppliants, in your hands
Branches of olive filleted with wool?
What means this reek of incense everywhere,

And everywhere laments and litanies?
Children, it were not meet that I should learn
From others, and am hither come, myself,
I Oedipus, your world-renowned king.

(Sophocles)

This play has been translated from the original Greek, of course, but you can see that the translator has retained the verse form. Just as a quick check, you can count the syllables in every line: you will see that there are ten.

Blank verse was a standard form for plays for many hundreds of years. Blank verse was introduced into English playwriting in the sixteenth century. Shakespeare joined his contemporaries who adopted the form: Thomas Sackville, Thomas Norton, Christopher Marlowe, Thomas Middleton and Ben Jonson. Shakespeare took that tradition and transformed it by developing a looser form of blank verse in which he varied the stresses and used **enjambment** (the connecting of lines together by running sentences from one line onto the next) and created a kind of blank verse that no other playwright has mastered. So we can see that Shakespeare's accomplishments arose from the writing tradition – the writing culture – in which he was writing.

Authors do not generate whole new forms out of nowhere; they build on existing conventions and the body of work in any given culture changes gradually over time. Understanding the tradition from which any given author's work arises helps us to understand the particular contributions to style, form and content that that author made.

The concept of culture applies particularly to the second area of exploration, Time and space, which will help you explore in great detail the effects of time and place on a work of literature.

It also has application for readers, writers and texts, in that so many important literary strategies require specific cultural knowledge in order to be interpreted well. And, the concept of culture also applies to intertextuality, as some of the most interesting comparisons and contrasts will come out of differences in the cultures in which the two works you are comparing to each other were written.

Creativity

Every literary text and every non-literary text is the result of an act of creation: the author, poet or playwright created the text itself. If the literary work is **fiction**, the writer created the characters, the actions, the **dialogue** and the setting. If the work is non-fiction, the writer still had to create the shape and structure of the piece. They had to use their creativity in order to develop metaphors and symbols and other figures of speech. We talk about some writers or texts as being particularly creative. J.K. Rowling, for instance, is renowned for her creativity in imagining the fictional world of the Harry Potter stories, including such features of setting as the Whomping Willow Tree; of actions, such as the magic spells Harry used to accomplish such feats as removing a wand from an opponent's hand or making people float; and the characters, such as Professor McGonagall, who can turn into a cat.

Colson Whitehead, in his 2016 novel *The Underground Railroad,* showed particular creativity in creating a living symbol by making the railroad an actual railroad that runs underground. (For those who are not familiar with the term 'underground railroad', it is the name of the secret chain of people who helped slaves to escape from the American South to states where slavery was not legal.)

Shakespeare is famous for the creativity of his language use. Consider, for example, some of his many insults:

> *'Would thou wert clean enough to spit upon!'*
>
> *Timon of Athens 4.3.402*

> *'The rankest compound of villainous smell that ever offended nostril.'*
>
> *Merry Wives of Windsor 3.5.91*

> *'Poisonous bunch-backed toad.'*
>
> *Richard III 1.3.255*

> *'I do desire that we may be better strangers.'*
>
> *As You Like It 3.2.263*

> *'There's no more faith in thee than in a stewed prune.'*
>
> *Henry IV Pt. 1 3.3.119*

All of these are more lively and more humorous than the narrow range of rather mean-spirited insults we tend to rely on in English today.

So we are quite used to the idea that authors are creative. Perhaps less familiar is the idea that readers have to be creative as well.

You have to be creative when you read both literary and non-literary texts because they communicate indirectly. We will investigate this fact in detail in Section 1 of this book, but for now, you can understand that authors of literature do not say directly what they mean: they convey ideas through myriad literary strategies, many of which you are no doubt familiar with. Consider this sentence, from the first line of TS Eliot's *Waste Land:*

> *'April is the cruellest month …'*

Such a claim seems a little odd. April is the beginning of springtime, and we associate it with blooming flowers and spring sunshine. For Christians, Easter, the holiday celebrating the rebirth of Jesus Christ into the world after his crucifixion, almost always occurs in April. April, it would seem, ought to be a happy month. And yet Eliot has called it not just cruel, but 'the cruellest' of all twelve months of the year. What are we to do with such a claim?

We could just dismiss the poet as something of a crackpot (that would be easiest – we wouldn't have to do anything!), but upon reflection, since this poet is TS Eliot, one of the giants of British literature, we have to accept that a great many people have appreciated his literary genius and so we probably have to also accept that he knew what he was doing when he gave us a claim about April that violates the stereotypical view. That in turn means that we now have to think creatively – to use our imaginations to figure out what he might have been thinking when he wrote that description.

ACTIVITY 1

Before you read the next paragraph, imagine at least three possibilities for what Eliot might have meant with this personification of April and write them down.

Probably once you thought about it, you realized that April, at least in the northern hemisphere where Eliot was writing, is an unpredictable month. Very often it is exactly what we think it is – the month which signifies rebirth. The soil warms, flowers bloom, trees come into leaf and birds build their nests. But not infrequently, once that promise of warmth and approaching summer is delivered, snow and ice storms appear, killing the flowers and dragging us back into winter. The cruelty of April then, lies in the fact that it so often breaks its promises, luring us into feeling hopeful and then smacking us with a powerful reminder that we cannot control nature or count on our expectations to be met.

This is the kind of creative thinking that you must do as a reader of any text. We saw with the Brexit cartoon on page 12, that one way in which readers must be creative is that they must be able to imagine themselves into the minds of readers and writers from other times and places. You must be alert for mention of anything that might mean more than it seems, and then you must use your imagination to work on the possibilities.

TOK Links: The nature of creativity

When you study individual knowledge-making in your Theory of Knowledge class, you may consider the ways in which our cognitive tools, the features of our minds which help us make knowledge, work together to create new ideas. We think of imagination as being the particular cognitive tool we use in order to think up something that we haven't thought before, or which hasn't been thought before by anyone. However, imagination is the result of the interaction of several different cognitive tools: certainly we need to be able to generate images and thoughts of possibilities, but for any creative act to be effective, the thoughts and images we generate have to be bounded by reason. There's no point, for example, in imagining that we could flap our arms and fly to the moon – except in fiction – because such an act is a physical impossibility in our universe.

Imagination also relies equally on memory. It is impossible to imagine something that is completely out of your realm of experience. Try it now: imagine a creature from outer space that has no feature that you have ever seen or experienced before. You can't do it. Your alien creature as a whole will be something you have never seen or experienced, but it will be made up entirely of shapes and colours and physical parts of people, creatures and objects that you have encountered sometime during your life.

Creative thinking in literature works the same way. You will find that you have to imagine possibilities for what things mean, but your interpretation will have to be based on what has been in your experience, and it will have to be bounded by reason.

Communication

The concept of communication relates to the concept of identity in that the communication we are considering is the communication between you and the author. As we have noted above, this communication is indirect. Rather than you and the author meeting and talking face-to-face, the communication is through the medium of the text. Even then, the text will not state directly what the author is thinking. Instead, the author will employ a wide range of tools to communicate to you through images, symbols, elements of settings, a variety of characters and actions, the meaning of which must be interpreted. In order for you to be able to receive the author's communication effectively, you must know how to use the technology, as it were. Imagine that the text is a machine and you have to learn how to run it, just as you learned to use your computer or your smartphone or your car.

The literary works and the non-literary texts you will study in school have been chosen in part because the assumption is that you cannot, at the beginning, read them effectively by yourself. Your teachers understand that you need assistance in learning how to use the tools in these texts; if you could read them on your own, you wouldn't need teaching. The most important thing you need to understand is that the knowledge and skills you lack when you begin studying a work of literature or a non-literary text can be learned. You can take conscious steps to develop your abilities as a reader, and every work you study helps prepare you for the communication in the next work.

American poet Elizabeth Bishop wrote a poem called 'The Fish', which can be read from a Christian perspective because it has several images which are, within Christianity, recognizable as religious symbols. Readers who are not familiar with standard Christian symbolism might not necessarily recognize the potentially religious elements of this poem. For example: The fish is a symbol, in Christianity, of Jesus. You can read the poem without knowing that, and it will make sense as a story about a fisherman reflecting on the significance of catching a fish that many others before have failed to catch. You would miss a great deal, however, of the author's message. Additionally, if you read the poem as nothing more than a poem about a fish, you might be somewhat confused by the mention, near the end, of a rainbow, which seems to be the thing which makes the fisherman decide to let the fish go. The rainbow is another religious symbol from Christianity: the rainbow comes from the story of Noah's Ark, in which God destroyed all living creatures in a 40-day flood, except those which were on the ark He commanded Noah to build. When the flood dries up, God sends the rainbow as a promise that He will never again send such a flood.

For readers who know the story, the poem can be seen as having a message about the need for people to remember God's mercy and to show mercy in their turn. If some readers do not know that story, however, they can learn it in order to increase their understanding of the poem. They could do some research on the symbolism of fish and of rainbows. Any time you read any text, you can be alert to anything that might be a symbol, and if you don't know what that object symbolizes, you can look it up. Symbolism is just one of the tools in a writer's toolbox; as you read more literary texts, you will learn to recognize and interpret more and more tools. One of the great satisfactions of studying literature is the satisfaction you feel when you have solved the puzzle of an author's strategy and, in so doing, broadened your own knowledge of the world.

The same process occurs when you are dealing with non-literary texts. Consider the Prada advertisement using the QR code on the right.

The communication between viewer and photographer must be developed deliberately, because this photograph consists of some elements that many viewers might not recognize. The head of the model in the television, for example, is Twiggy, whose real name is Dame Lesley Lawson. Twiggy was an instantly recognizable model – what we would now probably call a supermodel – in the 1960s. The advertisement here, which ran in *Tatler* in August of 2011, counts on the viewers' recognition of the iconic figure. It also counts on us recognizing the black and white television – something which many people today have never seen. That television gives us a sharp contrast between the bright colours of the dress (which is reminiscent of those that Twiggy herself modelled in) and the head, and it connects the past and present. It also counts on our recognizing that the laws of gravity have been violated here: although the model is upside down, her dress has not fallen around her head and shoulders. The advertisement is suggesting that Prada connects women across a 50-year divide, and it suggests, subliminally, both that anyone who wears the dress will be as iconic as Twiggy is, and that reality itself will alter in response to the level of such a woman's unique character.

You will be working on the skill of how to understand the author's communication throughout your IB English Language and Literature course, and all sections of this coursebook will help you to develop that skill. Section 1 Readers, writers and texts, will help you learn how to approach the communication act from the perspective of the immanent. Section 2 Time and space, will help you to approach the communication act from the perspective of understanding the influence of culture on any given text. Section 3 Intertextuality: connecting texts, will help you to understand the author's communication from the perspective of the influence of one text on another.

You will find it helpful to remember, as you work through the course, that the purpose of your study is ultimately communication from the author to you and that your work is aimed at closing the gap between your knowledge of the world and of literature and its features, and the author's.

Perspective

When we discussed the concept of identity, we pointed out that one difficulty in interpreting an author's identity is the fact that the author creates characters, each with his or her own perspective, and those characters' perspectives may or may not line up with the author's perspective. What this means for you as a reader is that you have to be aware, first of all, of the fact that multiple perspectives exist in every text and, second, that you must work to understand all of the perspectives and what they imply about what the author is trying to communicate. You must also work to be aware of your own perspective, and how your time and place and your personal knowledge influences what you are capable of understanding in any given text or how your assumptions and expectations might shape your interpretation of any given text.

A good example of a literary work with many different perspectives for which the modern reader might not be prepared is *Gulliver's Travels*, by Jonathan Swift. The book, published in 1726, is a satire on human nature. One of the most famous episodes in the book is Gulliver's visit to the land of the Houyhnhnms. The Houyhnhnms are a species of giant horse which is significantly more intelligent and cultured than humans, who are known in this land as Yahoos – creatures without any ability to reason. Gulliver describes Yahoos this way:

> *'… the* Yahoos *were a species of animals utterly incapable of amendment by precept or example.'*

As readers, we are not likely to be predisposed to accepting such a harsh judgement on human nature, so in order to understand Swift's perspective, we have to understand Gulliver's perspective, and we have to be open to the idea that human beings can sometimes behave in quite irrational ways, even in ways which work against their own best interests.

Similarly to literary work, some types of non-literary texts will likely have narrators who have perspectives similar to those of the author, while others will feature perspectives which are not similar to the author's at all. In some cases, the perspective demonstrated will be dramatically different from our own. The political cartoon opposite, for example, was published in *Klansmen Guardians of Liberty* in 1926 by the Pillar of Fire Church in Zarapeth, New Jersey.

THE BIBLE MUST BE PLACED IN EVERY SCHOOLROOM

This cartoon was published several decades before the Civil Rights Legislation was passed in the United States, and the Ku Klux Klan operated openly as a white supremacist organization. The image here presents the opinion that, as the caption says, the Bible must be included in classrooms. We know that the perspective presented is one shared by the creators and publishers of the cartoon because of the name of the publication and because the caption is not ironic. The perspectives here, then, are quite different from the perspective of most readers today. We have to consider the cartoon in the context of the times in which it was written. We also have to realize that even in the time in which it was published, this cartoon would not have been indicative of the perspectives of most people of its time. The magazine in which it was published appealed to a certain subset of the community which shared its perspective.

One of the most important skills in interpreting both literary and non-literary texts, in other words, is open-mindedness. We have to be ready for characters to have motivations and values we don't expect. We have to be ready for authors to push against stereotypical expectations and against easy understanding in an effort to make us think more deeply about something. We even have to be ready for authors or creators of texts to have values different from ours. Most works of literature require us to consider perspectives different from our own and potentially difficult to appreciate or respect.

TOK Links: Influence of perspective

The question of how your own perspective shapes your knowledge is an important one in your TOK class. Many factors shape your perspective, for example:

- The physical: Do you have poor eyesight? Extra sensitive hearing?
- The mental: What are your habits of mind? Are you quick to process, or to jump to conclusions? Are you inclined to take in a lot of data and think slowly before you decide what it means?
- The cultural: Do you live in a culture which admires and respects older people? Do you live in a culture in which independence is highly valued? Do you live in a culture which values the good of the community over the good of the individual?

One famous example of the question of whether and how someone's perspective shaped his knowledge is the example of Werner Heisenberg, the physicist who developed the Heisenberg uncertainty principle. When the Second World War broke out, Heisenberg chose to stay in Germany to work on Hitler's project to develop the atomic bomb. The Germans never did develop the bomb, and there has been speculation for many years about why not, given Heisenberg's undoubted genius as a physicist. Journalist Thomas Powers argued, in a 1993 book, that Heisenberg actually sabotaged the project so that Hitler would not build the bomb (Glanz). At the heart of the controversy is the question of Heisenberg's perspective. He was a German working for Germany during the war. He was also a scientist with full awareness of the implications of the power released by the split atom. People wonder whether Heisenberg's perspective as a scientist who might not want to give that power to any dictator was more important than his perspective as a German who would want to know whatever he needed to know in order to help his country.

Transformation

The concept of transformation refers to the variety of ways in which texts are transformed from one thing into another. One widespread and important way in which this transformation takes place is in the development of **intertextuality**, the reference in one text to an earlier one. Sometimes that kind of intertextuality takes the shape of an **allusion**, an explicit reference to another text. We saw, in the Prada advertisement, how the allusion to Twiggy shapes the meaning of that advertisement. We also saw how Elizabeth Bishop's poem 'The Fish', alludes to the Biblical story of Noah's Ark.

Another kind of intertextuality occurs when one work builds in a broader, deeper way on an earlier text. Shakespeare's *Romeo and Juliet* is a retelling of an earlier English poem written in 1562 called *The Tragicall Historye of Romeus and Juliet*, by Arthur Brooke. Brooke's work in turn was based on a 1554 Italian novella by Matteo Bandello called *Giulietta e Romeo* (Mabillard). Each author transformed his source into something quite different. Brooke took a novella and transformed it into a poem, while Shakespeare took that poem and transformed it into a play. At each transformation, the story changed to reflect the author's ideas.

A familiar kind of transformation of text is from text to film. This kind of change tends to be fairly substantial. For one thing, movies typically run about two hours apiece, while it might take 10 hours or more to read the book version. Much has to be cut. Screenwriters and directors make the choices about what bits of the book will not be included in the film, and they might choose things that the original author and/or the readers felt were essential to the effective representation of the book. Another point to consider is characters' appearance. When characters are described in books, readers form ideas in their minds of what those characters are like. The movie version necessarily makes one choice out of many when the casting director chooses a particular actor. Such a choice will always disappoint – or even anger – some readers whose ideas were quite different from what the film portrays.

The 2013 film version of F Scott Fitzgerald's *The Great Gatsby* caused a certain amount of controversy due to the music that the director, Baz Luhrmann, chose to include. The novel is set in the 1920s, an era when jazz was flourishing. Luhrmann, however, instead of filling the score with period music, chose to use modern music by hip-hop artists such as Jay-Z, Beyoncé, André 3000 and Kanye West. Such a choice displeases readers who prefer historical accuracy as being more true to the spirit of Fitzgerald's book, but pleases readers who feel that the modern songs create the kind of effect that Fitzgerald was going for. The point is that because the film director has made an interpretation, the effect of the medium is quite different than is the effect of reading a book which requires the reader to do the interpreting. *The Great Gatsby* has been transformed. Whether the transformation is effective or not is a different question.

Think of some examples of movies you have seen which were made from books that you had read. Were you happy with the transformation? Why or why not? An important point to realize with regard to the concept of transformation is that the film version cannot be substituted for the reading of the book. As with Brooke rewriting Bandello, and Shakespeare rewriting Brooke, the screenwriter transforms any novel or play into something new when she or he changes the form.

Another important kind of transformation is one that you will definitely encounter in your English Language and Literature for the IB Diploma course: translation from one language to another. Translation presents many difficulties. Among the problems for the translator to wrestle with are:

- words that exist in the original language but do not exist in the language of translation
- words which exist but which have significantly different connotations in the two languages
- line length and stress patterns when trying to preserve meter in poetry or plays
- sentence word order differs from language to language
- symbols do not mean the same thing in different languages
- idioms are different in different language.

There are other problems, but these will give you an idea of what the translator faces. Every translator must, therefore, settle for compromises. They must decide what is more important: the use of an exact word or the retention of implication? The number of syllables in a line or the number of lines? The rhyme scheme or the word choice?

One example of why word length and line length matter is the example of Boris Pasternak's translations of Shakespeare's plays into Russian. The average English word is 1.22 syllables long, while the average Russian word is 2.44 syllables long – double the length of an English word (France). That length difference matters when we consider that Shakespeare wrote predominantly in lines of ten syllables. If Pasternak wished to retain the ten-syllable line, he would need roughly twice the number of lines for the same content. For *Hamlet,* that would have meant increasing the line length from just over 4,000 lines (Open Source Shakespeare) to something over 8,000 lines. Kenneth Branagh filmed a complete-text version of *Hamlet* in 1996; it runs for 4 hours 2 minutes. That is already an extraordinary amount of time to expect an audience to sit still; imagine the effect of trying to stage an 8-hour performance.

The first line of Albert Camus' novel *L'Etranger* gives us an excellent example of the significance of the change in meaning that can occur when trying to translate a text into English. Camus' novel was written in French, and the first line reads: 'Aujourd'hui, Maman est morte' (Bloom). In 1946, Stuart Gilbert made the first translation into English, and he translated that line as 'Mother died today' (Bloom). In 1988, Matthew Ward's translation rendered the line 'Maman died today' (Ward 3). In a 2012 *New Yorker* article, Ryan Bloom provides a fascinating discussion of the difference. The word 'Mother', he argues, conveys a colder, more distant relationship than the French word 'Maman' does. He suggests that the English equivalent would be 'Mommy', but that this word is childish, and so conveys yet another kind of relationship between the son and the parent (Bloom). You can see that the particular decision about which version of this word to use, especially in the first sentence of the novel, will shape the reader's understanding of the main character and so will colour our attitude toward him throughout the novel. Bloom provides a further detailed argument about how the change in word order that happened when Gilbert decided to begin with the idea of the mother instead of the idea of 'today' eliminates a critical understanding of Meursault's relationship to time. You can read Bloom's insightful article about the analysis of the effect of translation on a literary work in full via the QR code in the margin.

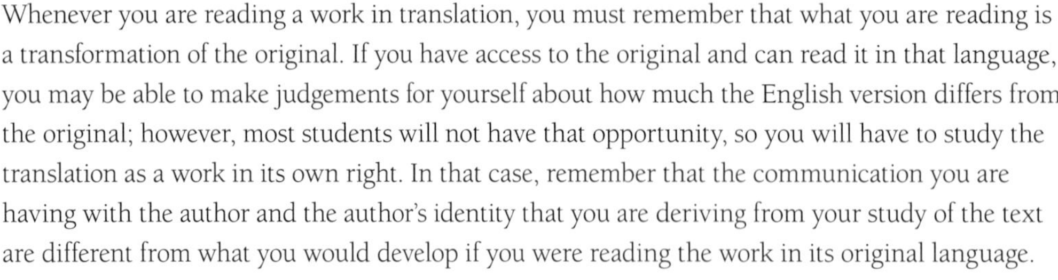

Whenever you are reading a work in translation, you must remember that what you are reading is a transformation of the original. If you have access to the original and can read it in that language, you may be able to make judgements for yourself about how much the English version differs from the original; however, most students will not have that opportunity, so you will have to study the translation as a work in its own right. In that case, remember that the communication you are having with the author and the author's identity that you are deriving from your study of the text are different from what you would develop if you were reading the work in its original language.

A final force that can transform texts is the readers themselves. As we saw in the discussions of identity and culture, the reader's identity – their background knowledge, beliefs, and values – inevitably influence what the reader is capable of understanding when engaging with any literary work or non-literary text. If you think back to the beginning of this introduction, you can identity for yourself the ideas that you were able to extract from the two poems, the cartoon of the sleeping person, and the fontspiece of the brochure about the flood. Your knowledge and vocabulary allowed you, no doubt, to understand some ideas quite readily, but might have led you to struggle with others. It's possible that you know something that the author did not know, and that, too, would cause you to transform the text. Shakespeare wrote *Henry IV Part 1* at the end of the sixteenth century. In Act 2, Scene 3, Lady Percy speaks to her husband, Hotspur, expressing her concern for his well-being. The speech begins this way:

LADY PERCY O my good lord, why are you thus alone?
For what offense have I this fortnight been
A banished woman from my Harry's bed?
Tell me, sweet lord, what is 't that takes from thee
Thy stomach, pleasure, and thy golden sleep?
Why dost thou bend thine eyes upon the earth
And start so often when thou sit'st alone?
Why hast thou lost the fresh blood in thy cheeks
And given my treasures and my rights of thee
To thick-eyed musing and curst melancholy?
In thy faint slumbers I by thee have watched,
And heard thee murmur tales of iron wars,
Speak terms of manage to thy bounding steed,
Cry 'Courage! To the field!'

(William Shakespeare, Henry IV Pt.1 *Act 2 Scene 3)*

In 1994, a medical doctor, Jonathan Shay, wrote a book about post-traumatic stress disorder (PTSD), in which he analysed the depiction of soldiers in classic works of literature in terms of the medical problems they exhibit in those works (Shay 165–66). He used this speech from *Henry IV Part 1* to do a line-by-line analysis comparing Lady Percy's descriptions with the modern medical symptoms typical of PTSD. PTSD did not become a recognized medical disorder until 1980. Clearly the author of this speech could not have known about PTSD, so we see that Jonathan Shay, a reader with a particular perspective as a medical doctor working with veterans of the Vietnam War, and with specialized background knowledge, was able to see something in the speech which the author himself could not have. Shay's perspective transformed the text by revealing how it can be seen as an accurate portrayal in twentieth-century terms of the kind of suffering that soldiers bring home with them from battle.

This is a fairly dramatic example of the way in which a reader can transform a text, but every reader transforms every text simply by bringing his or her own perspective to it. You will explore this process in greater depth throughout the book, but especially in Chapter 1.3

Representation

The concept of representation focuses your attention on the relationship of a literary work to reality. Fiction, by definition, is not 'true' in that the events described never actually happened. The obvious question, then, is the question of how something not true can convey any truth. The answer, of course, is that some aspect of every literary work does indeed represent reality. At a minimum, the themes and ideas must convey some truth about human experience, human nature, and/or human relationships. In fiction, the characters are not real people, but they represent real people. We can see, in the behaviours and motivations of the characters in the text, behaviours and motivations that we believe could happen in the real world.

An interesting aspect of representation in literary works is that the degree of realism will vary wildly. Some texts are highly realistic in their detail and descriptions. Consider for example this passage from the opening paragraph of *Middlemarch* by George Eliot:

Miss Brooke had that kind of beauty which seems to be thrown into relief by poor dress. Her hand and wrist were so finely formed that she could wear sleeves not less bare of style than those in which the Blessed Virgin appeared to Italian painters; and her profile as well as her stature and bearing seemed to gain the more dignity from her plain garments, which by the side of provincial fashion gave her the impressiveness of a fine quotation from the Bible,—or from one of our elder poets,—in a paragraph of to-day's newspaper. She was usually spoken of as being remarkably clever, but with the addition that her sister Celia had more common-sense. Nevertheless, Celia wore scarcely more trimmings; and it was only to close observers that her dress differed from her sister's, and had a shade of coquetry in its arrangements; for Miss Brooke's plain dressing was due to mixed conditions, in most of which her sister shared. The pride of being ladies had something to do with it: the Brooke connections, though not exactly aristocratic, were unquestionably 'good': if you inquired backward for a generation or two, you would not find any yard-measuring or parcel-tying forefathers—anything lower than an admiral or a clergyman; and there was even an ancestor discernible as a Puritan gentleman who served under Cromwell, but afterwards conformed, and managed to come out of all political troubles as the proprietor of a respectable family estate. Young women of such birth, living in a quiet country-house, and attending a village church hardly larger than a parlor, naturally regarded frippery as the ambition of a huckster's daughter. Then there was well-bred economy, which in those days made show in dress the first item to be deducted from, when any margin was required for expenses more distinctive of rank. Such reasons would have been enough to account for plain dress, quite apart from religious feeling; but in Miss Brooke's case, religion alone would have determined it; and Celia mildly acquiesced in all her sister's sentiments, only infusing them with that common-sense which is able to accept momentous doctrines without any eccentric agitation.

(George Eliot 4)

This passage is highly realistic. Despite having been published in 1871, it mentions objects of culture which are familiar even today to people familiar with the West: clothing with sleeves, Italian painters, the Virgin Mary, newspapers, parcels, clergymen and so on. The description of the young woman is detailed and believable. The setting, a quiet country-house in a village is also quite natural and realistic. This text, then, is highly representational.

Other texts are much less realistic. The following description of the life of a different young woman, Persephone, from the Greek myths, comes from the Homeric 'Hymn to Demeter':

I begin to sing of rich-haired Demeter, awful goddess – of her and her trim-ankled daughter whom Aidoneus rapt away, given to him by all-seeing Zeus the loud-thunderer. Apart from Demeter, lady of the golden sword and glorious fruits, she was playing with the deep-bosomed daughters of Oceanus and gathering flowers over a soft meadow, roses and crocuses and beautiful violets, irises also and hyacinths and the narcissus, which Earth made to grow at the will of Zeus and to please the Host of Many, to be a snare for the bloom-like girl – a marvellous, radiant flower. It was a thing of awe whether for deathless gods or mortal men to see: from its root grew a hundred blooms and it smelled most sweetly, so that all wide heaven above and the whole earth and the sea's salt swell laughed for joy. And the girl was amazed and reached out with both hands to take the lovely toy; but the wide-pathed earth yawned there in the plain of Nysa, and the lord, Host of Many, with his immortal horses sprang out upon her – the Son of Cronos, He who has many names.

('Hymn 2 to Demeter')

Persephone is described in some realistic terms: she has trim ankles and she is capable of amazement. But much of the description is quite unrealistic. Her mother, Demeter, is described as being an 'awful goddess', and 'lady of the golden sword and glorious fruits'. The Earth makes flowers grow at the will of Zeus. There is a flower with a hundred blooms that smells so sweet that it causes the earth and heaven and the sea to laugh. None of this is like what we see when we look out the window on a spring morning. We would say that this text, unlike *Middlemarch*, is not very representational.

The lack of correspondence between the facts of a literary work and the real world we are used to can extend beyond the characters and setting. We've already seen in this chapter how unrealistic Shakespeare's use of language was, in terms of the degree to which it sounds like everyday spoken English. The sonnet we examined is highly structured and the language formal and stylized. We've also seen, in the example of the Harry Potter books, that some stories contain actions which are not at all realistic in terms of whether they could actually happen in the real world.

Representation is an equally important element in non-literary texts. In the Twiggy Prada advertisement, we saw how the lack of representation – the fact that the dress does not comply with the laws of gravity – contributes to the message that the photographer was sending. In the dream cartoon, we explored both the representational and the non-representational elements of the image. The Brexit cartoon dealt with real political events in a distinctly non-representational way. Let's consider whether the following extract from Bill Bryson's book *Down Under* (which was published as *In a Sunburned Country* in the United States) is representational or not.

[Australia] is the home of the largest living thing on earth, the Great Barrier Reef, and of the largest monolith, Ayers Rock (or Uluru to use its now-official, more respectful Aboriginal name). It has more things that will kill you than anywhere else. Of the world's ten most poisonous snakes, all are Australian. Five of its creatures – the funnel web spider, box jellyfish, blue-ringed octopus, paralysis tick, and stonefish – are the most lethal of their type in the world. This is a country where even the fluffiest of caterpillars can lay you out with a toxic nip, where seashells will not just sting you but actually sometimes go for you. [...] If you are not stung or pronged to death in some unexpected manner, you may be fatally chomped by sharks or crocodiles, or carried helplessly out to sea by irresistible currents, or left to stagger to an unhappy death in the baking outback. It's a tough place.

(Bill Bryson 6)

The important thing for you to notice as you study the works in your Language and Literature course is the degree to which the authors use representational features in the text, and, if they do not, even if the texts are extremely unrealistic, how the authors nevertheless manage to convey some important idea about reality. Finally, you will be considering the author's choice to make the literature more representational or less so and what she or he gained by making that particular choice for that particular work.

TOK Links: The relationship between art and realism

The arts as a whole, including all the other media besides literature, span the whole range from highly realistic to extremely **abstract**. One of the central questions about how we make meaning in art revolves around the question of the function of realism. Much early art is considered highly realistic (naturalistic), but as the centuries have passed, the boundaries for what constitutes acceptable art have expanded dramatically so that now we accept as art, works that are so far removed from depicting the world in a representational way as to have virtually no connection at all. A good question for you to pursue is the question of what we gain either from clear representational techniques or from the rejection of those techniques and the adopting of such modes as expressionism, cubism or abstract art.

It will be important for you to remember that when you come across these concept connections, they are examples of how you might apply the concepts to your study of literature. Each chapter has a few concept connections, but that does not imply that those are the only concepts which are relevant in that chapter or to the particular literature being discussed. As you become more and more familiar with the concepts, you will be able to see ways in which they can all be applied in different situations and with different literature or non-literary texts and bodies of work. It's possible – indeed likely – that all seven of the concepts can be applied to any work or text you study. That is why they are identified as the core concepts for the course.

Global issues

The seven concepts for your IB English Language and Literature course are mandated by the IB curriculum. The global issues, on the other hand, are not as specifically required. You are required to consider the texts you read in terms of what they might reveal about global issues, and one of your assessments will require you to discuss two works in terms of a global issue, but you will have some freedom as to what global issue you choose, and it will not have to be one of those which are suggested in the curriculum guide.

The curriculum guide stipulates three characteristics which define a global issue:

- It has significance on a wide/large scale.
- It is transnational.
- Its impact is felt in everyday local contexts.

The guide suggests the following examples of areas of inquiry from which you can formulate global issues (International Baccalaureate 55–56):

- **Culture, identity and community**: this category might include investigation into the ways in which literary works depict gender, class, race, ethnicity or other cultural groups.
- **Beliefs, values and education:** this category could include consideration of how a text depicts the connection between education and values or beliefs, and the ways in which communities define and disseminate their beliefs and values.

- **Politics, power and justice:** this category includes all of the kinds of issues that arise in society – questions of equality, ruling classes, fair and unfair wielding of power, distribution of wealth, and the relationships among all of these. This category offers you the opportunity to consider what different societies consider to be the rights of citizens and how those rights are protected or undermined.
- **Art, creativity and the imagination:** this category provides you with the opportunity to consider what works themselves have to say about the role of art in people's lives. Art, in this case, is content, not medium. When you consider the course's core concepts, you are considering the texts as works of art themselves. When you are considering a work in the context of the global issue of art, you are noticing that the work is about art.
- **Science, technology and the environment:** if a work explores questions of science and nature, you can consider it in the context of this global issue. Questions that might arise could have to do with the relationship between science and society, science and nature or nature and society. You could look at what the work suggests about the importance or effectiveness of scientific developments.

In all of these categories, it would be useful to consider how different viewpoints come into conflict with each other.

As you consider your literary and non-literary texts in the context of global issues, you may notice that more than one global issue might be relevant to any given text. Within each of these general headings, you have quite a bit of freedom to choose what to discuss with regard to the works you study. The descriptions above are suggestions, and should not be considered to be definitive.

You are also free to develop a different global issue which is more relevant to the works you study than these are. You may find, also, that many other topics you might think of which meet all three of the requirements for defining a global issue already comes under one of these five umbrella headings. Poverty can be seen as an issue of politics, p[illegible] and justice, for example. Global warming could come under the heading of science, te[illegible] So long as you can clearly identify an issue as meeting all three [illegible] that issue as the defining feature for your individual [illegible]

Just as with the course concepts, this coursebook w[illegible] works and global issues in all three areas of explora[illegible] work in the context of one or more global issues ca[illegible]

How to use this book

The book has been structured around the three a[illegible] Literature for the IB Diploma curriculum. The g[illegible] and breaks it down into six questions to help yo[illegible] mirrors this structure: each section focuses on [illegible] each area of exploration, there is one chapter f[illegible]

Each chapter provides you with examples of how [illegible] the works that you study in your course. Each chapter also provides you with [illegible] in order to practise using the tools yourself. There are commentaries at the end of the book, but you should remember that the commentaries do not provide 'right' answers. A variety of answers is possible, so if you did not think of the particular interpretation the notes provide, that does not necessarily mean that your interpretation is wrong. If you can justify your response using specific evidence from the text as support, then you can feel confident about your interpretation. If your interpretation seems to have been way off, however, and you cannot really justify it using features of the text in support, then that simply means that you will need to keep practising! Learning to read literary works and non-literary texts effectively is a skill that takes time to develop; do not expect that you will necessarily get everything right the very first try.

ACTIVITY

Activities will be inside these boxes – look out for these to help you practise your skills.

Author profile

Extra information about the authors under discussion is provided in these boxes.

You should note that some works included in this coursebook include sensitive content and offensive or derogatory language. It is the nature of the IB's prescribed reading list to include texts that will challenge you intellectually, personally and culturally, and expose you to sensitive and mature topics. At times you or your classmates may find these works a challenge, but as readers it is up to us to consider not just how such language is used, but why. We invite you to reflect critically on various perspectives offered while bearing in mind the IB's commitment to international-mindedness and intercultural respect.

SENSITIVE CONTENT

Caution: this book contains extracts that use offensive and derogatory language.

In most cases, we have chosen to let the content remain as it originally appears, so you can consider the effects for yourself. This is central to understanding the themes of identity and human behaviour at the heart of this book. Any works that include such content will be prefixed with a sensitive-content box.

You will find a useful glossary on page 485 of this book, which you can refer to throughout each chapter. Note that glossary terms are in **purple**.

Using QR codes

Extra reading is recommended via the QR codes throughout the book. They are placed in the margin alongside the text for quick scanning, and look like the one on the right.

To use the QR codes to access the weblinks you will need a QR code reader for your smartphone/tablet. There are many free readers available, depending on the device that you use. We have supplied some suggestions below, but this is not an exhaustive list and you should only download software compatible with your device and operating system. We do not endorse any of the third-party products listed below and downloading them is at your own risk.

- For iPhone/iPad, Qrafter – https://apple.co/2Lx9H5l
- For Android, QR Droid – https://bit.ly/JKbRPO
- For Blackberry, QR Code Scanner – https://blck.by/2DD51Jo
- For Windows/Symbian, Upcode – https://bit.ly/2UJe7dt

Organization of the course

All three areas of exploration, along with the concepts and the global issues, are required to be investigated over the course of your two-year programme, but the course curriculum does not dictate to teachers the order in which each element is to be presented – or even that they be taught in an order. Teachers are free to touch on whichever one or more of the three areas of exploration is relevant to a given text. We have chosen to use the three areas of exploration as a starting point; however, your teachers may not have chosen to organize the course using those areas of

exploration, so it will be important for you to attend to your teacher's instructions about which chapters to read in what order.

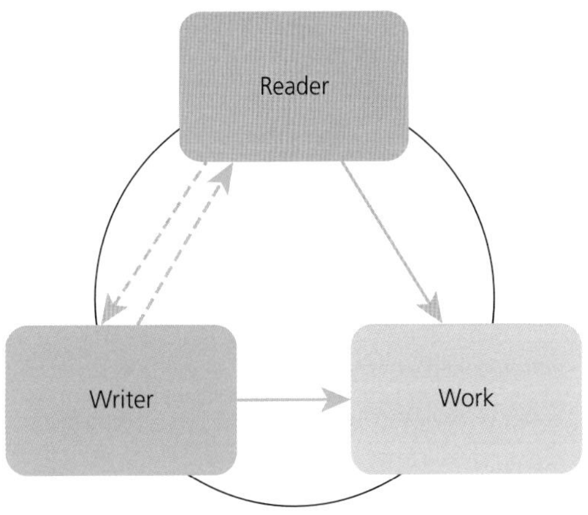

Even if your course is organized around the three areas of exploration, you will ideally be considering all of the literature and non-literary texts you study from all three perspectives, so from time to time, each section will point out some connections between and among both of the other areas of exploration. You may find it useful, while studying any particular work of literature or non-literary text, to refer to different chapters in the book as a refresher of how to use those tools to work on the present text.

Finally, you should be aware that because the range of choices available to your teachers for selecting literary works and non-literary texts for you to study is so wide-ranging, you are unlikely to encounter here works that you are studying in class. Therefore, you should not necessarily write about the works you learn from this book directly in your exams, Learner Portfolio or other assessments. Your IB assessments require you to use works and texts that you studied in your course. Instead, this book will help you to learn how to read any work of literature or text type you are given, because it will show you from a conceptual stance what is required of any reader approaching any work.

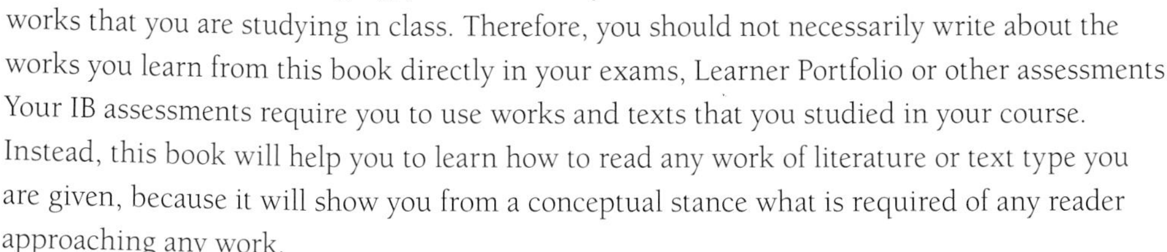

This diagram shows the relationships that we will investigate over the course of this book. The writer creates the literary work/non-literary text with which you, the reader, engages. The dotted lines show that the purpose of the exercise is for you to engage with the writer, but you cannot do that directly; your means of communication is through the written work. Once you understand the nature of your relationship to authors, how it is possible for you to communicate in this indirect fashion, and how authors expect you to approach that communicative task, it will be much easier for you to engage with any literary work. Once you understand the nature of literary works themselves, and once you have the tools to interpret them, you will be able to read any novel, short story, play, poem, or work of non-fiction you encounter equally well because you will know what to look for in any given work and you will know what to do with it when you find it.

Literary works *versus* non-literary texts

The English A language and literature IB Diploma guide identifies a text as being either a literary work or a non-literary text, and over the duration of your language and literature course you will be studying an equal measure of both. The IB's *Prescribed reading list* refers to four forms of literary works:

- **drama**
- **poetry**
- **prose non-fiction**
- **prose fiction.**

Note that prose fiction and prose non-fiction are both literary forms. The range of prose non-fiction authors and genres on the *Prescribed reading lists* is wide-ranging and includes literary memoirs by authors such as Primo Levi and George Orwell; (auto)biographical graphic novels by authors such as Marjane Satrapi and Alison Bechdel; and autobiographies, biographies, essays, travelogues and diaries by a range of authors. However, if an author is not on the *Prescribed reading list*, decisions regarding whether memoirs, biographies, letters, speeches and essays are a literary work or a non-literary text should be taken on an individual basis: your teacher will be able to advise you accordingly.

Texts that are characterized as non-literary text types are wide and varied. Table 0.1.1 includes some non-literary text types that the IB Language and Literature course identifies – but this list is not exhaustive.

■ Table 0.1.1

Non-literary text types		
advertisement	appeal	biography*
brochure/leaflet	cartoon	diary*
encyclopaedia entry	essay*	infographic
letter (formal and informal)*	magazine article	memoir
parody*	pastiche*	photographs
set of instructions	speech*	travel writing

**In some manifestations, these text types could be considered literary forms, usually within the category of prose non-fiction.*
(adapted from the Language A: Language and Literature guide, 21–22)

We will be exploring a wide range of literary works as well as non-literary text types throughout the coursebook and you will also be studying a wide range of both language and literature texts in class.

The nature of a text

Although there are some fundamental differences between a text that is considered a literary work and one that is a non-literary text, the essential nature of a text remains the same: to communicate with the reader. Chimombo and Roseberry define a text in the following way:

> *First consider* **discourse** *and what it is. Discourse is a process resulting in a communicative act. The communicative act itself takes the form of a* **text**. *A text is commonly thought of as consisting of written or printed words on a page; but a text may also consist of sign language or spoken words, or it may comprise only the thoughts of a writer, or speaker, on the one hand or a reader or listener, on the other. In addition to words, a text may consist of other symbols, sounds, gestures, or silences, in any combination that is intended to communicate information such as ideas, emotional states, and attitudes. It may fail to communicate, but if the intention to communicate is clearly there, it must be regarded as a text.*

(Chimombo and Roseberry ix)

In this coursebook, then, we will be closely exploring the plethora of ways a writer attempts to communicate with the reader. We will be exploring how discourse does not necessarily have to be written language, but it could also be visual language or even language that uses neither words nor visuals, but is more symbolic in nature. As well as the marks on the page, the way a writer has structured his or her text will also be explored, including how a writer may exploit the sounds and rhythms of a text's words, how a writer may manipulate the shape of his or her text and how a writer may decide to organize the text's written and visual language on the page to heighten the text's meaning.

Although the majority of literary works rely on the written word to communicate meaning, works such as graphic novels use illustrations as well as or instead of the written word to communicate, while poetry relies on the shape of the poem as well as the written word to communicate. In contrast, users of social media communicate meaning through an increasingly wide range of symbols such as emojis, emoticons and hashtags. Of course, a wide range of non-literary texts do not simply rely on the written word to communicate meaning: photojournalism, cartoon strips, advertisements, newspaper articles, magazine front covers and infographics are just a few examples that rely on photographic or other illustrative images to a lesser or greater degree.

Now that we understand the nature of a text we can start to distinguish between the nature of a non-literary text and the nature of a literary work. We have just seen what connects all texts, but we also need to be aware that there are some fundamental differences between a literary work and a non-literary text.

The nature of the non-literary text

Although not all non-fiction texts are considered non-literary, a text that is considered non-literary is usually non-fiction. Non-fiction means it is an account of the truth and deals with facts and information – it is based in the real world and is about real-life experiences. This does not mean all non-literary texts are objective, though – an encyclopaedia entry, a recipe from a cookery book or a set of instructions on how to change a bicycle tyre are likely to be objective, whereas an advertisement, a newspaper editorial or a politician's speech are likely to be subjective. A text's purpose is what will usually denote how objective or subjective a text is.

ACTIVITY 2

Here are six different text types with different purposes. Order them from 1 to 6 in terms of which you would expect to be the most objective (neutral, unbiased, impartial) to the most subjective (personal, biased, partial). When you have ordered the texts, compare your responses to those at the end of the book.

■ Table 0.1.2

Text type	Purpose	1 = extremely objective 6 = extremely subjective
Newspaper article	to report	
Restaurant review	to review	
Letter of application to university or for a job	to demonstrate your interest in and suitability for the course or job	
Propaganda poster	to persuade	
Set of safety regulations on an aeroplane	to inform	
Advice column in a magazine	to advise	

You may have found this activity problematic and your answers may have differed from the ones suggested at the back of the book. This is quite usual. Until we closely read a text or a body of work, we cannot always make assumptions about the objectivity of the writer. This, then, is one of the reasons why we need to hold a magnifying glass up to a text in order to deconstruct or unpick how the text has been put together and why. Being non-fiction and, therefore, about the real world in which we live, non-literary texts (similar to prose non-fiction works) have the potential to shape and change public opinion about real-life issues. It is important, then, to understand to what degree we may be being manipulated by a writer's personal views and to what degree we are being given a more objective viewpoint. Of course, sometimes, a text's purpose and meaning is obvious – this is what **explicit** means when we study texts. But sometimes, a text's purpose and meaning may be hidden and we have to work harder at unpicking the language of a text to find this hidden meaning – this is what **implicit** means when we study texts. In order to access the higher levels in this course, you will need to be able to show an understanding of a text's or a body of work's implicit meaning as well as explicit meaning.

The nature of the literary work

Although a literary work may be based on personal experience or real-life events (prose non-fiction), many literary works are fiction. Fiction is something that is imaginary and invented by the writer. Prose fiction is always fiction, drama is usually (almost always) fiction and while we do not classify poetry as fiction or non-fiction, its form of meter, rhyme and stanzas make it a symbolic rather than a literal representation of the truth. Some prose non-fiction, whilst being based on real-life experiences, uses a range of literary devices to engage the reader and shape the reader's understanding of the text's ideas that allow it to be characterized as a literary work.

Another common feature of a literary work is its purpose. Writers of literature use their imagination to entertain the reader. We are entertained two-fold: emotionally and also intellectually. Writers of literary works attempt to transport us, the reader, into a different reality, time or place, populated by often fictional characters or magical creatures, who are undertaking journeys or facing experiences that may be either similar or very different to our own. In order to appreciate these different realities, we need to believe in them while we are reading prose or poetry or watching drama. When English Romantic poet, Samuel Taylor Coleridge, explained the original intention behind *Lyrical Ballads, with a Few Other Poems*, a poetry anthology he co-wrote with William Wordsworth in 1789 which is now considered the seminal text that kick-started the English Romantic period, he coined the phrase 'willing suspension of disbelief' to describe this leap of faith a reader needs to take if a literary text is to be successful.

> *In this idea originated the plan of the 'Lyrical Ballads'; in which it was agreed, that my endeavours should be directed to persons and characters supernatural, or at least romantic, yet so as to transfer from our inward nature a human interest and a semblance of truth sufficient to procure for these shadows of imagination that willing suspension of disbelief for the moment, which constitutes poetic faith.*
>
> *(Samuel Taylor Coleridge, Chapter XIV)*

No matter how imaginative the work is or how removed from reality it is, the reader needs to believe in the work's reality when reading it. One of the tools a writer of literature uses to help us suspend our disbelief is language and as students of language and literature you will be investigating the ways writers use language to appeal to the reader and encourage a 'willing suspension of disbelief'.

Unlike non-literary texts which consist of a very wide range of text types, there are only four literary forms that you will be exploring on this course: drama, poetry, prose non-fiction and prose fiction. However, within each literary form, there is a range of different **genres**. For example, science fiction, gothic fiction, magical realism, science fiction and social satire are all types of prose fiction; comedy, history and tragedy are different types of drama; chivalric epic, lyric, mock heroic and narrative are different types of poetry; and, as we have already discussed, biographies, essays, letters and memoirs can all be types of prose non-fiction. We will be exploring the wide range of genres throughout this coursebook.

The toolbox of a writer

Because writers of literature are not necessarily bound by facts or keeping within the narrow parameters of what actually happened, this means that they can use their imagination and be creative in their construction of these literary works. The way a writer of literary works is creative is first and foremost through the language he or she uses to construct a text. A literary writer's toolbox, then, is full of literary features that are constructed primarily through language. Some of these literary features include the skilful use of:

- languag
- literary ... n, **imagery**
- phonolo ... hrases, including **alliteration**, **assonan**
- structur ... t and/or in a sentence and the type of v

We will be e ... oursebook and examining how these featur ... f a text's ideas.

Although n ... fically *literary* features, a writer of a n ... *terary* features that are equally important i ... features may include:

- photogr
- the use c
- organiza ... images have been organized on the page
- **typographical** features (size and type of font)
- other symbols including arrows, numbers and boxes as well as online features such as hyperlinks, emojis and emoticons.

In a similar way to our exploration of literary works, we will also be exploring the wide range of non-literary features throughout this coursebook and examining how they are used to affect a text's meaning and a reader's interpretation of a text's ideas.

Just as there is a range of different literary genres, as you saw from Table 0.1.1 there are also numerous non-literary text types and each text type has its own set of conventions. Throughout this coursebook, we will be identifying and exploring the conventions of different text types and the Key features boxes that are included within many chapters are a good resource to refer to as you begin to familiarize yourself with a wide range of non-literary text types.

Works cited

'1607. A true report of certaine wonderfull ouerflo shire, Norfolke, and other places of England d and children, ouerthrowing and bearing dow infinite numbers of sheepe and other cattle.' E 2019. **https://quod.lib.umich.edu/cgi/t/text/pa 596.0001.001;node=A12596.0001.001:2;seq= aJjiQK2CuKj5ifF83AnbyhT435ui1EdIUV2wRSu**

'Blank Verse.' *Ohio River – New World Encyclope* **www.newworldencyclopedia.org/entry/Blan**

Bloom, R. 'Lost in Translation: What the First Li 19 June 2017. Web. 25 Jan. 2019. **www.new what-the-first-line-of-the-stranger-should-b**

Branagh, K. (dir.) ***Hamlet***. Warner Home Video,

Bryson, B. ***In a Sunburned Country***. Broadway Books, 2001.

Camus, A. ***The Stranger***. Translated by M Ward, Knopf, 1993.

Bechdel, A. *Fun Home: A Family Tragicomic*. Jonathan Cape, 2006.

Chimombo, M, Roseberry, RL. *The Power of Discourse: An Introduction Analysis*. Routledge, 1998.

Coleridge, ST. Biographia literaria (1817) Chapter XIV. Web. 2 Feb. 2019. **www.english.upenn.edu/~mgamer/Etexts/biographia.html.**

Eliot, G. *Middlemarch.* Project Gutenberg, 14 May 2008. Web. 5 May 2019. **www.gutenberg.org/files/145/145-h/145-h.htm**.

Eliot, TS. 'The Waste Land.' *Poetry Foundation*. Web. 24 Jan. 2019. **www.poetryfoundation.org/poems/47311/the-waste-land**.

France, AK. *Boris Pasternak's Translations of Shakespeare*. University of California Press, 1978.

Frost, R. 'Nothing Gold Can Stay.' *Poets.org*, Academy of American Poets. Web. 27 Aug. 2019. **https://poets.org/poem/nothing-gold-can-stay**.

Glanz, J. 'Letter May Solve Nazi A-Bomb Mystery.' *The New York Times*, New York Times, 7 Jan. 2002. Web. 25 Jan. 2019. **www.nytimes.com/2002/01/07/us/letter-may-solve-nazi-a-bomb-mystery.html**.

'Hymn 2 to Demeter.' Edited by Hugh G. Evelyn-White, Hymn 2 to Demeter, Tufts University. Web. 24 Jan. 2019. **www.perseus.tufts.edu/hopper/text?doc=Perseus:text:1999.01.0138:hymn=2:card=1**.

Holder, S. 'Why the Amazon is on Fire.' Citylab, 22 Aug. 2019. Web. 12 Oct. 2019. www.citylab.com/environment/2019/08/amazon-rainforest-fire-map-burning-bolsonaro-deforestation-map/596605.

International Baccalaureate Organization. *Language A: Language and Literature Guide First Assessment 2021*. International Baccalaureate, 2019.

Klein, TM. *The Punch Escrow*. Inkshares, Inc., 2017.

'List of Natural Disasters in the British Isles.' *Wikipedia*, Wikimedia Foundation, 12 Aug. 2019. Web. 27 Aug. 2019. **https://en.wikipedia.org/wiki/List_of_natural_disasters_in_the_British_Isles**.

Mabillard, A. 'Sources for Romeo and Juliet.' *Shakespeare Online*, 21 Nov. 2009. Web. 24 Jan. 2019. **www.shakespeare-online.com/sources/romeosources.html**.

'NIH Fact Sheets – Post-Traumatic Stress Disorder (PTSD).' *National Institutes of Health*, U.S. Department of Health and Human Services. Web. 27 Aug. 2019. **https://report.nih.gov/nihfactsheets/ViewFactSheet.aspx?csid=58**.

Shakespeare, W. *Henry IV Part I*. Edited by Barbara Mowat, Paul Werstine, Michael Poston and Rebecca Niles, Folger Shakespeare Library. Web. 27 Aug. 2019. **www.folgerdigitaltexts.org**.

Shakespeare, W. 'Sonnet XLIV.' *Shakespeare's Sonnets*. Web. 6 Oct. 2019. **http://www.shakespeares-sonnets.com/sonnet/44**.

Shakespeare, W. *Hamlet*. Open Source Shakespeare. Web. 24 Jan. 2019. **www.opensourceshakespeare.org/views/plays/play_view.php?WorkID=hamlet&Scope=entire&pleasewait=1&msg=pl#a5,s2**.

Shay, J. *Achilles in Vietnam Combat Trauma and the Undoing of Character*. Scribner, 2003.

Sophocles. 'Oedipus the King.' Translated by F Storr, Project Gutenberg..7 March 2006. Web. 6 Oct. 2019. **http://www.gutenberg.org/files/31/31-h/31-h.htm**.

Spitzer, DR. 'What Is a Concept?' *Educational Technology*, vol. 15, no. 7, ser. 1975, pp.36–39. Web. 5 May 2019. **www.jstor.org/stable/44418021**.

Swift, J. *Gullivers Travels*, Dover Publications, 1996.

'Timeline of Shakespeare's Plays.' *Royal Shakespeare Company*, Royal Shakespeare Company. Web. 27 Aug. 2019. **www.rsc.org.uk/shakespeares-plays/timeline**.

Various Artists, *Music From Baz Luhrmann's Film The Great Gatsby*. Water Tower Music/Interscope, 2013.

Visual Journalism Team. 'No-deal Brexit: 10 Ways It Could Affect You.' *BBC News*, BBC, 1 Aug. 2019. Web. 27 Aug. 2019. **www.bbc.com/news/uk-politics-47470864**.

Wordsworth, W, Coleridge, ST. Lyrical Ballads, with a Few Other Poems. Printed for J & A Arch, Gracechurch-Street, 1798.

Readers, writers and texts

1.1 Why and how do we study language and literature?

OBJECTIVES OF CHAPTER

- To provide an overview of why we study language and literature.
- To provide an overview of how we study literary works.
- To provide an overview of how we study non-literary texts.
- To demonstrate ways to apply course concepts to specific works and texts.

This section focuses on the close reading of a wide range of literary works and non-literary texts and examines them from the perspective of the **immanent**. This means we will be exploring each text as an independent entity, without overly concerning ourselves with the time or place within which the text was produced or their relationship to other texts. Because we may at some points in the course be studying texts in isolation, when preparing for paper 1 mainly, we will be focusing primarily on how a text has been constructed by a writer and how a reader may interpret the text. We will be holding a magnifying glass up to each text in our attempt to identify and analyse the wide range of features each writer uses. This close reading of each text should then help us in our interpretation of each text's meaning. However, be aware that we may not come up with a definitive interpretation of the text or even the same interpretation as the writer intended. Because each reader is different with his or her own unique experiences, interests, values and beliefs it is likely that each reader may have a slightly different interpretation to a single text. This is fine, as long as we are able to explain our own interpretation based on evidence from the text – based on what is there. You will find in this chapter some detailed analyses of texts and you will also be expected to write your own in-depth analyses. It is through analysis that you are able to show your understanding of how a writer has consciously constructed a text but also show your understanding of a text's ideas and how it affects you as the reader.

The relationship between the writer, the reader and the text

Every text is written by a writer who has a reader in mind. This reader is the **implied reader** and they may not be you! One of the things you will be attempting to do in this section is working out who that implied reader may be and how they may be different to you. In the Introduction, the relationship between the writer, the reader and the text was explained and there was a simple but useful diagram that visually explains this relationship (see page 29). The writer is attempting to communicate with the reader through the text and the reader is attempting to understand the writer's message through the text. There is obviously no direct face-to-face communication between the writer and the reader; rather, the text is the communicative act. When constructing the text, it is up to the writer to communicate his or her message in a particular way that enhances the text's meaning. Once the text has been published and is out in the world to be consumed by the public, it is then the reader's responsibility to interpret the text and construct his/her own message in a particular way. You may have experienced a time when you did not fully comprehend someone who was speaking to you face-to-face – a friend, a teacher or a parent, perhaps. However, in this situation you are quite clearly able to ask that person to clarify exactly what they meant and to clear up any potential misunderstandings. Just as there is the potential for two speakers to misunderstand one another at times, there is obviously a much greater potential for a reader to misunderstand a writer's intention in a text. Because a reader is often unable to ask the writer directly to clarify a particular point, the reader of a text has to work out independently what the writer meant. Sometimes a reader can do this individually, but sometimes discussing a text with other people is a really important process in trying to understand a text's meaning and be aware of alternative viewpoints. This is one of the reasons why your English language and literature classes are so important: you should take full advantage of being in a class with other people and discussing the various ways a text can be interpreted. As we have already stated, a single text or body of work may have multiple interpretations and this is fine as long as you are able to support your ideas with evidence from the text.

Remember, also, that you may never fully understand what the writer's own ideas, values or beliefs are. Writers of both literary works and non-literary texts often create a **narrative persona** who may or may not represent the writer's own set of beliefs. For example, prose fiction and poetry can be written in the first person, but this does not necessarily mean that the first-person narrator of the work is the writer or indeed that the narrative persona's views and attitudes correlate with the writer's views and attitudes. Researching a writer's background, reading interviews with a writer and reading more texts by the writer may give you a fuller insight into the writer's own beliefs and values. However, you should remember that a literary work is a conscious construction and a writer's intention is for you as the reader to suspend your disbelief and just believe in the reality created, rather than necessarily getting an insight into the writer's personal reality. Likewise with both prose non-fiction and non-literary texts, a writer may have to create an **implied writer** due to being unable to share his or her real-life views with the reader as there may be other factors that restrict how a writer writes. For example, a journalist who writes for a particular newspaper may have to report in a way that reaffirms the owner's or readers, or, sometimes, the government's political stance rather than his or her own political stance; a journalist interviewing a celebrity for a magazine is likely to have to write a positive review to appeal to the celebrity's fans, irrespective of the writer's own personal views; a writer constructing an advertisement has a job to do – to sell a product through persuasive means, whether they believe in the product's worth or not. The skill of the writer is, of course, to make the reader believe in the reality created – all the more so as writers of non-literary texts are supposed to be reflecting the real world. This can get complicated! But this is the joy of using that magnifying glass on a text to deconstruct it and then sharing your ideas with others and listening to alternative interpretations. Just as you should never judge a book by its cover, you should never judge a text by its appearance. You need to read, analyse and discuss, and then you can start to understand and appreciate a text's meaning.

By the end of this section, you should feel more confident at closely analysing both literary and non-literary texts and at understanding how there can be more than one interpretation to any given text which may or may not reflect the writer's original intention. Many people would argue that a writer's toolkit is infinite and in this section we will be identifying and closely analysing a wide range of literary and non-literary features a writer may use in his or her attempt to heighten a text's meaning. We will be exploring texts through two reading strategies: a literary reading strategy and a non-literary reading strategy. These reading strategies can be applied to a wide range of both literary works and non-literary texts, particularly when studying texts using an immanent approach. These strategies should be especially helpful as you prepare for Paper 1.

You will find that this section contains a lot more close analysis than the other two sections and this is because we are primarily focusing on the text itself rather than exploring external factors that may affect a text's production and reception. The six guiding concept questions that we are exploring in this section introduce you to the various ways in which we can analyse and interpret texts. The skills and approaches you learn in this section can be applied to other literary and non-literary texts that you study in the other two sections of this coursebook as well as to the range of texts you will be exploring in your language and literature lessons.

Why do we study language and literature?

There is no one simple answer to the question of why we study language and literature; rather, we study language and literature for many reasons and these reasons may differ depending on the individual reader and depending on the text being read. However, we are going to attempt to break this question down into four key areas – we study language and literature:

- to gain an understanding of the self and our connection to others
- to gain an understanding of other cultures, other perspectives and other world views
- to gain an informed understanding of our changing world – now and in the past
- to appreciate the aesthetics of a text; for pleasure and enjoyment.

Gaining an understanding of the self and our connection to others

Language and literature often reminds us that we are not isolated individuals but that we are a part of the human race and we share humanity. This shared humanity can be referred to as the human condition and many literary and non-literary texts explore this idea. The English metaphysical poet, John Donne, expressed this idea well in his poem, *Devotions Upon Emergent Occasions and Seuerall Steps in my Sicknes – Meditation XVII* (1624). He used the metaphor of an island to suggest the importance of understanding ourselves as part of the human race if we are to thrive:

> No man is an Island, entire of itself;
> every man is a piece of the Continent,
> a part of the main.
>
> *(John Donne)*

These are very famous lines and even today, nearly 400 years later, 'no man is an island' has become a proverb, warning about the dangers of becoming too insular and inward-looking. Studying literary works and non-literary texts remind us of this and encourage us to look outwards and embrace others.

We are going to explore this idea through a poem that was published in 1994 called 'Perhaps the World Ends Here' by American Creek Indian, Joy Harjo. As you are reading this poem, what reoccurring everyday image is repeated throughout? When you have read the poem, read the commentary that follows.

Perhaps the World Ends Here

The world begins at a kitchen table. No matter what, we must eat to live.

The gifts of earth are brought and prepared, set on the table. So it has been
since creation, and it will go on.

We chase chickens or dogs away from it. Babies teethe at the corners.
They scrape their knees under it.

It is here that children are given instructions on what it means to be human.
We make men at it, we make women.

At this table we gossip, recall enemies and the ghosts of lovers.

Our dreams drink coffee with us as they put their arms around our children.
They laugh with us at our poor falling-down selves and as we put ourselves
back together once again at the table.

This table has been a house in the rain, an umbrella in the sun.

Wars have begun and ended at this table. It is a place to hide in the shadow
of terror. A place to celebrate the terrible victory.

We have given birth on this table, and have prepared our parents for burial here.

At this table we sing with joy, with sorrow. We pray of suffering and remorse.
We give thanks.

Perhaps the world will end at the kitchen table, while we are laughing and
crying, eating of the last sweet bite.

(Joy Harjo)

It is likely you will have recognised that the reoccurring image in this poem is an everyday kitchen table. Joy Harjo, a member of the Muscogee (Creek) Nation and a prominent writer in what is referred to as the literary Native American Renaissance, shows how literature can encourage us to transcend cultural differences and see the individual in a more universal and connected way.

She uses a simple and commonplace object – a kitchen table – which is instantly recognizable to readers of different cultural backgrounds and ages as an **extended metaphor** for our commonality: our shared humanity, set of preoccupations, hopes, fears and life experiences. Just as she literally starts the poem with 'The world begins at the kitchen table' and ends the poem with 'Perhaps the world will end at the kitchen table', she is also suggesting that life itself begins and ends there. The kitchen table, then, becomes life – something that connects us all no matter who we are or how old we are. She argues how the kitchen table represents the birth of new generations and the end of older generations (line 15). We see the elemental need for food (lines 1–2) and shelter (line 12), coupled with life described in all its facets, through the kitchen table. The small everyday things such as chasing chickens and dogs away (line 4) are done around the kitchen table, as are the big things in life such as giving children 'instructions on what it means to be human', creating men and women (lines 6–7). Sharing light-hearted moments, supporting each other when times are hard, experiencing both terror and victory are all experienced around the kitchen table. Harjo avoids figurative language which is culturally specific in the poem to emphasize her idea that ultimately wherever we are from we share a core humanity.

There is also a timelessness about the poem to emphasize this idea of universality – we are never told when the poem is set and there are no time markers to give us clues. Thus we can apply it to whatever time best suits us. The poem does not follow a rhyme scheme, regular meter or make use of regular stanzas. There is no obvious pattern. The only thing that appears to be consistent is the table that is anchored in the poem: both beginning and ending the poem and referred to in every line. The table, then, appears to transcend the unpredictability and irregularities of the poem itself – and perhaps life itself – and comes to represent the one constant which literally links each stanza and, metaphorically, links each of us reading the poem. This, then, allows us to understand ourselves better and be appreciative, perhaps, of the everyday items that are part of our lives.

Joy Harjo

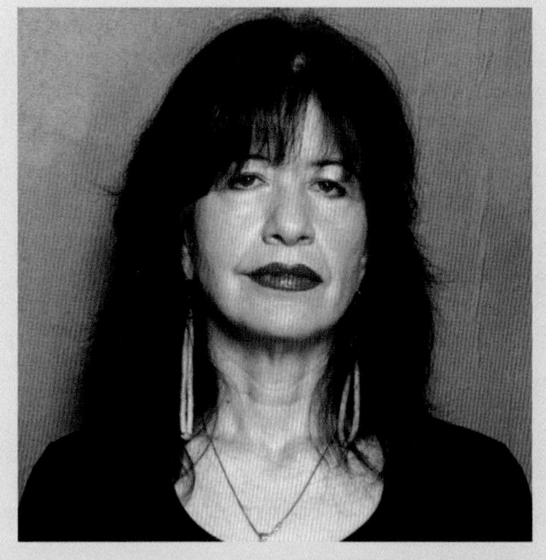

Joy Harjo, born Joy Foster, was born in Tulsa, Oklahoma, in 1951 and is a member of the Muscogee (Creek) Nation. She is an author, poet and musician and is an important figure in the second wave of the literary Native American Renaissance in the late-twentieth century. She has published several books of poetry and has won a number of awards, including the William Carlos Williams Award from the Poetry Society of America, the Lifetime Achievement Award from the Native Writers' Circle of the Americas and the PEN/Beyond Margins Award. She has also released highly acclaimed CDs of original music and in 2009 won a Native American Music Award (NAMMY) for Best Female Artist of the Year. Themes of Harjo's work include social justice, self and the arts.

To gain an understanding of other cultures, other perspectives and other world views

Non-literary texts can also do the same. While Harjo's poem embraces the universality of the human condition through the reoccurring image of the kitchen table, and thus allows us to better understand ourselves and our connection to others, we also study language and literature to gain an understanding of difference. Let us now explore this idea.

As well as giving us an insight into our own selves and our connection to others, we also read texts to understand other cultures, other perspectives and other world views. It is all too easy to think that our understanding of the world and way of looking at the world is the right one or even the only one. Of course this is not true! Studying texts can also give us an insight into the myriad of ways other people live their lives and view the world. This encourages us to look outside of ourselves, have an awareness that there are multiple perspectives different to our own and be aware of the significance of others.

The next text we are going to explore is a non-literary text, a satirical cartoon titled 'What's "Handwriting?"' by Canadian illustrator, Steve Nease. Satirical cartoons often give us an alternative view of a topical event which encourages us to reflect on the subject under scrutiny and perhaps change our perspective accordingly. Although non-literary texts may include literary features common to literary works, non-literary text types also have a particular set of key features or characteristics which a writer may conform to or deviate from. Although the IB emphasizes that you are not expected to learn the features or characteristics of every text type as the skills needed to analyse one text type are transferable to another text type (International Baccalaureate Organization 21), we have included key features boxes for some of the more common text types. Before we explore Nease's satirical cartoon, read the first of your key features boxes which summarises the main conventions of this particular text type. Remember that definitions for the words bolded in purple can be found in the Glossary at the back of the book.

KEY FEATURES SATIRICAL CARTOONS

- Employ humour – usually through exaggeration and/or **irony** and/or **satire** to mock an individual, institution or ideology.
- **Multimodal** texts – usually they use both **visual images** and written text. The visual images reinforce the written text and vice versa.
- Written text may include **captions, display lettering** and **word balloons**.
- Visual images may include **spatial mechanics, temporal mechanics, colour** and **shape** for effect.
- Focus on a topic that is **newsworthy** – a topic that is current and relevant to readers when the text is first published.
- Are dependent upon readers' knowledge of the event, individual, institution or ideology that is being mocked/satirized.
- Through humour, a serious point is made.

This is a **multimodal** text that uses a combination of **visual images** and written text to satirize different generational outlooks through the subject of handwriting. Structurally, it gives equal importance to both characters. **Spatial mechanics** are used in such a way that half of the panel is taken up with the image of the older man reading his newspaper and the other half of the panel is taken up with the younger man asking his question. This structural technique means that the reader has to decide which character's perspective is the most valid (see the concept connection box on perspective and communication for a discussion on this). The way in which the reader responds to this satirical cartoon reveals a lot about his or her values. It is perhaps how we respond to these stereotypes that shapes how we interpret the image and ultimately reveals something about ourselves and the judgements we make about other people. Although they take up an equal amount of space in the panel, the two characters are **juxtaposed** through both the visual images used to depict them and the type of written text that is applied to each of them.

Visual images are used to depict the man on the right of the panel, for example, wearing clothes associated with the younger generation - a hoodie and trousers that reveal his underwear. He is also holding a mobile phone. The **word balloon** makes it clear that he is actively speaking, asking the other man a question about the **headline** of the newspaper the older man is reading. We may feel that the young man in the cartoon with his style of dress, mobile phone in hand and questioning **tone** represents the idea of the 'ignorance of the youth' - his question in the **word balloon** astonishing us in much the same way as it affects the older man. In contrast, **visual images** are used to depict the man on the left wearing clothes stereotypically associated with the older generation - shirt-tucked-into-trousers and wearing glasses. He is reading the news from a more traditional mode of communication: a printed newspaper. He is not actively speaking but is reading, made obvious through the visual image of the newspaper as well as the **display lettering** on the back page of the newspaper. We may instinctively feel that the older man, visually depicted in this way, represents an older, wiser, more literate and better informed generation. In contrast, the younger man, whose hair covers his eyes, receives his information about the world on the tiny screen of his mobile device.

We could, however, look beyond this stereotype and consider that the young man's question is a valid and important one. Through both the visual images and the written text, we can observe that the older man receives his information about the world in a static way. **Proxemics** are used to depict him sitting down, rooted in a chair. He is passive, reading someone else's words in the newspaper and not actively communicating with the younger man. His view of what is going on in the world is to a large extent literally and symbolically obscured by the large newspaper. In contrast, the younger man is standing over the older man, able to look beyond his phone to read the newspaper headline and then actively question what has been written. We may feel that the younger man represents a curiosity about the world, willing to question values or ideologies of the past in order to make sense of the world around him at that moment. The older man, however, appears content with the way of the world and has no desire to question the values or attitudes of the past which, perhaps, are outdated and outmoded. This idea is accentuated through the use of the display lettering which depicts the newspaper's back page headline 'National Handwriting Day'. This can be interpreted as **irony** because the medium through which the older man reads about the world – and in this instance about National Handwriting Day – is not handwritten but makes use of the typed word. This, then, validates the young man's question in the word balloon. The fact that the headline is on the back page also suggests, perhaps, how outdated the concept of handwriting is. This would have had an additional impact on readers when it was first published in 2014, as it was published on National Handwriting Day of that year (23 January). This would have made the cartoon **newsworthy**, raising questions about the relevance of this particular day but also, of course, encouraging readers to question the validity of other traditional values and attitudes in an ever-changing world.

The combination of **spatial mechanics**, **visual imagery**, spoken words in a **word balloon** and written words in the **display lettering** combine to suggest that the younger man could symbolize how, while the older man sits in his chair, the world is changing.

This then helps us understand the other better. Neither individual is perfect and depending who we naturally gravitate towards should encourage us to laugh at ourselves, become aware of how flawed or ridiculous our perspective may be and how there are other perspectives and world views that are just as valid as our own and from which we can learn, particularly from other

CONCEPT CONNECTION

PERSPECTIVE AND COMMUNICATION

This is an interesting satirical cartoon as it seems initially to have multiple perspectives: the father's, the son's, the writer's and ours. However, because both the father and the son are being mocked to a certain extent, we are never sure which perspective the writer shares. This, then, affects how the reader responds to the text: whose perspective are we supposed to share? It is not clear and therefore the reader will have to decide independently, and it is likely that his or her decision will be based on their own background and first-hand experience of social media.

Moreover, as the commentary above shows, when we start deconstructing this text, we may feel that the writer, through **satire**, is actually making a serious point that transcends handwriting: that the world is changing at a fast pace and soon things we take for granted (like handwriting) will become redundant. This challenges the reader to look at their own perspective and that of others. This kind of an impact that texts can have on the individual in shaping or changing their perspective of the world is powerful and can be the instigating factor for changing attitudes and beliefs.

Handwriting is also a form of communication and, as we have explored, the text seems to be suggesting that this form of communication is redundant with both the younger generation, symbolized through the young man's question and his mobile device, and the older generation, symbolized through the older man reading a typed mode of communication, a newspaper. However, what about the text itself and how it has been created? It would appear the satirical cartoon itself seems to have been created by hand rather than being computer generated and the words in the word balloon seem to be handwritten rather than typed. This perhaps suggests that the cartoonist himself still views handwriting as a valuable mode of communication, which encourages us to reflect on where we stand on the importance of handwriting as a mode of communication.

generations. It is also interesting to think about the writer's perspective. This is a good example of how difficult it can be to have a definitive understanding of the writer's own viewpoint. Which side of the debate is he on? And what perspective is he encouraging us to take?

EE Links: English A – Language category 3

Satirical cartoons would make a good text type to analyse for an English A: Language category 3 extended essay. You would need to select a body of work of satirical cartoons, rather than just one or two. You could either study multiple satirical cartoons by the same author or you could study multiple satirical cartoons by different authors on the same subject. Some areas of research that you could consider include:

- **How does one particular satirical cartoonist either conform to or deviate from the typical conventions of satirical cartoons and to what effect?**
- **How do different satirical cartoonists use the genre of the satirical cartoon to offer alternative perspectives on the same subject?**

Remember you would need to include awareness of the key features of the text type, embed relevant terminology throughout and research your topic thoroughly in order to include a wide range of secondary sources. You are also highly recommended to make interconnections between the satirical cartoons you choose to study, rather than commenting on them as stand-alone texts.

The next two extracts are transcripts from two speeches from world leaders – Donald Trump and Jacinda Ardern – that were given at the United Nations General Assembly in September 2018 which also offer alternative perspectives on the same subject. Read the following extracts and then answer the questions that follow.

■ Table 1.1.1

DONALD TRUMP, President of the United States of America	JACINDA ARDERN, New Zealand Prime Minister
'America is governed by Americans. We reject the ideology of globalism and we embrace the doctrine of patriotism … We withdrew from the Human Rights Council and we will not return until real reform is enacted. For similar reasons the United States will provide no support and recognition for the International Criminal Court. As far as America is concerned, the ICC has no jurisdiction, no legitimacy and no authority … The United States is the world's largest giver in the world by far of foreign aid but few give anything to us … Thank you, God bless you and God bless the nations of the world.'	*'If I could distil it down into one concept that we are pursuing in New Zealand, it is simple and it is this: kindness … In the face of isolationism, protectionism, racism, the simple concept of looking outwardly beyond ourselves, of kindness and collectivism might just be as good a starting point as any. So let's start here with the institutions that have served us well in times of need and will do so again … New Zealand remains committed to doing our part, to building and sustaining international peace and security, to promoting and defending an open, inclusive and rules-based international order based on universal values, to being pragmatic, empathetic, strong and kind … Tena koutou, tena koutou, tena tatou katoa.'*

ACTIVITY 1

Each speaker clearly has a different world view. Respond to the following prompts and questions and then compare your answers with those at the back of the book.

1. Sum up each world view.
2. Which speaker do you agree with and why?
3. Why do you think two individuals in a similar position of power, one president and one prime minister, can have such diverse world views?
4. How are these transcripts different from and similar to satirical cartoons?

What is important here is that both speakers, with their very different world views, had their voices heard and by being aware that there are such diversities in the way individuals view the world, encourages us to reflect on our own world view and be aware that ours is not the only way the world is understood.

You should have a good understanding now, from the texts we have read, of how to gain an understanding of 'the other', whether that is a different culture, perspective or world view.

Let us now explore another reason why we study language and literature: to be informed about the world in which we live – both our world in the past and our world now.

To be informed about the world – now and in the past

To explore this idea, we are going to look at two texts in translation: an extract from twentieth-century Chinese travel writer, Pei Zhao, and a letter from Pliny the Younger, Ancient Roman lawyer, magistrate and politician, originally written in Latin in 79AD. The first extract we are going to explore is taken from an article called 'Water Town' which was originally published in the Winter 1986 edition of a Chinese literature quarterly magazine and then published in a selection of Chinese travel writing called *Yangtze River: The Wildest, Wickedest River on Earth*. This article was originally written in Chinese and translated by Song Shouquan. In this extract, Zhao is describing a village on the banks of the River Yangtze in China. Read the following extract and the commentary that follows.

> If the water is not polluted with filthy waste from factories, there will be frogs to be found lying on emerald duckweed, croaking at the ripples …
>
> Few of the channels can be dated. The locust, plane and sponge trees twisting out of the crevices in the river bank have grown two arm-spans round, and houses scattered here and there are advanced in years, some like hump-backs, others with knotty arms of distorted features. When a black-canopied boat in full sail slides through the shadowy channels, it seems to be a winged cherub who will carry you to the remote future. But for the television aerials glittering in the sunshine like the wings of dragonflies and the sweet music floating from records in flower-decked rooms, you would think it a deserted corner forgotten by the world …
>
> Under the quays there are always women with their trousers rolled up standing in the water washing rice and vegetables. Peasants' motorboats loaded with fragrant, sweet watermelons, musk-melons and thin-skinned, juicy peaches pass by. The peasants on deck, their heads held high and chests thrown out, look around smugly. They seem to hold not the engine bar but the lever of the times. The boats swish past like helicopters in flight …
>
> At the end of every bridge is usually a teahouse dignified with the name of 'The Moon-reaching Tower', 'The Star-plucking Pavilion' or 'The Orchid-viewing Hall'. In reality it is nothing but an ordinary stilt house, on whose roof yowling cats in heat scurry about. When it rains, fine raindrops from outside glimmer in the hazy smoke. Townsfolk who are tea addicts reck* little of the structural condition of the teahouse. Some, backs hunched, creep in before daybreak jabbering like garrulous old women and bustle around the smoke-blackened stove to help the staff do this and that. By the time the burning husks in the stove give off a greenish flame and the water in the pots on top is bubbling, there is no unoccupied seat in the L-shaped building, and the white steam impregnated with the fragrance of tea spreads throughout the ill-lit house …

The teahouse is very busy with many people going in and out. Women from the countryside bring baskets or trays of sunflower seeds or fried food to sell here. A quack doctor is making wild boasts about his skills and at the same time soliciting buyers for his sham tiger bones. In fact they are bones of an ox browned by smoke. Occasionally some girls from a cultural centre come here with their faces rouged red as strawberries and florid aprons round their waists and sing a song about the scenery around Lake Tai then perform an excerpt from a local opera before giving a slide show on changes in the countryside. At these times the whole teahouse is so quiet that even the moaning of a fly entangled in a spider's web can be heard.

***reck** *– archaic verb that means to pay heed to something*

(Pei Zhao 62–63)

What do we learn about this particular culture in the first four paragraphs?

In the extract we see a culture in the throes of change. The traditional way of life is slowly being lost to a more consumerist and modern way of life. This is a society whose lifestyle depends upon the river – the Yangtze – and we can see how industrialization symbolized by the 'filthy waste from the factories' (line 1) is contaminating this essential part of the peasants' world. The **adjective** 'emerald' (line 2) is used to describe the duckweed which suggests how valuable this natural water world is for those who live there.

How do we learn about this cultural change?

The idea that the rural world is being replaced by new technology is also highlighted through the **imagery** the writer uses. The natural world is described as having 'grown two arm-spans round' (line 4) and the traditional houses are described as being 'advanced in years, some like hump-backs, others with knotty arms of distorted features' (lines 4–5). **Personification** is used here to compare this ancient traditional world to the human world – suggesting, perhaps, a harmony between both worlds. In contrast, the new world which is taking over is compared to the natural world: 'television aerials glittering in the sunshine like the wings of dragonflies' (line 7). This **simile** suggests how the new world of technology is replacing and taking over the traditional world – but there is a beauty to the simile so perhaps the writer is suggesting that this is a natural process that needs to be embraced and accepted. The **metaphor** that describes how the peasants 'seem to hold not the engine bar but the lever of the times' (line 13) further suggests that this is a traditional community in transition, and that the peasants themselves are in charge of their own destiny.

ACTIVITY 2

Write a commentary on the final paragraph of this extract, similar to the commentary above. Examine *what* we learn about the culture described and *how* we learn about cultural change.

When you have written your commentary, read the one at the back of the book and compare your ideas.

This text was written just over 30 years ago and it describes the changing landscape of the land and the river for the Chinese community who work and live there. For readers who are not from this part of the world, we read this text to gain an understanding of a different culture and to recognise that industrialisation and globalization affect people all around the world. For readers of all backgrounds, the descriptions of the 'black-canopied boat' (lines 5–6) and the teahouses and their customers give us a glimpse into the traditional cultural world before it has changed beyond recognition.

The next text we are going to explore is a much older text than the Chinese travel writing extract. It is a letter, translated from Latin, originally written in 79AD. Letters are a text that the IB states can be either non-literary or literary. We are going to explore this letter as literary (prose non-fiction) and, as we will discover, this is partly because of the time it was written. This text is a letter written by Pliny the Younger to his friend, Cornelius Tacitus, describing his first-hand experience of the destruction of Pompeii by the eruption of Mount Vesuvius on 24 August 79AD. Tacitus was a historian who had requested Pliny write to him detailing the account of his uncle's death during the eruption so that he could include it in his own historical work. Pliny the Younger wrote the original letters in Latin but we are going to be reading an extract in English, translated by Betty Radice in 1969.

You may be asking yourself why we still read texts that were written such a long time ago. The reason, of course, is to help us understand our past better and in this way perhaps understand our present better.

Read the following letter and the accompanying commentary:

The letter which, in compliance with your request, I wrote to you concerning the death of my uncle has raised, it seems, your curiosity to know what terrors and dangers attended me while I continued at Misenum; for there, I think, my account broke off:

Though my shocked soul recoils, my tongue shall tell.

Ashes were already falling, not as yet very thickly. I looked round: a dense black cloud was coming up behind us, spreading over the earth like a flood. 'Let us leave the road while we can still see,' I said, 'or we shall be knocked down and trampled underfoot in the dark by the crowd behind.' We had scarcely sat down to rest when darkness fell, not the dark of a moonless or cloudy night, but as if the lamp had been put out in a closed room.

You could hear the shrieks of women, the wailing of infants, and the shouting of men; some were calling their parents, others their children or their wives, trying to recognize them by their voices. People bewailed their own fate or that of their relatives, and there were some who prayed for death in their terror of dying. Many besought the aid of the gods, but still more imagined there were no gods left, and that the universe was plunged into eternal darkness for evermore.

There were people, too, who added to the real perils by inventing fictitious dangers: some reported that part of Misenum had collapsed or another part was on fire, and though their tales were false they found others to believe them. A gleam of light returned, but we took this to be a warning of the approaching flames rather than daylight. However, the flames remained some distance off; then darkness came on once more and ashes began to fall again, this time in heavy showers. We rose from time to time and shook them off, otherwise we should have been buried and crushed beneath their weight. I could boast that not a groan or cry of fear escaped me in these perils, but I admit that I derived some poor consolation in my mortal lot from the belief that the whole world was dying with me and I with it.

(Pliny the Younger, translated by Betty Radice, 166)

What do we learn about our past?

We learn about both the physical and the human worlds of the past. This letter is written from the first person perspective, includes direct dialogue, refers to religious beliefs at this time – 'the gods' – and mentions Misenum, the ancient name for the Italian town, Miseno, which gives us a clear insight into the past both from a physical and a human point of view. It is an eye-witness account of the eruption of Vesuvius in 79AD, which destroyed Pompeii and is considered one of the most catastrophic natural disasters in European history. These elements situate the letter in a historical time and place and certainly give the historian an insight into a period of time and a place that no longer exist.

The details within the letter are evidence of how this ancient civilization both *differed* and was *similar* to our own. In terms of our *differences*, Pliny documents this event solely through descriptive language rather than scientific language; there are no facts or statistics regarding the eruption - and this is the reason we can discuss this letter as a literary work rather than a non-literary text. Today, the Volcanic Explosivity Index allows us to measure accurately different elements of volcanic eruptions: how much volcanic material is ejected, the height of the material thrown into the atmosphere and how long the eruption lasts. Using this data, we can measure the relative explosiveness of volcanic eruptions. If this eruption of 79AD occurred today, it is likely it would be reported in a different way. If you scan the QR code on this page you can read a report on the Amazon rainforest fires of August 2019. Notice how in this report a range of non-literary devices are included, such as: verifiable statistics, interviews with experts in the field, maps, graphs, satellite images and so forth.

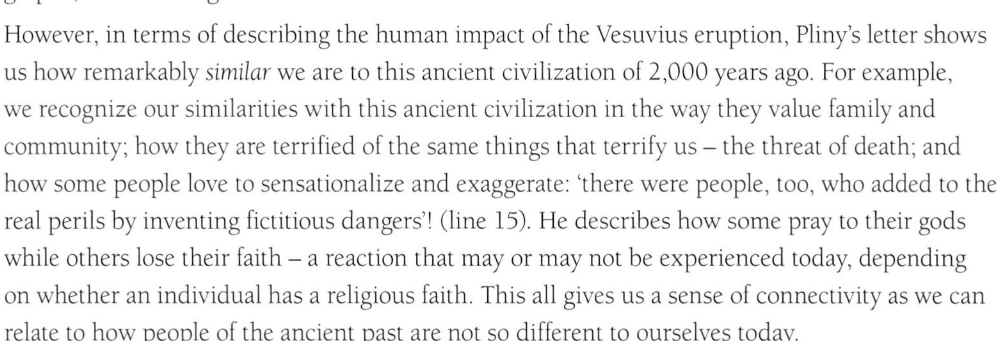

However, in terms of describing the human impact of the Vesuvius eruption, Pliny's letter shows us how remarkably *similar* we are to this ancient civilization of 2,000 years ago. For example, we recognize our similarities with this ancient civilization in the way they value family and community; how they are terrified of the same things that terrify us – the threat of death; and how some people love to sensationalize and exaggerate: 'there were people, too, who added to the real perils by inventing fictitious dangers'! (line 15). He describes how some pray to their gods while others lose their faith – a reaction that may or may not be experienced today, depending on whether an individual has a religious faith. This all gives us a sense of connectivity as we can relate to how people of the ancient past are not so different to ourselves today.

Thus, by reading a first-hand text from a different time and place, we are able to understand some of the ways civilization has changed and some of the ways we have remained the same. As well as giving us an insight into a past civilization, it also gives us a better understanding of ourselves – the ways in which we are connected to the past and the ways in which we are different.

Pliny the Younger

Gaius Plinius Caecilius Secundus, better known as Pliny the Younger, was a lawyer, politician and magistrate of Ancient Rome as well as an author. He was raised and educated by Pliny the Elder, a well-known author, philosopher, naval and army commander, who died trying to rescue people during the eruption of Vesuvius. Pliny the Younger wrote about this incident in a letter to his friend, the historian, Tacitus. He wrote hundreds of letters, including many to dignitaries. He published volumes of his letters, considered to be *litterae curiosius scriptae* (letters written with special care), during his lifetime. Popular themes of his letters include: social, literary, political and domestic current affairs relating to the Roman Empire.

How has Pliny given us an insight into this past world?

In terms of the language Pliny uses, rather than simply informing his friend about the volcanic eruption with **neutral language** and statistical facts, Pliny uses a range of literary devices to describe the eruption and encourage an emotional response. He uses the **simile** 'spreading over the earth like a flood' (line 7) to describe the cloud of ashes that is covering the town. This simile is appropriate because it is comparing one natural disaster with another natural disaster, and highlights how vulnerable the people are who are experiencing the eruption. Floods are generally more common than volcanic eruptions, so this simile helps Pliny's reader(s) in the past and now understand the chaos and fear that the eruption would have brought with it. Pliny also uses **tripling** to highlight how the eruption causes panic and terror throughout the whole community: 'You could hear the shrieks of women, the wailing of infants, and the shouting of men' (line 11). Pliny uses **onomatopoeia** here to echo the sounds and mimic the audible fear of the people which also helps transport us to a time and place 2,000 years ago and appreciate more fully the emotions experienced by these people. The **hyperbole**, 'the universe was plunged into eternal darkness for evermore' (line 15), accentuates the fear and vulnerability of the people, and the belief that the end of the world had come. This image has withstood the test of time – the fear that our world is being destroyed is a fear many people have today and has been used by environmental groups to persuade us to be more 'green' in our daily lives.

EE Links: English A – Literature category 2

An English A: Literature category 2 extended essay is a comparative study of two works. One work must be a work in translation and one must originally be written in the language studied (for English A students that means English). Pliny wrote many letters about life in Ancient Rome and as you can see from the extract we have just studied, his writing was descriptive and literary. You would need to explore a body of work by Pliny (10–15 letters) and comment on a number of his letters in your extended essay. There are many literary epistolary novels (novels written as a series of letters or other documents) that you could compare with Pliny's letters. Three famous epistolary novels include: Bram Stoker's *Dracula* (1897), Alice Walker's Pulitzer Prize-winning novel, *The Color Purple* (1982) and Aravind Adiga's Booker Prize-winning novel, *The White Tiger* (2008). However, there are many more. You could base a category 2 extended essay on a comparison of Pliny's letters (prose non-fiction) with an epistolary novel (prose fiction). Possible research questions could be:

- **To what extent does the letter-writer's purpose affect the tone and style of the letters?**
- **How and why does the reader respond to the letter-writer in a particular way?**
- **To what extent does the context within which the letters are written affect the content, diction and style used?**

Remember that this is a comparative extended essay, so you would need to make links – similarities and differences – between the two works. Remember, also, that one of the works chosen for study must be a text in translation.

To appreciate the aesthetics of a text for pleasure and enjoyment

Although we read language and literature to gain insights into the self, into other people's perspectives and into different times, we should never forget that texts are an artform and writers of texts use their imagination and creativity in their construction of a text. The following extract is from Arundhati Roy's Booker Prize-winning fictional novel, *The God of Small Things* (1997). This extract takes place when Rahel, one of the protagonists of the novel, enters a disused temple in her hometown of Ayemenem in Kerala, India, and watches a group of kathakali dancers perform shortly after they have performed to tourists. The excerpt clearly demonstrates one of the reasons why we read – to enjoy and be inspired by the beauty of art in all its forms. Read the following extract from Roy's novel and then read the commentary that follows:

Rahel, breathless, holding a coconut, stepped into the temple compound through the wooden doorway in the high white boundary wall ….

It didn't matter that the story had begun, because kathakali discovered long ago that the secret of the Great Stories is that they *have* no secrets. The Great Stories are the ones you have heard and want to hear again. The ones you can enter anywhere and inhabit comfortably. They don't deceive you with thrills and trick endings. They don't surprise you with the unforeseen. They are as familiar as the house you live in. Or the smell of your lover's skin. You know how they end, yet you listen as though you don't. In the way that although you know that one day you will die, you live as though you won't. In the Great Stories you know who lives, who dies, who finds love, who doesn't. And yet you want to know again.

That is their mystery and their magic.

To the Kathakali Man these stories are his children and his childhood. He has grown up within them. They are the house he was raised in, the meadows he played in. They are his windows and his way of seeing. So when he tells a story, he handles it as he would a child of his own. He teases it. He punishes it. He sends it up like a bubble. He wrestles it to the ground and lets it go again. He laughs at it because he loves it. He can fly you across whole worlds in minutes, he can stop for hours to examine a wilting leaf. Or play with a sleeping monkey's tail. He can turn effortlessly from the carnage of war into the felicity of a woman washing her hair in a mountain stream. From the crafty ebullience of a rakshasa with a new idea into a gossipy Malayali with a scandal to spread. From the sensuousness of a woman with a baby at her breast into the seductive mischief of Krishna's smile. He can reveal the nugget of sorrow that happiness contains. The hidden fish of shame in a sea of glory.

He tells stories of the gods, but his yarn is spun from the ungodly, human heart.

The Kathakali Man is the most beautiful of men. Because his body *is* his soul. His only instrument. From the age of three it has been planed and polished, pared down, harnessed wholly to the task of story-telling. He has magic in him, this man within the painted mask and swirling skirts.

(Arundhati Roy 228–230)

In this extract, Rahel is captivated by the Kathakali Man and the Great Stories he is relaying. The words 'mystery' and 'magic' (line 10) are used to describe these stories, suggesting they somehow transcend the ordinary and the everyday and enchant Rahel. In the same way that Rahel is enchanted and held 'breathless' (line 1), we too are held spellbound by the beauty of Roy's words also as a story-teller. Rahel is appreciating the aesthetic beauty of the graceful kathakali dancer and in these descriptions we can also appreciate the beauty of Roy's use of language. Roy, in the passage, seems to be exploring the importance of art in the world and how the creative form can uplift us and fill us with wonder. As readers, this idea is suggested predominantly in the description of the character of the Kathakali Man and the style of the writing. Stylistically, the writing is punctuated with lots of short sentences; sometimes paragraphs are only one line long and sentences often begin with conjunctions which create a sense of breathlessness and excitement as Rahel watches the kathakali perform. We as readers are directly addressed, drawn in and forced to feel part of what is being experienced. As readers, the study of Roy's language choices and literary techniques leads us to consider the aesthetic importance of all art forms including literature.

Roy draws us into this scene by elevating the kathakali stories' importance by giving them the proper name 'Great Stories' (line 4) which helps suggest they transcend time and place. She uses

figurative language to encourage the reader to make a connection between the stories themselves and Rahel, the fictional listener, and us, the reader: 'they are as familiar as the house you live in. Or the smell of your lover's skin' (lines 6–7). These **similes** and the use of the second person **personal pronoun**, 'you', suggest the stories are a part of each and every one of us and that there is a familiarity and, therefore, an intimacy that links us with the stories. This encourages us to participate in the extract and helps to make the extract all the more engaging and entertaining. The single sentence paragraph '*That* is their mystery and their magic' (line 10) stands out just as the stories stand out. The **alliteration** used in this sentence compounded with the meaning of 'mystery' and 'magic' connects these stories together and suggests they are other-worldly and offer knowledge above and beyond what we can learn from mortal man. The dancers are also elevated through the use of the singular proper noun 'Kathakali Man' (lines 11 and 22). This suggests there is something omnipotent about the dancers – almost as though they transcend time and place and have come to share the secrets of the universe with us. The significance of the stories to Kathakali Man is highlighted through the **metaphor** of them being 'his children and his childhood' (line 11). They have been a part of him since the beginning ('childhood') and will continue to be a part of his future ('his children'). The repeated use of simple sentences using a wide range of **verbs** suggest the simplicity yet the multi-faceted nature of both the story and the dancer: 'He teases it. He punishes it. He sends it up like a bubble. He wrestles it to the ground … He laughs at it …' (lines 13–14). This suggests that the stories are all-things and encompass every emotion man has. There are epic images combined with domestic images, 'the carnage of war into the felicity of a woman washing her hair in a mountain stream' (lines 16–17) which also suggest how these stories encompass all aspects of human life. The skill of Kathakali Man is also highlighted through the **listing** of verbs in the past tense, suggesting how this is very much a learned skill and accentuates the craftsmanship acquired through so many years of honing their skill: 'From the age of three it has been planed and polished, pared down, harnessed wholly to the task of storytelling' (line 23). Thus, Roy uses a wide range of literary devices to describe the kathakali dances and dancers in order to entertain us. She moves away from the purely informative to capture the essence of this artform and in this way encourages us to appreciate her aesthetic. Just as the dancers entertain Rahel and just as they bring the 'Great Stories' alive for her, Roy also entertains us and brings her fictional story alive for us, the readers. In this way she is imitating the dancers' skill through her own skill as a writer. Reading literature of this calibre fills us with joy and admiration. It is an enjoyable and pleasurable experience to appreciate the text's aesthetic and the beauty of this literary artwork.

Arundhati Roy

Arundhati Roy, born in 1961 in Shillong, India, has written two novels, *The God of Small Things* (1997, winner of the Booker Prize for Fiction) and *The Ministry of Utmost Happiness* (2017). She is also a political and social activist who has spoken and written extensively on human rights and environmental issues. Many of her political and environmental beliefs are embedded within her fiction writing as well as within her non-fiction writing.

Why would a reader study this text?

Studying literary works such as this prose fiction work not only gives us an insight into a culture and way of life with which we may be unfamiliar, but it also opens our eyes to the significance of story-telling and the universal and shared truths embedded within them. The content of the extract is about the power of storytelling – the 'Great Stories' – but Roy's writing itself is also evidence of the power of storytelling. As readers we are in awe of Roy's skill as a storyteller and are seduced by her ability to entertain us and transport us inside this fictional temple next to a fictional character called Rahel watching a fictional performance of kathakali dancers. This, then, is a very important reason why we study language and literature.

CHECK FOR UNDERSTANDING

Think of two or three literary works and two or three non-literary texts you have read. In which of these four 'why do we read language and literature' categories would you place them and why?

You should feel you have a better understanding now of the many reasons *why* we study language and literature. Some of the ideas explored here will be developed throughout the book and in your language and literature classes. The final part of this chapter focuses on the craft of the writer as we start thinking about *how* we study language and literature.

How do we study language and literature?

We study language and literature by paying close attention to the details of the texts being read and exploring why writers have made the linguistic, literary, structural and stylistic choices they have made. Each of these choices has an effect on the reader and how the text's meaning is conveyed.

During the course you will be studying a balance of literary works and non-literary texts. You will very quickly realize that there are some fundamental differences between the two. Literary works are of course *literary*, which means writers employ literary features to shape the text's meaning and entertain the reader. Non-literary texts, however, whilst attempting to engage the reader (otherwise you would not read them!) are generally written for a specific purpose (to inform, to persuade, to advise, to argue, etc.) and a specific audience. They use a different set of devices in order to achieve their purpose and appeal to their intended audience. In this part of the chapter, we are going to focus on two step-by-step reading strategies that you can use in your close reading skills. The first reading strategy can be applied when you are studying literary works and the second reading strategy can be applied when you are studying non-literary texts. There are overlaps, of course, but these two reading strategies should at least give you an overview of what to look for in your study of literary works and non-literary texts.

How do we study literary works?

There are three simple steps you can take to study a literary work. If you apply these in your studies, you should have a good understanding of what the author is trying to achieve and be able to put together a well-structured essay.

Step 1: Form and structure

Every literary work has a form. The IB identifies four literary forms: poetry, drama, prose fiction and prose non-fiction. As discussed in the Introduction, each literary form has its own genres. Here are just a few examples of the different genres each literary form can take:

- poetry – epic or lyric
- drama – comedy or tragedy
- prose fiction – novel; novella (or short story); science fiction; gothic fiction; romance
- prose non-fiction – autobiography, biography or memoir.

The writer of a literary work has consciously decided to use a particular form for his or her writing and it is a good idea to identify what the form is and, ideally, what the genre is within the form. Once you have identified the form and genre you need to decide *why* the writer chose to use it for the text under study. Once you have identified and discussed the work's form/genre, you could then move on to the title of the work – is there any significance behind the title, does it give you clues about what the text may be about or does it guide your reading in some way which is either confirmed or denied as you progress through the text?

The structure of the text is really about how it has been put together. What order do events occur? Where do you start and where do you finish? Has your understanding of a character or an idea changed at all from the beginning to the end? Are there any shifts in time, perspective, mood or place that affect how you respond to a character or idea? Has a chronological or a non-linear structure been used and what is its effect on the reader? You could also comment on the kind of sentence construction and register the writer has used and what is the intended effect on the reader. Many of these ideas are explored in detail in Chapter 1.5 but for now it is important to be aware that the decisions a writer has made regarding the text's structure is something you should be considering and thinking about.

Step 2: Language, Images and Features (LIF)

Now we can focus in more detail on the writer's craft. LIF is a useful acronym when you are trying to remember what devices to focus on.

<table>
<tr><th colspan="4">LIF</th></tr>
<tr><td>Language and its effect on the reader</td><td colspan="3">This is the diction – the words and phrases that you feel have been used for a particular effect. You should also look out for any semantic fields (groups of words that are connected to a particular subject).</td></tr>
<tr><td>Images and their effect on the reader</td><td colspan="3">There are lots of different kinds of images that writers use to shape the text's meaning and engage the reader. Often, an image appeals to one or more of our senses:
• auditory imagery – sense of hearing
• gustatory imagery – sense of taste
• olfactory imagery – sense of smell
• tactile imagery – sense of touch
• visual imagery – sense of sight.</td></tr>
<tr><td rowspan="3">Features and their effect on the reader</td><td colspan="3">There are so many literary features that writers can draw upon in their works that we cannot list them all here. Throughout this coursebook we will be exploring a wide range of literary features and there are definitions of these features in the glossary (page 485). Here are a few common literary features, but of course there are many more:</td></tr>
<tr><td>Figurative features (language or description that is not literal)</td><td>Phonological features (closely connected to auditory imagery – the sound of words used)</td><td>Other features, commonly used in literary works</td></tr>
<tr><td>Allusions
Metaphors
Personification
Similes
Symbols</td><td>Alliteration
Assonance
Sibilance
Onomatopoeia
Plosives/fricatives</td><td>Humour including irony, satire, parody
Listing
Tripling
Hyperbole</td></tr>
</table>

It is important, however, that you are not simply 'device spotting' but you are able to identify that a writer has used a particular type of language, image or literary feature in order to achieve a particular *effect*. Identifying the device is usually the easy part; explaining or analysing the effect of the device used is the more impressive skill and something you will be focusing on during this course.

Step 3: Reader response to ideas and message (RIM)

This is the final step that you should be able to comment on once you have understood the text's form, structure and LIFs. Once you have unpicked how the writer has put his or her text together, you should then have some idea about what the main ideas are within the text and what the text's underlying message is. Although your interpretation may differ from your neighbour's, as long as you are able to illustrate your ideas through the close analysis you did in steps 1 and 2 you should be okay. Remember that even if you understand a text's underlying ideas or message on first reading, you are unlikely to score highly in your assessments if you do not illustrate your ideas with evidence from the text – so doing steps 1 and 2 should give you lots of evidence to draw on when you comment on the text's underlying ideas and message.

CHECK FOR UNDERSTANDING

To prepare you for writing about step 2, specifically the other literary features of literature, consider the following questions:

- What is the difference between figurative and phonological features?
- Name at least three examples of figurative features and three examples of phonological features.
- What are three examples of humour used in literary works?

Once you feel comfortable with the terminology discussed in the 3-step literary reading strategy on the page above and at identifying literary devices, you can work on your analysis.

Putting it into practice

Let's try out this three-step reading strategy on an extract from Charles Dickens' prose fiction novella, *A Christmas Carol* (1843). Read the following extract from Stave 1 (Dickens replaces 'chapters' with 'staves') where Dickens describes one of his most famous characters, Ebenezer Scrooge. Read the following extract and then follow each step carefully:

CHARLES DICKENS

Charles John Huffam Dickens, (1812–1870), was an English writer and social commentator who used satire and caricature to criticize the class divisions and wealth disparity in Victorian England. He experienced hardship when he was growing up when his father was imprisoned in a debtors' prison and he had to leave school at a young age to work in a factory. Despite his lack of a formal education, he wrote fifteen novels, including *The Pickwick Papers*, *Oliver Twist*, *Great Expectations* and *David Copperfield* and many novellas, including *A Christmas Carol*, short stories and non-fiction articles. He became an international literary celebrity in his lifetime and travelled around the UK and the US performing readings of his novels. He created some of the most memorable characters in English literature including Oliver Twist, the Artful Dodger, Ebenezer Scrooge and Tiny Tim. Some of his characters are so well known that they have become part of English culture (for example, 'scrooge' is used to describe a miserly person).

Oh! But he was a tight-fisted hand at the grindstone, Scrooge! a squeezing, wrenching, grasping, scraping, clutching, covetous old sinner! Hard and sharp as flint, from which no steel had ever struck out generous fire; secret, and self-contained, and solitary as an oyster. The cold within him froze his old features, nipped his pointed nose, shriveled his cheek, stiffened his gait; made his eyes red, his thin lips blue; and spoke out shrewdly in his grating voice. A frosty rime was on his head, and on his eyebrows, and his wiry chin. He carried his own low temperature always about with him; he iced his coffee in the dog-days; and didn't thaw it one degree at Christmas …

Nobody ever stopped him in the street to say, with gladsome looks, 'My dear Scrooge, how are you? when will you come to see me?' No beggars implored him to bestow a trifle, no children asked him what it was o'clock, no man or woman ever once in all his life inquired the way to such and such a place, of Scrooge. Even the blindmen's dogs appeared to know him; and when they saw him coming on, would tug their owners into doorways and up courts; and then would wag their tails as though they said, 'no eye at all is better than an evil eye, dark master!'

(Charles Dickens)

Let's use our step-by-step approach to focus our close reading on this extract.

Step 1: Form and structure

This is an extract from a prose fiction novella – a long, short story or a short novel. Why did he use the form of a novella to structure this work? Although we may need to know more about the context of the work to answer this question effectively, we may feel that using the form of a novella suggests that the time period the story takes place over is short, or the pace with which the story is told is fast, or the message is a simple one which readers are expected to understand quickly. It is also interesting that staves are used rather than chapters. A stave is a musical term and seems to link in with the title of the novella, *A Christmas Carol*. This would appear to suggest that this story takes place during the Christmas period or perhaps the theme or message of the book is linked to ideas connected to Christmas in some way. The importance of context in informing our understanding of texts is explored in Section 2 Time and space.

The extract is structured in two paragraphs. The first paragraph focuses on Scrooge himself and the second paragraph focuses on other people's reactions to him. It is written in the third person and the narrator is omniscient. The sentences are long and very descriptive; numerous exclamatives are used that suggest this may be a caricature of the main character.

Step 2: LIF

A good way to identify the LIFs initially is to highlight them in the extract being studied and add annotations that explain their effect. Let's do this for paragraph 1:

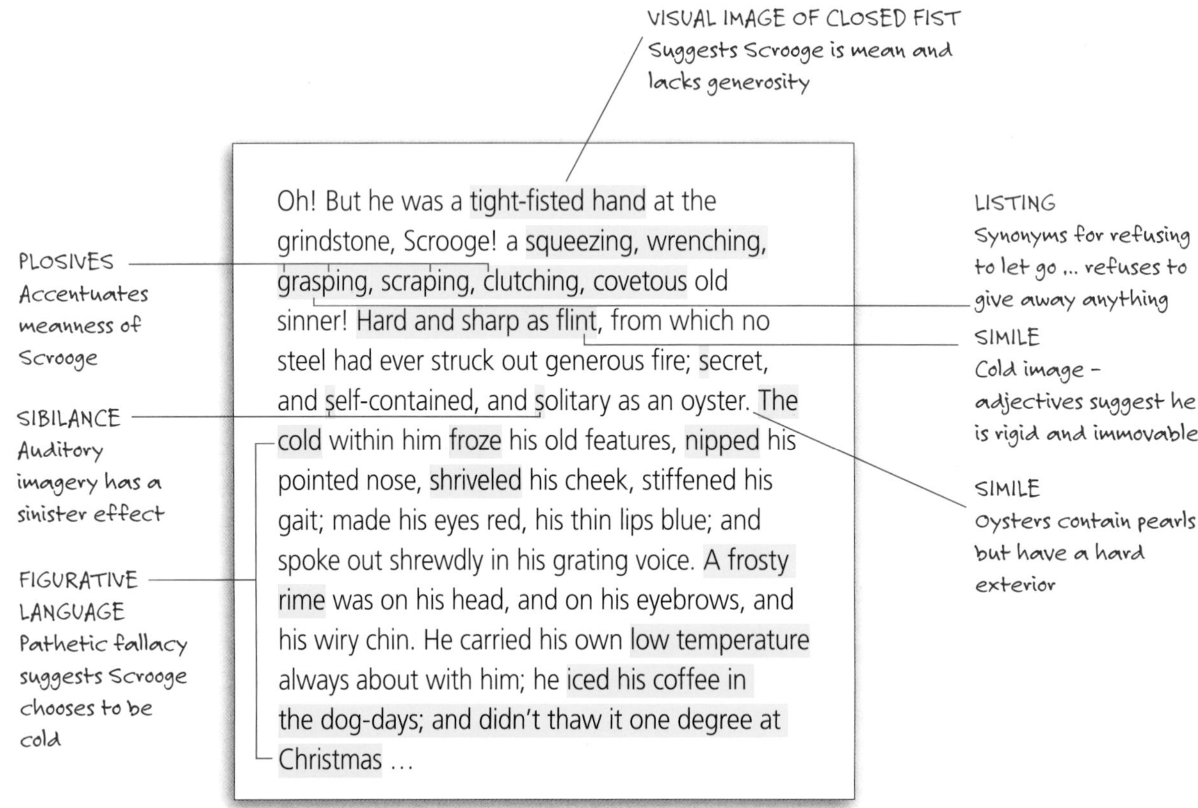

When you have highlighted and annotated your LIFs, you can attempt to write a commentary on the craft of the writer. Remember, it is not good enough simply to identify each device; you need to explain what the effect is on the reader and why the writer chose to use it. Here is a list of words you could include in your commentary that ensure you are explaining the *effect* of devices rather than simply device-spotting:

- accentuates
- emphasizes
- shows
- highlights
- demonstrates
- implies
- suggests
- symbolizes.

Let's see what a commentary may look like on paragraph 1 once we have highlighted the key devices and made some annotations. Notice how some of the words in the table above have been embedded throughout the commentary to ensure this is analytical rather than a simple device-spotting exercise:

The passage opens with a **visual image** of a closed fist in the 'tight-fisted hand' description. This **suggests** Scrooge is mean and lacks generosity. Dickens has used **synecdoche** here which reduces Scrooge to a hand and this helps to dehumanise him and encourage the reader to be repelled by him. The use of **listing** in the verbs, 'squeezing, wrenching, grasping, scraping, clutching' which immediately follows this visual image **accentuates** how Scrooge refuses to give away anything and keeps everything to himself. Each of the verbs also contains **plosive** sounds that heighten the sense of Scrooge's meanness and what a cold-hearted individual he is. The **simile** 'hard and sharp as flint' compares Scrooge to an inanimate mineral and the **adjectives** suggest further how unbending and inflexible he is. This comparison also dehumanises Scrooge and suggests he lacks compassion. Dickens uses **auditory imagery** to **imply** Scrooge is sly – the **sibilance** in the phrase 'secret and self-contained' heighten the sense that Scrooge is unpleasant precisely because he refuses to be sociable and chooses his own company over others. The simile 'solitary as an oyster' describes how even though Scrooge may have some goodness (pearl) inside him, it is clamped shut at the moment. Oysters have hard exteriors and this suggests that Scrooge, too, is callous and lacks compassion. It is also another image that is used to dehumanise Scrooge and it is quite unflattering to be compared to a shellfish! Dickens finishes this extract by using **pathetic fallacy** to describe Scrooge. He uses 'the cold' to **symbolize** Scrooge's cold attitude and lack of warmth or generosity to others and this is continued with the **repetition** of verbs connected to cold weather, 'froze ... nipped ... shrivelled ... stiffened'. All of these verbs suggest a lack of life or growth which implies that Scrooge, also, is dead inside. The final image uses **contrast** to **emphasize** how Scrooge's meanness is year-long – even in the 'dog-days' (summer) his office is 'iced' and this implies that rather than it being the weather that brings icy conditions, it is actually Scrooge himself who brings coldness everywhere he goes.

Step 3: Reader response to ideas and message (RIM) in first paragraph

Now you have identified a range of LIFs and understood the effect of them, you should be ready to interpret the extract's main ideas and the writer's underlying message. Your short commentary may look something like this:

Dickens makes it quite clear how Scrooge has turned his back on his fellow man and has lost his own humanity as a consequence. Dickens compares him to 'flint', an inanimate metal, and 'an oyster', a shellfish with a hard and calloused exterior. He may, like an oyster, have a pearl – something beautiful and pure – hidden inside him but in this extract from Stave I, it is well and truly buried beneath an impenetrable exterior. It is an unflattering picture of Scrooge and Dickens' underlying message seems to be that this is not a lifestyle we should aspire to. He seems to be condemning Scrooge for choosing such a selfish and solitary lifestyle through the negative language and images he uses to describe him.

ACTIVITY 3

Now you have a go! Attempt steps 2 and 3 (step 1 has already been done) on the second paragraph of this extract.

Step 2: highlight any LIFs and annotate the extract. Then write an extended commentary on the devices you have highlighted and annotated, embedding a range of words from the table above to ensure your commentary is analytical.

Step 3: write a short commentary showing your understanding of the extract's main ideas and underlying message. Because we have already analysed the first paragraph of the extract, you can refer to both paragraphs in your commentary.

When you have completed this activity, compare your responses to those at the back of the book.

GLOBAL ISSUES ***Field of inquiry:* Politics, Power and Justice**

UNEQUAL DISTRIBUTION OF WEALTH

In *A Christmas Carol* – and, in fact, in most of Dickens' fiction – he examines the global issue of the unequal distribution of wealth between the rich and the poor. Today, there is also a huge disparity in the way wealth and resources are distributed around the world and many would argue this is an injustice. You may be aware of this issue in your own local environment, too. For your individual oral, you need to compare a literary work with a non-literary text – *A Christmas Carol* is a literary work (prose fiction) and in Chapter 1.2, we will be exploring this global issue through another literary work (prose non-fiction), George Orwell's memoir, *Down and Out in Paris and London*. If you are interested in exploring this global issue of unequal distribution of wealth, related to the field of inquiry of politics, power and justice, you would also need to discuss it with a non-literary text.

SOCIAL RESPONSIBILITY

Another global issue explored in *A Christmas Carol* that relates to the politics, power and justice field of inquiry is social responsibility. In most of Dickens' novels, he condemns the lack of social responsibility shown to the working class in England during the nineteenth century. He is known as a social commentator and the moral that Scrooge learns in A Christmas Carol is that mankind as a whole has a social responsibility towards one another, rather than thinking it is someone else's responsibility.

As you read a range of literary works and non-literary texts in class, you may like to explore in more detail one of these global issues related to this field of inquiry.

Now that we have applied steps 1–3 to a literary work that is purely language based, let us explore one of the most well-known graphic novels of the twentieth century, *Maus*, and examine how we can apply these steps to a literary work that uses both visual images and language to communicate meaning.

Read the following key features box. Although some of the key features are similar to satirical cartoons, there are some differences, too.

KEY FEATURES COMIC BOOKS AND GRAPHIC NOVELS

- Considered literary works, even if autobiographical or biographical in nature.
- Written text, including use of **captions**, **word balloons** and **display lettering**.
- The inter-relationship between the visual image and the written text.
- Visual images, including use of colour, shading and shape.
- **Spatial mechanics** (how space is used within each panel).
- **Temporal mechanics** (how time is stopped, slowed down or speeded up).
- Use of **gutters** (the white space between the panels).
- Use of **panels** – the impact of their order, shape and size.

Maus by Art Spiegelman is a graphic novel that is based on interviews Spiegelman had with his father about his real-life experiences as a Polish Jew and a Holocaust survivor during the Second World War. It is biographical in nature and is, therefore, a prose non-fiction literary work.

Scan the QR code for some panels from *Maus*. Notice how Spiegelman uses graphic novel conventions (the written word and illustrations) to merge factual information with symbolism in these panels. Some of the features we will be discussing below can be seen very clearly in these panels.

This is a seminal graphic novel and we would recommend you borrow or buy a copy of it.

Art Spiegelman

Itzhak Avraham ben Zeev, known as Art Spiegelman, is an American illustrator, best known for his graphic novel, *Maus*. *Maus* is based on the conversations he had with his father, a Polish Jew and a Holocaust survivor, and it took him 13 years to write. It won a special Pulitzer Prize in 1992 and is credited with raising the profile of comics and graphic novels. He is an advocate for greater comic literacy and has also been a co-editor of comics magazines, a contributing artist for *The New Yorker* and a teacher at the School of Visual Arts in New York City.

Let us apply the step-by-step literary reading strategy to show our close reading skills of this work.

Step 1: Form and structure

Spiegelman uses the form of the graphic novel and uses written text and visual images to merge factual information with symbolism to tell his father's story. The panels conform to the graphic novel conventions of including both visual images (black and white illustrations) and written text (**word balloons** and **display lettering**) to tell the story. Spiegelman uses a **non-linear** structure which switches back and forth between the narrative present (1970s–1980s, New York City), the narrative long ago past (1900s–1940s, Central Europe) and the narrative recent past (1944–1945, Auschwitz) and the **narrative persona/voice** switches between two first person narrative voices: Art and Vladek, his father. This has the effect of showing how the past and present are interconnected whilst also suggesting that some memories are so painful that they cannot be revealed all in one sitting.

Step 2: LIF

(Based on page 34 from *The Complete Maus* (Book I: *Maus: A Survivor's Tale,* Chapter Two, 'The Honeymoon'.)

Highlighting and annotation

If you have access to this graphic novel, you could make a copy of a page, stick it on a sheet of A3 paper and highlight and annotate the LIFs. To study the language, you should focus on the written text in the word balloons and on the display lettering. To study the imagery, focus on the visual imagery (the illustrations); and in terms of the features, focus on the key features of comic books and graphic novels that are included in each panel.

Here is a commentary on page 34 of *The Complete Maus*:

In the top **panel**, the **caption** states the narrator is on a train travelling to a 'sanitarium ... inside Czechoslovakia'. One of the panels also states 'It was the beginning of 1938 – before the war'. This is, therefore, a retrospective memory of a past event and mentioning it was 'before the war' foreshadows events to come and creates an ominous **tone**. On the journey, the narrator sees a Nazi flag flying in the centre of one of the small towns the train passes through. The captions in these panels make explicit mention of this: 'hanging high in the center of town, it was a Nazi flag' and 'Here was the first time I saw, with my own eyes, the swastika.' Because it is explicitly stated that this is a retrospective memory, we understand the ominous meaning behind seeing a Nazi flag/the swastika hanging in the center of a European town in 1938. The words in the captions are also in the first person and in broken English – 'I remember when we were almost arrived ...' – that attempt to imitate closely the narrator's speech as he is retelling the story to us. This allows us to 'hear' the narrator's distinct **idiolect** and makes the story more authentic and personal. Through the language, readers feel many, if not all, of the details are factual – making this a non-fiction text.

However, Spiegelman uses typical graphic novel conventions that make the text literary and symbolic as well as factual which make it a literary work – prose non-fiction.

As you can see in the panels in the QR codes, Spiegelman uses **anthropomorphism** by depicting the Jews as mice. Mice are small mammals that have large litters of newborns up to three times a year and are a common prey for cats. By depicting the Jews as mice, Spiegelman seems to be suggesting their vulnerability and powerlessness during this time period and also referring to the large numbers of Jewish people who were killed during the Holocaust – alluded to in the 'before the war' caption. All the images are in black and white which perhaps suggests the lack of choices these Jews-as-mice have, even though in 1938 they are still 'free' to travel to Czechoslovakia. This stark colour scheme also tinges the panels with a bleakness and almost pits good (Jews-as-mice) against bad (Nazi swastika).

Other graphic novel features that Spiegelman uses for symbolic effect include the lack of lines that border the first panel illustrating the train travelling to another country which perhaps allude to the fact that at the beginning of 1938, Jews were still free to travel. The panels which illustrate the Jews-as-mice seeing the Nazi flag for the first time are bordered by a thick black line which perhaps foreshadows the lack of freedom they are soon going to experience – accentuated all the more as the Jews-as-mice are on a train, the mode of transport used to transport millions of Jews to concentration camps during the Second World War.

Although some of these comments are based on contextual knowledge about the Second World War, the fact that the date '1938' and the phrase 'before the war' are both explicitly stated in one of the captions anchors the panels in a certain time period. This means that even with an **immanent** reading, we can refer to this historical context.

Step 3: Reader response to ideas and message

The ideas in these panels relate to the Holocaust – despite these panels occurring in 1938 in Europe, most readers will be aware that in less than a year the Nazis will have invaded many European countries, including Czechoslovakia and its bordering countries, and the Jewish community will suffer persecutions throughout Europe.

Even if we just focus on the panels themselves, rather than bringing any external knowledge and influence to them (we are, remember, taking an immanent approach in this section), the visual image of the Nazi flag in one of the panels and the Jews-as-mice on a train in every panel on this page foreshadow their fate. The message of the panels is, perhaps, how vulnerable and intimidated the Jewish community were at this time and how there was very little they could have done to prevent the impending invasion and subsequent persecution.

CONCEPT CONNECTION

REPRESENTATION

This concept explores the way language and literature relates to reality. Some argue that texts should represent reality as accurately as possible, while others argue that art should have the freedom to represent reality in a more symbolic and creative way. *Maus* is an interesting text through which to explore this concept. Although *Maus* is biographical, based on the writer's father's personal experiences of being a Polish Jew during the 1930s and 1940s, these panels are focused on the ethno-religious group of Jews rather than on any one individual. Moreover, rather than depicting his father and the other characters in the graphic novel as recognizable people, Spiegelman uses the device of **anthropomorphism**, to depict different groups of people. Spiegelman represents his father and his Jewish companions with the same identity through illustrating them as mice. Using white mice to represent the Jewish population to a certain degree strips individuals of personal identity and rather accentuates their collective identity, specifically an identity associated with innocence and powerlessness, qualities associated with the Jewish community during their persecution by the Nazis during the 1930s and 1940s in Europe. Spiegelman draws the mice with rounded and delicate features to highlight further their vulnerability which helps create a sense of **pathos** for the group as a whole, rather than focusing on one individual.

The panel which depicts the Nazi flag uses **spatial mechanics** to represent the power of the Nazis versus the lack of power of the Jews. There are five mice in the foreground and one Nazi flag in the background. However, the mice are shaded and have their backs turned to the reader which perhaps alludes to their uncertain future while the Nazi flag takes central position, suggesting its importance and significance. The fact that a non-living object takes central position rather than a living being also suggests how this ethno-religious group will be persecuted in the near future throughout Europe. In these panels, Spiegelman is using symbolic illustrations – mice and a flag – to represent historical reality.

The words in the final caption are also used to represent the contrast in power between the Jews and the Nazis. The symbol on the flag is given a name, 'the swastika', which gives it a particular identity. The individual Jews, however, are not named in these panels – they are almost interchangeable in the way they have been illustrated and in the way they are referred to as 'everybody' and 'every Jew'. This suggests that, for their persecutors, their identity comes through their Jewishness rather than their individuality. This perhaps alludes to the millions of Jews who were killed during the Holocaust and how rather than individuals being persecuted during this time period, it was the Jewish population as a whole that was persecuted.

Spiegelman, therefore, represents historical reality through symbolic visual and linguistic features. This is an interesting concept you could perhaps explore in the literary works you study in class.

TOK Links: Knowledge and literature

Maus is based on Art Spiegelman's father's first-hand experiences of living in Poland during the Second World War and surviving Auschwitz concentration camp. The language and literature course, however, does not classify it as a non-literary text; rather it is classified as a literary work. In what ways is the kind of knowledge we gain from the study of a literary work such as *Maus* different from the kind we gain through the study of other disciplines, such as history? How reliable is the knowledge gained through literary works about historical events such as those illustrated in *Maus*? Do you think a historical event of such magnitude as the Holocaust can be or should be the focus of art?

EE Links: English A – Literature category 1

Even though *Maus* is based on Spiegelman's father's story, this is a literary work so an extended essay on this graphic novel would be an English A: Literature category 1 extended essay. Spiegelman depicts his father's real-life experiences in Poland during the Second World War using a range of graphic novel conventions as well as anthropomorphism to depict different ethno-cultural and political groups. This could form the basis of a research question such as: **How does Spiegelman use traditional graphic novel conventions to convey his father's experiences during the Second World War?** You would need to analyse the range of graphic novel conventions Spiegelman uses and explain their effect on the reader. You may also like to explore why Spiegelman chooses to use mice to represent the Jewish community, cats to represent the Nazis, pigs to represent the non-Jewish Polish community and dogs to represent the Americans.

It is clear, then, that the literary reading strategy we are using can be applied equally successfully to both wholly language-based literary works and to multimodal literary works, such as graphic novels.

We are now going to shift our focus onto a second reading strategy which you can apply to non-literary text types.

How do we study non-literary texts?

Step 1: Genre, audience and purpose (GAP)

As you are aware, there is a very wide range of non-literary text types, such as: advertisements, infographics, magazine features, opinion pieces, photojournalism, satirical cartoons, etc. It is important to identify the genre (or text type) you are exploring, as this will often denote the text's purpose – for example, non-literary texts are often aimed at a particular audience and this will affect the way they have been constructed. So, step 1 is identifying these three aspects of a text: genre (text type), audience and purpose. A useful acronym is GAP:

Genre	Advertisement, infographic, magazine article, online opinion piece, photojournalism, satirical cartoon, etc.
Audience	Can you determine the age or gender of the intended audience? The cultural or social group? The interest of the audience?
Purpose	To inform, to persuade, to advise, to mock, to educate, etc.

Step 2: Structure and style

Ideas associated with the text's structure are similar to those we discussed when exploring a literary work's structure. Just as a writer of literature has consciously constructed his or her work in a particular way, so has the writer of a non-literary text. More non-literary texts are multimodal than literary works, so you need to remember that if you are studying a text that is constructed with visual images or other non-verbal symbols and written text, the positioning of each on the page is important and has an effect on how we interpret the text's ideas.

The style of the text refers to the type of language used and the tone created. To try and discern this, you can ask yourself: has an informal or a formal register been used? Is the language neutral or emotive? Is there any specialist language (**jargon**)? Is the tone serious, critical, celebratory, light-hearted, etc. and how is this tone achieved? Often, the intended audience and purpose of the text will have a bearing on the style of the text.

Step 3: Typographical and graphological features

These features are generally unique to non-literary texts. You need to be able to identify them and explain how their inclusion shapes a reader's understanding of the text's purpose and/or meaning. Such features could be:

Typographical features	Refers to the appearance of the written text used and how it is used to shape the text's meaning. Some common typographical features include: font type (**sans-serif** or **serif** script), size of font used, colour or highlighting of words, use of bolding, italics, underlining or capitalization.
Graphological features	Refers to the visual elements of the text – how it appears on the page and how this shapes the text's meaning. Some common graphological features include: the placement of visual images on the page compared to the placement of written text; the use of space where there is neither a visual image nor written text; the inclusion of non-written symbols such as text boxes, arrows, graphs, bullet points, etc.

Step 4: Other features of text type

The other features of a text type may be dependent upon what the text type is you are studying. Although you are not expected to know all of the features and conventions of every text type, being aware that a satirical cartoon, for example, has different conventions to a newspaper article can be useful in your analysis of non-literary texts. Within this coursebook, we have included key features boxes on a range of non-literary text types which should support you in your analysis. However, other features you would want to explore will be dependent on the purpose of the text. If, for example, you are analysing a political speech, it is likely there will be a number of rhetorical devices; if you are analysing an informative leaflet, it is likely that features including facts and statistics will be embedded.

Step 5: Visual image and layout

Many non-literary texts include visual images or other non-verbal symbols and it is essential you analyse these in detail. Some techniques you may want to consider are:

- visual image reinforcing the written text (newspaper stories, infographics)
- the visual image taking the place of extended written text (cartoons and advertisements where there is minimal written text and the meaning is shaped through the visual images)
- interpreting the text's meaning through visuals alone where there is no written text (photojournalism, works of visual art)
- non-verbal symbols guiding a reader as to how to read the text (recipes, instructional texts, infographics, etc.).

Visuals can range in type, too, from hyper-real photographs to symbolic pictorial illustrations. It is essential, therefore, that you are able to analyse the visual aspects of a text and examine how they are used to shape the text's meaning and the reader's understanding in a particular way.

Step 6: Reader response to ideas, message and/or purpose

Similar to our response to literary works, once we have analysed the various features of a non-literary text we should be in a good position to respond to the underlying ideas, message or purpose of the text being studied.

CHECK FOR UNDERSTANDING

To prepare you for writing about these six steps, consider the following questions:

- What is the difference between typographical and graphological features?
- Name at least three examples of typographical features and at least three examples of graphological features.

Once you feel comfortable with the terminology and identifying techniques, you can work on your analysis.

Putting it into practice

SENSITIVE CONTENT

Caution: The photo here and on page 65 includes sensitive content and dehumanizing visuals.

The images show vulnerable children in extremely distressing circumstances but have been chosen as two widely circulated examples of photojournalism, to illustrate its effects on the themes of identity and human behaviour at the heart of this book. Furthermore, the IB recommends that your studies in Language A: Language & Literature should challenge you intellectually, personally and culturally, and expose you to sensitive and mature topics. We invite you to reflect critically on various perspectives offered while bearing in mind the IB's commitment to international-mindedness and intercultural respect.

Let's now apply these non-literary reading steps to a wholly visual non-literary text. **Photojournalism** is a non-literary text type that relies on the photographic image rather than the written word to inform the reader of something happening in the world. It is a powerful text type that has the potential to sway public opinion and change attitudes. One of the most iconic photographs that helped change public opinion and forced the US government to withdraw American troops from Vietnam in 1973 was the photograph originally known as 'Terror of War', now better known as 'Napalm Girl', taken by Nick Ut in 1972 during the Vietnam War. You will be analysing this photograph later on in this chapter.

Today, photojournalism is still a mode of reportage that can have a large impact on swaying public opinion and changing the course of world events. Look at the photograph above, taken by Turkish journalist, Nilüfer Demir, in September 2015 and which made headline news around the world.

Let us use our non-literary reading approach to analyse this photograph. As always, remember we are taking an **immanent** approach rather than focusing on contextual considerations.

Step 1: GAP

Genre	Photograph published in newspapers around the world
Audience	Millions of people globally who presumably are aware of current affairs if they read a newspaper
Purpose(s)	To inform readers of what is happening around the world; to elicit an emotional response

Step 2: Structure and style

This text includes no written language; it is just a photographic image. Being a photograph, it is a hyper-realistic image of a man in some kind of a uniform carrying a child (although we can only see the child's legs) on a beach. Because the child appears so inert and because the man is looking away from the camera (in shame? in embarrassment? to protect his and the child's identities?) we assume the child is either sick or even dead. The fact that this is a photographic image means we are viewing something tragic that actually occurred; we are viewing the truth. This not only informs the reader of an event that has occurred, but because of the subject matter of the photograph, it elicits an emotional response in the reader.

Step 3: Typographical and graphological features

There are no typographical features as the entire text is a photograph. If we could read the badge on the man's shirt, we may be able to place the image in terms of country.

The photograph consists of a man carrying a child on a beach. The child appears to be inert and the man is walking away from the camera lens. The background is taken up equally with the sea and the beach. The foreground is taken up with the man carrying the child. The photograph is skilfully laid out so that our attention is on the child being rescued. The man holding the child is placed just left of centre and although we can see him in his entirety, we can only see the child's legs which take central position. There is nothing else in the frame that takes our focus away from the subject of the image, therefore, we are forced to view this seemingly tragic event and reflect, perhaps, on why this has occurred. A closer analysis of the layout of the visual image will be explored in step 5.

Before we comment on steps 4 (other features) and 5 (visual image), let's annotate it:

Step 4: Other features of text type

Because this is a photograph, there is no written text. However, this makes the photograph universal in that it can be 'read' and understood by readers globally, irrespective of the language they speak. Although we may not know the nationalities of the man and child until we read outside of the photograph, the lack of language is also symbolic of how both individuals transcend culture – an adult carrying a child in his arms is a universal image of compassion and love. However, because the child appears not to be moving, we sense this child may either be seriously ill or possibly dead and the man is not looking directly at the camera, as if he is ashamed or embarrassed at the condition of the child in his arms. This also is a universal idea – children are supposed to outlive adults and when we see potentially a dead child in an adult's arms, we immediately feel that something has gone very wrong, that an injustice has taken place. The lack of language also accentuates the man's actions – his actions are more important than any words, particularly as the child may be dead and thus, for the child, words are now meaningless constructs anyway.

Step 5: Visual image and layout

This is a wholly visual image with a focus on a man carrying the inert body of a young child across a beach with the sea in the background. The man is dressed in a uniform that suggests some kind of professionalism or expertise, while the child is wearing shorts and shoes. **Juxtaposition** is used to contrast the man and child: the man is wearing a uniform, including heavy boots, whereas the child is wearing light-weight shorts and shoes; the man is standing, the child is lying; the man is walking across the beach, the child is inert; the man's face can be seen by the reader, the child's face is concealed. This makes the photograph unbalanced – all the power is with the man and even though he is treating the child with care and respect, we feel there is an injustice to the imbalance of power. The child appears to be either very sick or dead and because of the way the photograph has been framed, we feel that the child's sickness/death is also unjust. The fact that we cannot identify who the child is as we can only see his legs makes this image all the more universal. The hidden face also protects the child's identity, gives him some privacy in death, rather than sensationalising the tragedy that appears to have occurred. Moreover, by not being able to identify who the child is, whose son or daughter the child is, may result in some readers being reminded of their own children or family and thus create a personal connection between the reader and the image. Rather than being one specific child, the child could represent all children. The backdrop to this photograph is an idyllic scene: the sea and a long sandy beach. The photograph juxtaposes the serene natural world with a young boy's death – something unnatural and premature – and this creates an even more unsettling mood that jars with readers' expectations and values

Step 6: Reader response to ideas, message and/or purpose

If we just focus on the photograph itself, we can argue that two overriding ideas in this image are human compassion and shame. It is a shocking image of a man carrying an inert child across a beach. Although he appears full of shame that this child is either sick or dead (shown through his refusal to look directly at the camera), there is also a tenderness and care shown by the man to the small, unmoving body of the child and the way he is shielding the child's face from the camera lens. The fact that this scene is happening in what appears to be an idyllic setting suggests that nowhere is pain-free; that appearances can be deceptive. Perhaps one message we get from the image is that we should all be more aware of one another and show each other more humanity and care.

This photograph has multiple purposes. Because it is an example of photojournalism and was published in newspapers, its primary purpose is to inform readers of what is happening around the world. You would need to read the written news story that accompanies the photograph to understand the context of this image which may in turn give you another lens through which you could interpret the image. We may, for example, feel there are pertinent symbolic features associated with the particular image chosen to illustrate the news report – perhaps the image gives us an alternative viewpoint (the human story, for example) to a news report that may be focusing on the political ramifications and complexities of the event.

However, a secondary purpose is to elicit an emotional response in the reader. In this case, one of anger and shock that a child has seemingly died so young and also one of sorrow and **empathy** for both the child and his unseen family.

It is important to remember that photojournalists work under a strict ethical code and they are not allowed to edit their images to manipulate the truth. This means that this is a true image of what the photographer observed on the beach the day he took this photograph. Knowing this makes the image all the more powerful.

ACTIVITY 4

Now let's explore one of the most famous photographs of all time that is part of the genre of photojournalism. View the following image and follow the non-literary reading strategies as you analyse it.

This photograph, 'Terror of War', now known as 'Napalm Girl', was taken by the Vietnamese-American photojournalist, Huỳnh Công Út, better known as Nick Ut, during the Vietnam War on 8 June, 1972.

Focus on the following steps:

Step 1: Genre, audience and purpose

Step 2: Structure and style

Step 3: Typographical and graphological features

(annotate the image before you write about this)

Step 4: Other features of the text

Step 5: Visual image and layout

Step 6: Reader response to image, message and/or purpose

When you have completed your steps, compare your ideas to those at the back of the book.

As you can see, there are different approaches we should be taking depending on whether we are analysing a literary work or a non-literary text. However, the key to your analysis is explaining the effect of what you are analysing, rather than simply feature-spotting.

GLOBAL ISSUE ***Field of inquiry:* Politics, Power and Justice**

THE RIGHTS OF THE CHILD

The United Nations states that 'Every child has the right to health, education and protection, and every society has a stake in expanding children's opportunities in life. Yet, around the world, millions of children are denied a fair chance for no reason other than the country, gender or circumstances into which they are born.' Shortly after the Second World War, in 1953, UNICEF (United Nations International Children's Emergency Fund) became a permanent part of the United Nations and in 1959 the UN General Assembly adopted the Declaration of the Rights of the Child, defining the rights of every child to protection, education, health care, shelter and good nutrition.

Children's rights is, therefore, a global issue that affects billions of individuals around the world. Many literary works and non-literary texts focus on the rights of children. Although we explored Dickens' *A Christmas Carol* in this chapter, many of Dickens' other novels explore the rights of children in Victorian England (*Oliver Twist, David Copperfield,* for example). The two protagonists in Roy's *The God of Small Things* are 7-year-old twins who experience injustice first-hand in 1960s Kerala. The graphic novel, *Maus*, is about the Holocaust in Europe from 1939 to 1945 which affected millions of children. The two photographs that we analysed at the end of this chapter also focus on the effect of conflict on the child. You may like to explore this global issue in more detail through the literary works and non-literary texts you study in class and perhaps base your individual oral on this topic.

The following chapters in this section will continue to explore how writers construct texts and how we as readers construct meaning. However, this chapter should have given you an overview of why and how we study language and literature, and how we are able to explore in depth a text on its own merits, without needing to examine in too much detail the contexts surrounding its production and reception, or the texts that have influenced its inception.

Works cited

'Contrasting styles: Trump and Ardern speak at the UN – video.' *UN Web TV*, 28 Sept. 2018. Web. 3 Feb. 2019. **www.theguardian.com/world/video/2018/sep/28/contrasting-styles-trump-and-ardern-speak-at-the-un-video**.

Dickens, C. *A Christmas Carol*. Penguin English Library, 2012.

Donne, J. 'No man is an island.' Web. 1 Feb. 2019. **https://web.cs.dal.ca/~johnston/poetry/island.html**.

Harjo, J. 'Perhaps the World Ends Here.' *Poetry Foundation*. Web. 2 Feb. 2019. **www.poetryfoundation.org/poems/49622/perhaps-the-world-ends-here**.

Radice, B. (transl.) *The Letters of The Younger Pliny*. Penguin Books, 1969.

Roy, A. *The God of Small Things*. HarperCollinsPublishers, 1997.

Spiegelman, A. *The Complete Maus*. Penguin Books, 2003.

'The Destruction of Pompeii, 79AD.' *EyeWitness to History*, 1999. Web. 1 Feb. 2019. **www.eyewitnesstohistory.com/pompeii.htm**.

Zhao, P. 'Water Town.' Translated by Song Shouquan. *Yangtze River: The Wildest, Wickedest River on Earth*. Selected and edited by Madeleine Lynn, Oxford University Press, 1997.

1.2 How are we affected by texts in various ways?

OBJECTIVES OF CHAPTER

- Appreciate how texts can fill us with wonder and awe at the world in which we live.
- Encourage us to empathize towards those who are different to ourselves.
- Contemplate our inner selves as a result of the texts we read.
- Consider how texts educate us.
- Consider how texts can persuade us.
- Consider how texts can affect us intellectually and emotionally about topical issues.

As we have seen in the Introduction and Chapter 1.1, there are different forms of literary works and within each form, different genres; and a wide range of different non-literary text types, which follow different conventions and have different purposes. This chapter explores how, depending on the text we are reading, we are affected by texts in different ways. You may feel that no two readers are affected in the same way to any one text considering we are all individuals with different interests and passions, from different cultural backgrounds with different values, attitudes and beliefs. Once a work is published, it is down to the individual reader to respond in a particular way. We will be exploring this idea as well as exploring how a writer uses his or her craft to attempt to elicit a particular response in the implied reader.

As Chapter 1.1 has shown, there are some fundamental reasons why we study language and literature: to understand the self; to understand others; to gain an understanding of the world; and, of course, for enjoyment. We will explore many of these ideas in depth through the study of three literary works – poetry, prose non-fiction (memoir) and prose fiction (novella) – focusing particularly on *how* we are affected – the emotions that we experience when reading these texts. We will then move on to study three non-literary texts and explore how their particular genre (encyclopedia entry, opinion piece and infographic) and purpose (to inform, to persuade and a mixture of both) affect us in different ways.

Let's begin by exploring three literary works: a poem by William Wordsworth, 'I Wandered Lonely as a Cloud', an extract from George Orwell's literary memoir, *Down and Out in Paris and London* and an extract from Banana Yoshimoto's novella, *Kitchen*. Here is a quick overview of each text:

■ Table 1.2.1

Text	Form	Content	How we are affected
'I Wandered Lonely as a Cloud' by William Wordsworth (1807)	Literary work Poetry: lyrical ballad	The narrator describes a field of daffodils he experienced when walking alone one day. Focuses on the natural world.	Encourages a sense of wonder and awe at the world in which we live.
Down and Out in Paris and London by George Orwell (1933)	Literary work Prose non-fiction – memoir	The writer describes the treatment of homeless people in London who have stayed the night in a 'spike', a government institution that offers a bed for a night in return for work. Focuses on the other, in this case London tramps.	Encourages empathy for others different to ourselves.
Kitchen by Banana Yoshimoto (1988, translated into English 1993)	Literary work Prose fiction – novella (work in translation)	The first-person narrator is having an existential crisis following the loss of her grandmother.	Encourages us to reflect on our own feelings and realize that we are not alone when we experience similar internal crises.

Let's now read and analyse each text in detail and explore the various ways we are affected by each text.

■ Texts can fill us with wonder and awe at the world in which we live

Romanticism was a movement that encompassed art, literature and philosophy in the late-eighteenth and early-nineteenth centuries in Europe. It was a movement that in many ways rebelled against the previous age of the Enlightenment of the late-seventeenth and early-eighteenth centuries which focused on the pursuit of knowledge through using one's intellect and reason. For Romantics, this was an elitist philosophy and they attempted to show how knowledge could be acquired by anyone through using one's senses. For Romantics, rather than locking oneself away in a study or laboratory for years on end, studying sages of the past and using one's rational faculties to understand the world, they believed that wandering alone in nature and *experiencing* the world with our senses was the way to acquire knowledge. For Romantics, the natural world was both idyllic and wild, and could fill the observer with both utmost joy and terror. There was an understanding that the natural world was far greater than the human world – existing long before humanity and remaining long after we are gone. For Romantics, therefore, the natural world was a place of wonder that could teach us more than any fellow human being could. If you are interested in this aspect of Romanticism, Nicholas Roe's 1992 text, *The Politics of Nature: Wordsworth and Some Contemporaries*, explores this idea in more detail.

William Wordsworth (1770–1850) was an English Romantic poet who many consider to be the godfather of Romanticism. He wrote *Lyrical Ballads, with a Few Other Poems* in 1798 with his friend and fellow poet, Samuel Taylor Coleridge, and this is considered to be the start of the English Romantic movement in literature. In this anthology, he used what he called the

KEY FEATURES ROMANTICISM

- Late-eighteenth century and early-nineteenth century arts and literature movement in Europe.
- Challenged the Age of Reason which focused on logic, reason and rationality.
- Focused on the importance of individual experience to acquire knowledge.
- Nature was celebrated and elevated in Romantic poetry – it could fill you with awe and wonder at both its beauty and its power.
- Romantics often focus on the solitary individual, and a desire to escape the modern world.
- 'wise passiveness' (Wordsworth, *Expostulation and Reply*) was pursued rather than an active search for knowledge.
- Celebrated the 'everyday man' – the child, the labourer, the solitary reaper – rather than philosophers and intellectuals. Used a lyrical form and the 'language of conversation in the middle and lower classes of society' (Wordsworth, *Lyrical Ballads* i) rather than the overly flowery language of poetry of the past.
- Romantics were interested in the poetry of 'sensation' (Keats, *Selections* ...) – one's senses were as important in acquiring knowledge as empirical knowledge that could be measured through logic and reason.
- Romantic poets who explored these ideas include: William Blake (1757–1827), William Wordsworth (1770–1850), Samuel Taylor Coleridge (1772–1834), Lord Byron (1788–1824), Percy Shelley (1792–1822) and John Keats (1795–1821).

'language of conversation in the middle and lower classes of society' (Wordsworth, *Lyrical Ballads* i) to ensure everyone could understand his ideas and to represent how knowledge was accessible to everyone, not just learned philosophers and intellectuals. He is known as a 'nature poet' and much of his poetry is focused on his belief that there is a connection – physical and spiritual – between nature and man and that if man was able to experience nature with what he termed a 'wise passiveness' (ibid, 'Expostulation and Reply' 183), then nature could fill his soul with a nobility and purity that had been lost, he believed, due to the onset of industrialization and expansion of cities at the time he was writing. The aim of much of his poetry is to use his craft as a poet to fill his readers with a sense of wonder and awe at the power of nature and encourage readers to be more in tune with their senses rather than focus solely on their intellect.

Read the Key features of Romanticism to get an overview of this movement and then read Wordsworth's most famous poem, 'I Wandered Lonely as a Cloud' (more commonly known as 'Daffodils'), which was published in 1807 in his *Poems in Two Volumes* anthology. We are focusing in particular on how the reader is encouraged to be full of wonder and awe at the power of nature in this poem.

I Wandered Lonely as a Cloud

I wandered lonely as a cloud
That floats on high o'er vales and hills,
When all at once I saw a crowd,
A host of golden daffodils;
Beside the lake, beneath the trees,
Fluttering and dancing in the breeze.

Continuous as the stars that shine
And twinkle on the Milky Way,
They stretched in never-ending line
Along the margin of a bay:
Ten thousand saw I at a glance,
Tossing their heads in sprightly dance.

The waves beside them danced, but they
Outdid the sparkling waves in glee:–
A poet could not but be gay
In such a jocund company!
I gazed – and gazed – but little thought
What wealth the show to me had brought:

For oft, when on my couch I lie
In vacant or in pensive mood,
They flash upon that inward eye
Which is the bliss of solitude,
And then my heart with pleasure fills,
And dances with the daffodils.

(William Wordsworth)

William Wordsworth

William Wordsworth is an English Romantic poet who is credited with writing, with Samuel Taylor Coleridge, the first English Romantic literary work, *Lyrical Ballads, with a Few Other Poems*, in 1798. In this poetry anthology, Wordsworth explained in the Preface how he was experimenting with the everyday language of the lower and middle classes which was a new approach to poetry. Many consider his greatest work to be *The Prelude*, a long semi-autobiographical poem of 14 books, written in blank verse. In this poem, he explores his development from a child, surrounded and inspired by nature, to the Romantic poet he became. The poem was published three months after his death. He was the British poet laureate from 1843 until his death.

It is likely that you understood the overriding idea of this poem: a celebration of daffodils the narrator saw as he was wandering on his own one day. The main purpose of this poem is to describe the experience in such a way that readers will be encouraged to understand the power of nature and how not only does nature fill you with pleasure when you actually experience it, but the memory of it stays with you long after the experience and can bring you comfort and solace long after the actual moment has passed. This is an important idea and if Wordsworth is successful in conveying this, then we can see how we are affected by this poem: an understanding of how important our natural world is in the here-and-now but also in the future. In many ways it is a poem that attempts to offer us advice about the best way to live our lives but, unlike non-literary advisory texts, Wordsworth uses his literary craft as a poet to encourage this particular response in us. So how does he do it and how are we expected to respond? We are going to be using our three-step reading strategy from Chapter 1.1 to answer these questions. Read the following commentary, which focuses on how the reader responds and why.

Step 1: Form and structure

First, this is a **lyrical ballad**. This form of poetry was created by Wordsworth and Coleridge in their 1798 anthology and Wordsworth continued to use this particular poetic form in many of his other poems, including 'Daffodils'. A lyrical ballad can be defined as traditional verse that includes a harmonious **rhythm** (the tempo or pace of the poem) and **meter** (the beat of the poem, created through stressed/unstressed syllables) and usually a regular rhyme scheme. The combination of these features means when the reader is reading the poem, s/he has an auditory experience – the reader can hear the regular rhythm, meter and rhyme and this makes reading the poem easier and brings a sense of harmony and musicality to the poem. In 'Daffodils', Wordsworth uses a regular **iambic tetrameter** meter with regular unstressed/stressed syllables in each line. There is also a regular rhyme scheme of ABABCC which means lines 1 and 3 rhyme ('A'), lines 2 and 4 rhyme ('B') and the final two lines, lines 5 and 6 rhyme ('C') – otherwise known as a rhyming couplet. This is a particularly harmonious and melodic sounding poem – nothing jars or sounds out of place, everything flows fluently, almost as if it is following a subtle back and forth motion which ties in well with the gentle 'dancing' movement of the daffodils and waves that are referred to in the first two stanzas. Immediately, before we have even started thinking about the language used, the sound of the poem is appealing and allows the reader to be lulled by the sound of the poem and more likely to be seduced by it.

Step 2: LIF

Wordsworth is describing an everyday common English flower that his English readers would have been very familiar with. In order to achieve his purpose in raising awareness of the significance of nature, he needs to elevate a common flower beyond the commonplace, make something ordinary appear extraordinary. How does he do this? This is where his skill as a poet comes in. He uses a wide range of images and literary features to elevate the daffodils to an otherworldly (or transcendental) level and in doing so, encourages us to feel in awe of this common flower:

- Personifying the daffodils to a 'crowd' (line 3). The use of this collective noun elevates a common flower to the level of the human. Moreover, the 'crowd' of daffodils is **contrasted** with the narrative voice who is 'I' (line 3), one single individual. This imbues the daffodils with power: the collective is generally more powerful than the individual and the reader begins to feel that the daffodils' presence is more powerful than the individual's presence.
- The **metaphor/personification** of 'host' (line 4) again elevates the daffodils to the level of the human. This time, they are imbued with action. Just as a human host actively works hard to entertain and please his or her guests, the suggestion through this metaphor is so do the

daffodils. It is as if we are the passive guests and if we are open to the daffodils, they will actively entertain us and fill us with pleasure. This certainly elevates the daffodils and would fill many readers with a sense of wonder at how something so ordinary and commonplace can be so actively engaged in entertaining us.

- **Visual imagery** of 'golden' (line 4) appeals to our sense of sight. Not only is Wordsworth appealing to our sense of hearing through the meter, rhythm and rhyme, but he is also appealing to our sense of sight, so this is a multisensory poem that helps us experience the scene all the more effectively. The colour 'golden' is also something precious and valuable – it is the colour of money after all – but rather than the daffodils offering material wealth, we can interpret this adjective as suggesting the daffodils bring spiritual or emotional wealth to those who experience them. When Wordsworth wrote this poem, industrialization was beginning to take hold of the country and this perhaps would affect some contemporary readers to reflect on the true value of life: material wealth or spiritual wealth.
- **Verbs** associated with movement – 'fluttering and dancing' (line 6) – is also a visual image which ties in with the gentle flowing movement of the poem itself (through meter, rhythm and rhyme) and highlights a harmony and gentle beauty associated with the flowers. This would affect readers by highlighting how nature can bring peace, harmony and beauty to the world; qualities that Romantics felt were beginning to be lost with the onset of industrialization and technology. For readers today, this idea may also be relevant – particularly as we debate environmental issues and climate change around the world.

Step 3: Reader response to ideas and message

By the end of stanza 1, Wordsworth has worked his magic! A common everyday flower has been elevated to the divine (or at the very least, to the human), we can see them in their multitudes, in their glorious golden colour, gently swaying in the breeze everywhere we look. And the gentle rhythmic motion of the poem heightens their appeal all the more. Wordsworth wants us to experience the scene (hence the appeal to multiple senses) and appreciate it in the same way he did when he experienced it. By the end of stanza 1, readers are supposed to be affected by the daffodils, appreciating their power, beauty and harmony.

ACTIVITY 1

Now re-read stanzas 2 and 3 and attempt a close analysis, using step 2 of our reading strategy. Explore the ways Wordsworth uses language, images and literary features in his attempt to fill us with wonder and awe at this particular aspect of the natural world. You may like to use headings (similar to the model above) for each aspect of language, image and feature and then *analyse its effect on the reader.* Remember, this is not just a feature spotting exercise! The *analysis* part of this activity is absolutely essential.

Once you have done this, read the commentary at the back of the book and compare ideas.

So far, we have explored the wonder and awe of the natural world at the time it is experienced. One of the reasons 'Daffodils' is so famous and such an iconic Romantic poem is because of the final stanza. It is here that Wordsworth conveys the more philosophical nature of Romanticism. The power of experiencing nature not only nurtures you in the here-and-now when you actually experience it, but the memory of the experience becomes a part of the individual and can offer you comfort and solace in the future. So, experiencing nature becomes something timeless – and this is what makes nature so powerful. Let's use our reading strategy again to explore stanza 4 in more depth to get an understanding of these ideas that were so important to Romantic literature and explore how we are expected to respond.

Step 1: Form and structure

First of all, you should notice that the tense has changed from the past tense used in stanzas 1–3 to the present tense in stanza 4. The first three stanzas are describing the past experience itself, whereas the final stanza is explaining the effect of the experience on the narrator now, in the present.

Step 2: LIF

The stanza starts with the **prepositional phrase** 'For oft' (line 19) – the **archaic** 'oft' is a shortened form of 'often' and this immediately suggests that the experience of the daffodils was not a once-only experience, but something that has a continuous effect on him, an experience that often affects him. He explains how 'when on my couch I lie' (line 19) (notice the present tense), an ordinary and everyday occurrence that most readers will be familiar with, when 'in vacant or in pensive mood' (line 20), suggesting he is not thinking of anything in particular – again, something many readers will be familiar with – suddenly 'they flash upon that inward eye' (line 21). This suggests how when he is doing absolutely nothing – just relaxing – the daffodils 'flash' in his 'inward eye'. The **verb** 'flash' has connotations of speed and it is as if he is suggesting he has no control over this flashback of the daffodils. Notice how it is 'they flash', rather than him having a flashback. This implies the daffodils themselves still exist and have actively decided to 'flash' back in his mind's eye; the individual, however, remains passive and simply has to enjoy the experience. Again, Wordsworth is imbuing the daffodils with power and in this way elevating them. The last two lines of the poem are particularly effective in conveying a sense of wonder and awe at the daffodils' power:

> And then my heart with pleasure fills,
> And dances with the daffodils.

These final two lines are a rhyming couplet which makes them particularly memorable. He is comparing his heart to a cup and suggesting it is full to the brim with 'pleasure' as he remembers the daffodils. We could argue that without the daffodils, his heart would not be full, but would be empty. The final line even suggests that he becomes one with the daffodils by dancing with them – as if he has become part of the natural world or at the very least is nourished and full of joy because of the daffodils. The language he uses in these final lines is joyful – 'pleasure … fills … dances' – implying that the daffodils bring the beholder great happiness at the time of the experience and long after, too. Notice also how the last word of the poem is 'daffodils'. This is a clever way to end the poem – endings are powerful and we often remember the ending of a text better than we remember the beginning. So by ending the poem with 'daffodils', just as the memory of the daffodils stays with the narrator long after the experience no longer exists, the word or subject of the poem, daffodils, stays with the reader long after the poem has been read and finished! By ending the poem in this way, it should be clear to us how significant the daffodils are and this, also, encourages us to feel wonder at these flowers.

Step 3: Reader response to ideas and message

By the end of the poem, readers should be full with so much awe for the natural world that we are itching to get up and wander in nature to experience this first-hand! At the very least, we should be more aware of the beauty of our world and the powerful effect it can have on the individual, if we allow it to do so. From a literary perspective, we should also be full of awe and admiration for a poet who is able to create such a perfect poem – although Wordsworth may argue that this was because of the effect of the daffodils, his muse for this poem.

CONCEPT CONNECTION

IDENTITY

If we remind ourselves of the key features of Romanticism, we will see that Romantics, like William Wordsworth, believed in the importance of the individual experience to acquire knowledge and that they celebrated and elevated nature. The poem, 'I Wandered Lonely as a Cloud', is written in the first person and in the middle of stanza 3 (lines 15–16) the poet himself is mentioned in the lines 'A poet could not but be gay / In such a jocund company!' Throughout the poem, Wordsworth uses **sensory** imagery (auditory imagery through the harmonious meter and rhyme, and visual imagery through the description of the daffodils) and he elevates the daffodils through his use of **personification**. As the reader, we assume that the views in the poem mirror Wordsworth the writer's views and that the person who 'wandered lonely as a cloud' was Wordsworth himself. However, the relationship between the actual writer and the text is a complex one and this is true with this particular poem. Although the Romantic views articulated in the poem mirror Wordsworth the biographical writer's perspective, the person who 'wandered lonely as a cloud' was not Wordsworth and the 'poet' in line 15 was not Wordsworth, either. It was Wordsworth's sister, Dorothy, who experienced these daffodils when she was wandering in the Lake District and she wrote about them in her journals which she shared with her brother. It was her description of the daffodils which inspired Wordsworth to write this poem. In your reading of texts in class, be aware of the complex relationship between a writer and his or her text. The more texts by a single writer you read, the closer you may get to the biographical writer but it is rare that you will ever understand the true identity of the writer through reading their texts.

TOK Links: Validity of language

We have seen in Wordsworth's poem how he attempts to describe the scene by appealing to the reader's senses. In this way, he hopes we will feel we are experiencing the scene similarly to how the narrator experienced it.

Do we need to experience the world first-hand to acquire an understanding that is valid or can language give us an understanding of the world which is just as valid? How important is language in shaping our perception of the world?

We have explored how Wordsworth, a Romantic poet, wanted to affect his readers through this particular poem. However, once a text has been created it is out of the writer's hands and it is the reader who has the power to interpret it and be affected by it as she or he so wishes. A writer can only hope that a reader will be affected in a particular way, but of course this may not always be the case. The following poem by Welsh poet, Gillian Clarke, explores this idea. She wrote 'Miracle On St David's Day' in 1980, nearly 200 years after 'Daffodils' was written, and describes how one particular individual she met in a psychiatric hospital has been affected by this poem.

Miracle On St David's Day

All you need to know about this poem is that it is a true story. It happened in the '70s, and it took me years to find a way to write the poem.

'They flash upon that inward eye
Which is the bliss of solitude.'
(from 'The Daffodils' by William Wordsworth)

An afternoon yellow and open-mouthed
with daffodils. The sun treads the path
among cedars and enormous oaks.
It might be a country house, guests strolling,
the rumps of gardeners between nursery shrubs.

I am reading poetry to the insane.
An old woman, interrupting, offers
as many buckets of coal as I need.
A beautiful chestnut-haired boy listens
entirely absorbed. A schizophrenic

on a good day, they tell me later.
In a cage of first March sun a woman
sits not listening, not feeling.
In her neat clothes the woman is absent.
A big, mild man is tenderly led

to his chair. He has never spoken.
His labourer's hands on his knees, he rocks
gently to the rhythms of the poems.
I read to their presences, absences,
to the big, dumb labouring man as he rocks.

He is suddenly standing, silently,
huge and mild, but I feel afraid. Like slow
movement of spring water or the first bird
of the year in the breaking darkness,
the labourer's voice recites 'The Daffodils'.

The nurses are frozen, alert; the patients
seem to listen. He is hoarse but word-perfect.
Outside the daffodils are still as wax,
a thousand, ten thousand, their syllables
unspoken, their creams and yellows still.

Forty years ago, in a Valleys school,
the class recited poetry by rote.
Since the dumbness of misery fell

he has remembered there was a music
of speech and that once he had something to say.

When he's done, before the applause, we observe
the flowers' silence. A thrush sings
and the daffodils are flame.

(Gillian Clarke)

This is a powerful poem that explores how individuals are affected by poetry. Clarke makes it clear this is an actual experience and initially we see how she has a great belief in the power of poetry on the individual – perhaps because she, herself, is a poet. She is 'reading poetry to the insane' (line 6) on the 'first March' (line 12), the time of the year when winter thaws and spring arrives. The listeners respond differently: one old woman interrupts her with random remarks about 'buckets of coal' (line 8); one boy 'listens / entirely absorbed' (lines 9–10); another woman 'sits not listening, not feeling' (line 13). We wonder perhaps how effective poetry is – it appears only one boy is actually engaged. However, then the 'big, mild man' (line 15) with 'labourer's hands' (line 17) arrives – and it is through him that we understand the effect poetry can have on the individual. Initially, it is the sound of the poems that affect him and Clarke describes how 'he rocks / gently to the rhythms of the poems' (lines 17–18). However, there is then a shift in the poem as this man who, according to the nurses, 'has never spoken' (line 16), suddenly stands up and recites the poem. Clarke recalls how 'he is hoarse but word-perfect' (line 27). This detail helps us picture the scene and it is an incredible moment and perhaps fills us with wonder at the powerful effect this poem has had on this labouring man. We can also see the connection to Wordsworth's poem: just as the daffodils themselves stayed in the narrator's 'inward eye' long after the experience passed, the poem itself has stayed within this man's 'inward eye' long after he first recited it forty years ago at school. We are not told whether the man interprets the poem in the way Wordsworth had intended – is he filled with wonder and awe at the natural world? – but this is not important. The important thing is that he *has* been affected by the poem; it has stayed within him and in his moment of 'misery' (line 33), allows him to remember 'there was a music / of speech and that once he had something to say' (lines 34–35). Again, just as the daffodils bring solace and comfort to the narrator long after the experience is over, so does the poem remind the man of happier times and allows him to escape his misery temporarily.

This is an interesting poem as it clearly suggests that poetry *does* affect the individual and we can also see how a single poem may affect different readers differently. When you are studying poetry in class, you may want to explore this idea further – how a single poem may affect you differently to the way it affects your teacher or your other classmates.

Gillian Clarke

Gillian Clarke (born 1937) is a Welsh poet who speaks both Welsh and English. She has published a number of poetry anthologies and regularly performs her poetry for student audiences around Europe and at Poetry Live. She has translated poetry and prose from Welsh into English and has also written radio and theatre drama. In 1999 she was awarded the Glyndŵr Award for her outstanding contribution to the arts in Wales, in 2008 she became the third National Poet of Wales, in 2010 she became the second Welsh person to receive the Queen's Gold Medal for Poetry and in 2012 she was awarded the Wilfred Owen Award. She is the co-founder of a writer's centre in North Wales called Tŷ Newydd.

CONCEPT CONNECTION

TRANSFORMATION

This concept is about making connections between texts and how one text refers to another text. It is explored in greater depth in Section 3 Intertextuality: connecting texts. Gillian Clarke's poem is a good example of this concept, however, as she makes connections to Wordsworth's original poem. Clarke's poem is quite obviously based on Wordsworth's poem and she makes this clear before her poem starts by calling it 'Miracle on St David's Day'. St David's Day is the feast day of St David, the patron saint of Wales, and the daffodil is associated with this particular day being a Welsh symbol. Clarke also quotes two lines from Wordsworth's original poem before her first stanza which makes an explicit connection. There are other connections, too. The first two lines focus on 'yellow and open-mouthed' daffodils and we are immediately reminded of Wordsworth's poem which she herself refers to as 'The Daffodils' rather than its original title, 'I Wandered Lonely as a Cloud'. The poems she is reading to 'the insane' are clearly rhythmic, shown through the way the man 'rocks / gently to the rhythms of the poems' and this also reminds us of Wordsworth's original poem with its gentle musicality. However, it is the man's recitation of Wordsworth's poem that makes the connection absolutely clear – but, as already discussed, it is not only the fact that the man recites this particular poem, but it is the fact that Clarke herself is connecting this recitation with ideas in the original poem. Just as Wordsworth's narrator recalls the daffodils long after he first experienced them, so does this man recall the poem long after he first recited it. Just as the memory of the daffodils fills Wordsworth's narrator with 'pleasure' when he is 'in vacant or in pensive mood', so too does the memory of the poem remind the man 'there was a music / of speech and that once he had something to say' even though now 'the dumbness of misery' has befallen him.

Finally, just as the end focus of Wordsworth's poem is 'daffodils', so too is Clarke's poem which ends with 'the daffodils are flame'. Clarke manages to make clear connections to Wordsworth's original poem but manages to transform it, too. We are unclear whether the man is full of wonder for nature, Wordsworth's original intention, or whether it is the beauty and harmony of the poem itself that has filled him with wonder. Clarke's poem itself differs from Wordsworth's poem, too – her poem is not as musical as Wordsworth's. She uses an irregular meter and rhythm, there is no rhyme and there is an irregular use of stanza length – representing, perhaps, her audience's unpredictable reactions to her reading poetry. However, there is still a power to her poem as we are moved by the incredible effect poetry has had on this particular individual.

EE Links: English A – Literature category 1

This concept of transformation would make an interesting basis for an extended essay in which you compare Gillian Clarke's poem with William Wordsworth's poem. You could explore the ways in which Clarke's poem is influenced by Wordsworth's poem and compare the similarities and differences between them in terms of ideas, language, style and structure. A potential English A: Literature category 1 extended essay research question could be:

To what extent is Clarke's 'Miracle On St David's Day' influenced by Wordsworth's 'Daffodils' and to what extent do they differ?

CAS Links

Organize a fundraising activity at school and spend the money on small indoor plants, which you can either distribute to tutor rooms to make the school more green, or you could deliver to an old people's home. Alternatively, you could buy some outdoor plants and either plant in the school grounds or you could plant in the garden of an old people's home. If you buy outdoor plants, you could volunteer to look after them for a few months and use this as a service project.

Let's now move on to explore the effect texts have on us in understanding 'the other' and encouraging us to empathize with other people who are very different to ourselves. You may feel that Clarke's poem does this effectively, but we will explore this idea in more depth by studying an extract from a prose non-fiction work, a memoir by George Orwell.

Texts encourage us to empathize and be aware of others

As well as filling us with wonder about the natural world, texts also give us an insight into other people's experiences, thoughts and actions and in so doing help us experience empathy for those who are different to ourselves. Consider this famous quotation by philosopher, Hannah Arendt:

> *'The death of human empathy is one of the earliest and most telling signs of a culture about to fall into barbarism.'*
>
> *Hannah Arendt*

Before we start exploring the extract for this part of the chapter, it is important to understand the difference between 'empathy' and 'sympathy' as they are often confused. Although they are quite similar, they differ in their emotional meaning and intensity.

■ Table 1.2.2

empathy	The ability to understand and share what others are feeling; feeling an affinity with others, often because you have experienced it yourself or can put yourself in their shoes.
sympathy	Acknowledging another person's suffering and providing comfort and assurance.

To empathize, then, requires a more intense emotional reaction. Imagine a friend of yours has just finished her extended essay and then her computer crashes and she loses the entire essay. She did not back up her work. If this has never happened to you before, you can **sympathize** with her – you can imagine what she is going through and try to offer some kind of comfort. If, however, you have experienced something very similar – then you would be able to **empathize** with your friend as you really do know what she is going through, having gone through it yourself.

When we read texts, we often read about experiences of other people that we have not experienced ourselves. If a writer is successful, she or he will be able to use their craft as a writer to describe the experience in such a way that you really feel that you are experiencing it first-hand and are, therefore, able to **empathize** rather than simply **sympathize** with the character. The extract you are about to read employs a range of devices which encourages you to **empathize** with the protagonists of this extract.

The following extract is an example of the literary form of prose non-fiction. It is a memoir by George Orwell, an English writer who focused mostly on the flaws of society and attempted to elicit a response of shock, anger and, at times, fear in the reader. This extract comes from his memoir, *Down and Out in Paris and London* (1933), which is about his first-hand experiences of poverty when he was a young man living in Paris and London.

The following extract comes from the London section and Orwell is describing his experience of a London 'spike', the colloquial term for a workhouse where those who were unable to support themselves could work and have a bed for the night. Most readers – both now and back when it was published – would probably not have experienced first-hand conditions inside a spike. This extract, therefore, gives us an insight into the experience of 'others' – individuals who, unlike ourselves, have to depend upon spikes as they are unable to support themselves.

As you read this extract, think about how Orwell creates empathy for the tramps through his use of language, imagery and literary features (step 2 of our reading strategy). We are going to split the extract into three parts, focusing on the way Orwell depicts (a) the tramps collectively, (b) individual tramps and (c) the doctor.

The extract is an unflattering picture of this 'spike' – if it was set up to help tramps, it does not appear to have been successful in this respect. We are supposed to feel that the tramps are treated with a lack of compassion, dehumanized and discriminated against and that they are powerless to change anything. In fact, we could argue that the spike itself little benefits the tramps and even holds them back. Although Orwell is merely documenting what he experiences, he uses language effectively to encourage readers to feel shocked, angry and ashamed that this is how the tramps are treated and consequently empathize with them. So, how does he do this and how are we affected?

In the following model commentaries, notice how we are focusing our close reading on step 2 of our reading strategy, analysing the language, imagery and features. Notice, also, how each point is illustrated with a quotation and each quotation is analysed in detail, explaining the effect on the reader Orwell is attempting to have. All terminology is highlighted – any terminology with which you are unfamiliar should be looked up in the glossary at the end of the book.

So far, we have explored how texts can fill us with wonder and awe at the power of the natural world, and how they can encourage us to feel empathy for others who are very different to ourselves. The next part of this chapter explores how texts can also encourage us to look deep within ourselves and contemplate our inner self.

Naked and shivering, we lined up in the passage. You cannot conceive what ruinous, degenerate curs we looked, standing there in the merciless morning light. A tramp's clothes are bad, but they conceal far worse things; to see him as he really is, unmitigated, you must see him naked. Flat feet, pot bellies, hollow chests, sagging muscles – every kind of physical rottenness was there. Nearly everyone was under-nourished, and some clearly diseased; two men were wearing trusses*, and as for the old mummy-like creature of seventy-five, one wondered how he could possibly make his daily march. Looking at our faces, unshaven and creased from the sleepless night, you would have thought that all of us were recovering from a week on the drink.

The inspection was designed merely to detect smallpox, and took no notice of our general condition. A young medical student, smoking a cigarette, walked rapidly along the line glancing us up and down, and not inquiring whether any man was well or ill. When my cell companion stripped I saw that his chest was covered with a red rash, and, having spent the night a few inches away from him, I fell into a panic about smallpox. The doctor, however, examined the rash and said that it was due merely to under-nourishment.

**trusses: padded belt that is worn to support a hernia*

(George Orwell 157)

ACTIVITY 2

1 Read the two commentaries, **(a)** and **(b)** below, then write your own on the doctor – see **(c)** on the next page. When you have written your commentary, read the example at the back of the book and compare ideas.

(a) The tramps collectively

The extract opens with the emotive sentence, 'Naked and shivering, we lined up in the passage'. The two **adjectives** that open the sentence have **connotations** of defence-lessness and powerlessness and the fact that they are forced to line up, makes us feel they are being treated more like convicts who are guilty of a crime than individuals who are unable to support themselves because of some kind of hardship. This suggests that the institutions that have been set up to help the tramps lack compassion and rather than offering them care and support, humiliate them instead. This affects the reader, immediately encouraging us to empathize with the tramps and feel angry at the government that set up institutions such as spikes.

We are further forced to engage with the text through Orwell's use of the **second-person pronoun** 'you'. This has the effect of ensuring the reader does not look away but faces full-on what Orwell is documenting.

The tramps are now dehumanized through the **metaphor** 'ruinous, degenerate curs', which suggests they are closer to wild dogs than human beings. It also infers that just as a wild dog is aggressive because of the way it is rejected by mankind, the tramps also have become ungrateful because of the way they have been treated by society. This makes the reader feel guilty and reflect on his or her own attitudes towards the poor. Orwell also forces the reader to empathize with the tramps as he describes their physical appearance – now on public display as they are naked. He lists them as having: 'flat feet, pot bellies, hollow chests, sagging muscles – every kind of physical rottenness was there.' The way this sentence is structured highlights the overwhelming amount of sickness experienced by the tramps – from their feet to their bellies to their chests. We feel sickness is omnipresent and the **listing** suggests that every tramp is suffering from at least one physical illness. By focusing on body parts, the tramps are dehumanized too, only identifiable through their physical defect and this also makes us empathize with them. The **abstract noun** 'rottenness' also makes us feel the tramps are dying inside, like a piece of meat that is past its sell-by date and this heightens our empathetic feelings towards them. The fact that the tramps are naked means we see these ailments full-on, rather than pretending they do not exist when they are concealed underneath clothing, the usual way we view individuals. So, Orwell forces us to see the tramps as they truly are which in turn helps us empathize with them.

(b) Individual tramps

When Orwell shifts his focus from the group of tramps to individuals it is as if he is zooming his camera in to give us a close-up view. He describes how 'two men were wearing trusses' which could be a **metaphor** for the ineffectiveness of the spike. A truss is a padded belt that offers support for a hernia; however, it does not actually heal. It may ease the pain temporarily, but it does not get to the root of the problem. Likewise, the spike can be seen to offer temporary support – at least it offers the tramps a bed for the night – but it does not offer any permanent solution and Orwell appears to be criticizing this. When he zooms in on the 75-year-old man we are shocked that such an old man is in this position and still expected to 'march' the streets of London. This creates **pathos** for him. The **simile** 'mummy-like creature' that is used to describe him is also shocking as it degrades and dehumanizes him, suggesting he is more dead than alive. By zooming the camera in on individuals, we are forced to see them in detail, which also helps to heighten the sense of empathy we feel for these particular individuals.

c The doctor. Complete this commentary yourself , focusing on the LIFs (language, imagery, features).

Having described the tramps in general and honed in on two or three individual tramps, Orwell then moves on to describe the inspection and the doctor. Initially, we would feel having a doctor inspect the tramps is a good thing – perhaps now they will be offered treatment for their many physical illnesses. However ...

When you have completed this commentary, compare your ideas with the commentary at the back of the book. If you want to think further, consider the difference between sympathy and empathy. What are the similarities and differences?

GLOBAL ISSUES ***Field of inquiry:* Politics, Power and Justice**

UNEQUAL DISTRIBUTION OF WEALTH

We have already explored this global issue in Chapter 1.1 through our study of Dickens' prose fiction novella, *A Christmas Carol*. This is another example, this time through a prose non-fiction work, of how the unequal distribution of wealth is a global issue that transcends time. Orwell was a twentieth-century political writer and in this passage he is criticizing society where there is such a wealth gap and where the wealthy, including the government, are not helping the poor. Although the 'spike' exists and a doctor visits the tramps, Orwell is condemnatory of both: the spike treats the tramps inhumanely and the doctor is only concerned with illnesses that are contagious and may affect the larger community, rather than showing any compassion for the wide range of non-contagious but personally debilitating illnesses the tramps have. The memoir as a whole has as its theme 'poverty' and Orwell explores poverty in both Paris and London in the 1920s. He explores the workings and structures of institutions such as the pawnshop, the hotel industry, the 'spike' and the church and suggests rather than practically helping the poor, they humiliate them and make them feel worse than they already feel. As we explored in Chapter 1.1, this is similar to how Dickens focuses on poverty and social responsibility in nineteenth-century London. As we can see from Orwell's prose non-fiction and Dickens' prose fiction, exploring the distribution of wealth and the disparity between the wealthy and the poor is a topic that many literary works focus on. The disparity between the wealthy and the poor is a topic that many non-literary texts focus on as well and you may want to explore this global issue related to the field of inquiry of politics, power and justice in your oral through other literary works and non-literary texts you read in class.

George Orwell

George Orwell, born Eric Arthur Blair, was born in Motihari in British India in 1903. One year later, his mother took him and his two sisters to the UK where he grew up and lived for most of his life. He is an English writer of fiction and non-fiction, most famous for his novels *Animal Farm* (1945) and *Nineteen Eighty-Four* (1949) both of which are political in nature, warning of a dystopian future. Much of his work is based on his political views which were critical of colonialism and totalitarianism, and were formed through first-hand experience of working in colonial Burma as a police officer; living among the 'down and outs' in Paris and London during the interwar years; and experiencing the Spanish Civil War and the Second World War.

Texts encourage us to contemplate our inner self

Many people would argue it is easier to understand and empathize with the other, precisely because it is not the self. Understanding the self can be fraught with pain and angst because the self is such a personal, intimate and essential part of our own being. We will explore this idea in the next extract, which is from a work in translation, the Japanese prose fiction novella, *Kitchen*, by Banana Yoshimoto. Read the following extract and then read the accompanying commentary.

The next day was when I had to clear out of the old apartment for good; at last I got it cleaned out completely. I was feeling very sluggish. It was a clear, bright afternoon, windless and cloudless, and a warm, golden sunlight filled the empty rooms I had once called home.

By way of apology for taking so much time, I went to visit the landlord.

Like we often did when I was a child, we drank tea and chatted in his office. I felt very keenly how old he had become. Just as my grandmother had often sat here, now I was in the same little chair, drinking tea and talking about the weather and the state of the neighbourhood. It was strange; it didn't seem right.

An irresistible shift had put the past behind me. I had recoiled in a daze; all I could do was react weakly. But it was not I who was doing the shifting – on the contrary. For me everything had been agony.

Until only recently, the light that bathed the now-empty apartment had contained the smells of our life there.

The kitchen window. The smiling faces of friends, the fresh greenery of the university campus as a backdrop to Sotaro's profile, my grandmother's voice on the phone when I called her late at night, my warm bed on cold mornings, the sound of my grandmother's slippers in the hallway, the color of the curtains … the *tatami* mat … the clock on the wall.

All of it. Everything that was no longer there.

When I left the apartment it was already evening.

Pale twilight was descending. The wind was coming up, a little chilly on the skin. I waited for the bus, the hem of my thin coat fluttering in the gusts.

I watched the rows of windows in the tall building across the street from the bus stop, suspended, emitting a pretty blue light. The people moving behind those windows, the elevators going up and down, all of it, sparkling silently, seemed to melt into the half-darkness.

I carried the last of my things in both hands. When I thought, now at last I won't be torn between two places, I began to feel strangely shaky, close to tears.

The bus appeared around the corner. It seemed to float to a stop before my eyes, and the people lined up, got on, one by one.

It was packed. I stood, with my hand on the crowded strap, watching the darkening sky disappear beyond the distant buildings.

When the bus took off my eye came to rest on the still-new moon making its gentle way across the sky.

(Banana Yoshimoto 31–33)

Step 1: Form and structure

There is an intimacy about this extract that is created, to a certain extent, through its being written in a first-person narrative, which helps us to empathize with the narrator's situation. The narrator is in the throes of an existential crisis which we, as readers, can relate to – chiefly, the transient nature of all things. As the extract suggests, the narrator has lost her grandmother and she is now attempting to deal with a frightening and lonely present. Throughout the extract, minor sentences ('The kitchen window.' 'All of it.'), simple sentences and single-line sentences are embedded to great effect. They help to emphasize how uncomfortable and detached the narrator feels about the new life she is forced to confront as well as the harsh and sudden reality of losing those who are dear to us and trying to carry on with our lives. The use of a hyphen in the first section (line 9) and ellipsis in the second section (line 14) make the extract feel more authentic and less stylised. It gives the extract a sense of immediacy as if we are hearing the narrator reflecting spontaneously, helping to build a connection between the narrator and the reader.

In the extract, we are presented with a character who feels powerless, not wholly in control of her life and who is reluctant to accept change. Yoshimoto uses **contrasts** and time shifts between the past and the present to suggest how the narrator is caught between two worlds and cannot move on. The extract opens in the present, but the final paragraph of this first section makes it clear how the narrator has not voluntarily left the past for the present, but has been forced to leave the past behind: 'An irresistible shift had put the past behind me.' (line 8). The use of the passive tense here makes it clear that the narrator was not the active one in leaving the past behind. She blames it on 'an irresistible shift', suggesting that something beyond her powers had occurred, from which there was no turning back. The next section, starting 'Until only recently', (line 10) which is physically separated from the first section on the page, takes us back to the past. The way Yoshimoto has juxtaposed these paragraphs imitates how the narrator would rather escape the present and be back in the past, a more familiar and comfortable world. However, as we are all aware, we cannot turn the clock back and relive the past. Yoshimoto has structured the past section to be the shortest section, with the preceding and following sections which take place in the present being the longer passages. This seems to suggest how we can only relive the past in our memory, and only fleetingly. We are physically in the present and cannot escape this fact. Many readers will be able to identify with the narrator's anguish here – wanting to relive the past is a common desire, particularly if you have recently lost someone close to you (as the narrator has). The structure of the passage, therefore, encourages the reader to reflect on how the individual deals with grief and attempts to move on from the past to the present.

Step 2: LIF

Yoshimoto also **contrasts** the present and the past through the language she uses. The first paragraph describes a meeting between the narrator and the landlord. **Tripling** is used here to describe this meeting: 'now I was in the same little chair, drinking tea and talking about the weather and the state of the neighborhood.' (lines 6–7). There is nothing special about any of these things – they are unremarkable and impersonal. In contrast, when the narrator remembers her past, she recalls 'the smells of our life there … The smiling faces of friends, the fresh greenery of the university campus … my grandmother's voice on the phone … my warm bed on cold mornings, the sound of my grandmother's slippers in the hallway, the color of the curtains … the *tatami* mat … the clock on the wall.' (lines 10–14). This is a much longer list and our senses are awakened through the olfactory imagery ('the smells of our life there'), colour imagery ('greenery of the university campus', 'the color of the curtains'), auditory imagery ('grandmother's voice', 'the sound of my grandmother's slippers') and tactile imagery ('my warm bed on cold mornings', 'the *tatami* mat').

There is also a sense of belonging through the repeated use of the possessive pronoun 'my' which is missing from the previous section. However, there is a sadness to this description as it is clear that this has all gone and been replaced by a present that is cold and unremarkable. The only place where the past still exists and is validated is in her memories. We can understand how the 'irresistible shift' (line 8) that forced her to leave her past behind has caused her 'agony' (line 9). Again, we are encouraged to reflect on our own lives and compare our pasts with our presents.

Yoshimoto uses an **extended metaphor** of a window to explore some of these ideas. In the past, the 'kitchen window' (line 11) can be interpreted as a **symbol** through which the narrator can look to view her past life. It is a 'kitchen window' which suggests warmth and domesticity, traditionally a woman's place, perhaps, where food is cooked to nourish the body. The novella is titled *Kitchen* and this suggests that the kitchen is a place of significance, either literally or metaphorically. It is important, therefore, that it is a 'kitchen window' that offers her a glimpse into her past. However, a window is also a barrier, physically separating the narrator from her past life. This **metaphor** of the window is also used towards the end of the extract in the final section which takes place in the narrative present. When the narrator has finally left her old apartment to attempt to begin a new life, she watches 'the rows of windows ... suspended' (line 19) and 'people moving behind those windows.' (line 20). Unlike the 'kitchen window' of earlier, these windows offer no solace to the narrator. There is no warmth or feeling to what she observes through the windows. We feel she is an outsider, looking in on other people's lives from which she is detached and alienated. Additionally, the mechanical soulless 'elevators going up and down' (lines 20–21) accentuate this mood, suggesting how not only is the narrator unable to fully embrace the present but there is little worthwhile to embrace.

Yoshimoto uses setting to help us empathize with the narrator's existential crisis. When the narrator exits her apartment it is 'pale twilight' (line 17) – the time between light and darkness – which symbolizes the idea of the narrator being stuck between two worlds. She also uses **pathetic fallacy** to accentuate a discomforting and foreboding mood. As she is waiting for the bus, 'The wind was coming up, a little chilly on the skin' (line 17). Again, the present is associated with a lack of warmth or comfort. The bus can also be seen as a **metaphor** as it 'seemed to float' (line 24) in front of her eyes. It seems unreal with no definite sense of direction and does not offer the narrator safety, security or solidity. Ironically, the present here appears to be more dream-like than real even though it is of course happening and it is the memories of her past that are not happening. When the narrator boards, it could perhaps be seen as a **symbol** for how she feels about her life. She is standing, with her 'hand on the crowded strap' (line 26). There is no comfort in this description and we feel she is alone in a mass of people, having to hold on just in order to survive. As the bus begins its journey, she watches the 'darkening sky' (line 26) – another foreboding use of **pathetic fallacy**, suggesting she is heading towards darkness and hopelessness. The final image in this extract avoids the cliché of a new sun rising which would denote hope but rather Yoshimoto uses the image of a 'still-new moon' (line 28). She seems to be suggesting that the narrator's present and future will be largely predictable and a time of numbness and darkness with minimal light.

Step 3: Reader response to ideas and message

Many readers may have experienced this sense of alienation and powerlessness and will be able to recognise the narrator's feelings as resembling their own. It perhaps makes us feel less alienated, reading about someone else's sense of not belonging and craving that which has passed. Despite being a bleak passage, then, it can conversely offer hope to the reader knowing that we are not alone in our insecurities.

Banana Yoshimoto

Mahoko Yoshimoto was born in 1964 in Tokyo, Japan. Her pseudonym, Banana, was taken at university and comes from her love of banana flowers. She comes from an artistic family: her father, Takaaki Yoshimoto, is a famous poet and critic, and her sister, Haruno Yoiko, is a cartoonist. *Kitchen* was her first work to be published (1988) and it has had more than 60 printings in Japan, was translated into English in 1993 and has been made into two films in Japan and Hong Kong. Yoshimoto has written twelve novels and collections of essays, which together have sold over 6 million copies worldwide and won literary prizes in Japan and internationally. Recurring themes in Yoshimoto's works include how traumatic experiences can affect an individual's life and how exhaustion is ingrained within young Japanese people in modern-day Japan.

EE Links: English A – Literature category 2

Banana Yoshimoto's *Kitchen* is a work in translation and comparing this novella with a work originally written in English would work well for a literature category 2 extended essay. There are a range of topics you could base your extended essay on, including: alienation, gender, memory, nostalgia and identity. You would need to compare Yoshimoto's novella with another work (originally written in English) that explored a similar idea, and develop a focused research question that allowed you to research your chosen topic from a literary perspective.

So far, we have explored three forms of literary works – poetry, prose non-fiction and prose fiction – and seen how readers are affected in various ways by them. Of course, just as readers are affected in various ways by literary works, so are they affected by non-literary texts. We will now shift our focus onto three non-literary texts and explore how we are affected differently by each of them.

Texts that inspire curiosity and educate the reader

The literary works we have explored encourage an emotional response in the reader, either in terms of acknowledging the wonder of the natural world or in terms of empathizing with the other or understanding the self. The next text we are going to explore encourages a very different response in the reader. It is similar to the two poems we studied at the beginning of this chapter in the respect that it is about flowers and uses the daffodil as one of its examples. However, its approach differs from the poetry – and the other literary works – we have studied with the result that we are affected very differently. Before you read the extract, first of all read the key features box of informative texts:

KEY FEATURES INFORMATIVE TEXTS

- Uses **neutral language**, aimed at informing rather than eliciting an emotional response.
- Uses credible sources, including direct quotations from experts in the field
- Specialist language (**jargon**) can be embedded if aimed at specific audience.
- Clearly organized, often taking a step-by-step approach.
- An objective tone is used.
- Statistics, figures, percentages that can be verified and substantiated are used.
- May include **visual images** that reinforce the written text.
- **Typographical** and **graphological** features are often included to emphasize certain words or ideas.

Now read the following extract from *The Encyclopaedia Britannica: A Dictionary of Arts, Sciences, Literature and General Information, Volume X Slice V*, first published in 1910–11, and then read the accompanying commentary:

■ Table 1.2.3

FLOWER (Lat. *flos*, *floris*; Fr. *fleur*), a term popularly used for the bloom or blossom of a plant, and so by analogy for the fairest, choicest or finest part or aspect of anything, and in various technical senses. Here we shall deal only with its botanical interest. It is impossible to give a rigid botanical definition of the term 'flower'. The flower is a characteristic feature of the highest group of the plant kingdom – the flowering plants (*Phanerogams*) – and is the name given to the association of organs, more or less leaf-like in form, which are concerned with the production of the fruit or seed …

A sheathing bract enclosing one or several flowers is called a *spathe*. It is common among Monocotyledons, as *Narcissus* (fig. 4), snow-flake, *Arum* and palms. In some palms it is 20 ft. long, and encloses 200,000 flowers. It is often associated with that form of inflorescence termed the spadix, and may be coloured, as in *Anthurium*, or white, as in arum lily (*Richardia aethiopica*). When the *spadix* is compound or branching, as in palms, there are smaller spathes, surrounding separate parts of the inflorescence. The spathe protects the flowers in their young state, and often falls off after they are developed, or hangs down in a withered form, as in some palms, *Typha* and *Pothos*. In grasses the outer scales or glumes of the spikelets are sterile bracts (fig. 5, gl); and in Cyperaceae bracts enclose the organs of reproduction. Bracts are frequently changed into complete leaves. This change is called *phyllody* of bracts, and is seen in species of *Plantago*, especially in the variety of *Plantago media*, called the rose-plantain in gardens, where the bracts become leafy and form a rosette round the flowering axis. Similar changes occur in *Plantago major, P. lanceolata, Ajuga reptans*, dandelion, daisy, dahlia and in umbelliferous plants. The conversion of bracts into stamens (*staminody* of bracts) has been observed in the case of *Abies excelsa*. A lengthening of the axis of the female strobilus of Coniferae is not of infrequent occurrence in *Cryptomeria japonica*, larch (*Larix europaea*), &c., and this is usually associated with a leaf-like condition of the bracts, and sometimes even with the development of leaf-bearing shoots in place of the scales.

■ Fig. 4 – Flowers of Narcissus (*Narcissus Tazetta*) bursting from a sheathing bract *b*.

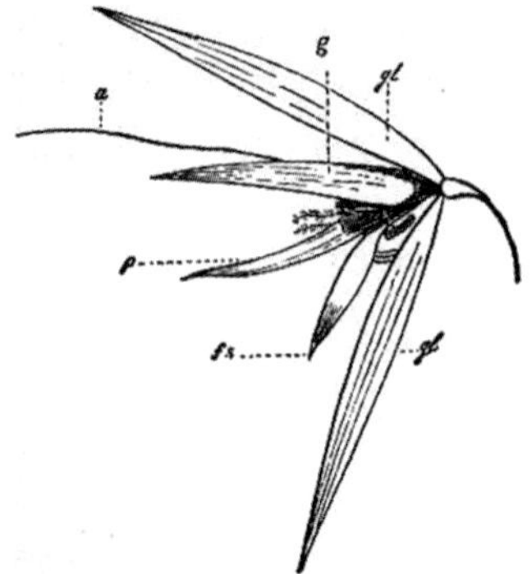

■ Fig. 5 – Spikelet of Oat (*Avena sativa*) laid open, showing the sterile bracts *gl*, *gl*, or empty glumes; *g*, the fertile or floral glume, with a dorsal awn *a*; *p*, the pale; *fs*, an abortive flower.

Encyclopaedia Britannica, 11th Edition, Volume 10, Slice 5, 554–5

Step 1: Genre, audience and purpose (GAP)

Genre (text type)	Encyclopaedia entry
Audience	Readers with a curiosity in the botany of flowers
Purpose	To inform

This is an extract from an encyclopaedia which gives the reader detailed botanical information about the item being described – in this case the 'flower'. The intended audience is readers who have a genuine curiosity in flowers from a scientific or botanical perspective. Its purpose is wholly informative: it aims to inform the reader about the general qualities of a flower as well as, in this particular extract, a specific part of the flower – the 'sheathing bract'. Unlike the Wordsworth poem, it is not attempting to elicit an emotional response, even though it discusses the same flower as Wordsworth, the daffodil (or 'narcissus'). By the end of the entry, the hope is that readers' curiosity about this flower has been satisfied through the wealth of information shared with the reader. Although we do not know who the author is, the writer appears credible and authentic due to their knowledge about the topic, grounded in scientific and factual statements that can be substantiated. The reader will, therefore, feel the knowledge being imparted is accurate and by the end of the entry, feel as though he or she has been educated in an area that he or she perhaps lacked understanding about prior to reading. This is a common feature of encyclopaedias making them a trusted source of unbiased and objective information for readers.

Step 2: Structure and style

The text is clearly structured by beginning with general information about flowers and then honing in on specific details – the sheathing bract. In the first paragraph, for example, the reader is immediately informed that 'flower' is a term 'popularly used for the bloom or blossom of a plant …' This is a direct statement that describes what 'flower' means - there is no ambiguity and readers will be clear about the general definition of this item. The second paragraph opens with 'A sheathing bract enclosing one or several flowers is called a *spathe*.' This is a similar way to begin the next paragraph, using a topic sentence to make a clear fact about the definition of a term. We have moved from the general 'flower' to the specific 'sheathing bract' and because of this step-by-step approach and unambiguous language, it is hoped the reader will follow and understand the more intricate details about the plant as the entry progresses. This structure allows the reader to build up his or her understanding of the flower in steps, making it an easy-to-follow informative text that directs the reader's learning in a manageable way. Most readers would appreciate this scaffolded structure – particularly if they are novices to botany. If they are able to follow and therefore learn about this part of the plant, it is likely the reader would be affected with pleasure or even pride as he or she widens his or her knowledge base.

Step 3: Typographical and graphological features

The entry is **foregrounded** with the sub-heading 'flower' which is in bold and capitalized with the effect that it stands out and allows the reader immediately to be clear about the subject matter of the text. After the sub-heading, 'flower', we are given its Latin and French etymologies which are italicised. By including the origin of the word, this immediately anchors the text in substantiated truths and creates an objective and trustworthy **tone**. The purpose of the text is made quite explicit in the first paragraph: 'Here we shall deal only with its botanical interest.' This immediately informs the reader that the extract is likely to be objective in tone, taking a scientific ('botanical') stance rather than a personal or emotional stance. The article is aimed at a particular reader: someone who is curious about this topic and genuinely wants to be educated about the different parts of the flower. If the text can achieve its purpose, then presumably the reader will feel fulfilled.

The second half of the first sentence could be argued to be subjective as three superlatives are used to describe a flower - 'the fairest, choicest or finest part or aspect of anything'. This description of the flower is a personal opinion rather than a fact that can be substantiated. However, this tone does not last. Immediately following this description, there is almost an apology by way of making it quite clear that this is not going to be the approach of the article – rather a 'botanical' approach is about to be taken. From this point onwards, a wholly scientific tone is used and the language is neutral and objective with a **semantic field** of specialist scientific lexis throughout.

In both paragraphs, **subject–specialist language** that few non-scientists would understand is embedded. However, all scientific terminology is italicised the first time the word or phrase is introduced:

> *A sheathing bract enclosing one or several flowers is called a* spathe. *It is common among Monocotyleddons, as* Narcissus *(fig. 4), snow-flake,* Arum *and palms.'*

The fact that these specialist words are italicised allows them to stand out and suggests to the reader that this is indeed a specialist term which perhaps the reader could learn. The italics then become a visual educational tool in terms of helping readers firstly identify and then remember each new scientific term. The article has certain expectations of the reader. Once the subject -specialist term has been used once and italicised, the next time it is used, it is embedded within the sentence in normal typeface. The implication with this is that the reader is encouraged to be an active reader who takes responsibility for his or her own learning. The reader is expected to 'learn' each new term and understand its meaning the next time it appears in the text. This, then, appeals to our intellectual understanding, encouraging us to engage in what we are reading and actively add to our knowledge during the reading process.

ACTIVITY 3

Step 4: Other features of text type

There are several features typical of informative text types that appeal to our intellectual understanding. Focusing on the extract, match up the feature, the quotation and the effect.

■ Table 1.2.4

Informative Features/Devices	Evidence	Effect
1 Embeds plants' **proper names** rather than their more commonly used names.	A 'In some palms it is 20 ft. long, and encloses 200,000 flowers.'	i This is a visual learning tool that identifies new vocabulary and encourages the reader to learn it.
2 **Typographical features**: such as italics for the Latin or Ancient Greek etymological names of the species.	B 'A sheathing bract enclosing one or several flowers is called a *spathe*.'	ii Allows additional information to be added, aimed at developing readers' knowledge base and understanding even more.
3 **Statistics** that can be verified.	C *Monocotyledons, Cyperaceae, Coniferae*	iii Assumes the reader has a certain knowledge base which appeals to readers. Even if reader is unfamiliar with these terms, the understanding is still clear.
4 **Diction**: subject-specialist language (jargon) is used	D *Narcissus, Richardia aethiopica, Typha, Pothos, Plantago, etc.*	iv The first time it is used it is italicised. This is a visual learning tool to encourage readers to (a) identify the word and (b) learn it before it is used again not italicised.
5 **Typographical features**: use of parenthesis for additional information	E *'Plantago major, P. lanceolata, Ajuga reptans,* dandelion, daisy, dahlia and in umbelliferous plants'	v To create objectivity with the intention of informing and educating the reader rather than eliciting an emotional response.
6 **Other features**: includes listing	F '(Fig. 4)', '(Fig. 5, gl)', '(*staminody* of bracts)'	vi This information can be substantiated and therefore gives the text credibility and authenticity.
7 **Tone**: uses neutral language	G *spathe, phyllody, staminody*	vii Implies the writer has a wide knowledge base which encourages the reader to trust the information.

When you have matched the feature with the evidence with the effect, check your responses at the back of the book.

These features, then, make the article overtly informative. Every sentence gives us another fact about a sheathing bract and in most sentences there is either a scientific term or a Latin name that readers are encouraged to learn and become familiar with. It uses neutral language throughout with the intention of informing and educating the reader about this particular subject.

Step 5: Visual image and layout

However, as well as the written text, the article includes two illustrations. Unlike the text, which is scientific and factual, the illustrations are not photographs but are hand-drawn sketches of 'Flowers of Narcissus' and a 'Spikelet of Oat'. Although the illustrations appear to be accurate depictions of the relevant plants, the fact that they are hand-drawn gives the article a personalised touch and helps prevent it from being too dry and dense. Both illustrations are an essential feature of this text as they clearly illustrate and, therefore, reinforce the written text. Each illustration contains labels in the form of letters ('b', 'gl', 'g', 'a', etc.) and in the caption underneath each illustration, each letter key is explained. Rather than needing multiple lengthy labels which could distract from the illustration itself, the letter key is precise and clear and gives the reader another route to understand the written text. Within the written text, each illustration is referred to in parenthesis which has the benefit of ensuring the reader knows exactly which part of the text the image is illustrating. The images are positioned to the right of the text which also makes it easy for the reader to move from written text to visual illustration when required quickly and without losing his or her place in the text.

Step 6: Reader response to ideas, message and/or purpose

By using a **multimodal** text to educate the reader about a specialized field – an aspect of botany – not only exposes the reader to a range of new facts, including scientific language, Latin names of flowers and statistics, but the illustrations enable the reader to visually recognise this information in the real world next time he or she observes a flower of Narcissus or spikelet of oat. This then gives the text a practical significance and relevance in the reader's everyday life. Readers are, therefore, affected both intellectually in terms of increasing their abstract knowledge about botany but also practically in terms of being able to recognise this new-found knowledge in the real world.

Texts that affect us emotionally

As well as affecting us intellectually, non-literary texts can also affect us emotionally. The next non-literary text that we are going to look at is an extract from an opinion piece that was published in a newspaper in August 2016, written by American writer, Ijeoma Oluo. Before we read this extract, let's have a look at the key features of opinion pieces:

KEY FEATURES **OPINION PIECES**

- Writer's personal opinion; subjective and one-sided.
- Uses first person **personal pronouns** ('I' and 'we').
- May include personal **anecdotes**.
- Uses **emotive language**.
- May acknowledge the opposite point of view and then use a longer counterargument to challenge it.
- May include a logical argument, often backed up by statistics (**logos**).
- May take the moral high ground to appeal to the reader's sense of right and wrong (**ethos**).
- May appeal to the reader's emotions (**pathos**).
- May include other persuasive features including **hyperbole**, **listing**, **anaphora**, direct address to the reader, rhetorical questions, etc.
- Structure – each paragraph develops the argument to construct a solidly argued point of view.

Now read the following opinion piece about Colin Kaepernick. Kaepernick was an American National Football League quarterback for San Francisco 49ers who, in 2016, knelt down while the US national anthem was being played before his preseason matches as a protest against police violence towards black Americans. His 'taking the knee' became global news and many people supported his action whilst many argued he was being disrespectful to the US. The following extract is Oluo's opinion piece about his action. After you have read the opinion piece, read the accompanying commentary.

Colin Kaepernick's national anthem protest is fundamentally American

Many are arguing that the footballer's refusal to stand is inappropriate, but it's what US values look like when all are included.

I was on family vacation when Colin Kaepernick decided to make me care about football. During Friday night's preseason game against Green Bay, the 49ers quarterback did what many black people have been waiting for more of our black football players to do for a long time – he protested. It was a quiet protest, the act of sitting during the national anthem, but it was heard around the world.

When interviewed after the game, Kaepernick explained: 'I am not going to stand up to show pride in a flag for a country that oppresses black people and people of color. To me, this is bigger than football and it would be selfish on my part to look the other way. There are bodies in the street and people getting paid leave and getting away with murder.'

In many corners, this didn't go over well, to say the least. Some people burned their Kaepernick jerseys. Many argued that, while Kaepernick may be right to be upset by the thousands of black and brown people killed by police in the US, protesting the flag was not the appropriate way to create change. Others asked why he hates veterans – still others, why he hates America. Yet more people asked why he can't just stick to football. But every argument against Kaepernick's protest is wrong. Every single one.

Furthermore, many of them are racist. And the backlash against Kaepernick displays how everyday Americans who would never consider themselves racist can get caught in acts of white supremacy.

For starters, there is nothing more American than protest. It's built into our history and our mythology. I imagine that those who think protesting during the National Anthem is un-American think that the Boston Tea Party was a literal tea party with tiny cakes and monogrammed napkins.

Just about every major change in this country to bring America closer to its ideals has been brought about by protest. The women's suffrage movement, the Montgomery bus boycott, labor protests, the Stonewall riots – how much time do you have? If someone can call a group of armed ranchers occupying federal buildings over cattle grazing rules 'patriots' while labeling one man sitting to protest the murder of thousands of American citizens 'un-American', it's time for them to examine their biases and priorities.

To those arguing that Kaepernick's protest insults veterans: soldiers did not fight and die for a song or a flag. They fought for many other reasons – American ideals of liberty and equality, access to education, economic opportunities, the draft.

And many of these veterans are people of color, who sacrificed overseas only to come home to a country whose service meant nothing to the police officers who only saw their black skin and deemed them a threat. Veterans like Kenneth Chamberlain Sr, who was shot and killed by police in 2011 when his medic alert necklace was accidentally triggered. Veterans like Anthony Hill, who was shot and killed by police this year while suffering from what relatives described as a nonviolent mental health crisis due to PTSD from serving in Afghanistan. Veterans like Elliott Williams, who was left paralyzed, naked and crying for help, unable to reach food or water, on a jail cell floor for six days in 2011 until he died from his injuries and dehydration. These men signed up to fight for us, and Kaepernick is fighting for them.

And to those who would argue that Kaepernick hates America when he should, as a rich sports star, have no complaints: this is one of the few lines that manages to be condescending, racist and ignorant all at once.

Most black people in America did not choose to be here. Most were brought here against their will and still suffer the socio-economic consequences of being treated for hundreds of years as cattle.

(Ijeoma Oluo)

ACTIVITY 4

Step 1: GAP

Complete the following GAP table for this extract. When you have completed it, check your answers with those at the back of the book:

Genre (text type)	
Audience	
Purpose	

This is a particularly interesting guiding question as although Oluo has a strong personal point of view regarding Colin Kaepernick's 'quiet protest', she also includes a range of different opinions which she then proceeds to challenge. We are encouraged to respond to these arguments on an emotional level and ultimately be persuaded to agree with Oluo's counterargument. Let's deconstruct this opinion piece and explore how we are affected in a particular way as a result of how Oluo has constructed her text.

Step 2: Structure and style

Being an opinion piece in a newspaper, the article is **foregrounded** with a **headline** that sums up what the article is about: 'Colin Kaepernick's national anthem protest is fundamentally American.' This is a **declarative** statement that makes it quite clear what the writer's point of view is. The statement is subjective and immediately would affect different readers in different ways: from those who agree with the statement to those who do not. The subheading beneath the headline is a compound sentence. The first independent clause acknowledges that not everyone will agree with the headline's statement, however, the writer introduces the second independent clause with the **co-ordinating conjunction** 'but' which implies there is another point of view – the point of view of the author. Immediately we are confronted with different perspectives but the fact that the author's perspective is repeated twice (in the headline and in the second part of the compound sentence) suggests this is the more valid perspective. Already we can see a strong personal perspective creeping into the article.

The article opens with a personal **anecdote**: we are transported to a 'family vacation' taken by the author during which she had a moment of epiphany – she made an emotional connection to American football. This opening creates an intimate **tone** as we feel we are being taken into the author's personal life as if we are her friend or close confidante. We immediately build a bond with the author which makes it easier to agree with her point of view. When referring to Colin Kaepernick and other 'black football players', she uses the plural possessive first personal **pronoun** 'our' to suggest we have a personal connection to these players, almost as if we own them and therefore have a personal interest in what they do and how they are treated. To further this feeling of ownership and close connection to the players, Oluo proceeds to include an extended quotation from Kaepernick himself, in which he explains his reasoning for protesting, rather than a short soundbite which may be misconstrued or misinterpreted. So far Oluo has structured the article to encourage readers to agree with her that Kaepernick's 'act of sitting during the national anthem' was a positive action, long overdue.

However, the following paragraphs acknowledge that there are alternative viewpoints regarding Kaepernick's action. The paragraph beginning 'In many corners …' is an extended paragraph **listing** all the ways in which people protested against Kaepernick's 'act of sitting'. She makes it clear that there were many different groups of people who did not support Kaepernick's actions and either took action themselves or verbally criticized him: 'Some people burned … Many argued that … Others asked why … Yet more people asked …' We are reminded that we are not all affected in the same way by a single event and it may be that some readers of this article responded to Kaepernick in precisely the way Oluo describes in this paragraph. However, the paragraph ends with the co-ordinating conjunction 'But' which, similar to the way it was used in the subheading, changes the tone and challenges the long list of alternative points of view we have just read.

The remaining six paragraphs are Oluo's counterargument. She challenges every criticism of Kaepernick using a range of techniques including **emotive language**, **sarcasm**, references to historical moments (**ethos**) and individual stories (**pathos**), rhetorical questions, **listing** and **tripling** and **figurative language** (which we will explore later on in this commentary). In terms of structure, what is significant is that much more article space is given to Oluo's counterargument rather than the opposing arguments she mentions. She is, therefore, able to build up an effective counterargument in the hope of persuading readers to agree with her perspective.

Step 3: Typographical and graphological features

As this is an online newspaper, a number of **typographical** and **graphological** features of this text type are included. The headline, for example, is in a much larger **serif** font than the rest of the text; the subheading is in a mid-size serif font; and the main body of the article is in a smaller serif font. This of course draws attention to the headline initially and then the subheading so that readers are aware of what the subject of the article is about and, moreover, what the author's own opinion is on the subject being discussed. This allows the reader to make his or her own decision whether to continue reading the article based on whether the subject and/or the writer's perspective is of interest to the reader. Similar to most newspaper articles, the initial letter of the main body of text is enlarged and in this case it is the pronoun 'I'. Being an opinion article, enlarging this particular pronoun is appropriate bearing in mind this is a personal piece of writing which is promoting the writer's own point of view. The final typographical and graphological features are unique to online texts. There are a number of **hyperlinks** within the article which stand out through the orange font colour (graphology) and underlining (typography). The effect of hyperlinks means the writer can just focus on her main line of argument rather than needing to explain any extraneous information. Readers who may want to investigate further about a particular idea mentioned in the text have the option to click on the hyperlink and be taken to another online location where that particular idea is explored or discussed in more detail. This makes the reading experience a personal experience and, moreover, one that takes account of the fact that we are all different readers with different interests and expertise that are catered for. The use of hyperlinks also suggests that there is a degree of objectivity to the writer's arguments and that they are well-researched and rooted in facts.

Step 4: Other features of online opinion pieces

Oluo uses a range of persuasive devices in her opinion piece. We are going to explore four of these features: **emotive language**, **ethos**, **pathos** and **figurative language**.

Being an opinion piece with the purpose to persuade, Oluo embeds **emotive language** throughout. Unlike the encyclopedia entry on Flowers, there is very little neutral or objective language. The article's first paragraph has a heavy use of emotive language. When describing Kaepernick's protest, Oluo describes it as a 'quiet protest'. Although it was literally a silent protest as Kaepernick sat down and said nothing, the adjective 'quiet' also has **connotations** of peacefulness and calmness. This is a subjective viewpoint as some would argue that although Kaepernick's actions may have been literally quiet, the way 'it was heard around the world' and the polarised responses to it made it far from 'quiet' or peaceful/calm. Other emotive language and phrases embedded throughout the article include 'hate', 'backlash', 'murder', 'suffer', 'condescending, racist and ignorant' all of which collectively work together to create an overall **tone** of anger and frustration at present-day America. Emotive language engages our own emotions and the inclusion of so much language that carries emotional weight encourages the reader to agree with the writer's sense of injustice and indignation.

Oluo also grounds the text in American historical protests, aiming to satirise those who criticise this recent American protest. She states that protest is 'built into our history and our mythology.' The language she uses here is loaded with gravity – 'history and mythology' suggests that she is going back to the forefathers of America who made the country the independent democracy it is today. This is an ethical argument which refers to a key moment of American history which most Americans would agree helped forge present-day America (**ethos**). She injects humour when she refers to the Boston Tea Party, a political protest by American colonists in 1773 who threw 340 crates of tea into Boston Harbour as a protest against the taxation of British imported tea. This was a key moment in the American Revolution and would be familiar to Oluo's intended audience, fellow Americans. By suggesting that those who are criticising Kaepernick today have no understanding of their own history, thinking that the 'Boston Tea Party was a literal tea party with tiny cakes and monogrammed napkins', satirises those people who have an alternative viewpoint to her, suggesting they are uninformed and 'un-American'.

As well as referring to the national landscape of American history, Oluo also zooms in on the individual, appealing to readers' sense of pity and sympathy (**pathos**). She refers to Kaepernick as 'one man sitting to protest the murder of thousands of American citizens'. By highlighting how he is 'one man' protesting about the unjust treatment of 'thousands of American citizens' places him on a pedestal. She **contrasts** this 'one man' with 'a group of armed ranchers', suggesting his 'quiet protest' is both brave and admirable whilst the latter are cowardly, only prepared to act in a group and, moreover, in an *armed* group.

Oluo of course wants to engage as well as persuade the reader to agree with her perspective and to this end she includes **figurative language**, more usually associated with literary works. The final sentence of this article is evidence of this. She argues how 'Most black people in America' did not choose to live in America voluntarily but were 'brought here against their will.' This of course alludes to America's past of slavery. She then points to present-day America, stating how 'black people in America ... still suffer the socio-economic consequences of being treated for hundreds of years as cattle.' This use of figurative language is unforgiving in tone and accentuates the deeply felt anger and indignation felt by Oluo and justifies Kaepernick's actions as a protest against historical as well as present-day racism in America.

Step 6: Reader response to message, ideas and/or purpose

As can be seen in this article, opinion pieces actively attempt to inspire the reader in order to affect his or her perspective to agree with the writer's point of view. In this instance, Oluo uses a range of devices to persuade us that Kaepernick's actions were justifiable and should be celebrated rather than condemned.

Texts that affect us intellectually and emotionally

So far we have explored two non-literary text types: one that aims to affect us intellectually and another that aims to affect us emotionally. There are also texts that aim to affect us in both of these ways. We are going to explore this idea through a **multimodal** text type, the infographic. With the increase in digital literacy, infographics that merge the written word, visual images and other symbols are a common non-literary text type that often affect us in various ways: intellectually, emotionally or even persuade us to take some kind of action. Before we look at the UN infographic, *Women and armed conflict*, read the following key features box on infographics to get an overview of this particular non-literary text type:

KEY FEATURES INFOGRAPHICS

- Brief but precise introduction that makes it immediately clear what the infographic is about.
- Focus on a topical subject.
- Often aims to elicit an intellectual response and an emotional response.
- Multimodal text that can use multiple modes of communication including visual images, **symbols**, **icons**, graphs, numbers and the written word.
- Colours are eye-catching and appealing and often link in with the topic being explored.
- Range of different graphics, which are clearly organized and easy to distinguish between. Use of icons or symbols are obvious to interpret without needing a key.
- Different typefaces and/or colour is used for different types of information.
- Use of arrows or numbers may be used to guide the reader as to what order to read the information.
- Use of reliable data that is up-to-date and can be substantiated; quoted sources should be reliable and trustworthy.
- **Declarative** sentences which are objective and factual.
- Simplicity: a complex topic needs to be understood quickly and clearly.

The text we are going to explore is an infographic that is found on the UNWomen website and its purpose is to inform readers about 'women and armed conflict'. Read the infographic with its annotations then read the commentary that follows.

■ Table 1.2.5

Genre (text type)	Online infographic
Audience	People around the world who have an interest in global affairs and/or gender issues. People who actively searched UNWomen on their digital devices
Purpose	To inform and to shock

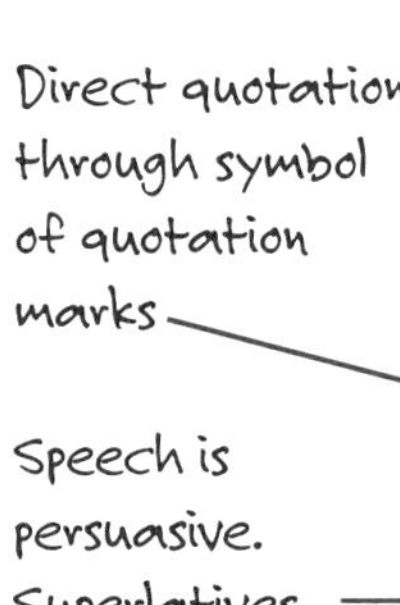

Typography and graphology: capitalization and large font for heading. Colour imagery stands out. Red connotes a warning.

Direct quotation through symbol of quotation marks

UN Women logo

Photographic image grounded in real life and fact

Speech is persuasive. Superlatives, tripling, alliteration used.

Contrast between red background and white typeface. Red connotes warning and white stands out

Captions explain pictorial images

Graphology: emotive language bolded in red (connotes warning)

Universal symbol representing 'female'

Facts as statistics, verifiable percentages

Alliteration – memorable

Blue matches the colour of the UN logo

Statistics that are verifiable

Superlative; shocking fact

Visuals: size of universal symbols reinforce written statistics

Listing of countries reinforces this is a far-reaching issue

Memorable slogan – alliteration

Pictorial image symbolizes peace and freedom

Graphology: multiple tick symbols show positive points and solutions

Direct quotation from UN Secretary General – gives authority to the text because of their status

Photographic image of Ban Ki-Moon – figure of authority, credibility. Connects to the UN visually (blue tie and background logo)

Pictorial image symbolizes topic

This infographic manages to achieve two purposes: to inform readers about the experiences of women in areas of conflict and to shock readers that so many women are affected in such a detrimental way due to this conflict. The effect on us is, therefore, twofold: we are affected *intellectually* in terms of being informed about a topic we may have been uninformed about before reading this infographic, and we are affected *emotionally* in terms of being shocked by the range of ways that conflict affects so many women and girls around the globe.

ACTIVITY 5

Write a detailed commentary on this infographic, using the key features of infographics box, the annotated text and the GAP table to help you. Use the following bullet pointed headings to structure your commentary. You may like to work with a language and literature student and write a commentary on two of these headings each. The first one has been completed for you.

- Text type, intended audience and purpose

> This is an online infographic that is aimed at a global audience who have an interest in global affairs, specifically gender issues. Its purpose is two-fold: to inform readers of the topic, Women and Armed Conflict, and to shock readers that so many women and girls experience harm and violence as a consequence of conflict. The infographic also seems to be attempting to persuade women to step forward into leadership positions in order to bring about sustainable peace.

- Structure and style
- Typographical and graphological features
- Other features of the text type
- Visual images and layout
- Reader response to ideas, message and/or purpose

When you have completed this activity, compare your commentary with the one at the back of the book.

In this chapter we have explored a number of literary works and non-literary text types to answer this guiding question. It is of course worth remembering that a literary work or a non-literary text type does not have exclusive ownership over how we are affected. Just as Wordsworth's 'Daffodils', for example, encourages us to experience the wonder and awe of the natural world, so can an article in a non-literary magazine such as *National Geographic*. Just as Oluo's opinion article attempts to inspire and persuade us to agree with a particular point of view, so can a literary prose non-fiction work such as Martin Luther King Jr.'s, 'I Have A Dream' speech (which we will be exploring in the next chapter).

CHECK FOR UNDERSTANDING

To summarise what we have discussed so far: consider the following questions:

- What do the following letters/acronyms stand for?

L		G	
I		A	
F		P	

- Which acronym can we apply to the study of literary works and which to the study of non-literary texts?

This chapter should have given you an insight into some of the different ways we are affected by texts. Remember, though, that the reader has a role to play in constructing meaning as well as the writer. The writer may have a fixed idea of how he or she would like us to be affected by his or her work but ultimately, the effect of a text upon a reader is often dependent on who the individual reader is.

Works cited

Arendt, H. 'The death of human empathy is one of the earliest and most telling signs of a culture about to fall into barbarism.' *Awaken the greatness within*. Web. 5 Feb. 2019. **https://awakenthegreatnesswithin.com/35-inspirational-quotes-on-empathy**.

Blake, W. *The Complete Poems*. Penguin Classics, 1977.

Byron, L. *The Major Works*, reissue edition. Oxford University Press, 2008.

Clarke, G. 'Miracle On St David's Day.' Web. 5 Feb. 2019. **www.gillianclarke.co.uk/gc2017/miracle-on-st-davids-day**.

Coleridge, ST. *The Major Works*. Oxford University Press, 2008.

'Fleury, Claude to Foraker'. *Encyclopaedia Britannica*, 11th Edition, Vol 10, Slice 5, 1 April 2011. Web. 5 Feb 2019. **www.gutenberg.org/files/35747/35747-h/35747-h.htm#ar55**.

Keats, J. *Selections from Keats's Letters. Poetry Foundation*. Web. 5 Feb. 2019. **www.poetryfoundation.org/articles/69384/selections-from-keatss-letters**.

Keats, J. *The Complete Poems*, 2nd edition. Penguin Classics, 1977.

Oluo, I. 'Colin Kaepernick's national anthem protest is fundamentally American.' *The Guardian*, 29 Aug. 2016. Web. 13 Sept. 2019. **www.theguardian.com/commentisfree/2016/aug/29/colin-kaepernick-national-anthem-protest-fundamentally-american**.

Orwell, G. *Animal Farm: A Fairy Story*, new edition. Penguin Classics, 2000.

Orwell, G. *Down and Out in Paris and London*. Penguin Modern Classics, 1986.

Orwell, G. *Nineteen Eighty-Four*, new edition. Penguin Classics, 2004.

Roe, N. *The Politics of Nature: Wordsworth and Some Contemporaries (Studies in Romanticism)*, 1992 edition. Palgrave Macmillan, 2014.

Shelley, PB. *The Major Works*. Oxford University Press, 2009.

Spiegelman, A. *The Complete Maus*. Penguin Books, 2003.

Wordsworth, W. 'I Wandered Lonely as a Cloud.' *Poetry Foundation*. Web. 5 Feb. 2019. **www.poetryfoundation.org/poems/45521/i-wandered-lonely-as-a-cloud**.

Wordsworth, W. *Poems in Two Volumes*. Longman, Hurst, Rees, and Orme, 1807.

Wordsworth, W, Coleridge, ST. *Lyrical Ballads, with a Few Other Poems*. Printed for J&A Arch, Gracechurch-Street, 1798.

Yoshimoto, B. *Kitchen*. Translated by Megan Backus, Faber and Faber, 2001.

1.3 In what ways is meaning constructed, negotiated, expressed and interpreted?

OBJECTIVES OF CHAPTER

- To deconstruct the key words of this concept question.
- To apply the concept question to a range of literary works, including concrete poetry, drama, prose fiction and graphic novels.
- To apply the concept question to a range of non-literary texts, including online texts, non-textual visual texts and formal letters of complaint.

Before we start picking apart this concept question, read the following poem by American poet, William Carlos Williams. He wrote it in 1923.

The Red Wheelbarrow

so much depends
upon

a red wheel
barrow

glazed with rain
water

beside the white
chickens.

(William Carlos Williams)

In what ways is meaning *constructed*?

Williams titled this poem 'The Red Wheelbarrow' so we assume the poem's meaning will be based on a red wheelbarrow. He constructed it without using any capital letters or punctuation (except the final full stop). However, there is a structure as each stanza is a couplet. Line 1 of each stanza has three words and line 2 of each line contains one word. Williams appears to have constructed this poem to give equal significance to each word. We are forced to slow down our pace of reading and take note of each word and how each word connects to the one before and the one after it. We are consequently making connections between words while at the same time being aware of the unique essence of each word. However, this is a meaning the reader is constructing as Williams is not here to ask. We are assuming there is a symbolic meaning to the poem, rather than it being a literal description of a red wheelbarrow and white chickens. It is likely we construct a symbolic meaning to this poem because of the way Williams has used an unconventional structure to construct the poem.

In what ways is meaning *negotiated*?

By closely analysing the language, features, stylistic and structural elements of the poem, we can start to negotiate meaning. Here are some ways students have negotiated meaning within this poem. You should note that each meaning differs, but each meaning is substantiated with evidence from the poem.

STUDENT A

The poem reminds me of a still-life painting of a red wheelbarrow and white chickens. The last three stanzas are describing the different parts of the still-life – the red wheelbarrow, the raindrops on the wheelbarrow, and the chickens beside the wheelbarrow. It is as if Williams is taking us round the painting, pointing out each part of the painting so we don't miss anything. The stanza that describes how the wheelbarrow is 'glazed with rain / water' makes me think this is a close-up picture of the wheelbarrow with every small detail included – like a still-life.

STUDENT B

I think the setting of this poem is really important. I think the poet is describing a simple scene in the countryside – on a farm, perhaps, because of the presence of a wheelbarrow and chickens. He seems to be idealizing the scene as there is a sense of peace and harmony. I think it is interesting how the poet has ended each stanza with something non-human ('barrow'), something natural ('water') and something alive ('chickens'). Each different object has a stanza to itself and perhaps this shows how although each thing is different and requires its own space, they all exist side-by-side harmoniously.

STUDENT C

The form and shape of the poem really stand out for me. The actual shape of each stanza could represent the shape of a wheelbarrow – the longer and fuller first line of each stanza may represent the main body of a wheelbarrow and the shorter one word final line of each stanza may represent the single wheel of a wheelbarrow. The title of the poem is 'The Red Wheelbarrow', so this suggests that the red wheelbarrow is the subject of the poem, and perhaps the way Williams has decided to shape the poem reinforces this idea, too.

STUDENT D

This poem could be read as an extended metaphor for the trials and tribulations that some people may go through in life. There could be a racial aspect to this poem's meaning as the wheelbarrow's identity seems dependent upon its colour. This could reflect how, in the past, the colour of one's skin signified your position in society. Since the 'red wheel / barrow' is 'beside' the 'white / chickens', this could be interpreted as coloured workers being 'beside' white landowners – but with different roles. In the same way that a wheelbarrow's function is to be used on the land, a coloured worker's function was also to work on the land; and just as the 'white / chickens' appear to be roaming free, a white landowner was also free.

ACTIVITY 1

Imagine you are **STUDENT E**. Closely read the poem again and write a paragraph in which you show how you would *negotiate* meaning. Make sure you support your ideas with evidence from the poem.

There is no end of book commentary on this activity; however, you may want to try this activity with a friend and compare ideas.

In what ways is meaning *expressed*?

Meaning is expressed in a very simple way. The language used is everyday language that everyone can understand and the structure of using couplets throughout is also simple. However, the poem's meaning appears to be hidden behind this simplicity. The use of **enjambment** between lines and between stanzas makes it difficult to know which ideas are connected.

In what ways is meaning *interpreted*?

We have a number of different interpretations which have been negotiated through closely reading the text. Here are some of the interpretations we have already discussed above:

- Williams is focusing on the essence of things (similar to mindfulness of today perhaps?).
- Williams is an artist, painting a still-life through his use of words.
- Williams is writing a pastoral poem in which he is idealizing the rural way of life.
- Williams is experimenting with the form of poetry to see whether he can recreate the form of a wheelbarrow through the way he structures his poem. (Similar perhaps to student A's interpretation – Williams as an artist.)
- Williams is exploring racial segregation through the poem.

All of these interpretations are valid because they are supported by textual evidence. Of course, there are also literary critics who hold the magnifying glass up to the text and share their interpretations with us. Some critics argue that this poem is an early example of **imagism**, an Anglo-American form of literature in the twentieth century that experimented with sharply focused images and precise language. And how did Williams interpret his poem's meaning? Although he did not 'interpret' it as such, he did explain that his friendship with an African-American man named Marshall inspired him to write the poem:

> *'He had been a fisherman, caught porgies off Gloucester. He used to tell me how he had to work in the cold in freezing weather, standing ankle deep in cracked ice packing down the fish. He said he didn't feel cold. He never felt cold in his life until just recently. I liked that man, and his son Milton almost as much. In his backyard I saw the red wheelbarrow surrounded by the white chickens. I suppose my affection for the old man somehow got into the writing.'*
>
> *(Sergio Rizzo 35)*

As we can see, then, there are various processes the writer and the reader go through before a text's meaning can be understood. And even when we go through these steps, we are never too sure whether the meaning we have given the text is the right one or not. This supports the idea that we have already discussed in previous chapters that there is no definitive meaning to a text, rather it is dependent upon the individual writer and the individual reader.

In order to further our understanding of this chapter's question, let's read the definition of each key word in the *Concise Oxford English Dictionary* and see whether these definitions give us any insight into how to respond to this question:

■ Table 1.3.1

Key word	Definition (from *Concise Oxford English Dictionary*)
Construct	1. build or erect. 2. form (a theory) from various conceptual elements. 3. *Grammar* form (a sentence) according to grammatical rules. (306)
Negotiate	1. try to reach an agreement or compromise by discussion with others; obtain or bring about by negotiating. 2. find a way over or through (an obstacle or difficult path). (959)
Express	1. convey (a thought or feeling) in words or by gestures and conduct. 2. press out (liquid or air). 3. *Mathematics* represent by a figure, symbol or formula. (502)
Interpret	1. explain the meaning of (words, actions, etc.); understand as having a particular meaning or significance; perform (a creative work) in a way that conveys one's understanding of the creator's ideas. 2. translate speech, either orally into another language or into sign language. (743)

Now let's apply each definition to a text's meaning.

Construct

According to the above dictionary definition, we can understand this to mean: how is meaning built? We may feel that a writer is responsible for **constructing** meaning – after all, a writer literally **constructs** the text. As the definition above states, forming sentences using grammatical rules is part of the **construction** process and this is the job of the writer. However, as we have already seen, it is not always this straightforward. Some writers consciously break the rules of grammar to **construct** meaning – as Williams did in 'The Red Wheelbarrow' poem we have just examined – and we will be exploring this idea further in the 'stream of consciousness' and 'textspeak' parts of this chapter. More importantly, though, as we have just seen, once a text is published, power transfers from the writer to the reader and it becomes the reader's responsibility to **construct** meaning out of the text. The meaning a reader **constructs** may be influenced by the reader's background, values or attitudes. It may also be influenced by what other people say about a text's meaning: friends, classmates or a teacher; as well as literary critics who may have **constructed** their own meaning to a text which may change over time (you will be exploring in more depth various literary theories in Chapter 3.4).

Negotiate

According to the above dictionary definition, to **negotiate** means to 'reach an agreement or compromise by discussion with others' and to 'find a way over or through (an obstacle or difficult path)'. How do we apply this to a text's meaning? Many texts deal with complex ideas, for example, philosophical, spiritual and/or political ideas, and the role of the writer is to guide the reader to an understanding of these ideas, or **negotiate** a way through for the reader – similar to how this coursebook is trying to guide you to an understanding of language and literature, in fact! Writers attempt to do this in various ways: for example, through their use of written and visual language; through their use of literary features and stagecraft; through their use of stylistic and structural features. The ways in which writers attempt to **negotiate** meaning for us, or guide us to an understanding of a complex idea, will be explored in this chapter.

The first part of the definition above concerns reaching an agreement or compromise about something through discussion. We can apply this to a text by thinking of the text as representing the 'discussion' and the 'something' we are discussing as representing the text's meaning. As we know, the writer has constructed the text. The writer has had his or her say in the discussion and has attempted to put forward one particular meaning. Now it is the reader's turn to take part in the discussion. How does the reader do this? By closely reading and analysing the text – and the reading strategies explored in Chapter 1.1 should help you as you negotiate a text's meaning.

As in all discussions, sometimes the writer and reader will agree on the text's meaning and sometimes they won't. That is absolutely fine. Different ways of understanding a text are viable, as long as the reader's understanding can be substantiated by what is in the text, rather than being some wild imaginings that are not actually based on the text itself. And that is what we are practising in our **immanent** reading of texts – negotiating a text's meaning by focusing on what is in the text.

This is one of the main differences between the arts and the sciences. A single artwork (and literature is an artwork) can have multiple interpretations; the arts, therefore, give the reader freedom to **construct** and **negotiate** his or her own meaning from a text. If the reader's meaning genuinely comes from the text, then that meaning is viable and valid. In science subjects, there is often one meaning or one truth. A single experiment, for example, has a single conclusion. If ten scientists perform exactly the same experiment under the same conditions, their conclusions will always be the same. If ten language and literature students all read the same poem, there could potentially be ten different interpretations and each interpretation could be valid – *if* supported with evidence from the poem. Some students may find this challenging and some may feel unsettled when there is not one definitive answer they can learn. Hopefully, by the time you have finished reading this coursebook and by the time you have finished studying your language and literature course, you will feel more excited than unsettled by this prospect. You as the reader should feel empowered in this **negotiation** process as you unpick a text to discover its meaning.

Express

According to the above dictionary definition, to **express** means to 'convey (a thought or feeling) in words or by gestures'. Applying this definition to a text's meaning is quite straightforward: for wholly language-based texts, meaning is expressed through words; for **multimodal** or **non-verbal** texts, meaning is expressed through words and/or visual images and other pictorial symbols and signs. As we know from our two reading strategies, a literary work's form and structure and a non-literary text's genre, audience and purpose can also be instrumental in expressing meaning.

Interpret

According to the above dictionary definition, **interpret** means to 'understand as having a particular meaning or significance', to 'perform (a creative work) in a way that conveys one's understanding of the creator's ideas' and to 'translate … into another language'. We can of course apply all of these definitions to our study of understanding a text's meaning. Let's take each definition separately and see how we can apply it to a text's meaning. The first idea relates to understanding a text's meaning. This is the job of the reader. A writer, through **constructing**, **negotiating** and **expressing** a text's meaning would hope that the reader would now be able to **interpret** the text's meaning, but as we already know, a writer cannot always predict who the reader is going to be and a reader brings his or her own set of values, attitudes and ideas to a text. Therefore, the way a reader interprets a text's meaning may not always coincide with the writer's intention. An added complication, which we have also alluded to, is that other readers construct their own meanings around a single text and this can influence how a new reader interprets the meaning of a text.

The second definition concerns how a text is performed and this idea is explored in the 'stagecraft' part of this chapter. It is the idea that sometimes a reader's **interpretation** of a text is influenced by a performer's interpretation of a text and so the negotiation of a text now becomes a three-way process between the writer, the performer and the audience. Finally, the dictionary defines interpretation as being linked to translation. During this course, you will be exploring texts in translation as well as texts originally written in English. Similar to how our interpretation of a play can be dependent upon how the performer interprets the original work, our interpretation of a text written in translation can be determined by how a translator interprets the original text and we will be exploring some of these ideas in the 'textspeak' part of this chapter. The discussion of the translation of Camus' *L'Étranger* in the Introduction also relates to this idea.

You should be beginning to realize that there is fluidity between **construction**, **negotiation**, **expression** and **interpretation**. Often, to understand one concept we have to understand another concept; often one concept is dependent upon one of the other concepts; and often a writer and a reader have equal responsibility for giving a text meaning through each of these concepts.

Let's start exploring some literary works and non-literary texts and see how we can apply these concepts to actual extracts. As we apply the concept question to a range of texts, notice how our reading strategies from Chapter 1.1 are embedded within our analyses.

The first text we are going to focus on is a literary work: a seventeenth-century poem by Welsh poet, George Herbert, called 'Easter Wings' which uses an unconventional lay-out to communicate meaning.

■ Communicating meaning through the shape of a text

Some writers not only use written language and/or non-verbal symbols or images within the text itself, but they also use the physical shape of the text to communicate meaning. **Concrete poetry** is a literary genre that uses **graphological** and presentational features to determine the shape of the poem. The writer who **constructs** the poem using shape as an essential feature of the text's form may do this to help **negotiate** or guide the reader to understand the content of the poem; may use shape (as well as words) to **express** a particular meaning; and ultimately hopes that the shape of the poem will help shape (no pun intended!) the reader's **interpretation** of the poem in a particular way. Some concrete poetry uses shape simply to entertain and engage the reader – Lewis Carroll, for example, in *Alice's Adventures in Wonderland* (1865), constructs his poem, 'A Long Tale', in the shape of a mouse's tail to represent who the speaker of the poem is and to visually illustrate how the poem itself is a **pun**, playing on the two meanings of tale and tail.

We are going to be exploring an even earlier example of concrete poetry that, while being visually interesting, uses the shape of the poem to negotiate and express meaning and in doing so helps to shape the reader's interpretation. Before we explore this poem, let's read the key features box to get an overview of the main conventions of this genre of poetry.

KEY FEATURES CONCRETE (OR SHAPE) POETRY

- A genre of poetry that arranges the words of the poem in a concrete way to create a shape that denotes the subject of the poem.
- The shape of the poem can be more significant in expressing meaning than the words themselves.
- As well as the words themselves, the spaces between words are also important in constructing meaning.
- Poetry that is first and foremost visual rather than verbal.

The first extract below from George Herbert's collection of poetry, *The Temple* (1633), is the way Herbert's poem 'Easter Wings' was first published.

Because shape is such an essential ingredient of concrete poetry, we are going to focus on the poem's form and structure (step 1 of our literary reading strategy) in our close reading.

Step 1: Form and structure

As you can see, the poem is laid out on two facing pages in the shape of a pair of wings. Initially, they may remind us of birds' or butterflies' wings. However, the poem's title, 'Easter Wings', is written above each pair of wings and above the poem's title is the page header, *The Church*. Because of the poem's title and the page header, the wings now take on the appearance of something more sacred: angel wings perhaps.

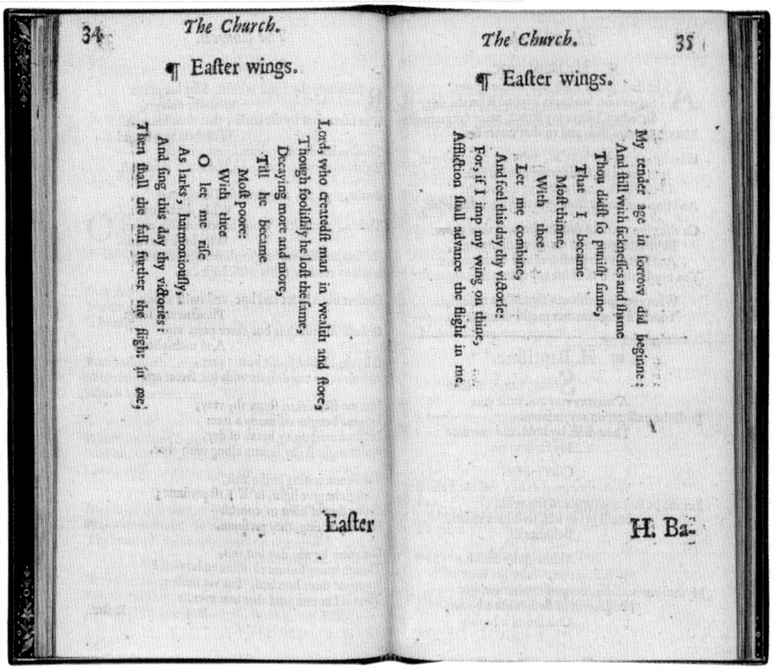

Before we read a word of the poem, we feel Herbert has **constructed** his poem as a pair of angel wings in order to **express** a religious idea – something connected to resurrection, perhaps, bearing in mind its title or at the very least, something uplifting and motivating: after all, wings are connected to flight, angels are associated with bringing good tidings and Easter celebrates the resurrection of Jesus Christ. Already, then, we are being guided as to how Herbert would like us to **interpret** this poem. Then there is an added layer of meaning that comes through the **construction** of the book itself. Because the wings have been printed on two facing pages, there is symmetry between each pair of wings: each pair of wings appears to be a perfect mirror image of the other pair of wings. Could Herbert be expressing his religious beliefs in the perfection of God or in the belief that God created man in his own image? Some readers may interpret the text's meaning in this way because of the way the text has been constructed or because of their own religious beliefs. Furthermore, by printing the text on two facing pages, we may feel that the stanzas of the text – or the wings – are constantly moving – or, being wings, flying. Whenever the page is turned or the book is opened/ closed, the wings also open and close and in this way they are literally moving, or flying. Rather than constructing a static poem, Herbert has constructed a poem that is constantly moving – and, being angel wings, perhaps we interpret this as meaning the text/wings are taking the reader closer to Heaven. Spirituality is a complex topic and we may feel that, if it is a religious poem, the way Herbert has constructed this poem is his attempt to negotiate meaning for us. We may also feel that, through the shape of the poem, Herbert is attempting to negotiate with us regarding how uplifting his faith is and in this way encourage us to interpret the text's meaning in a particular way.

■ George Herbert's collection of poetry *The Temple*

George Herbert

George Herbert, born in Wales, was a poet, speaker and Anglican priest. When he was at Trinity College, Cambridge University, he became known to James I, King of England, when he became the University's Public Orator. After serving in the English Parliament in 1624 and 1625, he became ordained by the Church of England (1629) and spent the rest of his life as a priest in St Andrew's Church in Bemerton, Wiltshire. Herbert wrote poetry in English, Latin and Greek and all of his surviving poems are on religious themes. He is known for his direct expression as well as a range of different formal devices he used to enhance his meaning: for example, his use of rhyme, different line lengths giving his stanzas a particular shape and presentational devices when printed on the page. He also played the lute and many of his poems have been set to music and many are now sung as hymns.

Now let's read the same poem presented in a more conventional manner:

Easter Wings

Lord, who createdst man in wealth and store,
Though foolishly he lost the same,
Decaying more and more,
Till he became
Most poore:

With thee
O let me rise
As larks, harmoniously,
And sing this day thy victories:
Then shall the fall further the flight in me.

My tender age in sorrow did beginne
And still with sicknesses and shame.
Thou didst so punish sinne,
That I became
Most thinne.

With thee
Let me combine,
And feel thy victorie:
For, if I imp my wing on thine,
Affliction shall advance the flight in me.

(George Herbert)

Even when the poem is not laid out as a pair of wings, Herbert plays with the shape of his poem through the length of each line and the shape of each stanza. He uses the shape of a triangle for each stanza: stanzas 1 and 3 start with the longer line (lines using an **iambic pentameter**) as the first line and then each line progressively gets shorter until the final line of both of these stanzas is the shortest (lines using one single **iamb**). Stanzas 2 and 4 are a mirror image: they start with the shortest line as the first line and each line progressively gets longer until the final line is the longest. If we read the words that make up each stanza, it is interesting to note that the meaning of each stanza is mirrored in the shape of each stanza. For example, stanza 1 opens by celebrating the 'Lord' for creating man 'in wealth and store' (line 1) – this is a celebration of the abundance Herbert's Lord has given mankind when he created him. Unsurprisingly, then, this is the longest line of the stanza – a long line to mirror abundance. The stanza then progresses to lament how mankind has 'foolishly' lost what their Lord gave them until they have almost nothing. Each line gets progressively shorter, visually representing mankind's depletion of everything the Lord gave them, until the final shortest line of the stanza which ends with the observation that now man is, 'Most poore' (line 5). The brevity of the line mirrors how far man has fallen from when he had everything to now when he has nothing. Herbert, therefore, **constructs** each line's length to help him **express** these ideas. Although most readers in seventeenth-century England would have been familiar with these ideas due to their Christian background, we could argue how Herbert's line construction helps guide modern-day readers who may not have this particular set of beliefs to better understand this Christian view of the world. Whatever our religious background, however, it is clear how Herbert **constructs** these lines to enhance an understanding of each line's meaning and in this way shape the way readers **interpret** the poem.

ACTIVITY 2

Re-read stanza 2 and write a short commentary explaining how Herbert **constructs** each line's length to express the stanza's meaning.

When you have written your commentary, compare it with the one below.

If we now take a closer look at stanza 2, which is the mirror image of stanza 1, we can see how he does something similar. The first line is the shortest – 'with thee' (line 6) – he is directly addressing his Lord and the shortness of the line suggests a simplicity and humility to his address. The stanza is about how, with help from his Lord, man can 'rise' again and sing the Lord's praises. He uses the **metaphor** of a lark – a songbird that also flies – to represent how praising their Lord through song (is the poem a song?) mankind can also fly and become closer to their Lord. He uses the shape of the stanza to visually represent this flight. As man flies higher and higher, each line becomes longer and longer until the final longest line represents how man's flight will be all the greater because he has fallen (line 10). Stanzas 3 and 4 use line length and stanza shape similarly to visually represent Herbert's meaning. We can see, then, Herbert's skill in **constructing** this poem in this particular shape to help **negotiate** his meaning with the reader, to **express** his ideas and ultimately to shape the way we **interpret** the poem's meaning.

The ideas Herbert is discussing are complex ideas – the very fact that faith cannot be proved with reason or logic make this topic particularly complicated for many people – but through the use of shape he is attempting to simplify his ideas so readers can understand the message and come to an interpretation of the poem in the way he intended. We could argue, then, that Herbert is using the form of concrete poetry to **negotiate** a way through a complex subject for the reader. Being an Anglican priest, it was important for Herbert that readers understood the religious message. However, even if we do not agree with or do not understand the religious message of the poem, we can still be motivated by the poem in a more secular way. This is part of the negotiation process. Herbert may be intending to express one particular meaning, but the reader brings his or her own understanding and sets of belief to the poem and in this way a compromise is negotiated. For a non-Christian reader, it is likely he or she will feel drawn to the longer lines of the poem – using the meter of **iambic pentameter** gives these long lines a harmony and fluidity to them which is further accentuated through much of the language and ideas in these lines that have positive **connotations**. As we know from our study of poetry in the previous chapter, the final line of a poem is significant. So let's apply this concept to the final line of Herbert's poem:

> Affliction shall advance the flight in me.
>
> *(line 20)*

Herbert has constructed this line to be the longest line in the stanza, to use the harmonious **meter** of iambic pentameter and to accentuate its uplifting message. Although the line starts in a negative way – 'affliction' (an illness or something that concerns us) is something we generally want to avoid – the line ends very positively with language including 'advance' and 'flight'.

Remember, Herbert has **constructed** the poem so that this is the last line and the final thought Herbert leaves us with is that although we may all face 'affliction' (and unless we are exceedingly fortunate, we all do!), this 'affliction' actually benefits us. How? By experiencing affliction, Herbert expresses how we are all the more able to take flight and soar. Different readers may **interpret** this line differently: a Christian reader may **interpret** this line as meaning the afflicted (the weak and suffering) will be the first to 'advance' to Heaven and join God (a Christian belief); a non-Christian reader may **interpret** this line as meaning those who suffer are better able to 'advance the flight', perhaps because they are in a better position to empathize with others who also suffer and, therefore, have a better understanding of humanity; perhaps some readers will **interpret** this line as meaning that through suffering, we better appreciate non-suffering and therefore enjoy life more, not taking it for granted. So even if we do not necessarily understand or agree with the religious sentiment in the poem, we **interpret** the overall message as being positive, uplifting and motivating which was Herbert's intention. A compromise, therefore, has been **negotiated** between the writer and the reader, and the compromise has been reached because of the way the writer has **constructed** the line.

As you can see, there are multiple interpretations to any single text and the reader's own interests, beliefs, attitudes and values have a huge part to play in how meaning is both **constructed** and **interpreted** by the reader. A writer can attempt to construct his or her text in a certain way to **express** their meaning, but ultimately the reader has the final say as to how she or he **interprets** a particular text. In the meantime, a process of **negotiation** has occurred and it is hoped that some form of compromise has been reached whereby at least some of the writer's original meaning is understood even though the reader may bring his or her own **interpretation** to the text, too.

■ Communicating meaning through stagecraft

One of the ideas we have been exploring is how a writer attempts to guide the reader into an understanding of a complex idea and in doing so helps to shape the reader's interpretation to an extent. We saw how Herbert used both verbal (words) and non-verbal (shape) elements in the construction of his poem in order to accomplish this. Another form of literary work that combines both verbal and non-verbal elements in its attempt to communicate a particular meaning to a reader and thereby shape a reader's interpretation is drama. Drama, of course, consists of language: with no dialogue, there would be no drama. However, a playwright does not just write dialogue. **Stagecraft** is an essential tool of a playwright and, although it is a non-verbal tool, is used to enhance meaning and shape a reader's understanding and interpretation of the work's meaning. Before we continue, read the key features box to get an overview of this essential non-verbal element of drama.

KEY FEATURES STAGECRAFT (non-verbal elements of drama)

- Use of lighting to create a particular mood or atmosphere.
- Use of props that may take on symbolic significance.
- Use of sound effects, including music.
- Staging, including a backdrop that denotes where the scene is taking place, positions of doors, windows, walls, furniture.
- Entrances and exits.
- Make-up and costumes.

Tennessee Williams was a twentieth-century American playwright who coined the phrase **plastic theatre** to describe the particular type of stagecraft he employed in his work. Read the following key features box to get an overview of this genre that applies to Williams' drama.

KEY FEATURES PLASTIC THEATRE

- Associated with Tennessee Williams.
- The use of props, lighting, sound and staging to represent **abstract** ideas such as characters' states of mind, emotions, memories or desires, central ideas or themes in a work or to heighten a particular mood or atmosphere.
- Metaphorical, expressionistic and symbolic rather than realistic or naturalistic.
- Expressing the mood is more important than creating a sense of realism.

We are now going to explore this chapter's concept question through Tennessee Williams' most famous play, *A Streetcar Named Desire* (1947), which employs **plastic theatre** features. Because we are taking an **immanent** approach, we are just going to focus on the extract rather than contextualising it within the play.

First, let's read the extract with no stagecraft and see how we can apply this concept question to the dialogue only:

BLANCHE [to STANLEY]: Don't come in here! Operator, operator! Give me long-distance, please. [...] I want to get in touch with Mr. Shep Huntleigh of Dallas. He's so well-known he doesn't require any address. Just ask anybody who – Wait! – No, I couldn't find it right now. [...] Please understand, I – No! No, wait! [...] One moment! Someone is – Nothing! Hold on, please!

STANLEY: You left th' phone off th' hook.

(Tennessee Williams, A Streetcar Named Desire Scene 10)

We can already see how Williams has constructed this dialogue to express a tense mood. Blanche's speech is peppered throughout with exclamatives, **ellipsis** and fragmented sentences, which expresses her increasing frustration as she is attempting to get hold of 'Mr Shep Huntleigh of Dallas' (line 3) on the phone. She appears to be having two conversations – one to Stanley and another to the operator – but both conversations seem to be going nowhere other than causing her exasperation. If this is what Williams was intending to express, then he has constructed Blanche's dialogue in such a way that this is indeed how we interpret it – assuming the actor performs accordingly, of course. Stanley's line does not seem to make sense in the context of this extract as we assume Blanche is on the phone so we do not understand why Stanley has said 'You left th' phone off th' hook.' (line 8). With no stage directions to guide us, we do not know what tone of voice Stanley uses either so it is difficult for the audience to interpret him in any particular way. Perhaps the contraction of 'the' gives us a clue that he is from a more working-class background than Blanche as Blanche does not use any **contractions**, suggesting she may be from a higher class than Stanley. Although we are able to interpret this scene to a degree, it is quite a superficial interpretation and there are lots of gaps in our understanding.

Now read the extract with the stage directions:

> BLANCHE [to STANLEY]: Don't come in here!
>
> *Lurid reflections appear on the walls around BLANCHE. The shadows are of a grotesque and menacing form. She catches her breath, crosses to the phone and jiggles the hook. STANLEY goes into the bathroom and closes the door.*
>
> Operator, operator! Give me long-distance, please. [...] I want to get in touch with Mr. Shep Huntleigh of Dallas. He's so well-known he doesn't require any address. Just ask anybody who – Wait! – No, I couldn't find it right now. [...] Please understand, I – No! No, wait! [...] One moment! Someone is – Nothing! Hold on, please!
>
> *She sets the phone down and crosses warily into the kitchen.*
> *The night is filled with inhuman voices like cries in a jungle.*
> *The shadows and lurid reflections move sinuously as flames across the wall spaces.*
> *Through the back wall of the rooms, which have become transparent, can be seen the sidewalk. A prostitute has rolled a drunkard. He pursues her along the walk, overtakes her and there is a struggle. A policeman's whistle breaks it up. The figures disappear.*
> *Some moments later the NEGRO WOMAN appears around the corner with a sequined bag which the prostitute had dropped on the walk. She is rooting excitedly through it.*
> *BLANCHE presses her knuckles to her lips and returns slowly to the phone. She speaks in a hoarse whisper ...*
>
> STANLEY: You left th' phone off th' hook.
>
> *He crosses to it deliberately and sets it back on the hook. After he has replaced it, he stares at her again, his mouth slowly curving into a grin, as he waves between BLANCHE and the outer door.*
>
> (Tennessee Williams, *A Streetcar Named Desire* Scene 10)

Williams' use of stagecraft enables the performers and in turn the audience to have a much deeper understanding of the scene's meaning while giving Williams an opportunity to **negotiate** more fully with the audience through the performance on stage. Let's analyse the scene in detail, paying particular attention to how Williams **constructs** meaning through his use of stagecraft; how he attempts to **negotiate** the scene's meaning with us through the performance; how he attempts to **express** a particular meaning through both verbal and non-verbal elements; and finally how we may **interpret** the scene's meaning.

Only two characters are on stage at any one time and most of the time it is Blanche on her own on stage. This means our attention is on Blanche constantly and we are aware that meaning is being constructed around Blanche. The actor playing Blanche, then, has a responsibility to express Williams' meaning through her performance – but of course the way she expresses Williams' meaning will depend on how she has interpreted his meaning during preliminary readings and rehearsals.

Initially, Williams uses a simple exclamative, 'Don't come in here!' (line 1) to express Blanche's viewpoint. She obviously wants to be left alone and does not want Stanley to enter the room. However, there are no stage directions to denote how these words are spoken so the actor playing this role will have to decide how to express the words, which of course will affect how we interpret Blanche's state of mind at this particular point. However, these words are immediately followed with stage directions that describe **non-verbal** elements – they are not of themselves dependent on how an actor performs and so perhaps they give us a better insight into Williams' intended meaning. The stage directions are as follows:

> *Lurid reflections appear on the walls around BLANCHE. The shadows are of a grotesque and menacing form ...*
>
> *(lines 2–3)*

We can think of these stage directions perhaps as Williams **negotiating** meaning with us. He cannot explain what he means through long descriptive passages as a novel can, so he includes stage directions to suggest his desired meaning. It is up to us how we **interpret** them although as a theatre audience, the way these stage directions are conveyed on stage is likely to vary, depending on the director's interpretation and this, of course, will have an effect on how we in turn interpret Williams' intended meaning. But if we take the stage directions at face value and analyse the language Williams uses we can perhaps gauge something of what Williams was hoping to **express**. First, the fact that 'lurid reflections' and 'shadows' suddenly appear on the walls 'around BLANCHE' make it clear this is *about* Blanche. The likely meaning **constructed** through these stage directions by both the playwright and the reader is that the reflections and shadows represent how Blanche is trapped in some way. However, because these reflections and shadows are obviously non-realist elements of Williams' stagecraft, this may affect our **interpretation**. Is Blanche literally trapped or, being non-realist, are the reflections and shadows merely in Blanche's imagination? It is an interesting question and because we are unable to ask Williams exactly what meaning he was attempting to **construct**, we will need to decide for ourselves.

What does appear clear though is that Williams was attempting to **express** that Blanche felt trapped, either physically in the real world or psychologically in her mind. Although the reader may **interpret** the scene differently, we can come to a compromise with the playwright – remember this is part of the **negotiation** process – and agree that a mood of claustrophobia is being created here and Blanche is the one who is affected by it in one way or another. Some readers may focus on how Stanley is still on stage at this point, and they may **interpret** these reflections and shadows as being a representation of him and how his presence is a nightmarish one for Blanche; other readers may **interpret** the stage directions as suggesting Blanche is simply paranoid and the nightmarish scenario is an internal one (inside her head) rather than an external one (Stanley's presence); other readers may **interpret** the stage directions as representing how Stanley's world is smothering Blanche's world. Of course, our **interpretation** is likely to be influenced by how the stage director stages this scene and how the actor playing Blanche responds to the reflections and shadows on the walls – there are no stage directions to explain Blanche's reaction to them which gives the director and actor artistic licence to **construct** their own meaning of what Williams was intending and in this way they are responsible for shaping the audience's **interpretation** to the scene's meaning rather than Williams himself.

Moving on, with Stanley's exit into the bathroom, Blanche is able to make her phone call. As discussed earlier, her dialogue here is peppered with exclamations, pauses, unfinished sentences and fragments. Although there are no explicit stage directions guiding us as to how Blanche should say these lines, the punctuation Williams uses is very useful in **expressing** how he intended these lines to be spoken. So he has **constructed** meaning through the punctuation and broken sentences to suggest Blanche's growing panic and even paranoia when she says 'One moment! Someone is – Nothing!' (line 7). She appears to think that someone is approaching or is listening in to her conversation, but then changes her mind when she exclaims 'Nothing!' This may support the **interpretation** that some readers may have had earlier regarding the reflections and shadows being inside Blanche's head and we may feel that Williams is attempting to **express** how she is simply paranoid and on edge. Again, depending on how the actor speaks these words and performs the scene will add an extra layer regarding how we **interpret** Blanche's state of mind but it seems likely that panic and fear, perhaps paranoia and desperation will be the overriding meaning constructed here.

It is the next long section of stage directions where we really see Williams' **plastic theatre** at its finest. So far he has constructed this scene using non-verbal visual imagery and verbal dialogue, which in turn attempts to construct a meaning that is unsettling and unnerving. Now – and remember Blanche is alone now – he merges **auditory** and **visual imagery** to accentuate this nightmarish mood even further:

> *The night is filled with inhuman voices like cries in a jungle.*
> *The shadows and lurid reflections move sinuously as flames across the wall spaces.*
>
> (lines 10–11)

Once again, each stage director will make his or her own decisions regarding how to stage this which will shape how an audience **interprets** this element of Williams' **stagecraft**, but focusing on the written text we can see how Williams is attempting to **construct** meaning that evokes terror. The 'inhuman voices like cries in a jungle' (line 10) suggest Blanche is in the middle of somewhere savage where the rules of civilization no longer apply. If you had read the rest of the play up to this point, you would know that Blanche's full name is Blanche Dubois which means White Woods and that Williams describes her as a 'moth' when we first meet her in scene 1. With this background knowledge, the reader may **construct** a meaning that points to Blanche's vulnerability – after all, how can a moth or someone connected to white woods survive in a jungle? Likewise, the **simile** that describes the shadows and reflections moving 'sinuously as flames across the wall spaces' (line 11) for most readers is likely to remind them of a hellish place or at the very least somewhere sinister and foreboding so the meaning **constructed** here seems to suggest Blanche's safety is at risk. Again, though, we are unsure whether she really is at risk, or whether this is simply in her mind. Has Williams **constructed** this scene to transport us inside Blanche's head to express her fragile state of mind or has he **constructed** the scene to **express** how the external world really is a threat to her? Again, compromise is needed. Just by focusing on this short extract, we may never be able to come to a definitive answer so **negotiation** is needed. Williams has **constructed** this scene in such a way to open up a dialogue with us, now we have to read (or watch) what he has created and **construct** our own meaning.

As we know, **constructing** our own meaning may depend on our own background. If we have experience of mental illness, perhaps we **interpret** these stage directions as pointing to Blanche's mental deterioration; if we have experience of a fraught reality, perhaps we **interpret** these stage directions as pointing to an external danger. Interestingly, Williams himself had experience of both: his sister was institutionalized and had a lobotomy and his father was an alcoholic who was violent. Having this contextual understanding to Williams' background, does this make it any easier to interpret the meaning? Perhaps it is a combination of both: Blanche's internal and external worlds are both threatening her, which makes it all the more difficult for her to escape this reality. Or perhaps we **construct** an entirely different meaning and **interpret** this scene as warning us about something more symbolic (the impossibility of two different worlds, Stanley's world and Blanche's world, co-existing side by side). However, one meaning we can all agree on and therefore construct is that Blanche is experiencing some kind of inner turmoil; the reason for her inner turmoil will depend on each reader's **interpretation** and/or each actor's **interpretation**. This then is the compromise the reader-actor-audience and playwright make through the **negotiation** process.

ACTIVITY 3

Now it is your turn. Re-read the second half of the extract again and write your own commentary, focusing on how meaning is constructed, negotiated, expressed and interpreted. Every time you use one of these keywords from the chapter's concept question, italicize or bold it (or underline if you are writing by hand). The extract you should focus on is below:

Through the back wall of the rooms, which have become transparent, can be seen the sidewalk. A prostitute has rolled a drunkard. He pursues her along the walk, overtakes her and there is a struggle. A policeman's whistle breaks it up. The figures disappear.

Some moments later the NEGRO WOMAN appears around the corner with a sequined bag which the prostitute had dropped on the walk. She is rooting excitedly through it.

BLANCHE presses her knuckles to her lips and returns slowly to the phone. She speaks in a hoarse whisper …

STANLEY: You left th' phone off th' hook.

He crosses to it deliberately and sets it back on the hook. After he has replaced it, he stares at her again, his mouth slowly curving into a grin, as he waves between BLANCHE and the outer door.

(Tennessee Williams, A Streetcar Named Desire Scene 10)

When you have written your own commentary, read the one at the back of the book and compare notes.

Tennessee Williams

Thomas Lanier 'Tennessee' Williams III was an American playwright who also wrote short stories, poetry, essays and memoirs. His early plays were one-act pieces, but his reputation was established with the publication of *The Glass Menagerie* (1944), and *A Streetcar Named Desire* (1947), which won the Pulitzer Prize for Drama in 1948. He used his personal experiences as the basis of much of his work, including living with an alcoholic and violent father when he was young and having a sister, Rose, who was sectioned into a mental institution and had a lobotomy from which she never recovered. Many of his plays have been adapted for the cinema, including *A Streetcar Named Desire* starring Marlon Brando and Vivien Leigh, which won four Academy Awards in 1951.

EE Links: English A – Literature category 1

Stagecraft could be the basis of an English A: Literature category 1 extended essay. You could either focus on just one play, such as *A Streetcar Named Desire*, and explore how Williams uses stagecraft to depict the abstract, or you could compare the way Williams uses stagecraft with another contemporary playwright you may be studying in class, who does not use plastic theatre. Two potential research questions could be:

- **How does Tennessee Williams employ plastic theatre conventions to depict the abstract in his play *A Streetcar Named Desire*?**
- **How do Tennessee Williams and** [name of other playwright] **use stagecraft differently to depict the abstract in *A Streetcar Named Desire* and** [name of other play]**?**

Constructing meaning through stream of consciousness

We have just explored how, through stagecraft, a playwright can attempt to transport the reader inside a character's head to experience, in this case, Blanche's inner turmoil. Another way that writers manage to transport the reader inside an individual's head is through **stream of consciousness**. Read the following key features box for an overview of this particular literary device.

KEY FEATURES STREAM OF CONSCIOUSNESS

- American philosopher and psychologist, William James, coined the term **'stream of consciousness'** in *The Principles of Psychology* in 1890.
- A narrative device that attempts to imitate an individual's internal thought processes, memories, desires and/or reactions to something.
- Usually follows the form of an interior monologue – unlike a dramatic monologue or a **soliloquy**, an interior monologue has no audience and is an individual's inner-most thoughts. As the reader is overhearing an individual's inner thoughts as they are thought, the thoughts are not ordered in any way when written down by the writer.
- Typically uninterrupted and continuous prose, often lacking punctuation, capitalization and grammatical accuracy.
- It was a popular narrative device used in the early-twentieth century by Marcel Proust (French), James Joyce (Irish) and Virginia Woolf (British) but is still used by contemporary writers.
- In terms of literary theory, this is an example of **modernism** which argues, 'the truth of the complex, non-linear workings of the human mind, are in stark contrast to the ordered language we often use to shape that vision of reality.'

(Sara Upston, Chapter 7)

Stream of consciousness, then, is an interior monologue that transports the reader inside an individual's head and allows us to listen in to an individual's thoughts as they are being thought. As we have seen with Williams' *A Streetcar Named Desire*, in drama, a playwright uses the tools of **stagecraft** to transport the audience inside a character's head. In prose fiction, a writer uses the tools of writing to do this. If you recall, one of the dictionary definitions of 'construct' was to form sentences according to grammatical rules. A writer is obviously very familiar with the rules of grammar, being one of the tools of writing. So when a writer breaks a grammatical rule, there tends to be a reason. This is one way a writer attempts to construct meaning when transporting a reader inside a character's head.

Read the following short extract from Toni Morrison's novel, *Beloved* (1987) and then read the accompanying commentary.

> I AM BELOVED and she is mine. I see her take flowers away from leaves   she puts them in a round basket   the leaves are not for her   she fills the basket   she opens the grass   I would help her but the clouds are in the way   how can I say things that are pictures   I am not separate from her   there is no place where I stop   her face is my own and I want to be there in the place where her face is and to be looking at it too   a hot thing
>
> All of it is now   it is always now   there will never be a time when I am not crouching and watching others who are crouching too   I am always crouching   the man on my face is dead   his face is not mine   his mouth smells sweet but his eyes are locked
>
> *(Toni Morrison 248)*

Step 1: Form and structure

Let's think about the **form** Morrison has used (step 1 of our literary reading strategy). You may have found this extract difficult to interpret – and this is the whole point! A stream of consciousness is not easy to follow as we are transported inside the speaker's head and given an insight into the speaker's thoughts as they happen. The speaker's thoughts may not happen in a logical order and because thoughts are thoughts rather than spoken language, rules of grammar, punctuation and sometimes spelling are not followed. Morrison has **constructed** meaning by using the form of a stream of consciousness by rejecting many of the rules of conventional writing: there is no punctuation; there are long gaps between certain words; there is very little capitalization; many sentences are fragments; the order of the phrases does not always follow a logical order. It is, therefore, difficult to **negotiate** a meaning when we are unable to understand exactly what has been written. But again this is the whole point. Morrison obviously wants us to recognize that this is a stream of consciousness and rather than being able to understand every thought process inside the speaker's head, the important thing is that we understand we are being transported inside the speaker's head. This then is part of the **negotiation** process. Now that we are inside the speaker's head, it is up to us to try to **interpret** some kind of a meaning but if this is not possible, at least we are where we are supposed to be (in this case, inside Beloved's head).

Step 2: LIFs

So, how do we **interpret** something that we do not fully comprehend? We have to pick our way through the language, images and other features of the extract (step 2 of our literary reading strategy) carefully and try to **construct** our own meaning, or try to think like the speaker thinks. Regarding this extract, we may start with the beginning statement 'I am Beloved' to place who the speaker is. It appears the speaker is someone called Beloved (the namesake of the novel so someone, we feel, who is significant to the narrative). The first few lines describe a scene we can interpret without too many problems. The speaker appears to be watching someone picking flowers. Although the sentences are short and simple, separated by large white spaces, the language used – 'flowers', 'leaves', 'a basket' and 'grass' – make this scene recognisable. However, this ordinary scene is broken by phrases that we find difficult to interpret. The speaker is unable to be physically present in this scene because 'clouds are in the way'. Additionally, she is unable to communicate with the woman picking flowers because 'how can I say things that are pictures', suggesting the speaker has no language. As we continue, the speaker states 'there is no place where I stop', suggesting an exhausting and never-ending journey of some kind. At this point, we feel we can **interpret** parts of her thoughts because of the **construction** of recognisable images, but there are parts we have difficulty **interpreting**.

The speaker moves on to think about the woman picking flowers – 'I am not separate from her' and 'her face is my own'. We feel a sense of connection between the two although their relationship is never explicitly stated. Perhaps we feel the speaker is a child – particularly as she thinks in pictures rather than using language. Some readers may pick up on the lack of grammar and punctuation and feel that as well as being a convention of stream of consciousness, this also makes the speaker sound childlike. If the speaker is a child, is the flower-picker her mother? This would make sense of some of the images, although we still do not understand completely why 'clouds' are preventing the speaker from being physically with her mother (if it is her mother).

The second paragraph appears to shift in time and place. We are no longer with the 'mother' picking flowers, but are with 'Beloved'. The **verb** 'crouching' is repeated numerous times in these lines – the speaker is 'crouching' but she also observes other people 'crouching'. She uses the present participle, 'I am always crouching', suggesting this is something she can never escape. It would appear she is in an enclosed place or somewhere she is unable to stand up straight. Perhaps in a prison – though imprisonment is not forever – or perhaps in a coffin from which there is no escape. Is this a dead child speaking? One of the final images in this extract is 'the man on my face is dead' which certainly links to the idea of death. We are attempting to **interpret** meaning by picking apart the language, images and other literary features Morrison has used to construct this stream of consciousness, but there are still aspects to our **interpretation** that do not make complete sense.

This is one example when using an **immanent** reading is not always sufficient. If we have read the novel, we will know Morrison dedicates it to 'Sixty million and more', an **allusion** to how many slave-related deaths there were during America's history of slavery. Once we know this, perhaps we can feel more certain in our **interpretation** that the speaker is one of the 'sixty million and more' and this is why she is unable to be with her mother picking flowers. However, even when we are able to contextualise, a stream of consciousness remains difficult to interpret fully. As for what Morrison is attempting to **express**, we can only surmise that she wants us to feel transported inside Beloved's head – and it does not appear to be a pleasant place to be. If we feel unsettled and confused about what the interior monologue means precisely, then Morrison has succeeded. We should be feeling very self-conscious as a reader here – almost as if we are being voyeuristic, listening into the speaker's inner-most thoughts that are supposed to be private rather than public.

We discussed earlier how a writer attempts to simplify complex ideas – a stream of consciousness is one of those times when a writer does not attempt to make things easy for us. Rather than the writer **negotiating** meaning for us, we have to **negotiate** meaning by ourselves with very little help from the writer.

Toni Morrison

Born Chloe Ardelia Wofford in 1931, Toni Morrison was an American writer of novels and essays, an editor, teacher and professor emeritus at Princeton University. She has won many awards for her writing, including the Nobel Prize for Literature in 1993, the Presidential Medal of Freedom (presented to her by President Barack Obama in 2012) and the PEN/Saul Bellow Award for Achievement in American Fiction in 2016. Her novels focus on the history and experience of African-Americans and *Beloved*, her most critically acclaimed novel, is based on the real-life experience of Margaret Garner, a runaway slave who killed her 2-year-old daughter when slave-hunters caught up with her.

Just as Morrison has broken – or deconstructed – the rules of grammar to construct meaning, with the advent of digital literacy and particularly with the rise in social media platforms many online writers are also breaking the traditional rules of writing. The author of the next text we are going to discuss is not a Pulitzer-winning novelist but is a 13-year-old Scottish girl, and her audience was not a global audience made up of millions, but her English teacher. Let's explore how the advent of digital literacy has had an impact on the way in which texts can be constructed to express meaning, and what happens when the negotiation process breaks down and a reader is unable to interpret the writer's intended meaning.

Communicating meaning through textspeak

The escalation in digital literacy has seen a change in the type of language used to construct and express meaning. The widespread use of communicating through digital devices began with the introduction of mobile phones, which allowed users to send SMS (short message service) or text messages. The language used for SMS/text messages, referred to as **textspeak**, is defined by its brevity, shorthand slang and use of **emoticons**. Telecommunication companies limited the number of characters per text message and charged users for every message sent. As a result, users communicated their messages using the least number of characters, often dispensing with punctuation, grammar and capitalization. Today, although mobile phones have changed so that texting has become easier and many telecommunication companies allow digital texts to be sent free of charge between users, brevity has remained the defining feature of textspeak. Before we explore this topic further, read the key features box below to give you an idea of the common conventions of this mode of communication – however, remember that this particular way of communicating is regularly changing as more **emojis** and **emoticons** are created. This form of communication allows for an individual and personal voice – or **idiolect** – to be heard and encourages users to break the rules precisely so that each user can construct their own unique and distinctive identity through their online voice.

KEY FEATURES TEXTSPEAK

- Use of abbreviations: tmr (tomorrow), ppl (people), txtspk (textspeak).
- Use of **acronyms**: gtg (got to go), LOL (laugh out loud), ttyl (talk to you later).
- Use of letter and number **homophones**: 2b (to be), b4 (before), gr8 (great).
- Use of shortened forms: k (OK), bb (goodbye).
- Use of less standard spelling: coz (because).
- Use of spelling based on sound: kewl (cool).
- Use of **emoticons**: :-) :-D :-* (symbols on the keyboard to denote emotions).
- Use of **emojis**: (pictorial images to denote feelings and emotions).
- Use of language mixing: in HK – *so ma fan ar* = so annoying/troublesome.

The emergence of textspeak has generated much debate regarding the topic of language change – and it is likely that you will have your own personal views about whether textspeak represents the latest exciting evolution in the changing English language or whether it is: 'butchering grammar [and] eroding literacy in young adults'. (Green)

Cast your mind back to when you were 12 or 13 years old. At the beginning of the new academic year, your English teacher may have asked you to write about your summer holidays, hoping you would include lots of description in your attempt to entertain and engage your teacher. The following extract is what one 13-year-old student wrote and handed in to her teacher in response to this assignment in 2012.

> My smmr hols wr CWOT. B4, we usd 2go2 NY 2C my bro, his GF & thr 3 :- kds FTF. ILNY, it's a gr8 plc. Bt my Ps wr so {:-/ BC o 9/11 tht thay dcdd 2 stay in SCO & spnd 2 wks up N, WUCIWUG - 0. I was vvv brd in MON. 0 bt baas & ^^^^^.
>
> AAR8, my Ps wr :-). they sd ICBW, & tht they wr ha-p 4 the pc&qt … IDTS!! I wnted 2 go hm ASAP, 2C my M8 again.
>
> 2day, I cam bk 2 skool. I feel v 0-:)
>
> BC I hv dn all my hm wrk. Now its BAU.
>
> *(Auslan Cramb)*

The student has **constructed** her assignment using textspeak. She is attempting to **express** what she did over her summer holidays to her teacher. As we have seen in the literary works we have already studied in this chapter, one way a writer attempts to **negotiate** with the reader is by using their craft as a writer to simplify complex ideas – to **negotiate** a way through a difficult topic for the reader. You may feel that this student has done the opposite: complicated a simple topic! As the reader, how do you **interpret** this student's writing? It may be that you feel parts of it are like a foreign language. Unless you are a fluent Russian speaker, it is unlikely, for example, you would be able to understand much of Tolstoy's *War and Peace* were you to read it in Russian, its original language. If this is a novel you would like to read it is highly likely you will read it in translation – and just as our interpretation of Williams' play is often determined by the way the director and actors **interpret** the play on stage, your understanding of Tolstoy's novel will be influenced by the translation you choose to read.

TOK Links

To what extent can a reader understand a text in translation's meaning that was written originally in a language different from their own? To what extent is the knowledge gained from reading a text in translation reliable compared to the knowledge gained from reading a text written in the reader's original language?

ACTIVITY 4

For this activity, you are playing the role of translator. Translate the essay above into Standard English. Just as texts that are translated into English often rely on more than one translator (a single translation of *War and Peace* often has more than one translator and as discussed in the Introduction, there have been many translators of Albert Camus' *L'Étranger*), you may feel you need to work with a friend on this task – he or she does not need to be an English language and literature student!

Once you have translated the text, you can read a full translation in the back of the book and compare translations.

It is likely that your background as a social media user will have influenced how successful you were in **constructing** meaning to this text, understanding what the writer was attempting to **express** and then **interpreting** the text so you could successfully translate it. The student had a meaning in mind when she **constructed** this text and attempted to **express** her meaning through a combination of **Standard English** words, **contractions** and **emoticons**. This is her response to the assignment and she is presumably hoping that her teacher will **interpret** it in the same way she does. However, we can argue there was a gap in her **negotiating** skills! Her teacher did not understand her meaning – but more than that, he was unable to **construct** his own meaning that made any sense. In that sense, the text she had **constructed** failed because she had been unable to **express** her meaning in a way that her teacher could understand or even **construct** his own meaning.

Who then is at fault? Some readers may argue that the writer is at fault for not being clear enough, other readers may argue that the reader is at fault for not being imaginative enough to squeeze some kind of meaning from the text. Hopefully, you will have been able to **construct** some kind of meaning yourself when you translated the text – and if this was too challenging for you, you could have read a translation at the end of the book. However, the translation is *a* translation – it is not *the* translation. Only the writer can explain what the definitive translation is – and this is only if she has a clear understanding herself of how to translate **emoticons** such as {:-/ into **Standard English**.

So here we see how a text's meaning can be fluid – my translation of {:-/ may well have differed from your translation of {:-/ which in turn may differ from the writer's translation of {:-/ if she were ever asked to translate it. Some readers would argue that a translation never manages successfully to **express** the precise meaning of the original text and having attempted this activity, you may agree with this sentiment.

CONCEPT CONNECTION

CREATIVITY

We can view the student's response to the assignment, using textspeak, as being creative. She is combining standard English with non-standard English to describe what she did over the summer holidays and the use of emoticons make the writing look visually appealing. If you compare her response with your standard English translation, it is likely you will agree that her original text is more creative than your translated version using conventional language. Her use of textspeak also forces the reader to interact in an imaginative way with the text in order to comprehend the writer's meaning. You may have translated the text differently to the translation in the back of the book – after all, there is no one definitive translation of {:-/. The text itself is also original. It is unlikely anyone would have used exactly the same emoticons this student has used were they to write an essay about their summer holidays using textspeak.

Likewise, George Herbert's use of the physical shape of his poem to enhance the religious meaning of the text, Tennessee Williams' use of stagecraft to represent a character's psychological decline and Toni Morrison's rejection of traditional written language to represent a character's thoughts are all examples of how literature is an artform that uses creativity and the imagination to explore a range of ideas. In each of these literary works, readers are encouraged to engage creatively and imaginatively with the text in order to understand potential meanings.

As you continue to explore texts in class, think about how writers use both their own creativity to express meaning and encourage readers to interact creatively with the text to interpret meaning.

Just as writers of literary works and non-literary texts can deconstruct language in order to **construct** meaning, so can writers deconstruct the form they are using in order to **construct** meaning. The next extract we are going to be exploring in this chapter is from Shaun Tan's graphic novel, *The Arrival* (2006) and we will be discussing how he deconstructs the conventions of a graphic novel to **defamiliarize** the reader in his attempt to **construct** a particular meaning and challenge and shape the reader's **interpretation** of the text's meaning.

Communicating meaning through *defamiliarization*

Before we explore Tan's text, read the following key features box which gives an overview of this convention.

KEY FEATURES DEFAMILIARIZATION ('OSTRANENIE')

- Russian Formalist literary critic, Viktor Shklovsky (1893–1984), coined the phrase **defamiliarization** or **ostranenie** in his 1917 essay 'Art as Technique', later published in his 1925 book, *Theory of Prose* (Chapter 1).
- He used this phrase to describe the way literary writers use language to transform what is over-familiar and ordinary into something strange or unfamiliar.
- A writer may use defamiliarization for different reasons: to satirize social or political conventions; to raise awareness of an issue that has lost its impact due to over-familiarity; or to force a reader out of his or her comfort zone and to take action.
- Ultimately, a writer uses defamiliarization to attempt to shape and challenge the way a reader perceives the world in which they live.

In terms of literary theory, this is an element of **formalism**, which awakens the reader 'not by a new idea, but rather by the new linguistic presentation of something familiar'.

(Sara Upston, Chapter 2)

The Arrival is a fascinating literary work by Chinese-Australian graphic novelist, Shaun Tan. Tan's graphic novel employs many traditional graphic novel conventions to **construct** meaning, but it also subverts a number of these conventions in order to defamiliarize the reader and challenge the way she or he views the protagonist of the graphic novel, an immigrant. Before we explore an extract from Tan's graphic novel, let's remind ourselves of some of the Key features of comic books and graphic novels.

KEY FEATURES COMIC BOOKS AND GRAPHIC NOVELS

- Considered literary works, even if autobiographical or biographical in nature.
- Written text, including use of **captions, word balloons** and **display lettering**.
- The inter-relationship between the visual image (illustration) and the written text.
- Illustrations, including use of colour, shading and shape.
- **Spatial mechanics** (how space is used within each panel).
- **Temporal mechanics** (how time is stopped, slowed down or speeded up).
- Use of **gutters** (the white space between the panels).
- Use of **panels** – the impact of their order, shape and size.

We are going to explore eight panels from Tan's literary work in detail, which depict the protagonist arriving for the first time in the new land. We will be exploring how Tan uses defamiliarization to **construct** meaning, how meaning is **negotiated** between the writer and the reader, how Tan's meaning is **expressed** and how the reader **interprets** the text's meaning. First, read the following eight panels closely – although there is no written text, take your time to 'read' each panel, fully exploring each **visual image** and the inclusion of **display lettering** in as much detail as you can.

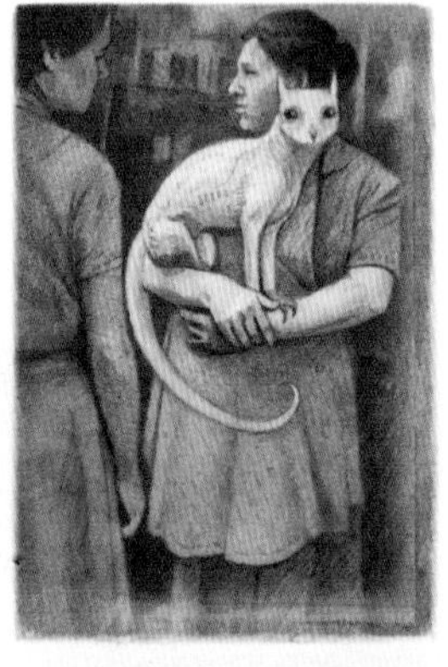
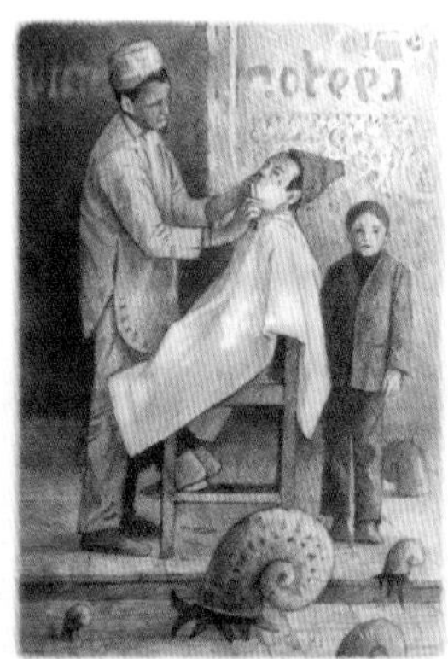

Tan attempts to **construct** meaning through each of the visual panels. There are eight rectangular **panels**, all the same size and equidistant from one another. Initially, we feel we are able to **interpret** them quite successfully. The first panel depicts a newspaper boy selling newspapers; the third (or it may be the fifth one, depending on the way you read the page) depicts someone having a shave at the barber's; the next panel depicts a pair of musicians playing in the street; one of the panels depicts a couple at a market stall buying and selling eggs, and so on. However, on closer inspection, there is something decidedly unfamiliar about each panel: **display lettering** which denotes writing on the newspaper in panel 1 is incomprehensible; we have never seen the giant-like snail creature in the foreground in the barber panel; the instruments the musicians are playing are also unfamiliar; and we have certainly never seen eggs *that* size before. Tan has used **spatial mechanics** to merge the familiar with the unfamiliar – in seven of the eight panels, between one-third to one-half of each panel contains images of the unfamiliar and this helps to defamiliarize us. We are not sure where we are or even what time we are in. The colouring he uses throughout is sepia, which usually denotes a time in the past; however, the scenes we are looking at seem more futuristic than historical. However, they are certainly not scenes from a science fiction novel because we recognize the land and people as being familiar to us.

Through using the traditional graphic novel convention of illustrations, Tan has **constructed** a place that is both familiar and unfamiliar. The fact that there is absolutely no language we can understand adds further to our confusion – Tan is **expressing** himself solely through images and we now have to work at **constructing** and **interpreting** the text's meaning. Our confusion is heightened because we are not even sure which order to read these panels. Do we read them from top left to top right, then bottom left to bottom right; or top left, second top left, bottom left, second bottom left, third top left, top right, third bottom left, bottom right? And does it actually matter which order we read the panels? From a young age, we are taught that there *is* a correct order to read words on a page, but these panels seem to defy that. There are other ways that Tan attempts to defamiliarize us which are not so obvious. For example, his use of **guttering** is unusual – he uses very wide white spaces between each panel which has the effect of slowing down the process of reading, slowing down time. It takes us time to pass our eyes from one panel to the next and this makes the panels seem disconnected in some way. He also uses **temporal mechanics** to defamiliarize us. We are unsure whether time has stopped, slowed down or speeded up within the sequence of panels and we are unsure whether each moment occurs at the same time or whether they are disconnected. And of course, the main reason we are defamiliarized is because there is no writing that we recognize. There *is* **display lettering** in a number of the panels, so presumably communication through the written word does occur in this land, but it is no lettering we understand so we feel disconnected, powerless and unsettled. It would appear Tan has **constructed** these panels to make full use of defamiliarization, but why? What is he attempting to **express**? And how do we **interpret** his meaning?

It is not until we reach the final **panel** that we begin to **construct** an understanding of the text's meaning and begin to appreciate Tan's skill in his **construction** of these panels. Whatever order we decide to read these panels, the newspaper boy is always the first panel and the man with the suitcase is always the last panel. As soon as we read this final panel, we feel relieved. Why? Because there is absolutely nothing about this panel which is unfamiliar. We can probably understand every part of it. There is no strange lettering, no weird creatures, no gigantic eggs. Everything about this panel makes sense and this is a relief. And what is the image in the panel? A solitary man, wearing everyday clothes, holding a travelling case, looking confused. We may not be holding a travelling case, but everything else about this man is similar to us as we, too, are feeling confused about the previous seven panels we have been trying to make sense of. Then it crosses our mind that this man is looking towards the panels we have just read – he, too, appears confused by the same scenes that confused us. We are beginning to feel a connection with him – empathy even, as we have just experienced the same sense of confusion that he appears to be experiencing. So who is this man? He is the protagonist of Tan's graphic novel, an immigrant who has been forced to leave his homeland and has just arrived in this new land. Now we are beginning to understand what Tan is attempting to **express**: he is attempting to **express** how displaced an immigrant arriving in a new land feels and through his use of defamiliarization in the seven panels prior to the 'immigrant' panel, he attempts to force us to stand in the immigrant's shoes and experience his displacement first-hand. He has used his craft as a graphic novelist to **construct** a particular meaning and **express** a particular point of view.

The meaning he has **constructed** is that an immigrant feels an outsider when he first arrives in a new land. The point of view he is **expressing** is that we should attempt to see things through the immigrant's eyes in order to empathize with him (and other immigrants). Most adult readers would understand this meaning and would also, maybe for the first time in their lives, feel as if they had experienced this sense of displacement an immigrant is likely to experience when he arrives in a new land. How are we supposed to **interpret** this message? It is likely that as well as understanding the literal meaning of the panels – feeling empathy for this particular fictional character in a graphic novel – we understand the bigger picture. Most adult readers would **interpret** these panels in the way Tan had intended: in reflecting on immigration in our own world and perhaps rethinking how we view those images of immigrants we see in our newspapers or on our television screens regularly. So, meaning has been **constructed**; Tan's viewpoint has been **expressed**; and it is likely that most (adult) readers will have **interpreted** the meaning accordingly.

However, how has meaning been **negotiated**? Let's think of the definition of negotiation being how we are guided by the writer through a complex subject (similar to the way Herbert guided us at the beginning of the chapter). We could argue that immigration is a complex topic and Tan attempts to simplify this for us through his visuals and lack of language. An immigrant, for example, becomes an immigrant for a myriad of reasons and trying to understand the topic of immigration can be quite daunting. Moreover, understanding an individual immigrant's experience can also be difficult for many people, primarily because of the language barrier. Many newly arrived immigrants to one's country do not speak one's language so it is difficult to form a relationship with them and consequently difficult to feel much empathy. Through these panels, Tan has attempted to **negotiate** a way through these problems for us. The images themselves are quite simple – simple sepia is used, there is one thing going on in each panel and the panels themselves are quite large. The final panel depicting the immigrant is particularly easy to comprehend as every part of it is so familiar to us. Perhaps this is Tan suggesting that actually the topic of immigration is not so complex, or does not have to be complex. Anyone who is an immigrant experiences the same sense of displacement and it is this that Tan is attempting to raise our awareness of. We can perhaps also see why Tan has consciously decided not to include any comprehensible language. This is also a way he attempts to **negotiate** meaning with us. He is trying to raise our awareness of how difficult it is for the immigrant who very often has no shared language with the new people in the new land. It is rare that in our everyday lives we actually experience this sense of being unable to communicate with anyone, so by removing language from his novel Tan is making it easier for us to understand what that feels like – and as we have just seen, it unsettles us and makes us feel quite powerless and vulnerable. So, through both using (visual images) and not using (language) conventional graphic novel features, Tan has helped guide us in our understanding of this complex topic – and this is part of the **negotiated** meaning.

Shaun Tan

Shaun Tan's father was a Chinese-Malay immigrant who moved to Australia from Malaysia when he was a young man. Shaun Tan was born in Perth, Australia, in 1974 and much of his work centres around the idea of the outsider. He is a writer, artist and filmmaker and in 2011 he won an Academy Award for Best Short Film (Animated) for the animated film adaptation of his graphic novel, *The Lost Thing* (2000). His wordless graphic novel, *The Arrival* (2006), has won many prizes throughout Australia and in 2011 the Swedish Arts Council awarded him the Astrid Lindgren Memorial Award for his contribution to children's and young adult literature.

How do different readers interpret these panels?

Tan would hope that the reader would **interpret** the panels in the way we have just explored them. However, the way a reader **interprets** the text does, as we know, depend on the reader themselves. Precisely because it is a wordless graphic novel, it is popular with many young children. It is unlikely they will **interpret** the text as attempting to raise their awareness of immigrants and displacement. They may feel some connection to the protagonist but it is unlikely they will be able to intellectualize the protagonist as representing immigrants worldwide throughout time. Some readers may find the book appealing because of its sepia-coloured illustrations – entering a semi-surreal world which is not too surreal that we cannot recognize it, but surreal enough to offer some kind of adventure. As we know, once the book is published and is in the domain of the reader, the reader takes over. These are all valid interpretations; however, with this particular work, we do know what Tan's intention was. In an interview with Rick Margolis in September 2007, Tan himself explained how he was hoping readers would interpret and respond to this graphic novel:

> *'In Australia, people don't stop to imagine what it's like for some of these refugees. They just see them as a problem once they're here, without thinking about the bigger picture. I don't expect the book to change anybody's opinion about things, but if it at least makes them pause to think, I'll feel as if I've succeeded in something.'*
>
> *(Rick Margolis)*

Now that we have explored how meaning is **constructed**, **negotiated**, **expressed** and **interpreted** in these eight panels that depict the protagonist's arrival, 'read' the panel on next page. It is a double-page panel that depicts the protagonist in his old land just prior to his departure. This panel comes from early on in the graphic novel. Closely 'read' the panel and then attempt the activity that follows.

ACTIVITY 5

Copy and complete the following table on this double-page panel – try to include a short paragraph for each key word. Because you are only analysing one panel, you are not expected to write as much as the model commentary above. When you have completed your table, compare your ideas with those at the back of the book.

■ Table 1.3.2

In what ways is meaning ...	Write at least one paragraph for each key word
Constructed?	
Negotiated?	
Expressed?	
Interpreted?	

GLOBAL ISSUES *Field of inquiry:* Culture, Identity and Community

MIGRATION

The Arrival is a graphic novel about immigration and the difficulties faced by migrants who arrive in a new land. Although there is much that they recognize in the new land, there is also much that is unfamiliar – particularly the ability to communicate. This graphic novel, through its use of sepia colouring, merging familiar with unfamiliar images and, primarily, through its lack of any recognizable language makes it clear that immigration is a global issue that affects people around the world throughout time. It is likely you will be aware of immigration both through the news media and also perhaps in your own local community. You may like to focus on the field of inquiry of culture, identity and community through the global issue of migration, exploring how both the non-literary texts you study in class and literary works such as *The Arrival* discuss issues concerning immigration and the ways in which immigration impact both the individual and larger societies. This global issue is also explored in Chapter 2.1 through the poetry of Vietnamese-American poet, Ocean Vuong.

If there is a refugee centre in your area, you may like to volunteer to teach small groups of refugee children English. You could also get a group of IBDP students together and either offer sports coaching lessons (for example, football or basketball) or organize a friendly match in mixed student/refugee teams. If you worked with this group of your community on a regular basis, this could be either a Service or an Activity project.

■ Constructing meaning through non-textual visual language

We have just explored how different readers may interpret Tan's text differently depending on their age. Knowing Tan's intention this suggests that certainly for a writer there may be a right and a wrong way to interpret a text. So far, we have answered this concept question using texts that include written language, even if some of that written language is incomprehensible. The final text we are going to explore attempts to express meaning through a wholly visual image.

The wholly visual text we are going to be exploring this concept question through is a seventeenth-century painting by Spanish painter, Diego Rodríguez de Silva y Velázquez called *Las Meninas* (translated as *The Ladies in Waiting*), painted in 1656. Similar to the other texts we have explored so far, we are viewing the painting through an **immanent** lens. It is an extremely ambiguous painting which has been constructed in such a way that its meaning can be interpreted in a number of different ways. Before you read the commentary, view the painting on the next page closely and read the annotations. The annotations focus on how Velázquez has constructed his artwork.

Because this is a wholly visual text, we are going to use Step 5 of our non-literary reading strategy to try to interpret the painting's meaning, focusing in particular on the visual images and their placement within the frame. There are a number of ways a viewer can interpret this artwork. Let's explore some of them now.

Step 5: Visual image and layout

In one sense we can interpret this artwork as Velázquez challenging preconceptions of what good art should be. The painter in the artwork (is it Velázquez himself or a fictional painter?) peers around his canvas at the subjects he is supposedly painting. We assume they are extremely wealthy aristocrats, partly because of the palatial setting with its high ceilings and walls covered with artwork and partly because of the other figures in the painting – a girl and her waiting women, all dressed in full splendour; two dwarves dressed in luxurious clothes; a personal painter. However, the subjects of the painting are off-frame and are reduced to a barely noticeable reflection in a mirror at the back of the room. Their significance is, therefore, diminished as they are a mere reflection in contrast to the painter and the other figures in the artwork who, ironically, are not the subjects of the painting being painted. What Velázquez seems far more interested in **expressing** is a snapshot of the moment rather than the couple themselves. In the artwork, we are confronted with what is happening beyond the couple and the painting being painted. We view a man bathed in light leaving or entering the room, two adults in conversation in the shadows, a sleeping dog almost the same size as the two dwarves in the foreground, a splendidly dressed young girl of 5 or 6 years old who takes centre stage and is waited on by her two meninas. Although we may not know who these figures are, they now become the subject of Velázquez's artwork, rather than the wealthy couple 'sitting' for the (fictional) painting. Do we **interpret** this as Velázquez **expressing** through his artwork that the function of art is to imitate real life

Where is the viewer? Placed in same position as subject of painting. Is artist painting our picture? Is girl gazing at us?

Couple in mirror: is this a reflection of couple who are the subject of the painting? Reflection; diminishes power of couple.

Setting – palatial. High ceilings, paintings adorn walls. Private painter.

Easel: larger than life – significance of art?

Man in doorway – entering or exiting? Ambiguous. Bathed in light – given prominence.

The painter – is this self-portrait of Velázquez or fictional painter/scene? Prominent position of painter ... depicting the importance of art?

Two adult figures in shadows – who are they?

Two dwarves: dressed up.

Las meninas (ladies in waiting). Why is the painting named after them? Attending to 5- or 6-year-old child ... power imbalance? Looks like submission to child. Menina on right: about to curtsy. Menina on left: kneeling.

Girl is central position – who is she? 5–6 years old, dressed in full splendor. Who is she gazing at – the subject of the painting? Her parents? Us, the viewer? Someone/something else?

Dog: sleeping? Same size as dwarves.

rather than a forced, artificial 'sitting' of subjects? Has he **constructed** his artwork in this way to challenge our preconceptions regarding what or who is significant?

If we look at how Velázquez has used colour in the **construction** of his artwork, it is interesting that the man in the doorway in the background is bathed in light. This then forces us to be drawn to this part of the artwork even though it is in the background and the man seems apart from the figures in the foreground. He has been captured mid-movement, about to either exit or enter the room. We will have to **negotiate** this meaning as it is ambiguous whether he is leaving the group or joining them. However, his presence is accentuated due to the use of lighting and also because he has been positioned just off centre. His presence is certainly more apparent than the reflected couple in the mirror in the shadows, positioned immediately to the left of the man. How do we **interpret** this? Perhaps Velázquez is deliberately contradicting stiff and very formal portraiture as being artificial and striving for what he perceives to be a higher degree of realism capturing movement, interaction and spontaneity. This interpretation becomes valid, also, when we look at the figures in the foreground. Although the child who we may assume is the daughter of the couple seems still, almost as if she is 'sitting' for a painting herself (which ironically perhaps she was, bearing in mind she is the subject of this artwork), the other figures are captured mid-movement or mid-interaction. The *menina* to the girl's right is about to curtsy, the menina to the girl's left is kneeling, attempting to engage the girl in some way; the two figures in the shadows appear to be in mid conversation; the dwarf on the far right of the frame is playing with the dog, placing a leg on its back. Movement and interaction with others therefore seem to be more significant to **express** in this artwork than an artificial stilted 'sitting' of individuals, irrespective of how wealthy or powerful they are.

Velázquez has also **constructed** his artwork around a 5- or 6-year-old girl. She takes centre position and her ivory dress **contrasts** with the dark background, ensuring she stands out as the focal point. Why would Velázquez consciously choose to **construct** his artwork around a young girl? She appears to be gazing at the couple who are 'sitting' for the painting but she is definitely not joining them. Is she resisting the menina's cajoling to join her parents for the painting? Again, we are **negotiating** meaning and will never know the definitive answer to this. However, we could **construct** a meaning from these questions that inevitably arise once we view the artwork: has Velázquez included her to symbolize a new generation and a new way of thinking which rejects the conventional art of still portraits? The fact that Velázquez includes a working painter – who may or may not be himself – in the artwork suggests that the artist is very aware of himself as a constructor of an art form which **expresses** meaning/truths to the viewer.

So much for the constructor of the artwork, but what about the artwork itself? **Spatial mechanics** have been used to accentuate the canvas' prominence. It is huge, both in terms of scale within the setting (it is three or four times as tall as the painter himself) and in terms of how much space it takes up within the artwork itself (it takes up almost one-quarter of the entire artwork and the majority of the canvas is off-frame due to its size). What meaning is Velázquez **expressing** by including such a vast canvas? We could **negotiate** meaning and **interpret** this as Velázquez **expressing** how significant art is/should be in our lives – to entertain us, to educate us, to inform us of the world in which we live? Additionally, both the constructor (the painter) and the constructed (the painting) are prominent in the artwork, suggesting perhaps that both are of equal significance and one would not exist without the other.

We might also **negotiate** and **interpret** meaning by looking at the distance between and positioning of the mirror, the painter's easel and the rich couple not directly visible who we can assume are 'sitting' somewhere in front of the artwork (possibly where we would be standing if we were viewing the artwork hanging on a wall). We could **interpret** the positioning of these objects as symbolic. The painter could be making an arrogant statement about his power and prowess as an artist. The easel in the foreground is closer to the couple 'sitting' than the image that we see in the mirror on the back wall. Rather than reflecting the 'sitting' couple, could the mirror be a reflection of the painting? Is Velázquez **expressing** the idea that he is so skilled that his portrait is closer to reality than a reflection that could be offered by a mirror? If we agree with this **interpretation** of the painting being a medium which the artist is consciously using to demonstrate his greatness, we could also argue that he knowingly constructs other textual clues to guide us towards this interpretation. This can be seen through the inclusion of other paintings on the back wall. These works of art which may have been painstakingly created by other artists are almost an afterthought – decorative and ornamental pieces that Velázquez has effortlessly copied and assigned to the darkest part of the room. We could also **interpret** the man entering/leaving via the backdoor as the artist's testament to his own powers. The open door looks almost like a picture frame. The man is metaphorically entering (or leaving) the picture; the gap between reality and art is symbolically blurred, such is the power of the artist.

ACTIVITY 6

There are even more ways we can interpret this painting. Write a short commentary on how Velázquez has constructed this artwork to express the following ideas:

- questioning hierarchy and/or class inequality
- questioning our own interpretation of and involvement with art
- any other ideas?

When you have written your commentaries, compare them with the ones at the back of the book.

Velázquez has consciously **constructed** this highly ambiguous artwork so that we **negotiate** between different ideas in our attempt to **interpret** meaning and understand what he was attempting to **express**. Of course, we will never come to a definitive truth; we cannot ask Velázquez and, therefore, perhaps each viewer will ascribe his or her own particular and individual interpretation, depending on who the viewer is.

GLOBAL ISSUES ***Field of inquiry:* Art, Creativity and the Imagination**

THE FUNCTION OF ART IN SOCIETY

As we have seen, one interpretation of Velázquez's *Las Meninas* is to raise awareness of the significance of the artist and his or her artwork in challenging our perceptions of what or who we value in society. It challenges us to consider whether art is purely an aesthetic form, constructed to entertain or please us or whether it has another function – to raise awareness of the social, cultural and/or political constructs we may take for granted. Velázquez's painting forces us to consider some of these ideas whilst also forcing us to acknowledge the significant role the artist and art in general play in the way we understand the world and participate within it. You may like to consider this global issue about the function of art in society from the field of inquiry of art, creativity and the imagination in your reading of literary works and non-literary texts and compare how different creators of texts view the function of art in society.

TOK Links: Interpreting texts

(a) To what extent is the knowledge we gain from the study of visual-based texts different from the knowledge we gain through the study of language-based texts?
(b) Is there a wrong and a right way to interpret a text?

Constructing meaning through explicit and implicit language

The final text we are going to be exploring in this chapter is a letter of complaint. Unlike Velázquez's painting which has been constructed to be interpreted in a number of ways, the letter of complaint is usually a written text constructed in a way that the writer's intention is quite clear: to complain about something. There may also be a secondary purpose: to encourage change or to persuade the recipient to take some kind of action. Before you read the letter, read the key features box below.

KEY FEATURES FORMAL LETTERS OF COMPLAINT

Generally formal letters of complaint are structured as follows:

(a) begin with background information about the complaint
(b) identify the problem early on
(c) include a proposed solution or a request for a solution
(d) include a warning (although note that (d) can come before (c))
(e) formal closure to the letter.

Formal letters of complaint may also include:

- facts and figures that can be substantiated
- personal story or **anecdote**
- **personal pronouns**, especially first and second person pronouns
- **emotive** and/or hyperbolic language
- **sarcasm** or **irony**
- exclamatives and/or rhetorical questions
- **standard English** and formal **register**.

Now read the following letter of complaint, written by Mrs G.H. Cope, who has recently eaten at a restaurant with her family:

Dear Manager

My family and I visited your restaurant on Monday 22nd August for what we thought was going to be a relaxing family outing to celebrate our son's birthday. Your 'Healthy and Happy Hunger Busters' sounded appealing – especially to the birthday boy who was celebrating his 9th birthday. My husband and I were also looking forward to visiting your restaurant, especially after reading in your promotional literature how it was 'a welcome oasis off the beaten track'. I now truly understand why you are off the beaten track! The staff were totally disinterested in serving us and when we did manage to catch the attention of the waitress, who seemed to be having a relationship crisis with a man called Barry in an expletive-laden 20-minute phone conversation, she made us feel extremely uncomfortable grunting and mumbling as she took our order.

The food, when it arrived, was absolutely disgusting. The birthday boy's meal looked as if it had been cooked by his 5-year-old brother and tossed onto a plate. The eggs that were supposed to be the Benedictine variety made us all want to scramble out of the premises and the chicken wings were so undercooked we were worried they might take flight. I politely asked the waitress to ask the 'chef' if he could re-cook the meals. Ignoring her raised eyebrows and tuts, I eventually persuaded her to take our plates away and pass my message on. To be fair, we were promptly served new food – but, to be fair again, it wasn't much better. Either the 'chef' was in a bad mood, or the microwave that was clearly being used to reheat our meals was having an off day. My second complaint was met with further raised eyebrows and tuts but, again, I persisted. And so it continued. The evening, rapidly descending into night, transformed from a family birthday celebration into a game of tennis – serve and return.

We finally finished our meals and returned home, relieved that the evening had finally come to an end. However, the trauma was yet to continue. Not one of us (did I mention we were a family of five?) was able to sleep. Why not? Severe stomach cramps. Our poor children (5, 7 and 9 years old) were in absolute agony and neither my husband nor myself were able to offer them any support or care as we, too, were suffering the most extreme discomfort. So much for your 'Healthy and Happy Hunger Buster' meals. It is appalling that you see yourselves fit to call your food outlet a restaurant. Your food is neither healthy nor does it bring happiness nor does it satiate hunger! In fact, it is the opposite of everything you advertise it of being.

One of the top physicians at our local hospital diagnosed us all with acute food poisoning and has prepared a report. She claims that it is a certainty that we were exposed to campylobacter bacteria at your establishment. I work in the area's local government offices and have been talking to my colleagues, many of whom work in Health and Safety. It is surprising how supportive my colleagues have been, and how quickly word gets around. I know that my husband, who is a lawyer, has also been discussing how our dining experience became so hazardous with his work colleagues.

We feel that it is now incumbent on you to address the problem we experienced in your restaurant. As a family, we have had to pay huge medical costs, suffered distress and anxiety as well as loss of earnings and the children have had to miss three days from school resulting in us having to employ a private tutor so they can catch up on all of their missed work.

I look forward to hearing from you in the very near future.

Yours faithfully,

Mrs G.H. Cope

Step 1: GAP

Let's first of all complete the GAP table:

Genre	Formal letter
Audience	Restaurant Manager
Purpose	To complain; to seek compensation

Step 2: Structure and style

This letter follows a typical letter of complaint structure which makes it easy for the recipient to follow the customer's complaint. It follows a **chronological** order and the (a) to (e) structure identified in the key features box of formal letters of complaint. The writer of the letter is not only negotiating in a financial sense for some form of compensation, but she is also negotiating with the Manager of the restaurant in a more linguistic sense. It has been carefully constructed to communicate the writer's anger in a controlled, polite but threatening manner.

Step 3: Typographical and graphological features and Step 4: Other features of text type

There are moments of explicit outrage but the writer attempts to appear rational and reasonable through her formal **register** and **standard English. Emotive language** such as 'absolutely disgusting', 'appalling' and 'distress' are somewhat balanced with the repeated phrase 'to be fair'. The letter writer has also constructed the letter in such a way that she makes the letter very personal, targeting the individual Manager rather than the company or the brand, thus attempting to make the Manager feel personally responsible and even ashamed. She does this initially in her salutation by her 'Dear Manager' direct address and then throughout the letter by repeatedly using the **personal pronoun** 'your'. To achieve her aim of making the Manager feel guilty, she uses the **typographical feature** of parenthesis successfully. For example, in the third paragraph, she includes additional general information about her family: '(did I mention we were a family of five?)' and specific details about her children: '(5, 7 and 9 years old)'. The inclusion of this additional information forces the Manager to be confronted with personal information about the writer and her family as if they might know the family personally, rather than them being anonymous customers. In addition, she uses **emotive language** in her reference to her 'poor children' to add to the sense of shame she is hoping the Manager is experiencing.

The letter also forces the Manager to interpret meaning through what is left unsaid in the fourth paragraph. The letter writer is indirectly threatening the Manager through her carefully chosen language. For example, she mentions the physician her family saw was 'one of the top physicians' and she uses **subject-specific language** when she uses the scientific term 'campylobacter bacteria'. These details suggest that the letter writer will not be fooled easily or brushed aside. This idea is developed by letting the Manager know that her husband is a lawyer and that the matter has been discussed 'with his work colleagues' who are, presumably, also lawyers or know the legal profession well. She also mentions that she has many supportive colleagues who work in Health and Safety. The letter, therefore, has been constructed carefully to indirectly suggest the threat of legal action if a favourable solution is not reached. The letter writer not only attempts to exert authority and a sense of power by revealing both the nature of her and her husband's work and their professional connections, but also by threatening to ruin the reputation of the restaurant. In each of the last three sentences of this paragraph, she constantly reinforces the idea that she is making her grievances known about the restaurant to as many people as possible. She has been 'talking', her husband has been 'discussing' and 'word gets around'. Each sentence builds on this idea with the aim of scaring and threatening the restaurant Manager.

The writer also attempts to make the Manager feel ashamed in the penultimate paragraph when she says, 'we have had to pay huge medical costs, suffered distress and anxiety as well as loss of earnings and the children have had to miss three days from school resulting in us having to employ a private tutor so they can catch up on all of their missed work.' The use of **tripling** here, combined with the **adjective** 'huge' and **emotive language** serves to evoke feelings of guilt and shame and convey the letter writer's predicament concisely and powerfully. It is interesting to note that the final point she expresses in the tripling within the sentence is to draw attention to the suffering of the children, focusing on them as victims and their vulnerability rather than on the suffering of her and her husband.

Within the letter, there are also shifts in **tone**. As we have seen within paragraph four where veiled threats are made, the reader has to look beyond the literal meaning of the text to interpret the writer's purpose in writing. The letter is full of **sarcasm**. We see this when the writer suggests that perhaps the 'microwave … was having an off-day' and how she 'now truly understand(s) why you are off the beaten track!' Throughout the letter, there are attempts at humour. There is also a playful use of language in the 'scramble' and 'serve and return' passages and the reader is forced into interpreting the function of using humour in the text. It would seem to go against the objective of the letter if the writer was trying to make the Manager laugh, so we have to ask ourselves the question, why is humour being used? We can interpret this playful use of language in a number of ways as we negotiate with the text. The writer may be expressing that the experience at the restaurant was so poor that it borders on the ridiculous. The writer is left feeling incredulous and cannot help but laugh at the situation in sheer disbelief. Closely linked to this idea is that the writer is mocking the restaurant and the people who work there and thus conveying her anger through humour.

Step 6: Reader response to ideas, message and/or purpose

The use of playful language can also be interpreted as a demonstration of the letter writer's feelings of power and authority. Although she is angry, she is rational and in control and this is reflected in the way that she demonstrates control over her language. She is using language as power. Indeed, if we look at the closing of the letter, there is a real **contrast** in tone with the earlier more humourous parts of the text. The closing is very formal and there is an underlying threatening tone that is humourless and ominous. The final phrase 'in the very near future' as opposed to 'the near future' suggests that the letter writer is expecting a satisfactory outcome to her complaint much sooner rather than later. It is clear that the purpose of the writer's letter is to formally complain but also to seek some kind of compensation.

CONCEPT CONNECTION

COMMUNICATION

This concept is all about how a writer communicates to the reader through the text. This chapter has explored how writers have attempted to communicate to their reader not just through the words but also through the stylistic choices they have made. We have explored concrete poetry, stagecraft, stream of consciousness, textspeak defamiliarization, artwork and formal letters of complaint which are all different styles writers have consciously employed to communicate with their readers in their attempt to enhance meaning and shape interpretation. As you study other texts in class, you may like to explore this concept of how a writer makes particular choices about a text's style in order to communicate with the reader and encourage a particular interpretation or understanding of the text.

This chapter has explored the wide range of ways a literary work or non-literary text attempts to **construct**, **negotiate**, **express** and **interpret** meaning. You should be aware now of how **constructing** meaning is a two-way process between the writer and the reader. Initially, meaning is constructed by the writer and she or he **expresses** the meaning through the form or style of the text. Once published, however, the reader constructs his or her own meaning onto the text. The text contains the meaning and there follows a **negotiation** between the writer and the reader until an **interpretation** is reached, which may or may not coincide precisely with what the writer intended. Meaning, therefore, is not static – it changes depending on the writer, on the reader and after discussion with others. A text's meaning can also change, of course, with the passage of time – but this will be explored in Section 2.

Works cited

Carroll, L. *Alice's Adventures in Wonderland and Through the Looking-Glass*. CreateSpace Independent Publishing Platform, 2018.

Concise Oxford English Dictionary, 12th edition. Edited by Angus Stevenson and Maurice White, Oxford University Press, 2011.

Cramb, A. 'Girl writes English essay in phone text shorthand.' *The Daily Telegraph*, 3 March 2003. Web. 8 Feb. 2019. **www.telegraph.co.uk/news/uknews/1423572/Girlwrites-English-essay-in-phone-text-shorthand.html**.

Green, E. 'Why text messaging is butchering grammar.' quoted in 'Tech is upending the ways we write, speak, and even think.' *Digital Trends*, 5 Dec. 2016. Web. 7 Oct. 2019. **https://www.digitaltrends.com/features/dt10-language-and-tech**.

Herbert, G. 'Easter Wings.' *Poetry Foundation*. Web. 9 Feb. 2019. **www.poetryfoundation.org/poems/44361/easter-wings**.

Herbert, G. *The Temple. Penguin Clothbound Poetry*. Penguin Classics, 2017.

James, W. *The Principles of Psychology, Vols 1–2 Illustrated*. CreateSpace Independent Publishing Platform, 2017.

Joyce, J. *A Portrait of the Artist as a Young Man*. CreateSpace Independent Publishing Platform, 2019.

Margolis, R. 'Stranger in a Strange Land: Interview with Shaun Tan.' School Library Journal, Sept. 2007, Vol. 53 Issue 9, p.34.

Morrison, T. *Beloved*. Pan Books, Picador, 1988.

Proust, M. *In Search of Lost Time (Proust Complete – 6 Volume Box Set)*, Slp edition. Modern Library, 2003.

Rizzo, S. 'Remembering Race: Extra-poetical Contexts and the Racial Other in "The Red Wheelbarrow".' *Journal of Modern Literature*, 29 (1): 35. 2005. Web. 9 March 2019. **https://muse.jhu.edu/article/192243**.

Shklovsky, V. 'Art as Technique', *Theory of Prose*. Translated by Benjamin Sher, Dalkey Archive Press, 1990.

Tan, S. *Lost Thing*. Hodder Children's Books, 2010.

Tan, S. *The Arrival*. Arthur A. Levine Books, 2007.

Tolstoy, L. *War and Peace*. Wordsworth Editions, 2001.

Upston, S. *Literary Theory: A Complete Introduction (Complete Introductions)*. Teach Yourself, Hodder Education, 2017.

Williams, WC. 'The Red Wheelbarrow.' *Poetry Foundation*. Web. 9 March 2019. **www.poetryfoundation.org/poems/45502/the-red-wheelbarrow**.

Williams, T. *A Streetcar Named Desire*. Penguin Classics, 2009.

Williams, T. *The Glass Menagerie*. Penguin Classics, 2009.

Woolf, V. *Orlando*. Vintage Classics, 2016.

1.4 How does language use vary among text types and among literary forms?

OBJECTIVES OF CHAPTER

- Exploring the way language varies amongst prose non-fiction and non-literary text types, focusing on:
  - the language of persuasive speeches
  - the language of informative texts
  - the language of advisory texts.
- Exploring the way language varies between literary forms.
- Exploring the effect of evolving language through emoji books and informal social media texts.

There is no doubt that the language used by writers varies among text types and literary forms. In this chapter we will be exploring how the language choices made by writers vary depending on a number of things: the purpose of the text, the context within which the text was created, the intention of the writer, the conventions of the text and the audience for whom the text is written. We will be exploring, for example, how the language of a persuasive speech follows certain conventions that are different to those conventions followed by a text that aims to inform. We will also be exploring how, not only does language vary amongst text types and literary forms that are different, but language also varies between text types and literary works that are similar. To explore this idea, we will be reading extracts from two literary works that share the same form – drama – but that differ drastically in terms of the language used. By the end of this chapter you should have a clear idea of the many ways in which language varies among and between text types and literary forms and should be better placed to analyse the language a writer uses, explaining how and why a writer has used the language s/he has. You should be able to apply these skills to the non-literary texts and literary works you study in class.

Let's start off by exploring one of the most famous prose non-fiction texts of the twentieth century: Martin Luther King Jr.'s 'I Have a Dream' speech.

Literary forms that persuade

A powerful prose non-fiction that persuades is the spoken speech. It is a particularly popular mode of communication by politicians who use oration to persuade their countrymen and women to vote for them and to persuade governments to agree with their policies. A politician is often remembered not by their policies, but by their words. A politician who is regarded as one of the most powerful speakers of the twentieth century is British Prime Minister, Winston Churchill. The following lines are spoken in the Academy Award-winning film, *Darkest Hour* (2018), following one of Churchill's speeches to the British Parliament when he successfully persuaded the British government to announce war against Nazi Germany in 1939, at the beginning of the Second World War:

> *'What just happened?'*
>
> *'He mobilized the English language and sent it into battle.'*
>
> *(Darkest Hour)*

American broadcast journalist, Edward R Murrow (1908–1965), coined this phrase when he introduced excerpts from some of Churchill's war speeches in a recording he made for Columbia records in 1940: 'Now the hour had come for him to mobilize the English Language, and send it into battle, a spearhead of hope for Britain and the world' ('I Can Hear It Now 1933–45' recording). This describes well how powerful the English language can be to inspire, motivate and persuade.

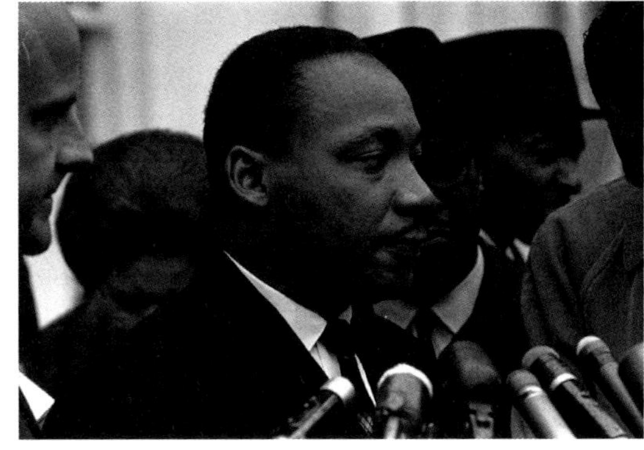

■ Martin Luther King Jr.

Two decades after Churchill's famous war speeches, another powerful speaker 'mobilized the English language' to inspire another generation, this time not to go into war but to achieve equality for all people at home. We are going to read a transcript of what many consider to be the most famous speech of modern history, Reverend Martin Luther King Jr.'s 'I Have a Dream' speech (1963), and explore how the language King used was shaped by the speech's purpose as well as the speaker's background.

On 28 August 1963, 250,000 Americans made their way to the Lincoln Memorial in Washington DC to listen to American civil rights activist, Reverend Martin Luther King Jr. deliver a speech during the 'March on Washington for Jobs and Freedom'. The speech they heard not only became a defining moment for the civil rights movement in America but has also gone down in history as one of – if not *the* – most persuasive speeches in modern history. By 1963, slavery had been abolished in the United States and President Abraham Lincoln had, 100 years earlier, delivered his Gettysburg Address in which he spoke the famous words:

> *'Four score and seven years ago our fathers brought forth on this continent, a new nation, conceived in Liberty, and dedicated to the proposition that all men are created equal.'*
>
> *(Abraham Lincoln)*

However, racism continued to be institutionalized, particularly in the southern states of the United States that advocated for racial segregation in many aspects of public life. It was in this climate that Martin Luther King Jr., an African-American Baptist minister and civil rights activist, gave his speech arguing for civil and economic equality for all people, irrespective of their race. He was attempting to persuade the American nation to change its attitudes and bring an end to the overt racism that pervaded so many areas of American society.

Before we read the opening of Martin Luther King Jr.'s literary speech, let's take a look at how the Ancient Greek philosopher, Aristotle, defined the art of persuasion. Although he defined the key ingredients in the fourth century BCE, they are still considered today as the defining features of persuasion. Read the key features box below:

KEY FEATURES PERSUASIVE SPEECHES

Aristotle, in his *The Art of Rhetoric* (fourth century BCE), argued there were three key ingredients needed to be a successful persuasive speaker. The three ingredients he identified were:

- **Ethos** – speeches need to have an ethical appeal. How?
  - Through the speaker's credibility.
  - By alluding to a spiritual or moral leader with whom listeners cannot disagree.
  - By alluding to a universally accepted premise that few can disagree with.
- **Logos** – speeches need to have an intellectual appeal. How?
  - Through a clear, logical, reasonable and easy to follow argument.
  - Through the use of facts and statistics.
  - By quoting an expert in the field.

- **Pathos** – speeches need to have an emotional appeal. How?
  - Through encouraging the audience to identify with the speaker's own pain and/or suffering.
  - By encouraging the audience to imagine the pain and/or suffering of others, especially the most vulnerable in society – the young and the old.

Let's now read a transcript of the opening of Martin Luther King Jr.'s speech and then read the accompanying commentary which explores how King's language was shaped by his own background as a Baptist minister and his overriding purpose to persuade. Although this speech is non-fiction, it is categorized as a literary prose non-fiction speech as Martin Luther King Jr. is on the IB's prescribed reading list of authors.

> I am happy to join with you today in what will go down in history as the greatest demonstration for freedom in the history of our nation.
>
> Five score years ago, a great American, in whose symbolic shadow we stand today, signed the Emancipation Proclamation. This momentous decree came as a great beacon light of hope to millions of Negro slaves who had been seared in the flames of withering injustice. It came as a joyous daybreak to end the long night of their captivity.
>
> But one hundred years later, the Negro still is not free. One hundred years later, the life of the Negro is still sadly crippled by the manacles of segregation and the chains of discrimination. One hundred years later, the Negro lives on a lonely island of poverty in the midst of a vast ocean of material prosperity. One hundred years later, the Negro is still languished in the corners of American society and finds himself an exile in his own land. And so we've come here today to dramatize a shameful condition.
>
> *Delivered 28 August 1963, at the Lincoln Memorial, Washington DC (Martin Luther King Jr.)*

Martin Luther King Jr.'s background

Although, to an extent, Martin Luther King Jr. was 'performing' on stage to a live audience of 250,000 Americans and a secondary national and international audience of millions who listened to his speech on the radio or watched it on television, what makes this speech different to speeches that are performed in the theatre, is that this speech was real. Martin Luther King Jr. was addressing a topic that was grounded in reality for him and for the 250,000 people who had travelled all over America to hear him on 28 August 1963 in Washington DC. He spoke using **prose** and he spoke using the language that his audience could understand and remember. However, the speaker was *Reverend* Martin Luther King Jr., an African-American Baptist minister who was used to preaching to congregations from the pulpit in church, using his voice to accentuate the rhythms of the Bible and the musicality of the psalms. Being aware of the rhythms of language is deeply entrenched in African-American congregations. In Harper Lee's *To Kill A Mockingbird* (1960), Chapter 12 describes a scene from the church Calpurnia, an African-American, regularly attends. It is the 1930s in the fictional town of Maycomb, Alabama, and many in the congregation are illiterate and unable to read the words of the hymns. The way they are able to actively participate in the church service is by 'lining':

> Zeebo cleared his throat and read in a voice like the rumble of distant artillery,
>
> 'There's a land beyond the river.'
>
> Miraculously on pitch, a hundred voices sang out Zeebo's words. The last syllable, held to a hum, was followed by Zeebo saying, 'That we call the sweet forever.'
>
> Music again swelled around us: the last note lingered and Zeebo met it with the next line.
>
> *(Harper Lee, Chapter 12)*

One member of the congregation who can read – in this instance it is Calpurnia's son, Zeebo – reads or sings a line and then the congregation repeats the line and so on until the hymn has been sung by the entire congregation. What makes this easier for the congregation is the rhythm of the lines and the musicality of the speaker's voice. This focus on rhythm and musicality – even if 'lining' is not such an integral part of services today – is still an important part of many African-American church services. In May 2018, at the royal wedding of the UK's Prince Harry and Meghan Markle, the African-American bishop, the Most Rev. Michael Curry, spoke using this rhythmic and musical style to engage the guests at St George's Chapel at Windsor Castle. This tradition of using language for its rhythm and musicality was part of Martin Luther King Jr.'s background. Not only was he a practising minister for the African-American Baptist church but his father, Martin Luther King Senior, was also an African-American Baptist church pastor. When we listen to Martin Luther King Jr. speaking – and the QR code below is a video of him delivering this speech – we can hear the way he uses his voice to emphasize certain words, to change the pace, to pause so that his meaning is fully grasped and to give his audience an opportunity to respond.

Scan the QR code opposite to watch Martin Luther King Jr. deliver his 'I Have a Dream' speech on 28 August 1963. We are focusing on how language varies amongst text types and literary forms. As this speech is a literary prose non-fiction text, let us focus on step 2 of our literary reading strategy: **language, images and other literary features**.

Step 2: LIFs

The strong rhythm and musicality of the speech is evident in the language King uses – this is shown particularly clearly in the final paragraph of this extract when he uses **anaphora** by repeating the phrase, 'One hundred years later …' Later on in the speech, when he repeats the now famous phrase, 'I have a dream', this becomes almost like a refrain in a song or a hymn and many in his audience repeat it after him, accentuating it all the more. Thus, the language he uses that creates such a strong rhythm and musicality is shaped by his background.

But how does the purpose of his speech also shape the language he uses? Just in this short extract, we can see how he employs Aristotle's three defining features of persuasion (**ethos**, **logos** and **pathos**) through the language he chooses to use. Let's take each persuasive feature and explore how King uses language to appeal to his audience's ethical (ethos), intellectual (logos) and emotional (pathos) judgement.

Ethos

Ethos means when the words spoken have an ethical impact on the audience. One way a speaker can appeal to the audience's ethical judgement is by alluding to a universally regarded moral or spiritual leader – someone with whom the audience unanimously agrees with and holds in high esteem. Following this speech, Martin Luther King Jr. himself became such a leader and he is often alluded to in other people's speeches in their appeal to ethos. Martin Luther King Jr.– unable to allude to himself! – foregrounds his speech by alluding to President Abraham Lincoln, the American president who led the country through the American Civil War and is considered by many Americans as one of the greatest presidents the country has ever had. Martin Luther King Jr. opens his speech with the famous words: 'Five score years ago …' (line 3). For Americans, this phrase was a reminder of the words used by Lincoln in his famous Gettysburg Address in 1863: 'Four score and seven years ago …' The fact that Martin Luther King Jr. was giving this speech at the Lincoln memorial in Washington DC and, as he explicitly remarks, 'in whose symbolic shadow we stand today' (line 5), makes the **allusion** all the more pertinent. This, then, is one way Martin Luther King Jr. uses language to appeal to ethos. At the same time as referring to Lincoln, this opening phrase also elevates Martin Luther King Jr. himself as, rather than using ordinary everyday language, he uses the language of the past, which implicitly connects him to the sages of the past, such as Lincoln.

Logos

Logos means when the words spoken have an intellectual impact on the audience. In order to achieve this, the speech needs to be clearly argued and the audience needs to feel it is grounded in fact. This persuasive feature appeals to the audience's reason and logic. Martin Luther King Jr. includes logos early on in the speech by repeatedly referring to the date Lincoln made his Gettysburg Address. First of all, Martin Luther King Jr. refers to the date using Lincoln's own language: 'Five score years ago …' (line 3). One score year denotes 20 years, so five score years denotes 100 years. Lincoln made his Gettysburg Address in 1863; Martin Luther King Jr. made his speech in 1963. One hundred years separates both speeches and so the 'five score years' reference not only reminds audiences of their past president's words, but it is also grounded in fact. Later on, Martin Luther King Jr. repeatedly refers to 'One hundred years later …' (lines 7–9). This time phrase is comparing the present (1963) with the past (1863) and suggesting that nothing has changed: the African-American is still not free. Again, Martin Luther King Jr. is grounding his speech on a time period that can be substantiated – his audience would be aware of this undisputed fact with which he **foregrounds** his speech and therefore everything else he says is more likely to sound credible. Martin Luther King Jr. has immediately created a trustworthy persona for himself and in this way appeals to his audience's logic, reason and intellect.

Pathos

Pathos means when the words spoken have an emotional impact on the audience. A speaker can appeal to pathos by describing their own or someone else's pain and suffering in such a way that the audience can imagine it themselves. Martin Luther King Jr. is particularly successful at using language that appeals to this idea of pathos. In the final paragraph, for example, he directly addresses the pain and suffering experienced by African-Americans and the language he uses acknowledges how great this suffering has been. In 1963, many African-Americans assumed they would experience segregation and racism; it was 'old news'. However, having Martin Luther King Jr., a highly respected civil rights activist, publicly acknowledge this 'old news' using such elevated language made their suffering seem important for the first time. Phrases describing how the African-American 'still sadly crippled by the manacles of segregation and the chains of discrimination' (lines 7–8) is poetic in the language he uses. He uses emotive language, 'sadly crippled', metaphorical language, 'manacles of segregation and the chains of discrimination' and **sibilance**, 'still sadly … segregation …' to create a heightened image of how the African-American is still not free. Manacles and chains would remind many in the audience of how their parents and grandparents were treated during the days of slavery, and by using this imagery Martin Luther King Jr.'s is suggesting that little has changed since those days. The rest of the paragraph uses equally emotive images and allows him to appeal to this idea of pathos, encouraging an emotional response in the audience.

In this short extract, then, it is clear how Martin Luther King Jr.'s. language has been shaped by both the background of the speaker and also by the purpose of the speech. However, although ethos, logos and pathos have been key features of persuasive speeches since the fourth century BCE, there are a number of other literary features used that encourage listeners to be persuaded by the speaker. Here is a list of ten features that writers often use to persuade – of course many of these techniques are used in non-literary texts as well as literary works and many of these features may also be used by writers for purposes other than persuasion.

■ Table 1.4.1

Technique	Meaning	Effect
Alliteration	Words that have the same letter repeated. **Plosive alliteration**: harsh sounding letters (b, d, p); **fricative alliteration**: longer sounding letters that are softer (l, f, m); **sibilance**: repeated 's' or 'sh' sound.	Reinforces the meaning of the words; can be used to heighten an emotive image; plosive sounds can create an angry tone; fricative sounds can create a harmonious tone; sibilance can create either a gentle and romantic tone or a sinister tone.
Anecdote	A story that is personal to the speaker.	Can create a more intimate tone by the speaker sharing a personal story; can appeal to pathos; can encourage the audience to sympathize with the speaker.
Antithesis	Words or phrases that have the direct opposite meanings. Two words next to each other that have opposite meanings (bitter sweetness) is an **oxymoron**; two ideas that are placed close to each other is called **juxtaposition**.	This technique can be used to strengthen the speaker's argument and also to make his argument more memorable with the audience.
Emotive language	Usually **adjectives**; words that are loaded and describe how the writer feels about something (e.g. 'atrocious', 'disgusted', 'outrageous').	Encourages the audience to respond emotionally and to agree with the speaker's point of view.
Inclusivity	Language that is used to include everyone – especially the listeners. This is often achieved through using the **personal pronoun**, 'we'.	Can be used to close the gap between the speaker and the listener; can be used to directly involve the reader in the speech; can be used to encourage the opposition to feel welcome in the speaker's eyes.
Metaphor	A device that compares one thing to another thing without using the words 'like' or 'as'. If the same metaphor is repeatedly used, this is an **extended metaphor**.	This can appeal to the audience because it makes the speech more interesting; it can create a visual image so that the audience can understand a complex idea easier; it can highlight or heighten the importance of a particular idea.
Onomatopoeia	When the sound of a word imitates the word's meaning.	This is an example of auditory imagery and encourages the audience to actually hear what is being described.
Personal pronouns	Here are the **personal pronouns** in the English language: **Narrative voice** | **Singular** | **Plural** 1st person | I | we 2nd person | you | you 3rd person | he, she, it | they	Using personal pronouns can have different effects: 1st person: 'I' encourages the reader to feel this speech is heartfelt and genuine; 'we' closes the gap between the speaker and the reader and encourages inclusivity. 2nd person 'you' is a direct address to the audience and encourages the audience to feel they are an essential part of the speech. 3rd person is generally more impersonal. Can be used to create a split between 'them' and 'us'.
Relevance	This is when the speaker ensures what they are saying is directly relevant and applies to the audience. It can be similar to inclusivity.	This encourages the audience to feel that the speaker is speaking on their behalf or that the speaker really understands what they are experiencing.
Repetition	This is when a word, phrase, sentence pattern or idea is repeated. If it is repeated three times, we call this **tripling**. If the first few words of a sentence are repeated, we call this **anaphora**.	This is usually used to emphasize a particular point; it can have a cumulative effect whereby the tone builds up and becomes more intense; it can also be memorable, encouraging the audience to remember a particular word, phrase or idea.

ACTIVITY 1

Now let's read another extract from Martin Luther King Jr.'s speech. This extract comes towards the end of his speech and includes his famous 'I have a dream' words. Read the following extract and then complete the table below:

I have a dream that one day on the red hills of Georgia sons of former slaves and the sons of former slave-owners will be able to sit down together at the table of brotherhood. I have a dream that one day even the state of Mississippi, a state sweltering with the heat of injustice, a state sweltering with the heat of oppression, will be transformed into an oasis of freedom and justice.

I have a dream that my four little children will one day live in a nation where they will not be judged by the color of their skin but by the content of their character. I have a dream … I have a dream that one day in Alabama, with its vicious racists, with its governor having his lips dripping with the words of interposition and nullification, one day right there in Alabama little black boys and black girls will be able to join hands with little white boys and white girls as sisters and brothers.

I have a dream today … I have a dream that one day every valley shall be exalted, every hill and mountain shall be made low. The rough places will be made plain, and the crooked places will be made straight. And the glory of the Lord shall be revealed, and all flesh shall see it together. This is our hope. This is the faith that I go back to the South with. With this faith we will be able to hew out of the mountain of despair a stone of hope. With this faith we will be able to transform the jangling discords of our nation into a beautiful symphony of brotherhood. With this faith we will be able to work together, to pray together, to struggle together, to go to jail together, to stand up for freedom together, knowing that we will be free one day.

(Martin Luther King Jr.)

Now copy and complete the following literary features table in as much detail as you can. A few of the boxes have already been completed. Once you have completed every box, compare your answers to the table at the back of the book.

■ **Table 1.4.2**

Technique	Quotation from the extract	Effect
Alliteration	'a **state sweltering** with the heat of **injustice**, a **state sweltering** with the heat of **oppression'**	This use of sibilance – the repeated 's' and 'sh' (oppre**ss**ion) sounds – creates a sinister and harsh atmosphere, imitating the meaning of the language he has used.
Anecdote		By referring to his own children, this makes the speech deeply personal to MLK and closes the gap between him and his audience; his own family are experiencing the same injustice that his speakers are experiencing.
Antithesis	'The **rough** places will be made **plain**, and the **crooked** places will be made **straight'**	
Emotive language		
Inclusivity		
Metaphor		
Onomatopoeia	'the **jangling** discords of our nation'	

Technique	Quotation from the extract	Effect
Personal pronouns		
Relevance		By naming an actual place that many of his audience would have come from and by describing a geographical feature of that place encourages the audience to feel that MLK understands who he is speaking to, their background and their experiences.
Repetition (anaphora)		

CONCEPT CONNECTION

CULTURE

The concept of culture relates to how a text is influenced by the context of its production and reception, and to the respective values, beliefs and attitudes prevalent in them. This speech is very much rooted in its cultural context: Martin Luther King Jr. was an active supporter of the civil rights movement in America in the 1950s and 1960s and he gave this speech to the 250,000 people who had taken part in the 'March on Washington for Jobs and Freedom', a civil rights march demanding economic and social equality for all Americans irrespective of the colour of their skin. King's speech alluded to the culture of slavery in America's past and how still in 1963, when he gave the speech, African-Americans experienced inequality, injustice and segregation. It was very much influenced by the cultural experiences of the time and the people who were listening were very aware of what King was alluding to, many of whom were experiencing first-hand the inequalities King was addressing. When King repeatedly referred to 'I have a dream …', many in the audience repeated these words, showing their support and assent that the future could – and hopefully would – be better than the present. This is one way the production and reception of this speech were affected by the concept of culture.

The concept of culture also refers to the relationship a text has on the tradition that precedes it. With regards to Martin Luther King Jr.'s speech, past traditions are clear. First, by appealing to pathos, ethos and logos King is showing his connection to the ancient tradition of rhetoric from where these elements originate. However, he shows his connection to a more recent and personal tradition: his own background (and his father's background) as a Baptist minister who used the rhythms of language and the musicality of the voice to heighten his message. The influence of lining that many African-Americans may also have been familiar with can also be seen in the way many in the audience repeated the 'I have a dream' phrase. Again, we can see the importance of culture and how it affected both the production and the reception of this speech.

The concept of culture is central to the study of language and literature – as you study texts in class, be aware of how this concept can affect both the production and the reception of the text you are studying.

ACTIVITY 2

Connect the persuasive feature to the appropriate definition and example. The first one has been done for you:

Persuasive	Definition	Example
Ethos	Has an emotional appeal	Uses facts and/or statistics
Logos	Has an intellectual appeal	Alludes to moral or spiritual leader
Pathos	Has an ethical appeal	Refers to the young and/or old

Once you have completed this activity, you can check your understanding by looking at the key features of persuasive speeches earlier on in this chapter.

You should be clear then that the purpose of this prose non-fiction speech has had a large influence on the language used. What makes this such a powerfully persuasive speech is that Martin Luther King Jr. seamlessly integrates a number of persuasive and literary techniques throughout his speech as well as using the rhythms of language to make it all the more memorable for his audience. We are now going to move on to a non-literary text type that has a very different form and purpose which, as we shall see, also shapes the language the writer uses.

■ Text types that inform

A text that aims to inform covers many different non-literary text types and literary forms including essays, letters, autobiographies and newspaper articles. These texts, while aiming to inform the reader about something, may include **emotive language** in their attempt to shape the reader's view of the information being shared. We have already seen this to a certain extent in the literary prose non-fiction extracts we have explored so far in this section, for example in Pliny the Younger's letter to his friend following the eruption of Vesuvius (Chapter 1.1) and in George Orwell's description of the spike in *Down and Out in Paris and London* (Chapter 1.2). Both of these texts were literary non-fiction texts and their aim was to inform the reader about something she or he had not experienced first-hand, but they also had the intention of evoking a particular emotional response in the reader, which shaped the kind of language each writer used.

There are also other types of informative texts that aim to instruct the reader about how to do something without necessarily attempting to shape the reader's opinion about something. The purpose of these text types is to share some practical information with the reader with the intention of teaching the reader a new skill. Informative text types such as these are non-literary and include: instructional manuals, 'how to' guides, road signs, lists of rules and regulations, recipes etc. We are now going to explore how the purpose of a Korean recipe shapes the language the writer uses. This extract comes from a book of recipes by South Korean illustrator and writer, Robin Ha; if you studied multiple recipes from this book, this would be classified as a non-literary body of work.

Read the following extract from Robin Ha's *Cook Korean!* recipe book (2016), 'Green Onion Kimchi'.

Step 1: GAP

To deconstruct this text, we are going to apply our non-literary reading strategy from Chapter 1.1.

Genre:	Page from a recipe book
Audience:	Readers interested in cooking, not necessarily Korean readers
Purpose:	To inform

Step 2: Structure and style

The first thing that would have struck you as you read this extract is that it is a **multimodal** text that uses a range of **non-verbal** features including illustrations, **word balloons**, arrows, colour and different sized font as well as the written word to achieve its purpose of informing. Remember that 'language' includes non-verbal visual language as well as written language. So how does the purpose of the text – to inform the reader how to cook a particular Korean recipe – shape the language used?

Step 3: Typographical and graphological features

Being an informative text, the reader needs to know immediately what information is being shared. The text is foregrounded with the words 'Green Onion Kimchi' to fulfil this function. **Typographical features** have been used to emphasize the words at the top of the page, 'Green Onion Kimchi'. These words are in a larger font and act as a heading, informing the reader what recipe this text is for. In addition the **non-verbal language** such as the use of colour imagery in the green lettering, together with the illustrations of green onions, reinforce the written text to accentuate the subject of this recipe. **Graphological features** have also been used here as an informative tool: the illustrations of the green onions have been placed behind the written text which informs readers what the main ingredients of the recipe look like. Positioned underneath the name of the recipe in English, is its name in Korean, 'Pa Kimchi', and this has a dual function:

informing the reader of what this dish's Korean name is as well as highlighting its specific Korean cultural heritage.

Step 4: Other features of text type

The first section of text, immediately underneath the title, is also informative. It informs the reader how 'you can also use this recipe to make chive kimchi by substituting chives for green onions'. As well as being informative, this also suggests the reader is getting two recipes within one. The reader is also informed that 'green onions are packed with vitamins and help boost the immune system' which as well as being a fact that can be substantiated, also suggests this recipe has health benefits and would be beneficial for the reader to cook. There is an overtly informative **tone** to this text, but there is also a subtle persuasive tone through the **emotive language** 'packed with' and 'boost'. This is not **neutral language** and it has the effect of encouraging the reader to read on, actively follow the instructions and cook the recipe due to its health benefits.

Other ways in which the purpose of the text has shaped the language is through the inclusion of the ingredients box. This is another **graphological feature** that helps draw attention to a key point – in this case, the ingredients needed. Here language is overtly instructional: it is a list of the amounts of ingredients needed using precise, clear and completely **neutral language**. **Non-verbal features** have also been included in the use of contrasting colour imagery to make key informational facts stand out. For example, the words 'Prep time:', 'Fermentation time:' and 'Makes:' are printed in a red colour while the 'answers' of '1 hour', '2 days' and '12 cups' are printed in the contrasting colour of black. Although a question/answer format has not literally been used, the red colour acts as a question and the black colour acts as the answer.

In line with informational texts that aim to instruct, the verb forms used are all commands. 'Rinse', 'put', 'turn', 'whisk', 'crush' and 'combine' are examples of this use of language and its effect is to clarify what needs to be done. There is no room for discussion – to create this dish successfully, the reader needs to follow the instructions precisely. The **verbs** used are also precise. Many consider cooking an artform and the **listing** of verbs in a **chronological** order suggest that many skills are required to prepare even the 'simplest' of dishes. Rinsing, whisking and crushing, for example, are all examples of **subject-specific language** and thus we can see how the text's genre – a page from a recipe book – shapes the specific language used.

Step 5: Visual image and layout

As we have already noted, this is a **multimodal** text, which means it uses more than one mode of communication – in this case, it uses both visual and written language. As well as including written instructions that inform the reader what to do, visual language is used throughout to reinforce the written language. Each written instruction is printed in either a green or a gold box, gold arrows indicate which order to read the instructions and gold dotted lines separate one instruction from another. There are also many colourful illustrations that function as a set of visual instructions to illustrate each written instruction. Thus, the informative nature of the text is doubly reinforced: through both the written language and the visual language. It is also interesting that all of the illustrations, arrows and dotted lines are hand-drawn and slightly irregular, and all of the written text is handwritten. This also reinforces the purpose of the text – teaching the reader how to cook a *homemade* recipe. The use of colour imagery also makes the text easy to follow as well as making a potentially dry and humourless text type into something that is more engaging and fun for the reader. Earlier we said that many people consider cooking an artform – this idea is perhaps highlighted through the combination of visual language and written language which is both creative and imaginative.

Although most of the language used is neutral, in line with the informative purpose of the text, there is an intimacy created between the writer and the reader through the inclusion of the illustration of the girl and the speech bubble. Not only do the colours of the girl's dress match the colours used throughout the text and the ingredients she is using but she is smiling and obviously enjoying cooking this dish. The reader feels there is a synergy and harmonious connection between the girl and the food she is preparing which makes this all the more appealing to the reader. Happiness is visually connected to the act of cooking this particular recipe, which is later reinforced by the golden scroll at the end of the text which states in capital letters 'ENJOY'. The reader also feels the girl is speaking directly to them and, while the words in the **word balloon** are completely neutral and instructional – in line with the text type – there is a connection made between the 'implied' writer and the reader. The reader may assume this is an illustration of Robin Ha herself but, if she or he has read the earlier sections of the book, they will know this is actually 'Dengki', a female Korean character created by Ha to share her expertise and instruct the reader in the art of Korean cooking.

Step 6: Reader response to ideas, message and/or purpose

Ha merges the factual (the precise amount of ingredients, the recipe's name in Korean, step-by-step instructions), with the fictional (the character of Dengki, the hand-drawn illustrations and handwritten script). Thus, although the language may be informative, instructional and appropriate for a text whose purpose is to inform, there is also a sense of creativity that is both engaging and appealing to readers.

CONCEPT CONNECTION

CREATIVITY

We could argue that this recipe page from Robin Ha's cookbook is creative in the way it merges visual language with written language and embeds an understanding of Korean culture. Rather than simply following a set of instructions that are placed in chronological order, Ha forces the reader to engage their imagination when responding to this text. Perhaps we could interpret the text itself as encouraging the reader to perceive the subject of the text, cooking, as an artform that is both creative and imaginative. This could be an area you may like to explore further: how a text that is overtly creative and engages the reader's imagination challenges the reader to perceive the subject matter being explored in the text as something that is also creative and imaginative.

So far we have seen how language varies amongst literary forms that aim to persuade and non-literary texts that aim to inform. We are now going to explore another non-literary text – an advisory text – and explore how language is used differently as a result of its purpose.

■ Text types that advise

If you need advice about something, who are you likely to approach? It is likely you would approach someone you feel is qualified to give you advice: someone you can trust, someone who is an expert in the area you need advice about, possibly someone who is older than you or a friend whose opinion you value. Advisory texts have been a popular text type as early as the fifth century BCE when Chinese general and military strategist, Sun Tzu, wrote an advisory guide on bamboo strips called *The Art of War.* This text has had a large influence on both Eastern and Western military strategists and tacticians throughout history and is regarded as the most influential military strategist text in East Asian warfare. Its influence continues to grow and it is now widely read as much by business leaders interested in its guiding principles, as military historians. You will be writing a commentary on this advisory text later on in this part of the chapter.

Today, many newspapers and magazines feature an advisory section to answer readers' letters requesting advice on a particular topic. The advice columnist was often referred to with the

English **colloquial** term, 'agony aunt' or 'agony uncle'. The term itself suggests that the person we are asking advice from is a trusted relative or friend of the family who is happy to listen to our 'agonies' or things that are causing us anxiety, and will try to advise us appropriately. Anything colloquial is informal, so this term suggests a relationship that is not necessarily hierarchical or formal, but a more relaxed relationship where you can say whatever you want without the fear of there being any repercussions. Before we look at an extract from an advisory text, let's read the following key features box to get an overview of this particular text type.

KEY FEATURES ADVISORY TEXTS

- Early advisory texts include *Sun Tzu on the Art of War* (fifth century BCE) and ancient religious texts.
- The first known advice column is the 'The Athenian Gazette', published in London in 1690.
- The person offering advice is: trustworthy, wise, an expert in the subject, perhaps an older person or a confidante.
- British **colloquial** term 'agony aunt' or 'agony uncle' suggests an intimacy between advisor and advisee; suggests advisor is older.
- **Tone** is reasonable and credible; opinion may be disguised as fact.
- Credibility may be achieved through quoting an expert with whom one cannot disagree.
- Use of modal verbs and **imperatives**.
- Organization – an easy to follow, step-by-step structure.
- Use of **personal pronouns** – especially first and second person pronouns.
- May include a warning if advice is not followed.

Of course, not all advisory texts follow the question/answer format. We are going to be reading an extract from *Mrs Beeton's Book of Household Management* (1861), edited by Mrs Isabella Beeton, which offers advice to the 'mistress' of a Victorian household even though Mrs Beeton has not received any letters from mistresses of Victorian households requesting such advice. Mrs Beeton's advisory book offered advice on a wide range of household matters, especially culinary matters. We are going to be looking at one extract from this advisory text – however, remember that were you to read multiple extracts or chapters from this text, you would be studying the text as a non-literary body of work. The book had been published in sections prior to its 1861 publication when it formed part of a series of guidebooks published by her husband, Samuel Beeton. The first source is a copy of the front cover and the extract is from the opening chapter entitled 'The Mistress'. Read the following two sources and then read the commentary that follows.

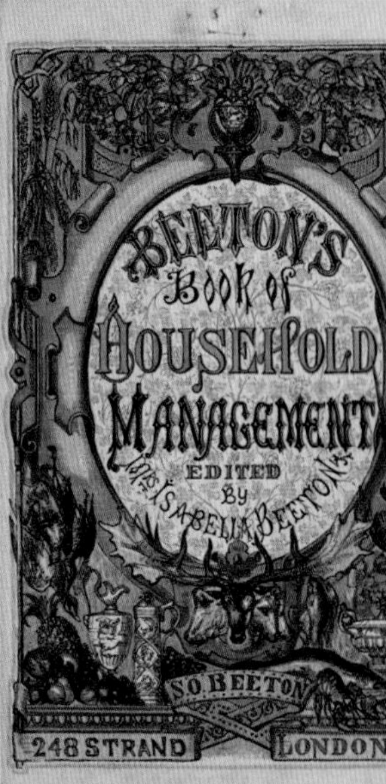

Front cover of *Beeton's Book of Household Management*, edited by Mrs Isabella Beeton

'Strength, and honour are her clothing; and she shall rejoice in time to come. She openeth her mouth with wisdom; and in her tongue is the law of kindness. She looketh well to the ways of her household; and eateth not the bread of idleness. Her children arise up, and call her blessed; her husband also, and he praiseth her.'—*Proverbs*, xxxi. 25-28.

I. AS WITH THE COMMANDER OF AN ARMY, or the leader of any enterprise, so is it with the mistress of a house. Her spirit will be seen through the whole establishment; and just in proportion as she performs her duties intelligently and thoroughly, so will her domestics follow in her path. Of all those acquirements, which more particularly belong to the feminine character, there are none which take a higher rank, in our estimation, than such as enter into a knowledge of household duties; for on these are perpetually dependent the happiness, comfort, and well-being of a family. In this opinion we are borne out by the author of 'The Vicar of Wakefield,' who says: 'The modest virgin, the prudent wife, and the careful matron, are much more serviceable in life than petticoated philosophers, blustering heroines, or virago queens. She who makes her husband and her children happy, who reclaims the one from vice and trains up the other to virtue, is a much greater character than ladies described in romances, whose whole occupation is to murder mankind with shafts from their quiver, or their eyes.'

2. PURSUING THIS PICTURE, we may add, that to be a good housewife does not necessarily imply an abandonment of proper pleasures or amusing recreation; and we think it the more necessary to express this, as the performance of the duties of a mistress may, to some minds, perhaps seem to be incompatible with the enjoyment of life. Let us, however, now proceed to describe some of those home qualities and virtues which are necessary to the proper management of a Household, and then point out the plan which may be the most profitably pursued for the daily regulation of its affairs.

3. EARLY RISING IS ONE OF THE MOST ESSENTIAL QUALITIES which enter into good Household Management, as it is not only the parent of health, but of innumerable other advantages. Indeed, when a mistress is an early riser, it is almost certain that her house will be orderly and well-managed. On the contrary, if she remain in bed till a late hour, then the domestics, who, as we have before observed, invariably partake somewhat of their mistress's character, will surely become sluggards. To self-indulgence all are more or less disposed, and it is not to be expected that servants are freer from this fault than the heads of houses. The great Lord Chatham thus gave his advice in reference to this subject:—'I would have inscribed on the curtains of your bed, and the walls of your chamber, "If you do not rise early, you can make progress in nothing."

(Isabella Beeton)

Step 1: GAP

Genre	Advisory text about household management
Audience	Young housewives of the nineteenth century
Purpose	To advise

Step 2: Structure and style

It is important that advisory texts are easy to follow and this also shapes the type of language used. In this particular text, there are three sections and each section is a different point. Each section is relatively short, is numbered and the first few words of each section are capitalized. Throughout the text transitional words, phrases and connectives – such as 'we may add' (line 16), 'let us … now proceed' (line 19), 'indeed', 'on the contrary' (lines 24–25) and 'invariably' (line 26) – are used to create the sense of a logical relationship between sentences and ideas. This gives the extract a clarity that is easy to follow as well as giving readers the impression that Mrs Beeton's argument is objective, impartial, logical and well-reasoned. The language used is also formal, ensuring readers take this advice seriously and there is no ambiguity in terms of colloquial or idiomatic phrases. The 'expert' voices are clearly demarcated using quotation marks and the *Proverbs* quotation that opens the entire chapter is printed using a different typeface.

In our commentary of this extract, we are going to focus on:

Step 4: Features of text type

The key areas we will be discussing include:

- the language of the front cover and title of the text
- language that gives the writer authority
- repetitive language to emphasize a point
- language that is used to disguise opinion as fact
- language that is used to warn if advice is not followed
- other ways language is shaped by the text type.

The language of the front cover and title of text

The book is called *Beeton's Book of Household Management, edited by Mrs Isabella Beeton*. By referring to herself as 'Mrs Isabella Beeton', this infers she is a married woman with experience of managing a household. Immediately, this suggests that the writer is knowledgeable and experienced in the subject she is advising on. Interestingly, her husband, Samuel Beeton, was responsible for publishing a number of guidebooks (including his wife's) and it may well be that her readers would have been more familiar with her husband's name than with her own name. Perhaps she is using her marital status as the wife to the well-known Samuel Beeton to her advantage by using the vocative 'Mrs' rather than simply referring to herself as 'Isabella Beeton'.

Language that gives the writer authority

Readers of advisory texts expect the person giving advice to be an expert in the field of advice being given. One way Mrs Beeton does this is by quoting other well-known and respectable sources in order to give her own words authority. The text is **foregrounded** with a quotation from a Biblical passage, Proverbs xxxi 25–28 (lines 1–4). For most of her readers, the Bible would have been considered a moral text that offered spiritual guidance. By foregrounding her advisory text with a quotation from the Bible, it suggests that her text, too, will be offering similar guidance and gives it authority from the outset. This of course should remind you of **ethos**; she is appealing to her readers' ethical and moral values, which also steeps the text with authority. The quotation that is used uses **archaic** language from the Bible such as 'she openeth her mouth …', 'she looketh well … and eateth not'. This gives Mrs Beeton's text a gravitas and suggests that the knowledge she is about to impart is a timeless truth also. The *Proverbs* quotation also includes language such as 'blessed' and 'praiseth' and these two specifically Biblical words suggest that this will be the reader's reward for heeding Mrs Beeton's advice that follows. Therefore, Mrs Beeton is using the authority of the Bible to create a moral imperative that her readers follow her advice.

Mrs Beeton also quotes 'the author of "The Vicar of Wakefield"' (line 11) and it is interesting that although we may initially think this is another spiritual source that she is using to give herself authority, in actual fact 'The Vicar of Wakefield' was a popular and widely read prose fiction novel, published in 1776, nearly 100 years prior to Mrs Beeton's advisory text. Although she attempts to give her own words status by quoting Oliver Goldsmith, the author of this novel, it is interesting that her authority is coming from the author of a work of fiction. It is neither scientific nor factual but rather the opinion of someone who has written a popular fiction book. The final 'expert' she refers to is 'the great Lord Chatham' (line 28) who her readers would have known as William Pitt the Elder (1708–1778) who was Prime Minister of Great Britain in the mid-eighteenth century. He would have been a respected leader and Mrs Beeton is using his authority in order to corroborate her own words.

Mrs Beeton uses the language of other texts and individuals, all of whom were strongly connected to the establishment at the time she was writing. It is interesting that Mrs Beeton herself identifies the role of a good housewife with the upkeep of the 'establishment' (line 6) in section 1. The word establishment as used here could refer to either the household itself or the wider nation.

Language that is repeated to emphasize a point

Mrs Beeton is offering advice to young women on how to be a 'good housewife'. To emphasize that this is the purpose of the text, Mrs Beeton repeatedly uses language that is connected to this topic: 'mistress of a house' (lines 5–6), 'household', (line 9), 'good housewife', (line 16), 'management of a Household' (line 20) and 'good Household Management', (line 22). Repeatedly using language that is so obviously linked to the topic being discussed, grounds the text in this subject and ensures the writer does not get distracted or go off topic.

Military language is also repeatedly referred to in the extract. Section 1 starts with the **simile**: 'As with the commander of an army, or the leader of any enterprise, so is it with the mistress of a house.' (lines 5–6). Mrs Beeton **foregrounds** the text with this simile and by linking the mistress of a house with an army commander, she appears to be challenging the preconceived ideas regarding the stereotypical female position in society at this time. By suggesting a housewife is on an equal footing with a commander of an army is elevating the role of a housewife and immediately makes the reader feel that her role as a housewife is valued and important. It is also suggesting that the moral upkeep of the nation begins in the home and is the foundation of a successful nation. Just as a commander leads his soldiers into battle to defend his country's values, it is the job of a housewife to battle with her domestics and family to protect these same values upon which the nation is ultimately built. This idea is repeatedly alluded to throughout section 1 by Mrs Beeton's use of military language: 'duties' is repeated a number of times and the phrase 'higher rank' is also included. Throughout this section, then, Mrs Beeton is flattering her audience by elevating their role as a housewife to the level of an army commander; and by doing this she is also forcing her readers to take their role as housewives seriously and, in turn, take her advice as to how to carry out this role seriously, too. This is another way Mrs Beeton manages to imbue her words with moral authority and encourage her readers to look up to her and think of her as a virtuous and knowledgeable voice whose words must be read carefully and applied appropriately.

Language that is used to disguise opinion as fact

Although an advisory text is often written by an 'expert' in the field, that expert does not always have official credentials or qualifications that prove him or herself as a definitive 'expert'. However, the language a writer uses can often help disguise opinions as facts and thus encourage the reader to assume the writer is in fact an expert and therefore qualified to offer advice on this particular subject. In this extract, the language Mrs Beeton uses does this at times. In section 3, for example, Mrs Beeton states that: 'To self-indulgence all are more or less disposed, and it is not to be expected that servants are freer from this fault than the heads of houses.' (lines 26–28). The language used in this sentence infers that this is a fact; however, it is not a fact that can be definitively proved and consequently can be viewed as pseudo-science. There are phrases embedded throughout the extract such as 'in our estimation' (lines 8–9), 'we think it the more necessary ...' (line 24), 'it is almost certain that ...' (line 24), which make it clear that Mrs Beeton's judgements are value-based rather than factual statements.

Other value judgements that are disguised as facts are found in the quotations Mrs Beeton chooses to include. For example, the author she quotes reminds women that they are one of three types: 'the modest virgin, the prudent wife, and the careful matron' (line 11) and that these roles are 'much more serviceable in life that petticoated philosophers, blustering heroines, or virago queens' (lines 12–13). The language the author uses is fabulously **hyperbolic** and today we may well laugh. However, Mrs Beeton includes this not for her female readers to laugh at, but for them to take note of and follow accordingly. These ideas, however, are personal opinion rather than definitive facts. It is possible that the author's viewpoint, for some of her readers, even in 1861, may have sounded exaggerated and old-fashioned. Contextually, Mary Wollstonecraft had published her *Vindication of the Rights of Woman* in 1792 (nearly 70 years before Mrs Beeton's advice) which argued for the full education of women, so they could take part in discussions with their husbands rather than be mere passive listeners. Wollstonecraft's text is known as one of the earliest feminist philosophy texts. Her daughter, Mary Shelley, had also published *Frankenstein; or the Modern Prometheus* (1818), 40 years before Mrs Beeton's text was published. Although it is most famous for being a gothic fiction novel, Shelley also criticizes 'modern' man for whom the pursuit of knowledge has become the most important thing, irrespective of the outcome. It is likely that many of Mrs Beeton's readers would have been familiar with both of these texts. Perhaps, by deciding to quote the author's criticism against 'petticoated philosophers' (line 12) and those women 'whose whole occupation is to murder mankind' (lines 14–15), this is a veiled criticism of Wollstonecraft, her daughter and other women who had ambitions outside the domestic realm. Again, if it is, the criticism is spoken by one man, the author of 'The Vicar of Wakefield', and it is his supposition rather than a scientific fact.

At times, the text focuses on non-tangible ideas relating to being a good housewife, such as 'her spirit will be seen through the whole establishment …' (line 6) and how the domestics will 'partake somewhat of their mistress's character' (line 26). These are not measurable qualities and are opinion-based judgements rather than factual-based judgements that can be definitely measured through science or mathematics. Even the use of the **personal pronoun** 'we' and 'our' is ambiguous: who is the 'we'? It could be a linguistic feature that elevates Mrs Beeton from a single individual to representing the voice of many; or it could refer to her and her husband; or even to her and the 'experts' she has quoted throughout the text. However, the ambiguity of the pronoun links in with the pseudo-scientific tone which is a feature of this text type. This, then, is a personal advisory text; unlike the previous informative text, there are no precise facts or information that can be substantiated.

Language that is used to warn if advice is not followed

The final section of the extract is a warning to her readers of the disasters that will follow if her readers do not follow her advice. The advice she is focusing on here is the consequences that will follow should the mistress 'remain in bed till a late hour' (line 25). To make this point all the more emphatic, she personifies getting up early to being 'the parent of health' (line 23). This **metaphor** may have extra weight with her readers who are, perhaps, young mothers themselves or hoping to be, soon. As you will have noticed, however, this is not a scientific fact; only an emotive argument that is opinion-based. However, Mrs Beeton uses language effectively here by suggesting that should the mistress of the household rise late, then her domestics will follow her lead and become 'sluggards' (line 26). She uses **emotive language** here to shock her readers to such an extent that they will be sure to follow her advice and rise early. This technique of warning readers of the dire consequences that will follow should the advisor's advice not be taken is a common feature of advisory texts and we can see here how it shapes the language used.

Other ways language is shaped by the text type

Perhaps to show her own craftsmanship of writing, having quoted Proverbs and the author of 'The Vicar of Wakefield' in her first advisory point, Mrs Beeton includes a lot of alliterative language in her second advisory point. She starts off by saying 'Pursuing this picture …' (line 16), mentions 'proper pleasures' (line 17), refers to 'performance' (line 18), uses the verb 'proceed' (line 19) and finishes the section by 'point[ing] out the plan … most profitably pursued' (lines 20–21) – and all this in under seven lines! Being an advisory text, Mrs Beeton would want her message to be memorable and maybe she was thinking by using so much **alliteration**, this would make it snappier. In this section, she suggests that although being a good housewife is of great significance, it 'does not necessarily imply an abandonment of proper pleasures or amusing recreation' (lines 16–17). However, it is interesting that Mrs Beeton mentions this just once and then moves on to use her military **semantic field** again, reminding her reader of the 'qualities' (line 19) needed for the 'proper management of a Household' (line 20) and the 'daily regulations of its affairs' (line 21). The language she uses in this section continues the **extended metaphor** of the Commander of an army she began the text with and the preponderance of the 'p' sound gives this section a precision which tends to elevate Mrs Beeton herself to the rank of General giving orders to her commanding officers (readers). This is another way Mrs Beeton assumes authority – she leaves the reader in no doubt that she is the one in charge who has the wisdom and she expects to be listened to and followed.

You should now have a clearer understanding of how the language of an advisory text is shaped by its purpose and the writer's intention of creating a persona of authority that the reader finds credible, trustworthy and believable. Now it is your turn to read and explore the ways in which language is shaped in an advisory text.

Read the following extract which is a translation of what many consider to be the first advisory text, written in the fifth century BCE. The extract is taken from *Sun Tzu on the Art of War.* Underneath the title, on the front cover of the Classic Reprint Series, the text is introduced as: *The Oldest Military Treatise in the World; Translated From the Chinese With Introduction, and Critical Notes.* The extract below comes from Chapter III, titled 'Stratagem'. When you have read the extract, attempt the questions that follows:

Chapter III. Attack by Stratagem

1. Sun Tzu said: In the practical art of war, the best thing of all is to take the enemy's country whole and intact; to shatter and destroy it is not so good. So, too, it is better to recapture an army entire than to destroy it, to capture a regiment, a detachment or a company entire than to destroy them.

2. Hence to fight and conquer in all your battles is not supreme excellence; supreme excellence consists in breaking the enemy's resistance without fighting.

3. Thus the highest form of generalship is to balk the enemy's plans; the next best is to prevent the junction of the enemy's forces; the next in order is to attack the enemy's army in the field; and the worst policy of all is to besiege walled cities.

4. The rule is, not to besiege walled cities if it can possibly be avoided. The preparation of mantlets, movable shelters, and various implements of war, will take up three whole months; and the piling up of mounds over against the walls will take three months more.

5. The general, unable to control his irritation, will launch his men to the assault like swarming ants, with the result that one-third of his men are slain, while the town still remains untaken. Such are the disastrous effects of a siege.

6. Therefore the skilful leader subdues the enemy's troops without any fighting; he captures their cities without laying siege to them; he overthrows their kingdom without lengthy operations in the field.

7. With his forces intact he will dispute the mastery of the Empire, and thus, without losing a man, his triumph will be complete. This is the method of attacking by stratagem. [...]

18. Hence the saying: If you know the enemy and know yourself, you need not fear the result of a hundred battles. If you know yourself but not the enemy, for every victory gained you will also suffer a defeat. If you know neither the enemy nor yourself, you will succumb in every battle.

(Sun Tzu)

ACTIVITY 3

Remind yourself of the features we explored in Mrs Beeton's advisory text:

- the language of the front cover and title of the text
- language that gives the writer authority
- language that is repeated to emphasize a point
- language that is used to disguise opinion as fact
- language that is used to warn if advice is not followed
- other ways language is shaped by the text type.

Choose four of these language features and write a short commentary on each one, referring to the extract from *Sun Tzu on the Art of War.*

When you have written your commentaries, compare your ideas with the commentaries at the end of the book.

EE Links: English A – Language category 3

We have just explored three non-literary texts: the informative recipe text by Robin Ha and the two advisory texts by Mrs Beeton and Sun Tzu. These would be appropriate text types to explore for a language category 3 extended essay. You could either focus on a non-literary body of work and analyse how the writer embeds a range of non-literary features to achieve his or her purpose and appeal to the intended audience, or you could compare two different advisory texts, for example, and explore the similarities and differences in how each writer achieves their purpose and appeals to the audience. You could use your non-literary reading strategy to help you structure your analysis.

GLOBAL ISSUES ***Field of inquiry:*** **Beliefs, Values and Education**

HOW INDIVIDUALS AND COMMUNITIES ARE SHAPED BY THEIR VALUES AND BELIEFS

Both Mrs Beeton's and Sun Tzu's advisory texts aim to educate their readers about some of the beliefs and values they deem are central in their societies. Mrs Beeton educates her readers as to what her society considers to be the perfect housewife; Sun Tzu educates his readers as to what his society considers to be the perfect military leader. Neither text allows for alternative viewpoints – on the contrary, both texts warn their readers of the dire consequences if their advice is not followed. Both writers use credible sources to educate their readers that the beliefs and values being promoted in their texts are unquestionable: Mrs Beeton through quoting the Bible, a well-known author and a politician; Sun Tzu by quoting himself, a well-known and highly successful military leader! In your individual oral, you may like to explore the field of inquiry, of beliefs, values and education through the global issue of how a society's values and beliefs shape individuals and communities. Alternatively, you could explore the tensions that arise when there is conflict between beliefs and values within a society. This global issue is also explored in more detail in Chapter 1.5, through a range of literary works.

CAS Links

Either on your own or in a group, think about a problem that students in your school community are concerned about. For example, it may be a concern regarding bullying (physical, verbal or digital bullying); meeting deadlines; revising; academic honesty; being more eco-friendly around school; having a more balanced lifestyle. Create a poster or a number of posters (either physical or digital) that you can share with your student body that (a) informs the students of the concern/problem and (b) offers practical advice to help students resolve the problem. You may like to run an assembly or visit tutor groups where you share your advice. Try to use some of the key conventions of informative and advisory texts in your poster. This could potentially fulfil all three CAS strands.

So far, we have explored how language, both visual and written, is shaped and varies in literary prose non-fiction works and non-literary text types which have different purposes: a speech to persuade, a recipe to inform and an advisory text. We have seen how each writer uses language to achieve their particular purpose and how, sometimes, the background of the writer and the context of the text also have an effect on how language varies among text types. We are now going to explore how language varies *between* literary works that share the same form: drama. We are going to be studying two extracts from two different literary works: an extract from a Shakespeare play, *King Lear*, which uses verse to communicate; and an extract from a modern American play, *Oleanna*, which uses prose to communicate.

Shakespearean drama: *King Lear*

We are going to explore the language used by King Lear in Shakespeare's tragedy, *King Lear*, first performed on 26 December 1606. We will follow the literary reading strategy (Chapter 1.1) in our analysis of King Lear's speech, focusing on how the form and structure of the text (step 1) shape the language (step 2) he uses. Before we read and analyse the extract, let's firstly explore the way characters typically spoke in a Shakespearean drama.

Blank verse and iambic pentameter

In most of Shakespeare's drama, he used two forms for characters' dialogue: prose and verse (either rhyming verse or blank verse). **Prose** is used to imitate everyday speech – it does not rhyme and has no meter. Shakespearean verse is used to elevate a character's speech – it may rhyme or it may not rhyme but it has a regular **meter** of **iambic pentameter**. Generally, the characters who had little power or were of a low social status (the messenger, servant, nurse) spoke in prose and the characters who were powerful and had a high status in society (the king, nobleman, merchant) spoke in verse. This was one way audiences were able to distinguish a character's social status in the play. Of course, sometimes a character with a low social status may revert to **blank verse** if addressing a character with a high social status and sometimes a character of high social status may revert to prose if speaking informally among friends of an equal social status. Shakespeare wrote many plays with a king as the protagonist (*King Henry IV Parts 1 and 2, King Henry V, King Lear, Macbeth* to name a few) and it is rare for the king to break from the stylized blank verse and regular iambic pentameter meter. However, King Lear does. In order to understand how he breaks from this form and why, let's first explore what blank verse and iambic pentameter are.

Blank verse means it is verse (rather than prose) but it is 'blank' which means it does not rhyme. Iambic pentameter means there are five iambs per line (one iamb = two syllables) and each iamb is made up of an unstressed syllable and a stressed syllable. The sound of each line would sound something like this:

da-**dum** da-**dum** da-**dum** da-**dum** da-**dum**

Shakespeare is very famous for using iambic pentameter in his plays – perhaps because it is easier for actors to remember the lines if there is a regular meter, perhaps because it is easier for audiences to follow long speeches or perhaps because it naturally suits the English language. Of course, it also sounds a lot grander than prose and Shakespeare wrote much of his protagonists' dialogue using blank verse and iambic pentameter. As his protagonists were always from a noble background, using this form of speech also helped give them an air of importance and grandeur, elevated from those on-stage and those off-stage.

CHECK FOR UNDERSTANDING

Match the dialogue with the correct form:

Once more unto the breach, dear friends, once more Or close the wall up with our English dead. [King Henry V]	Verse
For never was a story of more woe Than this of Juliet and her Romeo. [Romeo and Juliet]	Prose
If to do were as easy as to know what were good to do, chapels had been churches, and poor men's cottages princes' palaces. [The Merchant of Venice]	Blank Verse

We are now going to read and explore an extract from Shakespeare's tragedy, *King Lear.* The extract comes from Act III, scene ii. King Lear, the aged king of Britain, has recently divided his kingdom up between two of his three daughters, Goneril and Regan, as they have flattered him with compliments. His third daughter, Cordelia, simply tells him that she loves him as much as a daughter should. The scene you are about to read takes place after both Goneril and Regan have refused to shelter him even though there is a storm raging outside. Read the extract below and the commentary that follows:

Another part of the heath. Storm still.
Enter *KING LEAR and FOOL .*

KING LEAR: Blow, winds, and crack your cheeks! rage! blow!
You cataracts and hurricanoes, spout
Till you have drench'd our steeples, drown'd the cocks!
You sulphurous and thought-executing fires,
Vaunt-couriers to oak-cleaving thunderbolts,
Singe my white head! And thou, all-shaking thunder,
Smite flat the thick rotundity o'the world!
Crack nature's moulds, an germens spill at once,
That make ingrateful man!

FOOL: O nuncle, court holy-water in a dry
house is better than this rain-water out o'door.
Good nuncle, in, and ask thy daughters' blessing:
here's a night pities neither wise man nor fool.

KING LEAR: Rumble thy bellyful! Spit, fire! spout, rain!
Nor rain, wind, thunder, fire, are my daughters:
I tax not you, you elements, with unkindness;
I never gave you kingdom, call'd you children,
You owe me no subscription: then let fall
Your horrible pleasure: here I stand, your slave,
A poor, infirm, weak, and despised old man:
But yet I call you servile ministers,
That have with two pernicious daughters join'd
Your high engender'd battles 'gainst a head
So old and white as this. O! O! 'tis foul!

FOOL: He that has a house to put's head in has a good
head-piece.
The cod-piece that will house
Before the head has any,
The head and he shall louse;
So beggars marry many.
The man that makes his toe
What he his heart should make
Shall of a corn cry woe,
And turn his sleep to wake.
For there was never yet fair woman but she made
mouths in a glass.

KING LEAR: No, I will be the pattern of all patience;
I will say nothing.

(William Shakespeare, King Lear *Act 3 Scene 2)*

Step 1: Form and structure

Let us first of all explore the effect of using the conventions of blank verse and iambic pentameter on the language Lear speaks.

Following the conventions of blank verse and iambic pentameter

As we have already discussed, the form of a king's speech usually follows the stylized conventions of blank verse and iambic pentameter. This helps to elevate the king and gives him authority over the ordinary prose-speaking individuals of lower social status (including us off-stage!). However, this is a restrictive form as each line can only contain 5 iambs and the meter of each iamb is unstressed stressed. This has a great impact on the language used and the order the words are placed within the line. Let's look at lines 2 and 3 from Lear's speech. He is addressing the storm itself and describing the impact the storm is having on the country:

> You cataracts and hurricanoes, spout
> Till you have drench'd our steeples, drown'd the cocks!

Here are the same two lines, split up to identify the iambic pentameter:

> You **cat** / a **racts** / and **hurr** / i **can** / oes, **spout**
> Till **you** / have **drench'd** / our **steep** / les, **drown'd** / the **cocks**!

How does this form affect the language used? Remember each line only consists of 5 iambs and this means Shakespeare is restricted in terms of how many syllables he can include in each line. He has to be precise with the language he uses, as he cannot afford to waste any words due to the restrictions he is placing on himself by using this particular form of verse. In these two lines, it is clear he has chosen his language precisely – if you notice most of the nouns and verbs he has used are words connected to the storm itself ('cataracts', 'hurricanoes', 'spout', 'drench'd', 'drown'd'). The subject matter of this speech, then, shapes the language used. However, what is particularly interesting about the way these two lines have been constructed, is the way words have been placed to exploit sound imagery. Not only do the words themselves denote the storm, but the way they sound imitate the sound of the storm. This is accentuated through those sounds that are stressed as the syllables that are stressed tend to be those syllables that have harsh **plosive** sounds. For example, the first stressed syllable of 'cat' starts with a hard 'c' sound and ends with a spitting 't' sound; the second stressed syllable of 'racts' repeats and therefore emphasizes both of these harsh 'c' and 't' sounds by having them side-by-side at the end of the syllable. If we look at the second line, **monosyllabic** verbs are stressed including 'drench'd' and 'drown'd'. The impact of this is that the verbs that are being stressed denote something destructive, and the sounds of the words imitate something forceful and discordant – both verbs begin and end with a plosive 'd' sound and this heightens the impact of the words' literal meaning, bringing the sound of the storm onto the stage through Lear's language. Thus, we can see how when Lear speaks using **iambic pentameter**, not only does this shape the language used but it also shapes the order of the language spoken.

Subverting the conventions of iambic pentameter

King Lear's speeches in this play are quite unusual for a king. You may have noticed in this extract that although some of the lines scan well in terms of following an iambic pentameter meter, many lines do not. There are lines that are too short (line 1), lines that are too long (line 16) and many lines that are fragmented and broken with multiple exclamatives and one word sentences (lines 1, 14 and 24). The effect of this is that Lear does not always sound fluent, in control or even rational. By subverting the regular iambic pentameter form we are expecting King Lear to use can suggest a number of ideas:

- Lear's anger and frustration at the way he has been treated by his two daughters, resulting in his overwrought emotions that results in him being unable to speak or think rationally
- Lear's inner turmoil and sense of powerlessness at the situation in which he finds himself
- Lear's confusion at how he is being treated leading to his gradual descent into madness
- Lear's falling in status; he is no longer king having given away his kingdom to two of his daughters

- the anger of the natural world at Lear's renouncing his kingship and at the chaos this has brought to the country.

As the play progresses, all these ideas come into play – but this is the first time that we begin to see so clearly the larger impact of Lear's hollow values when he so quickly gives away his kingdom to those daughters who flatter him with niceties. It is through the use of language, of course, that Shakespeare is able to subvert the traditional conventions of a king's speech – conventions that he himself created – and by doing so infer so many ideas that will become important as the play progresses. Let's look at the first line and explore how Shakespeare manipulates language to this end:

> Blow, winds, and crack your cheeks! rage! blow!

This line only contains 4 iambs. As we know, an iamb in poetry is two syllables that follow an unstressed stressed meter. Each word in this first line of Lear's speech is **monosyllabic** and is broken up with an abundance of **caesura**. Because there is so much punctuation, which fragments the line into many single monosyllabic words, it is not clear which syllables should be stressed. We would think – because of the word's meaning and sound – that the first word, 'blow', should be stressed as well as the final two words, 'rage! blow!' but this would disrupt the iambic meter. Perhaps this is the intention as after all the number of iambs has been reduced by one. The entire line consists of monosyllables, the majority of which are verbs and most of which have a **plosive** sound. This appears to imitate the storm itself – the **verbs** suggest how it is something that is active and the plosives suggest it is wilfully destructive. The preponderance of monosyllables has the effect of fragmenting the line further, suggesting both the turmoil of the external world and the inner turmoil Lear is experiencing.

This line, then, clearly shows how language has been chosen for its syllable length, for its meaning, and for its sound to suggest particular ideas. Furthermore, the way each word has been separated by punctuation has also been shaped to heighten a sense of breakdown, fragmentation and turmoil in the external world as well as in Lear's inner world.

Step 2: LIFs

Language is shaped by the context during which the play was written

Shakespeare was writing during the late-sixteenth and early-seventeenth centuries and most of his plays were performed at The Globe theatre, a large circular open-air theatre, in Southwark, London. Unlike theatre today, which is able to employ many visual and auditory special effects, Shakespeare was restricted by the special effects he was able to use. Having minimal special effects had a huge impact on the way language was used by Shakespeare. One of the attractions of going to the theatre was that audiences were transported from the drudgery of their daily existence, to a time and place that was fundamentally different to their present. As we know from Chapter 1.1, audiences needed to suspend their disbelief to fully appreciate the theatrical experience. How then could Shakespeare transport an audience in seventeenth-century London to the middle of a battlefield in France (*Henry V*), or to the Rialto in central Venice (*The Merchant of Venice*), or to a heath in the middle of a tempestuous storm (*King Lear*)?

The answer remains the same for each of his plays: through language, imagery and other dramatic features.

ACTIVITY 4

The stage directions at the start of the extract are minimal: 'Another part of the heath. Storm still.' It is through the language, imagery and other dramatic features (LIFs) Shakespeare uses in Lear's speeches that he is able to transport the off-stage audience to this heath in the middle of a raging storm. The following table identifies a number of different ways LIFs have been used to recreate the storm on stage. The first half of the table has been completed for you. Complete the rest of the table with an appropriate quotation from the extract and a short explanation of the effect of this literary feature. When you have completed the table, check your ideas with those at the back of the book.

■ Table 1.4.3

Use of language	Quotation	Effect
Alliteration	'... drench'd our steeples, drown'd the cocks!'	Repeated harsh 'd' sounds imitate the meaning of the words. To drench and to drown are negative effects of a storm, something we want to avoid. The alliterative 'd' sound heightens the negative mood. This sentence uses parallelism to suggest that nothing is safe from the storm. Steeples were associated with church buildings, so this suggests the storm is evil and that even the church is not immune from the storm.
Assonance	'... cataracts ...'	The hard 'a' vowel sound (assonance) compounded with the harsh 'c' consonant recreate the sounds of the storm. There are no soft or gentle sounds here, suggesting the storm is relentless. Cataracts has two meanings: a waterfall and an eye condition which affects one's sight. This suggests then that as well as rising waters in waterfalls, the storm has the effect of blinding people. (We will return to this idea later.)
Contrast	'You sulphurous and thought-executing fires ...' 'Spit, fire! spout, rain!'	The language used contrasts in terms of its syllable count. Some words have many syllables (**polysyllabic**) and some only have one syllable (**monosyllabic**). This suggests that the storm is omnipotent – there is nothing it cannot do or destroy.
Listing	'Nor rain, wind, thunder, fire ...'	By listing the different elements of the storm, highlights how the storm represents many dangers.
Loaded language	'Vaunt-couriers to oak-cleaving thunderbolts'	**'vaunt-couriers'** is a military term meaning a soldier who is sent out in advance of the army. By using this military term, it is suggesting the storm is at war with Lear/with the country. **'oak-cleaving'** is a loaded term also: by suggesting the storm has the power to cleave in two (split) oak, this suggests how all-powerful the storm is. Oak symbolizes longevity, strength and power but if the storm is able to cleave an oak in two, then this suggests how powerful the storm is. This line also recreates the powerful sounds of the storm through the different plosive sounds, 'v', 'c', 'd' and 'b'.
Onomatopoeia		
Personification		
Plosive sounds		
Violent verbs		

Language is shaped by the writer's intention

In this extract, as well as attempting to recreate the storm on stage, Shakespeare also wants us to understand the disastrous effects Lear's past actions have had and the inner turmoil he is experiencing. Language is shaped by this intention. First, the storm represents **pathetic fallacy** whereby the natural environment is being used to enhance a particular mood. Lear has acted irresponsibly by giving away his kingdom to his two daughters because they were able to appeal to his vanity and as a consequence the kingdom itself is suffering. The storm can be explained as representing a greater power than man that is battering both the king and his kingdom to show its anger at Lear's foolishness. The ways in which language, imagery and other features have been used, as shown in Table 1.4.3, reinforces this idea.

Language is also used to give us an insight into Lear's character. We have already discussed how we can view this scene as representing the start of his mental decline. Other ways this idea is suggested through the use of language is the way Lear continually addresses the storm as if it were a living being and attempts to command the storm to do his own bidding. He uses the **personal pronouns** 'you', 'your', 'thou' and 'thee' which heighten this idea but which also, ironically, elevate the storm's power, suggesting it is a conscious being that is purposefully attacking Lear, making his commands all the more absurd.

Shakespeare also uses language in this extract to suggest Lear's powerlessness and vulnerability. The reference to how the storm is 'singe(ing) my white head' is a **visual image** that reminds us that Lear is an old man – making it all the more difficult for him to survive the power of this storm. In his second speech, this idea is continued as Lear pronounces:

> … here I stand, your slave,
> A poor, infirm, weak, and despised old man:

The language used here emphasizes Lear's vulnerability and audiences are encouraged to pity him, despite his past foolishness. Interestingly, Shakespeare plays with iambic pentameter in the second line to also emphasize Lear's weakness. The first two iambs and the final two iambs scan perfectly. The middle iamb, consisting of the words 'weak, and' are subverted. The stress should be on 'and' but when you read this line, the stress naturally falls on 'weak'. The **meter** then has been broken – or **weakened** – in the middle which also heightens the sense of Lear's lack of authority and power. This is a clever way Shakespeare manipulates the meaning of language in terms of where it is placed in the line.

EE Links: English A – Literature category 1

Here are two possible extended essay questions based on *King Lear*.

- **How is King Lear's descent into madness depicted through language?**
- **How does Shakespeare use the natural world to explore key ideas in *King Lear*?**

Remember that for all English A extended essays, you need to explore and include secondary research. You should read what other critics and academics have said about your chosen topic before you start planning your extended essay.

For a literature-based extended essay, you may find your literary reading strategy useful in structuring your close reading skills.

The Fool

The Fool is an interesting character: he is of low social status but Lear treats him as a friend and a confidante throughout the play. The Fool's name is ironic – although it may appear he speaks foolish and nonsensical words, in actual fact he uses riddles to reveal the truth. Unlike Lear, who is clearly losing his sanity and is in the middle of an internal turmoil that is affecting his rational judgement, the Fool speaks honestly and truthfully. In order to highlight how the two characters are contrasted, Shakespeare uses form, structure, language, imagery and other dramatic features to this end:

- The Fool's first speech is in **prose** – the opposite of verse. It is a more down-to-earth and ordinary way of speaking, in **contrast** to Lear's more stylized way of speaking and which, as we have seen, he is unable to sustain.
- The Fool uses **antithesis** in his first speech: 'water … dry' and 'wise … fool' which also highlights the idea of **contrast** and opposites.
- In the Fool's second speech, from lines 27–34, he uses a strict rhyme scheme (ABABCDCD), which contrasts with Lear's **blank verse**.
- Although we have to work at what the Fool's words mean due to his riddles, they are spoken in a more fluent manner than Lear's due to the lack of **caesura** when he speaks.

William Shakespeare

William Shakespeare is widely considered the world's greatest dramatist and writer in the English language. He wrote plays that were comedies (including *A Midsummer Night's Dream, Much Ado About Nothing*), tragedies (including *Macbeth, Hamlet, Othello, King Lear*) and history plays (including *Henry IV Parts 1 and 2, Henry V*). Most of his plays were performed in The Globe theatre in London, a circular open-air theatre which was built by his performing company, The Lord Chamberlain's Men. His performing company changed their name to The King's Men when King James I of England took the throne in 1603 and many of his plays were performed at court in front of the king. Shakespeare also wrote two narrative poems and 154 sonnets. The sonnet form he used (three quatrains followed by a rhyming couplet) is now referred to as a Shakespearean sonnet. Many of his sonnets centre around the lust the narrative voice feels for a married woman with a dark complexion and many centre around the love the narrative voice feels for a fair young man. Critics are uncertain as to whether the narrative voice represents Shakespeare himself or not – although Wordsworth thought it did – an interesting link to our concept of authorial identity!

We are now going to explore an extract from a play called *Oleanna,* which premiered on the stage in 1992. It is interesting to compare this play with *King Lear,* which was written nearly 400 years earlier. By comparing these two plays we can see very clearly how language can vary not only *among* text types and literary forms but *within* the same literary form. One could rightly argue that the differences in language between *King Lear* and *Oleanna*, for example, is the result of the fact that language is constantly evolving and we no longer speak English in the same way that people spoke English during Shakespeare's day. We could also argue that with technological advancements, we can use special effects more convincingly and so there is less of a need to use figurative language to create mood or to bring complicated scenes such as huge battle scenes or storms to life. However, there seems to be something else going on that is shaping the language in *Oleanna*.

Modern American drama: *Oleanna* by David Mamet

Oleanna is a two-act twentieth-century play written by American playwright, David Mamet, first performed in May 1992. Just as when it was first performed, the play is still controversial today in terms of its subject matter and the way it divides audiences' responses to the two characters: John, a university professor, and Carol, one of his students who has come to see him because she is failing his course.

In the following extract from Act 1, John is on the phone when Carol enters his office. Let's read the extract – hopefully you will immediately notice that the language used differs dramatically from that used in the extract from *King Lear*:

JOHN: Yes. No, no, I'll meet you at the new … That's a good. If he thinks it's necc … you tell Jerry to meet … All right? We aren't going to lose the deposit. All right? I'm sure it's going to be … (Pause) I hope so. (Pause) I love you, too. (Pause) I love you, too. As soon as … I will. (He hangs up.) (He bends over the desk and makes a note.) (He looks up.) (To CAROL:) I'm sorry …

CAROL: (Pause) What is a 'term of art'?

JOHN: (Pause) I'm sorry …?

CAROL: (Pause) What is a 'term of art'?

JOHN: Is that what you want to talk about?

CAROL: … to talk about …?

JOHN: Let's take the mysticism out of it, shall we? Carol? (Pause) Don't you think? I'll tell you: when you have some 'thing'. Which must be broached. (Pause) Don't you think …? (Pause)

CAROL: … don't I think …?

JOHN: Mmm?

CAROL: … did I …?

JOHN: … what?

CAROL: Did … did I … did I say something wr …

JOHN: (Pause) No. I'm sorry. No. You're right. I'm very sorry. I'm somewhat rushed. As you see. I'm sorry. You're right. (Pause)

What is a 'term of art'? It seems to me a term, which has come, through its use, to mean something more specific than the words would, to someone not acquainted with them … indicate. That, I believe, is what a 'term of art', would mean. (Pause)

CAROL: You don't know what it means …?

JOHN: I'm not sure that I know what it means. It's one of those perhaps you've had them, that, you look them up, or have someone explain them to you, and you say 'aha', and, you immediately forget what …

CAROL: You don't do that.

(David Mamet 2–4)

It is likely when you read this, it felt more 'realistic' – and it's not just because the language feels more modern. Drama, as an artform, is constantly changing and evolving. The conventions, rules and expectations of drama have changed and out of this have sprung different theoretical movements. Playwrights, although they are writing using the same literary form – drama – have often sought new ways to convey their ideas and this has invariably shaped the language used. Classical, Modernism, Postmodernism and the Theatre of the Absurd are just some of the labels that have been used to distinguish different types of theatre and the ways they have deviated and established new conventions on stage.

Step 1: Structure and form

In the extract above, Mamet is clearly interested in and intent upon recreating 'real' speech on stage. He has included pauses and **filled pauses** – where uncomfortable pauses are 'filled in' with sounds such as John's 'Mmm' (line 16). We also have **false starts** where the grammatical constructions of the sentence is not completed and another grammatical construction simply replaces it. We see this when John is on the phone at the beginning of the extract and shifts topics mid-sentence (lines 1–4). We also have the characters interrupting each other. In fact, we can interpret the extract as Mamet exploring the form and structure of characters' dialogue as a form of power; a similar idea, perhaps, to Shakespeare's drama which, at times, uses blank verse rather than prose as a way to denote position and nobility. When Mamet's characters interrupt each other in the extract, for example, we could interpret this as them attempting to take control of the conversation and disempower the other.

Step 2: LIFs

The language Carol and John use also denote their positions of power. When Carol asks John, 'What is a "term of art"?', if we look at John's response in lines 21–25, many of his words and phrases sound very impressive but he is not really answering the question:

> What is a 'term of art'? It seems to me a term, which has come, through its use, to mean something more specific than the words would, to someone not acquainted with them … indicate. That, I believe, is what a 'term of art', would mean.
>
> *(David Mamet)*

Words and phrases such as 'through its use', 'mean something more specific', 'acquainted' and 'indicate' are examples of how John, as an academic, is able to hide behind language and make it sound sophisticated and knowledgeable which gives him power and authority. We could even go as far as to suggest that because this is a play and there is obviously an audience, that Carol's question is not just directed at John but also at us. Mamet might be using his play to ask us, through Carol, to think about whether what we are watching is art. Is art really reality – the everyday observation of real communication from which we then create meaning – or should art be something different? This is a question you can take further in the TOK link later on.

One of the important features that seems to shape Mamet's language use in this play seems to be the unreliability of language to communicate clearly. John, in his attempt to explain the 'term of art', has simply replaced it with another vague set of words. When John says, 'Don't you think …?' (line 14) this is a strategic bid to use a rhetorical question to get Carol to agree with him. Carol misunderstands it, thinking that John is suggesting that she is stupid and unable to think. Maybe this is in actual fact what John does mean which is why he does not finish his sentence! We could also argue that perhaps Carol is deliberately misconstruing what John says to engage him in an argument! We, as the audience, are caught up in this unreliability of language. We have to negotiate the text with all its ambiguities and decide who, if either, is the innocent party in this exchange. We, as members of the audience, have to fill in the gaps and construct our own narrative to explain what is going on on-stage. Mamet symbolizes this idea through the telephone conversation at the beginning of the extract. We cannot hear John's wife on the phone and in between the pauses between John's words we attempt to guess what she is saying!

The language used by Mamet in this play is shaped by his philosophical concerns and ideas about language. Although he is exploring his ideas through the same form as Shakespeare was using, he is following a different set of dramatic conventions and these two factors undoubtedly shape the language used in this play.

David Mamet

David Mamet is an American playwright and author who has also written and directed many films, including the film adaptation of his play, *Oleanna*. His play *Glengarry Glen Ross* (1984) won a Pulitzer Prize and in 2002 he was inducted into the American Theater Hall of Fame. He made his name in the 1970s with plays, including *The Duck Variations* (1972) and *American Buffalo* (1975). He is a regular contributor to *Huffington Post,* drawing satirical political cartoons. He is famous for his distinctive style of dialogue: fast-talking, street-wise, jargonistic, cynical and manipulative. This style of writing dialogue which has been imitated by other playwrights and screenwriters is known as 'Mamet – speak'.

TOK Links: Art and reality

Can and should art recreate reality? How true is an artform's recreation of real life?

Can the knowledge gained through art (including literature) teach us anything about reality?

CONCEPT CONNECTION

COMMUNICATION

This concept revolves around the relationship that is built between the writer and the reader through the text. As we have seen, Mamet's use of language is often ambiguous and we have to construct our own narrative. Mamet appears to have consciously not facilitated communication that can be interpreted in one particular way. The way we interpret the language used may also be affected by the way performers interpret Mamet's language, as well. Some members of the audience may sympathize with Carol, while others may sympathize with John. Communication, therefore, can differ between audiences and between performances.

This particular text was also written following a high profile case in 1991 when Anita Hill, a university professor, accused Clarence Thomas, nominee for the US Supreme Court, of sexual exploitation. More recently, it may remind audiences of a similar case in 2018 when Christine Blasey Ford, a psychology professor, accused Brett Kavanaugh, nominee for the US Supreme Court, of sexual assault. Depending upon an audience member's knowledge and attitudes to these cases may also affect how engaged or open the audience is to Mamet's play and to each of the characters.

In a text such as *Oleanna*, communication is rarely **univocal**, making the concept of communication both productive and problematic. You may like to explore this idea further in the texts you read in class.

As we have discussed, the conventions of a particular literary form constantly evolve in the same way as language evolves. In both the Shakespeare play and Mrs Beeton's advisory text, for example, you will have come across certain words that are no longer commonly used. This is one of the challenges of reading texts from the past and will be explored in more detail in the next chapter. As already explored in this chapter, language can be interpreted as meaning visual language as well as written language. In Chapter 1.3, we discussed how social media has had an impact on the type of language we use in recent years, looking particularly at the use of emoticons in certain modes of communication. This brings us to our final point regarding how, due to language evolving, language varies among text types.

The emoji

According to the Oxford Dictionaries, visual symbols are words. The Oxford Dictionaries have chosen a 'Word of the Year' since 2004 to 'reflect the ethos, mood or preoccupations of that particular year and to have lasting potential as a word of cultural significance'.

Here are the words of the year for the last five years.

■ Table 1.4.4

Year	Word of the Year	Definitions from: **https://en.oxforddictionaries.com/word-of-the-year**
2018	Toxic	The adjective toxic is defined as 'poisonous' and first appeared in English in the mid-seventeenth century from the medieval Latin toxicus, meaning 'poisoned' or 'imbued with poison'.
2017	Youthquake	The noun, youthquake, is defined as 'a significant cultural, political, or social change arising from the actions or influence of young people'.
2016	Post-truth	An adjective defined as 'relating to or denoting circumstances in which objective facts are less influential in shaping public opinion than appeals to emotion and personal belief'.
2015		For the first time ever, the Oxford Dictionaries Word of the Year is a pictograph: , officially called the 'Face with Tears of Joy' emoji, though you may know it by other names. There were other strong contenders from a range of fields … but was chosen as the 'word' that best reflected the ethos, mood, and preoccupations of 2015.
2014	Vape	The verb means 'to inhale and exhale the vapour produced by an electronic cigarette or similar device', while both the device and the action can also be known as a vape.

The word of the year for 2015 should have stood out! For the first time, an **emoji** was chosen as the 'word of the year' – so, it's official, emojis are words! Just as your background may have played a part in the way you interpreted and responded to the student's use of textspeak in Activity 4, Chapter 1.3, so too may your background influence how you respond to the concept of an emoji being a word. If an emoji is a word, does that mean each emoji needs a definitive definition? The *Oxford Dictionaries* have defined this particular emoji as meaning 'Face with Tears of Joy' but have also noted that 'you may know it by other names'. This is an interesting concept – if individuals have different definitions of one single emoji, how are we expected to 'translate' the emoji accurately? There are of course online 'emojipedias' where you can find the meanings of a wide range of emojis but when writers use emojis in textspeak it tends to be a way to communicate quickly and an emoji becomes a shorthand to express a particular emotion. It defeats the object of speed-texting if you have to look up the meaning of every emoji you are using! When a writer uses an emoji rather than traditional words to express an emotion, the writer is assuming the reader will 'translate' the pictograph appropriately; without needing to resort to an emojipedia! However, we can see how there is a potential for mistakes to be made in the translation process. This is why, then, emojis are generally used in informal communication between friends – the writer makes the assumption that their reader knows them well enough to know intuitively what they are intending to express when they use any particular emoji.

Although there may be 'other names' for each emoji, it is supposed to be a universal language. The emoji 😂 is, therefore, cross-cultural: it can be used and understood whether you speak English, Japanese, Russian, Chinese or Hebrew. To date, there have been three 'emoji books' written and published: two paper books and one online book. *Emoji Dick* (2010) by American emoji aficionado, Fred Benenson, is the first emoji translation of a book originally written using **standard English**. It is a translation – in emojis – of Herman Melville's 1851 epic adventure novel, *Moby Dick*. The other two emoji books are original texts: *Book from the Ground* (2014) is a book written by Chinese artist, Xu Bing, using pictographs similar to emojis; and *The Book Written Entirely Out Of Emojis* (2017) is an original story written entirely with emojis and punctuation which is published on the social storytelling platform, Wattpad, by YarnStore. In theory, because of the universal language of emojis used, these books should be understood by anyone, irrespective of their native language. Below are short extracts from each of these emoji books – your success in understanding them is likely to depend, not on your **mother tongue**, but upon your knowledge of emojis.

Here is the opening page of *Emoji Dick*. The first line of 'words' is the text in emojis by Benenson; the lines in traditional English is the original text by Melville.

Call me Ishmael.

Some years ago--never mind how long precisely--having little or no money in my purse, and nothing particular to interest me on shore, I thought I would sail about a little and see the watery part of the world.

It is a way I have of driving off the spleen and regulating the circulation.

Whenever I find myself growing grim about the mouth; whenever it is a damp, drizzly November in my soul; whenever I find myself involuntarily pausing before coffin warehouses, and bringing up the rear of every funeral I meet; and especially whenever my hypos get such an upper hand of me, that it requires a strong moral principle to prevent me from deliberately stepping into the street, and methodically knocking people's hats off--then, I account it high time to get to sea as soon as I can.

This is my substitute for pistol and ball.

With a philosophical flourish Cato throws himself upon his sword; I quietly take to the ship.

Below are the first three chapters as listed in the contents page from *Bing's Book from the Ground*.

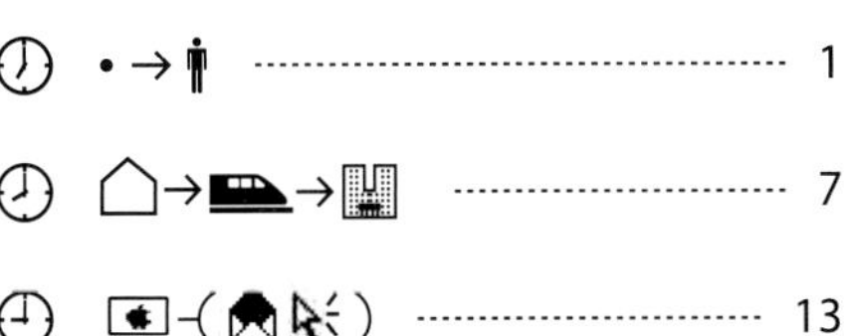

Scan the QR code alongside to read *The Book Written Entirely Out Of* Emojis from YarnStore.

Currently, despite emojis being a universal language, writing a book entirely using emojis is rare because of their limited audience. Few readers are able to read fluently an emoji book and they are still considered novelty books. This of course may change if our written language evolves to such an extent that emojis are used to express ourselves to a greater extent than the traditional written word. Once this happens, you may find yourself reading a translated version of this IB Language and Literature coursebook written entirely in emojis! However, until then, emojis are a form of language that writers use alongside traditional written words on social media when sending informal messages to people they know.

ACTIVITY 5

Either translate the lyrics from one of your favourite songs (or at least the opening verse) using just emojis. Then share your translation with a friend and see if they can work out what song you have translated.

Or translate the first few lines of a text you are studying in class using just emojis. Then share your translation with a classmate and see if she or he can recognise the text you have translated.

There is no end of book commentary for this activity.

To conclude, then, this chapter has shown how language does vary among text types and among literary forms, but how it also varies within text types and literary works of the same form. The aspects of a text that shape the language that is used include:

- a text's purpose
- a writer's intention
- the context in which a text is produced and received.

Of course, the same language device can be used in different text types and literary forms, but what is important is that you are able to identify why language has been used in a particular way depending on the text being read.

Works cited

Aristotle. *The Art of Rhetoric*. Translated by Hugh Lawson-Tancred, Penguin Classics, 1991.

'A View on Culture.' *Emoji Dick by Anja*. Web. 12 Feb. 2019. **https://aviewonculture.wordpress.com/2014/05/18/emoji-dick**.

Beeton, I. *Mrs Beeton's Book of Household Management*. CreateSpace Independent Publishing Platform, 2018.

Beeton, I. *The Book of Household Management*. Web. 9 Feb. 2019. **www.gutenberg.org/cache/epub/10136/pg10136-images.html**.

Benenson, F. *Emoji Dick*. (Creative Commons Attribution 2.0) 7 Sept. 2010. Web. 12 Feb. 2019. **www.emojidick.com**.

Bing, X. *Book from the Ground: from point to point*. The MIT Press, 2014.

King, ML Jr. 'I Have a Dream ...' speech at the 'March on Washington', 1963. Web. 10 Feb. 2019. **www.archives.gov/files/press/exhibits/dream-speech.pdf**.

Lee, H. *To Kill A Mockingbird*, 50th anniversary edition. Arrow, 2010.

Lincoln, A. 'The Gettysburg Address.' Web. 16 Feb. 2019. **www.abrahamlincolnonline.org/lincoln/speeches/gettysburg.htm**.

Mamet, D. *Oleanna*. Methuen Drama, 1993.

Melville, H. *Moby Dick*. Wordsworth Editions, 1992.

Murrow, ER. 'I Can Hear It Now 1933–1945.' Format: vinyl, Columbia Records, International Churchill Society. Web. 10 Feb. 2019. **https://winstonchurchill.org/resources/quotes/quotes-faq**.

'Previous Words of the Year.' *Oxford Dictionaries*. Web. accessed 8 Feb. 2019. **https://en.oxforddictionaries.com/word-of-the-year#hb-previous-words-of-the-year**.

Rich, F. 'Mamet's New Play Detonates The Fury of Sexual Harassment.' *The New York Times*, The New York Times, 26 Oct. 1992. Web. 17 Feb. 2019. **www.nytimes.com/1992/10/26/theater/review-theater-oleanna-mamet-s-new-play-detonates-the-fury-of-sexual-harassment.html**.

Shakespeare, W. *King Henry V*, 2nd edition. Edited by Andrew Gurr, *The New Cambridge Shakespeare*, Cambridge University Press, 2005.

Shakespeare, W. *King Lear*. Edited by Prof. Cedric Watts and Dr Keith Carabine, Wordsworth Editions, 1994.

Shelley, M. *Frankenstein: Or, the Modern Prometheus*. Wordsworth Editions, 1992.

Tzu, S. *Sun Tzu on the Art of War: The Oldest Military Treatise in the World; Translated From the Chinese With Introduction, and Critical Notes*. Translated by Lionel Giles, Classic Reprint Series, Forgotten Books, 2018.

Wollstonecraft, M. *A Vindication of the Rights of Woman (with an introduction by Millicent Garrett Fawcett)*. Digireads.com Publishing, 2018.

'Word of the Year.' *Oxford Dictionaries*. Web. 8 Feb. 2019. **https://en.oxforddictionaries.com/word-of-the-year/word-of-the-year-2015**.

Wright, J. (dir.) *Darkest Hour*. Universal Pictures UK, 2018.

YarnStore. *The Book Written Entirely Out Of Emojis*. Wattpad, 2017. Web. 12 Feb. 2019. **www.wattpad.com/105027268-the-book-written-entirely-out-of-emojis-the-book**.

1.5 How does the structure or style of a text affect meaning?

OBJECTIVES OF CHAPTER

- Consider the structure of literary works, including:
  - chronological vs non-linear structure
  - plot structure and endings.
- Consider the structure of non-literary texts, including:
  - the chronological structure of a newspaper sports report
  - the non-linear structure of magazine front covers.
- Consider the different styles used in prose fiction.
- Consider the style of non-literary texts, particularly style used in advertising.

How does the structure or style of a text affect meaning?

Just as language varies among and between text types and literary works, so does the structure and style of a text. The structure or style used by a writer is important as it has an impact on how readers negotiate and interpret a text's meaning. We are going to explore both features of literary works and non-literary texts. The first half of this chapter will explore different structural choices a writer may make and what impact this has on how we interpret a text's meaning. The second half of this chapter will explore the different stylistic choices a writer may make and, again, what impact this may have on how we interpret a text's meaning.

Structure of literary works

Plot structure: chronological vs non-linear

The structure of a text refers to the way ideas have been organized. In particular, we may focus on how a text is **foregrounded**, what its **end focus** is and what kind of a journey we have been on from the beginning to the end. A writer may decide to start at the beginning and end at the end, using a strictly **chronological** structure. A number of literary works may follow a chronological structure: Charles Dickens' *A Christmas Carol* (Chapter 1.1, prose fiction), George Orwell's *Down and Out in Paris and London* (Chapter 1.2, prose non-fiction), Shaun Tan's *The Arrival* (Chapter 1.3, graphic novel) and Tennessee Williams' *A Streetcar Named Desire* (Chapter 1.3, drama) are examples of different forms of literary works which employ this structural feature. Using a chronological structure means the text is generally easy to follow and writers may opt to use this structure if they are attempting to offer instruction or guidance to the reader about something or attempting to explain the cause and effect of something.

Many children's stories use a chronological structure, not just because it is easier to follow the narrative, but because it is easier to educate the reader. *Aesop's Fables*, a collection of fables with an ethical message written by the ancient Greek storyteller, Aesop, between 620 and 564BCE, follow a chronological structure which makes their moral message easier to understand. Initially, these fables were aimed at adults but because of their strong ethical message they became popular texts to use to educate children. Fairy tales, too, often had a strong moral message, which a chronological structure helped to make clear. French author, Charles Perrault, wrote many fairy tales in the seventeenth century, all of which employ this particular structure. The beginning to *The Sleeping Beauty in the Wood* (1697), for example, is typical of a traditional fairy tale, using the famous 'Once upon a time …' opening that we now associate with this genre of storytelling:

> Once upon a time there lived a king and queen who were grieved, more grieved than words can tell, because they had no children. They tried the waters of every country, made vows and pilgrimages, and did everything that could be done, but without result. At last, however, the queen found that her wishes were fulfilled, and in due course she gave birth to a daughter.
>
> *(Charles Perrault)*

The opposite of a chronological structure is a **non-linear** structure. This is when we are taken on a journey that jumps backwards and forwards in time and may have flashbacks or shifts in perspective, time or place. Art Spiegelman's *Maus* (Chapter 1.1), Arundhati Roy's *The God of Small Things* (Chapter 1.1), Banana Yoshimoto's *Kitchen* (Chapter 1.2) and Toni Morrison's *Beloved* (Chapter 1.3) are all literary works that use a non-linear structure. Although each of these works start in the **narrative present**, a text following a non-linear structure will include regular shifts in time, place and perspective. The effect of using a non-linear structure is that the reader has to work harder at negotiating and interpreting meaning. Initially, there may be gaps in the reader's understanding as the reader tries to make sense of different time periods or narrative voices or physical places and it is often not until the whole story has been told that the reader has a full understanding of the text's meaning.

Rather than starting at the beginning, some texts may start **in medias res** – in the middle of things. Homer's epic poem *The Odyssey* (eighth century BCE) is a famous text that starts in medias res. The poem recounts Odysseus' adventures travelling back to Greece after the end of the Trojan War. Rather than starting immediately after the end of the Trojan War, Homer starts mid-adventure and the poem then includes flashbacks to some of Odysseus' earlier adventures, making it follow a non-linear structure. Here are the opening lines of the poem:

> All the other Greeks
> who had survived the brutal sack of Troy
> sailed safely home to their own wives – except
> this man alone. Calypso, a great goddess,
> had trapped him in her cave; she wanted him
> to be her husband. When the year rolled round
> in which the gods decreed he should go home
> to Ithaca, his troubles still went on.
>
> *(Homer)*

The effect of using this structure is that it plunges the reader into the middle of the action and can be a dramatic hook to encourage the reader to continue reading. Other texts may start at the end and then follow either a chronological or a non-linear structure to construct the narrative that explains how the ending occurred. In Gabriel García Márquez's *Chronicle of a Death Foretold* (1981), for example, the narrator is attempting to piece together what exactly happened when his friend, Santiago Nasar, was murdered 27 years ago. The following lines come from page 1 of this South American prose fiction work.

> 'He was always dreaming about trees.' Plácida Linero, his mother, told me twenty-seven years later, recalling the details of that unpleasant Monday. 'The week before, he'd dreamed that he was alone in a tinfoil aeroplane and flying through the almond trees without bumping into anything,' she told me.
>
> *(Gabriel García Márquez 1)*

Shakespeare's *Romeo and Juliet* (1597) is another text that starts at the end. It starts with a Prologue, spoken by the Chorus, that tells the audience in 14 lines exactly what happens. For many people, one of the most irritating things about book or film reviews is when there are spoilers – so why would we want to stay in the theatre to watch the performance if we know the ending? The craft of Shakespeare is that even though we know what happens, we want to know *how* it happens and are hooked by knowing that this play is going to be about feuds, love and death. So the spoilers actually entice us to watch – we want to go on the journey to find out how this all happens, who is to blame and whether it could have been avoided. Once the play starts, Shakespeare will follow a strictly chronological structure but, of course, other writers who may start with the end may opt to follow a non-linear structure.

Plot structure and endings in literary works

Aristotle in his *Poetics* (335BCE) deconstructed the structure of tragedy, arguing that there were basically two parts to a tragedy: the complication and the unravelling. The complication is when the problem is revealed and the unravelling is when the problem is resolved. There are two turning-points in Aristotle's definition: the reversal when there is a change of fortune; and the revelation when the protagonist finally comprehends the truth and has his or her eyes opened, even though it may be too late to avert the tragedy. In the nineteenth century, German writer and critic, Gustav Freytag, wrote *Die Technik des Dramas* (1863) in which he argued a slightly different approach. The following diagram is a simplified version of Freytag's Pyramid:

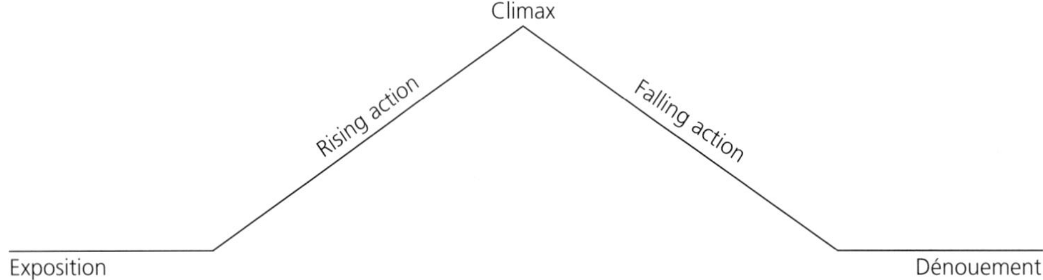

■ **Freytag's Pyramid**

Although Freytag's Pyramid defines a five-act drama, it is also used to explain the structure of other works of literature. This pyramidal approach argues that a text's structure includes the following plot developments:

- **Exposition:** the opening where characters, place and time are introduced.
- **Rising action:** following an inciting incident which disrupts the harmonious opening, a series of events follows in which the action rises to a crescendo.
- **Climax:** the crescendo. The climax is the turning point from which there is no return. If the play is a comedy, a turning point which promises a change for the better will ensue; if the play is a tragedy, a turning point which promises a change for the worse will ensue.

- **Falling action:** this is the opposite of rising action. The relationship between the protagonist and antagonist is likely to unravel, events leading to the protagonist's change either for the better (comedy) or the worse (tragedy) until a final resolution which can be positive or negative is arrived at.
- **Dénouement:** following the resolution – which can be happy (through the protagonist's marriage, for example) or sad (through the protagonist's death, for example) – a sense of normality is returned to and characters (and the audience) can return to their everyday lives knowing order has been restored.

Many works of literature follow a structure similar to this. Let's focus on *Death and the King's Horseman*, a play written by Nigerian playwright Wole Soyinka, which you will be studying in more detail in Chapter 2.5. Let's plot the play using Freytag's Pyramid:

■ Table 1.5.1 Plot structure of *Death and the King's Horseman*

Exposition Act 1	We are introduced to Elesin, the King's Horseman, and his constant companion, the praise-singer. We discover that this is Elesin's last evening on earth as he has to commit a ritual suicide, following the death of his King. He plans to spend his last night enjoying himself among the women in the marketplace: dancing, singing, being dressed in fine clothes and marrying a young woman he has just met. Iyaloja, the 'Mother' of the market arranges his wedding even though she has misgivings. However, tradition is upheld and celebrated.
Rising action Acts 2–3	Simon Pilkings, the local District Officer, and his wife, Jane, discover what Elesin is about to do. Thinking it barbaric, particularly at a time when the prince from England is visiting, Pilkings sends local policemen to arrest Elesin in order to prevent his suicide. This then represents an affront to local tradition by the colonisers. To make this clear, the local police are mocked and harassed by the women in the market and accused of working for the English. They eventually leave without Elesin. When Elesin emerges from being with his new bride, he starts dancing in a trance towards his death.
Climax Act 4	Later that evening, Simon Pilkings is entertaining the Prince at a ball when he is told Elesin is about to commit suicide. He leaves to prevent the suicide. Elesin's son, Olunde, who has returned from England where he has pursued a Western education, calmly listens to the drums that denote his father's suicide and explains to Pilkings' wife why his father's suicide is honorable. When Pilkings returns, Olunde explains to Pilkings why it would have been a tragedy had Pilkings prevented his father's death. At that moment Elesin arrives on stage, handcuffed. When he sees his son, he falls to his feet knowing he has disgraced the family and the community. Olunde insults his father and walks off stage.
Falling action Act 5	Although the Pilkings feel they have averted a barbaric act from taking place, they cannot understand why there is so much anger throughout the local community. Initially Elesin blames his new wife for reminding him that there are pleasures still to enjoy on earth, however, Iyaloja, the 'Mother' of the market who arranged his marriage, berates him for failing to fulfil his duty as the king's horseman and bringing dishonour to himself and to the rest of the world.
Dénouement Act 5	The women of the market arrive at Elesin's cell, carrying something covered on their shoulders. They tell Elesin that, to right the wrong, someone else has fulfilled his duty to appease the king: his son, Olunde, has killed himself. Elesin, in shame and horror, strangles himself with his chains. The play ends with Iyaloja telling Elesin's new bride to think about her unborn child. The death of the protagonist, Elesin, is his punishment for not fufilling his duty. The death of his son, Olunde, attempts to undo the disaster Elesin has brought upon the family and the world as a consequence of his inaction. Although it is unclear whether the death of Olunde will avert disaster, we are reminded of the next generation – symbolizing hope, perhaps, in being able to put right the wrongs of the current generation.

Here are the final words of the play, spoken by the 'Mother' of the market, Iyaloja:

> IYALOJA: Now forget the dead, forget even the living. Turn your mind only to the unborn.
>
> *She goes off, accompanied by the Bride. The dirge rises in volume and the Women continue their sway. Lights fade to a blackout.*
>
> *(Wole Soyinka 84)*

These final words are given to the 'Mother' of the market and her final words are about 'the unborn'. This suggests that focusing on the future – the next generation – is essential. Audiences can interpret this as being hopeful; the next generation can put right the wrongs of the current generation and bring peace to the world. Although the play is about the 'King's horseman', the final words are given to the matriarch of the community, and the final stage directions explicitly mention the 'Bride' and the 'Women'. This suggests that women are a powerful force even when men may disgrace themselves and the community. After a play concerned with 'Death', the focus of the ending on new life and 'the unborn' is positive, which brings a resolution – a dénouement – to this tragedy. Audiences can leave the theatre in the knowledge that, even though tragedy has not been averted, the future is hopeful.

Wole Soyinka

Wole Soyinka, born in 1934, is a Nigerian poet, playwright and essayist and the first black African to win the Nobel Prize for Literature, doing so in 1986. He was born into a Yoruba family and spent time studying in the UK before working with the Royal Court theatre in London. He had strong political views and encouraged Nigeria's eventual independence from Great Britain. He frequently writes about the misuse of power and particularly his disregard for authoritarian rule in Africa. In 1967, during the Nigerian civil war, he was arrested and put into solitary confinement for two years. Decades later, in the 1990s, a price was put on his head and he was forced to escape Nigeria on a motorcycle. He is now welcomed back there and has also taught in a series of American, British and African universities.

However, literature is creative and creativity cannot be contained! This makes it difficult to apply a single rule to all works of literature. Let's have a look at a play that precedes Soyinka's play by almost two thousand years – Euripides' tragedy, *Medea* (431BCE).

Medea is based on the Greek mythological character, Medea, whose grandfather was Helios, the Sun god and father was King Aeëtes of Colchis. When Jason arrived at Colchis in his quest to find the Golden Fleece, Medea fell in love with him, helped him achieve each of her father's tasks through her magical powers and eloped with him back to Greece. The play starts in Corinth, Medea and Jason have been married for a number of years and they have two sons. However, as Medea's old nurse explains to us at the beginning of the play, Jason has recently 'betrayed his own sons and my mistress' (Euripides, 3) by marrying the King of Corinth's daughter. Medea is inconsolable and plans how to take revenge. This is an overview of how *Medea* fits into the first four elements of Freytag's Pyramid:

■ Table 1.5.2 Plot structure of *Medea*

Exposition Prologue, first episode and first choral ode	Through Medea's nurse, we are told about Medea and Jason's past, and the present situation Medea finds herself in. We meet Medea's children, Medea and the Chorus of women who sympathize with Medea for being betrayed by her husband and support her plans to take revenge, arguing how: *'We women shall have honour,* *And ugly slander hold us down no more.'* (Euripides, p29)
Rising action Second–fifth episodes	We meet Jason who reproaches Medea for the way she is behaving and her threats to his new wife. Medea then meets Aegeus, the King of Athens, who promises her she can live in Athens freely whenever she so chooses. With this promise in hand, Medea then reveals her plans to the Chorus: she plans to use her children in a 'plot to kill the princess' (p55) – and once the princess has been killed, she will commit 'the most unholy crime, the murder of my dearest sons' (p57). Medea will then have taken revenge on Jason, reasoning: *'He will never see alive again the sons* *He had by me; nor will he father children* *With his new bride'* (p57) and no-one, she argues, will ever be able to think her weak. The Chorus are shocked by Medea's plans and in a direct address to her, use emotive language to try to dissuade her from taking this action:

	'We beseech you, at your knees, *Entreat and plead with you:* *Do not kill your children.'* (p61) The Fourth and Fifth episodes see Medea being impervious to the Chorus' pleas, and putting her plan into action.
Climax Sixth episode and fifth choral ode	We hear through a messenger's monologue that the princess and her father have suffered a long and painful death. The princess' death is described as follows: *'… Blood dripped from her head in flaming drops:* *Her flesh, torn by the poison's hidden jaws,* *Melted from her bones like resin tears.* *It was a gruesome sight.'* (p83) The King's death is described: *'… as ivy clings to laurel stems,* *So he stuck to the fine-spun dress.* *A dreadful wrestling match began.* *He tried to lift his knee, she pulled him down.* *When he used force, he tore his old flesh* *Off his bones …'* (p85) Even by today's standards, these are gruesome descriptions of the princess' and her father's deaths. We then hear Medea's sons' screams off stage as Medea murders the children off-stage.
Falling action Exodus	Jason attempts to save the boys but is too late.
Dénouement …	A chariot is sent by the Sun that saves Medea and she flies off to Athens, unpunished for the murders of the princess, Creon and her two sons. Jason is left alone in anguish. This is problematic … there is neither resolution nor dénouement.

Let's now read two extracts from the Exodus – the final part – to this problematic play. The first extract occurs just after Medea has murdered her sons:

JASON: Undo the bolts there, servants! Quickly!
Open up! Let me see the double horror –
The children's bodies and … take my vengeance on her.

MEDEA: Why do you rattle and batter the doors here?
Are you looking for the corpses and me, who did it?
Stop it. If you want me, say what you wish.
You will never lay hands on me again.
This chariot the Sun has given to me,
My father's father, to save me from the hands of enemies.

JASON: Hateful creature! O most detestable of women
To the gods and me and all the human race!
You could bring yourself to put to the sword
The children of your womb. You have taken my sons
And destroyed me. And can you still face the Sun
And this Earth, guilty of the most unholy crime?

(Euripides 93)

The extract above begins with Jason desperate to see his murdered sons and to take vengeance on Medea. His words, 'the double horror' (line 2), highlight the appalling nature of Medea's murder and Medea's response, 'Why do you rattle and batter the doors?' (line 4) seems to be mocking Jason which makes the crime all the worse. We know why Jason wants the doors open – to see his dead children but more than that, to 'take my vengeance on her' (line 3). The next lines of Medea mock him further: 'You will never lay hands on me again. / This chariot the Sun has given to me, / My father's father, to save me from the hands of enemies.' (lines 7–9) This is the moment we realize Medea will not be punished: she is out of reach of her husband and out of reach of us, the audience, who may be feeling similar to Jason at this point! She is in a chariot above the stage. Throughout literature, we often have characters who stand above others to denote their power and this is a good example of how Euripides uses **proxemics** – positions on stage – to denote who is victorious and who is not. The fact that the Sun god has sent her a chariot also empowers her and makes it clear she is out of any mortal's reach and will evade punishment for her crimes. We call this kind of ending whereby a problem that appears unsolvable is suddenly solved in an unlikely way, **deus ex machina** (translated as 'god from the machine'). This device was popular in ancient Greek drama and used by playwrights including Aeschylus and Sophocles as well as Euripides. We can see Euripides using it clearly in the extract above. Its purpose is to save Medea from certain punishment after she has committed four murders, including regicide and infanticide, by having her fly away in the Sun's chariot. Of course, not only does she evade punishment, but we feel she is being rewarded for her crimes. She has been rescued by the Sun god and she has secured herself a free life in Athens, the centre of civilization at this time. Jason's question at the end of this extract may reflect how many in the audience – ancient and modern – perhaps respond to this unexpected plot twist.

The second extract is how Euripides ends his play.

JASON: Zeus, do you hear how I am driven off,
How treated by this loathsome murderer
Of children, this savage lioness?
As long as I have opportunity and strength,
I will lament and call the Gods to witness
That you killed my children and refuse
To let me touch or bury them.
I wish I had never had children and lived
To see them destroyed by you.

CHORUS: Many are the destinies that Zeus in Olympus ordains,
Many things the Gods bring to unexpected ends.
What seemed likely does not come to pass
And, for the unlikely, God finds a way.
So ended this story.

(Euripides 101)

Here we see Jason alone on stage just with the Chorus as company. His final speech is an emotional appeal to first Zeus and then the Gods, one of whom has quite clearly sided with Medea. It is Jason, not Medea, who has the final words before the Chorus and his final lines are increasingly desperate, futile and anguished. Jason's metaphorical language, referring to Medea as a 'savage lioness' (line 3), accentuates the ferocity and ruthlessness of Medea's actions and most audiences – again, both ancient and modern – are likely to sympathize with his plight and wonder how to make sense of an ending that seems to condone so much violence, particularly the cold-blooded murder of one's own sons. We feel at this point that Jason's punishment has outweighed his crime and for many in the audience, the **pathos** initially felt for Medea is now transferred to her husband, Jason.

The final words by the Chorus seem to echo what the audience is thinking – the **repetition** of 'unexpected' (line 11) and 'unlikely' (line 13) suggest that this is not an ending we could have predicted, blaming the Gods for ending the story in such a way.

As we know, readers have different interpretations to texts depending on their own context; however, this particular ending – saving a mother who has just killed her two innocent sons – is difficult to interpret in terms of restoring order and regaining harmony. Most audiences would be in agreement that it is not a harmonious ending, order is not restored and there is no clear resolution that allows us to make sense of what we have just watched. Perhaps, as some scholars have argued, Medea's rescue represents Euripides' sympathy for women who had little freedom or power in this male-dominated society. Perhaps her rescue is a warning to the ancient Greeks that if women are not treated as equals or with respect, then the oppressed woman will be within her rights to take revenge, however bloody that revenge may be. However, even if we feel this is an early feminist play, few audiences – ancient or modern – condone infanticide and this makes it a problematic ending. The way Euripides has structured his play, then, affects the way we respond and it is likely that our responses today would be similar to Euripides' audiences' responses in 431BCE, such is the universal and timeless condemnation we have regarding infanticide.

CONCEPT CONNECTION

PERSPECTIVE

Medea offers a multiplicity of perspectives which may, or may not, reflect the views of Euripides. At times we sympathize with the protagonist, Medea; at times we sympathize with the princess, King of Creon and the two young children; and at times we sympathize with the antagonist, Jason. Like the Chorus, initially we feel outraged by how Medea has been betrayed, but later we feel horrified by Medea's vengeance. The ending is problematic and we are unsure how to interpret the play that appears to have the perspective that vengeance at any cost is permissible and will be rewarded. Although we may interpret the play taking a feminist perspective this, also, fills us with unease because of the brutal murders committed by the female protagonist. Although the play was written over 2,000 years ago, infanticide, especially filicide, is a taboo subject that we feel shocks us now in the same way it would have shocked Euripides' audiences. By the end of the play, we are unsure what Euripides' perspective is and whether he wants us to finally pity Jason or feel relieved that Medea has escaped punishment.

We wonder how far the contexts of production and reception influenced and shaped the perspectives within *Medea*, or whether they transcend historical and cultural contexts because of the universal and timeless perspective that states infanticide/filicide is wrong.

You may also like to think about this concept with regards to Soyinka's *Death and the King's Horseman*. In this play there are alternative perspectives, too: the local community, symbolized by the Praise-singer, Iyaloja and the other women in the market who uphold and celebrate the tradition of ritual suicide following the death of their king versus the colonial perspective, symbolized by the Pilkings', who abhor suicide and attempt to prevent it from happening despite it being such an important part of the local cultural tradition. Interestingly, Olunde, Elesin's son, who has been educated in the Western tradition returns home when his king dies, in order to honour and support his father's duty as the king's horseman which dictates he accompany the king in the afterlife.

Exploring the different perspectives of a text read in class is a useful way to interpret a text's meaning and to engage personally with a text as you reflect on your own perspective towards a given subject that is explored within the text.

Euripides

Euripides was an Ancient Greek playwright, famous for his tragedies, including *Medea, Electra* and *Bacchae.* He is well known for sympathizing with those who are usually sidelined, including women such as Medea who takes revenge on her husband by murdering her young sons. His characters resembled everyday Athenians rather than mythical heroes, which was a departure from his contemporaries. He is only one of three Ancient Greek tragedians whose plays have survived: the other two being Aeschylus and Sophocles. His plays won the famous Athenian dramatic festival five times.

Another playwright who defies Freytag's Pyramid in the way he structures his plays is Irish playwright, Samuel Beckett. Beckett is associated with the 'Theatre of the Absurd' – a phrase coined by Martin Esslin in his 1962 book, *Theatre of the Absurd:*

> *'The Theatre of the Absurd strives to express its sense of the senselessness of the human condition and the inadequacy of the rational approach by the open abandonment of rational devices and discursive thought.'*
>
> *(Martin Esslin 5)*

This idea of 'the Absurd' is a philosophical idea that argues although it is the human condition to find meaning and value in existence, in actuality there is no meaning or value in existence. Existence simply *is* rather than having a purpose. This contradiction in what we are conditioned to do versus our inability to find any purpose because there is no purpose is what philosophers term 'the Absurd'. Many twentieth-century European writers including Jean-Paul Sartre, Albert Camus, Eugène Ionesco, Jean Genet and Samuel Beckett explored this idea through many of their writings.

Before reading any Beckett, knowing his plays have been categorized as examples of 'Theatre of the Absurd', may make you predict that it is highly unlikely Beckett is going to structure his plays with a dénouement whereby order and harmony are restored. The 'senselessness of the human condition' and the meaninglessness of existence would appear to preclude this kind of an ending! And you would be right. Beckett's most famous play, *Waiting for Godot* (1953), is a typical example of 'Theatre of the Absurd' and a play that Esslin explores in depth in *Theatre of the Absurd.* In Beckett's play, there are two main characters, Vladimir and Estragon, and they are 'waiting for Godot'. The play is in two acts and each act follows a similar structure.

Let's look at the way Beckett structures the endings of each act and explore what this suggests about the text's meaning. Read the following extracts – the first is the ending of Act 1, the second is the ending of Act 2. Just prior to each of these extracts – so towards the end of Act 1 and towards the end of Act 2 – a boy arrives to say that Godot will not be arriving today.

VLADIMIR: We can still part, if you think it would be better.
ESTRAGON: It's not worthwhile now. *Silence.*
VLADIMIR: No, it's not worthwhile now. *Silence.*
ESTRAGON: Well, shall we go?
VLADIMIR: Yes, let's go.
They do not move.

(Waiting for Godot, *end of Act 1 47)*

ESTRAGON: Well? Shall we go?
VLADIMIR: Pull on your trousers.
ESTRAGON: What?
VLADIMIR: Pull on your trousers.
ESTRAGON: You want me to pull off my trousers?
VLADIMIR: Pull ON your trousers.
ESTRAGON: *(realizing his trousers are down).* True. He pulls up his trousers.
VLADIMIR: Well? Shall we go?
ESTRAGON: Yes, let's go.
They do not move.

(Waiting for Godot, *end of Act 287)*

You may have felt that both endings were quite similar – it is the same two characters on stage, their dialogue is stark and unemotional and there is a lack of action. The ending of Act 1 is punctuated with the stage direction '*Silence*' (lines 2 and 3), which makes this ending all the more expressionless. Negative language is repeated when first Vladimir and then Estragon states 'it's not worthwhile now' (lines 2 and 3) and this creates a sense of futility, suggesting the present time ('now') is infused with nothingness. Although the final words by Vladimir may appear to contradict this idea as he makes a positive statement, 'Yes, let's go' (line 5), the final stage directions '*They do not move*' (line 6) cancels out any positivity we may have felt following the final words of the act. When the curtain falls at the end of Act 1, there is a sense of hopelessness and pointlessness – in line with the philosophical ideas associated with the Absurd.

Beckett has structured the end of Act 2 similarly. At the beginning of the second extract, the two characters are initially talking about Estragon's trousers. Estragon repeatedly uses the interrogative tone as he attempts to make sense of Vladimir's instructions. However, the fact that Vladimir's instruction is so simple and obvious makes it appear ridiculous that Estragon is unable to comprehend what Vladimir is saying. Eventually, when he does make sense of the instruction and accordingly pulls up his trousers, they are (in theory) able to leave. However, they do not leave which then makes a mockery of Estragon's attempts to make sense of Vladimir's instructions. Was there any purpose in Estragon struggling to comprehend Vladimir's question and then pulling up his trousers? The answer is supposed to be no! This ties in with the 'absurdity' of existence – there is no purpose or meaning. This scene, then, is one of many examples from this play that supports Esslin's argument that Beckett's plays can be categorized as being 'Theatre of the Absurd'.

The final two lines of Act 2 are exactly the same as the final two lines of Act 1: 'Well, shall we go?' 'Yes, let's go' but the speakers differ. In Act 1, Estragon asks the question and Vladimir responds affirmatively; in Act 2, Vladimir asks the question and Estragon responds affirmatively. This seems to suggest that there is little that distinguishes us; individual identity is something else perhaps that is meaningless. The affirmative, 'Yes, let's go' (line 9) is again contradicted at the end of Act 2 with the stage direction '*They do not move*' (line 10). This ending parallels the ending of Act 1 and suggests that there is actually nothing worthwhile to move for – so therefore doing nothing is the best – or only – way to exist. We can also see how Beckett uses a **circular structure** in this play which accentuates how nothing has changed and each day is a **repetition** of the day before and so on *ad infinitum*. The fact that they are still 'waiting for Godot' and are likely to be 'waiting for Godot' for eternity, if he even exists, highlights this idea, too. By the end of Act 2, the audience assumes that Godot will never appear and yet Estragon and Vladimir continue waiting.

Their waiting is the only purpose they have in their life but it is a monotonous and purposeless purpose because Godot will never arrive! This, then, is the Absurd: our lives are absurd as we constantly attempt to find purpose in something that has no purpose.

Beckett's structure, then, imitates the text's meaning: that existence is meaningless or, as Esslin would argue, it reflects a 'sense of the senselessness of the human condition'. Like Euripides' play, Beckett's play does not end with resolution or order restored and there is no dénouement. For many, this is a bleak view of human existence and contrasts with the more hopeful ending we explored in Soyinka's *Death and the King's Horseman* where there was dénouement.

Samuel Beckett

Samuel Barclay Beckett was born in Ireland but lived most of his adult life in Paris, France. He wrote essays, novels, short stories and poems as well as tragicomic plays that explore the absurdity of human existence. Later in his life he became a theatre director, directing his own plays on stage. He won the Nobel Prize for Literature in 1969 for writing novels and drama that depicted 'the destitution of modern man' (The Nobel Prize in Literature 1969). He was a linguist and wrote in both English and French. He translated his works, including his most famous play, *Waiting for Godot*, which was originally written in French as *En attendant Godot*. He was a close friend of fellow Irish writer, James Joyce, who also lived in Paris. In his biography of Beckett, Knowlson argued that whereas Joyce focused on man as 'knowing more' in his literary works, Beckett focused on man as a 'non-knower' and a 'non-can-er' (Knowlson 352). Beckett has been cited as being a major influence on a number of twentieth-century playwrights, poets and novelists.

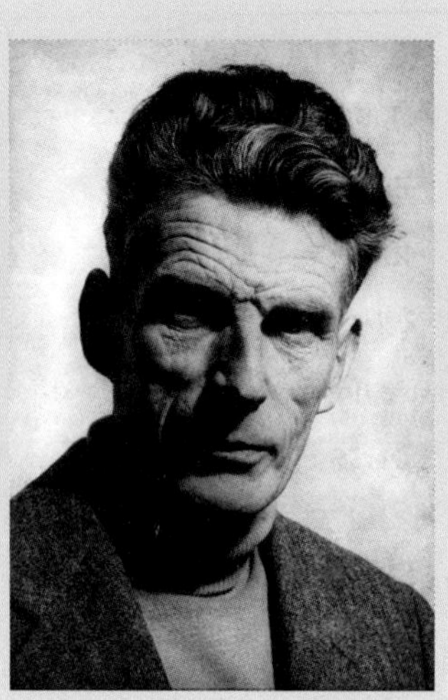

TOK Links Knowledge that is philosophical

Beckett's play *Waiting for Godot* is a fictional play grappling with a philosophical idea, the Absurd. In what ways is the kind of knowledge we gain from the study of language and literature different from the kind we gain through the study of other disciplines, such as philosophy? Can the study of language and of literature be considered philosophical?

EE link: English A – Literature category 2

Whilst Euripides' *Medea* is obviously a work in translation, Beckett's play is not quite so easy to categorise. It was originally written in French as *En attendant Godot* but Beckett himself translated it into English as *Waiting for Godot*. You could, therefore, use this play as either a work in translation or as a work written in English. English A: Literature category 2 extended essays are comparative essays in which you compare a work originally written in a language other than English with a work originally written in English. You could compare *Medea* with *Waiting for Godot* although you would need to make it quite clear that the Beckett version you were using was the English version. A possible research question could be:

How do Euripides and Beckett use unconventional structures to shape meaning in their plays, *Medea* and *Waiting for Godot*?

Alternatively, you could compare a play that follows a more conventional structure with a play that does not – a possible research question could be: **What is the effect of using a conventional structure in Soyinka's *Death and the King's Horseman* and an unconventional structure in Euripides' *Medea* [or Beckett's *En attendant Godot*]?**

In order to respond to either of these questions, you may like to research Freytag's Pyramid and explain how this is a more conventional structure that many playwrights have traditionally followed.

ACTIVITY 1

Choose one of the prose fiction or drama works you are studying in class and complete the following table, showing the plot structure of your chosen work using Freytag's Pyramid. In the left hand column, add where we see this part of the structure occurring in your chosen work and in the right hand column summarise the plot outline, similar to the charts completed on *Death and the King's Horseman* and *Medea*.

Although there is no commentary at the back of the book for this activity, you may like to ask a friend in your class to attempt this activity on the same text you are exploring and then compare ideas with one another.

Copy and complete this table on your chosen prose fiction or drama text.

■ Table 1.5.3

Exposition	
Rising action	
Climax	
Falling action	
Dénouement	

Structure of non-literary texts

Chronological structure of non-literary text types

Just as literary works can follow a chronological or a non-linear structure, so can non-literary texts. Many writers of non-literary texts opt to use a chronological structure to make the text's purpose clearer. Essays, reports, instructions, recipes, diaries and memoirs are some examples of text types that often use this type of structure. A chronological structure works well for writers who are attempting to argue a certain position, as it makes their argument appear more logical and well thought-out. Similarly, texts that aim to instruct are likely to use this structure to make the instructions easier for readers to follow; writers of memoirs may also use this kind of a structure so readers are better able to understand the cause and effect of certain pivotal moments that have influenced the writer's life in some way. Text types we have already explored that use a step-by-step chronological structure include *The Encyclopedia Britannica* entry (Chapter 1.1) and Robin Ha's 'Green Onion Kimchi' recipe (Chapter 1.4). As seen with Mrs Beeton's and Sun Tzu's advisory texts (Chapter 1.4), some non-literary writers who may not necessarily follow a chronological narrative, use numbers to imply a linear structure in order to give their writing an order that readers can follow.

Let us look at the following non-literary text, a sports review of a boxing match between John L Sullivan, the Boston champion, and Paddy Ryan, his Irish opponent. This report was published on the front page of *The Indianapolis Leader* on Saturday 11 February 1882. As you read the review, take particular note of the strictly chronological structure the writer uses throughout.

SENSITIVE CONTENT

Caution: the extract below includes violent content.

We have included this extract from a boxing match report in order to engage with the structure of a typical sports newspaper report, but we do not condone violence in any form. The IB recommends that your studies in Language A: Language and Literature should challenge you intellectually, personally and culturally, and expose you to sensitive and mature topics. We invite you to reflect critically on various perspectives offered while bearing in mind the IB's commitment to international-mindedness and intercultural respect.

PADDY POUNDED

The Sullivan-Ryan Fight at Mississippi City.

The Troy Giant Knocked Out of Time in Twenty-Six Minutes.

SULLIVAN WINS.

Boston Pugilist Knocks Ryan Out of Time in Nine Rounds, Fought in Twenty-six Minutes.

MISSISSIPPI CITY, Feb. 7. – Trains run from New Orleans with people to witness the fight between Ryan and Sullivan arrived here about 11 o'clock. The crowd consisted of sporting men from all sections of the country and many prominent citizens of New Orleans. A large number of newspaper correspondents, representing prominent papers of the North and West, were also in attendance. Sullivan arrived on the ground at 10:30, and took a room at the hotel opposite Ryan's, within 100 feet of the ring, which was pitched in front of the Barnes Hotel, in a grove of live oaks. Sullivan cast his cap into the ring at 11:45 by the Judges' time, amidst great enthusiasm. [...]

Ryan entered the ring at 11:55 amid enthusiastic cheers ... The men were ready to commence business. [...]

THE FIGHT.

At exactly 11:58 the men toed the scratch and shook hands for the first round. Both men sparred cautiously for the opening. Ryan led with his right, which fell short, catching in return a hot one from Sullivan's left in the face. The changes then became short and quick. Sullivan finally knocked him down with a severe right-hander on the cheek. Time, 30 seconds.

Second round – Sullivan at once rushed to his man and let go his left, which caught Ryan on the jaw. Ryan closed with him and they wrestled for the fall, which Ryan won, falling heavily on his opponent. Time, 25 seconds.

Third round – The men came together with a rush, and Sullivan after making three passes, knocked Ryan down with a terrible right-hander on the chest. Time, 4 seconds.

Fourth round – The men sparred for perhaps a second or two; both feinted, and then Sullivan went for Ryan's face, putting in stinging blows on his head before they closed. The slugging then commenced and continued until Ryan was forced onto the ropes, where he went to grass. Time of round, 20 seconds.

Fifth round – This was a repetition of the above round, both men closing and putting in their best licks, the attack of both being confined to the face. Ryan succeeded in bringing Sullivan to his knees at the close.

Sixth round – Sullivan came up smiling, but it was evident Ryan was not only suffering, but was somewhat afraid of his antagonist. Sullivan lost no time, but went in to win. Ryan, however, closed and downed him.

Seventh round – This round was a short one, and the men closed. The slugging continued for a few seconds, when Ryan went to the grass a wreck. Sullivan came to his corner smiling. Ryan, however, had grit to come up for another round.

Eighth round – The men, on call of time, came up promptly. Ryan was decidedly weak, but made a gallant struggle. Sullivan fought him all over the ring and into the umpire's corner and over the ropes. Getting off ropes he rallied, but went down on a knee and hand. A foul was looked for, but, though Sullivan had his hand raised to strike, he restrained himself as Ryan rose. Both men were returning to their corner, when the seconds of each cried, 'Go for him,' and, the men responding, came together. They closed and clinched, and, after a short struggle, both men went down.

Ninth and last round – Ryan came up groggy, and Sullivan at once forced him into his corner, delivering one heavy blow, but Ryan recovered and drove Sullivan out, and just beyond the middle of the ring Sullivan got in a right-hander under the left ear, and Ryan went down senseless. When time was called Ryan did not respond, and the fight was declared in favor of Sullivan amid great cheering. Time, 26 minutes.

AFTER THE BATTLE.

Ryan and Sullivan were visited after they had gone to their quarters. Ryan was lying in an exhausted condition on his bed, badly disfigured about his face, his upper lip being cut through and his nose disfigured. He did not move, but lay panting … At the conclusion of the fight Sullivan ran to his quarters at a lively gait, and, laughing, he lay down for a while, a little out of wind, but there was not a scratch on him. He chatted pleasantly with his friends. […]

WHY RYAN LOST THE FIGHT.

Immediately after the fight Ryan was visited in his quarters by a well-known physician with the intention of giving him medical assistance if any was needed … After an examination the doctor stated that Ryan was suffering from hernia, and must have been in great pain during the fight. He advised him to forsake the ring. Ryan stated he intended giving up pugilism as he did not think he was suited by nature for that kind of business. He said he considered Sullivan a born prize fighter, and a very formidable opponent in the ring. […]

SULLIVAN'S FIGHTING QUALITIES.

The result was in accordance with the expectations of many keen observers of the two men. They relied upon Sullivan's wonderful hitting powers and remarkable skill as a two-handed fighter to win him the battle.

('Paddy Pounded')

Being a non-literary text, let's first of all identify the text's GAP:

Genre	Newspaper report of a boxing match
Audience	People with an interest in sports, particularly boxing
Purpose	To inform

Now let's focus on how this sports report has been structured and how it achieves its purpose.

The article is **foregrounded** with a headline, 'Paddy Pounded', which uses **emotive language** ('pounded') and **alliteration** to hook the reader. The **plosive** repeated 'p' and 'd' sounds imitate the sound of boxing, in line with the subject of this report. The next three subheadings give us more information about who fought ('Sullivan-Ryan'), what happened ('Sullivan Wins'), where ('Mississippi City'), and how it happened ('The Troy Giant Knocked Out of Time in Twenty-Six Minutes') – the key points readers want to know. Newspaper articles generally follow an inverted pyramid structure, as illustrated below, and it is interesting that many of the '5 W's' are contained in the report's subheadings, as well as in the lead paragraph:

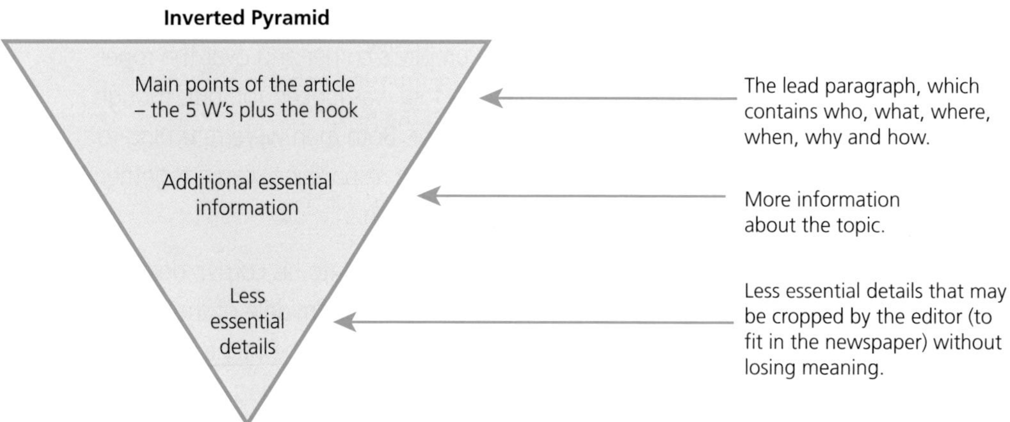

The lead paragraph is one sentence only and reaffirms these main points. The subject of this sentence is 'The Boston Pugilist', which immediately gives him more significance and accentuates how he was the champion of this fight. The title that he is given also empowers him – rather than using his everyday name, he is elevated to a national heroic status in contrast to the very ordinary 'Ryan'. The fact that the report is foregrounded with this vocative also suggests that the readers are aware of who this title belongs to and that Sullivan's reputation and celebrity status goes before him. This appeals to the fascination we have with celebrities and is another way readers are hooked to read on.

A sense of anticipation is created in the next paragraph by describing the build-up to the fight, before describing the fight itself. It is clear this was an important fight as 'sporting men from all sections of the country and many prominent citizens of New Orleans' attended. Quite clearly, people have travelled long distances in order to watch the fight. Moreover, because 'sporting men' are amongst those who have made the long journey suggests this particular sporting event is something extra special – a fight, perhaps, between two equally matched and highly-skilled boxers. In addition, there are many newspapers from the 'North and West' in attendance which also suggests this is a sporting event that is newsworthy and of interest to many readers in many parts of the country. Before the fight has started, then, a great sense of occasion is alluded to which also acts as a hook, arouses the readers' curiosity, and encourages them to read on to find out more about the fight. Many readers reading this report would not have watched the fight first-hand, however, including details such as where each fighter was staying, the times each fighter arrived in the ring and the crowd reaction to each fighter's arrival helps transport the reader to the ring-side, waiting for the fight to begin. Atmosphere has been created before the fight has even begun.

The report uses headings to introduce each new section, and the first heading is 'The Fight.' This is a clear structural device that divides each part of the report into separate sections and is a clear indicator to the reader what the main topic of each section is. After the preliminary paragraphs of setting the scene and creating a mood of anticipation, now the fight itself is described. Again, precise details are included that make the writer appear credible and trustworthy – if he knows, for example, what time the fight began ('at exactly 11:58') – then this is surely a first-hand account of what happened. In this section, boxing **jargon** is included such as 'toed the scratch', 'sparred', 'right-hander', 'slugging', 'best licks', etc. which also gives the report a sense of authenticity. The first paragraph in this section begins at the precise moment the fight begins, with the men shaking each other's hands and then describing how they 'sparred cautiously for the opening'. Structurally, the writer is taking a **chronological** approach, being sure not to miss out any minute details, so readers can follow the fight as it happened and picture themselves at the ringside. The writer's sentence constructions also imitate the fight. The longer, complex sentence describes a series of moves: 'Ryan led with his right, which fell short, catching in return a hot one from

Sullivan's left in the face.' This describes a spar between the two men and the structure imitates both men's moves. This is then followed by a simple sentence which speeds up the pace: 'The changes then became short and quick.' The two **adjectives**, 'short and quick', are **monosyllabic** and help imitate the speed of each man's punches. The end of this paragraph includes more precise information: 'Time, 30 seconds.'

The next paragraph opens with 'Second round –' and from now until the final paragraph in this section, each paragraph will begin similarly: 'Third round –', 'Fourth round –' and so on until 'Ninth and last round –'. These discourse markers make it quite clear the writer is following a strictly chronological structure which makes it easy for the reader to follow and helps build up tension as we are waiting for the moment that Sullivan finally achieves victory. Many of the sections also end with how long the round took: 'Time, 25 seconds.', 'Time, 4 seconds.', 'Time, 20 seconds' and so forth. Note how the length of each paragraph is moreorless in line with how long the round lasted. For example, the 30-second round is a considerably longer paragraph than the 4-second round. This is another structural device the author has used that gives us an insight into the fight and helps us imagine we are there.

Not only does the writer take us on the journey of the fight, round for round in the order it happened, but the writer also gives us an indication of the qualities of each man. Sullivan, for example, is described as having a 'severe right-hander', a 'terrible right-hander' who puts in 'stinging blows' and delivers 'one heavy blow' before he 'got in a right-hander under the left ear'. His skill and strength as a boxer is referred to throughout the article and he is even described as 'smiling' at the end of some of the rounds, suggesting Ryan's blows are having no impact on him. In contrast, Ryan is described as being 'knocked … down', 'forced onto the ropes', 'afraid of his antagonist', 'decidedly weak' until he 'went down senseless.' Despite his relative weakness when compared to Sullivan's strength, Ryan is described in a number of paragraphs as having 'grit to come up for another round' and making a 'gallant struggle.' Respect is shown to Ryan and this helps the reader empathize with him and respond emotionally to the sports report.

After 'The Fight' section, which has followed a strictly chronological structure, we move on to 'After the Battle'. The metaphorical language here elevates the boxing match to an epic war and we are now given an insight into what happens now the fight has been fought and won. We first see Ryan who is 'in an exhausted condition on his bed'. His injuries are described in graphic detail – 'badly disfigured about his face, his upper lip being cut through and his nose disfigured' – and the use of **tripling** emphasizes the extent of his injuries whilst the **repetition** of 'disfigured' highlights the gravity of his physical beating. In contrast, Sullivan 'ran to his quarters at a lively gait' and laughs with his friends. Rather than being confined to his bed, he has an excess of energy and, moreover, 'there was not a scratch on him.' We see both sides of the post-battlefield – the injured and suffering contrasted with the victorious.

The penultimate section of the report is 'Why Ryan Lost the Fight.' We are now given an insight into the findings of the 'well-known physician' who visited Ryan after his defeat. It transpires Ryan had a hernia that affected his performance in the ring which, it is inferred, was one of the reasons he lost against Sullivan. We are reminded of his 'grit' and 'gallant struggle' of the earlier paragraphs and he is now elevated in our minds to almost heroic proportions. When he acknowledges that he 'intended giving up pugilism as he did not think he was suited by nature for that kind of business' we agree with his prognosis and have a new-found respect for him. This respect deepens when, rather than using his hernia as an excuse for why he lost, he is full of praise for Sullivan, describing him as 'a born prize fighter and a very formidable opponent in the ring.' Leaving this information until the penultimate paragraph forces us to reevaluate which of the two men was heroic and which one we admire most. Again, a **chronological** structure has been used – although, presumably, Ryan knew about his hernia before the fight, we only discover this fact after the fight, along with everyone else.

However, the final paragraph of this extract ends with 'Sullivan's Fighting Qualities' and just as the report began with 'The Boston Pugilist', it ends with him also. This is appropriate bearing in mind he was the winner. Just as Ryan has described him as being formidable in the ring, the 'many keen observers of the two men' are also in agreement that it was his 'wonderful hitting powers and remarkable skill as a two-handed fighter' that brought him victory. These observations were made after the fight and, again, we can see how a **chronological** structure has been adhered to throughout. The final two sections are interesting: one section is focused on Ryan and the final section is focused on Sullivan. By the end of the report, we are meant to feel both men are worthy of our respect and admiration.

The structure is chronological in terms of the timeline followed and this allows the reader to experience the fight as it is occurring, as well as to get an insight into the aftermath of the fight. We could also argue this loosely follows the structure of Freytag's Pyramid: the **exposition** is introducing the two men to us; the **rising action** is the fight; the **climax** is the knock-out; the **falling action** is the exhaustion and injuries experienced by Ryan compared to Sullivan's energy and lack of injuries post-fight; and the **dénouement** is discovering that actually both men are worthy of our admiration and respect.

Non-linear structure: magazine front covers

There are, however, non-literary text types that do not follow a chronological structure – the infographic (Chapter 1.2) is a typical text type that uses a **non-linear** structure. Magazine front covers and advertisements are other non-literary text types that do not follow a chronological structure. The purpose of a magazine front cover is not necessarily to convey information in an ordered way, but to display information in an appealing way that allows the reader to first identify the magazine and second to buy the magazine. In order to achieve this purpose, a structured approach is taken which is often non-chronological. Before we explore the next extracts, read the following key features box to familiarize yourself with some of the terminology.

KEY FEATURES MAGAZINE FRONT COVERS

- **Masthead** – the name of the magazine (usually at the top of the page).
- **Tagline** – memorable phrase that readers may apply to magazine.
- **Headline** – text that reveals the main article (usually in large font or a different font to stand out).
- **Main image** – a large **visual image**, often a photograph, that promotes the main article in the magazine. Often this will be the central feature of the cover.
- **Subtitle** – text that advertises the other big stories (usually denoted through larger font than the cover lines).
- **Cover lines** – text that reveals the other stories.
- **Pull quote** – a quotation from the main article – words are surrounded with quotations marks.
- **Buzzwords** – words that promise there is even more in the magazine ('plus' and 'exclusive').
- **Strapline** – a narrow strip of text at the bottom of the cover.
- **Puff** – an incentive to buy the magazine, usually put in a different shaped 'box' or 'balloon' to stand out.

We are now going to explore three magazine front covers from a single magazine, UK music magazine, *Q*, to see how a similar structure is applied to help create a particular identity (brand) for the magazine and to encourage the reader to buy the publication. The following three magazine front covers were all published in 2015: January 2015 (Ed Sheeran), May 2015 (Paul McCartney) and September 2015 (Florence and the Machine).

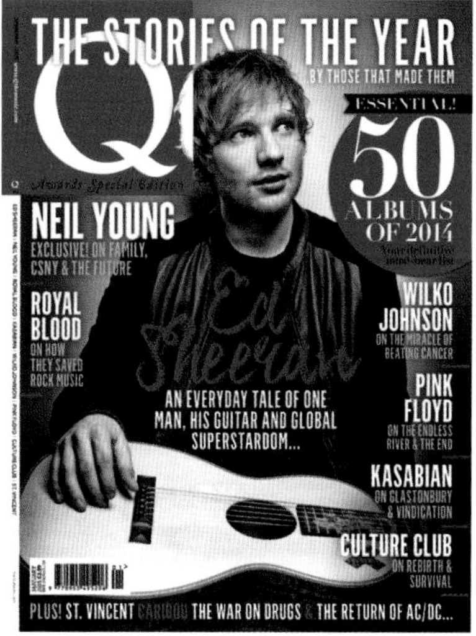

■ 'Ed Sheeran' front cover, January 2015

■ 'Paul' front cover, May 2015

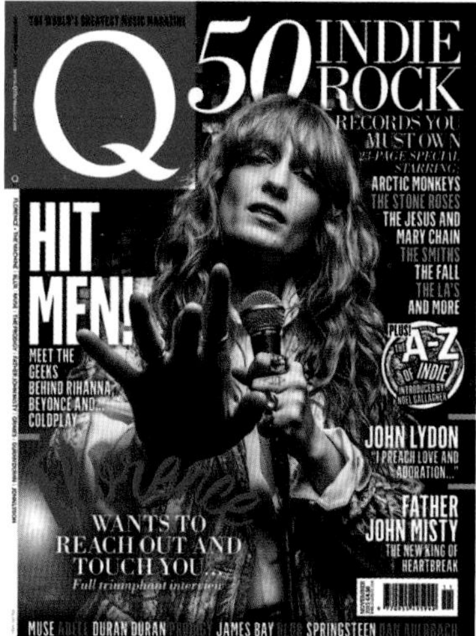

■ 'Florence' front cover, September 2015

Before we start deconstructing the magazine front covers, let's complete our GAP table, step 1 of our non-literary reading strategy:

Genre	Music magazine.
Audience	Music fans who want to stay in touch with current popular music trends. Perhaps older music fans rather than 'cutting-edge' music fans.
Purpose	To entertain, to inform.

You should immediately be able to identify similarities between each of these magazine front covers. Although four months separate each cover and the contents differ, the structure (and style) is remarkably similar, presumably because it is the same magazine with the same intended audience. Here are some of the structural similarities you may already have identified:

- The **masthead** – the title of the magazine, *Q*, is positioned in the same place for each front cover: the top left-hand corner in a large font. Not only do the contrasting colours, white on red (which is part of the magazine's *style*), help the logo to stand out but its positioning also is essential in fulfilling this purpose.
- The May and September editions include *Q's* **tagline**: 'The World's Greatest Music Magazine'. Placing the tagline at the top of *Q's* logo makes it clear this hyperbolic statement refers to *Q* and readers subconsciously make the connection between the magazine and global greatness.
- All three editions include a simple **headline**: the name of the musician who is the lead story in the magazine. In terms of **graphology**, 'Ed Sheeran' and 'Paul' are positioned centrally which highlights the central position these musicians will have in the magazine's pages. Although 'Florence' is positioned towards the bottom left, the fact that this musician's name is written in a stylized script and is the only text in red, similar to the way 'Ed Sheeran' and 'Paul' are written, ensures the name stands out. In terms of **typography**, the cursive script used for the musicians' names is more expressive and creative than using a non-cursive script. This perhaps highlights that each musician is a *real* musician and, by virtue of their profession, is indeed creative. Moreover, we are encouraged to feel each musician has signed

the front cover as if they are giving their fans an autograph – although when we compare the January and September editions, it is quite clear that this is not the case as the same cursive script has been used. By using only the first names 'Paul' and 'Florence' an added layer of intimacy and informality is constructed, suggesting we are on first name terms with these performers, as well as implying that they are so famous that they do not need a surname. Perhaps the designer of the January issue felt that just using the two letter name 'Ed' would not have stood out enough – in the May edition, 'Paul' which is twice as long as 'Ed' has been written using an extra-large typeface to ensure it stands out. This may have been difficult to achieve with a much shorter name, hence using the full name, 'Ed Sheeran'.

- All three editions include a large photographic **image** of the musician who is the magazine's main feature, which takes up the majority of the space on the front cover. Each of the images is placed centrally and each musician is photographed with the tools of his or her trade: both Ed Sheeran and Paul McCartney are holding their signature instrument, the guitar, and Florence, singer from Florence and the Machine, is holding a microphone.
- There is **additional text** below the **headline** which sums up the focus of the main feature article. This gives the reader a quick taste of what the article will be about in the hope that it will act as a hook and entice the reader to want to read more. Here is the additional text for each cover:
    - ☐ January 2015: 'AN EVERYDAY TALE OF ONE / MAN, HIS GUITAR AND GLOBAL / SUPERSTARDOM ...'
    - ☐ May 2015: 'FROM WRITING YESTERDAY ... / ... TO COLLABORATING WITH KANYE / AT HOME WITH A POP GENIUS'
    - ☐ September 2015: 'WANTS TO / REACH OUT AND / TOUCH YOU ...'
- The **headline** and **additional text** are the only words which are placed directly on top of the **image**, partially covering the photographic image. This positioning then encourages the reader to subconsciously connect the headline and additional text with the image. The skill in the graphic designer who put each cover together is that the image that has been chosen reinforces the written text and in this way the text's meaning is accentuated all the more. For example, the additional text for the January edition is 'An everyday tale of one man, his guitar and global superstardom ...' These words are positioned directly on top of an image of 'one man' (Ed Sheeran) and 'his guitar'. The clothes this 'one man' is wearing are ordinary, everyday clothes linking in with the beginning of the additional text, 'an everyday tale'. The **ellipsis** after 'global superstardom ...' suggests how unlikely it is that 'one man' and 'his guitar' could attain 'global superstardom' and this acts as a hook – persuading readers to read the article to discover *how* such an ordinary individual with a guitar has managed to reach such heights of global superstardom.

ACTIVITY 2

Comment on the additional text used in the May and September editions, explaining how its meaning is reinforced by the particular photographic image that has been used.

When you have written your explanations, compare your ideas with the commentaries at the back of the book.

- The **subtitle** which is placed in the left-hand margin is written in a larger text type, but in white and not in cursive so as not to take away from the headlining text that promotes the lead article. It may be, of course, that not all readers are interested in the lead article, so the subtitle is used to reveal that month's other main articles. The subtitle in the January edition reveals that Neil Young will feature, in the May edition it is Muse and in the September edition there is an article on Hit Men.

- Each front cover includes numerous **cover lines** – all printed in white and positioned either side of the main image. The cover lines reveal to readers the other articles that are featured in the magazine and this is effective for a number of reasons. First, the reader can very quickly get an overview of what is inside the magazine, and second, it makes it clear that there are numerous articles – surely there will be at least one article that will appeal to the reader! The numerous cover lines suggest why, perhaps, *Q* has the **tagline** it has!
- The January and September editions both include a **puff** – text in a circular 'balloon' that give the reader an added incentive to buy the magazine. The January edition uses the **buzzword** 'Essential!' to introduce the '50 albums of 2014' in the red circular balloon; and the September edition uses the **buzzword** 'Plus!' to introduce the 'A–Z of Indie' in the yellow circular 'balloon'.

As we can see, a number of similar structural features have been included in these three magazine front covers and, combined, they help fulfil the purpose of reinforcing the unique *Q* identity as well as encouraging their reader base to buy the magazine. Although there are fixed structural conventions that are used by this magazine, a chronological structure is not used. Chronology suggests a step-by-step order and a logical progression from one point or idea to the next. The meaning of a text is dependent upon reading the information in a particular order. The magazine front covers have not been structured in this way. Of course, the main story takes precedent through a large and central photographic image and headline. However, the cover lines are in no particular order; they can be read in any order and the meaning of the text does not change. The reader can decide which order the cover lines are read and that is likely to depend on the reader's own interests rather than an expectation that a particular order is followed. Of course, the magazine front covers also use a similar *style* – including similar colour imagery and types of words, phrases and punctuation – and we will be exploring stylistic features in more detail in the second half of this chapter.

ACTIVITY 3

Collect three to four magazine front covers of the same magazine. Comment on the structural features that have been used and discuss how they create a particular identity for the magazine, how they appeal to a particular reader and how they achieve their purpose. In particular, comment on how the use of visual images and written text work together to reinforce a particular meaning. Use the key features of magazine front covers box in this chapter to focus your commentary.

There is no commentary at the back of the book for this activity.

Style

The style of a literary work or textual non-literary text refers to the **diction** a writer uses – the words and phrases a writer chooses to use. This includes whether a writer uses formal or informal language, **figurative language** or **neutral language**, **jargon** that may be considered exclusive or more universally accepted language that is more inclusive. Style also refers to the way the words are put together, the order and arrangement of words on the page as well as the sentence construction used and grammatical and punctuation choices made. Some writers may choose to use a very simple style that aims to include a wide readership, other writers may choose to use a more complex or experimental style that may exclude some readers. The choice of the **narrative voice** is also part of a writer's style. The historical and cultural context during which a text was written can affect the style a writer uses as can the form or genre of the work. Poetry, for example, is usually written in verse (rhymed or unrhymed) while prose fiction is usually written in prose. This, also, is part of a text's style. We are going to focus on prose fiction in this section and explore how the stylistic choices made by a writer has an impact on the text's meaning.

Prose fiction

The first two texts we are going to explore are *The Scarlet Letter: A Romance* (1850) by Nathaniel Hawthorne and *Like Water for Chocolate* (1989) by Laura Esquivel. As we shall see, each writer uses a very different style which affects our understanding of each text's meaning.

The Scarlet Letter: A Romance is a historical fiction novel that was written in 1850 by American writer, Nathaniel Hawthorne, but takes place in a Puritanical Massachusetts during the seventeenth century. The following extract comes from the opening few pages of the novel.

The Prison Door

A throng of bearded men, in sad-coloured garments and grey, steeple-crowned hats, intermixed with women, some wearing hoods, and others bareheaded, was assembled in front of a wooden edifice, the door of which was heavily timbered with oak, and studded with iron spikes.

Before this ugly edifice, and between it and the wheel-track of the street, was a grass plot, much overgrown with burdock, pigweed, apple-Peru, and such unsightly vegetation, which evidently found something congenial in the soil that had so early borne the black flower of civilized society, a prison. But on one side of the portal, and rooted almost at the threshold, was a wild rose bush, covered, in this month of June, with its delicate gems, which might be imagined to offer their fragrance and fragile beauty to the prisoner as he went in, and to the condemned criminal as he came forth to his doom, in token that the deep heart of Nature could pity and be kind to him.

This rose bush, by a strange chance, has been kept alive in history ... Finding it so directly on the threshold of our narrative, which is now about to issue from that inauspicious portal, we could hardly do otherwise than pluck one of its flowers and present it to the reader. It may serve, let us hope, to symbolize some sweet moral blossom that may be found along the track, or relieve the darkening close of a tale of human frailty and sorrow ...

It was a circumstance to be noted, on the summer morning when our story begins its course, that the women, of whom there were several in the crowd, appeared to take a peculiar interest in whatever penal infliction might be expected to ensue ...

'Goodwives,' said a hard-featured dame of fifty, 'I'll tell ye a piece of my mind. It would be greatly for the public behoof, if we women, being of mature age and church-members in good repute, should have the handling of such malefactresses as this Hester Prynne. What think ye, gossips?* If the hussy stood up for judgement before us five, that are now here in a knot together, would she come off with such a sentence as the worshipful magistrates have awarded? Marry, I trow not.'

**at the time this meant acquaintance or friend*

(Nathaniel Hawthorne 37–40)

Keeping our focus on the extract's style, we are going to explore the following aspects of Hawthorne's writing style:

- diction that is old-fashioned
- long, complex sentences
- figurative language
- intrusive narrator.

Let's take each stylistic feature and explore how it has been used and how it affects our understanding of the text's meaning.

Diction that is old-fashioned

Throughout this extract Hawthorne has made the stylistic choice of including a number of words or phrases that are either old-fashioned or whose meaning has changed. Even for a nineteenth-century reader, much of Hawthorne's language would have been unfamiliar. Here is a list of some of the words and phrases that readers in the nineteenth century and readers now no longer use:

■ **Table 1.5.4**

Paragraph in extract	Word/phrase in extract	Original meaning
1 (lines 1–3)	steeple-crowned	Describes the shape of the hats worn in the seventeenth century – a hat that is tall like a church steeple. These types of hats were no longer worn in the nineteenth century.
2 (lines 4–10)	came forth	To come forward
3 (lines 11–14)	which is now about to issue	Which is now about to begin
5 (lines 19–23)	Goodwives	Female head of the household
5 (lines 19–23)	dame	Elderly or mature woman
5 (lines 19–23)	ye	you
5 (lines 19–23)	behoof	Benefit, advantage
5 (lines 19–23)	malefactress	Female version of malefactor: someone who commits a crime
5 (lines 19–23)	gossips	Acquaintance or friend – this is a changed meaning to what 'gossip' means today
5 (lines 19–23)	Marry, I trow not	Really, I don't think so

What is the effect of having so much **diction** that is old-fashioned, **archaic** or has changed in meaning? The most obvious answer is that this use of language places the text in the past – although Hawthorne wrote this novel in the nineteenth century, he places the narrative in the seventeenth century. By using so much language that was not used at the time he wrote the novel, Hawthorne manages to transport his readers back in time to the seventeenth century. This is one way readers are able to suspend their disbelief and fully immerse themselves in the time period within which the story takes place. As the table above shows, most of the archaic language occurs in the final paragraph of the extract, in the dialogue of the 'hard-featured dame of fifty' (line 19). By including **direct speech** and then by imitating the language that would have been spoken in seventeenth-century Massachusetts, Hawthorne's narrative appears all the more authentic and realistic.

Long, complex sentences

How many sentences are there in the first two paragraphs? Three! It is likely that if you were to write two paragraphs of an equal length to those in the extract but only used three sentences, your English teacher would advise you to go back to your writing and include more full-stops. But Hawthorne, in a novel that is considered a 'classic' today, uses overtly long and complex sentences throughout. What is the effect of this stylistic feature? Hawthorne's overly long sentences allow him to (a) merge ideas about this particular society with (b) vivid description of characters and setting and (c) create a mood of tension. If we take the first sentence, for example, we can see how these three elements are all interwoven in just one sentence. Here is the opening sentence again:

> A throng of bearded men, in sad-coloured garments and grey, steeple-crowned hats, intermixed with women, some wearing hoods, and others bareheaded, was assembled in front of a wooden edifice, the door of which was heavily timbered with oak, and studded with iron spikes.
>
> *(Nathaniel Hawthorne 37)*

Hawthorne **foregrounds** the sentence (and the novel) with the 'throng of bearded men'. By beginning the entire novel with 'men', this in itself suggests there is an importance to men in the society during which the narrative takes place. We then have a detailed description of what these men are wearing: 'sad-coloured garments and grey, steeple-crowned hats'. This description is wonderful in creating a sombre mood through the colour imagery ('sad-coloured ... grey'). Notice also, how Hawthorne has constructed these two clauses in a perfectly balanced manner. Both clauses contain a **compound adjective**: 'sad-coloured' and 'steeple-crowned'. Each compound adjective is like a mirror image of the other in terms of both sounds ('s-c') and syllables. In between each compound adjective is a word beginning with a hard-sound 'g' ('garments ... grey'), which adds further to the balanced construction. Perhaps the combination of the diction (words) and order of the words suggests that these men are united in their sombre attitude, that appears so rigid and severe. Following the description of the men, we have a description of the women – they very much take second place in the way Hawthorne has structured this sentence imitating, perhaps, their position in society. The description of what they are wearing is less detailed, suggesting also how they are of less significance to the men. Notice how the men wear 'steeple-crowned hats' – a tall hat that is associated with a church steeple. The hat itself imbues the men with a sacred power, which elevates them all the more. In contrast, the women simply wear 'hoods' or are 'bareheaded' – a representation, perhaps, of the lack of power they hold within this society. The final part of this sentence describes the door to the 'wooden edifice'. Because of the chapter's title, we are assuming the 'wooden edifice' is a prison but it is not explicitly stated that this is the function of the 'edifice'. This then is an example of delay tactics and helps build up a mood of suspense. It is not until the final word of the second complex sentence that the edifice is explicitly referred to as a 'prison'. The opening sentence describes the door in detail. It is 'heavily timbered with oak' and is 'studded with iron spikes'. The language used has negative **connotations** with the **end focus**, in particular, suggesting violence, brutality and even torture. Whatever the door is a door to, we are under no illusions that it is not a place we would want to enter. The descriptive 'iron spikes' are the final words of this long sentence and they do fill the reader with curiosity as well as discomfort as we still do not know for sure what the door is a door to or, more importantly, who is behind the door. This again is Hawthorne using delay tactics and creating suspense for the reader.

As you can see, Hawthorne's stylistic decision of using a long complex sentence and ordering the words in a particular way within the sentence enables him to make a wide range of points about both the society in general and characters as well as build a mood of suspense. It also forces the reader to slow down our reading so that we can follow the sentence and this in itself encourages us to become more involved with the writing and actively work at interpreting the many ideas inherent within each sentence.

ACTIVITY 4

Write a similar commentary on the second sentence. Try to explain how the long complex sentence:

(a) gives the reader an idea about this particular society

(b) describes characters or setting

(c) creates suspense.

> Before this ugly edifice, and between it and the wheel-track of the street, was a grass plot, much overgrown with burdock, pigweed, apple-Peru, and such unsightly vegetation, which evidently found something congenial in the soil that had so early borne the black flower of civilized society, a prison.
>
> *(Nathaniel Hawthorne 37)*

Once you have written your commentary, compare your ideas to the commentary at the back of the book.

Figurative language

In this extract there is an extended description of a 'wild rose bush' (line 7). It is first mentioned in the second paragraph and then the entire third paragraph focuses on this rose bush. Hawthorne uses this rose bush to contrast with the prison, in particular with its 'portal' (line 7) – or door – which, as we have just explored, is an intimidating door with 'iron spikes' (line 3) and fills the reader with fear. The **co-ordinating conjunction** 'But' (line 7) is used to introduce the rose bush and this conjunction in itself implies the rose bush will be different to what has gone before. Immediately before this conjunction is the metaphorical phrase, 'the black flower of civilized society, a prison' (line 6). You may have analysed this **metaphor** in the activity above and hopefully explained how this is a negative image, implying the prison is a dark and evil place. By using 'But' to introduce the rose bush implies, then, that the rose bush is opposite to the prison – something light and good, perhaps. In contrast to the prison, which is constructed by man, this is a 'wild rose bush' and this suggests that even though man may attempt to take away the liberty of individuals, freedom and beauty does exist in the natural world. The **adjectives** Hawthorne uses to describe the rose bush also **juxtapose** with the language used to describe the prison. The rose bush is 'delicate' and 'fragile' in contrast to the 'heavily timbered' and 'iron spikes' (line 3) of the prison. However, although there is a fragility to the rose bush, it 'has been kept alive in history' (line 11) which suggests it has an inner strength which cannot be destroyed. The final sentence of the third paragraph explicitly refers to the rose bush as a symbol: 'It may serve, let us hope, to symbolize some sweet moral blossom that may be found along the track, or relieve the darkening close of a tale of human frailty and sorrow …' (lines 13–15) The narrator is suggesting here that the rose bush is a hopeful **symbol** and that although we are about to read a story of 'human frailty and sorrow', perhaps there will be a hopeful ending. Because Hawthorne has spent an extended time describing this rose bush, this becomes an **extended metaphor** and helps the reader understand that even in the midst of intolerance, oppression and darkness there is hope and light.

Intrusive narrator

The **narrative persona** of a text is part of a writer's style. In this extract, the narrator has a strong presence and not only describes the setting and characters but also comments on what she or he is describing and in this way encourages a particular response in the reader. We call a narrator who stops the story to address the reader with a personal comment, an **intrusive narrator** and this was a common stylistic device in many eighteenth- and nineteenth-century works of literature. In this extract, the narrator addresses us directly which is most clearly seen in the third paragraph when the narrator states, 'we could hardly do otherwise than pluck one of its flowers and present it to the reader' (lines 12–13). This helps build an intimate tone, we feel the narrator is directly talking to us, confiding in us a story perhaps and offering us his or her own personal opinions on the action and/or the characters. The effect of this stylistic device is that the narrator is able to encourage the reader to interpret the text in a certain way (although of course remember that the narrator is *not* the writer and may not share the same views as the writer). In this extract, we also feel the narrator is mocking certain characters – especially the women who 'take a peculiar interest in whatever penal infliction might be expected to ensue …' (lines 17–18). This suggests that the women enjoy seeing who is being punished and moreover enjoy watching the punishment itself. There is a voyeurism attached to these women and an implication that they are gossips, using this word in its modern meaning. It is not a flattering image and we feel the narrator is being critical of the women and encouraging us also to be judgemental.

We can see, therefore, how Hawthorne's style not only transports us to the seventeenth century, but how it also encourages the reader to interpret the text's meaning and respond in a particular way. Although Hawthorne's work is fiction, its style is still realistic, transporting us to a particular historical time and place where we can follow the narrative. The next text we are going to explore comes from a work in translation, the prose fiction novel, *Like Water for Chocolate*, written by Mexican writer, Laura Esquivel, in 1989. Esquivel makes very different stylistic choices to Hawthorne. Let's read the following extract which also comes from the opening chapter of the novel:

Tita was so sensitive to onions, any time they were being chopped, they say she would just cry and cry; when she was still in my great-grandmother's belly her sobs were so loud that even Nacha, the cook, who was half-deaf, could hear them easily. Once her wailing got so violent that it brought on an early labour. And before my great-grandmother could let out a word or even a whimper, Tita made her entrance into this world, prematurely, right there on the kitchen table amid the smells of simmering noodle soup, thyme, bay leaves and coriander, steamed milk, garlic and, of course, onion. Tita had no need for the usual slap on the bottom, because she was already crying as she emerged; maybe that was because she knew then that it would be her lot in life to be denied marriage. The way Nacha tells it, Tita was literally washed into this world on a great tide of tears that spilled over the edge of the table and flooded across the kitchen floor.

That afternoon, when the uproar had subsided and the water had been dried up by the sun, Nacha swept up the residue the tears had left on the red stone floor. There was enough salt to fill a ten-pound sack – it was used for cooking and lasted a long time. Thanks to her unusual birth, Tita felt a deep love for the kitchen, where she spent most of her life from the day she was born.

(Laura Esquivel 9–10)

You should have noticed that this is a very different style to Hawthorne's realist style. In the very first sentence of this extract, we can see how Esquivel combines the natural – 'Tita was so sensitive to onions, any time they were being chopped, they say she would just cry and cry' – with the supernatural – 'when she was still in my great-grandmother's belly her sobs were so loud that even Nacha, the cook, who was half-deaf, could hear them easily.' The merging of the natural and the supernatural is accentuated because they both appear in a single sentence. Something similar occurs in the second paragraph, too. The natural image of 'when … the water had been dried up by the sun' is juxtaposed with the following sentence's hyperbolic image of 'There was enough salt to fill a ten-pound sack'. Again, two different realities are merged: the real and the unreal. We are transported to this magical world which is, nevertheless, grounded in reality.

The reader is likely to be slightly astonished by the story of the birth, but the narrator, Tita's great-niece, simply sums it up as an 'unusual birth'. She does not appear to think it is in any way extraordinary, just simply 'unusual'. The point of the story is not to dwell upon its strangeness, but to explain why 'Tita felt a deep love for the kitchen'. The effect of this is that we are immediately transported to this alternative reality and are able to suspend our disbelief, mirroring the narrator who clearly suspends hers, by describing it in such a matter-of-fact way.

Rather than focusing on the extraordinariness of the actual birth, we focus on the symbolic imagery – her 'wailing … (that) got so violent'; the 'great tide of tears that spilled over the edge of the table and flooded across the kitchen floor'; the 'uproar'; and 'residue of tears'. We would usually associate the birth of a new child with joy, happiness and hope for the future, but a **semantic field** associated with anger and grief is used, and this jars with the reader. This birth seems to foreshadow the life of Tita: 'that it would be her lot in life to be denied marriage'.

The setting of Tita's birth – the kitchen – is also emphasized in this extract with 'kitchen' being repeated three times and 'cook' and 'cooking' being mentioned twice. Her birth, then, is intrinsically linked with where she is born. To accentuate this further, the narrator describes how her great-aunt was born 'amid the smells of simmering noodle soup, thyme, bay leaves and coriander, steamed milk, garlic and, of course, onion'. Olfactory imagery and listing are used here to create a vivid sense of place: the kitchen. The ingredients described – herbs, garlic and onions – all add strong flavours to food to make it more palatable. We may feel that they are being used symbolically, suggesting perhaps that Tita will also be a strong presence in the kitchen and in her relationships with others. Through the hyperbolic salt image, we may feel that Tita represents something that is essential and that without her, perhaps the story we are reading would be very different or even non-existent. What we are doing here is putting to one side the magical elements of her birth, and attempting to make sense of the symbolic images and figurative language that we recognise as being conventions of prose fiction. However, we should never forget that, even if the narrator does not appear surprised by aspects of her grand-aunt's birth, it is nevertheless not an everyday or an ordinary birth.

So why does Esquivel use this particular style of writing? The stylistic device that Esquivel uses in this opening extract and continues to use throughout her novel is known as magical realism and was a popular style of writing in Latin America during the twentieth century. Many Latin American magical realist writers were living in countries ruled by dictatorships and their work is seen as a political act of defiance against censorship. The creation of a different reality by merging the ordinary with the magical and the extraordinary, is seen as a symbol of their defiance, suggesting there is another reality to that created by an oppressive regime.

In Esquivel's novel, the protagonist, the narrator's great-aunt Tita, whose birth in a kitchen opens the novel, is repressed by her tyrannical mother by not being allowed to marry. She is the youngest daughter and has a duty to look after her mother. Tita spends her life in the kitchen but the meals she cooks are infused with magic and affect people who eat them physically and emotionally. We can see this as a form of empowerment for Tita. The author seems to be suggesting that, through the kitchen that is traditionally a female domain, a woman can have a voice, be creative and exercise control over her destiny. At the end of the novel, when her lover, Pedro, has died, she eats matches to literally set her passion alight so that she is able to join her lover in death. The extract here uses magical realism to explain Tita's affinity and power in the kitchen, which becomes a motif throughout the novel.

There are many styles in works of literature – in fact, some may argue that each writer has his or her own style. We are now going to read two more short extracts from prose fiction to give you an idea of the wide range of styles writers can employ and sum up how each style affects the text's meaning.

■ Table 1.5.5

Extract	Commentary
riverrun, past Eve and Adam's, from swerve of shore to bend of bay, brings us by a commodius vicus of recirculation back to Howth Castle and Environs. Sir Tristram, violer d'amores, fr'over the short sea, had passencore rearrived from North Armorica on this side the scraggy isthmus of Europe Minor to wielderfight his penisolate war: nor had topsawyer's rocks by the stream Oconee exaggerated themselse to Laurens County's gorgios while they went doublin their mumper all the time: nor avoice from afire bellowsed mishe mishe to tauftauf thuartpeatrick: not yet, though venissoon after, had a kidscad buttended a bland old isaac: not yet, though all's fair in vanessy, were sosie sesthers wroth with twone nathandjoe. Rot a peck of pa's malt had Jhem or Shen brewed by arclight and rory end to the regginbrow was to be seen ringsome on the aquaface. *(James Joyce 3)*	**James Joyce, *Finnegans Wake* (1939)** **Experimental style** – This is the opening and it does not even start with a capital letter! Every conventional rule of standard written English is broken (except Joyce's use of letters). **Meaning of text** – Some critics feel this is Joyce attempting to recreate the language of sleep and dreams. This style then attempts to transport us inside our dreams and raises questions regarding whether we dream in language and how we are able to understand our dreams when we are not conscious. Although this is overtly experimental, we automatically attempt to construct meaning from the words used. Joyce is forcing us to negotiate with the text in order to construct meaning. This perhaps represents how we are conditioned to make sense of our world – or, if we think this is a representation of our dreams, how we attempt to understand our dreams. The effect of using this experimental style, however, is that it is Joyce's least read book!
His mother's only comment? You need to worry about your grades. And in more introspective moments: Just be glad you didn't get my luck, hijo. What luck? his tío snorted. Exactly, she said. His friends Al and Miggs? Dude, you're kinda way fat, you know. His abuela, La Inca? Hijo, you're the most buenmoso man I know! Oscar's sister, Lola, was a lot more practical. Now that her crazy years were over – what Dominican girl doesn't have those? – she'd turned into one of those tough Jersey dominicanas, a long-distance runner who drove her own car, had her own checkbook, called men bitches, and would eat a fat cat in front of you without a speck of vergüenza. *(Junot Díaz 24)*	**Junot Días, *The Brief and Wondrous Life of Oscar Wao*, (2007)** Code switching – **characters switching between languages:** This novel is written from different perspectives and there is code switching throughout, particularly between (a) Caribbean dialect (including **slang** and profanity) and English (often eloquent and academic) and (b) English and Spanish (shown in this extract). There is no translation or glossary of the non-English words or phrases so readers have to interpret the Caribbean dialect and Spanish independently. **Meaning of text**: The text takes place in both New Jersey, USA and the Dominican Republic, and has multiple narrators. The code switching imitates the Dominican-American speech as well as helps to identify each different narrator's unique vernacular. We can interpret this text as exploring ideas about cultural identity and different voices. Code switching represents a fluidity in identity and how culture and identity are deeply rooted in language. Díaz's style, like Joyce's, challenges the traditional conventions of what a novel originally written in English looks like and who the reader is through the prevalence of code switching.

GLOBAL ISSUE *Field of inquiry:* **Beliefs, Values and Education**

TENSIONS THAT ARISE WHEN THERE ARE CONFLICTS OF BELIEFS AND VALUES

Many of the literary works explored in this chapter link in with the field of inquiry of beliefs, values and education. *The Scarlet Letter*, for example, explores how the rigid Puritanical set of beliefs and values that are the basis of seventeenth-century Massachusetts society, shape individuals and the community as a whole. A punitive rather than a forgiving ideology is ingrained in this society and the novel explores the effect of this on the protagonist, Hester Prynne, her daughter, Pearl, and other members of the community. Nathaniel Hawthorne was the great-great-grandson of John Hathorne, the Judge during the Salem witch trials of 1692 – one of the historical figures who plays a part in Arthur Miller's *The Crucible* (explored in further detail in Chapter 2.4). Nathaniel Hawthorne himself was born in Salem and was influenced by his family's history and connection to the witch trials. Some critics believe he added a 'w' to his surname in order to distance himself from Judge Hathorne. We can perhaps see the conflict between the world views of Judge Hathorne and writer Hawthorne in the imagery Hawthorne uses in this novel. The natural image of the rose bush that survives and blooms despite the 'black flower' of the prison represents, in the novel, the conflict that exists between the theocratic society and its prohibitive rules, and the beauty of Hester Prynne who represents love and loyalty. However, knowing Hawthorne's family history, perhaps it also symbolizes how the uncompassionate world view of Judge Hathorne will come to an end and be replaced by a more compassionate and loving world view in the future. In the novel, it is symbolic that the scarlet letter that is embroidered on Hester's dress as a mark of her shame will become a symbol of beauty. This seems to suggest that a community that is based on a belief system of oppression, punishment and prohibition is unnatural and will eventually be overcome by the individual who does not give in but who celebrates life, love and beauty. This idea would have had an added resonance with Hawthorne's American readers when it was first published as it was only 80 years after the United States Declaration of Independence was adopted (1776) that declared:

> *We hold these truths to be self-evident, that all men are created equal, that they are endowed by their Creator with certain unalienable Rights, that among these are Life, Liberty and the pursuit of Happiness.*

Hawthorne's novel, which explores how a rigid and unforgiving society can adversely affect the individual, would have been a reminder to his contemporary readers of how far society had progressed since the Declaration of Independence which valued the 'Life, Liberty and the pursuit of Happiness' of the individual.

Many of the other works of literature we have studied in this chapter also relate to this global issue: Soyinka's *Death and the King's Horseman* explores the tragic consequences when different cultural beliefs and values clash; *Medea* explores a similarly tragic outcome when different personal beliefs and values clash; magical realism is used by Esquivel to show the possibility of alternative realities when the present-day reality oppresses an individual's freedom; and Díaz's Dominican-American narrative voices in *The Brief Wondrous Life of Oscar Wao* refuse to conform to speaking standard English, constantly code switching to assert their cultural identity. This is an interesting global issue you could explore in the literary works and non-literary texts you may be studying in class that relates to the field of inquiry, of beliefs, values and education.

Advertising

Style is of course also important in non-literary texts. The style employed by a writer often depends on the purpose of the text type. As we have seen in the previous chapter, a recipe will use lots of commands and avoid using emotive language; a persuasive speech will use a range of rhetorical devices to appeal to pathos, logos and ethos; an advisory text will couch opinion as facts and use language to elevate the status of the person giving advice. In this final section of the chapter, we are going to look at a non-literary **multimodal** text, an advertisement, and explore how stylistic features are employed to fulfil the purpose of the text. Before we analyse the advertisement in depth, read the key features box below.

KEY FEATURES ADVERTISEMENTS

- **Target audience**: this is the particular audience the advertiser is attempting to persuade or elicit a particular response. An advertisement is rarely aimed at 'everyone'!
- Values inherent within an advertisement are supposed to reflect those values shared by the target audience, or those values the target audience finds appealing.
- The purpose is usually to persuade – either to persuade the target audience to buy a particular product or to raise awareness about an organization or **ideology**.
- **Presentational features** are important – this is the lay-out/organization of the text: where the visual image, the written text and/or the brand name/logo are placed on the page and how this promotes a particular viewpoint.
- **Typographical features** are also important – this refers to the way the written text is presented in terms of its size, font, use of capitalization or bold or italics.
- Written text: some advertisements include a lot of written text – a **slogan** or headline and additional text about the product or brand which is persuasive in nature; other advertisements have no written text, relying on the visual image for effect.
- Visual image: most advertisements include a visual image which is aimed at persuading the target audience to buy the product being advertised. The visual image may or may not include the actual product.
- **Multimodal texts**: this is a text that includes both written text and a visual image. Usually the written text and visual image work together – the visual image may reinforce the written text or it may give the target audience a more in-depth understanding of the product and why it is essential for the reader to purchase.
- Colour imagery: colour(s) of written text and visual image are often chosen because of the **connotations** of certain colours.

Similar to literary works, style in advertising includes the type of written language used – including the text's diction, sentence construction and figurative language. However, being a multimodal text, an advertisement's stylistic features also include its non-verbal language – including the image used, the colours used and the size and font of the typeface used.

Before we start exploring this advertisement, let's identify the GAP (step 1 of our analysis):

Genre	Advertisement
Target audience	Men in their 20s–30s who are aware of their body image.
Purpose	To advertise a man's cleansing product and persuade readers to purchase it.

The advertisement is advertising an *Old Spice* product, a man's cleansing item that is both a body wash and a moisturizer. The style that is employed through both the written and the non-verbal visual language plays on the idea that the product is two things in one. First of all let's explore the written language used.

Written text

The written text we are immediately drawn to is the **slogan**, 'IT'S TWO THINGS.', due to its position in the top third of the advertisement. The advertisement's structure, then, guides the way we read this text. The language used in this slogan is simple and its simplicity is accentuated through the **monosyllabic** words and the simple sentence construction that have been used. The full-stop at the end of the sentence makes the statement definitive, suggesting there is no question about what has been stated – it is so obviously true. The construction of the sentence is quite playful as the words 'It is' have been combined into one word, 'It's'. This contracting two words into one is symbolic, perhaps, of the product being advertised: two things in one.

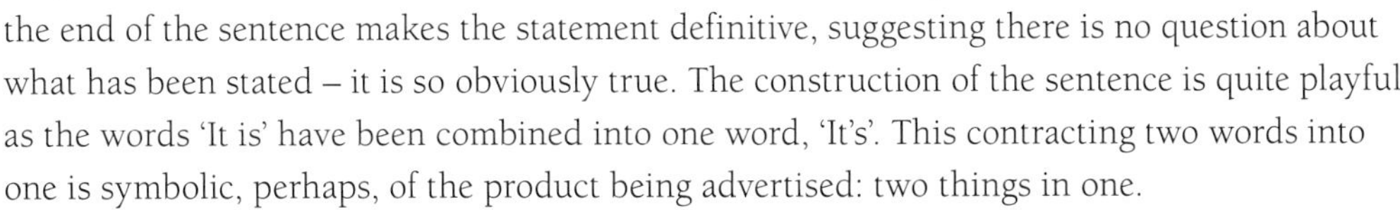

The additional text in the bottom third of the advertisement acts like a sub-heading and accentuates the 'two things' quality of the product through the word 'DOUBLE'. The language used in this additional text is also straightforward, but it builds on the monosyllabic slogan we have already read. The words 'DOUBLE IMPACT.' have double syllables which perhaps is playing with the **denotation** of the word 'double'. This is another definitive statement made clear through the use of the full-stop. The **verb** 'INTRODUCING' suggests this is a new product and perhaps makes the reader feel, being new, this may be innovative and worth trying out. The smaller additional text underneath this sub-heading builds still further on the 'two things' idea. The additional text states:

> BODY WASH. MOISTURIZER. STRIPED TOGETHER. IT'S TWO PRODUCTS
> IN ONE AWESOME PRODUCT.

The simple style is continued in this additional text – each new piece of information is separated by a full-stop which makes each statement appear of equal importance and worthy in its own right. The single phrase 'striped together' combines two words that both mean merging two things ('striped' and 'together') and they are obviously used to highlight the **motif** of two things (striped/together – two words) in one (single phrase). It is another playful and creative stylistic feature that the writer of this advertisement has used to highlight what appears to be the main selling point of this product.

The typeface used is a classic style and all the lettering is in white. This suggests that the product itself is classic, needing no fancy lettering or colours to promote it. The lettering of the slogan and additional text also **contrasts** with the lettering of the logo, 'Old Spice'. This is a recognizable logo with the image of the old sailing ship above the brand name. The combination of this cursive style of lettering together with the old style tall ship suggests the brand has longevity and is also exotic. The **denotation** of 'Old Spice' links in to this idea further: 'old' is an **adjective** that suggests this is a product that has a past and a history, it has withstood the test of time which is a selling point; 'spice' is something we add to our food to make more appealing and appetising so this word has positive **connotations**. When read with the tall ship, we are also reminded of the past when ships sailed around the world selling and buying goods such as spices that were viewed as exotic which is also a positive idea attached to the product. So, by combining a classic style of font with an old-fashioned cursive style of font not only links in with the two things in one motif but also appeals to readers on many levels.

Non-verbal visual language

The visual language of this advertisement has to be read together with the written text that we have just analysed. The main image is of a centaur in a shower using the product to wash himself. A centaur of course continues the **motif** of two things in one, being half-man and half-horse. The style of image used is a photograph – it would appear that a photograph of a man has been Photoshopped with a photograph of a horse and the effect of this is that it looks authentic and real. This also plays with the dual motif of the advertisement: a centaur is quite obviously *not* real being a mythical creature and yet the use of a photograph gives the illusion that this *is* real. A centaur is also a clever image to use for this product as centaurs are associated with being strong and powerful creatures, suggesting therefore that if you buy this product you, too, will be strong and powerful.

The colours used in this advertisement also link in with the dual motif. The tiles surrounding the bath are two colours, blue and white; the background colours are also two colours, beige and red; and the colours of the product itself are primarily two colours, red and blue.

We can see, therefore, that the stylistic features that have been used for both the written and the visual language cleverly tie in with the main selling point of the product and thus would fulfil the purpose of the advertisement – to persuade readers that this product's dual nature makes it a worthy product to buy.

ACTIVITY 5

Remember that in your individual oral, you need to refer to a non-literary body of work. In terms of advertising, this means you are expected to refer to the advertising campaign from which your chosen advertisement comes from. The advert below is an example of an advertisement from an advertising campaign in July 2012, advertising *Old Spice* cosmetics called 'After Hours'. The slogan for each advertisement in this campaign is the same:

SOMEWHERE IN THERE
THERE'S A
MAN IN THERE
Old Spice
SMELL BETTER THAN
YOURSELF

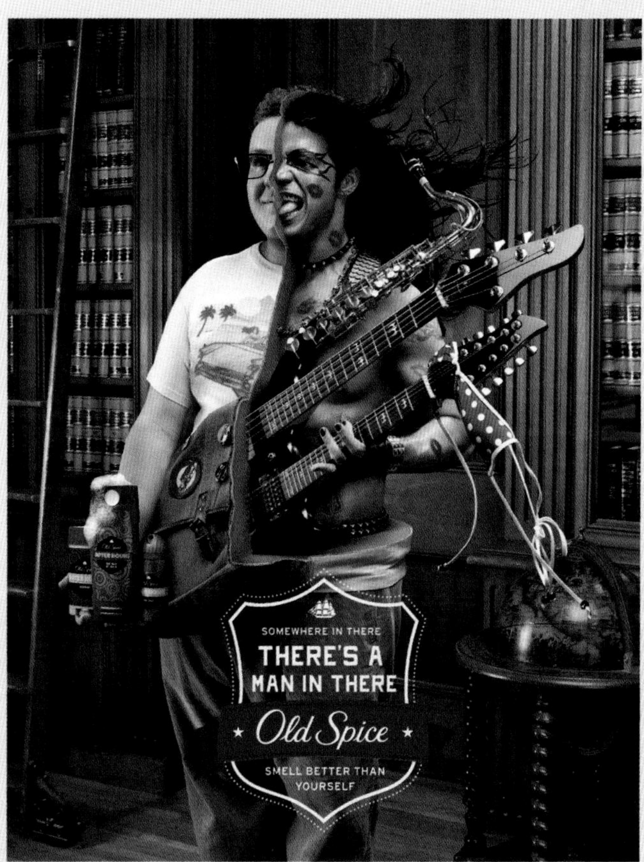

■ Old Spice Rocker, July 2012

Write a commentary, focusing on the **stylistic features** that have been employed. Similar to the commentary above, write a paragraph on the written language used and a paragraph on the non-verbal visual language used. How does the style of the written language and the visual language help to sell the product by persuading the reader to buy the product?

Once you have written your paragraphs, compare your ideas to the commentary at the back of the book.

EE Links: English A – Language category 3

We have compared the structural and stylistic features employed by magazine front covers for the same magazine and different advertisements for the same product. You may like to research this idea further for an English A: Language category 3 extended essay. You could **either**:

- compare the structural and stylistic features employed by *different* magazines of the same genre or *different* brands advertising a similar product (for example, music magazines or men's health magazines; brands advertising cosmetics or sportswear)

or

- compare the structural and stylistic features of the *same* magazine or the *same* brand (for example, *Cosmopolitan* magazine or *Old Spice*) over a period of time.

Possible research questions could be:

- **To what extent do music magazines** [you could replace this with a different genre of magazine] **published in 2019 use similar or different structural and stylistic features to appeal to their target audience?**
- **In what ways have the advertisements of the male cosmetics brand *Old Spice*** [you could replace *Old Spice* with another cosmetics brand] **combined language and visual images to reinforce a particular message about the advertised product in the last 20 years?**
  You may like to use your non-literary reading strategy to structure your analysis.

In this chapter, we have studied a range of literary works and text types and explored how the structural and stylistic features employed have an impact on how we interpret a text's meaning. Of course, the ideas explored in this chapter are not definitive – although literary critics attempt to define literary works through the structure or style the writer has used, some would argue that the joy of reading literature is that each writer has his or her own style which makes it difficult to define. However, you should have a better understanding now of some of the structural and stylistic choices writers are able to employ and how these choices affect a text's meaning.

You will have noted that poetry has not been explored in this chapter despite structural and stylistic features being key to our understanding of a poem's meaning. Our next chapter focuses on a range of poetry from different time periods and we will be addressing how language, structure and style are employed by writers of poetry in order to offer insights and challenges to the reader.

Works cited

Aesop. *Aesop's Illustrated Fables*. Barnes & Noble, 2013.

'All Of The Stars – Get Q342 For Ed Sheeran, 50 Albums Of 2014 & Much More.' *Q*. Web. 21 Feb. 2019. **www.qthemusic.com/articles/the-latest-q/q342-ed-sheeran-and50-albums-of-2014**.

'At Home With A Pop Genius – Paul McCartney Is On The Cover Of Q.' *Q*. Web. 21 Feb. 2019. **www.qthemusic.com/articles/the-latest-q/paul-mccartney-q346**.

Aristotle. *Poetics*. Penguin Classics, 1996.

Beckett, S. *Waiting for Godot: A Tragicomedy in Two Acts*. Grove Press/Atlantic Monthly Press, 2011.

Díaz, J. *The Brief Wondrous Life of Oscar Wao*. Kindle Edition, Faber & Faber, 2008.

Esquivel, L. *Like Water for Chocolate*. Translated by Carol Christensen and Thomas Christensen, Black Swan, 1993.

Esslin, M. *The Theatre of the Absurd*, reissue edition. Bloomsbury Academic, 2014.

Euripides. *Medea*. Translated by John Harrison, Cambridge University Press, 2016.

Faeder, S. 'More Than Just Two Things.' Old Spice, 6 May 2015. Web. 24 Feb. 2019. **https://oldspicenewblog.wordpress.com**.

Hawthorne, N. *The Scarlet Letter*. Alma Classics, 2015.

Homer. *The Odyssey*. Translated by Emily Wilson, WW Norton & Company, 2018.

'Independent Spirit! Florence + The Machine Is On The Cover Of Q.' *Q*. Web. 23 Feb. 2019. **www.qthemusic.com/articles/the-latest-q/florence-and-the-machine-q352**.

Joyce, J. *Finnegans Wake*. Wordsworth Editions, 2012.

Knowlson, J. *Damned to Fame: The Life of Samuel Beckett*. Bloomsbury Publishing PLC, 1997.

'Paddy Pounded.' *The Indianapolis Leader*, 11 Feb 1882, Library of Congress. Web. 12 Oct. 2019. **https://chroniclingamerica.loc.gov/lccn/sn84027490/1882-02-11/ed-1/seq-1**.

Márquez, GG. *Chronicle of a Death Foretold*, reissue edition. Translated by Gregory Rabassa, Penguin Books, 2014.

Morrison, T. *Beloved*. Pan Books, Picador, 1988.

Orwell, G. *Down and Out in Paris and London*. Penguin Modern Classics, 1986.

Perrault, C. *Perrault's Fairy Tales*. Translated by AE Johnson, Dodd Mead and Company (1921), Dover Publications, Inc., 1969.

Roy, A. *The God of Small Things*. HarperCollinsPublishers, 1997.

Shakespeare, W. *Romeo and Juliet*. Heinemann Shakespeare, 2010.

Soyinka, W. *Death and the King's Horseman*. Methuen Drama, 1998.

'Story Design (Freytag's Pyramid).' Rook Reading, 12 Aug. 2018. Web. 22 Feb. 2019. **https://rookreading.com/2018/08/12/story-structure**.

'The Constitution of the United States and The Declaration of Independence.' Delegates of The Constitutional Convention, Racehorse Publishing, 2016.

'The Nobel Prize in Literature 1969.' Nobel Prize. Web. 23 Feb. 2019. **www.nobelprize.org/prizes/literature/1969/summary**.

1.6 How do texts offer insights and challenges?

OBJECTIVES OF CHAPTER

- Explore unfamiliar narrative voices in prose: fiction and poetry.
- Consider the role of the extended metaphor in poetry and drama.
- Consider the role of a range of non-literary features in animated explainer videos, recruitment posters and online science magazines.

How do texts offer insights and challenges?

By focusing on how texts offer insights and challenges, we will be referring to many of the ideas we have explored in previous chapters in this section. As we know from the literary works and non-literary texts we have studied in the previous five chapters, a text may encourage readers to see the familiar world in a different way or, alternatively, to see the unfamiliar world in a familiar way. This in itself offers insights to readers whilst of course the unpicking of these features may offer challenges to the reader, even when applying one of our two reading strategies!

One of the ways texts may offer insights is by making our familiar world unfamiliar. We have explored many literary works and non-literary texts that encourage us to do just this: Joy Harjo, for example, in her poem, 'Perhaps the World Ends Here' (Chapter 1.1), attempts to give us new insights into the human condition through an everyday object, a kitchen table; and Wordsworth's 'Daffodils' (Chapter 1.2) encourages us to view a common flower, the daffodil, as having the power to fill the human heart with joy in the present and future. Art Spiegelman's *Maus* and Shaun Tan's *The Arrival* are two graphic novels that, through their visual illustrations, make the familiar world unfamiliar, using **anthropomorphism** (*Maus*, Chapter 1.1) or **defamiliarization** (*The Arrival*, Chapter 1.3); George Herbert, Toni Morrison and Tennessee Williams, also, merge the familiar with the unfamiliar by subverting the conventions of their literary form. Reflecting on the non-literary texts we have analysed, our familiar world is made unfamiliar in the satirical cartoon in which the young man asks 'What's Handwriting?' (Chapter 1.1); through the use of emojis and other non-verbal symbols in textspeak (Chapter 1.3); and through the visual imagery employed in some advertisements (Chapter 1.5).

Each author, then, uses **defamiliarization** in some way in order to give us an *insight* into their texts' meanings. Of course, whenever something familiar is made strange, it is always a *challenge* to unpick the strange and try to make sense of it. It may take us a while to understand what Harjo and Wordsworth are doing: giving an ordinary and everyday object a power that can teach us about something as essential as the human condition is not something we are used to. We usually think the human condition needs something far more abstract or 'deep' to make sense of it. Literature does not always agree! And this can be challenging as it forces us to re-think how we view ourselves and the world. Attempting to make sense of something incomprehensible in texts such as Tan's graphic novel, Morrison's prose fiction and Williams' drama is supposed to challenge the reader. It is not supposed to be easy to comprehend any of these texts and that really is the point: an immigrant's experience is unsettling; making sense of another person's internal stream of consciousness is not easy; experiencing someone else's psychological trauma is difficult. However, once we have overcome the challenges of understanding why the author has written in such a way and how these features of the text enhance the text's meaning, then we are filled with a much deeper insight into the text's meaning and our journey to learning about ourselves, others and the world in which we live really begins.

Of course, texts do not always make the familiar world unfamiliar. Many texts do precisely the opposite. Some texts explore the unfamiliar world and attempt to demystify this world by making it familiar. We saw this in our discussion of George Orwell's prose non-fiction memoir, *Down and Out in Paris and London* (Chapter 1.2), which helped to give his predominantly English middle class readers an insight into a world of abject poverty in both Paris and London during the 1920s. Likewise photojournalism (Chapter 1.1) brings the world of conflict which many do not experience first-hand into our living rooms. Works such as *Death and the King's Horseman* (Chapter 1.5) also give us an insight into the disastrous consequences that occur when an individual or culture does not understand the traditions of another individual or culture - when the unfamiliar world remains unfamiliar. Soyinka attempts to give us an insight into how there are other perspectives which may be challenging but nevertheless need to be understood. Likewise non-literary texts such as informative and advisory texts attempt to demystify what may be unfamiliar to their readers. Robin Ha, Sun Tzu and Mrs Beeton (Chapter 1.4) all attempt to do precisely that in their respective texts. Whether it is defamiliarizing the familiar or demystifying the unfamiliar, the effect is similar: to give the reader an insight into our world and/or the experiences of others as well as the self and by doing so challenge us to reflect on the world in which we live, our shared humanity and who we are as individuals.

As we have also explored in this section, writing is a craft with specific tools, and the craft of a writer is to use these tools in such a way that helps us understand a text's meaning. We explored these tools in Chapter 1.1 through our two reading strategies. However, although a writer will employ these tools in order to enhance the text's meaning, once a text is published, it is then up to the reader to make sense of the ways in which the writer has used their tools and come to their own understanding of the text's meaning. It is this interpretation of a text's language, style and structure that can be challenging. A writer is a skilled craftsperson in the same way that an architect or neurosurgeon or painter is. Just as we do not see the foundations of a building an architect has designed, or the inside of a person's head that a neurosurgeon has operated on, or the artist's palette that he has used to mix colours, so we do not always see immediately the writer's craft. We know a building has foundations, we know a person who has had brain surgery has been operated on and we know an artist has mixed colours and often layered paint on the canvas. This is true of a text. A writer uses his or her craft to construct a text but it is not always obvious how she or he has constructed it. It is the job of the reader to unpick the text and discover the skill of the writer and in this way we can then start to understand the text's meaning and in turn recognize the insights the text is offering us. Our two reading strategies help us with this.

We are going to explore our final concept question of this section by bringing together many of the ideas already explored in this section. The first part of the chapter will focus on how literary works such as a short story, drama and poetry offer insights and challenges whilst the second part will focus on how non-literary texts including an animated explainer video, a recruitment poster and an online science magazine article do likewise.

Literary works that offer insights and challenges

Kholstomer by Leo Tolstoy

The first text we are going to explore is a work in translation by Russian novelist, Leo Tolstoy (1828–1910). Although he is well known for his epic literary works such as *War and Peace* (1867) and *Anna Karenina* (1877), he also wrote novellas and short stories. One of his short stories, *Kholstomer* (1886), is particularly famous for its use of **defamiliarization**, which we explored in Chapter 1.3. Read the following short extract from this work in translation and see if you can work out who the **narrative voice** is and what the narrative voice is talking about:

> I was quite in the dark as to what they meant by the words 'his colt', from which I perceived that people considered that there was some connexion between me and the head groom. What the connexion was I could not at all understand ... I could not at all understand what they meant by speaking of *me* as being a man's property. The words 'my horse' applied to me, a live horse, seemed to me as strange as to say 'my land', 'my air', or 'my water'.
>
> But those words had an enormous effect on me. I thought of them constantly and only after long and varied relations with men did I at last understand the meaning they attach to these strange words, which indicate that men are guided in life not by deeds but by words ... Such words, considered very important among them, are my and mine, which they apply to various things, creatures or objects: even to land, people, and horses. They have agreed that of any given thing only one person may use the word *mine*, and he who in this game of theirs may use that conventional word about the greatest number of things is considered the happiest. Why this is so I do not know, but it is so. For a long time I tried to explain it by some direct advantage they derive from it, but this proved wrong ...
>
> Later on, having widened my field of observation, I became convinced that not only as applied to us horses, but in regard to other things, the idea of mine has no other basis than a low, mercenary instinct in men, which they call the feeling or right of property. A man who never lives in it says 'my house' but only concerns himself with its building and maintenance; and a tradesman talks of 'my cloth business' but has none of his clothes made of the best cloth that is in his shop.
>
> I am now convinced that in this lies the essential difference between men and us. Therefore, not to speak of other things in which we are superior to men, on this ground alone we may boldly say that in the scale of living creatures we stand higher than man. The activity of men, at any rate of those I have had to do with, is guided by words, while ours is guided by deeds.
>
> *(Leo Tolstoy)*

You would have worked out quite quickly that the narrative voice of this short story is a horse! You would, also, have understood that the horse is discussing man's obsession with private property and ownership. By using a horse as the narrative voice, Tolstoy is attempting to make a familiar topic – private property and ownership – unfamiliar by being discussed by a horse! The purpose of this is that Tolstoy is attempting to encourage his readers – nineteenth-century Russians – to reflect on the social values that prized private ownership through new eyes and understand it in a different way. Most critics agree that Tolstoy was using the narrative voice of the horse to express his own views about man's obsession with ownership and property. Although Count Tolstoy was born into an aristocratic Russian family, by the time he wrote this short story he had rejected the idea of private property and ownership. These beliefs are alluded to in this extract, starting with the first paragraph when the horse tries to make sense of man's obsession with ownership: 'I could not at all understand what they meant by speaking of *me* as being a man's property. The words "my horse" applied to me, a live horse, seemed to me as strange as to say "my land", "my air", or "my water".' (lines 3–5). We are encouraged to interpret this as just as it is absurd for a horse to own land, air or water, so is it absurd for a man to own a 'live horse'. As the extract progresses, this idea is developed until the horse's final observation that, regarding man's obsession with owning property, horses 'are superior to men … and we stand higher than man' (lines 20–21). By subverting the dominant ideology that states men are superior to horses, Tolstoy forces the reader to reflect on society's values and whether they are noble and meaningful or simply absurd and arbitrary.

So how is this text challenging?

First, being encouraged to see the world through the eyes of a horse is challenging! Usually, the reader makes a connection with the **narrative persona** and is encouraged to understand the narrator's world view in some way. Once we realize Tolstoy's narrative persona is a horse, this has its own challenges and we are then forced to reflect on whether this animal may be speaking more sense than man. If the horse *is* speaking sense, then this devalues man and this obviously challenges the reader to reflect on how we view the world and whether there is an alternative world view.

Second, although Tolstoy uses humour to criticize private ownership which makes his criticism less harsh, there would be some readers who would find this perspective challenging as it is in direct opposition to their own world view.

And how is this text insightful?

Once we understand the narrative persona is a horse, we are forced to reflect on an alternative perspective – a perspective that few men would have posited: that horses are superior to men! When we are encouraged to view the world through different eyes, this offers us an insight into the world that we have not examined before. We saw this in Shaun Tan's *The Arrival* when, through his visual images, Tan forced us to view the new land (the reader's land) through the eyes of the immigrant and thus understand how someone other to us views something with which we are familiar.

The text also offers us an insight into the writer himself. We are encouraged to gain an understanding of Tolstoy's own personal world view and if we research his life, it is clear that the horse's views on private ownership mirror his own as he renounced private ownership in his later life. Researching the writer's life may have given us an understanding into Tolstoy's pacifist ideology and how he advocated change should come through discussion and debate and non-violent action. The text you have just read, then, can perhaps be interpreted as his attempt to instigate change through pacifism. Writing is not violent; however, it is a powerful means that has the potential to change and shape readers' perspectives. Throughout history we have examples of books that have been banned, burnt or censored because they posit an alternative world view and are seen as a potential danger to individuals or political parties that are in positions of power and challenge the political status quo. This short story, then, encourages readers to open their eyes to an alternative perspective to the one posited by those in power in the hope that readers may, like Tolstoy, also reject private ownership and thus force a change to society's values in an entirely non-violent manner.

Finally, we also gain an insight into Tolstoy's craftsmanship as a writer. His creation of an unfamiliar narrative persona as well as his inclusion of humour are skilful and creative ways to explore real-world political and social issues. By being aware of this, we are more likely to find Tolstoy's work entertaining and take the time to understand why he has used these devices and in this way gain an even deeper insight into the text's meaning.

Leo Tolstoy

Count Lev Nikolayevich Tolstoy, better known in English as Leo Tolstoy, was born into an aristocratic Russian family in 1828 and is regarded as one of the greatest Russian writers of all time. Following his experience in the army during the Crimean War (1853–56) and two trips around Europe (1857 and 1860–61), he changed his views drastically and became an advocate for rejecting personal property, nonviolent resistance and, later on in his life, a spiritual anarchist. His epic novels including *War and Peace* (1869) and *Anna Karenina* (1877) are realist prose fiction. The former follows the impact of war on Russian aristocratic families through several generations and the latter focuses on the extramarital affair the titular character has that scandalizes Russian society and forces the two lovers into exile. He also wrote novellas, short stories, plays and non-fiction. In 1901, Tolstoy was awarded the Nobel Prize for Literature but he turned it down because he felt the prize money would bring unwanted complications to his life.

Just as Tolstoy uses an unconventional voice to challenge readers and ultimately to offer us insights, so does Korean-American poet, Suji Kwock Kim, in her 'Monologue for an Onion'. This time it is an onion which takes on the role of the narrative voice.

'Monologue for an Onion' by Suji Kwock Kim

The next poem we are going to explore is a poem by Korean-American poet, Suji Kwock Kim, which was published in her first poetry anthology, *Notes from the Divided Country*, in 2003. Kim is a Korean-American writer who, although born in the United States, is influenced by her cultural background and her 'divided country', Korea. The title of the poem we are about to read is 'Monologue for an Onion'. The title itself sounds absurd! We are immediately ***challenged***! What ***insight*** could a talking onion give us into life, the universe and everything?! Although the poem sounds humorous in its absurdity, it has a serious side to it. Read the poem, paying particular attention to its form and structure and LIFs from our literary reading strategy:

Monologue for an Onion

I don't mean to make you cry.
I mean nothing, but this has not kept you
From peeling away my body, layer by layer,

The tears clouding your eyes as the table fills
With husks, cut flesh, all the debris of pursuit.
Poor deluded human: you seek my heart.

Hunt all you want. Beneath each skin of mine
Lies another skin: I am pure onion – pure union
Of outside and in, surface and secret core.

Look at you, chopping and weeping. Idiot.
Is this the way you go through life, your mind
A stopless knife, driven by your fantasy of truth,

Of lasting union – slashing away skin after skin
From things, ruin and tears your only signs
Of progress? Enough is enough.

You must not grieve that the world is glimpsed
Through veils. How else can it be seen?
How will you rip away the veil of the eye, the veil

That you are, you who want to grasp the heart
Of things, hungry to know where meaning
Lies. Taste what you hold in your hands: onion-juice,

Yellow peels, my stinging shreds. You are the one
In pieces. Whatever you meant to love, in meaning to
You changed yourself: you are not who you are,

Your soul cut moment to moment by a blade
Of fresh desire, the ground sown with abandoned skins.
And at your inmost circle, what? A core that is

Not one. Poor fool, you are divided at the heart,
Lost in its maze of chambers, blood, and love,
A heart that will one day beat you to death.

(Suji Kwock Kim)

Like Tolstoy's *Kholstomer*, Kim uses **defamiliarization** in her use of an unconventional **narrative voice**. Let's use our literary reading strategy to try to make sense of this poem.

Step 1: Form and Structure

The poem is constructed as ten triplets, with neither a regular rhythm nor a regular rhyme. The first stanza starts 'I don't mean to make you cry' and the final stanza ends with 'A heart that will one day beat you to death'. Immediately, we sense that the poet may be exploring dark ideas. There is certainly a lack of harmony in the odd number of lines in each stanza and in the lack of a regular meter or rhyme. The language used in the first and last lines suggest pain and death. This, combined with the poem's title which suggests the narrative voice is an onion, immediately challenges us whilst acting as a hook, encouraging us to read on.

Step 2: LIFs Language

If we look closely at the poem, there are lots of words used that connect to the cutting of an onion: 'cry', 'peeling', 'layer by layer', 'skin', 'husks', 'stinging shreds', 'inmost circle' and 'core' which, together, suggest something serious and introspective. The process of chopping an onion is being defamiliarized. The opening stanza **challenges** us. It suggests that the person chopping is metaphorically on a quest for some kind of truth and that the process of peeling back the layers of the onion only leads to more crying and by extension more suffering. As the onion says in this stanza, 'I mean nothing' (line 2). The person cutting the onion is later referred to as:

… you who want to grasp the heart
Of things, hungry to know where meaning
Lies. …

(lines 19–21)

Kim plays with language in these lines, creating a humorous tone which many readers would find entertaining as well as offering an **insight** into one of the poem's main ideas: the pursuit of knowledge. For example, 'hungry' links to the idea of food and presumably the woman is cutting the onion so she can eat it – a concept the onion seems unaware of and which creates a layer of **irony** as we are aware of why the woman is cutting the onion. The onion, therefore, seems unaware of the truth regarding why the woman is cutting it even though he is criticizing the woman for her pursuit of the truth. This links in to the other meaning of 'hungry' – the meaning the **narrative voice** is suggesting – hungry for knowledge. This meaning also links in to the word 'Lies', which has been shifted on to the next line where it is isolated from the line above and from the following phrase due to the full stop. In the context of the sentence, the word is used as a **verb** – suggesting the position of something – however, it is also a play on words if we think about its meaning as a noun – deception. The onion might, therefore, be suggesting that belief in the pursuit of meaning is a deception. Indeed, the onion describes the layers that the cutter removes to arrive at the core (another play on words) as 'veils'. Just like a veil, the layers of an onion are not translucent – we cannot see completely through them as they are opaque. In their opaqueness, they obscure rather than reveal.

The witty use of language, which perhaps disguises a deeper, darker and more **challenging** aspect to the poem, is also seen in the substitution of the letter 'o' for the letter 'u' in the word 'onion' to create the word 'union' (lines 8 and 13). Is the poet suggesting that we take an object and essentially turn it into something else without ever arriving any closer to understanding what it was – we just replace it with another word? This interpretation would point to how the pursuit of understanding is just a semantic game of shifting words. Is this what we are doing right now – peeling back the layers of Kim's poem in our attempt to arrive at a meaning? This idea is both insightful and challenging – is Kim mocking us, the readers, in our close analysis? If we turn back to the poem itself, we are also challenged in the sense that we want to know what it is the cutter is searching for. The poem seems deliberately ambiguous. Perhaps the cutter is searching for nothing and is simply cutting the onion to satiate hunger, which would mean the onion is either deliberately misrepresenting the cutter or the onion lacks understanding itself. Or perhaps the cutter *is* searching for something but is either unaware of what it is she or he is searching for, or is attempting to conceal their quest for knowledge from others. This makes the poem challenging because the meaning is not explicit; in fact we have to search deeply in order to understand the poem's meaning!

This of course makes the poem really clever. We are forced to step into the shoes of the cutter as we peel back the layers of this poem to find its core, its hidden meaning. The process can be quite frustrating – causing tears, perhaps, similar to the cutter's tears. Again, depending on the reader, this interpretation can either be highly **insightful**, as we are forced to experience the challenges and frustrations of finding meaning, or **challenging** in itself as we feel the author may be mocking us. Whichever interpretation we construct, it is entertaining and forces us to engage with the poem in a creative way.

Images (figurative language)

An alternative interpretation that the text may be offering an **insight** into is that perhaps the onion is an **extended metaphor** for a partner in a relationship. Is the onion suggesting the cutter is over-analysing their relationship in an attempt to find out who the onion/partner really is, dissecting the onion/partner and slowly destroying the lover and in turn their relationship? Language which would lead us to this interpretation includes: 'peeling away my body' (line 3), 'lasting union' (line 13) 'a blade / Of fresh desire' (line 25–26) and 'divided at the heart' (line 28). A further interpretation is that perhaps the poem is offering us an insight into the futility of attempting to understand and make sense of the world around us. As the onion describes it, the cutter is obsessed with 'the fantasy of truth.' (line 12). To some extent we are given an insight into perhaps the 'futility' of the pursuit of meaning. As we know, when we read the poem we are involved in analysing the language, structure and style of the text in an attempt to arrive at a 'core' understanding of the text. However, as we have seen throughout Section 1 of this coursebook and will continue to see in Sections 2 and 3, our understanding is shaped by so many variables. What we bring to the text as an individual reader affects the way we interpret a text and my 'core' understanding of a particular text may be different to yours, which may be different to the writer's. The poem appears to be offering us an insight into the role of the reader here and how this relates to the quest of meaning.

Other features (irony)

The onion is dismissive of the idea that we can arrive at a singular meaning. The language used by the onion to describe the cutter is quite disparaging. The cutter is described as a 'poor deluded human' (line 3), an 'Idiot' (line 10) and a 'Poor fool' (line 28). Indeed the poem can be seen as ironic in tone. The more the cutter attempts to cut away the layers of the onion in the pursuit of truth, not only does the cutter destroy the onion but the cutter also makes themselves even more unhappy. Language associated with unhappiness is repeated throughout the poem: 'cry' (line 1), 'tears clouding your eyes' (line 4), 'weeping' (line 10), 'tears' (line 14) and 'grieve' (line 16) which accentuates this idea. By causing the cutter's eyes to sting, ironically the clarity of the cutter's vision is obscured or clouded which makes the cutter mourn all the more. There is also an added **irony** in the idea that each new layer of an onion is exactly the same as the previous layer – no progress is made by the cutter. The cutter remains 'lost in its maze of chambers' (line 29). The cutter is no more wiser than when they first started cutting the onion – which makes the action absurd! It is also interesting that when the cutter arrives at the 'core', the core is described as 'Not one' (line 28). These words are emphasized as they are the opening words of the final stanza. Their meaning – that the 'core' has no meaning – is highlighted through the way Kim structures her stanzas and lines. Similar to the 'Lies' of earlier, the words 'Not one' have been isolated from the 'core' as they are not only separated from the core being on a new line, but are separated from the core all the more as they are in a new stanza. The structuring of the words on the page is a clever way Kim attempts to offer us insight into her meaning here. We wonder whether the poet is suggesting that when we analyse the world around us, that we will never arrive at a singular unifying meaning and that there will always be different ways of interpreting the same object.

As readers, this **challenges** our ideas about knowledge. We are conditioned to believe that knowledge exists in the world – is this not why you study such a range of subjects in the IB and revise so hard for your end of course examinations?! This raises questions as to whether we should be studying the world in which we live. Is the process of analysis a futile and ultimately pointless act? Should we just experience the world around us and simply enjoy the good things in life whenever possible rather than try to make sense and understand the components that make up our existence? Was Romantic poet, Wordsworth, right when he said in his poem, 'Expostulation and Reply', 'we murder to dissect'? If we follow Wordsworth's advice, will this lead to ignorance and the end of progress? Is it part of the human condition to analyse and is it a necessity? These then are some of the questions and considerations that this poem challenges us to reflect on.

Step 3: Reader response to ideas and message

Kim's poem is quite informal in terms of the language used and does not include a regular meter or contain rhymes. One could argue that the three-line stanza structure mirrors the slicing of the onion in terms of every layer of the onion is exactly the same as the previous one. One could also argue that using the odd number of three lines per stanza combined with a lack of a rhyme scheme ultimately **challenges** the idea that there is a harmonious, logical and satisfying pattern that can be deciphered when we analyse the world around us, which complements the message in the poem. The use of the **personal pronoun** 'you' is also ambiguous. It could be directed at a specific person who is cutting the onion, but at the same time we feel that we are being directly addressed and challenged.

Thus, this poem uses form, structure, language, images and other features to offer insights about the pursuit of knowledge as well as challenging the reader.

Suji Kwock Kim

Suji ('Sue') Kwock Kim is a Korean-American poet and playwright who was the first Asian-American to win the Walt Whitman Award from the Academy of American Poets for her first poetry publication, *Notes from the Divided Country*, in 2003. Kim was born in the United States but much of her poetry focuses on the theme of Korea: nation, isolation and community. She is influenced by her cultural background and often uses the voices of her parents to describe their experiences in a country divided between North and South Korea. The title of her first poetry anthology also alludes to this idea. However, she also explores themes that are universal as seen in her 'Monologue of an Onion' explored here. Kim has won a number of awards for her poetry and was a Fulbright Scholar at Seoul University. She has also co-written *Private Property,* a multimedia play, which was performed at the Edinburgh Festival Fringe in the UK and appeared on BBC television.

TOK Links: The fantasy of truth

As you will know from your TOK lessons, there are different ways of knowing. One of the main functions of TOK of course is to be aware of what we **can** know, rather than just what we cannot know. The idea of the 'fantasy of truth' as conveyed in Kim's poem is in direct opposition to TOK. In what ways does the study of knowledge and an awareness of what we know improve our lives?

ACTIVITY 1

Hopefully this next task should be a fun and creative activity. Think about a global issue that concerns us. **Either** use an unfamiliar narrative voice (similar to Tolstoy's horse or Kim's onion), **or** use a familiar object as an extended metaphor (similar to Kim's cutting the onion) to give your reader an insight into your global issue. You can either write a poem or a short story. Whichever task you attempt, think in particular about:

- the form and structure you are using
- the language you are using
- The images you are using
- other literary features you are using.

Possible pairings could include:

A tree in the Amazonian rainforest reflecting on the destruction of the natural environment;

An artist's canvas reflecting on the function of art.

When you have completed this task, ask a friend or a classmate – it would be better if your friend was a language and literature student – to read and analyse your work, using our literary reading strategy. Is your partner able to understand what global issue you are exploring? Is their interpretation the same as yours or have your ideas and use of techniques been interpreted differently to how you intended?

There is no end of book commentary for this task.

'The Thought Fox' by Ted Hughes

Now that you have read the commentary on Kim's poem, it is your turn at analysis! The following poem is written by British poet laureate, Ted Hughes, and was first published in 1957 in his anthology *The Hawk in the Rain*, Hughes's first poetry anthology. In this poem, Hughes uses an animal as an **extended metaphor** to represent a key idea in the poem. Read the following poem, 'The Thought Fox', and when you have read the poem, attempt the following activity.

The Thought Fox

I imagine this midnight moment's forest:
Something else is alive
Beside the clock's loneliness
And this blank page where my fingers move.

Through the window I see no star:
Something more near
Though deeper within darkness
Is entering the loneliness:

Cold, delicately as the dark snow
A fox's nose touches twig, leaf;
Two eyes serve a movement, that now
And again now, and now, and now

Sets neat prints into the snow
Between trees, and warily a lame
Shadow lags by stump and in hollow
Of a body that is bold to come

Across clearings, an eye,
A widening deepening greenness,
Brilliantly, concentratedly,
Coming about its own business

Till, with a sudden sharp hot stink of fox
It enters the dark hold of the head.
The window is starless still; the clock ticks,
The page is printed.

(Ted Hughes)

In this poem, Hughes is exploring the notion of creativity through the **extended metaphor** of an animal – a 'thought fox'. In a writing programme he recorded for school children on 'Capturing Animals' and later published in *Poetry in the Making* (1967), Hughes explains how he views this 'thought fox':

> *So you see, in some ways my fox is better than an ordinary fox. It will live for ever, it will never suffer from hunger or hounds. I have it with me wherever I go. And I made it. And all through imagining it clearly enough and finding the living words.*
>
> *(Ted Hughes,* Poetry in the Making *19)*

A little bit like Wordsworth's daffodils (Chapter 1.2), this thought fox is a part of Hughes' consciousness and it inspires him to find the 'living words' to create his poetry. The thought fox then is a metaphor for his imagination and the creative process – it is elusive and cannot be hurried, but it is there and if you are patient and let it be, it will show itself and suddenly 'the page is printed.'

ACTIVITY 2

Now that you have an overview of the poem's meaning, fill in the following table on how the poem offers us challenges and insights. Use the literary reading strategy to guide your thinking, and then compare your answers with those at the back of the book.

■ Table 1.6.1

How does Hughes' 'The Thought Fox' offer us insights and challenges?
Step 1: Structure and form You may want to think about the length of Hughes' stanzas, use of meter and/or rhyme. You may like to discuss his use of enjambment.
Step 2: LIFs **Language** Now move on to any interesting language that Hughes includes. You may like to think about any repeated images he uses as well as any puns you can discover. **Images** Hughes uses an extended metaphor throughout this poem. Explain what the extended metaphor is and how it works. **Other features** Finally, think about Hughes' style. Does he use formal or informal language? Can you explain why he has used this particular narrative voice?
Step 3: Reader's response to ideas and message Now explain what the poem's meaning is. The short blurb underneath the poem should help you with this.

Remember to tie all your thoughts together and keep answering the question: in what way does the poem offer us insights and/or challenge us? Once you have written your own paragraphs, compare your ideas with the responses at the back of the book.

GLOBAL ISSUES ***Field of inquiry:* Art, Creativity and the Imagination**

AESTHETIC INSPIRATION AND THE CREATIVE PROCESS

Ted Hughes' poem, 'The Thought Fox', is considered an example of **ars poetica**. This translates as the 'art of poetry' and is a term that is used to describe literature that reflects on the aesthetic inspiration, creation, craft and beauty of the artform of poetry, through the artform itself. If you undertook Activity 2 above and read the commentary at the back of the book, you will be aware of how Hughes attempts to explain aesthetic inspiration, the creative process and the role of the writer through his comparison of the imagination with a fox. As the commentary at the back of the book discusses, not only is the content of the poem about aesthetic inspiration, but the poem's form, structure and wealth of poetic/figurative language are also used symbolically to help the reader understand the imaginative process that a poet experiences when creating a poem.

Ars Poetica (15BCE), sometimes known as *Epistle to the Pisos*, was used by Roman poet, Horace, as the title for his letter to the Roman senator and consul, Lucius Calpurnius Piso, and his two sons in which he offers practical advice as to how to write poetry and drama. The letter is written in **hexameter verse** (lines with six feet). Unlike his predecessors, Plato and Aristotle, who took a theoretical approach when discussing literature, Horace took a more practical approach and lists 30 maxims for would-be poets – including his recommendation that poets should begin their works **in medias res** while warning against the use of **deus ex machina** which – as we saw with Euripides' play, *Medea* (Chapter 1.5) – resolves a plot by having a god intervene.

In your exploration of literature and non-literary texts, you may like to explore the field of inquiry of art, creativity and the imagination through the global issue of aesthetic inspiration and the creative process and use it as the basis for your individual oral.

You may also like to remind yourself of this field of inquiry which we looked at in Chapter 1.3 when we were discussing Velázquez's painting, *Las Meninas*. Remember that you would need to choose your extracts carefully as you need to contextualize both your literary and your non-literary extracts within the work/body of work they have come from.

EE Links: English A – Literature Category 1

Much of Hughes' poetry uses natural imagery. **How does Hughes depict the natural world to explore aspects of the human condition?** You could focus on a number of Hughes' poems from a single anthology such as *The Hawk in the Rain* or you may want to explore a number of his poems from his different works. For a poetry extended essay, you should be focusing on between three to five poems, depending on their length and complexity. You could use our literary reading strategy as a way to structure your close analysis of Hughes' poems.

Ted Hughes

Edward James Hughes (1930–1998) was born in Yorkshire, England, and was a poet, playwright and children's writer. He was Poet Laureate of the United Kingdom from 1984 until his death in 1998. His first poetry anthology, *The Hawk in the Rain*, was published in 1957 and his final poetry anthology, *Birthday Letters*, was published months before Hughes' death. Hughes' first wife was American poet, Sylvia Plath, and his final poetry anthology explores his relationship with Plath, who committed suicide in 1963. Hughes' earlier work is influenced by his love of nature and his poetry often explores how beauty and savagery can exist side by side. His later poetry is influenced by his interest in myths and one of his final works, *Tales from Ovid*, a retelling of many of Ovid's tales from *Metamorphosis,* won the Whitbread Book of the Year Award in 1997. Hughes also wrote many children's books, including the fantasy fictional story, *The Iron Man,* published in 1968 for his own children. The Ted Hughes Award was set up in 2009, which awards new and innovative poetic work in the United Kingdom.

'Master Harold' … and the boys by Athol Fugard

The final literary work we are going to analyse comes from *'Master Harold' … and the boys*, a drama written in 1982 by South African playwright, Athol Fugard. The play takes place in South Africa during the 1950s, during the apartheid era. The extract we are about to read is between Hally, a white South African who is the 'Master Harold' of the title, and Sam, a middle-aged black South African who works in a tea shop owned by Hally's mother. Sam is an accomplished ballroom dancer and is teaching Willie, another middle-aged black South African, who also works in the tea shop. Hally has just asked Sam to share some 'facts' about ballroom dancing competitions. Read the following extract and the accompanying commentary:

HALLY When you're dancing. If you and your partner collide into another couple.

(HALLY can get no further. SAM has collapsed with laughter. He explains to WILLIE)

SAM If me and Miriam bump into you and Hilda …

(WILLIE joins him in another good laugh)

Hally, Hally … !

HALLY *(Perplexed)* Why? What did I say?

SAM There's no collisions out there, Hally. Nobody trips or stumbles or bumps into anybody else. That's what that moment is all about. To be one of those finalists on that dance floor is like … like being in a dream about a world in which accidents don't happen.

HALLY *(Genuinely moved by SAM'S image)* Jesus, Sam! That's beautiful!

WILLIE *(Can endure waiting no longer)* I'm starting!

(WILLIE dances while SAM talks)

SAM Of course it is. That's what I've been trying to say to you all afternoon. And it's beautiful because that is what we want life to be like. But instead, like you said, Hally, we're bumping into each other all the time. Look at the three of us this afternoon: I've bumped into Willie, the two of us have bumped into you, you've bumped into your mother, she bumping into your Dad … None of us knows the steps and there's no music playing. And it doesn't stop with us. The whole world is doing it all the time. Open a newspaper and what do you read? America has bumped into Russia, England is bumping into India, rich man bumps into poor man. Those are big collisions, Hally. They make for a lot of bruises. People get hurt in all that bumping, and we're sick and tired of it now. It's been going on for too long. Are we never going to get it right? … Learn to dance life like champions instead of always being just a bunch of beginners at it?

HALLY *(Deep and sincere admiration of the man)* You've got a vision, Sam!

SAM Not just me. What I'm saying to you is that everybody's got it. That's why there's only standing room left for the Centenary Hall in two weeks' time. For as long as the music lasts, we are going to see six couples get it right, the way we want life to be.

HALLY But is that the best we can do, Sam … watch six finalists dreaming about the way it should be?

SAM I don't know. But it starts with that. Without the dream we won't know what we're going for …

HALLY *(A little surge of hope)* You're right. We mustn't despair. Maybe there's some hope for mankind after all. Keep it up, Willie. *(Back to his table with determination)* This is a lot bigger than I thought. So what have we got? Yes, our title: 'A World Without Collisions.'

SAM That sounds good! 'A World Without Collisions.'

HALLY Subtitle: 'Global Politics on the Dance Floor.' No. A bit too heavy, hey? What about 'Ballroom Dancing as a Political Vision?'

(The telephone rings. SAM answers it)

SAM St George's Park Tea Room … Yes, Madam … Hally, it's your Mom.

HALLY *(Back to reality)* Oh, God, yes! I'd forgotten all about that … Remember my words, Sam? Just when you're enjoying yourself, someone or something will come along and wreck everything.

(Athol Fugard 45–47)

Athol Fugard

Harold Athol Lanigan Fugard was born in 1932 in the Eastern Cape of South Africa and is a playwright as well as a novelist, actor and director. Much of his writing is political and many of his works are anti-apartheid, criticising the racially segregated politics that governed South Africa for nearly 50 years. During the apartheid years, Fugard was a prominent supporter of the Anti-Apartheid Movement and formed The Serpent Players in the 1960s, a theatre company comprizing of black actors for whom he directed and wrote plays. The national government of South Africa were critical of Fugard and as a consequence his plays were produced and published outside of South Africa. In 1982 he wrote *'Master Harold' ... and the boys* which, whilst being semi-autobiographical, was fiction rather than memoir. Many of his plays have won multiple awards and/or been made into films starring Fugard himself. The film *Tsotsi* was an adaptation of his novel with the same name and won an Academy Award for Best Foreign Language Film in 2006.

Let's use our literary reading strategy as we explore how this extract offers us insights and challenges:

Step 1: Form and Structure

It is quite clearly an extract from a work of drama and there are two main characters who are speaking. Willie, the third character, is dancing in the background during the majority of the conversation. Because the conversation is about ballroom dancing, audiences are able to visually experience the ideas Sam is expressing to Hally through watching Willie's dance. Sam appears to be the more knowledgeable of the three characters as he speaks at length about how ballroom dancing transcends reality. Willie takes an active part in the scene through his dancing whilst Hally takes a more passive role, listening and only interjecting occasionally.

The play was first performed in 1982 and although it takes place during the 1950s, apartheid – a system of institutionalised racial segregation in South Africa – was still the political system in South Africa until 1994. Fugard has given Sam, the black cleaner, considerably more lines to speak than Hally, the white owner's son, which suggests Sam is the one who holds more power at this particular moment. Furthermore, the content of what he is saying is philosophical, suggesting he has empathy and a deep understanding of the world despite his lack of opportunities, certainly compared to Hally. Sam is also using ballroom dancing as an **extended metaphor** to explain to Hally how imperfect the real world is and this, in itself, is a sophisticated technique that Sam is using effortlessly. One of the **challenges**, therefore, that some South African audiences living during the apartheid era may have experienced was the way Fugard clearly conveys Sam, who is both knowledgeable and articulate, as the intellectual superior to Hally. Even today, although Sam is much older than the 17-year-old Hally (which would explain his more comprehensive worldliness), the fact that he has a menial position in society may, for some audiences, create the idea that he is less educated compared to Hally who is in the middle of writing an English assignment for school. The roles Fugard gives to each character then challenges audiences to reflect on their own prejudices and ways of viewing individuals, predicated perhaps by one's position within society. As well as challenging us, the content of Sam's speeches offers us an **insight** into the real world and enlightens us as to why something as perfectly executed as ballroom dancing is appealing to many – especially, perhaps, those who have suffered as a consequence of political, social and/or cultural attitudes at any particular time or place.

Step 2: LIFs Language

Contrasting language is used in this extract to accentuate and juxtapose the two worlds being described. The real world is repeatedly described with the verb 'bump'. Both past and present tenses of the verb are used, implying bumping into one another has been a core element of the real world for a long time and continues to be so. The verb 'bump' also denotes a clumsiness and lack of care and Sam is suggesting, therefore, that this has been a characteristic of the real world for many years.

Sam uses the more emotive noun, 'collisions', to describe how individuals from different backgrounds and whole countries with different political systems collide. He explains how 'Those are big collisions, Hally. They make for a lot of bruises. People get hurt in all that bumping …' The language he uses here, 'bruises' and 'hurt', is the language of pain and suffering, implying that the world is a dangerous and violent place and people are not prepared to compromise or accept the idea of difference. It is a selfish world Sam is describing – almost a survival-of-the-fittest world – if you are not strong enough to withstand the knocks, then you will get hurt.

In contrast, the language Sam uses to describe ballroom dancing is much more positive. He maintains 'Nobody trips or stumbles or bumps into anybody else'. The indefinite pronoun 'nobody' accentuates how collisions on the dancefloor are non-existent; there is space for everybody and respect is afforded to all. In contrast to the clumsiness and carelessness of the real world, on the dancefloor there is an elegance and perfection that transcends the real world. He also uses language such as 'dream' to imply that although the dancefloor may be perfect, it is not real; 'beautiful' to emphasize how what people crave is not the ugliness of collisions, but the beauty of a harmonious world; and 'champions' that suggests on the dancefloor everyone is equal and has the opportunity to become a champion – it is your skill as a dancer that will be judged, rather than the colour of your skin or your social standing. There is **juxtaposition** between the collisions in the real world where both people and countries are unable to 'get it right', constantly bumping into one another, and the phrase 'six couples get it right', which suggests that multiple people are able to dance together in harmony without colliding. The fact that they are 'couples' also denotes a sense of harmony and togetherness, rather than the selfish society Sam has been describing earlier. Finally, the verb phrase 'get it right' has obvious positive connotations, suggesting that not colliding or bumping into one another is 'right' and, conversely, that the opposite must be wrong.

The language Sam uses **challenges** us to reflect on the world in which we live and how we as individuals and as a society treat others. Are we able to compromise with those who may have different opinions to ourselves? Are we able to treat all people as equals and give everyone opportunities, space and respect in order to succeed? These may be quite challenging questions for some in the audience and certainly challenging questions for people in authority who have to balance domestic and international relationships. However, the language Fugard uses also offers us **insights** into what an ideal world could look like and perhaps inspires us to change our own way of doing things and demand others to do the same in our attempt to achieve a more harmonious world, free of bumps and collisions.

Images

The main image used in this extract is that of ballroom dancing. Sam is using ballroom dancing as an **extended metaphor** to symbolize what an ideal world could look like. This is made clear when Sam describes 'To be one of those finalists on that dance floor is like … being in a dream about a world in which accidents don't happen.' The **simile** of 'being in a dream' makes it clear that this is an idealistic world, a world where the act of ballroom dancing is so perfect that perhaps it could never exist. It is at this point that Willie 'can endure waiting no longer' and starts dancing. Willie's dancing in the background is a visual representation of the elegance and beauty of ballroom dancing which, Sam argues, is lacking in the real world. It is interesting that Willie, a black South African cleaner, is dancing in his work place. He is surrounded by everything that represents his oppression and inequality (tables, chairs, his employer's son) and yet in the middle of this he is able to demonstrate what a 'beautiful' existence could look like. In a similar way to how Sam uses language eloquently to express the beauty of ballroom dancing, Willie uses his love of ballroom dancing to physically express this idea. It is almost as if Sam's dialogue accompanies Willie's dancing, much in the same way as music accompanies the dancer. This elevates Sam's words, suggesting they are music to the ears, and helps keep the audience enthralled and hooked to what he is saying. When he maintains that 'None of us knows the steps and there's no music playing', there is a sense of **irony** as we feel Willie does know the steps (or, even if he doesn't, can still dance beautifully) and although there may not be any literal music playing, Sam's voice takes the place of music. Although he acknowledges that 'I've bumped into Willie, the two of us have bumped into you …' we nevertheless feel that, perhaps, Willie and Sam are best placed to teach others how to live a bump-free existence (such as Hally and his mother, perhaps). He states ballroom dancing is 'beautiful because that is what we want life to be like'. This statement has additional power as we can see Willie effortlessly illustrating Sam's words here and we can understand the metaphor Sam is using all the better; how beautiful life would be were it as elegant and bump-free as dancing clearly is.

Sam continues to use this metaphor when he mentions how 'there's only standing room left for the Centenary Hall in two weeks' time'. He argues that this is because 'everybody' wants to watch the dancers 'get it right, the way we want life to be'. Not only is he using the same extended metaphor of ballroom dancing being 'right' but he is also suggesting that everyone craves this perfect and harmonious existence – which, one could argue, makes his current situation of being a racially discriminated against menial worker for Hally's mother an absurdity. Hally picks up on the extended metaphor Sam has been using by applying it to his English essay: 'A World Without Collisions'. Sam affirms that Hally has understood his analogy by agreeing that this title 'sounds good'. The **extended metaphor** that Sam uses, together with Willie's dancing in the background, offer audiences an **insight** into what an ideal world could look like and perhaps **challenges** audiences, also, to reflect on whether such a world can become reality or whether it will remain a dream.

Other features

There are a number of other features throughout this extract that offer us insights and challenges. Sam, for example, uses **repetition** of 'bumping' throughout his long dialogue to highlight the continued lack of awareness afforded to others. He also uses **listing** to accentuate how everyone is to blame for the collisions in life: 'I've bumped into Willie, the two of us have bumped into you, you've bumped into your mother, she bumping into your Dad' and **tripling** to emphasize how it is not only individuals that collide, but countries and groups of people: 'America has bumped into Russia, England is bumping into India, rich man bumps into poor man.' This is a **challenging** concept as Sam is making it quite clear that none of us are guilt-free.

Initially, however, we feel that Sam is making a difference with his speech. Hally is clearly inspired by it, shown through his exclamatory interjections: 'Jesus, Sam! That's beautiful!' and 'You've got a vision, Sam!' and his enthusiasm to use Sam's **extended metaphor** about the world as the basis of his English assignment. However, the mood is broken by the telephone ringing and it being Hally's mother – Sam and Willie's employer. Hally's final words in this extract are ominous. The stage directions make it quite clear he is 'back to reality' when he bemoans, 'Just when you're enjoying yourself, someone or something will come along and wreck everything.' He uses the language of collision – 'wreck' – and the suggestion is that this 'World Without Collisions' will indeed remain a dream and 'reality' will remain a 'wreck'. This is a challenging concept as it is a negative world view which offers audiences a pessimistic view of the future.

Step 3: Readers response to ideas and message

In this extract, Fugard is not suggesting that we literally bump into each other, rather he is using the idea of 'bumping' and 'colliding' to suggest that our lives are based on conflict. The ballroom dancing extended metaphor is symbolic; if you know the steps and there is music, conflict is completely avoided and every couple has the space to move around as they so wish. The idea here is that if we learn to understand others' needs and desires (the 'steps'), and if there is a will or justice or regulation (the 'music' the dancers are following) then the world could be a much more peaceful place, with far fewer conflicts. Those who achieve success (becoming the 'champions' of the dancefloor) will do so based on their own merit rather than based on their racial or social background. As this was written during the apartheid era of South Africa, this would appear to be a direct criticism of that particular political system, which centred on institutionalised segregation based on an individual's race. It is likely that the audience's background and personal experiences will affect how they respond to the ideas embedded within this extract. Some audiences may find Sam's speech and Willie's dance so inspiring that, despite Hally's pessimistic outlook, they may feel change is possible and be inspired to take the first step. Others may agree with Hally, that Sam's vision is too idyllic and in reality it can never exist. However, as Sam states 'Without the dream we won't know what we're going for'. Similar to Martin Luther King Jr.'s 'dream' (Chapter 1.2), Sam is suggesting that without a dream there will be no chance of future change, so it is better to dream than not to dream. Again, this **challenges** us to have our own dreams in order to at least 'try for something real' and make reality better.

Of course it is not just literary works that offer us insights and challenges; non-literary texts can also offer us insights and challenges and we are now going to focus on three different text types: a video from an animated web series; a recruitment poster; and an online science magazine article about de-extinction.

Non-literary text types that offer insights and challenges

Animated video: The Smith Family children's charity

Our first non-literary text is an animated video published on the website of an Australian children's charity, The Smith Family. There are six videos in the series, *Tales of the One in Six*, and this one, 'Jess and the Mighty Journey: A True Story', is the third episode in the series. The animated video follows the journey of Jess from when she was about 5 years old to her present 25-year-old self, and tells the story of her challenging childhood.

However, as well as focusing on this particular 'true story', the video also gives us an insight into The Smith Family, the children's charity that supported her in her time of difficulty. We can, therefore, view this video as being both an autobiographical story of Jess' life but also an 'animated explainer video' – a video whose purpose is to explain to viewers about, in this case, the charity itself. Before we watch and analyse the video, read the following key features box.

KEY FEATURES ANIMATED EXPLAINER VIDEOS

- Short animated video that explains a business idea or the work of a charity, etc. in a simple and straightforward way.
- Uses simple and concise language.
- Focuses on a specific target audience.
- Uses high quality graphics and sound.
- Includes animated characters that are appealing to the viewer.
- May use colour imagery that connects with the brand's identity.
- Includes music or sound effects that match the mood of the narrative.
- Includes a professional voice-over.

Scan the QR code and then watch the animated video on the right-hand side of the webpage underneath the headline 'Jess and the Mighty Journey'. It is 2 minutes and 27 seconds in length.

We are going to use our non-literary reading strategy to analyse how this video offers us insights and challenges.

Step 1: GAP

Genre	Animated video about a child's challenging childhood and how she has overcome it; animated explainer video explaining how The Smith Family charity supports disadvantaged children in Australia.
Audience	Potential Australian donors and/or sponsors for this children's charity; possibly other disadvantaged families in Australia.
Purpose	To inform us about Jess' story; to explain to us about The Smith Family charity; to persuade viewers to donate money to the charity or sponsor a child.

Step 2: Structure and style

The video follows a narrative arc, starting with Jess when she is about 5 years old and finishing when she is 25. It follows a strictly **chronological structure** which makes it a straightforward narrative to follow. The animated video is structured in two halves: the first half narrates the challenging childhood Jess has experienced and the second half tells us how her life was turned around due to The Smith Family charity's support. The video ends on a positive note, looking forward to the future when Jess will be a qualified doctor able to help other people suffering from multiple sclerosis, the illness her mother was diagnosed with. It is a simple narrative, told through simple language, animated visuals, music and other sound effects which would appeal to many viewers, including children.

The voice-over is a female Australian voice who uses the first person pronoun throughout and constantly refers to 'my mum'. We assume, therefore, that this is Jess in the present narrating her life story using simple language and sentence structures which make her story clear, concise and personal. There is no **figurative language** in the spoken word, but the non-textual **visual images** used, such as the dark swirling circles in the first half and the rhombus-shaped image in the second half, are symbolic. There are no subtitles so this encourages the viewer to listen to the words spoken and the female narrator's tone of voice.

The video is animated throughout and is reminiscent of a children's fairy tale. We are following a rags-to-riches narrative with Jess playing the role of a modern-day Cinderella and The Smith Family charity taking on the role of a fairy godmother/saviour figure. This is appropriate as the subject of the video is a child and it may also remind viewers of their own childhoods, challenging them to step into the shoes of Jess in order to experience what she has experienced. Because it is an animated video, not only are the identities of Jess and her mother concealed ensuring confidentiality is maintained, but this also infers that the story we are listening to and watching is a story experienced by many other children, not just this one particular child.

It is quite clear where we are supposed to be **challenged**: Jess' early disadvantaged childhood is through no fault of her own and, just as Jess finds it challenging to remain upbeat, so do the viewers. There appears no support network to help Jess and her mother initially which also challenges us. However, half–way through the video The Smith Family are mentioned by name and we are given an **insight** into the way this charity supports children like Jess. We are relieved, inspired and motivated, it is hoped, to donate to the charity and/or sponsor a child.

Step 3: Typographical and graphological features of the text

There are four frames that contain written text. The first frame of the video contains details of the series.

Tales of the

One In Six

Episode 3

The Smith Family logo

The typography used for the first line, 'Tales of the', is a cursive script, reminiscent of a child's handwriting. This ties in with the fact that the video we are about to watch is one particular child's personal and intimate story, rather than, for example, a corporate business story. This offers us an **insight** into the kind of video we are about to view.

The second line of text, 'One In Six', is in a much bolder capitalized font so that it stands out. If you read the additional information on the website's page where the video is published, you will discover that Jess represents just one child from the one in six children who are living in poverty in Australia. This is a statistic that is verifiable; it is a shocking statistic and using a bold typeface ensures viewers are unable to ignore it. This, then, offers us an **insight** into child poverty in Australia whilst challenging us due to the high number of disadvantaged children in the country.

The third line of text, 'Episode 3', is in another font and makes it clear this video is part of a series. If you were to watch all six videos you could classify this as a body of work.

The final line of text is The Smith Family logo: two stylised red hands hugging a blue rectangle which could symbolize a child's torso. It is the only colour on this page – all the other text is white on a black background – so the red and blue of the logo stand out and we are likely to recognise the charity through their memorable branding.

The next frame of text occurs in about the third frame, after the introductory animated frame introducing the child and where she used to live. The text on this frame is again white font on a black background and it acts like the title page of a book:

JESS

& The Mighty Journey

A True Story

The first line of text is 'JESS' and it is in a large blocked font. This is the child's name and represents her own unique identity. Jess is often a shortened version of Jessica so by being introduced with her abbreviated name creates an intimacy as if we know her, and thus we are immediately emotionally involved with her story.

The second line of text, '& The Mighty Journey', is capitalized and the font chosen uses elongated letters. This perhaps is a visual representation of how Jess' journey through childhood is also long due to the challenges she faces. Using the ampersand '&' rather than the word 'and' creates an informal **tone** – again, this is a child's personal story rather than a formal corporate story.

The final line of text, 'A True Story', is in smaller typeface, but still capitalized, and makes us aware that this is not a fictional fairy tale but is in fact 'true'. Perhaps this line of text is required because what we are about to watch may feel like a fairy tale (a tale of rags-to-riches) and serves as a reminder to us that Jess' story is autobiographical and, moreover, applies to 'one in six' children in Australia. This again offers us an insight into the true situation of child poverty in the country whilst being a challenging fact to come to terms with.

There are two additional frames of text that occur after the narrative has been told. The penultimate frame is:

> Helping Young Australians Create Better
>
> Futures For Themselves

This is in a slimline capitalized font and is a **declarative** statement. The statement is motivational in tone, uses positive language, 'helping', 'better' and 'futures', and focuses on the subject of the video and the people Jess represents ('Young Australians'). In contrast to the text at the beginning of the video, this text is inspiring and offers us an insight into the work of the charity and the positive effects it has on children's lives in Australia. Note that the nouns and pronouns are all in the plural – 'Australians', 'Futures' and 'Themselves' – which give us an insight into how the charity supports multiple children and that Jess' story is just one of many. Thus, the typographical features used in the written text help to offer us both **insights** and **challenges**.

ACTIVITY 3

The final frame is also text-based. What is the effect of the typographical features used (you will need to view the final frame at 2:23 of the video) and how do they offer viewers insights and challenges?

When you have completed this activity, check the response at the end of the book.

> Sponsor An Australian Child Today
>
> THESMITHFAMILY.COM.AU
>
> The Smith Family logo
>
> everyone's family

In terms of **graphological features**, the rest of the video is animated with each frame taken up entirely with animated moving visuals. There is a mixture of long-shot and close-up frames, and recognisable animated characters and cityscape scenes with symbolic swirling black circles and shining golden rhombus shapes. The range of animations included not only ensure the viewer's interest is maintained but they are used in such a way that we are offered insights and challenges through the rags-to-riches narrative arc we are viewing. We will analyse the visuals used in more detail in **steps 4 and 5** of our non-literary reading strategy.

Step 4: Other features of the text type

You may like to remind yourself of the key features of animated explainer videos on page 219 before you read this section. This particular video includes all of the conventional features of this particular text type. It is relatively short at 2:27 and by the end of the video we have an insight into who The Smith Family charity work with (disadvantaged Australian children), what they do (offer financial support to Australian children experiencing poverty) and how they do it (through sponsorships from viewers like you and me).

The video uses simple and concise language throughout. The voice-over uses simple **declarative** sentences and the vocabulary she uses is straightforward so that a wide range of viewers, including children, can fully comprehend and access her story. She is telling us the story of her childhood and we feel she is using the language of her younger self to reflect this. She does not use any **figurative language** or literary features and this makes her story all the more powerful. The only **subject-specific language** she uses is 'multiple sclerosis' and towards the end of the video, she explains how she is now researching 'MS'. Most viewers would understand that 'MS' is an **acronym** for multiple sclerosis, particularly as she makes this statement immediately after she acknowledges that 'Throughout my entire childhood my mum has been my role model.' The structure of the narrative means we associate 'MS' with her mother. If we are unsure what multiple sclerosis (MS) is, the visuals give us an insight into some of the effects of this illness: tiredness, shaking and an inability to work for long periods of time. This is one of the ways the spoken language and the animated visuals support one another to ensure viewers have a full understanding of Jess' story.

We are also **challenged** by the way Jess clearly cannot escape what she is experiencing: neither she nor her mother can cure her mother's illness and we feel it is unfair that a child so young as Jess should experience so much hardship through no fault of her own. The fact that she is clearly an innocent child creates **pathos** and is one way the viewer is encouraged to respond emotionally to Jess' story. The only other **subject-specific language** is 'outback' which the **target audience** – Australian viewers – would recognise as being the remote parts of their country. This places the text in a particular region as well as giving us an insight into Jess' background. The video's audience are also targeted through the voice-over itself. It is clearly a female with a strong Australian accent speaking, similar perhaps to the accent of many of the viewers. This is another way an emotional connection may be forged between the narrator and the narratee, by making 'Jess' appear similar to many of the viewers.

All the animations are simple but high quality, accompanied by music and other sound effects. The voice-over itself has been recorded so that every word is clearly enunciated. We may feel the narrator is sitting in the same room as us, so clear and precise is the recording of her voice. Music and other sound effects are also an integral part of the video and they are used to accentuate the mood of the story. The first frame includes light piano music and the sound of birds singing which give us an **auditory image** into Jess' early childhood before her mother becomes ill: she is happy, living in the rural outback and has no worries. When Jess discovers her mother is not well, the music changes to a darker mood through lower notes and a slower pace. In addition, a number of sound effects are included so that we can literally hear as well as see the story being told through the voice-over. For example, we hear someone crying during the close-up of Jess crying (0:32); we hear the sounds of something being dragged along the floor as we see an animated image of Jess dragging a huge bag of rubbish out to the rubbish bins one night (0:43); we hear marching feet as we see multiple grey silhouettes of people walking through the city (0:48). At 1:21 (just under half-way) when Jess admits 'it was overwhelming', the music changes again to a haunting soundtrack full of sounds that echo and repeat, imitating how overwhelming and inescapable Jess' poverty has become. Huge black circles swirl around Jess' small figure at this point in the video and the combination of symbolic **visual images** and **auditory images** are powerful in giving us an insight into Jess' physical and emotional distress during the period she is living in a car with her mother.

Ten seconds later, both the visuals and the music change. A shining rhombus-shape flashes through the darkness and the music becomes lively and upbeat. The voice-over is saying 'It was at that time mum found The Smith Family' and we subconsciously link the rhombus that is full of light and movement with the charity. For the rest of the video the music remains upbeat and the animated images include many recognisable symbols of music and dance: in one frame the rain appears to be dancing to the music; musical notes fly through some of the frames; the rhombus twirls in Jess' mother's hands like a dancer; and Jess is seen skipping up the animated book-steps to the door that represents education and her future career as a doctor. The final frame when Jess looks at her image dressed as a doctor in the doorway of learning is accompanied by a burst of singing and a spinning rhombus. Music and sound effects, therefore, offer us an **insight** into how to interpret the voice-over as well as engaging us and offering us an auditory as well as a visual experience.

In terms of colour imagery that connects to the brand's identity, the fact that Jess is always wearing a blue top during her childhood years is a reminder of the charity's blue rectangular logo, which is supposed to symbolize a child's torso. There are many times throughout the video where Jess' mother is hugging Jess and offering her emotional support despite her illness. She is unable to offer her financial security, due to her illness, and this perhaps suggests that The Smith Family's hands of their logo do not replace the child's family's hands, but they are an extra pair of hands to turn to in financial need. In this way, the brand's identity is constantly embedded, albeit subtly. The logo itself is placed at the beginning and the end of the video, which denotes its significant role in turning Jess' story of hardship and poverty into a story of hope and success. It is a powerful reminder to the viewer that it is this particular charity that has such a positive impact on children's lives.

Step 5: Visual image and layout

As has already been discussed, the visual images and other non-textual visual symbols are obviously an integral part of this animated video. The animated characters are symbolic rather than literal representations of the narrator and her mother but we find them appealing, perhaps because they remind us of fairy tale characters from our childhood. Mother and child are juxtaposed throughout which helps create **pathos** for Jess. In the first frame, for example, Jess is peering over the window sill of her bedroom window with a ladybird on her hand. The voice-over tells us 'I grew up in a very tiny little town'. The girl herself appears 'very tiny' and 'little' so although the voice-over is describing the place she grew up in, we can also apply the language to the child herself. The ladybird is enlarged which also accentuates how small Jess is when this story begins. We are reminded of the child's young age, also, in the animated frames showing us the extra responsibilities she takes on around the house to help her mother. One frame shows her standing on tiptoe on a stool attempting to reach a cupboard and one frame shows her dragging a bag of rubbish that is as big as Jess herself. **Spatial mechanics** and **proxemics** are used, therefore, to remind us of her young age which in turn creates **pathos**. We are challenged by these images which, the charity would hope, would motivate us to sponsor a child to ensure other disadvantaged children are able to escape the poverty trap.

Throughout the video, Jess is always dressed in a blue top and skirt. She is easily identifiable, reminding us that she is the protagonist of this story, she is telling her own story. As already discussed, her blue top may also remind us of The Smith Family's blue logo, a constant reminder of the charity's brand. Her mother is dressed in a yellow dress in the early frames which is a positive colour, giving us an insight into the happy relationship Jess and her mother had prior to her illness. However, the moment Jess realizes her mother is ill (0:21), the mother's dress becomes dark grey. For the rest of the video this is the clothing she wears, a constant reminder that happiness and joy have been stripped from their lives due to something beyond their control. At 2:04, after her mother has found The Smith Family and Jess' life has been turned around, we have one final image of Jess' mother, dressed once more in her yellow dress. The voice-over that accompanies this image is how Jess' mother has always been a role-model to her. The yellow dress symbolizes the positive impact the mother has had on the child despite her illness and inability to financially support her child. Colours, therefore, are used symbolically and help give us an insight into the emotions experienced by Jess and her mother at different points in their lives together.

Other non-textual visual images are used throughout the video to enhance the mood. At certain points, an entirely black frame appears with neither text nor visuals. The black frame is almost used like a **volta** in a poem: it denotes a shift in mood, situation, perspective or time.

ACTIVITY 4

Complete the following table. Fill in the middle column with the appropriate shift(s). In the final column explain the shift that occurs in the video in your own words. The first one has been completed for you.

Time of shift	Shift in mood, situation, perspective and/or time	Explanation
0:19	Shift in mood	Trouble-free and happy mood to troubled and sad mood
0:34		
1:25		
2:12		

When you have completed this table, check the table at the back of the book.

Two other symbolic uses of non-textual visual imagery are the large, black swirling circles that are used in the first half of the video and the rhombus-shaped symbol that at times glows and spins which is used in the second half of the video. The black, swirling circles, as already discussed, are used to symbolize Jess' physical and emotional trauma as a consequence of poverty and they give viewers an insight into how poverty affects the individual. In **contrast** to Jess, the circles are huge and Jess is depicted as a small figure being consumed by these dark circles. This is a challenging image for viewers and the charity would hope this **visual imagery** would encourage viewers to become a sponsor for another disadvantaged Australian child.

In the second half of the video, a golden-coloured rhombus is used that reminds viewers of a shining star or a diamond. It is in direct contrast to the dark swirling circles and represents hope and success. The first time it appears it is a small speck in the middle of a dark circle but by the end, it has grown to a huge presence and envelops the Jess-as-a-doctor image. This obviously gives viewers an insight into how The Smith Family charity represents hope even for the most disadvantaged children and how, over time, they make a huge impact on the individual. This idea is reinforced throughout the second half of the video. For example, in some frames, rays of light emanate from the shape, suggesting it represents light in a dark place; in some frames it twirls and spins, suggesting it can offer you an exciting alternative to the dead-end existence you may have found yourself in; and in some frames it takes the position of either the mother's or the girl's heart, suggesting it is a positive life-force that can offer emotional support. Ultimately, it is a visual symbol for The Smith Family charity, suggesting this is what the charity can offer disadvantaged children.

Step 6: Reader response to ideas, message and/or purpose

Through visual and auditory imagery, this video fulfils its two main purposes. Firstly, it tells the story of one particular Australian girl's journey from hopelessness to hope. This offers viewers an insight into some of the specific experiences children in Australia suffer as a consequence of poverty. Many viewers would find this a **challenging** story, particularly as it is foregrounded with the fact that this is 'A True Story' and the voice-over appears to be the actual voice of the girl in question. Secondly, the video successfully explains to viewers the role The Smith Family charity plays in supporting disadvantaged children in Australia. We are given an **insight** into the charity through the written text which details the charity's website and logo; the voice-over which mentions by name The Smith Family; the visual image of the rhombus-star-diamond that becomes a symbol for the charity; the music which is used to symbolize the positive impact the charity has on disadvantaged children; and the subtle branding that is embedded throughout, through the colouring of Jess' clothes. The final text we read is a request to sponsor an Australian child and this is a direct **challenge** to viewers to become actively involved in supporting this charity and becoming part of The Smith Family's family.

CONCEPT CONNECTION

REPRESENTATIONS

In this animated video, Jess and her mother are represented as non-realistic animated characters. Although we can identify them as people, neither character has a mouth and they are cartoon-like animated illustrations rather than real-life depictions of people. The video purposely misrepresents reality for a number of reasons: it keeps individuals' identities concealed; it suggests that this story could be any child's story; it reminds viewers of children's fairy tale animations; it engages a wide range of viewers; it offers both insights and challenges about child poverty in Australia and about the charity itself. We have explored a number of literary works in this section which also misrepresent reality through non-textual visual images including Art Spiegelman's *Maus* (Chapter 1.1) and Shaun Tan's *The Arrival* (Chapter 1.3).

This is an interesting concept that you could explore further in the texts you study in class. How do writers represent or misrepresent reality and how does this offer us an insight or challenge us to view the world or our values differently?

Recruitment posters

The next non-literary text type we are going to explore that offers insights and challenges is the recruitment poster. Recruitment posters are frequently used during wartime to encourage civilians to support the war effort or to sign up to fight. This text type often offers readers an insight into attitudes of a particular country during wartime and challenges readers to reflect on their own role in supporting the war effort. Before we look at a British recruitment poster from the First World War, read the key features box below.

KEY FEATURES RECRUITMENT POSTERS

- Can be wholly visual, wholly textual or multimodal.
- Persuasive techniques including emotive and hyperbolic language, exclamatives and rhetorical questions, second person personal pronouns, etc.
- Striking visual images, using colour effectively.
- Emotional appeal by making the target audience feel guilt if he or she does not sign up.
- Patriotic appeal by praising/celebrating one side whilst demonising the enemy.
- Often aimed at a particular target audience in terms of gender, background, social status, etc.
- May include an explicit or implicit warning – what will happen if you do not sign up.

The recruitment poster on the following page was produced in 1915 in Britain during the First World War. Firstly, read the poster's GAP table:

Genre	Recruitment poster.
Audience	British fathers with young children.
Purpose	To persuade fathers with young families to sign up to the war effort.

Now look at the recruitment poster and read the annotations. The blue annotations identify a particular feature, whilst the red annotations focus on how the feature offers insights or challenges:

Daughter's gaze: looking at father for guidance and inspiration.

Father's gaze: cannot meet her gaze.

Challenge: if father wants to feel worthy of his daughter's gaze, he needs to join the war effort.

Background colours: co-ordinating patterns on curtains and armchair suggest a comfortable and domestic setting – but the father is unable to enjoy it.

Challenge: to enjoy home life, he needs to take part in the war effort. Sense of guilt: he's unable to enjoy domestic bliss while other fathers are fighting to secure peace.

Visual symbolism of the book: white pages represent purity, clear conscience. Daughter wants father to contribute to the story, but he has no story to tell. Does the book recount tales of heroism?

Challenges father: does he feel empty and ashamed?

Absent mother, where is she? Has she left him because she is ashamed? Has she joined the war effort herself?

Challenge: father will have to face children alone with no support from their mother.

Son's gaze: looking at soldiers rather than at his father.

Challenge: if father wants son to look him in the eye he has to join the war effort.

Spatial mechanics/ simplified visual image:

- soldiers are small
- dressed smartly in red uniforms
- all standing
- no enemy.

Challenges: simplifies and sanitises war; injuries and death are avoided.

Colour imagery: father's suit and boy's shorts are the same colour, suggesting they are 'cut from the same cloth', inextricably linked.

Challenge: son's identity is shaped by his father's actions.

Typographical features:

- cursive script – personal and intimate tone
- personal pronoun YOU capitalized and underlined for emphasis
- unanswered interrogative – cannot answer if you didn't go to war.

Challenges any father directly who did not go to war.

ACTIVITY 5

Find another recruitment poster (it does not have to be a First World War or a British recruitment poster). If you can, make a copy of the poster. Complete a GAP table and annotate the poster in a similar way to the poster above. Use two colours in your annotations: one colour identifies and examines a particular feature and another colour explains how this feature offers insights or challenges. There is no back of book response to this activity but if you do this activity with a friend or classmate on the same recruitment poster, you could compare ideas when you have both finished.

Cosmos, online science magazine on 'de-extinction'

Our final non-literary text comes from an online magazine, *Cosmos*, an Australian science magazine. *Cosmos* is a magazine that attempts to popularize 'the science of everything' by making its stories accessible to everyone. This article is published in the online magazine of *Cosmos* and is about an aspect of biology called 'de-extinction'. Read the following article, focusing on how the writer offers us insights into this particular scientific area of knowledge but also challenges us to consider the consequences of actively applying this knowledge in the real world. The following article was published on 8 March 2017:

What is de-extinction and how do you do it?

Lately there's been a lot of talk about bringing back mammoths from the dead, using a process called de-extinction. How is that possible, and is it a good idea? Stephen Fleischfresser explains.

In February of this year, scientists from Harvard University in the US announced their plans to create a live woolly mammoth in just two years.

Wait, what? A woolly mammoth? The massive elephant-like creature with long fur and huge tusks, last seen roaming the frozen tundra in the Ice Age (both the time period and the movie)? Aren't they extinct?

Well, yes, they are extinct, but that doesn't seem to matter anymore!

We've all heard of extinction. It's when a species of plant or animal no longer exists, and is normally marked by the death of the last living individual of that species. Extinct species are even famous, like the dodo of Mauritius, or 'Benjamin' the last Tasmanian tiger, which died in 1936.

So what's 'de-extinction' then? Well, if you listen to George Church of Harvard University, it's the process of bringing an extinct species back to life, and this is exactly what he intends to do with the mammoth!

But how on earth do you do it? Every living organism has tiny molecules that contain instructions on how each organism will look and function. These molecules are called deoxyribonucleic acid, or DNA, and are unique to every living being. Church and his team plan to take DNA from the bodies of mammoths that were trapped in ice or permafrost somewhere between four and 10 thousand years ago, and mix it with the DNA of its nearest living relative, the Asian elephant.

There are many mammoths that have been frozen in the ice in Siberia that modern scientists have preserved in laboratories. Scientists can extract the DNA from these to de-extinct the species! The problem is that after an organism dies its DNA tends to break up and degrade.

So how do you fix that? Here comes the Asian elephant to the rescue!

By using the DNA of the elephant, scientists can patch up the holes in the mammoth DNA to produce a whole DNA sequence that can be used to create a live mammoth. The Harvard team are using the new and incredibly exciting gene-editing technology called CRISPR to do this. CRISPR is short for 'clustered regularly interspaced short palindromic repeats' (now we know why they just call it CRISPR!), and is the most precise, easiest and least expensive way to take genes and put them wherever you like.

This amazing technology will enable scientists to take the mammoth genes and insert them into the DNA of Asian elephants to produce a complete sequence. After that, the DNA will be placed inside an egg cell of an Asian elephant, and from this will grow a live mammoth.

Church and his team believe they can do this by 2019, just two short years away. Not long after that, we hope, there will be mammoths wandering around all over the place! But, hold on! If you're mixing mammoth and elephant DNA together, do you really get a woolly mammoth?

Well, sort of. What you really get is a 'mammophant', a hybrid of a mammoth and an elephant. It would totally look like a mammoth though, with long tusks, small ears and long shaggy fur. It would even have some other mammoth traits, such as blood that is adapted to very cold weather. So, although it might not be exactly like the woolly mammoths of the past, it will be pretty close, and half a mammoth is better than no mammoth at all, right?

So perhaps we can de-extinct species that have died out, but should we? Should we bring back the mammoth? It's a tricky question. Mammoths, like elephants, were a social species: they need the company of other members of their own species. If we only bring one individual back to life, won't they get terribly lonely? Well, perhaps over time scientists can create a large number of mammoths so they can have friends to socialise with. But then we'd have a huge herd of big, powerful, hungry mammoths. Where will they live?

There actually might be an answer to that. There is already a place called Pleistocene Park in north-eastern Siberia where scientists have recreated much of the environment of the last Ice Age. This is exactly the environment which mammoths lived in 10 thousand years ago. So it is here that scientists are thinking of releasing mammoths into the wild.

So maybe we can de-extinct mammoths and thylacines, but the big question is: can we de-extinct a dinosaur? Can we finally make *Jurassic Park* a reality? Unfortunately, the answer seems to be 'no'. Where the mammoth has been extinct for 4,000 years and the thylacine for less than 100 years, the dinosaurs have been extinct for 65.5 million years. Given the half-life of DNA is 521 years, it is nearly impossible that enough genetic material would remain intact for us to be able to use to de-extinct a dinosaur.

Sadly, *Jurassic Park* must remain on our movie screens for now. Instead, we will have to make do with Pleistocene Park. It might not have a T-rex, but it could have mammoths – and that's pretty awesome.

STEPHEN FLEISCHFRESSER is a lecturer at the University of Melbourne's Trinity College and holds a PhD in the History and Philosophy of Science.

(Fleischfresser)

ACTIVITY 6

Complete the following GAP table on the article:

Genre	
Audience	
Purpose	

When you have completed the table, check your responses to those at the back of the book.

Insights in the online article

'De-extinction' is an area of science also known as resurrection biology or species revivalism. In this article, the writer, Stephen Fleischfresser – who is also a lecturer at the University of Melbourne and has a PhD in the History and Philosophy of Science – attempts to demystify this scientific area of knowledge and in this way he is able to offer insights to readers who may not have a scientific background or understand some of the scientific **jargon** that is often used when discussing science. Let us first look at the ways in which Fleischfresser attempts to familiarize us with this topic and offer us insights into this scientific domain.

Insights offered by Fleischfresser:

- Early on in the article, he explains clearly what the scientific term 'de-extinction' means. First, he explains what 'extinction' means by using examples many readers would be familiar with (the dodo and 'Benjamin' the last Tasmanian tiger). Then he moves on to explain quite simply that de-extinction is 'the process of bringing an extinct species back to life' (lines 9–10). This is like a stepped approach and it means that every reader is likely to be able to follow this simple two-pronged approach.
- The article is structured in relatively short paragraphs which also helps us follow Fleischfresser's explanation. It is almost as if each new piece of information which builds up

our understanding of the topic is reduced to a small soundbite which is memorable and easy to understand and follow.

- He uses a key feature of online articles, the **hyperlink**, to enable readers to find out more about de-extinction if they so wish. George Church from Harvard University has talked about this scientific area of knowledge and we are given the option to click on the hyperlink 'listen' (line 11) if we would like to find out more in-depth information about the topic. This gives the reader a sense of power and independence – we have enough insight into de-extinction to continue reading and understanding this article, but if we would like to further our insight into the topic, we have the option to do so.
- Fleischfresser includes some scientific **jargon** but he explains in layman's terms what each term means. For example, 'These molecules are called deoxyribonucleic acid, or DNA, and are unique to every living being.' (lines 14–15). You will be able to find other examples of this throughout the article. He either uses simplified language to explain the meaning of scientific terms or he uses an **acronym** that we may be familiar with which also simplifies the far more complex specialist scientific language. The effect of this is that we feel the writer is knowledgeable and credible about this particular subject, we feel he is teaching us about a complex topic and, most importantly, we are able to understand the topic as well as understand the scientific jargon. This is a feel-good factor for the reader!
- Fleischfresser uses a question and answer format that both challenges the reader but also offers insights. First, the questions the writer asks may challenge us as we try to answer them ourselves: 'The problem is that after an organism [like a mammoth] dies its DNA tends to break up and degrade. So how do you fix that?' (lines 19–21). For the non-scientist, this is a difficult question and one we are supposed to be challenged by. However, in the next sentence, Fleischfresser answers this challenging question for us: 'Here comes the Asian elephant to the rescue!' (line 19). And then the next paragraph develops his answer. This question and answer format encourages the reader to become actively involved and engaged in the article, but by including the answers, offers the reader insights and a fuller understanding of the topic.
- Fleischfresser even includes clues as to how we are supposed to respond emotionally to some of the information and attempts to add humour to lighten the mood when explaining some particularly in-depth scientific term: 'CRISPR is short for "clustered regularly interspaced short palindromic repeats" (now we know why they just call it CRISPR!)' (lines 24–25). Although the writer is discussing a serious topic, he does not appear to take himself too seriously which many readers will find appealing. However, he is sharing scientific **jargon** with us here and so he is offering us insights into the world of science. But he is doing it in a fun way.
- Fleischfresser also includes simple facts that the reader can understand: the number of years ago when the last living mammoth died, how many years DNA lasts for before it begins to break up, the year the last Tasmanian tiger died. This factual information can of course be substantiated and also fills us with insight and knowledge.
- Finally, Fleischfresser mentions popular culture – films such as *Ice Age* and *Jurassic Park* – that makes the article appear relevant, less elitist and allows the readers to feel more involved as most of them will be familiar with at least one of these films, if not both. We feel that having watched these films actually helps us understand the article more and this also is a way we are offered insights into the topic.

Challenges in the online article

However, the text also raises challenges about this area of scientific knowledge. Fleischfresser himself makes explicit mention of some of the ways we are supposed to feel challenged by this information, but by the end of the article it is likely that there may be other ways we feel challenged now that we understand what de-extinction is and what it could mean for our future. Here are some of the ways the text challenges us:

How does Fleischfresser's article challenge us?

- In the sub-heading underneath the headline, Fleischfresser poses this question about de-extinction: 'How is that possible, and is it a good idea?' The article is **foregrounded** with a question that challenges us. We are about to go on a journey of discovery to learn about a new scientific area of knowledge; however, the final question, 'is it a good idea?', suggests that there may be evidence to support it is not a good idea.
- As already discussed, there are multiple questions peppered throughout the text and this forces the reader to engage with the text and attempt to answer the questions. Initially, we may feel challenged to answer them in a particular way, but almost immediately after raising a question, the writer answers them. The challenge, then, does not last too long!
- We are challenged to follow through Fleischfresser's explanation. He is attempting to explain a complex scientific new area of knowledge and he uses quite a lot of scientific **jargon**. Although, as discussed, he does simplify this knowledge and jargon, we have to focus and concentrate in order to fully comprehend the meaning behind the article.
- Towards the end of the article, Fleischfresser explicitly challenges us to reflect on what the consequences may be if this scientific knowledge to de-extinct certain species is put into practice. He raises a number of questions in quick succession: 'So perhaps we can de-extinct species that have died out, but should we? Should we bring back the mammoth? … If we only bring one individual back to life, won't they get terribly lonely? Well, perhaps over time scientists can create a large number of mammoths so they can have friends to socialize with. But then we'd have a huge herd of big, powerful, hungry mammoths. Where will they live?' (lines 35–39). These are challenging questions that deal with the ethics of bringing back to life a species that has become extinct. However, like the other questions Fleischfresser has raised, in the following paragraph, he answers most of these questions and so puts the reader's mind at ease …
- … or does he? Although he does answer the final question he has raised regarding where they will live, he doesn't really answer the question about whether it is ethically right to do this. For some readers, we may feel de-extincting creatures is an attempt at playing the role of some almighty creator. There may be readers that would feel just because we may be able to de-extinct a creature, does that give us the right to do so? This is a topic that has been explored in much literature – including Mary Shelley's gothic fiction novel, *Frankenstein* (1823), and H.G. Wells' science fiction novel, *The Island of Doctor Moreau* (1896). But there may also be scientists who disapprove about this, too. Charles Darwin in his scientific book, *On the Origin of the Species* (1859), maintained that evolution was down to natural selection and many people may feel that de-extinction is not natural and, therefore, ill-advised.
- There will, of course, be other people who will feel that in order to progress, we need to be continually experimenting and putting into practice our new-found knowledge. This is how we learn. Without taking risks, we stand still.
- However the reader responds, one thing is quite clear. The topic that has just been explained and filled us with insights, is not simply an academic subject of the intellect. There are ethical considerations that are raised and this of course challenges us to reflect on progress and the future.

GLOBAL ISSUES *Field of inquiry*: Science, Technology and the Environment

SCIENTIFIC DEVELOPMENT AND PROGRESS

The Fleischfresser article makes a connection between science (biology/DNA), technology (CRISPR) and the natural world (de-extinction) and the implications this has to our future world. He suggests that the combination of scientific and technological knowledge means that man can bring back to life extinct creatures. This could change the world as we know it – both globally and locally. If de-extinction applies to a woolly mammoth that became extinct 4,000 years ago, the possibilities of de-extincting a wide range of other creatures from around the world are high. The article also discusses how a hybrid creature could be created: half-mammoth, half-Asian elephant. This would suggest that with advances in science and technology, man could potentially create new species. Some may celebrate this as evidence of man's progress; others may have ethical concerns. The idea of scientific development and progress combined with technological know-how has been the topic of both literary works (gothic fiction and science fiction) and non-literary texts (like this magazine article) for many years. You may like to explore these global issues that relate to the field of inquiry of science, technology and the environment further in the texts you study in class and base your individual oral on this issue. Remember that your oral needs to be a literary exploration and an analysis of how meaning is shaped in non-literary texts relating to your chosen global issue, rather than a social issues discussion. It is not required that you defend a particular position of how science or technology affects the progress of civilization in general. Remember, also, that any extracts you use need to be contextualized within a body of work.

CAS Links

Organize a visit to your local science museum or science and technology museum and research the progress man has made in one area of science or technology in which you are interested. If you organized this with a group of students, you could each explore a different area. For example, you may want to explore how science and technology have been used in the exploration of space, or in the medical field, or in robotics. You could then visit either a local Junior School or a lower school science class and do a short presentation on your chosen area of study. This would be a Service experience.

TOK Links: Knowledge about creation

We can see some connections between man as a creator in this non-literary text and Hughes' poem. In the non-literary text, we are encouraged to view science and technology as helping man create; in Hughes' poem, he uses the metaphor of a thought fox to symbolize the imaginative process of creating an original work. In what ways do interpretative strategies vary when reading a literary work and when reading a non-literary text? Is one way of creating better than the other?

This chapter has brought together many of the ideas discussed throughout this section to explore how literary works and non-literary texts can offer us insights and challenge us. As we know by now, whether a text offers us an insight or challenges us may be down to the individual reader and what his or her experiences are. However, it is important to be aware that writers' creativity is a discipline and a craft. Creating an original work is not a random thing that occurs – just like the final article we have read, writing also is like a science with its own set of skills and tools and as Hughes explores, the writer may need to wait patiently until that thought fox leaps into his or her head and inspiration is formed. The writer's toolbox is varied and each writer – whether writing literature or a non-literary text – has his or her own tools that they apply in a certain way. To uncover the insights and challenges that are hidden within a text is the job of the reader and, hopefully, this chapter has given you some insights into how to go about this as well as challenged you to dig deeper.

Works cited

Darwin, C. *On the Origin of Species*. Oxfod University Press, 2008.

Fleischfresser, S. 'What is de-extinction and how do you do it?' Cosmos The Science of Everything, 8 March 2017. Web. 4 March 2019. **https://cosmosmagazine.com/biology/what-is-de-extinction-and-how-do-you-do-it**.

Horace. 'Essay on Poetic Theory Ars Poetica by Horace.' *Poetry Foundation*. Web. 17 March 2019. **www.poetryfoundation.org/articles/69381/ars-poetica**.

Hughes, T. *Poetry in the Making: A Handbook for Writing and Teaching*. Faber & Faber, 2008.

Hughes, T. 'The Thought Fox.' *The Poetry Archive*. Web. 1 March 2019. **www.poetryarchive.org/poem/thought-fox**.

'Jess and the Mighty Journey.' Animation, *The Smith Family*. Web. 12 Oct. 2019. **www.thesmithfamily.com.au/stories/tales-of-the-one-in-six/jess**.

Kim, SK. 'Monologue for an Onion,' *Notes from the Divided Country: Poems*. Louisiana State University Press, 2003.

Shelley, M. *Frankenstein: Or, the Modern Prometheus*. Wordsworth Editions, 1992.

Tolstoy, L. 'Kholstomeer: The Story of a Horse by Leo Tolstoy.' *The Long Riders Guild Academic Foundation The world's first global hippological study*. Web. 2 March 2019. **www.lrgaf.org/training/kholstomer.htm**.

Wells, HG. *The Island of Doctor Moreau*. William Collins, 2017.

Wordsworth, W, Coleridge, ST. 'Expostulation and Reply.' *Lyrical Ballads, with a Few Other Poems*. CreateSpace Independent Publishing Platform, 2015.

Time and space

2.1 How important is cultural or historical context to the production and reception of a text?

OBJECTIVES OF CHAPTER

- To understand the difference between 'cultural' and 'historical' context.
- To understand the meaning and implications of 'context of production'.
- To understand the meaning and implications of 'context of reception'.
- To explore a variety of texts and understand how their production and reception is influenced by their cultural and historical contexts.

In the previous section, we were concerning ourselves with the area of exploration referred to as Readers, writers and texts. This means that we were primarily exploring the **immanent** and focusing on the information contained within the confines of the text. In doing so, we have largely been treating the text as an isolated entity, without putting much focus on how it might reflect the world it was created in.

This first chapter in Time and space is instead focused on the fact that texts are *not* isolated entities, but are connected to **time** and to **space**. First, we need to consider what we mean by 'time' and 'space'. **Time** is temporal – essentially the historical time we inhabit. **Space** is a little more complicated – we inhabit a *geographical* space in that we live in a particular place, and we inhabit a *cultural* space in that we are within a particular culture. Of course, we exist at the point of intersection between all these factors: we inhabit a particular **time**, **place** and **culture**. This affects the kind of text we might **produce**, but also how we interpret another's text when we **receive** it.

We term these connections to time and space **context**. The word is derived from the Latin *contextus* – 'con' means 'together' and 'textus' is the conjugated form of *texere*, which means 'weave' – essentially a 'weaving together' of influences that affect the **creation** of a text by a writer and the **interpretation** of a text by its reader.

These influences are many: no text is written or read in a vacuum. Both the historical *time* and the geographical and cultural *space* a text is written in has an enormous influence on its content and delivery, something we will refer to as the **context of production**. Similarly, no text is interpreted in a vacuum – the historical *time* and geographical and cultural *space* the reader finds themselves in has an enormous influence on a text's interpretation, something we will refer to as the **context of reception**. These terms will be explored more fully later in the chapter.

How does context affect the writing and reading of a text?

Now, let's break down this chapter's specific **guiding conceptual question**. In simpler terms, we are being asked the following: **How does context affect the writing and reading of a text?** The term **context** is very broad, but thankfully the guiding conceptual question narrows it down to **cultural** and **historical** context.

It is therefore useful to begin by defining the following key terms:

- **cultural context**
- **historical context**
- **context of production**
- **context clues**
- **context of reception**

As we introduce these terms, we will try a few activities to test our understanding. Then we will put the terms into practice by applying them to longer extracts, and consider how these extracts demonstrate that cultural and historical context is important to the production and reception of texts.

Defining 'cultural' and 'historical'

To begin, let's define what we mean by 'culture' and 'history' when dealing with context.

Cultural context (space) is what the inherent values, beliefs and attitudes of the time and place actually are. These are shared by a distinct group of people and affect how they view the world and interact with it. They are formed through influencers like education, religion, language, family, shared beliefs and customs.

However, many of these aspects of culture do not remain static: they change with time. This means that the **cultural context** is, more often than not, also tied in with the **historical context**.

Historical context (time) can be defined as the historical time at which the text is being produced or received. This can impact the production and reception of texts in two main ways:

- **Historical events:** The texts themselves may be inspired by major events that are usually on a national or international scale. An example of this is the First World War, with its horrors inspiring powerful words by poets like Wilfred Owen and Siegfried Sassoon.
- **Historical attitudes and values:** As previously mentioned, culture changes over time. This is often driven by historical events or historical figures. An example of this is the dramatic change of cultural attitudes towards race caused by the Civil Rights Movement in America – the way society viewed African-American people in the 1930s was very different to how they were viewed in the 1990s, for example, and this will have been reflected in texts created in those time periods.

Clearly, the cultural context and historical context have a profound effect on how texts are **produced** and on how texts are **received**; this influence is referred to as the **context of production** and the **context of reception**, terms that will now be explored in more detail.

What is meant by 'context of production'?

The cultural and historical factors that affect the content and style of a text is called its **context of production**. A text's context of production is fixed – it is written by a particular person, in a particular place, over a particular time period. This, as you would expect, has an influence on not only what is written about, but how it is written.

Cast your mind back to Chapter 1.3; there, we explored how texts are **constructed** by a writer. This point of origin, the writer, is (or was) flesh and blood – a human being like you or me. It is sometimes easy to forget this when you are reading a text from a distant time or place – everything from *The Odyssey* to *Harry Potter* was written by someone undergoing all the chaos of human experience. This human experience, usually termed 'the human condition', is the essentials of human life. This includes birth, growth, emotionality, aspiration, conflict and morality. These experiences form who we are, and every one person has different experiences to the next. These differences can sometimes be subtle: we may assume, broadly speaking, that someone growing up in modern Paris will have pretty similar experiences to someone growing up in modern London. Conversely, these differences can be much more pronounced: someone growing up in rural Mongolia will almost certainly have had very different experiences to those growing up in London and Paris. These differences arise from a multitude of factors, including, but not limited to, the following: race, gender, sexuality, religion, location, time and relationships – the 'historical' and 'cultural' factors we previously discussed.

The fingerprints of this context and its influence on a writer can be found all over a text, and these fingerprints need to be studied by us as students of Language and Literature. Through close reading of the text and research of the **context of production**, we can gain a better understanding of not only *what* the writer was trying to communicate, but often *why* they felt compelled to communicate their ideas in the first place.

This all centres on the fact that texts, as discussed in Section 1, are **acts of communication**. They are fascinating but imperfect windows into the minds and experiences of others, and, if you look carefully, they reveal an incredible amount of rich detail about the time and space they were produced in.

Context clues

These fingerprints of context that we can find on the text are what we will term **context clues**. In literary works, these can often be found in the characters, dialogue, language, style and narrative. In more visual texts, these can often be found in the clothing, models, props, layout, graphic design and the elements of language used. These features were being analysed in Section 1 using the literary and the non-literary reading strategies, but with a focus on what could be found *within* the confines of the text. In this section, these strategies can still be used to analyse our texts, but we are more concerned with how these features both reflect and communicate the **context** *beyond* the confines of the text itself.

CHECK FOR UNDERSTANDING

Can you remember each of the steps from the non-literary reading strategy? Try writing them down and then turn back to Chapter 1.1 to see if you remembered them correctly.

Consider the adverts on the following page – you will immediately recognize one is much more modern than the other. We come to this conclusion through noticing various **context clues** that reflect the culture and historical time in which they were produced, often without even having to consciously think about it. To break down the clues we are picking up on, we will apply some of the steps of the non-literary reading strategy: **typographical and graphological features** (step 3 from the strategy), the **product and props** and the **model** (these are more specific examples of step 5 'visual imagery and layout') and the use of **language** (from step 2 'structure and style').

Though the clues in these two adverts are fairly obvious (you would obviously need much more subtle detail in an exam response or individual oral), they illustrate how **context clues** can help you narrow down the time and place a text was produced.

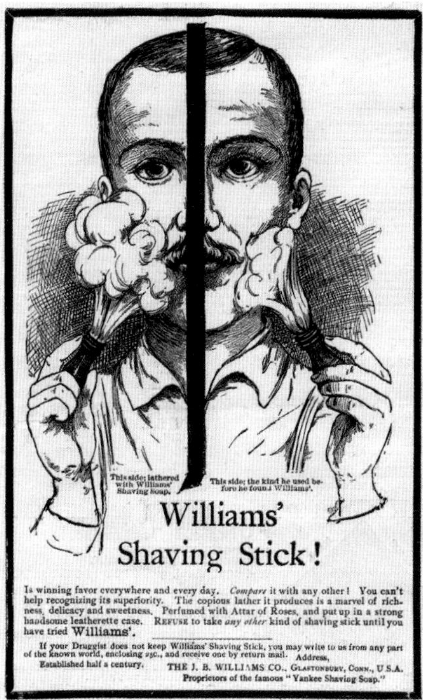

Typographical and graphological features:

Typographically, this advert uses an old-fashioned, formal font throughout.

Visual image and layout:

- Layout: The advert is clearly and simply organized, with an illustrated image at the top, captions below, and the name of the product and detailed copy at the bottom of the advert. This formal simplicity is typical of older adverts that often mimicked the style of conventional newspaper articles. This helped lend the adverts an air of authority and trustworthiness that would appeal to the readership of the time.
- Product and props: The product itself, a shaving cream that is applied with a brush, is something we associate with the past.
- Model: The clothing of the model is formal and old-fashioned, suggesting a context of production in the past.
  He also has the hair-style and facial hair of a kind that was common in the late nineteenth and early twentieth centuries. The model is showing no emotion so as not to draw focus away from the product itself.
- Illustration: The imagery in the advert is illustrated, suggesting modern techniques such as colour photography were unavailable for the production of the advert. The image is split with a line to show the differing amounts of lather produced by the product being advertised (on the left) and competing products (on the right). This black and white illustrated style was common in the late nineteenth and early twentieth centuries due to the limitations of printing technology.

Structure and style:

The copy is long and detailed, a characteristic of older adverts as they tended to demand the focus of the reader. A formal register is used. The complexity of the vocabulary ('copious', 'leatherette') suggests this advert is of the past as modern adverts tend to value clear, straightforward language over advanced lexis. Various rhetorical techniques are used, including tripling and imperatives.

Context:

From all of the context clues above, you will almost certainly have gathered this advert is from the past. It was printed in the USA in 1890.

Typographical and graphological features:

- Compared to the advert on the left, the font is bolder and more stylised. It uses the same font as the brand logo, typical of the modern emphasis on creating a cohesive brand image. There are some small illustrations that look like app icons to make the product appear high-tech and to convey information without resorting to the extensive use of text that can be seen in the other advert.

Visual image and layout:

- Layout: The advert is creative in its use of layout, with text and an image of the product layered on top of the main photo of the model. This complexity of layout is typical of modern adverts and is possible due to advanced publishing software.
- Product and props: The product comes in a plastic container with a modern looking shape and design. The shaver in the man's hand looks sleek and modern, in clear contrast to the brush and shaving foam in our other advert.
- Model: Though the model is not wearing clothes, often a useful contextual clue, his style of hair and 'designer stubble' suggest a more modern context of production.
  The expressive model is the focus of the advert. This is typical of modern adverts that often show an aspirational image of a life that readers would find appealing and then link it to the product, rather than focusing entirely on the mechanics of the product itself.
- Photography: The main image uses high quality colour photography, suggesting a more modern context.

Structure and style:

The website is a clear sign of a modern context and an American origin as it is a 'US' site. The copy is persuasive yet concise, typical of modern adverts that understand modern consumers are busy and do not have time to read detailed product descriptions.

Context:

Based on the context clues, you should have ascertained this advert is from the recent past. It was printed in the USA in 2009.

SENSITIVE CONTENT

Caution: This advert includes sensitive content and dehumanizing visuals.

The advert includes a caricature of a person of colour to exaggerate skin tone, which was a perception held at the time of production. We have chosen to include the advert as it originally appeared, so you can consider for yourself its dehumanizing effect as well as its context of production. This is central to understanding the themes of identity and human behaviour at the heart of this book. Furthermore, the IB recommends that your studies in Language A: Language and Literature should challenge you intellectually, personally and culturally, and expose you to sensitive and mature topics. We invite you to reflect critically on various perspectives offered while bearing in mind the IB's commitment to international-mindedness and intercultural respect.

ACTIVITY 1

Below you can find an advert for 'Pears Soap' and a QR code linking to Dove soap adverts. List the context clues and how they reflect their contexts of production. An example comparison between the Pear's Soap advert and Dove's 'As tested on real curves' advert can be found in the back of the book.

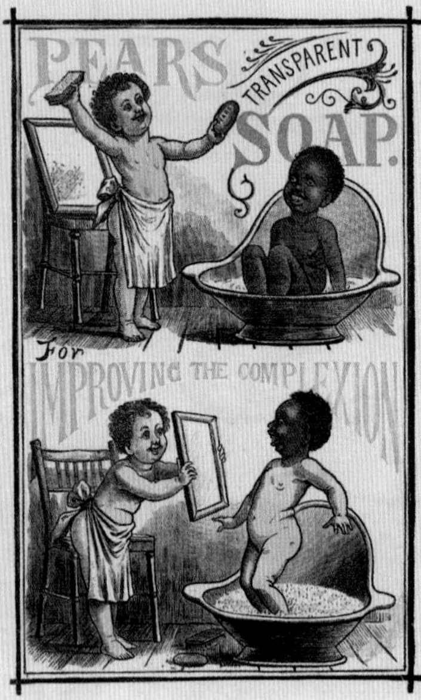

These examples should have concentrated your mind on how you use context clues to gain insight into the context of production of texts. As students of Language and Literature, this is an essential skill that will help guide you through your studies and the unseen texts in the exam.

Now that we have introduced the idea that history and culture have an impact on the texts produced by writers, it is time to consider how they affect the person at the other end of the act of communication: the reader.

What do we mean by 'context of reception'?

The historical and cultural factors that affect how a text is **interpreted** by a reader is called its **context of reception**.

Unlike the fixed context of production, the context of a text's reception can vary dramatically. This shift in context of reception can be extreme – a text written today will, if the writer is lucky, still be being read in one hundred years by audiences unimaginable to the writer. That future readership will almost certainly **decode** and interpret the text differently to a contemporary readership. This shift in meaning is something we will explore in this chapter by looking at texts like *The Diary of Samuel Pepys*, a personal diary written as far back as the 1660s. What to Pepys was a 'modern' everyday diary has now become a fascinating historical document due to a shift in its context of reception. This is once again down to **time** and **space** – the reader's historical time and geographical and cultural space affect how they interpret his diary and respond to its ideas. As another example, imagine an advert from the 1950s that depicts a household with the woman as a subservient housewife and the husband as the dominant breadwinner. A modern reader would interpret this as sexist, even if this was not the intent of the writer. The writer will have merely been reflecting the attitudes and values of their **context of production**. These attitudes and values have changed dramatically for the modern reader, who interprets the advert as offensive in their **context of reception**.

DISCUSSION

Problems caused by changes in context of reception can even be found in day-to-day life. For example, a teacher or parent may overhear language you use when speaking to your friends and interpret it as offensive or inappropriate.

Can you think of any examples in your own life when a change in context of reception has had an impact on how something you have said or written has been interpreted?

There are terms we can use to describe this gap in interpretation between writer and reader. A reader who interprets and accepts the ideas as the writer intended has what is called a **dominant reading**; a reader who partly interprets and accepts the ideas as the writer intended has what is called a **negotiated reading**; a reader who rejects the intended interpretation and ideas the writer intended has what is called an **oppositional reading**. These ideas will be explored more fully in Chapters 2.2, 2.4 and 3.4.

Additionally, readers may sometimes struggle to understand everything contained in a text. You will almost certainly have experienced this when you have had to search for a word or a reference on the internet to understand what the writer was communicating. This is because a writer has in mind what we refer to as an **implied reader**: a member of a target audience who will understand and accept all the references, ideas and symbols in a text. The easiest way to imagine this is to envision a letter you write for a close friend – it may well contain in-jokes, allusions to things they have experienced with you, slang you have created and **esoterica** that only they and you will fully understand. This is an example of an **implied reader** – the letter is written with them in mind, and they have all the tools needed to fully decode your text.

However, once a text is out in the world, the writer no longer has control of it. Your letter to your friend may get passed around and interpreted in contexts you did not expect. To another reader, a reference you intended to mean X to your close friend may be interpreted as meaning Y to someone else. We are doing this all the time as students studying texts – analysing poetry, for example, we do not check with the poet whether our interpretation of their poem ties in perfectly with their intention (most of the time, it is not even possible to ask them!), we instead back our interpretation up with evidence and argue our point. Reasoned interpretations are valid and our teacher or examiner gives us a pat on the back. This is the beauty of both language and literature – its ability to mean many different things to many different people. And as the **context of reception** shifts, so does the way the text is interpreted – no one person's interpretation is the same as anyone else's. This ability for a text to have many different interpretations, or 'voices', depending on who is reading and the time and space they find themselves in is called **multivocality** (this term will be further explored in Chapter 3.4).

ACTIVITY 2

The following letter has a British context of production, and is consequently written using a mix of British English and British slang. Look for the **bold** British English and British slang words and find out their Standard English equivalents (answers can be found in the back of the book).

Consider how the context of reception switching from a British teenager well-versed in this slang to an American teenager who is unfamiliar with British slang would affect the meaning of the text.

Hi **Mate**,

I've been **skiving** off school because the stuff we've been doing is **pants**. That new English teacher is **well dodgy**, so I'm glad I'm not sat listening to that **pillock** - he's **lost the plot!**

Skiving has been great - I've been able to watch **footy** on the **telly**, get **plastered** whenever I like, and I even **nicked** some **bloke's peng trainers**.

Anyway, **give me a bell** when you get the chance,

All the best,

David Linquent

As you can imagine, this shift in context of reception has a dramatic impact on the interpretation of the text. Sometimes even shared words like 'pants' have completely different meanings due to the changed **context of reception**. When the letter says that what the writer has been doing is 'pants' (in this context meaning schoolwork that is not very good), an American person may misinterpret and think they have been creating items of clothing in school. When the writer says 'give me a bell' (meaning phone call), an American reader may wonder why the writer is asking for a physical bell of the type that is a hollow metal object that can be struck to make a noise. When the writer says 'some bloke's peng trainers', words like 'bloke' and 'peng' may mean nothing to the American reader unless they have had exposure to British slang elsewhere, and 'trainers' may well be misinterpreted as meaning personal trainers who help you with physical exercise. Clearly, the context of reception can affect the way a text is interpreted in many unexpected ways.

TOK Links

If texts can have multiple interpretations, their meaning is not fixed. What implications does this have for the notion of 'truth'?

We have already covered a lot of terms: **cultural context, historical context, context of production, context clues** and **context of reception**. Don't feel overwhelmed, you will become more comfortable with them as you work through this section of the book. We will be applying them to a variety of works and texts, and every time we do you will become more comfortable with using these terms and linking texts to their respective contexts.

To begin with, we will look at a couple of extracts from Pepys' diary and look for some **context clues** that tell us about its **context of production**. Afterwards, we will think about how the context of reception affects the reading of a text like a diary.

KEY FEATURES DIARIES

- **Non-fiction:** A personal form of writing recording both daily events and the thoughts and feelings of the writer.
- **Day, date and time:** Writers include the day, date and occasionally the time of each entry. This aids in the diary's function as a record and reflection on a day's particular events.
- **First person**: Diaries are personal and, as such, are written from the first person perspective in order to best express the writer's thoughts and feelings.
- **Informal register:** Though this is not set in stone, diaries are generally written using an informal to semi-formal register. This is because the implied reader is also the writer of the text. Consequently, the writer often uses the language they are most at ease and expressive with rather than, say, the particular and formal register of a public speech.
- **Private:** Diaries are written to be private rather than public, so they are often very confessional and open about the writer's thoughts, feelings and experiences.

The Diary of Samuel Pepys (1660–1669)

Samuel Pepys

Samuel Pepys was born in London, England, in 1633. Although now best known for his frank and insightful diaries, during his lifetime he was primarily an administrator for the navy of England and, later, a Member of Parliament. He had an eventful 70 years of life, experiencing the coronation of King Charles II in 1661, the Great Plague of 1665, and the Great Fire of London in 1666 – events documented in his famous diaries. A talented administrator, he oversaw broad and successful organizational changes to the navy and, towards the end of his life, wrote the only work published during his lifetime: *Memoires Relating to the State of the Royal Navy of England.* His diary, first published in 1825, has provided historians with valuable insights into seventeenth-century life.

Pepys' diary was written between January 1660 and May 1669, years that encompassed three important historical events: the Restoration of the English monarchy with Charles II being crowned in 1661, the Great Plague of 1665, and the Great Fire of London in 1666. Though not written for public consumption by his contemporaries, it was eventually published in 1825 and has become one of the most celebrated and best-known English language diaries.

Its appeal is in no small part due to the frank and colourful descriptions of seventeenth-century life, providing valuable insight into 1660s Britain. Its 1.25 million words chronicle an incredibly turbulent and exciting time in Britain's history, but also describe aspects of 1660s British culture: Pepys' marital affairs, culinary habits and even the weather.

To provide a flavour of the kinds of things described in his diary, we have a few interesting quotes to look at before getting to our full extract. If you feel inspired to look up the full entries, they can be found easily online (visit www.pepysdiary.com).

> Did mightily magnify his sauce, which he did then eat with every thing, and said it was the best universal sauce in the world, it being taught him by the Spanish Embassador. *(10 February 1668)*

Cultural insight: Here, Pepys is writing about cuisine. He reveals the recipe for what was deemed 'the best universal sauce in the world' – for the curious, it involves parsley and dry toast being beaten in a mortar before being mixed with vinegar, salt and pepper. This is primarily cultural context because it relates to the customs of the time.

> The crowne being put upon his [King Charles II] head, a great shout begun. *(23 April 1661)*

Historical event: Here, Pepys is referencing a historical event – the Restoration of the British monarchy. Of course, this also shows aspects of British culture through their tradition of having a King or Queen as head of state.

> I did in Drury-lane see two or three houses marked with a red cross upon the doors, and 'Lord have mercy upon us' writ there – which was a sad sight to me. *(7 June 1665)*

Historical event: Here, Pepys is referencing the Great Plague of 1665. This is a historical event that caused great suffering in London and beyond.

> And do so towse [kiss] her and feel her all over, making her believe how fair and good a skin she had; and indeed she has a very white thigh and leg, but monstrous fat. *(29 June 1663)*

Cultural insight: Here, Pepys is writing about an encounter with Betty Lane, the wife of a linen-draper. This provides insight into his culture's attitude to relationships and fidelity.

> A long cassocke close to the body, of black cloth, and pinked with white silke under it, and a coat over it, and the legs ruffled with black riband like a pigeon's leg; and, upon the whole, I wish the King may keep it, for it is a very fine and handsome garment. *(15 October 1666)*

Cultural insight: Here, Pepys' sartorial commentary provides insight into the fashions of the time – an aspect of culture and customs. This is, of course, also historical, as fashions change dramatically over time.

> All over the Thames, with one's face in the wind you were almost burned with a shower of firedrops. *(2 September 1666)*

Historical event: Here, Pepys is writing about a specific historical event, the Great Fire of London in 1666.

Now you have a sense of Pepys' writing, let's look at a more substantial extract. As you read it, consider what context clues there are and what they tell you about the context of production.

Before doing so, we need to clarify the **genre**, **audience** and **purpose** of the text (the GAP from step 1 of our non-literary reading strategy). However, as this section of the book is primarily concerned with context, each non-literary text will instead include a CGAP table (**context, genre, audience, purpose**) to provide a neat summary of the essentials of the text. Whenever you are confronted with a new non-literary text, remember to establish the CGAP as early as possible, as this has a bearing on the content of the text.

Context	England – 1666
Genre	Diary
Audience	As it is a personal diary, Pepys himself
Purpose	To record and reflect

2 September [1666]. Lords Day. Some of our maids sitting up late last night to get things ready against our feast today, Jane called us up, about 3 in the morning, to tell us of a great fire they saw in the City. So I rose, and slipped on my nightgown and went to her window, and thought it to be on the back side of Markelane at the furthest; but being unused to such fires as fallowed, I thought it far enough off, and so went to bed again and to sleep. About 7 rose again to dress myself, and there looked out at the window and saw the fire not so much as it was, and further off … By and by Jane comes and tells me that she hears that above 300 houses have been burned down tonight by the fire we saw, and that it was now burning down all Fishstreet by London Bridge. So I made myself ready presently, and walked to the Tower and there got up upon one of the high places, Sir J. Robinsons little son going up with me; and there I did see the houses at that end of the bridge all on fire, and an infinite great fire on this and the other side the end of the bridge – which, among other people, did trouble me for poor little Michell and our Sarah on the Bridge. So down, with my heart full of trouble, to the Lieutenant of the Tower, who tells me that it begun this morning in the King's bakers house in Pudding Lane, and that it hath burned down St Magnes Church and most part of Fishstreete already. So I down to the waterside and there got a boat and through bridge, and there saw a lamentable fire. Poor Michells house, as far as the Old Swan, already burned that way and the fire running further, that in a very little time it got as far as the Stillyard while I was there. Everybody endeavouring to remove their goods, and flinging into the river or bringing them into lighters* that lay off. Poor people staying in their houses as long as till the very fire touched them, and then running into boats or clambering from one pair of stair by the waterside to another. And among other things, the poor pigeons I perceive were loath to leave their houses, but hovered about the windows and balconies till they were some of them burned, their wings, and fell down …

Having seen as much as I could now, I away to Whitehall by appointment, and there walked to St James's Park, and there met my wife and Creed and Wood and his wife and walked to my boat, and there upon the water again, and to the fire up and down, it still increasing and the wind great. So near the fire as we could for smoke; and all over the Thames, with one's face in the wind you were almost burned with a shower of firedrops – this is very true – so as houses were burned by these drops and flakes of fire, three or four, nay five or six houses, one from another. When we could endure no more upon the water, we to a little alehouse on the Bankside over against the Three Cranes, and there stayed till it was dark almost and saw the fire grow; and as it grow darker, appeared more and more, and in corners and upon steeples and between churches and houses, as far as we could see up the hill of the City, in a most horrid malicious bloody flame, not like the fine flame of an ordinary fire. We stayed till, it being darkish, we saw the fire as only one entire arch of fire from this to the other side the bridge, and in a bow up the hill, for an arch of above a mile long. It made me weep to see it. The churches, houses, and all on fire and flaming at once, and a horrid noise the flames made, and the cracking of houses at their ruine. So home with a sad heart, and there find everybody discoursing and lamenting the fire …

**lighter: a flat-bottomed barge*
(Samuel Pepys 162–166)

Let's break down some of the **context clues** present in the text and consider what they tell us about the **context of production**.

Pepys' diary – context of production

Context clue 1: '2 September' (line 1)

- This is an interesting case study because its historical and cultural context is so clear – every entry contains a clear date and then records the events experienced by Pepys on that particular day. Our extract begins '2 September' which is not only evidence of the text type, but also makes clear the content has a direct link to its historical context – it records his experience on that fateful day in London in 1666.

Context clue 2: 'Lords Day' (line 1)

- As part of the date, we find 'Lord's Day'. With either prior knowledge or research, we can ascertain that this is a reference to the Christian faith. England at the time was an almost entirely Christian country, and Sunday was considered a day of worship. This provides insight into the time and space the text was produced in, and shows that religion played a big part in people's daily lives.

Context clue 3: 'Markelane' (line 4), 'Fishstreet' (line 8), 'St Magnes Church' (line 14)

- These are all very specific references to location. They provide insight into specific areas Pepys lived near to and provide a clear idea of the 'space' in which the text was produced. These places still exist today: St Magnes church has since been rebuilt as St Magnus the Martyr, Fishstreet exists as Fish Street Hill, and Markelane exists as Mark Lane; unsurprisingly, they are all close to the Monument to the Great Fire of London.

Context clue 4: 'an infinite great fire on this and the other side the end of the bridge' (lines 10–11)

- The date, the location references and this quote about a 'great fire' make abundantly clear this entry was influenced by the historical event of the Great Fire of London. Without the fire, this entry may have ended up being far more mundane, but Pepys found himself in the middle of a historically significant event. It burned for five days, consumed 13,200 houses, 87 churches and even St Paul's Cathedral.

Predictably, as it is a diary, we can clearly see the cultural and historical context has had a strong influence on the production of this text. Various context clues allow us to pinpoint the day and location in which it was produced, something fairly easy to do with a diary entry. Next, it is time to focus on how the **cultural** and **historical context** have an impact on how this text is **received**.

Pepys' diary – context of reception

Implied reader

Pepys' implied reader was himself – his diaries were not written to be published at the time, but instead were a personal space for him to record and reflect upon the events of his life. This had a clear influence on his writing style as well as the content of the text. We can see evidence of this in references to 'Michell and our Sarah' (lines 11–12) – to anyone else reading the text, who these people are is likely to be a mystery. Pepys does not feel the need to elaborate as this is assumed knowledge the implied reader will have; unsurprising as this implied reader is himself.

In reality, his style was even more personal than in our extract. He actually wrote the originals in a type of shorthand and code that would prevent prying eyes from learning of his opinions and experiences. However, he ensured his diaries would be left in his library after his death along with a shorthand guide that could be used to decipher the text. This suggests that he was somewhat aware of the significance of his writing as a historical artefact, and that he suspected it may be of interest to future generations.

Other contexts of reception

His diaries have since had a very different context of reception – they were published, in part, in 1825, and the more sexually explicit entries were first published in the 1970s as cultural attitudes towards sex became more open. This is another example of attitudes and values shifting over time, and this changing how readers react to a text. A contemporary of Pepys receiving the text would have been scandalized by his frank descriptions of sex and affairs, but a modern reader is far less shocked as they live in a society that is more open about these aspects of our lives.

As we have established, the implied reader was Pepys himself, with his personal knowledge of who he is referring to, where he is describing and what he is describing. His new readership often lacks this background knowledge needed to fully understand the text. Consequently, his diary now often includes additional explanatory notes to flesh out the contextual knowledge of the reader. In more recent times, his diary entries have been published online, and include hyperlinks within the diary entries which, when hovered over, provide explanatory notes on archaic references. You can have a look at one such site using the adjacent QR code.

The function of the text has also changed through its new context. Though for Pepys the diary was to allow for personal rememberings, in modern times the diary is seen as a historical document and has been used by historians to glean insights into seventeenth-century life. This is an excellent example of a different context of reception having a profound effect on the reading of a text. To his implied reader (himself), the text would have been received as a means to remember events in his life and to reminisce. To readers outside this implied readership, we get a fascinating insight into a fascinating man living at a fascinating time – we read the text with a historical curiosity and receive the text in a very different way to Pepys himself.

Summary

Through Pepys' diary, we have explored how its production was influenced by the **historical** and **cultural context**. We have also seen how a change in **context of reception** can fundamentally alter the function of a text – for Pepys, the diary was a personal reflection, but for subsequent readership, the text served as a historical artefact offering insights into seventeenth-century life.

Our next text is Ibsen's *A Doll's House*. We will examine how this text is very clearly a product of its time, and how its context of reception can affect how it is interpreted. First, consider the key features of realism in the box below.

KEY FEATURES REALISM (THEATRE)

- **A focus on the everyday:** Theatre had previously focused on heightened dramatic content, such as gods, kings, queens and regicide like Shakespeare's *Macbeth*. Realism instead focuses on plots related to the everyday lives most people are living, dealing with issues such as poverty, personal relationships and gender roles.
- **Believable dialogue:** In the realism genre, characters neither use heightened language nor speak in dramatic monologues and soliloquies. Instead, playwrights more closely emulate real-life speech patterns and manners of talking.
- **Everyday settings, costumes and props:** Plays are usually set in relatable settings such as inside middle-class households, as opposed to grand palaces and castles. Furniture, props and costumes are similarly realistic and everyday.

- **A focus on behaviour and psychology:** Characters have psychological depth and their actions and motivations seem realistic and believable.
- **A social message:** Plays of this genre both reflect and comment on society. They often draw attention to problems in society in the hope that they will be ruminated on by the audience and will prompt social change.

A Doll's House by Henrik Ibsen (1879)

Henrik Ibsen

Henrik Ibsen was a Norwegian playwright who has had an enormous impact on the world of theatre. Often referred to as the 'father of realism', he produced plays that more closely resembled real-life as the majority of the public experienced it. In doing so, he presented theatre as a means to reflect on the world in which the audience lived. Many of his plays were considered scandalous at their time of production as Ibsen, through his drama, questioned many deeply-held societal notions about issues such as a woman's role in society and the consequences of moral judgement. He won the Nobel Prize for Literature three times and influenced the writings of many future playwrights such as Arthur Miller and George Bernard Shaw.

Ibsen's *A Doll's House* is a three-act play first performed in Copenhagen, Denmark, 21 December 1879. Ibsen set the play in a typical middle-class household. The man of the house is Torvald Helmer, a newly promoted bank manager. He is married to Nora Helmer, a mother of three who spends her days looking after their children and seeing to the upkeep of their house.

The play focuses on Nora and her role as both a wife and mother. The Norway of Ibsen's time was a heavily **patriarchal** society, with women having little opportunity or agency. Throughout the play, the audience witness the damaging effects this patriarchal world has on Nora. She is both infantilized and patronized by her husband, who sees her more as a beautiful possession than an equal. Nora, in assuming this subservient role, is shown to be immature and underdeveloped, often acting more like a child than an adult. Both husband and wife appear to be in a hollow, loveless and imbalanced marriage. However, this was typical of marriages at the time, and each of them persists in their role as husband and wife as it was convention to do so.

Ultimately, at the end of the play, Nora recognizes her position and abandons her husband and children, thus rejecting the roles of wife and mother forced on her by society. However, Ibsen was told audiences in Germany would not respond well to this conclusion, and was forced to write an alternative ending to get it staged. In this alternative ending, Nora argues with Torvald before being led to her children, at which point she collapses in tears and the curtain falls. The implication is that the sight of her children convinces her to stay, and she instead gives her husband a second chance. It was an ending Ibsen would later call a 'barbaric outrage'.

In the following extract, we can see the original ending alongside the alternative ending Ibsen was forced to write to cater for German audiences' sensibilities.

■ Table 2.1.1

Original ending	Alternative German 'conciliatory' ending
NORA: Both you and I would have to change to the point where ... Oh, Torvald, I don't believe in miracles any more. HELMER: But I *will* believe. Name it! Change to the point where …? NORA: Where we could make a real marriage out of our lives together. Goodbye. [*She goes out through the hall door.*] HELMER: [*sinks down on a chair near the door, and covers his face with his hands*]. Nora! Nora! [*He rises and looks around.*] Empty! She's gone! [*With sudden hope.*] The miracle of miracles …? [*The heavy sound of a door being slammed is heard from below.*]	NORA: Both you and I would have to change to the point where ... Oh, Torvald, I don't believe in miracles any more. HELMER: But I *will* believe. Name it! Change to the point where …? NORA: Where we could make a real marriage out of our lives together. Goodbye. [*Begins to go.*] HELMER: Go then! [*Seizes her arm.*] But first you shall see your children for the last time! NORA: Let me go! I will not see them! I cannot! HELMER: [*draws her over to the door, left*]. You shall see them. [*Opens the door and says softly.*] Look, there they are asleep, peaceful and carefree. Tomorrow, when they wake up and call for their mother, they will be – motherless. NORA: [*trembling*]. Motherless …! HELMER: As you once were. NORA: Motherless! [*Struggles with herself, lets her travelling bag fall, and says.*] Oh, this is a sin against myself, but I cannot leave them. [*Half sinks down by the door.*] HELMER: [*joyfully, but softly*]. Nora! [*The curtain falls.*]

A Doll's House – context of production

This play is clearly reflecting the cultural attitudes of nineteenth-century Norway, which were largely aligned with attitudes in much of Europe and beyond. Divorce was rarely seen or discussed, and wives were obedient to their husbands and utterly devoted to their children. Ibsen wished to bring these attitudes into question by presenting the problems of marriage and motherhood on stage.

In our extract, we can see a revolutionary role reversal between husband and wife in the original ending of the play. Below is a model of analysis focused on the cultural significance of the **original ending**. Consider how the response focuses on technique and effect, the deeper symbolism of aspects of the work, and how it links the analysis to the audience's response.

Torvald, who up until this point has controlled Nora, suddenly falls apart. In contrast to Nora's confident dialogue, he speaks in exclamatives, interrogatives and even has a sentence impudently completed by his wife. This interruption from Nora shows her new-found assertiveness and willingness to challenge her husband. Torvald's desperate repetition of 'Nora! Nora!' (lines 10–11) shows a heightened emotional response that audiences of the time would have associated with women rather than men. The intent is to provoke the audience into reflecting on their expectations of men and women - if Nora can be strong and independent, perhaps other women can. Conversely, if Torvald can be reduced to an emotional breakdown, perhaps men are not so different from women after all.

Nora speaks with determination and resolution, shown in her steely 'Goodbye' (line 7) before going 'through the hall door' (line 8). Doors have a symbolic significance in their ability to prevent or allow access to the outside world. Nora spends the play confronted with symbolically closed doors, representing the opportunities denied to her by society. In actively opening the door and moving beyond the threshold of the heart of the house, she is transgressing the domestic boundaries enforced upon her. The final 'heavy sound' of a 'slammed' (line 14) front door would reverberate in theatres full of people shocked into silence. Ibsen's use of the verb 'slammed' in the stage directions made clear his intent for this separation of Nora from her roles to be determined, sudden and visceral. Witnessing an assertive woman leave her roles behind to be independent will have scandalized some, and inspired others. Audience members will have wondered whether the expectations of being a wife and a mother need to change if they are as inhibiting and stunting to others as they are to Nora, driving her to such extremes as abandoning her children. They will also wonder whether, like Nora, more women should reject the ideas of loveless matrimony and motherhood outright.

A Doll's House – context of reception

Ibsen famously stated that a 'dramatist's business is not to answer questions but only to ask them'. Ibsen was clearly questioning the attitudes and values of his contemporaries with his play. This is not uncommon; works of literature are often used to hold a mirror up to society, forcing audiences and readers to examine aspects of their way of life that they otherwise accept unquestioningly. Ibsen knowingly created a provocative and challenging ending to create debate in Norwegian society about gender roles and the institution of marriage. He knew his implied readership would see the play and be shocked, but this was by design. He wished to jolt them out of their comfort zone in order to make them question convention and, hopefully, change their ways.

Ibsen's ideal audience member would be shocked by the play, undoubtedly, but also be open-minded and willing to reflect on gender roles and marriage. Some felt this implied reader did not exist and predicted audiences would reject the message of the play. This is how the alternative ending came into being. When staging the play in Berlin, Ibsen was forced to cater to the cultural attitude of German audiences (and a particular actress who refused to play Nora as he intended) by toning down his scandalous dènouement. This is an unusual example of the context of reception forcing a writer to adapt their work, in this case due to cultural attitudes held by those receiving the work.

ACTIVITY 3

Using the model commentary of the original ending to help you, analyse the alternative ending to the play by responding to the below prompts. Example responses can be found in the back of the book.

1 Compare how Ibsen characterizes Nora as less confident and assertive in the alternative ending, and explain what impact this will have had on the audience.

2 Compare how Ibsen takes away Nora's sense of independence and agency while increasing Torvald's assertiveness in comparison to the original ending.

3 Explain how the reconciliation between Nora and Torvald is conveyed to the audience and explain what their response would have been.

Other contexts of reception

CONCEPT CONNECTION

PERSPECTIVE

This work is a good opportunity to consider the importance of perspective and how a text can have multiple meanings depending on who is interpreting it and their respective contexts. The fact that the act of reading (or in this case, seeing a play) happens in a given place and time poses the question of how far the reader's perspective on the text is influenced or even shaped by their **context of reception**. Below is a summary of differences in culture between past and modern Norway – consider how these differences would impact their perspectives on the original play.

■ Table 2.1.2

Ibsen's Norway	Modern Norway
Patriarchal society: Women could not vote, and therefore had little to no influence on laws that were drafted and decisions that were made – even those that directly impacted women's lives.	**Comparatively non-patriarchal society:** Though there are still problems with female representation, women can vote, hold positions of power, and have often powerful positions within the workplace.
Marriage: Women were entirely dependent on their fathers until marriage, at which point they became dependent on their husbands. Because of this financial dependency, marriages were far more transactional, and were based on practical concerns such as money, reputation and family.	**Marriage:** The institution of marriage has changed dramatically. For example, since 1 January 2009, gay and lesbian couples have had the same marriage rights as heterosexual couples. Marriages are now between equals rather than favouring the man, and promote foundations of love and respect. Marriages between people of different races, financial backgrounds and cultural backgrounds have become normalized and accepted.
Education: Beyond basic schooling, girls were focused on learning household management and childcare. In being denied a full education, they were destined to a domestic life and a financial reliance upon their fathers and husbands.	**Education:** Women have equal access to education and training as men. This ensures independence from men and lessens the need to be married in order to lead a comfortable and fulfilling life.

The factors shown above have a profound impact on a modern audience's perspective on the play. Ibsen was reflecting his contemporaneous culture and its attitudes towards gender and marriage, but those attitudes in places like Norway have clearly changed. Let's consider a modern Norwegian audience and their **negotiated reading** of this work. To this audience, it is not Nora's assertiveness and independence that is shocking, but the power imbalance within the marriage. To see the character of Nora infantilized and controlled on stage now serves as a reminder of how far we have come as a society, and as a warning to not regress back to the inequalities of the past. To a modern audience, marriage can often be seen as an emotional connection between equals, so Nora's once shocking decision to leave her cold and imbalanced marriage appears natural and obvious. The play still resonates, but contemporary audiences interpret the play differently due to their more modern **context of reception**. For such audiences, social progress has made inroads in ensuring the ability of once oppressed groups such as women and minorities to assert agency and individuality, in part spurred on by plays like *A Doll's House* forcing people to face up to their society's failings.

This extract illustrates that texts clearly reflect their **context of production**, often focusing on the faults of the society in which they originate. Beyond this, we have seen that when the text is not being received by the **implied reader** the playwright had in mind, it can be received and even rejected in unexpected ways. Unusually in this case, we have seen how a text may be forced to fundamentally change to prevent rejection, even at the cost of the play's overall message.

DISCUSSION

1 Why do we continue to engage with works that were written about societies that have since changed dramatically?

2 Should works like *A Doll's House* be updated to reflect social problems of the present day?

'Aubade with Burning City' by Ocean Vuong

Our next text is a poem that reflects the cultural background of the writer, and refers to historical events that played an important part in the writer's family history: 'Aubade with Burning City' by Ocean Vuong.

The poem describes the 1975 evacuation of US civilians and south Vietnamese refugees from Saigon towards the end of the Vietnam War. The code to signal the start of the daring evacuation was broadcast on the radio. It was 'the temperature in Saigon is 105 degrees and rising' followed by Irving Berlin's song 'White Christmas'. Vuong refers to this through switching from poetic description of the scene on the ground to the lyrics of the song. His use of poetic form allows him to layout his lines like falling snow, and their lack of cohesion also echoes the chaos of an evacuation that signalled the end of the Vietnam War.

Ocean Vuong

Ocean Vuong is a Vietnamese-American poet and essayist who was born on a rice farm outside Saigon in 1988 (now known as Ho Chi Minh City), spent a year in a refugee camp in the Philippines before moving, aged 2, to Hartford, Connecticut, USA. He was named Ocean after his mother learned the English word's meaning and felt it reflected the oceanic connection between the USA and her native Vietnam. His mother ensured Ocean became the first literate member of their family thanks to the opportunities the USA provided. He went on to win the 2018 TS Eliot Prize and was a 2011 'Over the Rainbow' selection for notable LGBTQ books by the American Library Association. His work has been translated into Hindi, Korean, Russian and Vietnamese. He is currently Assistant Professor of the Modern Fine Arts for Poets and Writers at the University of Massachusetts at Amherst.

Aubade with Burning City

South Vietnam, April 29, 1975: Armed Forces Radio played Irving
Berlin's 'White Christmas' as a code to begin Operation Frequent
Wind, the ultimate evacuation of American civilians and Vietnamese
refugees by helicopter during the fall of Saigon.

Milkflower petals in the street
like pieces of a girl's dress.

May your days be merry and bright ...

He fills a teacup with champagne, brings it to her lips.
Open, he says.
She opens.
Outside, a soldier spits out
his cigarette as footsteps fill the square like stones
fallen from the sky. *May*
all your Christmases be white
as the traffic guard unstraps his holster.

His fingers running the hem
of her white dress. A single candle.
Their shadows: two wicks.

A military truck speeds through the intersection, children
shrieking inside. A bicycle hurled
through a store window. When the dust rises, a black dog
lies panting in the road. Its hind legs
crushed into the shine
of a white Christmas.

On the bed stand, a sprig of magnolia expands like a secret heard
for the first time.

The treetops glisten and children listen, the chief of police
facedown in a pool of Coca-Cola.
A palm-sized photo of his father soaking
beside his left ear.

The song moving through the city like a widow.
A white ... A white ... I'm dreaming of a curtain of snow

falling from her shoulders.

Snow scraping against the window. Snow shredded

with gunfire. Red sky.

Snow on the tanks rolling over the city walls.
A helicopter lifting the living just
out of reach.

The city so white it is ready for ink.

The radio saying run run run.
Milkflower petals on a black dog
like pieces of a girl's dress.

May your days be merry and bright. She is saying
something neither of them can hear. The hotel rocks
beneath them. The bed a field of ice
cracking.

Don't worry, he says, as the first shell flashes
their faces, *my brothers have won the war*
and tomorrow ...
The lights go out.

I'm dreaming. I'm dreaming ...
to hear sleigh bells in the snow ...

In the square below: a nun, on fire,
runs silently toward her god –

Open, he says.
She opens.

(Ocean Vuong)

'Aubade with Burning City' – context of production

GLOBAL ISSUES ***Field of inquiry:*** **Culture, Identity and Community**

MIGRATION

There have been movements of people across the globe for millennia, and with this has come a wider and deeper cultural diversity as people of different backgrounds mix and live together. There are many global issues that can be linked to migration, and one of them is the increasing complication of people's 'cultural identity' as cultures mix and feed off of each other. For the children of immigrants and refugees, their cultural identity can sometimes be complicated. They often find themselves straddling two cultures, in part reflecting the culture of their parents, in part reflecting the culture of the country their parents emigrated or fled to. In looking at the context of production of this text, we will see that Vuong uses the poem to explore his own particular identity and his culture. Poetry can be used as a means to explore such complex cultural identities, as Vuong explained in an interview:

> *'We're singing of solitude, but we're singing it to each other. The poem is for self-preservation, but it is also written in the hopes of speaking to these private fears and joys that we all share, but that we don't get to talk about in public spheres. In that sense, it is also communication between people in order to build a space where we can recognize one another ... it's always important for me to say, "This is where I came from", and that my making of this art is both an act of creation and survival at once.'*
>
> *(Kaveh Akbar)*

This is an interesting thought. Poems are often a form of exploring oneself and one's identity, a 'singing in solitude', but they are also a method of communication and attempts at building understanding so that we can 'recognize one another'. Vuong suggests that in having such intensely personal poems published, they are shared with others as an act of communication and a sharing of his identity and experience. We, as readers, gain insight into his Vietnamese-American identity and cultural background. Through being exposed to such works as readers, we can build an understanding of the world as others outside our specific cultural background see and experience it, an increasingly important process in a globalized, multicultural world.

There is a range of other texts that deal with this global issue, including many written by first and second generation descendants of immigrants. We have seen examples of this already with texts like 'The Arrival' by Shaun Tan, and similar texts will also be looked at in Chapter 2.5.

SENSITIVE CONTENT

Caution: the poetry discussed in the following section includes sensitive content.

The lines quoted from Ocean Vuong's poem 'Notebook fragments' includes an expletive. We have chosen to use this extract in order for you to consider the effect of such words and why the author may use them. Furthermore, the IB recommends that your studies in Language A: Language and Literature should challenge you intellectually, personally and culturally, and expose you to sensitive and mature topics. We invite you to reflect critically on various perspectives offered while bearing in mind the IB's commitment to international-mindedness and intercultural respect.

Vuong's particular **cultural** and **historical context** is a fascinating one. He was born of an immigrant family in a country that caused devastation to their ancestral Vietnam. In our poem, Vuong explores this identity and culture by looking to the past rather than the present. This is because historical events had an enormous bearing on Vuong's life, and thus on the poetry he creates. His grandfather was an American soldier who fell in love with an illiterate Vietnamese girl who worked in the rice paddies. As he puts it in his poem 'Notebook Fragments', 'An American soldier f****d a Vietnamese farmgirl. Thus my mother exists. Thus I exist. Thus no bombs = no family = no me. / Yikes.' Here, through a simplified historical equation, he is expressing that his entire existence is predicated upon dark historical events like bombings and warfare. This historical context is a part of his story of origin, and something he wished to capture in poetic form. This desire was magnified by the functional illiteracy of his family and their consequent inability to do so themselves.

Vuong's 'Aubade with Burning City' centres on the Americans fleeing Saigon in Vietnam, an event his grandmother was a part of. In mixing this second-hand experience with his imagination and wider research, he has created a poem that explores an event that is both historically and personally significant. He makes sense of who he is and where he is in the present by writing of the past, of events with repercussions that include his very existence, decades later, in a foreign land.

He constructs a poem that is a product of Vietnamese-American cultural context, expressing the feeling of having a mixed cultural heritage that has its origins in conflict and warfare. He is also writing of family history in an attempt to capture the essence of a personal experience that cannot be written down by the grandmother who experienced it. It is a fascinating **context of production** that explores the culture and identity of being part of a refugee family in the United States.

ACTIVITY 4

For your benefit, some contextual research has been completed for you. Below, you will find some context clues. With this new contextual knowledge, you will be prompted to analyse parts of the poem. The first question is completed for you, and you can find example responses to questions 2 and 3 in the back of the book.

1 Why does Vuong compare the 'milkflower petals' to 'pieces of a girl's dress' in lines 5 and 6?

- **Context clue 1:** Milkflower petals
  The milkflower is common in Vietnam and blossoms in late autumn, often carpeting the streets in tiny white flowers as they fall and leaving a beautiful aroma. Songs such as 'Milk Flower' by Hong Dang (1978) is further evidence of their cultural significance in Vietnam and their often romantic connotations.

'Milkflower petals' are foregrounded by the poet at the beginning of the poem. In doing so, Vuong opens with an image of beauty as these petals have strong romantic connotations in his ancestral country of Vietnam. However, he then jarringly juxtaposes this image of beauty with the simile 'like pieces of a girl's dress'. The image of a dress torn into 'pieces' suggests violence and destruction. This is accentuated through the dress belonging to a 'girl', with the implied age connoting innocence and purity that has been corrupted by an act of violence. This comparison immediately introduces the motif of innocence and beauty being destroyed by violence and destruction, a recurring theme throughout the poem.

2 Why does Vuong juxtapose the lyrics of 'White Christmas' with images of war and violence throughout the poem?

- **Context clue 2:** 'White Christmas' lyrics
'White Christmas' is an incredibly successful Irving Berlin song written in 1942. It has taken many forms, but the Bing Crosby version is the world's best selling single, cementing its iconic status. To millions of people, its lyrics and tuneful melody puts them in mind of a romanticized Christmas, with snow falling, families coming together, and presents under the tree.

3 In lines 34–39, how is the rescue of American civilians and Vietnamese refugees conveyed?

- **Context clue 3:** Helicopters
The evacuation of Saigon was the largest helicopter evacuation in history. It was referred to as 'Operation Frequent Wind' and involved 7,000 people being evacuated by helicopter from various parts of Saigon.

'Aubade with Burning City' – context of reception

Now we need to think about the reception of a work such as this. The vast majority of his readers would likely not be Vietnamese-American, and most would not have been refugees. For these readers, the poem is an education as they engage with a work by someone with Vietnamese heritage describing events that caused his family to flee their country. In providing historical context at the beginning of the poem, Vuong clearly expects many readers to be ignorant of the history of the evacuation of Saigon. The poem was published in 2016, a full 41 years after the event, and, despite its portrayal in documentaries like 'The Fall of Saigon' (1995), it is not a historical moment that is especially well known around the world. In raising the readership's awareness of the event, Vuong is encouraging them to learn more about the Vietnam War and its impact on Vietnamese people. His **implied reader** would pick up on the conflict between the lyrics and the reality of the evacuation, and consider how it reflects the conflicted identity Vietnamese people may feel growing up in the United States. It increases their understanding of those who have been forced to flee, and those who have grown up with mixed cultures.

Other contexts of reception

Let us consider how immigrants and people of mixed cultural background may interpret this text. In exploring a clash of cultures through his juxtaposition of American music with Vietnamese history, Vuong is exploring notions of identity. As discussed, he himself has a shared Vietnamese-American heritage, and vast numbers of other Vietnamese people emigrated around the world as a consequence of the Vietnam War. By including contextual references related to both countries, Vuong explores the history of the two sides of his identity. Though readers without a mixed cultural background will be able to understand his portrayal of this cultural duality, it will particularly resonate with those who have similar backgrounds. For them, it may conjure up feelings about their own mixed cultural backgrounds and remind them of times when these cultures came into conflict. Seeing such ideas in a poem could be a powerful experience for them, as the voices of immigrants and refugees are often marginalized. Vuong himself spoke of the importance of voices like his being published, particularly for people of colour.

> *'I was also glad the piece spoke of my background – how someone like me came into writing. The recognition of another life existing within these spaces is important because, as writers of color, we don't have a solid*

literary foundation to build on, whereas white writers enjoy the perpetual presence of a canon where their faces are faithfully reflected. For POC, the lineage is more tenuous, fractured, erased, cut out, and ghosted. So it's always important for me to say, "This is where I came from", and that my making of this art is both an act of creation and survival at once.'

(Kaveh Akbar)

For such readers, seeing themselves represented amid a **canon of literature** that is predominantly white gives the poem added power and significance.

CAS Links

Service and Creativity: Both the migrant and the refugee experience is an underrepresented one. Research if there are any refugee or migrant support centres near you. If so, go and meet them. See if there is anything you can do within school to raise money or provide supplies to help the organization. You could even organize a poetry workshop or write a poem about their experiences.

This poem illustrates that texts often reflect **cultural context**. Vuong is expressing his cultural background through looking at a historical event that, though he did not experience it first hand, still expresses his sense of who he is and why he is in the present moment. In having a context of production that involves a Vietnamese-American family living in the United States decades after the war that forced them there, Vuong has written a poem that deals with a past in a way that informs the present and shares his thoughts on his cultural identity with a wide audience.

Advertising – car adverts

We briefly looked at advertising and how it can contain contextual information at the beginning of this chapter. Now, we will explore a case study that focuses on gender and examine how this reflects its **context of production**. We have two car adverts: one an advert printed in a magazine, the other an advert sent as a Tweet. (It is worth noting that individual non-literary texts such as adverts need to be studied as part of a wider advertising campaign by the same company or agency to qualify as a 'non-literary body of work' for the individual oral, whereas looking at individual non-literary texts in isolation is good practice for the unseen texts in Paper 1). We will see how much information we can glean from **context clues** before finding out the real origin of the adverts. First, read through the following key features box.

KEY FEATURES TWEETS

- **Character limit of 280:** The defining factor of Tweets is their tight character limit. They require concision and often result in a breakdown in grammar to squeeze in content.
- **Public:** Outside of direct messages (or 'DM's), Tweets are public and available to everyone. This means you can engage in public commentaries on events and get insights into people's lives, thoughts and opinions across the globe.
- **Emoji:** To help get around the character limit, emojis (you should remember these from Chapter 1.4) can help get across information in just one character. If a picture is worth a thousand words, imagine how many characters an emoji is worth.

- **Hashtags:** Essentially a way of labelling or tagging a Tweet. People can follow #hashtags and get a feed of all Tweets using that hashtag. This aids in public debate around ongoing events and issues.
- **Links:** Rich media, such as videos and images, can either be embedded or linked to in Tweets.
- **@:** tagging usernames causes your Tweet to appear in a special feed on their Twitter client, usually engaging that user in conversation or highlighting a Tweet for them.
- **Tone:** Though this is often up to the user, Tweets generally have an informal tone. This is in part due to the character limit, and in part due to the typical register used online on social media platforms. Political institutions and news organizations often retain a formal tone on Twitter to suit their image and reputation.

Car adverts – context of production

Take a look at the advert below and scan the QR code.

We are now primarily looking for visual **context clues**. Even the most seemingly insignificant elements of adverts can contain cultural or historical information, so let's break down the adverts into small elements.

■ Table 2.1.3

Mini advert	Ford advert
Context clues: Models, body language, facial expression, clothing	
Model: The woman in the advert is white and is shown with a bob haircut, a style particularly popular in the 1960s and 1970s. This helps us date the advert, and suggests the advert is perhaps from Europe or North America. **Clothing and makeup:** She is wearing makeup, bold nail varnish, big rings that seem impractical for driving, and a dress that reveals cleavage – this suggests she is in a liberal country and is perhaps dressed up for a night out. The mascara emphasizing her eyes accentuates the look of shock and surprise. **Body language:** Her body language shows her leaning towards the steering wheel as if she is anxious about driving. She holds the steering wheel incorrectly (her hands are too close together), and her fearful eyes look directly at the viewer of the advert as if she is about to drive into you. Her bitten lip further suggests how nervous she is about driving. Combined, this seems to imply that women find driving challenging and stressful. This suits the message of the advert as it is encouraging such drivers to buy their new car with an automatic transmission, something they believe will take the stress and fear out of driving. **Summary:** Having established the advert originates around the 1970s due to the styling of the model, the other features that suggest women are poor drivers make a lot more sense. Sexist attitudes were far more common in the past, and the fact that an advert like this would be published certainly suggests there was an accepted stereotype that women were often poor drivers. The advertisers focus on this stereotype to help sell their new easy-to-drive car.	**Model and body language:** Little of the woman is revealed – we are just shown her eyes in the rear view mirror. Her skin tone suggests she is perhaps of Middle Eastern appearance, and her makeup and expression suggest a confident woman behind the wheel. However, as we will analyse in more detail later, the use of the black background behind the mirror makes the image look like a niqab, suggesting this is from a Muslim country. **Summary:** Unlike the Mini advert, the Ford advert shows a confident driver. This is primarily conveyed through the eyes; unlike the woman in the Mini advert and her wide-eyed shock, she directs a determined and confident gaze towards the viewer. This reflects a change in attitude towards women and their driving ability. The suggestion of a niqab locates this advert as perhaps being Middle Eastern.
Context clues: Setting	
In the background, we can see the inside of a car. The rear window is close to the woman, making clear the car is a Mini, but the main focus of the advert is the woman holding the steering wheel.	The Ford advert features a particularly interesting background – a black cloth. This is a surreal element to the advert, as if it were a real car it would be covering the windscreen and preventing the driver from seeing. The layout places the eyes in-front of the blanket, and combined they resemble a niqab, a common item of clothing in some Muslim countries. In comparison to the Mini advert, this reveals different cultural attitudes towards women's clothing, and also helps locate the advert.
Context clues: Language	
The Mini advert is lauding its automatic transmission, a relatively common feature of cars today – this helps us date the advert. The adjective 'simple' in 'simple driving' has a surface meaning of relating to the ease with which you can drive the Mini. However, when placed on the image of a confused woman, it may also be interpreted as being for 'simple' people who find driving a challenge. The copy features a lexical set of conflict with words like 'fight' and 'battle' to remind the audience of how driving can be difficult, and then contrasts this with words such as 'effortless' and 'safer' to show the benefits of the automatic Mini.	The Ford advert is a Tweet, showing it has a more recent context. Tweet advertising is generally aimed at younger people and, through Retweeting, has the ability to go viral – a powerful modern advertising technique. The Tweet itself has the hashtags #SaudiWomenMove and #SaudiWomenCanDrive. This gives us the clearest signal of historical context – the advert was prompted by Saudi Arabia lifting its ban on women driving. Up until June 2018, Saudi Arabian women were forbidden to drive motor vehicles, an obvious cultural difference to the Mini advert from the 1970s showing a woman behind the wheel.

Though contingent upon some background knowledge of the Saudi driving ban, we have been able to learn a lot about the context of production through various context clues. Look at the CGAP tables below to find out the true context of the advert and the Tweet.

Mini Advert CGAP

Context	United Kingdom – 1970s
Genre	Advert
Audience	Particularly targeted at female drives
Purpose	To inform and persuade

Ford Tweet CGAP

Context	Saudi Arabia – 2018
Genre	Tweet
Audience	Saudi Arabian women
Purpose	To persuade

Context of reception

The Mini advert is clearly aimed at people who struggle with driving, and the prominent use of a woman suggests it is appealing to women who would like driving to be less of a challenge. Though there would undoubtedly have been women who would have had **oppositional** and **negotiated** readings and seen it as patronising and sexist, Mini were clearly confident that the majority would accept the **dominant reading** of the advert and take on board the message of the Mini being an easier car to drive, especially for women.

The Ford advert was targeting women of Saudi Arabia who could now drive – an obvious target market as they may now want to buy cars. In including the hashtags, Ford was hoping to ride the wave of excitement at a newly won right for women. This is known as **brand activism** – when a brand integrates a social movement into its advertising.

Other contexts of reception

If we imagine a modern British woman reacting to the Mini advert, they would likely have an **oppositional reading** and would consider it insulting and sexist – statistically, after all, women are safer drivers. In fact, it is hard to imagine the advert being run at all in a modern context as it would almost certainly damage Mini's brand, risking them losing half of their potential buyers.

The Ford advert is so recent and specific to its historical moment, it is hard to imagine it having any other context of reception. To a past audience, it would not make sense as it is so clearly tied with a future lifting of the Saudi Arabian ban on women driving.

EE Links: English A – Language category 3

Advertising is always an interesting and – dare we say it! – fun topic for an extended essay. The above example shows how advertising on similar products but with vastly different contexts of production can open up fascinating avenues of analysis and insight. You could look at adverts for cigarettes from the 1950s (such as Camel's famous 'More doctors smoke Camels than any other cigarette' tagline) versus adverts for e-cigarettes and vaping today. Another interesting comparison would be around body image and body positivity, comparing adverts for bathing suits or weight loss products in the 1950s versus today. For example, a Protein World advert with the tagline 'Are you beach body ready?' launched on the London Underground in 2015 caused such outrage that a petition was launched to get the advert banned in the UK, though the reception in the USA was much more muted.

Introduction to social satire

Our final extract of this chapter is an example of **social satire**. This genre of literary fiction has a fundamental link to its **context of production** as it is using humour to mock an individual, an ideology or an idea from its **cultural** and **historical context**. Within this genre, the writer often emphasizes the problems with people or society in order to put them up for ridicule. This leaves the reader unable to take the person or aspect of society seriously, and often leads to them changing their opinion about the issues raised.

Jane Austen

Jane Austen (1775–1817) was an English novelist born into a respectable middle-class family during the Regency period. She was known as a social commentator who used wit, gentle irony and satire to mock traditional middle-class sensibilities regarding romance, marriage and social status. She published her novels anonymously to moderate acclaim. It wasn't until the 1920s that her novels were more widely hailed as masterpieces. In recent years, there have been many film adaptations of her novels which has brought further popularity to her works.

Austen's novels were based on her own personal observations of middle-class attitudes during her lifetime in the Regency period. She is well known for satirising many of these attitudes, particularly those relating to romance and marriage. The narrators of her novels make frequent use of **satire** to mock the conventions of her class, clearly suggesting she herself was critical of them.

The following extract comes from the opening of *Pride and Prejudice* which was published in 1813. Read the following extract and, as you do so, consider what you can gather about the **context of production**:

> It is a truth universally acknowledged, that a single man in possession of a good fortune, must be in want of a wife.
>
> However little known the feelings or views of such a man may be on his first entering a neighbourhood, this truth is so well fixed in the minds of the surrounding families, that he is considered as the rightful property of some one or other of their daughters.
>
> 'My dear Mr Bennet,' said his lady to him one day, 'have you heard that Netherfield Park is let at last?'
>
> Mr Bennett replied that he had not.
>
> 'But it is,' returned she; 'for Mrs Long has just been here, and she told me all about it.'

Mr Bennet made no answer.

'Do not you want to know who has taken it?' cried his wife impatiently.

'You want to tell me, and I have no objection to hearing it.'

This was invitation enough.

'Why, my dear, you must know, Mrs Long says that Netherfield is taken by a young man of large fortune from the north of England; that he came down on Monday in a chaise and four to see the place, and was so much delighted with it that he agreed with Mr Morris immediately; that he is to take possession before Michaelmas, and some of his servants are to be in the house by the end of next week.'

'What is his name?'

'Bingley.'

'Is he married or single?'

'Oh! single, my dear, to be sure! A single man of large fortune; four or five thousand a year. What a fine thing for our girls!'

(Jane Austen 1)

Pride and Prejudice – context of production

The extract has clear links to its context of production, but without contextual knowledge, these links can be much harder to spot. Below, you will find information about the context of production paired with explanations of how this links in with the work itself.

Context fact 1: Women of the time were dependent on men for financial security.
The opening sentence of the entire work foregrounds a central theme of the novel: 'It is a truth universally acknowledged, that a single man in possession of a good fortune, must be in want of a wife.' (lines 1– 2). In making such a bold declarative statement, Austen is clearly signalling this issue will be explored in the story to come. This statement obviously implies that, for women after a husband, wealthy men are extremely eligible and sought after. The use of the adverb 'universally' is clearly hyperbole – the narrator cannot know for sure that this how every single person feels – and this heightened tone is often used in satirical writing to exaggerate and ridicule. This foreshadows the novel's later explorations of different motivations for marriage, particularly through the character of Elizabeth Bennet and her desire to marry for love, not just material gain and social acceptance.

Context: Parents often arranged marriages for their children, particularly if it meant improving a family's status or financial situation.
Mrs Bennet is also used as a device for Austen to satirise further these attitudes. She is overly excited about the new arrival to Netherfield Park solely because he is a 'single man of large fortune' which makes him 'a fine thing for our girls!' (lines 25–26).' Austen is mocking Mrs Bennet who quite clearly equates Bingley's money, rather than any other qualities he may possess, with making him a suitable marriage partner for one of her daughters. The fact Mrs Bennet mentions how many horses pull his carriage and focuses on how much Bingley earns – 'four of five thousand a year' (line 25) – before she has even met him makes it quite clear that his financial

status is the overriding factor in Mrs Bennet's high opinion of him. The abundance of exclamation marks in her final speech is used to further mock Mrs Bennet and her materialistic values. Her function in the novel is to represent traditional middle class parents and their enforcement of social conventions. In satirising her, Austen is also satirising the transactional nineteenth-century attitudes towards marriage in general.

Pride and Prejudice – context of reception

Satirical writing is often very much of its time and space as it is mocking attitudes tied to the context of the writer. When it was first published, readers could clearly interpret the text as a criticism of their particular contemporaneous society. Despite these close ties to its context of production, the novel has had an enduring success that has long outlasted the Regency period. Elements of the text clearly still resonate with modern readers, and this is due to some universal themes (a term that will be fully explored in our next chapter). Modern readers read the novel less as a social satire and more as a romantic comedy, focusing on the relationships of the characters and the trials and tribulations of their love lives. Its Regency period setting has now become history, and this aspect of the novel appeals to modern readers as a form of escapism.

However, in some segments of society and in some parts of the world, the transactional approach to marriage that is criticized in the novel still holds true. A good example of this is the movie adaptation 'Bride and Prejudice', an British-Indian movie released in 2004. This movie still follows Austen's general plot of parents trying to marry off their daughters to the 'perfect husbands' rather than for love, but adapts it to explore the tradition held by some Indian families of arranged marriages. There are clear parallels with the transactional nature of many Regency period marriages, and in this context its satirical message is given new life and continued relevancy.

This is an excellent example of the context of reception affecting the interpretation of the text - for some modern readers the text is read merely as a romantic comedy, for others it can still act as a social commentary on attitudes to love and marriage that may persist in their particular context.

Conclusion

In this chapter, we have only just begun our exploration into how time and space affect texts. The terms used here will be used throughout the next few chapters, and with each subsequent chapter our skills at spotting **context clues** and understanding **contexts of reception** and **production** will improve.

Works cited

Akbar, K. 'We're singing of solitude, but we're singing it to one another.' divedapper, 6 June 2016. Web. 12 March 2019. **www.divedapper.com/interview/ocean-vuong**.

Austen, Jane, Pride and Prejudice, CGP, 2010.

Ibsen, H. *Four Major Plays*. Oxford University Press, 1998.

Pepys, S. 'a long cassocke close … handsome garment,' *The Diary of Samuel Pepys*. Web. 10 March 2019. **www.pepysdiary.com/diary/1666/10/15**.

Pepys, S. 'all over the Thames … of firedrops.' *The Diary of Samuel Pepys*. Web. 10 March 2019. **www.pepysdiary.com/diary/1666/09**.

Pepys, S. 'and do so towse … but monstrous fat.' *The Diary of Samuel Pepys*. Web. 10 March 2019. **www.pepysdiary.com/diary/1663/06/29**.

Pepys, S. 'I did in … sight to me.' *The Diary of Samuel Pepys*. Web. 10 March 2019. **www.pepysdiary.com/diary/1665/06/07**.

Pepys, S. 'the best universal sauce in the world.' *The Diary of Samuel Pepys*. Web. 10 March 2019. **www.pepysdiary.com/diary/1669/02/10**.

Pepys, S. 'The crowne being … shout begun' *The Diary of Samuel Pepys*. Web. 10 March 2019. **www.pepysdiary.com/diary/1661/04/23**.

Pepys, S. *The Illustrated Pepys from the Diary*. Selected and edited by Robert Latham, Bell & Hyman Limited, Book Club Associates, 1979.

Vuong, O. *Night Sky with Exit Wounds*. Random House, 2017.

2.2 How do we approach texts from different times and cultures to our own?

OBJECTIVES OF CHAPTER

- To understand what is meant by 'time' and 'culture'.
- To consider the universality of texts.
- To consider the importance of contextual research when interpreting texts from cultures other than our own.
- To look at a variety of texts considering their universal text features, universal themes.

Guiding conceptual question break down

How do we approach texts from different times and cultures to our own? Once again, let's break down the **guiding conceptual question**. We are clearly being asked to consider our ability to be confronted with texts from other times and/or cultures yet still able to interpret them and understand them. The more different the time and/or culture to our own, the harder the text may be to interpret and understand.

The two key terms here are '**culture**' and '**time**'. You should remember our exploration of '**culture**' in the previous chapter: the values, beliefs, and attitudes of a distinct group of people. '**Time**' is essentially the same as our exploration of 'historical' in the previous chapter: the time at which the text is produced, and the influence this has on its content and style.

This **guiding conceptual question** emphasizes consideration of how we, as readers, are able to approach and interpret texts despite them not being from the same time and culture as ourselves. This will, of course, also involve thinking about *why* we approach texts from other times and cultures at all.

First, let's consider why approaching texts from a different time or culture to our own can sometimes be difficult.

CONCEPT CONNECTION

IDENTITY – SIMILAR YET DIFFERENT

We must remember that texts are acts of communication, and it is no surprise that it is easier to communicate with those who have grown up at the same time and in the same place – this creates a shared historical and cultural background. If you speak the same language, went through the same education system, consumed the same media growing up and took part in the same cultural traditions, you have a lot that links you. This gives you what we call a shared frame of reference – what a gesture, symbol or word means to you will mean the same to others from the same context; you have a shared sense of identity.

However, there are billions of people on the planet currently living different lives in different cultures, added to the multitude of people who lived in different *times* as well as different cultures. People often speak a different form of the language, have been educated differently, consumed different media growing up, and have taken part in what, to you, are strange and unusual cultural traditions – there might be a lot that separates you. Their frame of reference is different – and their understanding of a gesture, symbol or word could be different to your own.

It is far easier to approach a text created at the same time and in the same culture as your own because of this shared frame of reference. A shared cultural background means you share aspects of your identity with others, and texts that appeal to this identity will particularly resonate with you.

ACTIVITY 1

Consider your own cultural identity. If a library were to have a shelf of books that best reflect your shared culture and identity, what would they be? Research some texts and create a list, considering how someone outside your culture may react to the texts differently.

Time and culture

Being from a different time or culture to a writer can cause confusion and miscommunication on two levels:

- Times and cultures sometimes have the same words and symbols, but attach different meanings to them – take 'pants' meaning 'trousers' in America but 'underwear' in Britain.
- Times and cultures sometimes have references and ideas that readers from a different time or culture may struggle to understand as they rely on knowledge exclusive to that time and culture.

ACTIVITY 2

To illustrate the first type, let's consider the confusion that attaching different meanings to words and symbols can cause. You will find below a series of hand gestures and their typical meanings. However, each has a very different meaning in particular cultures. Can you match the unusual cultural meaning to the gesture? Answers can be found in the back of the book.

A In Latin America, this gesture can be interpreted as 'your anus' and all its various negative associations.

B This gesture can be considered a rude and offensive gesture in some Middle Eastern and Asian countries, being more associated with an 'up yours'.

C In the UK, this gesture is considered offensive if it is mistakenly performed with the back of the hand towards the receiver. It apocryphally represents the bowfingers of longbowmen who took part in Anglo-French wars throughout the ages. If English or Welsh longbowmen were captured, these particular fingers would be severed by the French. This led to the fingers being raised towards the French as an offensive gesture before battle.

D In Greece, this gesture is known as the *moutza* and suggests the smearing of excrement on the person it is directed towards.

■ Table 2.2.1

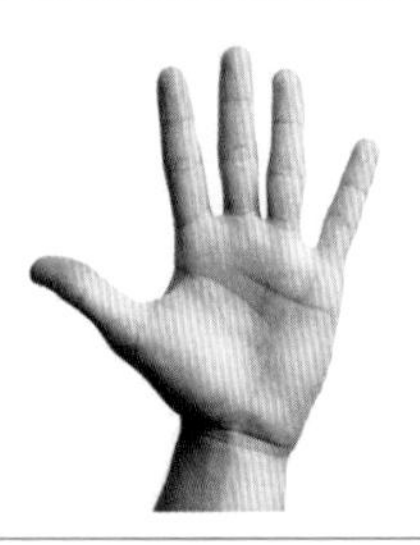	**Typical meaning:** In most cultures this gesture can be seen as a type of welcome or a way of saying 'hi'. **Specific cultural meaning:** A, B, C or D?
	**Typical meaning:** In most cultures, this gesture means things are 'okay' or 'going well'. **Specific cultural meaning:** A, B, C or D?

	**Typical meaning:** In most American and European cultures, this gesture signals things are going well and is a friendly gesture. **Specific cultural meaning:** A, B, C or D?
	**Typical meaning:** This gesture is often associated with peace and is a gesture of openness. In Asia it has also moved beyond this meaning to be a typical fun pose for photos. **Specific cultural meaning:** A, B, C or D?

As this demonstrates, approaching texts from other cultures, even if they are simply gestures, opens up the possibility of miscommunication. Without growing up with this cultural background and its shared frame of reference, you cannot always accurately interpret the gesture – that Greek fellow on holiday may not have been giving you a friendly wave!

To illustrate the second type of problem – having references and ideas that are particular to a time or culture – let's look at this extract from Amitav Ghosh's *River of Smoke*:

> From the Malay and Chinese parts of town people came in perahus and hired twakow rivercraft, while sailors and lascars usually came directly from their ships, in brightly painted tongkang lighters
>
> *(Amitav Ghosh 107)*

Without an understanding of the terms 'perahu', 'twakow', 'lascar' and 'tongkang lighters', this is a confusing description. A reader would need the cultural and historical knowledge of Asian ships to be able to accurately picture the scene, meaning that readers without this specific knowledge would have to rely on context clues such as 'rivercraft' to assume they refer to boats of some sort. (For the curious, a 'perahu' is a small sailboat, a 'twakow' is a single-masted boat, a 'lascar' is an archaic term for an Indian or south-east Asian sailor and a 'tongkang lighter' is a barge.)

These differences in **time** and **culture** clearly present a challenge for us as readers. How can we possibly approach a text that is not from our time and culture? Surely it is going to result in misinterpretation and misunderstanding? The answer is that it inevitably will – miscommunication is a reality of life. Even when we interpret texts from our *own* time and culture we do not always interpret things exactly as the producer intended. It is no surprise, then, that when the gap between producer and receiver is magnified by *differences* in time and culture, it can become harder for the reader to approach and interpret a text.

In Chapter 1.6, we saw how texts can present challenges in a variety of ways, from being written from the perspective of a horse to utilizing archaic language and complicated poetic styles. The challenges in this chapter will be more specifically focused on how time and culture can make texts hard to approach, and will demonstrate that there are steps we can take as readers to make it easier for us to connect with and interpret these texts. In doing so, we open up avenues of cross-cultural and cross-temporal understanding that help broaden our understanding of the world we inhabit and our place within it.

Before looking at these approaches, let's sum up what we've explored so far.

- We are all formed within a particular time and culture, helping shape our identity and how we see the world.
- When encountering texts from other times and cultures, we can struggle because of:
  - ☐ words, symbols and gestures having different meanings
  - ☐ content being closely tied to a particular time and place.

Universality

Despite this capacity for miscommunication, there is still more that connects us than divides us, regardless of our time and culture.

To introduce what we will call **universality**, let's first consider inter-generational communication. Do you ever feel you don't understand your parents? Have your parents ever felt equally bewildered by you? It seems every generation decries the state of the next one coming up, as you can see in the next quick activity.

ACTIVITY 3

Look at the following complaints from the older generation about the new generation. See if you can guess which year each is from – we'll be generous and allow you to be within a hundred years of the correct answer. You can find the answers in the back of the book.

1 'Modern fashions seem to keep on growing more and more debased … The ordinary spoken language has also steadily coarsened. People used to say "raise the carriage shafts" or "trim the lamp wick", but people today say "raise it" or "trim it". When they should say, "Let the men of the palace staff stand forth!" they say, "Torches! Let's have some light!"'

(History Hustle)

2 'The free access which many young people have to romances, novels, and plays has poisoned the mind and corrupted the morals of many a promising youth …'

(History Hustle)

3 '[Young people] are high-minded because they have not yet been humbled by life, nor have they experienced the force of circumstances […] They think they know everything, and are always quite sure about it.'

(History Hustle)

4 'Never has youth been exposed to such dangers of both perversion and arrest as in our own land and day. Increasing urban life with its temptations, prematurities, sedentary occupations, and passive stimuli just when an active life is most needed, early emancipation and a lessening sense for both duty and discipline …'

(History Hustle)

5 'Millennials are lazy and think basic tasks are beneath them.'

(Ruggeri)

Notice anything similar? In our examples above, you can see the same ideas being communicated by writers in vastly different times and places. There is a common sentiment, regardless of context, that the younger generation is rebellious and lazy, and that the previous generation was wiser and harder working. As these demonstrate, there are certain aspects of life that **transcend** the contextual; truths that are more related to the human condition rather than the technology we surround ourselves with or the culture we find ourselves in.

How can this be so? It is because certain things **transcend time and culture**, and are so closely tied in with the human condition and experience that they happen to all of us. Some are due to biology – we are all born, we all go through puberty, many of us reproduce, and we certainly all die. Regardless of where and when these moments are happening, the fundamentals will largely be similar and we will largely feel the same way about them. Others are due to emotions that we all share as a species due to our evolutionary background – we all feel the entire spectrum of emotions, including hate, love, anxiety, desire. Also, we have some broadly similar experiences: we have a nervous first day at school; we experience hierarchy when someone is in charge of us; we see inequality within our society. When texts deal with these **universals**, we can understand the intent of the writer regardless of how different their culture or time may be – they speak to us on a human level. We will refer to these as **universal themes**.

Further to this, you will have been noticing universal aspects of texts in terms of the way they are written. Similar literary features, for example, will appear in texts from very different times and cultures. These shared tools of expression used by writers provide us, as receivers of the text or work, with something to grasp onto. As a species, we are adept at spotting patterns, and many of these patterns within texts and genres have been highlighted in this textbook in the key features boxes. We will look in even more detail at these connections in Section 3 when we focus on **intertextuality**. These connections illustrate the common tools of the trade, the tried and tested methods of communication that are largely the same between time and culture. For example, novels make use of description, of dialogue, of symbolism, regardless of time or culture. Advertising uses persuasion, imagery and layout similarly across time and culture. Recognizing these common patterns eases us into the works and texts, and provides a foundation from which we can begin to approach and interpret the ideas and messages contained within them. We will refer to these as **universal text features**.

To sum up, there are two areas of universality you can look for in a text to help you approach it:

- **Universal text features**: writers using similar literary features, conventions and text types regardless of their time and culture.
- **Universal themes**: texts dealing with issues and ideas that are tied in to the human experience that we can all relate to.

These universals are the key to approaching texts from different times and cultures to our own – focusing not on what is different, but what is similar. Once we have the similar to grasp on to, we are able to more fully consider and explore the different, enriching our understanding of times and cultures alien to our own.

To explore this notion of **universality**, we will now revisit a work from Charles Dickens and introduce a text by Nelson Mandela.

A Christmas Carol by Charles Dickens (1843)

We looked at an extract from *A Christmas Carol* in Chapter 1.1 focusing on the presentation of the character of Scrooge. This time, we are going to focus on how Dickens uses literary features such as symbolism to communicate universal ideas that can be understood and related to by people regardless of time or culture. As you read, consider why this text resonates with you despite it having been written nearly two hundred years ago.

> They were a boy and girl. Yellow, meagre, ragged, scowling, wolfish; but prostrate, too, in their humility. Where graceful youth should have filled their features out, and touched them with its freshest tints, a stale and shrivelled hand, like that of age, had pinched, and twisted them, and pulled them into shreds. Where angels might have sat enthroned, devils lurked, and glared out menacing. No change, no degradation, no perversion of humanity, in any grade, through all the mysteries of wonderful creation, has monsters half so horrible and dread.
>
> Scrooge started back, appalled. Having them shown to him in this way, he tried to say they were fine children, but the words choked themselves, rather than be parties to a lie of such enormous magnitude.
>
> 'Spirit! are they yours?' Scrooge could say no more.
>
> 'They are Man's,' said the Spirit, looking down upon them. 'And they cling to me, appealing from their fathers. This boy is Ignorance. This girl is Want. Beware them both, and all of their degree, but most of all beware this boy, for on his brow I see that written which is Doom, unless the writing be erased. Deny it!' cried the Spirit, stretching out its hand towards the city. 'Slander those who tell it ye! Admit it for your factious purposes, and make it worse. And abide the end!'
>
> 'Have they no refuge or resource?' cried Scrooge.
>
> 'Are there no prisons?' said the Spirit, turning on him for the last time with his own words. 'Are there no workhouses?'
>
> *(Charles Dickens 61–62)*

Looking for the universal

Dickens is writing primarily for his implied readership of Victorian Britain, yet his is a work that is still being studied and enjoyed today. This is because of the **universal themes** of his work. It deals with issues that transcend Dickens' particular time and place, and they are conveyed in a way that we can still engage with and enjoy because of his method as a novel writer – **universal text features**. We can do this because we have seen and studied such techniques before in other novels. We can recognize Dickens' use of **symbolism**, **microcosm** and **allegory**, and thus understand that Scrooge is not just Scrooge, but a representative of a wider, greedy ruling class. We can encounter the novel's characters like Tiny Tim and Bob Cratchit and recognize them as the poor and exploited, understanding that they represent issues like inequality that always have and almost certainly always will exist. This allows readers to apply the novel's universal theme of sharing and community to their own particular time and culture and recognize the power of such a sentiment. Due to their **universal themes**, works such as these often go on to be regarded as 'classics'. (We will explore what we mean by a 'classic' and the 'literary canon' in Chapter 3.3.)

In this particular extract Dickens makes use of description, symbolism and contrast – **universal text features** typical of the novel text type – to convey the damage inequality can wreak upon the vulnerable and needy.

ACTIVITY 4

Complete the responses to the following two prompts before referring to the table of analysis below to compare your answers.

1 How does Dickens use universality to create an emotional response in the reader?

2 How does Dickens use universality to convey a universal message about inequality in society?

Analysis: Dickens confronts the reader with a boy and a girl. He describes them as 'yellow, meagre, ragged, scowling, wolfish' (line 1). This **asyndetic listing** of adjectives creates a relentless succession of horrifying details for the reader. 'Yellow' suggests neglect, illness and a sense of decay that is jarring in people so young. 'Meagre' suggests the children are malnourished, and 'ragged' reminds the readership of their poor clothing and lack of material comforts. Though they are young, an age associated with innocence, they are 'scowling' to suggest they are already damaged and filled with anger and resentment. 'Wolfish' animalizes the children, and suggests a lack of humanity that would horrify readers.

Universality: So what about this is easy for all readers to grasp? Well, regardless of culture or time, children have an inviolable link to purity. This is a consequence of them being recently born and the logical understanding that they have not had any influence on the world they have been brought into. Throughout the world and throughout history, children have been seen as innocent and worthy of protection and care; in presenting a 'girl' and a 'boy' in such poor condition, and in using such detail in doing so, readers of all times and cultures will be moved and will empathize with their state. Dickens has used his skill as a writer to create a universal response in readers.

Analysis: Dickens uses religious imagery to convey the wasted potential of the children. He writes 'Where angels might have sat enthroned, devils lurked, and glared out menacing' (line 4). The **binary opposition** of 'angels' and 'devils' relates to the symbolic degradation of the children. 'Angels' is a reminder to his largely Christian readership that we are made in the image of God, and in treating poor children so badly, we are treating God badly. Instead, the children's lurking devils 'glared out menacing'. This suggests the trouble these children may cause now and when they grow older, and reflects the sinfulness and crime that was rife in London at the time, in large part thanks to poverty.

Universality: Though on the face of it this is heavily tied in with Christian cultural background, there is still a **universal theme** that can be understood. All cultures around the world have a sense of good and evil, and these can often be found in religious and cultural imagery - yin and yang in Chinese philosophy and the concept of Dharma in Hinduism, for example. Despite the specific cultural dressing of angels and devils, the opposition of good and evil and the corruption of the former by the latter is an idea we can understand regardless of our time or culture.

Analysis: The boy and the girl have symbolic significance. Dickens presents them as the abstract notions of 'Ignorance' and 'Want' (line 11) manifest. He has chosen to personify them as children to emphasize the destruction society is causing to the innocent, but also to imply that these problems will only become worse in the future as the children grow up. If society is vandalizing the innocence and potential of its youth through inflicting ignorance and want, it is clear that society is destined for collapse. The remedy for the former is education and for the latter is both charity and providing opportunity - an implication that will not have been lost on Dickens' Victorian readership.

Universality: In writing about notions such as ignorance and want, Dickens is addressing issues that are prevalent in all societies, regardless of time or culture. His message was relevant in 1843 but would have been just as relevant in 1743 and 1943. Poverty and poor education are perennial human problems - there may have been progress, but even today they are still being battled by governments and leaders. Struggling with ignorance and want will resonate with all readers, regardless of time and culture, thanks to it being a **universal theme**.

In approaching the text with an awareness of the **universal text features**, in this case literary devices to convey deeper meanings, we are able to interpret broader **universal themes** being conveyed by Dickens. The messages themselves deal with universals, issues that transcend that particular moment in 1843 in London, and we are still learning from them today. In approaching this text by looking for the universals in terms of text features and messages, we are able to respond to the text on a human level and empathize with the children, even without a detailed background knowledge of Victorian London in 1843.

We will next look at another text that transcends its specific context – a letter by an imprisoned Nelson Mandela to the Head of Prison.

The Prison Letters of Nelson Mandela (2018)

Nelson Mandela

Nelson Mandela, born in 1918, was a South African revolutionary, political leader and philanthropist. He is famous for fighting for equality and against apartheid. Apartheid was a legal separation and systematic oppression of black people over white people in South Africa and was in place from 1948 until the early 1990s. It severely limited opportunities for education, jobs and living space in South Africa; concentrated non-white people into ghettos, or 'townships': and separated the races in schools, public facilities like swimming baths and even in personal relationships. Due to his rebellion against the government and its apartheid policies, he spent 27 years in prison for attempts to 'overthrow the state'. He became a globally known figure due to his dignity, patience, self-belief and principles. After his release from prison and the fall of apartheid, Mandela became the President of South Africa between 1994 and 1999. After this, he focused on philanthropy until his eventual death in 2013.

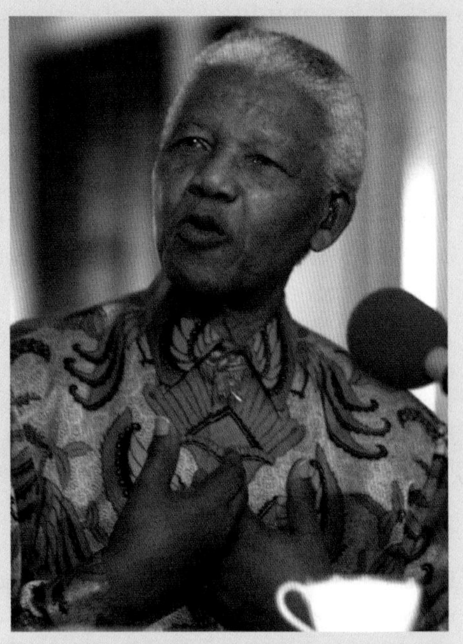

Dickens called on his readers to fight the evils of ignorance and want to provide for the needs of the poor and destitute. This focus on universal human needs crops up in a variety of texts and works throughout human history. They have inspired generations of writers due to their inherent drama and emotional resonance – when people are in need, they are suffering, and when they are suffering, we feel intense emotion. It is these intense emotions we often want to communicate through works and texts. In the following extract, we see these same needs appearing in a very different form and with a very different purpose.

The following text is a letter from Nelson Mandela to the person in charge of the administration of Pollsmoor Prison in Tokai, Cape Town, the prison he found himself incarcerated in. In the letter, he describes the inadequacy of his cell in quite some detail and politely requests better conditions in order to avoid illness. It was a prescient request, as he later developed tuberculosis, an infectious disease caused by bacteria which attack the lungs and can spread to other parts of the body. This infection was undoubtedly exacerbated by the damp conditions in his cell. Though he was subsequently moved to another prison, his damaged lungs meant he was more susceptible to lung infections, and he suffered further infections in later life.

KEY FEATURES FORMAL LETTERS

- **Addresses:** Traditional formal letters are physically transported to the recipient, so they usually contain the address of the person/business/institution they are intended for. Conventionally, the sender's address comes first on the right hand side of the letter with the date below it, allowing the recipient to reply if necessary and providing clarity regarding who sent the letter and when it was written. The recipient's address comes below this on the left hand side, before the main body of the letter begins.
- **Formal:** Unlike more modern forms of communication like emails, letters take time. They were traditionally handwritten, although typing is now more common. They are generally to be posted, and thus do not get instant responses. Because of this slower process both in terms of writing and response, they tend to be carefully structured and written in a formal register. (It is worth nothing that, for this course, informal letters that use an informal register are considered a different non-literary text type.)
- **Flexible purpose:** Formal letters generally have a functional or transactional purpose, including to persuade, to complain and to appeal. Each of the many functions has its own particular stylistic conventions. More personal letters, such as a letter to a loved one, are generally considered 'informal letters'.
- **Salutation:** Formal letters begin with a direct address to the recipient. Depending on the context, they can vary from a specific 'Dear _____' followed by the name of the recipient to a more general 'To whom it may concern'.
- **Signing off:** Similarly, the sign-off depends on the recipient. As a general rule, 'Yours sincerely' is used if the letter was written for someone whose name is used, and 'Yours faithfully' is used when the writer does not know the name of the recipient (for example, 'To whom it may concern').

As ever, let's first consider the CGAP and then analyse the extract.

Context	South Africa – 1986
Genre	Formal letter
Audience	Head of Pollsmoor Prison
Purpose	To appeal and complain

To the head of prison, Pollsmoor Maximum Security Prison

D220/82: NELSON MANDELA

6.10.86

Head of Prison

Pollsmoor Maximum Security Prison

Attention: Major Van Sittert

I would like to be transferred, at the earliest possible convenience, from my present cell to the opposite and empty cell across the passage primarily on health grounds.

My present cell has proved to be quite unhealthy and, if I continue staying in it, my health will eventually be impaired. At no time of day does the cell get the natural light, and I am accordingly compelled to keep the electric lights burning throughout the day.

The interior window panes are opaque and thick and the exterior fittings are made of louvre boards, all of which make the cell dark and depressing. Six panes have been removed and the cell becomes unbearable on cold and windy days.

Part of the wall and floor are perpetually damp and, during the ten months of my stay here, I have had to endure this inconvenience. You will readily appreciate, I trust, that it is not desirable that I should be compelled to live under such unwholesome conditions when there is a far better cell right in the same unit in which I could stay with relative comfort.

I must add that the dampness, as well as the metal fittings on the walls, also affect the reception in both the wireless and television set, resulting in uncontrollable flickering on the screen. I believe that I would get a better performance in a dry and properly ventilated cell which is not cluttered with metal material. I accordingly suggest that you allow me to move to the opposite cell …

(Nelson Mandela)

On the face of it, this is a situation that is incredibly alien to the typical reader. Mandela is a historical figure who has had an enormous impact on politics, race relations and poverty. Certainly for readers outside South Africa, it should be difficult to imagine being a black freedom fighter and political prisoner imprisoned in a white-minority ruled country that has racism hard-coded into the political and legal system. Thankfully, this is outside the experience of the majority of people, and truly understanding what such an experience of oppression would be like is a near impossibility.

Despite this incredibly alien **context of production**, the letter is something we can connect with. Much like Dickens' *A Christmas Carol*, we can approach it by relating to its **universality**: the aspects of the letter that transcend history and culture and speak more to the human experience.

The text includes **universal text features** as it is both a letter of complaint and of appeal and is addressed to the 'Head of Prison' (line 4). Though we cannot necessarily relate to the specifics of this context without having being imprisoned ourselves, we certainly can relate to the situation of writing to a superior who will not necessarily grant our request – another example of universality. It is likely all of us, at some point, have written a letter to a headteacher, a parent or a figure of authority whom we need to appeal to in order to be granted something. The tone of the letter reflects this situation: it is formal, polite, and contains subtle examples of **rhetoric** to gently win over the recipient to Mandela's perspective on his conditions. He reflects his inferior position to the Head of Prison by not writing with **imperatives** (saying things like 'you *must*' transfer me), but instead making use of **conditional verbs** such as 'would' in 'would like' (line 7) to both be polite to the recipient and to recognize the imbalance in power between himself, as a prisoner, and Major Van Sittert, as the Head of Prison. These features are common in formal letters of appeal. Such letters often recognize the imbalance of power between the writer and the recipient by avoiding forceful language, instead relying on being polite and using gentle explanation and persuasion.

ACTIVITY 5

In Chapter 1.3 we looked at the key features of letters of complaint. See if you can list those key features from memory and then research the following further types of formal letters: letter of persuasion, letter of appeal. Find an example of each, and complete a 'key features' box for each type, focusing on language features that suit their differing purposes.

The content of the letter is also something we, as readers, can find the **universal** in. Mandela's detailed and largely objective descriptions of his poor conditions in the cell are things we can relate to as a universal theme. When he describes that 'part of the wall and floor are perpetually damp' (line 15) it is easy for us to imagine the discomfort of being locked in a room in damp conditions. The adverb 'perpetually' helps reinforce the reality of it being a condition that is inescapable – unlike the reader, who could simply leave a damp room behind, this is a permanent reality for the writer. Even with no contextual knowledge of who Mandela is or why he was in prison, this letter in isolation creates empathy. Whatever our time or culture, we value freedom and comfort, and to read about it being taken away has an impact on us all.

These universal aspects of the text give the reader something to grasp on to. The **universal text features** help the reader recognize it as a letter of complaint and appeal. The **universal theme** of suffering discomfort allows the reader to approach it on a human level. Regardless of the history and culture surrounding the text, there are aspects that are related to the human condition that transcend both time and place and speak to us as fellow humans. These features of human life and experience are beyond effects of local cultural and historical conditions, and are relatable to by people regardless of the time and culture they find themselves in.

ACTIVITY 6

Below is a love letter from the First World War. It is from Emily Chitticks to her fiancé Private William Martin. What universal text features and universal themes can you spot in this letter? Answers can be found in the back of the book.

My Dearest Will, I feel I must write you again dear altho there is not much news to tell you. I wonder how you are getting on. I shall be so relieved to get a letter from you. I can't help feeling a bit anxious dear. I know how you must have felt darling when you did not get my letters for so long. Of course I know dear you will write as soon as ever you can, but the time seems so dull and weary without any news of you, if only this war was over dear and we were together again. It will be one day I suppose.

Don't think dear I am worrying unnecessarily about you, because I know God can take care of you wherever you are and if it's his will darling he will so are you to come back to me, that's how I feel about it dear, if we only put our trust in Him. I am sure he will. I wonder how your Cousins are getting on dear. We are feeling very anxious about George, as no news has come from him yet. We can't understand why his wife doesn't write.

How are your hands now dear? Mine are very sore, so chapped, and my left hand has got several chilblains on it and they do irritate. I could scratch it to bits. Have you been receiving the books I have sent you dear. I am very pleased to say dear I am keeping very well indeed, and I trust you are the same.

There has been a bit of a fuss over Arthur this week. He has been trying to get in the Army unbeknown to his parents, but Mrs T. thought his parents ought to be informed about it, so she wrote and told them about him and he had to go home in hot haste last night. I guess he got in a fine row, but he won't say today. He is as miserable as anything. Really Will I never saw such a boy as he is. I am afraid he is going to the bad. I don't know if Mrs T. will keep him on or not. He says he has to join up in a fortnight, but as he is under age I suppose his parents could stop him. I don't know whether they will or not. For my part I hope he does go, he will be a jolly good riddance for there is nothing but rows and deceitfulness going on where he is.

Well darling I don't know much more to say now, so will close with fondest love and kisses from your loving little girl. Emily.

(Amanda Mason)

Approaching texts of a different time – changing perspectives

TOK Links

We often judge people of the past for their moral failings, but should we? It is easy to pass judgement in hindsight, but they were a product of their time and culture. Has morality shifted, or are there moral absolutes?

Both Mandela's and Chitticks' letters were easy to relate to because of their **universal themes** but there are texts that contain messages that are not always as easy to relate to and are far more closely tied to time and place.

To explore this, we will look at a couple of texts from different time periods that focus on **attitudes and values** that we find repugnant today. When dealing with texts from the past, we are often brought into contact with **ideologies** that go against our modern sensibilities of equality and community. To approach such texts can sometimes be challenging and alienating as they go against so much of what our current ideologies stand for. In reading such texts, we can reflect on how much attitudes and values have changed over time. They can also help us hold a mirror up to our own time and culture, causing us to reflect on what our current attitudes and values are and whether they will have aged as badly when looked back on by future generations.

The Life and Strange Surprising Adventures of Robinson Crusoe by Daniel Defoe (1719)

The Life and Strange Surprising Adventures of Robinson Crusoe was first published in 1719 and is a work of fiction presented as an autobiography of the titular character, Robinson Crusoe. An Englishman who sets out on an adventurous sea voyage, he experiences shipwrecks and piracy before eventually finding himself on an expedition to bring slaves from Africa to Brazil. After settling in Brazil, Crusoe then sets sail to Guinea to buy slaves of his own, but is shipwrecked off an island near the coast of modern day Venezuela. On the island, he encounters cannibals. A prisoner of the cannibals escapes and is encountered by Crusoe. Crusoe names him Friday and converts him to Christianity; together, they kill most of the cannibals and eventually escape to England.

Daniel Defoe

Best known for his work *The Life and Surprising Adventures of Robinson Crusoe*, Daniel Defoe was an English trader, writer, pamphleteer, journalist and spy. He was born in 1660 and lived at the time of the transatlantic slave trade – the act of trading goods for captured people in Africa, then selling these people in the Americas or Caribbean in exchange for goods such as sugar, rum and tobacco. He was one of the earliest English novelists, helping popularize the form in Britain; he also wrote many influential political pamphlets regarding politics and society. A prolific writer, he wrote over 370 published works including a series of famous novels including *Moll Flanders*, *Captain Singleton* and *Memoirs of a Cavalier.*

In the extract below, Crusoe has recently encountered the prisoner he will soon name 'Friday'.

In a little time I began to speak to him, and teach him to speak to me; and, first, I let him know his name should be Friday, which was the day I saved his life; I called so for the memory of the time. I likewise taught him to say Master, and then let him know that was to be my name; I likewise taught him to say Yes and No, and to know the meaning of them. I gave him some milk in an earthen pot, and let him see me drink it before him, and sop my bread in it; and gave him a cake of bread to do the like, which he quickly complied with, and made signs that it was very good for him. I kept there with him all that night; but, as soon as it was day, I beckoned to him to come with me, and let him know I would give him some clothes; at which he seemed very glad, for he was stark naked. As went by the place where he had buried the two men, he pointed exactly to the place, and showed me the marks he had made to find them again, making signs to me that we should dig them up again and eat them. At this I appeared very angry, expressed my abhorrence of it, made as if I would vomit at the very thoughts of it, and beckoned with my hand to him to come away, which he did immediately, with great submission. I then led him up to the top of the hill, to see if his enemies were gone, and pulling out my glass, I looked and saw plainly the place where they had been, but no appearance of them or their canoes; so that it was plain they were gone, and had left their two comrades behind them without any search after them.

But I was not content with this discovery; but having now took more courage, and consequently more curiosity, I took my man Friday with me, giving him the sword in his hand, with the bows and arrows at his back, which I found he could use very dexterously, making him carry one gun for me, and I two for myself; and away we marched to the place where these creatures had been – for I had a mind now to get some fuller intelligence of them. When I came to the place, my very blood ran chill in my veins, and my heart sank within me at the very horror of the spectacle, indeed, it was a dreadful sight; at least it was so to me, though Friday made nothing of it. The place was covered with human bones, the ground dyed with the blood, and great pieces of flesh left here and there, half-eaten, mangled, and scorched; and, in short, all the tokens of the triumphant feast they had been making there, after a victory over their enemies. I saw three skulls, five hands, and the bones of three or four legs and feet, and abundance of other parts of the bodies; and Friday, by his signs, made me understand that they brought over four prisoners to feast upon; that three of them were eaten up and that he, pointing to himself was the fourth; that there had been a great battle between them and their next king, of whose subjects, it seems, he had been one, and that they had taken a great number of prisoners; all of which were carried to several places by those who had taken them in the fight, in order to feast upon them, as was done here by these wretches upon those they brought hither.

(Daniel Defoe 174–175)

The content of works such as this are problematic for the modern reader. The colonial-era attitudes to slavery and race are shocking and offensive in a modern **context of reception**. Though slavery is far from eradicated in modern times – sex slavery, people trafficking, forced migrant labour and bonded labour are persistent problems that still exist today – the accepting attitude towards it in this work causes undoubted offence in a contemporary context. Being under someone's control or supervision is certainly a **universal theme** all readers will be able to understand – we all experience some sort of hierarchy of power – but the extreme horror of slavery is nearly impossible to imagine. Not only this, but the positive **attitudes and values** shown towards slavery in the text are alien, offensive and make the work difficult to approach. Though shocking, it is often the texts that challenge us that are the ones that are more valuable and insightful in terms of understanding the history and development of human attitudes through the ages. If we ignore such texts, we are failing to face up to our past and risk repeating the same mistakes again.

We must, therefore, approach such texts as ideological historians, performing a **negotiated** and occasionally **oppositional reading** of the work or text. We at once attempt to understand the intent of the **implied author**, the response of the **implied reader**, but also inevitably compare the text to our modern time and context. We see the text as a product of its time and a window into the attitudes and values of the past. These works and texts are as close as we can get to a time machine, allowing us to step into different eras and communicate with writers who were living and breathing in periods of history that are often fundamentally different to our own. As we do not live in the same time and space as the writer, and as we cannot speak directly to the writer, we have to find connections to them through the text itself: the text is our means of communicating with the past.

With such works and texts, it is necessary to approach them on a more practical level with a degree of knowledge about their time. If we were ignorant of the slave trade and European colonization of Africa and the Americas, the events in *Robinson Crusoe* would lose a lot of their **subtext**. We would fail to realize that the act of Crusoe controlling Friday and enforcing upon him **Western** beliefs and ways of life is symbolic of a wider attitude and reality of the time – Western countries were doing much the same to non-Western countries through colonization. This, of course, requires us to perform research around the context of production of the text we are interpreting. **Research** is another useful tool when approaching texts from different times and cultures to our own. The advent of the internet has made this far easier than it used to be – we have an almost infinite library of resources, artefacts, insights and documentaries at our fingertips. Through online video platforms we can watch university lectures on the slave trade; through online encyclopediae we can read about Daniel Defoe and the novel itself; through digital libraries we can access academic papers on the work and its background.

With such background knowledge, we can then more clearly spot **context clues** and **subtext** that would otherwise be harder to recognize. The broader significance of the moment Crusoe 'taught him to say Master' (line 3) before he had even taught him the meaning of 'yes' and 'no' becomes more apparent. The self-identification of the white Crusoe as 'Master' sets up a hierarchy that is seen as natural, introducing a master-slave relationship that is indicative of wider historical attitudes of the time. This is the European attitude to non-Europeans in microcosm – non-Europeans are seen as inferior, subservient and need to be 'civilized' by learning the ways of Europeans. In not even knowing the English terms for 'yes' and 'no' before this system is established, Friday is denied agency and the ability to accept or reject this imposition of ownership. This is further emphasized through the dehumanization of the native peoples of the island. Referred to as 'these creatures' (line 20), the view of native peoples outside Europe as uncivilized and, in many ways, subhuman is clearly apparent.

The idea of forcing other cultures to conform to your own goes against the idea of global citizenship in all its varieties and forms. In reading works like *Robinson Crusoe*, we are able to face up to the attitudes, values and beliefs of the past and put our present time and space in context. To a modern British reader living in multicultural Britain, for example, this text puts their present context in stark relief. It not only shows the progress that has been made in terms of attitudes to other cultures and races, it also helps remind such a reader of how those attitudes and actions of the past affected their current context. Britain's history of colonization eventually led to the settlement of many of those colonized peoples in Britain, and their descendants are part of its current multicultural demography.

In approaching texts from other times and cultures from our own as ideological historians, we can recognize this journey of historical development and we can learn much about the world as it is in our current time by peering into the past. This is the power of texts such as *Robinson Crusoe* – they can prompt us to reflect on our rights and responsibilities, consider how they did not always exist, and remember that they may not continue to exist unless we protect them. In a world where white-supremacism, anti-immigration and far-right politics persist, texts like *Robinson Crusoe* give readers an ability to broaden their perspective beyond the current time, and see the horrors we can inflict upon each other if we do not fight hate with love and understanding.

GLOBAL ISSUES ***Field of inquiry:* Politics, Power and Justice**

SLAVERY

Within the politics, power and justice field of inquiry, this work is closely tied in with notions of power, race, human rights and inequality. We must remember that a global issue needs to persist in everyday contexts today, be transnational, and have a wide significance. Despite its age, many of the issues *Robinson Crusoe* deals with fulfil these criteria.

Texts that deal with the global issue of slavery are an obvious point of comparison. Though in most parts of the world slavery has become less explicit, it still exists in areas like domestic servitude, prostitution, agricultural slave labour, forced marriages and factory labour – this is termed 'modern slavery'. As it is often 'hidden in plain sight' (meaning that people may encounter modern slaves without realizing their plight), there have been recent campaigns to raise awareness of the issue so that people can spot and report it. Advertising campaigns and speeches can be found that deal with this issue, and these texts can be an interesting companion piece to *Robinson Crusoe*.

Other possible global issues are imperialism and cultural imperialism. *Robinson Crusoe* focuses on one country imposing its systems and control over another, and examples of this can be found in propaganda texts of the past that supported colonialism. The denial of Friday's human rights also opens up other avenues of non-literary comparison to texts relating to human rights abuses and impositions of inequality.

Hoover advertisements

Attitudes and values are constantly shifting. To recognize this constant change, another way of approaching texts from a different time is by **comparing** them with more modern examples (looking at connections between texts will be explored in far more detail in Section 3 Intertextuality: connecting texts). This is another approach beyond looking for the **universal themes**, **universal text features** and **research**. In approaching texts by comparing them, we can put them in historical context. We can see how attitudes and values have developed, and also recognize how text types may have changed over time. In our next example, a more modern advert has been used to compare and contrast with the text from a different time. By **juxtaposing** them, it is easier to identify changes in attitudes and values from the past to the present.

Both advertisements are for a particular type of consumer product: the vacuum cleaner. In our last text, the difference in time between ourselves and the context of production was hundreds of years – this made the text harder to approach and the attitudes vastly different to those of today. Our next texts were both produced within the past hundred years. You may well think this would make the attitudes and values far closer to our own, but you will often be surprized at the differences. Even with a relatively recent context of production, a lot can have changed – remember, it was around 60 years ago that black people were still being segregated from white people in parts of the USA. This clearly illustrates not only the pace of change, but also the consistency of change – at no point do attitudes and values stand still, they are constantly shifting and adapting as time moves on.

To illustrate this, we will look at two adverts from a wider non-literary body of work: Hoover's advertising campaigns. As ever, we will begin by looking for **universal text features** and **universal themes** in our advert from a different time to our own. The universal text features are immediately apparent: it is an advert; it features imagery of products and people; it makes use of graphic design and layout; it uses persuasive language in the copy. There is also a universal theme: material goods are things you desire and can make you happy.

ACTIVITY 7

Below, some key features of the two adverts have been identified for you. Write a brief explanation of how these features show a shift in attitudes and values before reading the example commentary on the next page.

■ Table 2.2.3

Origin and purpose: 1948 USA. Print advert aimed at adult women to inform and persuade.	**Origin and purpose:** ~2000 USA. Print advert aimed at adults to inform and persuade.
Models: Illustrations of two women. Both look directly at the viewer of the advert. The upper model is wearing heels, a long skirt, and a red top; she is wearing makeup and vacuuming. The lower woman is also in heels and makeup; she is in a posed position to model the vacuum and is wearing an elegant and stylish dress.	**Models:** A young girl smiling and in a relaxed pose looking directly at the viewer; she is missing milk teeth to emphasize her youth. She is dirty from having been playing baseball outside (evidenced by the prop of a baseball in her hand and a baseball glove nearby). She wears a baseball cap with mud stains, dungarees, a pale green top and white socks covered in mud stains. Next to her is a father looking lovingly at his daughter; his watch suggests he is successful.
Copy: Ideological language such as 'The name women prefer 2 to 1 over any other cleaner'. Persuasive language such as use of direct address ('you'), technical jargon ('Mothimizer'), anaphora ('you'll').	**Copy:** Little ideological language. Persuasive language through direct address ('you'll'), technical jargon ('Windtunnel Technology'), heightened language ('powerful').
Product imagery: The products are in use by the two female models. A range of vacuum cleaners are shown and they are made to look sleek and stylish.	**Product imagery:** Products are shown separately from the main image; a range of vacuum cleaners are shown; they look sleek, stylish, and appear to be coming towards the viewer.

Comparing features

In this course, we are looking at texts with our three different lenses: **immanent**, **contextual** and **comparative**. Though this coursebook gives each a delineated section, all three methods of exploring texts are complementary and using them together allows a fuller exploration and understanding of a text. The following activity requires the immanent by looking at the inherent features of the adverts; the contextual by considering the attitudes and values of the time; and requires comparison, a method of exploration that will be more fully explained in Section 3 Intertextuality: connecting texts. The below analysis examines first the modern advert, then the old advert, and finally compares them to comment on how they reflect changes in representation.

Modern: Though there are striking similarities between the adverts in terms of layout and colour, the more specific details reveal the attitudes and values of their context of production. In the modern advert, the young girl is in dungarees and a baseball cap, clothes that, in the past, were associated with boys. She is also holding a baseball prop, implying she has been playing baseball and getting dirty, shown by the stains on her clothes. This image of a girl having enjoyed the rough and tumble of a baseball game shows a modern attitude towards femininity as it suggests girls can be just as active and adventurous as boys. Next to her is her father, with the caption 'time for a little spring-cleaning' implying that the father will be using the vacuum cleaner to clean up after his daughter. This shows a modern attitude towards housework as something that can be done by men and not just women. This is reinforced by the products being shown on their own, with neither a man nor woman using them. This suggests they can potentially be used by anyone, regardless of gender.

Old: Contrastingly, the 1948 advert genders the product by only showing it being used by women. This is reinforced in the copy with the statement that their brand is 'The name women prefer 2 to 1 over any other cleaner'. In having surveyed only women, the producer has women in mind as the implied reader, suggesting they are the ones interested in products used for housework. The women's clothes also show a focus on the superficial - they are wearing makeup and impractical heels while doing the housework, implying a need to focus on beauty regardless of the situation. One of them is also in an elegant dress and both women have skirts, gendered clothing that reinforces the image of what women wear and how they should look.

Comparison: In comparing the two adverts, shifts in attitude are clearly present. Females in the old advert are in skirts and dresses, whereas the modern advert features a female in far more casual dungarees and baseball cap. This more gender-neutral clothing in the modern advert reveals notions of femininity having shifted, and that girls are no longer expected to wear the stereotypical dress. The modern advert suggesting the father will clean as opposed to the old advert's portrayal of women cleaning shows a shift in terms of gendered domestic work. Unlike the old advert, housework is being shown to also be the domain of men, and the gender-neutral language in the copy ensures that the product appeals to both genders rather than just women. The pairing of these adverts suggests that notions of femininity and gender roles have developed significantly since 1948, and that the gendering of everything from clothing to jobs has become more neutral.

ACTIVITY 8

Practise using comparison to approach texts from different times and cultures by writing a commentary for these two detergent adverts. You can find an example response in the back of the book.

■ Table 2.2.4

<table>
<tr>
<td>
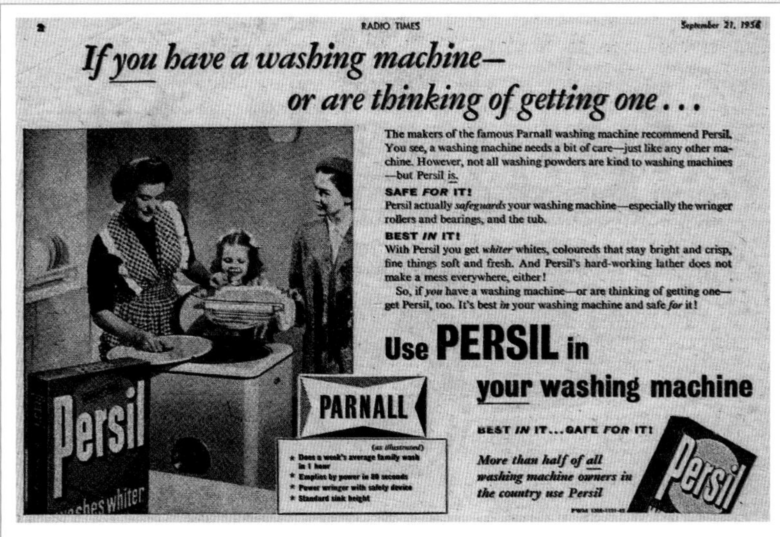

</td>
<td>
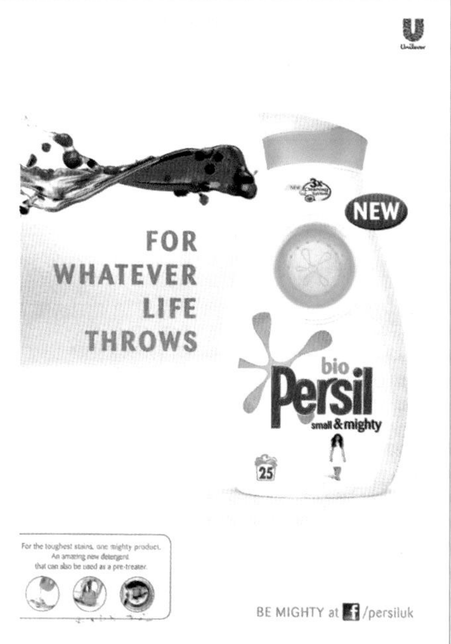

</td>
</tr>
<tr>
<td>Origin and purpose: 1950s UK. Print advert aimed at housewives to inform and persuade.</td>
<td>Origin and purpose: 2000s UK. Print advert aimed at adults to inform and persuade.</td>
</tr>
</table>

As your commentary should have shown, approaching texts of a different time by comparing them to modern counterparts can put differences in attitudes and values into stark relief, allowing a better understanding of how changes over time are reflected in texts.

Having looked at texts that are primarily from a different time to our own, we are now going to consider a text that is most probably from a different *culture* to our own. Different cultures can be both exhilarating and alienating. Anyone who has travelled widely will have had moments of sheer bewilderment, as we have already discovered earlier in the chapter when looking at how even something as simple as a gesture can have implications we do not expect. When approaching texts with distinct cultural differences, the approaches in the previous part of the chapter still apply – you can look for **universal themes**, you can look for **universal text features**, you can **research**, and you can **compare** to a text from a context you are more familiar with.

The Famished Road by Ben Okri (1991)

Ben Okri

Ben Okri is a Nigerian poet and novelist. He was born in Minna, Nigeria in 1959, and moved with his family to London at the age of 18 months. He grew up in Peckham until he was 7 years old, when he moved back to Nigeria with his parents and three siblings. When he was eight, a 3-year conflict called the Biafra war broke out. He witnessed horrific acts of violence during the war. At the age of 14 he left school and wrote journalism as well as poetry and stories. He moved back to England at the age of 19 to study at university, but his funding from the Nigerian government failed to materialize. He consequently spent time homeless, living in parks and the homes of friends. At 21 his first novel *Flowers and Shadows* was published, the beginning of an upturn in his fortunes. In 1991 his magical realism novel *The Famished Road* won the prestigious Booker Prize for Fiction, making him the youngest ever winner of the prize.

To demonstrate how approaching texts from cultures other than our own can be alienating and challenging, the following extract by Ben Okri is placed before our usual introduction. Read the extract without the introductory contextual information and consider how this lack of context affects your interpretation and understanding. After the extract, you will find an introduction that should help unlock the meaning of the extract.

With our spirit companions, the ones with whom we had a special affinity, we were happy most of the time because we floated on the aquamarine air of love. We played with the fauns, the fairies, and the beautiful beings. Tender sibyls, benign sprites, and the serene presences of our ancestors were always with us, bathing us in the radiance of their diverse rainbows. There are many reasons why babies cry when they are born, and one of them is the sudden separation from the world of pure dreams, where all things are made of enchantment, and where there is no suffering.

The happier we were, the closer was our birth. As we approached another incarnation we made pacts that we would return to the spirit world at the first opportunity. We made these vows in fields of intense flowers and in the sweet-tasting moonlight of that world. Those of us who made such vows were known among the Living as abiku, spirit-children. Not all people recognised us. We were the ones who kept coming and going, unwilling to come to terms with life. We had the ability to will our deaths. Our pacts were binding. Those who broke their pacts were assailed by hallucinations and haunted by their companions. They would only find consolation when they returned to the world of the Unborn, the place of fountains, where their loved ones would be waiting for them silently.

Those of us who lingered in the world, seduced by the annunciations of wonderful events, went through life with beautiful and fated eyes, carrying within us the music of a lovely and tragic mythology. Our mouths utter obscure prophecies. Our minds are invaded by images of the future. We are the strange ones, with half of our beings always in the spirit world ...

How many times had I come and gone through the dreaded gateway? How many times had I been born and died young? And how often to the same parents? I had no idea. So much of the dust of living was in me. But this time, somewhere in the interspace between the spirit world and the Living, I chose to stay. This meant breaking my pact and outwitting my companions. It wasn't because of the sacrifices, the burnt offerings of oils and yams and palm-nuts, or the blandishments, the short-lived promises of special treatment, or even because of the grief I had caused. It wasn't because of my horror of recognition either. Apart from a mark on my palm I had managed to avoid being discovered. It may simply have been that I had grown tired of coming and going. It is terrible to forever remain in-between. It may also have been that I wanted to taste of this world, to feel it, suffer it, know it, to love it, to make a valuable contribution to it, and to have that sublime mood of eternity in me as I live the life to come. But I sometimes think it was a face that made me want to stay. I wanted to make happy the bruised face of the woman who would become my mother.

(Ben Okri 4–5)

So far, you should have been able to notice some universal themes and some universal text features.

- **Universal themes:** We have the idea of birth and the mystery of where we come from, as well as an expression of love for a mother.
- **Universal text features:** As this is a novel, it is rich with descriptive language and symbolism, but what is being symbolized is a little unclear. We have descriptions of emotion and feeling.

On first reading, then, we are able to interpret some of the text by looking for universals. We have a child that appears to come from a 'spirit' world to be born into the material world, but much of the significance is lost on us. As with *Robinson Crusoe*, a little contextual research should greatly enhance our understanding of the work. In reading the following introduction to the text, our understanding of it should be greatly enhanced.

The Famished Road is the story of Azaro, a spirit child living in an unnamed but most likely Nigerian city. Spirit children are known as 'Abiku', a Yoruba word meaning 'pre-destined for death'. Abiku are part of Yoruba mythology, and are the spirits of children who die before reaching puberty. They are believed to be killed by hungry spirits who wish for the child's spirit to return to the spirit world. Once they have entered the spirit world, they soon return to their mother to be reborn in human form once again. Each time they are born, they are marked by their parents on their chest, back, face or palm. Unless the spirits are appeased, they are then dragged back into the spirit world by dying before puberty, creating a cycle of grief for the mother. In Okri's novel, Azaro stubbornly refuses to die and re-enter the spirit world due to his love for his mother and father, despite the best efforts of his sibling spirits. This coexistence of the spiritual and material worlds is a fundamental part of Yoruba culture.

ACTIVITY 9

You should now have a better understanding of the culture the text is focused on. Re-read the extract with this new knowledge, and then respond to the following prompts. The first is done for you. Example responses can be found in the back of the book.

1 How is the beauty and glory of the spirit world conveyed by Okri in the opening paragraph?

Okri introduces the spirit world inhabited by the Abiku as a place of almost-unqualified beauty and joy. The dynamic verbs 'floated' and 'played' (line 2) convey the leisurely experience of the spirit world, and the metaphysical 'aquamarine air of love' (line 2) on which they float introduces the fantastical experience of this realm. The physicality of 'love' being something which they can lightly float over emphasizes the Yoruba belief that the spirit world is one of ecstasy. Further fantastical imagery, shown with the tripling of 'the fauns, the fairies, and the beautiful beings' (lines 2–3), uses the fricative alliteration of 'fauns' and 'fairies' paired with the plosive alliteration of 'beautiful beings' to create a rhythmic quality that accentuates the beauty and harmony they experience. A lexical set of peaceful adjectives such as 'tender', 'benign' and 'serene' (line 3) make clear the tranquility of the setting and how free from suffering the Abiku are when they are in the spirit world. This heightened sense of peace and beauty is later contrasted with the pain experienced by the Abiku in the human-world.

2 How does Okri present the suffering created by Abiku spirits?

3 How does Okri present the connection between the spirit world and the material world?

'The Stress of a Night During Wartime' by Sivaramani Sivanandan

Our final text is a poem in translation by Sivaramani Sivanandan, a Sri Lankan poet who committed suicide on 19 May 1991 after burning all the copies she had of her poetry. Her suicide was driven, in part, by her experiences during the Sri Lankan Civil War which took place between 1983 until as recently as 2009.

Read the poem and consider what **universal themes** and **universal text features** you can identify.

The stress of a night during wartime

The stress of a night during wartime
will make adults
out of our children.
Because of
every blood-soaked, faceless human corpse
that's hurled across
the passage of their mornings
lovely as a tiny sparrow's
and the smashed ramparts falling
on their lively laughter,
our little boys have

ceased to be little boys.
The report of a lone gun
on a star-lit night,
smashing the silence and exploding,
reduced to naught
the meaning of all children's stories.
And in the brief daytime remaining,
they forgot how to make chariots
from thorn apple seeds
or to play hopscotch.
To shut the wicket gate before nightfall,
to recognise any unusual barking of the dogs,
to refrain from asking questions
and to remain silent when
the question had no reply –
later, in herd-like fashion,
they learnt it all.
Wantonly ripping out a moth's wings
and turning staves and twigs into guns
to kill a friend, thinking of him as the enemy,
became our children's sport.
Amidst the stress of a night during wartime,
our children had
turned into 'adults'.

(Sivaramani Sivanandan)

Universal themes and text features

Even without extensive knowledge of the Sri Lankan Civil War or the poet's life, the message and significance of the poem remains largely intact.

One obvious universal text feature used throughout the poem is **juxtaposition**. Words and phrases such as 'children' (line 3) and 'tiny sparrow' (line 8) are in clear contrast to 'adults' (line 2) and 'smashed ramparts' (line 9). The meaning behind this can be unlocked by analysing the opening of the poem, 'the stress of a night during wartime / will make adults / out of our children' (lines 1–3). Wartime is described to be changing children into adults, a transition that is symbolic of lost innocence and corruption of purity. This idea is expanded on through this use of juxtapositional imagery – the adjective 'tiny' in 'tiny sparrow' contrasts with 'smashed' in 'smashed ramparts' to show that the small and fragile are being faced with destruction. The 'ramparts' could symbolize the defences of innocence that have been destroyed by war, and that many children of Sri Lanka were forced to grow up very quickly in the face of death and destruction. This should put you in mind of the extract from *A Christmas Carol* earlier in the chapter – the universal theme of childhood losing its innocence is being used once again, but this time in a very different space and a very different time. This connection between texts is called **intertextuality** and will be focused on in more depth in Section 3.

Another universal text feature is the poet's use of **enjambment**, a common technique in poetry. Throughout the poem, lines flow into the next such as lines 12–13, 'our little boys have / ceased to be little boys'. Speaking broadly, the enjambment conveys the quick and enforced transition from childhood into adulthood despite the children not being ready for it, in much the same way the lines suddenly change mid-clause before being fully developed. In our particular example, the parallel construction draws contrast between the two lines, emphasizing the suddenness of the change. The use of the verb 'ceased' makes clear that this is an ending of childhood and implies that the children caught up in the war had to become men in order to survive. This coming-of-age is a universal theme that we can all understand, but the particular situation it happens in is harder for us to grasp.

Our final universal text feature is **visual imagery**, a common feature of prose and poetry. The final section of the poem describes children 'wantonly ripping out a moth's wings / and turning staves and sticks into guns' (lines 29–30). The adverb 'wantonly' emphasizes how needless and unprovoked the violent act of the children is as they rip out the wings of a delicate 'moth'. From this, it can be inferred that the violence during the civil war started to affect how children played as they began to mimic the violence around them. This is reinforced by them being described as having turned sticks into 'guns' on the next line. The reader picks up on the dark subtext to their childhood games because of the earlier parts of the poem describing the very real violence that has been taking place in Sri Lanka. In ending the poem with the violent games of children, it is suggested that the next generation will grow up to continue this violence, creating a cycle of aggression that in reality played out until 2009 when the war finally came to an end.

As this poem demonstrates, sometimes without the added detail provided through detailed research and understanding of context, the meaning of a text can still be understood through a focus on **universals**. This relies on the skill of the writer in constructing a universal text that can speak to people regardless of time or place through their avoidance of specific references to particular historical or cultural context.

Conclusion

In this chapter, we have considered how we approach texts from different times and cultures to our own. First of all, we look for **universal themes** and **universal text features** to give us something to grasp onto as a reader. We may then **research** more background information, or **compare** it to another text to highlight similarities and differences that put the text in a wider context. With these approaches, we can better understand a variety of texts from any time or space.

ACTIVITY 10

To put all this into action, you are about to be confronted with a text from another time and culture. Feel free to look for **universals** and to **research**, and then create a commentary on what you think the text is conveying about time and place.

Coronation of Queen Victoria

Originally published in the Saturday Evening Post, July 28, 1838

[...] The Archbishop then placed the crown on her Majesty's head, and the peers and peeresses put on their cornets, the bishop their caps, and the king-of-arms their crowns. The effect was magnificent in the extreme. The shouts which followed this part of the ceremony was really tumultuous.

After this followed the anthem, 'The Queen shall rejoice in thy strength O Lord'; at the conclusion of which the Archbishop and Bishops and other peers lifting up her Majesty into the throne, when the peers did homage. The solemnity of the coronation being thus ended, the Queen went down from her throne to the altar, made her second oblation, and returned to the chair. The Archbishop then read the prayers for the whole estate of Christ's Church militant here on earth, etc. and the chorus, 'Hallelujah! For the Lord God omnipotent reigneth', having been sung, her Majesty proceeded to the altar, when the Archbishop read the final prayers. The whole coronation office being thus performed, the Queen proceeded, crowned, to King Edward's Chapel, where she delivered the scepter with the (dove) to the Archbishop, who laid it on there altar there. His Grace then placed the orb in the Queen's left hand, and the procession returned in the same state and order.

The night presented a scene of indescribable luster from the illumination throughout all the principal squares and streets in the metropolis, the inhabitants viewing with each other in doing honor to this interesting occasion. There was also a brilliant display of fireworks in Hyde Park.

(Jeff Nilsson)

Works cited

Defoe, D. *The Life and Strange Surprising Adventures of Robinson Crusoe, of York, Mariner: Who Lived Eight and Twenty Years Alone in an Uninhabited Island on the Coast of America, Near the Mouth of the Great River Oronoko.* Palala Press, 2015.

Dickens, C. *A Christmas Carol*. Penguin Classics, 2012.

Ghosh, A. *River of Smoke*. Farrar, Straus and Giroux, 2011.

Mandela, N. *The Prison Letters of Nelson Mandela*. Liveright Publishing, 2018.

Mason, A, Parton, E. 'Letters to Loved Ones.' IWM, 4 Jan. 2018. Web. 12 March 2019. **www.iwm.org.uk/history/letters-to-loved-ones**.

Nilsson, J. 'The Coronation of Queen Victoria.' *The Saturday Evening Post*, 13 Jan. 2017. Web. 12 March 2019. **www.saturdayeveningpost.com/2017/01/coronation-queen-victoria**.

Okri, B. *The Famished Road*. Vintage Publishing, 1992.

Ruggeri, A. 'People have always whinged about young adults. Here's proof.' BBC, 3 Oct. 2017. Web. 12 March 2019. **www.bbc.com/capital/story/20171003-proof-that-people-have-always-complained-about-young-adults**.

Sivanandan, Sivaramani. 'The stress of a night during wartime'. Web. 29 October 2019. **https://scroll.in/article/915511/how-were-we-done-for-in-this-war-three-poems-by-women-poets-from-sri-lanka-ask-the-same-question**.

'The 2,500-Year-Old History of Adults Blaming the Younger Generation.' History Hustle, 17 April 2018. Web. 12 March 2019. **https://historyhustle.com/2500-years-of-people-complaining-about-the-younger-generation**.

2.3 To what extent do texts offer insight into another culture?

OBJECTIVES OF CHAPTER

- To consider the difficulties of representing the complexity of cultures through texts.
- To consider the importance of different perspectives within cultures.
- To explore the differing insights offered by outsiders and insiders to a culture.
- To examine how global brands adapt to suit different cultures.

In the previous chapter, we looked at different ways to approach texts from times and cultures other than our own. In this chapter, we are going to consider more fully how texts **offer insight into other cultures**, and explore the extent to which that insight is offered.

Every one of us reading this coursebook is immersed in a particular time and culture. Some of us may be in a bustling Asian city like Hong Kong, with its mixture of Cantonese and Western culture. Some of us may be in Paris, with its French culture and its *liberté*, *égalité* and *fraternité*. Some of us may be third culture children – people who are influenced by a mix of cultures growing up – and could be a person of mixed Indian and English descent living in Peru; the possibilities are near endless. It is this complexity that affects the texts we create and the way we interpret texts written by others.

As cultural boundaries blur and intercultural relationships become more common, an openness and understanding of other cultures is increasingly important. As explored in the previous chapter, one of the most powerful ways of understanding another culture is through a work or text that has been produced within it.

Our guiding conceptual question asks us to consider the extent to which we are given insight through such texts. It is true that texts have their limits. Let's first consider some of the **limitations** of texts providing insights into culture.

- **The complex nature of culture:** It is a good time to remember that cultures are fuzzy, complex and often contradictory constructions. An overall culture often broadly encompasses other cultures within it, sometimes grouped by religious beliefs, race, or geography. American culture is a good example: African-American culture has certain distinctions from Southern US American culture which has certain distinctions from Native American culture, yet they all contain a lot of overlap and often feed off each other. This 'melting pot' of cultures contains a variety of experiences and contradictions, but these will not always be evident in isolated texts, which leads on to our next point …
- **Narrow perspective:** The insights into culture you gain from a particular text are narrow. A single text is one voice among many, and often reflects specific parts of a much wider and diverse culture. This is because a text is almost always created by one writer, and they are communicating their one perspective and experience. Representation can also be an issue – it is often the oppressed who have their voices silenced or minimized, and this can extend to texts. To gain a better understanding, a range of texts needs to be engaged with, providing a range of perspectives. In doing so, a much broader picture of a place is painted, with the complexities and subtleties that can offer true insight.

- **Texts are reproductions:** Without being physically immersed in a culture – tasting the food, taking in the smell of a city, seeing the sights, and hearing the musicality of the language – it is hard to truly understand what life is like there. This essence of a culture cannot be produced in a text, it can only be *re*produced. Any act of communication, particularly through a text, is an act of reproduction – an imperfect attempt to capture an essence of a place, a culture, a feeling, an experience. When a text describes the markets of Istanbul, we cannot smell the aroma of the spices ourselves, we can only have it described to us through the craft of the writer and experienced through our imagination. It is better than nothing, but it is always a second-hand experience.
- **Language barrier:** This course focuses on texts in English. We look at texts in translation, but translating the native words of a culture into English is an imprecise science and never truly retains the entire original meaning of a text. Reading a Russian classic like Dostoevsky's *Crime and Punishment*, for example, is often said to lose a little of its magic and power when divorced from the original Russian – even the word 'crime' itself is an imprecise translation of *prestupleniye*, which literally means 'stepping over' in English.

Despite all of these deficiencies, texts can still provide valuable insight into a culture; it may be at best a facsimile, but a text opens up cross cultural understanding that is important in an increasingly globally connected world. The Language and Literature course is designed with this in mind – it is no accident that you are confronted with texts from a variety of times and places and in a variety of forms.

In this chapter we will consider the following:

- the insights offered by different perspectives within a culture by looking at texts from Australia
- how outsiders and natives to a culture can offer different insights and perspectives by looking at texts about and from India
- how different sides to a culture can be explored by looking at a text from Spain
- the insights offered by brands adapting to different cultures by looking at some advertising by multinational corporations.

Different perspectives within a culture

The Australia of today is a very different one to that of its past. To a modern reader, Australia likely conjures images of golden beaches, surfing, barbecues and modern, multicultural cities. However, Australia at the time of early European settlement was a much harsher and unforgiving place – a landmass consisting mostly of desert and containing exotic wildlife that could often maim, poison and kill. Still further back in history, Aboriginal people developed a distinct culture and learned to live in a place that seemed so inhospitable to life.

To see how texts can offer insight into Australia, we will look at two poems: one by a European settler and another by an Aboriginal poet. In doing so, we will consider that a culture is made up of many different voices, a fact that needs to be kept in mind when making assumptions about cultures based on reading texts.

The first poem, 'Past Carin'' is a bush poem by poet Henry Lawson. Read through the following key features box and then the poem itself.

KEY FEATURES **BUSH POETRY**

- **The bush:** Poems are focused on the life, character and scenery of the Australian bush. The bush is a largely Australian term used for the sparsely populated rural areas of the country outside the main urban centres, unlike the more remote 'outback' which generally refers to the even more remote and arid areas of the country.
- **Oral tradition:** Began by early European settlers influenced by the folk music of their homelands, poems were often shared orally rather than written down, and bush poems lend themselves to expressive performance. (You can find some particularly evocative performances of 'Past Carin'' online.)
- **Straightforward rhyme:** The genre does not feature formal rules, but poems generally feature simple rhymes reflecting the oral and folk music origins of the genre.
- **Colloquial style:** Language is typically colloquial and colourful, using Australian vernacular and slang.
- **Patterns:** Again due to its oral tradition, bush poems tend to follow a pattern, often featuring repetition, consistent stanza length, and the aforementioned consistent rhyme pattern.
- **Ballads:** Bush poems are often referred to as bush ballads, as they tend to narrate colourful stories that reflect Australian identity.

'Past Carin'' by Henry Lawson (1899)

'Past Carin'' is an example of a bush poem that evokes a sense of the cruel, unforgiving nature of life in the Australian bush. Written from the perspective of a woman who has suffered a seemingly unrelenting life of grief, loss and despair, we see Lawson capturing the difficulties of life in nineteenth-century Australia and the constant, draining battle between humanity and nature. Modern Australian culture was formed through such hardships, with the sense of community built through battling such an unforgiving landscape often referred to as 'mateship', a deep camaraderie formed through adversity that has lived on in spirit to Australia's much more prosperous and forgiving present.

Henry Lawson

Henry Archibald Hertzberg Lawson, to give him his full title, was an Australian writer and bush poet born in 1867. He had a troubled life, marked by periods of alcoholism, destitution, spousal abuse and mental illness. An ear infection in his youth left him entirely deaf by the age of 14. His first poem was published when he was 20 years old, and soon after he began a career as a journalist. His journalism took him to the inland parts of Australia, experiencing the harsh realities of life there. Life in these inhospitable areas was a common theme of his writing, and he dispelled many of the romanticized notions people had of life in the bush and the outback. He is considered an incredibly important figure in Australian literature as he wrote prolifically of the Australian experience. He was the first Australian writer to be granted a state funeral and was even featured on the paper version of the Australian ten-dollar note, affirming his importance to Australian culture.

Past Carin'

(1) Now up and down the siding brown
The great black crows are flyin',
And down below the spur, I know,
Another `milker's' dyin';
The crops have withered from the ground,

The tank's clay bed is glarin',
But from my heart no tear nor sound,
For I have gone past carin' —
Past worryin' or carin',
Past feelin' aught or carin';
But from my heart no tear nor sound,
For I have gone past carin'.

(2) Through Death and Trouble, turn about,
Through hopeless desolation,
Through flood and fever, fire and drought,
And slavery and starvation;
Through childbirth, sickness, hurt, and blight,
And nervousness an' scarin',
Through bein' left alone at night,
I've got to be past carin'.
Past botherin' or carin',
Past feelin' and past carin';
Through city cheats and neighbours' spite,
I've come to be past carin'.

(3) Our first child took, in days like these,
A cruel week in dyin',
All day upon her father's knees,
Or on my poor breast lyin';
The tears we shed — the prayers we said

Were awful, wild — despairin'!
I've pulled three through, and buried two
Since then — and I'm past carin'.
I've grown to be past carin',
Past worryin' and wearin';
I've pulled three through and buried two
Since then, and I'm past carin'.

(4) 'Twas ten years first, then came the worst,
All for a dusty clearin',
I thought, I thought my heart would burst
When first my man went shearin';
He's drovin' in the great North-west,
I don't know how he's farin';
For I, the one that loved him best,
Have grown to be past carin'.
I've grown to be past carin'
Past lookin' for or carin';
The girl that waited long ago,
Has lived to be past carin'.

(5) My eyes are dry, I cannot cry,
I've got no heart for breakin',
But where it was in days gone by,
A dull and empty achin'.
My last boy ran away from me,
I know my temper's wearin',
But now I only wish to be
Beyond all signs of carin'.
Past wearyin' or carin',
Past feelin' and despairin';
And now I only wish to be
Beyond all signs of carin'.

(Henry Lawson)

We are presented here with insight into the culture of Australia inasmuch as we learn about the struggles encountered by a settler trying to forge a living in the bush. The form of the poem itself reflects Australian bush culture, with its lack of formality, ballad-like qualities, and straightforward rhyme reflecting the directness of the people who were capable of living in such challenging conditions. For Lawson, the bush was the embodiment of Australia, a place where hardship could only be overcome with grit, humour and community. His choice of writing from the perspective of a woman is an interesting one – women were often left alone on ranches while their husbands spent long periods away from home, herding livestock in the vast open plains of Australia.

DISCUSSION

This lonely life, full of worry and cares, is an evocative topic for a poem – but would a text written directly by one of these women have been a more accurate insight into this culture? Can and should men offer insight into the female experience, whatever the culture may be? It is an issue that has been argued over by critics for decades. (More feminist theory will be explored in Chapter 3.4.)

The first stanza immediately sets the tone of the poem by introducing the suffering and death that is part and parcel of living in the Australian bush. The 'siding brown' (line 1) the narrator looks out on reveals the landscape to be arid and inhospitable to life. This is further emphasized by the flight of the 'great black crows' (line 2), carrion birds that symbolize death and conjure images of carcasses being picked clean. The determiner 'another' in 'another milker's dyin'' (line 4) shows the stark reality of existence in this landscape – it is a constant struggle and death appears to be a common occurrence. Beyond livestock, the crops are also 'withered' (line 5) and decaying, with the 'clay bed' (line 6) of the tank reiterating the lack of water and aridity of the land. Not only does this stanza include farming imagery that reflects the primary way of life in the bush, it also provides a powerful sense of the struggle and grind that came along with it. The wearing impact of this life is emphasized in the **refrain** of the poem, 'Past worryin' or carin'' (line 9). The narrator's only defence against the loss and pain is to be beyond caring, for to care would make the losses unbearable. This characterizes bush farmers as gritty but broken people, hardened by loss.

The second stanza deals less in specific details and instead uses heightened language to express the scale of suffering of those who struggled through life in the bush. The lexical set of abstract nouns related to suffering, such as 'Death', 'Trouble' and 'desolation' (lines 13–14), expresses the grim realities of life there. The use of 'flood and fever, fire and drought' (line 15) echoes language of the Old Testament, as if the bush is a cursed place suffering from biblical plagues. The slow, sibilant alliteration of 'slavery and starvation' (line 16) provides emphasis on a hyperbolic description of farming there – with no crops and little income, they feel they are enslaved and dying. Amid this lexis of suffering, 'childbirth' (line 17) is striking, with its juxtapositional effect emphasizing the horrors within which an innocent new life has been brought into the world, foreshadowing the later descriptions of infant mortality.

ACTIVITY 1

The stanzas in the poem are numbered. Each stanza provides insight into Australian bush culture. You have just read commentaries on the first two stanzas, so try your hand at the next three and then compare your responses to those in the back of the book. Focus on how the writer explores life in the bush and the attitudes and values of the people living there. You could try applying the literary reading strategy from Chapter 1.1 to help you with your analysis.

This poem provides powerful insight into a particular aspect of Australian culture – its bush pioneers and their determination in the face of adversity. It allows the modern reader insight into the hardy women and men who built the foundations on which modern Australia today rests. It includes universal themes of loss, with historical detail specific to the time and place to provide insight. In researching Lawson, we have seen that he has first-hand experience of such a life, adding credence to the insightfulness of the text.

But this is not the entire story of the continent; it is one very particular perspective in a particular moment on a particular part of Australia. These European settlers were taking over a land already inhabited by Aboriginal and Torres Strait Islander people (sometimes referred to as indigenous people). If we just listen to the voices of Europeans, we neglect other aspects of the Australian story, and silence aspects of its culture such as the problematic relationship between indigenous peoples and the white settlers. Our next poem provides that voice, and shows the importance of reading a variety of texts in order to get a better and rounder understanding of a culture. Much like in the previous chapter, you will find that the researched context combined with the universal themes of the text allow you to interpret the poem with some understanding. This allows you insight into the experience of an Aboriginal Australian and her suffering at the hands of the Australian government – a different suffering to that of the previous poem, and just as much a part of Australian history.

KEY FEATURES **DRAMATIC MONOLOGUE**

- **Persona:** The poem is written from the imagined perspective of a character.
- **Speech:** The content of the poem is entirely the words of the persona speaking in a specific situation or about a crucial moment.
- **Address:** The persona is addressing other people, but we often do not know who they are and how they react as we only hear the persona's side of the conversation.
- **Allusion** and **inference:** We, as the reader, pick up on clues and learn about the psychology of the persona, who they are talking to, what the situation is, and what they are talking about.

'A Letter to My Mother' by Eva Johnson (1985)

Eva Johnson

Eva Johnson was born in 1946 and is an Aboriginal poet, actor, director and playwright. She is part of what is known as the 'stolen generation'. Between 1910 and 1970, the Australian government forcibly removed indigenous children from their families in order to assimilate them into white Western culture. She is of the Malak-Malak people and, aged 2, she was taken away from her mother and placed in the care of a Methodist Mission. Once she was 10 years old, she was placed in an orphanage in Adelaide before being adopted. Her plays and poetry often focus on the oppression of Aboriginal people, and address themes of cultural identity and women's rights. She has received a number of awards for her works, including the Red Ochre Award in 1996.

This poem expresses Johnson's feelings on being reunited with her mother – an unusually autobiographical perspective for a dramatic monologue. As a member of the Stolen Generation – children who were taken from indigenous families and adopted by white families – she spent most of her life knowing nothing about her birth mother. This is because neither birth parents nor children were given information about each other, and they were never intended to reunite. However, Johnson was featured on a television show and was recognized by her birth mother who was watching TV in a nursing home. They soon reconnected. In the poem, Johnson asserts her rediscovered heritage and provides insight into another aspect of Australia's culture.

A Letter to My Mother

I not see you long time now, I not see you long time now
White fulla bin take me from you, I don't know why
Give me to Missionary to be God's child.
Give me new language, give me new name
All time I cry, they say – 'that shame'
I go to city down south, real cold

I forget all them stories, my Mother, you told
Gone is my spirit, my dreaming, my name
Gone to these people, our country to claim
They gave me white mother, she give me new name
All time I cry, she say – 'that shame'
I not see you long time now, I not see you long time now.

I grow as a woman now, not Piccaninny* no more
I need you to teach me your wisdom, your lore
I am your Spirit, I'll stay alive
But in white fulla way, you won't survive
I'll fight for Your land, for your Sacred sites
*To sing and to dance with the Brolga** in flight*
To continue to live in your own tradition

A culture for me was replaced by a mission
I not see you long time now, I not see you long time now.

One day your dancing, your dreaming, your song
Will take me your Spirit back where I belong
My Mother, the earth, the land – I demand
Protection for aliens who rule, who command
For they do not know where our dreaming began
Our destiny lies in the laws of White Man
Two Women we stand, our story untold
But now as our spiritual bondage unfold
We will silence this Burden, this longing, this pain
When I hear you my Mother give me my Name
I not see you long time now, I not see you long time now.

**piccaninny: a racial slur used to describe small black children; **brolga: an Australian crane, the focus of many traditional Aboriginal legends*

(Eva Johnson)

ACTIVITY 2

Passages of the poem have been italicised and are shown below. Write a paragraph about each, explaining how the poet expresses her cultural identity. The first two have been completed for you. You can find example responses in the back of the book.

1 *White fulla bin take me from you, I don't know why* *(line 2)*

The poet writes **phonetically** and with broken grammar in phrases like 'White fulla bin take me' (a white fellow has taken me) in order to mimic the Aboriginal English dialect, making clear the intent of the poem to be from an Aboriginal perspective. In using this voice, the persona is showing a separation from the typical white Australian manner of speaking that she was brought up with, and instead is using a voice that asserts her stolen Aboriginal heritage. The declarative 'I don't know why' highlights the cruelty of taking children at such a young age and the senselessness of the act. In emphasizing the bewilderment children feel at being separated from their parents and their culture, we empathize with the narrator of the poem and view the situation through her lens. The second-person pronoun 'you' suggests direct address to the narrator's mother, creating a personal and emotive tone that involves the reader in a moment of intimacy. It also allows the reader to take on the perspective of the mother, as it is as if we the reader are being addressed, prompting us to reflect on the horror of having a child of our own torn from us.

2 *I forget all them stories, my Mother, you told*
Gone is my spirit, my dreaming, my name
Gone to these people, our country to claim *(lines 7–9)*

The forgetting of the 'stories' - orally transmitted Aboriginal tales - symbolizes the forgetting of the narrator's culture and identity. This is reinforced by the tripling of 'my spirit, my dreaming, my name'. The first-person possessive pronoun 'my' makes clear these belonged to her, and they have been taken away in order to erase not just her identity, but her spirit as an Aboriginal child. The reference to 'these people' creates a degree of separation between the white people and the Aboriginal people, asserting their cultural distinctiveness. These people have claimed 'our country', with the first-person plural possessive pronoun 'our' making clear that Aboriginal people see Australia as a land stolen by Europeans. The sense of loss permeating these lines makes clear that it is not just a mother the child has lost, but an even broader loss of self and of a different life she could have led had she not been stolen away from her birth mother.

I'll fight for Your land, for your Sacred sites
To sing and to dance with the Brolga in flight
To continue to live in your own tradition
A culture for me was replaced by a mission (lines 17–20)

We will silence this Burden, this longing, this pain
When I hear you my Mother give me my Name (lines 30–31)

This poem provides insight into both Aboriginal culture and the broader Australian culture in which it now exists. It illustrates a point of conflict between the peoples of Australia and uses the writer's personal experience to show a wider schism that is still present in modern Australian culture.

CONCEPT CONNECTION

PERSPECTIVES WITHIN A CULTURE

In looking at these two texts, we can see that every culture has multiple stories and perspectives, and they often contain similarities and differences. Our first mother has children taken away by the harshness of the land, and our second is a child who herself was taken from her mother in a much more deliberate way. Though connected in loss, they say very different things about attitudes and values that have existed in Australia. Both poems are true to particular experiences, and both are part of the shared Australian story and culture. Our insight into this culture as a reader is enhanced by hearing this variety of different voices and experiences.

CAS Links

Think about your own culture. Can you think of any interesting perspectives that may be distinct? Are there any perspectives within your own culture that you think would show very different sides to it? Are there any voices that are often ignored and silenced? You could research and reach out to these people, and document their experiences to allow their voices to be heard. You may be surprised what you learn. This could become a CAS project that involves building links with the local community and blending creativity and service. Presenting your work in an assembly would be a powerful way to raise awareness of marginalized people within your community.

EE Links: English A – Literature category 1

Comparing different voices within cultures can be a rich area to analyse, and the parallels and points of difference can reveal a lot about a culture. Comparing the diary of a plantation owner like Thomas Thistlewood with that of a slave like Adam Plummer, for example, can show insight into the early history of the USA. These comparative examinations within cultures, particularly when looking at the oppressors and the oppressed, can be revealing.

From the outside looking in

Cultures are not always explored in texts by writers that grew up immersed in them. Sometimes, outsiders to a culture can provide a fresh perspective and insight that other outsiders may find easier to relate to. At other times, they may offer a reductive or stereotyped insight of that culture that may be considered offensive. Our following two texts provide two different perspectives on the same issue. One is from an outsider looking in, and the other is from an insider looking around them. Both are focused on the Indian slums, and both show different insights into Indian culture.

Shantaram by Gregory Roberts (2003)

Gregory David Roberts

Australian Gregory David Roberts, born 1952, has had an eventful life. After divorce and losing custody of his daughter, he became addicted to heroin. To fund his drug habit, he became known as the 'Gentleman Bandit' and robbed banks that he ensured had adequate insurance, sometimes wearing a three-piece suit and always being sure to say 'please' and 'thank you'. After being caught and jailed, he escaped from Pentridge Prison in 1980 and went on the run, spending many years living in India. He was caught in Frankfurt in 1990 smuggling heroin, extradited to Australia and jailed for six years. It is during this imprisonment that he began writing his famous novel *Shantaram*. He has since moved around the world continuing with his writing career and supporting charity work.

Shantaram is a novel loosely based on the eventful life of the author, Gregory Roberts. Lindsay, the main character, has escaped prison in Australia and fled to India. While travelling through the country to Bombay, he is robbed and ends up having to live in the slums. Despite being wanted for crimes elsewhere, he is sheltered by the people he encounters. He learns the language and becomes part of the community, falls in love, and embroils himself in an underworld crime syndicate.

In considering this text, we must ask ourselves how and to what extent does an outsider's perspective offer insight into a foreign culture? Though it has its challenges, writers often write of cultures they themselves are not a part of, in the same way they may write of historical times they did not experience. To do so is fraught with danger, as it is easy to misrepresent a culture, or to show a lack of cultural sensitivity and understanding (*Memoirs of a Geisha* by Arthur Golden, for example, was accused by some of exoticizing and stereotyping elements of Japanese culture). But it does offer some advantages:

- **Wider perspective:** It allows a wider perspective as the writer is able to compare it to their own culture and other cultures they may have experienced.
- **Fresh insight:** It allows a fresh point of view as the writer may have an unusual perspective on a culture or see beauty in things that would otherwise be ignored by people native to that culture.

Shantaram is, of course, a novel. This allows what is often referred to as 'poetic licence' – an ability to deviate from true reality and to add imagined detail for artistic effect. In addition to this, Roberts is only a partial outsider; he may not have grown up in the slums, but he did spend time living there. With these things in mind, the description of the slums may be exaggerated, romanticized or heightened for descriptive impact. It is not always the writer's intent to create a truly accurate reflection of a place or culture, but one that suits their story or their intended readership. However, these texts are sometimes the only exposure a reader has to a culture, and texts can sometimes help generate stereotypes and reductive impressions in the minds of their readers. This means a critical eye must always be used when reading texts that relate to culture: Has the writer exaggerated aspects of this culture? Is the writer exoticizing the descriptions to make them more appealing? Am I only being presented this culture from a Western perspective? What aspects of this culture is the writer *not* describing? Any assumptions about culture garnered from texts should always be tested with further research and reading, particularly when that writer was born an outsider. With this in mind, consider the following extract and the extent to which Roberts is able to provide insight into another culture.

> Like brown and black dunes, the acres of slums rolled away from the roadside, and met the horizon with dirty heat-haze mirages. The miserable shelters were patched together from rags, scraps of plastic and paper, reed mats, and bamboo sticks. They slumped together, attached one to another, and with narrow lanes winding between them. Nothing in the enormous sprawl of it rose much above the height of a man.
>
> It seemed impossible that a modern airport, full of prosperous and purposeful travellers, was only kilometers away from those crushed and cindered dreams. My first impression was that some catastrophe had taken place, and that the slums were refugee camps for the shambling survivors. I learned, months later, that they *were* survivors, of course, those slum-dwellers: the catastrophes that had driven them to the slums from their villages were poverty, famine, and bloodshed. And five thousand new survivors arrived in the city every week, week after week, year after year.
>
> As the kilometres wound past, as the hundreds of people in those slums became thousands, and tens of thousands, my spirit writhed. I felt defiled by my own health and the money in my pockets. If you feel it at all, it's a lacerating guilt, that first confrontation with the wretched of the earth. I'd robbed banks, and dealt drugs, and I'd been beaten by prison warders until my bones broke. I'd been stabbed, and I'd stabbed men in return. I'd escaped from a hard prison full of hard men, the hard way - over the front wall. Still, that first encounter with the ragged misery of the slum, heartbreak all the way to the horizon, cut into my eyes. For a time, I ran onto the knives.
>
> Then the smoulders of shame and guilt flamed into anger, became fist-tightening rage at the unfairness of it: *What kind of a government,* I thought, *what kind of a system allows suffering like this?*
>
> But the slums went on, kilometre after kilometre, relieved only by the awful contrast of the thriving businesses and crumbling, moss-covered apartment buildings of the comparatively affluent. The slums went on, and their sheer ubiquity wore down my foreigner's pieties. A kind of wonder possessed me. I began to look beyond the immensity of the slum societies, and to see the people who lived within them. A woman stooped to brush forward the black satin psalm of her hair. Another bathed her children with water from a copper dish. A man led three goats with red ribbons tied to the collars at their throats. Another man shaved himself at a cracked mirror. Children played everywhere. Men carried water in buckets. Men made repairs to one of the huts. And everywhere that I looked, people smiled and laughed …
>
> I looked at the people, then, and I saw how *busy* they were - how much industry and energy described their lives. Occasional sudden glimpses inside the huts revealed the astonishing cleanliness of that poverty: the spotless floors, and glistening metal pots in neat, tapering towers. And then, last, what should've been first, I saw how beautiful they were: the women wrapped in crimson, blue, and gold; the women walking barefoot through the tangled shabbiness of the slum with patient, ethereal grace; the white-toothed, almond-eyed handsomeness of the men; and the affectionate camaraderie of the fine-limbed children, older ones playing with younger ones, many of them supporting baby brothers and sisters on their slender hips. And half an hour after the bus ride began, I smiled for the first time.
>
> *(Gregory Roberts 4)*

Wider perspective

The protagonist, our narrator of the story, initially has a strong reaction that someone used to such a slum may not have. He shows this with the emotive metaphor describing the 'smoulders of shame and guilt' that 'flamed into anger' (line 19). The abstract nouns 'shame', 'guilt' and 'anger' demonstrate a sequence of emotion that an outsider may feel: shame that they were not aware of the problem; guilt that they have lived in relative comfort while people elsewhere in the would live in such poverty; anger that it is a problem that exists. His anger is directed towards the Indian government, asking, 'What kind of a system allows suffering like this?' (line 20). This simplistic reaction is the luxury of an outsider, someone without deep knowledge of the complex ways a country works. It is also looking at India through a **Western** lens. This outrage in an Indian writer may not be quite as stark, as the reality of the slums would be something they may have grown up with. They may have a clearer understanding of the historical, political, economic and cultural reasons the slums exist. This demonstrates how outsiders can often make broad comments about other cultures despite a shallow knowledge and understanding of the place they are describing. However, this often means they are reflecting questions and perspectives the reader may share as the reader is often an outsider themselves.

Our character is also able to provide commentary on inequality. He speaks of feeling defiled by his 'health' and 'money' (line 13) – symbols of his Western lifestyle. The metaphorical 'lacerating guilt' (line 14) conveys the almost physical response he has to seeing such poverty that was hitherto unimaginable. In writing as an outsider, he is able to express sentiments that other outsiders may feel, but insiders to the culture being described may not. This outsider's perspective, though instinctive and fresh, still has value when looking for insight into another culture. It is easy for those within a culture to become used to the status quo, and an outsider can sometimes ask questions that people of that culture have stopped asking.

Fresh insight

Outsiders also have an ability to see beauty in the mundane. Sometimes we take our own culture for granted until an outsider visits and is full of praise for the things we see as everyday. When writing in such a way, there is always a danger of this falling into what we call **exoticizing** other cultures – describing them in romantic terms, falling back on stereotypes, focusing on the unusual and simplifying them to fit an outsider's narrative. This is not always intentional, and not always negative, but it can sometimes cause offence to people of that culture. A text that exoticizes can reduce 'foreign' characters to stereotypes, or describe things that to a cultural insider would be 'normal' in exaggerated, heightened language that emphasizes the foreignness of the place. Historically, this most often happened when Western writers have been writing about non-Western cultures – meaning the reader is provided with a Western perspective on the wider world and fails to empathize and understand what these cultures are truly like. In the past, many writers of cultures around the world have been marginalized, or if they have been published, their works have not been translated into English. This is why reading texts in translation is particularly important; it allows non-Western voices to be heard through texts written by non-Western writers about their non-Western cultures.

There is, perhaps, evidence of **exoticization** in our extract. The people of the slums are described as 'beautiful' and the women wear 'crimson, blue, and gold', carrying themselves with 'ethereal grace' (lines 33–34). There is also a 'white-toothed, almond eyed handsomeness' (line 35) of the men. These heightened physical descriptions reinforce stereotypical views of India as a place of exotic colour and beauty; there is a focus on the superficial 'otherness' of life there. Rather than focusing on the reality of day-to-day life in the slums, the writer focuses on a noble beauty he perceives in the people. In describing the slum and its inhabitants in such an exotic, enchanting and intoxicating way, it is easy to sideline how problematic their plight is. Nevertheless, the writer successfully creates vivid and evocative imagery in the reader's mind, which is of paramount importance when writing a novel, and is perhaps an example of the poetic licence we mentioned before. And, of course, we are being a little unfair to Roberts: the rest of the novel gives a far more nuanced perspective on the slums, and our extract deliberately shows an outsider's initial reaction to them.

GLOBAL ISSUES *Field of inquiry:* **Politics, Power and Justice**

WEALTH INEQUALITY

As we have seen, this work explicitly deals with income inequality through the lens of an Australian man viewing the slums of Bombay, now known as Mumbai. For him, such poverty had previously seemed distant and foreign, but physically experiencing the slums triggers a wave of shame and anger he describes as a 'lacerating guilt' (line 14). Though the life, energy and beauty of the slums is explored later in the novel, this initial reaction conveys a guilt that many privileged people share when faced with the poverty that much of the world's wealth is built on.

Many bodies of work can be found that explore the same issue. An increasing awareness of global supply chains has made the public ever more conscious of the conditions in factories that produce much of the world's goods. Various anti-sweatshop advertising campaigns can be found that raise awareness of the issue, and a series of infographics have been produced to emphasize the scale of the problem. Searching for terms such as 'sweatshop political cartoon' also brings up a series of cartoons that deal with the suffering behind the manufacturing of products bought in wealthier countries. Beyond this, many films, photographs, articles and appeals also relate to the global issue of wealth inequality.

Shantaram is an interesting example of a text by an outsider. It contains autobiographical elements but is, at its heart, a novel. Fiction is not primarily concerned with accuracy in the same way a painter is not concerned with creating a precisely accurate image of a place. By its nature, the text-type allows imaginative detail, exaggeration and a focus on feeling. We cannot read all texts as if they are neutral passages in an encyclopaedia, there to provide factual insight into a culture, and this is something we need to be aware of as readers. This is similar to writers setting stories in the past or in space – they can often just be convenient backdrops for the deeper messages of the text, which often transcend such cultural concerns. For many in India, however, it can be frustrating that poverty is so often the focus of film and literature set in their country, and that other aspects of India are often sidelined by outsiders. *Shantaram*, it appears, has elements of truth, but it needs to be considered a voice among many rather than giving definitive insight into India and the Mumbai slums.

TOK Links

These are issues writers and critics often wrestle with: if a writer deals with a culture other than their own, is it their responsibility to portray it accurately? Should we expect documentary-level accuracy in works of fiction? Do writers outside cultures even have the right to write about them, or is this a form of cultural appropriation?

Times of India (2013)

By contrast, our next text is written by a writer within Indian culture. This article is an op-ed from the *Times of India* giving a positive spin on the slums that exist in most major cities in the country. The *Times of India* is a broadsheet newspaper and is the third-largest in the country in terms of circulation. Consider how the text provides insight into the culture, and how similar or different it is to Gregory Roberts' novel extract.

KEY FEATURES OP-ED

- **Expresses opinion:** An article in a newspaper in which newspaper staff or guest writers convey their opinions on an issue. The name originally came from the page **op**posite the **ed**itorial page, but is now often understood as meaning 'opinion editorial'.
- **Solid foundation:** Op-eds are usually backed up by research or well-thought-through points in order to make the opinion more compelling.
- **Clear structure:** Op-eds have a clearly organized structure and may make use of features such as bullet points and imagery. They are reasonably short and provide a clear argument.
- **Rhetoric:** They sometimes feature persuasive techniques to make the opinion more impactful.
- **Strong ending:** Op-eds, much like speeches, often end with some sort of a call for action or an imperative demanding change.

https://timesofindia.indiatimes.com/blogs/Swaminomics/slums-are-hubs-of-hope-progress-and-dignity/

Slums are hubs of hope, progress and dignity

The Census Commissioner has released a new report showing that 64 million people, representing one in six urban residents, live in slums with unsanitary conditions 'unfit for human habilitation'. This has caused much moaning and groaning. But conditions are far worse in most villages. Romantic pastoralists may fantasize about happy green villages as opposed to filthy urban slums. But migration of millions proves that villagers see slums, warts and all, as the way forward.

Yes, slums are dirty, but they are also entrepreneurial hubs where India's poor are climbing up the ladder of opportunity and income. The census report shows that 16.7% of slum households are factories, shops and offices. These are humming commercial centres, not dead-ends.

Dharavi in Mumbai, India's largest slum, has an estimated business turnover of $650 million. It has created slumdog millionaires aplenty. They should be objects of envy, not objects of pity.

Dalit writers like Chandhra Bhan Prasad and Milind Kamble have highlighted how cities are hubs of opportunity and dignity. Ambedkar rightly denounced villages as cesspools of cruelty and prejudice. Dominant castes continue acting like feudal rulers in many rural areas. Social barriers make it difficult for dalits and shudras to raise their heads in many villages. But once they migrate to towns, they escape the caste discrimination and landowner-dependency of rural India. They earn far more in towns than in villages, and the money they send home frees their relatives from historical dependence on village feudatories.

Slums are the entry point of the poor into cities. Insane tax and urban land policies have encouraged a never-ending avalanche of black money into real estate. Urban land prices have skyrocketed, and bear no relationship to the income they generate. Land is unaffordable by most of the middle class, let alone the poor. This is one reason why urbanization has been so slow in India.

The poor can enter cities only through existing or new shanty-towns. This is illegal, yet fully accepted by politicians as a legitimate form of entry. So, shanty-towns are frequently regularized before election time.

No politician dares raze them. Rather, they are improved through supplies of water and electricity. Many slums simply steal electricity, with the tacit backing of politicians plus bribes to linesmen.

The census description of slums as 'unfit for human habitation' is highly misleading. In fact census data prove that slums are much better off than villages, which are presumably fit for habitation! No less than 70% of slum households have TVs, against only 47% of total Indian households. The ratio is just 14.5% in Bihar and 33.2% in UP. Even Narendra Modi's shining Gujarat (51.2%) and Pawar's Maharashtra (58.8%) have a far lower rate of TV ownership than our slums!

True, 34% of slums don't have toilets. Yet the ratio is as high as 69.3% in rural India. Ratios are worst in rural Jharkhand (90%) and Bihar (82%). But even Modi's Gujarat (67%) and Pawar's Maharashtra (62%) are far worse off than urban slums.

Similar stories hold for access to tap water, education, healthcare, electricity or jobs. As many as 90% of slum dwellers have electricity, against barely half of rural households. Ownership of cellphones (63.5%) is as high among slum dwellers as richer urban households, and way above rural rates. One-tenth of slums have computers, and 51% have cooking gas (not far short of 65% of total urban households). Amazingly, more slum households (74%) have tap water than total urban households (70.6%).

So, let nobody misinterpret the Census report on slums as a terrible indictment. The report does indeed highlight unsanitary, cramped conditions, and the need to improve these. Yet it also provides a wealth of data showing how slums are better off than villages, and how on some counts slum-dwellers are as well off as richer urban dwellers. The report fails to highlight the extent to which slums have generated thousands of thriving businesses. It also fails to highlight the role of slums in helping conquer rural caste and feudal oppression.

Forget tear-jerkers about our filthy slums. Instead, see them as entry-points of the poor into the land of urban opportunity. See them as havens of dignity for dalits and shudras. See them as hubs of rising income and asset ownership, which have already generated several rupee millionaires.

This means we need more slums, more hubs of opportunity. The urban gentry want to demolish slums, but they are plain wrong. Instead we should improve slum sanitation, water supply and garbage disposal. We need more improved slums, upgraded slums, but slums nevertheless.

DISCLAIMER : Views expressed above are the author's own.

(Swaminathan Aiyar)

Context	India – 2013
Genre	Newspaper article – op-ed
Audience	Adults in India, particularly those with an interest in social issues
Purpose	To inform and persuade

In this text we get a far more practical perspective of the slums. While the *Shantaram* extract gives an outsider's first reaction to them, the writer of this op-ed gives a far more considered explanation of how, in many ways, slums provide better conditions than the countryside. This demonstrates a more in-depth understanding of India and its demography of a kind that an outsider would struggle to possess.

ACTIVITY 3

Can you find examples of the key features of an op-ed and explain how they are used to provide a positive perspective on the slums? Here are some hints to get you started. Answers can be found in the back of the book.

- **Expresses an opinion:** *Sum up the opinion of the writer and explain how it may be considered surprising.*
- **Solid foundation:** *Look for examples of statistical and factual evidence used to back up the writer's opinions.*
- **Clear structure:** *Explain how the points the writer makes are ordered to keep the ideas clear and effective for the reader.*
- **Rhetoric:** *Look for persuasive techniques in the article.*
- **Strong ending:** *Explain how the article ends with a call to arms and a clear sense of how things need to change.*

This type of text has a very different function to a novel and is far more grounded in the practicalities and realities of slum life. We get a more subtle and less descriptive sense of the slums, and the writer provides surprising insight into a place that may be dismissed by outsiders as an appalling place to live. Such nuance is often beyond the grasp of outsiders to a culture, whereas a writer from within the culture can provide perspectives that are sometimes surprising and almost always better informed.

In looking at the culture of India, we have explored how insights from people within and without the culture can vary. Writers writing about a culture that is not their own can provide fresh insight, and their perspective can often resonate with other outsiders. Writers from within a culture can often write with more detail and capture its essence and subtleties. Both have value, and we can get a rounder picture of a culture by reading a variety of texts from a variety of perspectives.

Cultural complexity

Cultures are complex and often contradictory constructions. Writers frequently try to explore these contradictions in their work, and Federico Garcia Lorca was no exception. His native Spain had a stark divide between traditionalist conservatives and progressive liberals. Despite his liberal background, he was fascinated by the conservative side of Spain, particularly the music and folklore of the rural areas of his homeland. He produced a series of plays that sought to provide insight into this part of Spanish culture.

Blood Wedding by Federico García Lorca (1932)

Federico García Lorca

Federico García Lorca, born in 1898, was one of the most important Spanish poets, playwrights and theatre directors of the twentieth century. He was a Republican with strongly liberal views in a divided Spain, where liberal Republican views clashed with conservative Nationalist views. After spending some time in New York, he travelled the countryside of Spain with his theatre company 'La Barraca', giving free performances of Spanish classics. With this group, he also produced the three 'rural tragedies' which cemented his theatrical reputation: *Blood Wedding*, *Yerma* and *The House of Bernarda Alba*. In 1936, he was tragically shot by a Nationalist and anti-Communist death squad during the Spanish Civil War for being a liberal, a Republican and a homosexual, all of which were considered to be unforgivable. He was buried in an unmarked grave.

The Spanish countryside was highly religious, conservative, and had clear social rules, particularly regarding women and honour. García Lorca's play explores what happens when those rules are broken, and how society reacts. Based on a true story from the Almeria province of Spain, the bride of the play gets married to the groom – the son of the mother in our extract. However, she does not love him, and eventually runs away with a married man called Leonardo. The two lovers flee to the forest, a symbolic escape from the stifling rules of the village into the wild and raw expanse of nature. The groom and a vigilante group of villagers head to the forest, where Leonardo and the groom kill each other in battle. Our extract shows the reaction of the mother of the now-dead groom when confronted with the source of the conflict: the bride who abandoned her son.

The BRIDE enters. She comes without the orange-blossom and wearing a black shawl.

NEIGHBOUR *(angrily, seeing the BRIDE)*: Where are you going?

BRIDE: I'm coming here.

MOTHER *(to the NEIGHBOUR)*: Who is it?

NEIGHBOUR: Don't you know her?

MOTHER: That's why I'm asking who she is. Because I mustn't know her, so I shan't sink my teeth into her neck. Serpent!

She moves towards the BRIDE threateningly; she stops.

(To the NEIGHBOUR): You see her? There, weeping, and me calm, without tearing her eyes out. I don't understand myself. Is it because I didn't love my son? But what about his name? Where is his name?

She strikes the BRIDE who falls to the ground.

NEIGHBOUR: In the name of God! *(She tries to separate them)*

BRIDE *(to the NEIGHBOUR)*: Leave her. I came so that she could kill me, so that they could bear me away with them. *(To the MOTHER)*. But not with their hands; with iron hooks, with a sickle, and with a force that will break it on my bones. Leave her! I want her to know that I'm clean, that even though I'm mad they can bury me and not a single man will have looked at himself in the whiteness of my breasts.

MOTHER: Be quiet, be quiet! What does that matter to me?

BRIDE: Because I went off with the other one! I went! *(In anguish.)* You would have gone too. I was a woman burning, full of pain inside and out, and your son was a tiny drop of water that I hoped would give me children, land, health; but the other one was a dark river, full of branches, that brought to me the sound of its reeds and its soft song. And I was going with your son, who was like a child of cold water, and the other one sent hundreds of birds that blocked my path and left frost on the wounds of this poor, withered woman, this girl caressed by fire. I didn't want to, listen to me! I didn't want to! Your son was my ambition and I haven't deceived him, but the other one's arm dragged me like a wave from the sea, like the butt of a mule, and would always have dragged me, always, always, even if I'd been an old woman and all the sons of your son had tried to hold me down by my hair!

A NEIGHBOUR enters.

MOTHER: She's not to blame! Nor me! *(Sarcastically.)* So who's to blame? A weak, delicate, restless woman who throws away a crown of orange-blossom to look for a piece of bed warmed by another woman!

BRIDE: Be quiet, be quiet! Take your revenge on me! Here I am! See how soft my throat is; less effort for you than cutting a dahlia in your garden. But no, not that! I'm pure, as pure as a new-born child. And strong enough to prove it to you. Light the fire. We'll put our hands in it: you for your son; me for my body. You'll be the first to take them out.

Another NEIGHBOUR enters.

MOTHER: What does your honour matter to me? What does your death matter to me? What does anything matter to me? Blessed be the wheat, for my sons lie beneath it. Blessed by the rain, for it washes the faces of the dead. Blessed be God, for He lays us side by side so we can rest.

Another NEIGHBOUR enters.

BRIDE: Let me weep with you.

MOTHER: Weep. But by the door.

The LITTLE GIRL enters. The BRIDE remains by the door. The MOTHER, centre-stage.

(García Lorca, Blood Wedding Act 3 Scene 2)

In this play, García Lorca explores how the repressive, conservative social norms can come into conflict with the raw emotions and passions of two lovers.

ACTIVITY 4

Using the literary reading strategy to help you, answer the following questions, and then compare them with the provided commentary below.

1 How does this moment in the play explore cultural notions of honour?

2 How does the daughter demonstrate how passion and emotion can conflict with the conservative values of rural Spain?

A society built on strong notions of honour is evident in the extract. The mother's son went out to kill Leonardo to restore his honour after his wife's unfaithfulness, and Leonardo fought back for the honour of his love: both have ended up dying. These honour-bound deaths show how destructive rigid conformity to honour can be. It leads to hatred, suffering, and the bereavement of those left behind. The bereaved mother relates imagery of her lost son, saying 'blessed is the wheat, for my sons lie beneath it' (line 40), an image of peace that contrasts with his past suffering and shame at the hands of the dishonourable bride. His death is shown to be a bittersweet one: he has had an honourable death, but it is a death all the same, and the mother is left without any sons. The bride then offers her own life, in part to be with Leonardo in the afterlife, and in part as a sacrifice to help restore the honour of the mother character. García Lorca thus presents the audience with an image of female suffering due to the repercussions of honour: both women are grieving and forced to face uncertain futures without men. In doing so, García Lorca presents the dangers of traditional honour codes and the difficulties faced by many rural women.

The strong, passionate emotions of the bride are a source of conflict with the society she is a part of. The hyperbole used in her description of being 'a woman burning, full of pain inside and out' (line 21) emphasizes the depth of feeling she was suffering when she was in her fruitless marriage with the groom. The groom is metaphorically described as a 'drop of water' (line 21) in contrast to the 'dark river' (line 22) of her lover, suggesting her strength of feeling for him but also the mysterious power with which he was able to carry her, much as a river can carry you away to places unknown. In a society that focused on control, repression and transactional marriages, this broke many unspoken rules and caused irreparable conflict with the rest of the village. We see the outcome of the desires of the individual coming into conflict with the desires of the community.

With this text, we can see how writers can often come into conflict with aspects of their own culture. García Lorca, a liberal, often clashed with some of the more conservative aspects of his native Spain. Through this work, he is able to show what happens when the needs and feelings of the individual are at odds with the needs and feelings of the community. He also presents an exploration and criticism of aspects of conservative society – a prescient and ominous message given his later execution by conservative Nationalists. When writers such as García Lorca explore the contradictions in their cultures, we can gain insight into the internal struggles and debates that can sometimes express themselves as events such as the Spanish Civil War.

Cross-cultural texts – going global

Another way of gaining insights into other cultures is looking at how they sell and promote products. In our globalized world, businesses often operate within a variety of cultures. This can lead to some interesting localized advertising that caters to that market's particular culture. You will certainly see some of the **universal text features** when dealing with adverts, but you will also find many **context clues** that reveal more specific details about the origin of the adverts.

CHECK FOR UNDERSTANDING

Can you find any examples of adverts that say something about your culture? Find some examples and annotate them with how they reflect the place you come from – use the non-literary reading strategy with particular focus on models, props, layout, colour, language and setting.

Cultures are increasingly mingling and feeding off each other. Our global world means cultural elements such as cuisine, fashion and even language are increasingly mixed. K-pop is an excellent example of this: it is wildly popular outside South Korea and is a vehicle for promoting Korean culture. Teenagers around the world are learning Korean to become more involved in the music; Korean fashion has become increasingly popular; and there are increasing numbers of YouTubers demonstrating how to get the 'Korean look' in their makeup tutorials.

HSBC 'local knowledge' adverts

As part of this globalizing process, many companies find themselves operating in a wide variety of cultures. To make a point of how they understand and respect these different cultures in which they operate, they often make it a focus of their advertising. The HSBC 'local knowledge' adverts are an interesting example of a non-literary body of work. In being a global bank, HSBC want to project a global image by showing they understand their various markets. To do so, their adverts show how they understand that different cultures approach things differently. Scan the QR codes in the margin to take a look at these adverts.

The first advert features the same image three times, but for each it provides a different interpretation depending on the cultural context. The carpet could, to some, be seen as simply a way of decorating the house, to another it could be seen as an exotic souvenir from a country like Morocco, and to a Muslim it may be seen as a prayer rug. This brings us back to our examples of hand gestures in the previous chapter – what an object, gesture or word is associated with may vary depending on the cultural context it is received in. HSBC is showing it understands its markets to build the reader's trust – an important quality in a bank.

Hot Fuzz film posters

Film posters also provide interesting insights into cultural attitudes as they are advertising the same film, but to sometimes very different audiences. These examples of *Hot Fuzz* make this very clear – they provide very different imagery to promote the same movie.

KEY FEATURES FILM POSTERS

- **Informative**: Film posters contain factual information such as the name of the film, its release date and its cast. Some may contain producer credits, website addresses, lists of awards and quotes from critics.
- **Striking visual imagery**: Film posters aim for impact. This is often provided through a complementary colour palette (blue and orange is very common) and an image of the stars of the film or of an exciting moment to entice potential cinema goers.
- **Film title**: The title is prominently displayed and often makes use of typographical and graphological elements that tie-in with the theme and tone of the film.
- **Tagline**: A slogan that gives a brief and catchy summary or theme of the film.

ACTIVITY 5

Much like in the previous chapter, bullet-point a comparison of the two film posters for *Hot Fuzz*, explaining how they are trying to appeal to their target audiences. The UK poster is filled in for you. You can find answers in the back of the book.

■ Table 2.3.1

CGAP: UK 2007. Film poster aimed at a general audience to inform and entertain.	**CGAP:** Japan 2007. Film poster aimed at a general audience to inform and entertain.
Models: We get a close-up of Nick Frost and Simon Pegg, two actors with a cult following in the UK, thus grabbing the attention of fans of their work. Neither particularly fits the typical, square-jawed action hero convention of the assumed genre.	**Models:**
Visual image and layout: Humour is generated through juxtaposition of action movie tropes (such as the smoking gun, the serious facial expressions, the mirrored sunglasses and the chewing of toothpicks) and images of English rural life (the bunting, the fields and the reflection of a village church in their sunglasses). This clash of American action movie culture and British rural life is reinforced with the tagline 'they are going to bust your arse' – the addition of the Britishism 'arse' subverts the typical 'bust your ass' slang of cool, slick American action heroes. Through this contrast, humour is generated and the receivers of the text understand that the film is a parody of the action movie genre. The poster is also reasonably simple and focused, typical of modern advertising in the West.	**Visual image and layout:**

Conclusion

If we go back to our original question, '**to what extent do texts offer insight into another culture?**', we can now provide more of an answer. As all texts are made within a culture, they are always replete with both implicit and explicit cultural information, and these elements can be examined by students of Language and Literature to understand the context and intent of a writer. However, this is not without qualification. The complex nature of cultures themselves, as well as the varied purposes of texts and backgrounds of writers, can complicate how accurate and wide these insights might be. It is important as students of Language and Literature to look at texts with a critical eye, and to consider how the **text type**, **context of production**, and **context of reception** have influenced the content and interpretation of texts. All this aside, texts are an invaluable tool for learning about other cultures and promoting an intercultural understanding that helps us bond as an increasingly global community. Think back to the texts in this chapter – you will almost certainly have learned something about cultures that you were otherwise relatively ignorant of: this is the power and importance of texts. With them, we have the key to a better global understanding; without them, we risk ignorance and division that can have disastrous consequences.

Works cited

Aiyar, SA. 'Slums are hubs of hope, progress and dignity.' *The Times of India*, 31 March 2013. Web. 13 March 2019. **https://timesofindia.indiatimes.com/blogs/Swaminomics/slums-are-hubs-of-hope-progress-and-dignity**.

'Australian Bush Poetry and Verse.' Australian Bush Verse. Web. 13 March 2019. **www.bushverse.com**.

Johnson, E. 'A Letter to My Mother.' Web. 13 March 2019. **https://carolyngage.weebly.com/blog/eva-knowles-johnson-and-the-stolen-generations**.

Lawson, H. 'Past Carin'.' Australian Poetry Library. Web. 13 March 2019. **www.poetrylibrary.edu.au/poets/lawson-henry/poems/past-carin-0002014**.

Lorca, F. *Lorca Plays 1: Blood Wedding; Yerma; Dona Rosita the Spinster.* Methuen Drama, 2008.

Roberts, Gregory David, *Shantaram: A Novel*. St. Martins Griffin, 2005.

How does the meaning and impact of a work change over time?

OBJECTIVES OF CHAPTER

- To understand that texts reflect their contexts of production.
- To explore the relationship between texts and their changing contexts of reception.
- To consider how the universal aspects of texts allow them to gain new resonance in changing contexts.
- To consider how texts can be appropriated for purposes far outside the original intent of the writer.

We have discussed how meaning does not simply reside in a text, ready to be consumed by the person receiving it, but is an **act of interpretation** on the part of the reader. When a text is read, a relationship is drawn between the writer and the reader through the medium of the text. The writer has their intent and writes for an **implied reader** in producing the text, but that implied reader may be very different to the one who reads it in real life. The actual reader's own **context of reception** will affect how they interpret the text, often in ways that the producer did not intend. One of the biggest factors in this change of interpretation can be **time**. Essentially, the time or era in which we live shapes the way we see and understand texts.

These ideas have cropped up in the previous chapters, but this chapter will particularly focus on texts and works that have had very distinct **changes in impact and meaning over time**. We already know that texts like Charles Dickens' *A Christmas Carol* can still make people think about poverty whatever their context may be, but how might an American slave song from the 1800s become an English national rugby anthem in the modern era? This, and other changes of meaning and impact, are going to be examined in this chapter. For each, we will first examine its original meaning and impact, before travelling through time to see various other interpretations that created new and often surprising meanings.

First, let's consider how time affects meaning.

Changes over time

Changes in meaning can be specific, in that the meanings of words used by the writer can change in interpretation, or broad, in that the generally accepted interpretation of a work can change. This has been a common theme of the Time and space section of this coursebook: meaning is malleable and fluid, and temporal shifts have an impact on interpretation and meaning.

Below are some examples of words in common use that have had their meanings shift over time.

■ Table 2.4.1

Word	Modern meaning	Historical meaning
Gay	Homosexual	To be happy
Clue	A piece of evidence or information to help solve something	A ball of yarn
Naughty	To be badly behaved	To have nothing
Silly	Having a lack of common sense	Something that is blessed
Cheater	Acting dishonestly to gain an advantage	The person in charge of land that would be handed to the king if the current owner died with no heirs

Word	Modern meaning	Historical meaning
Terrible	Extremely bad	To inspire great fear or dread
Flirt	To behave as though attracted to someone	A sudden, sharp movement
Spinster	An unmarried woman	A woman who spins yarn or thread
Fantastic	Something that is very good	Belonging to the imagination

These changes in meaning are very specific and isolated, but it is not just word meanings that can change. In some cases, the wider meaning and significance of a text can shift over time too. We have been seeing this shift in various examples throughout the Time and space section – think back to examples like the 1950s adverts that now signify sexism. This is because texts are constantly being reinterpreted by **new readers** with **new ideas and contexts**. These changes in meaning and impact can be very distinct, as we are about to find out by looking at our first work, *The Merchant of Venice*.

The Merchant of Venice by William Shakespeare (~1598)

The Merchant of Venice is a comedy written by William Shakespeare. The play revolves around a character named Antonio taking a loan from a Jewish moneylender called Shylock. The terms of the loan are that Shylock can take a pound of flesh from Antonio if he fails to repay the debt on time. Due to Antonio's fleet of ships later being lost at sea, he cannot afford repay the debt. He is taken to court by Shylock who insists on the pound of flesh as payment. However, it is argued that the agreement specifies he is entitled only to flesh and not blood, and in having sought a payment that would have led to the death of a Christian he is in violation of Venetian law on penalty of death. His life is instead spared but, as a Jew, he is classed as an 'alien' under Venetian law and can be ordered to give half of his property to the government and half to Antonio. Shylock is ultimately forced to convert to Christianity and give his estate to his daughter and her Christian lover.

Our primary focus with this work is the character of Shylock. He is a fascinating fictional character and has generated intense academic debate. He has the most powerfully emotive speeches in *The Merchant of Venice* and, many would argue, in any Shakespeare play. However, over the centuries he has been performed in a myriad of ways. There are no stage directions from the playwright advising the director or the actor how to depict Shylock, so directors and actors have artistic freedom to depict him however they so wish. Below, you can see how he has been made to look in various productions of the play – what impression does each one give you of the character?

■ Guy Masterson as Shylock in Gareth Armstrong's *Shylock* (2011)

■ Jonathan Pryce as Shylock in the Globe theatre (2015)

■ Sarah Finigan as Shylock in the Globe theatre (2018)

First, we will look at an extract that demonstrates how Shylock is vilified and shown to suffer. In the following monologue in Act 3 Scene 1, we can see how Shylock has suffered at the hands of anti-Semitism and how he tries to humanize himself.

SHYLOCK [...] He hath disgraced me and hindered
me half a million, laughed at my losses,
mocked at my gains, scorned my nation, thwarted my
bargains, cooled my friends, heated mine
enemies—and what's his reason? I am a Jew. Hath
not a Jew eyes? Hath not a Jew hands, organs,
dimensions, senses, affections, passions? Fed with
the same food, hurt with the same weapons, subject
to the same diseases, healed by the same means,
warmed and cooled by the same winter and summer as
a Christian is? If you prick us, do we not bleed?
If you tickle us, do we not laugh? If you poison
us, do we not die? And if you wrong us, shall we not
revenge? If we are like you in the rest, we will
resemble you in that. If a Jew wrong a Christian,
what is his humility? Revenge. If a Christian
wrong a Jew, what should his sufferance be by
Christian example? Why, revenge. The villainy you
teach me I will execute [...]

(William Shakespeare, The Merchant of Venice Act 3 Scene 1)

Shylock begins with a listing of his suffering at the hands of Antonio, describing having been 'disgraced', 'hindered', 'laughed', 'mocked', 'scorned' and 'thwarted' (lines 1–3). The seemingly endless description of acts committed against him makes clear his suffering is not only at the hands of Antonio, but also because of a more general mistreatment by society as 'I am a Jew' (line 5). Having been described using dehumanizing language throughout the play, he reasserts his humanity in the famous line 'hath not a Jew eyes?' (lines 5–6), an attempt to create a sense of common humanity between himself and the Christians that populate Venice. He then pointedly describes the hypocrisy of Christians and simultaneously provides his motivation for desiring a pound of Antonio's flesh: 'If a Jew wrong a Christian, / what is his humility? Revenge.' (lines 15–16). In pointing out how un-Christian the acts of the other characters of the play have been, he declares 'The villainy you / teach me I will execute' (lines 18–19). He is simply reflecting the cruelty the Christians have shown him, and he is grasping his chance at revenge with both hands. However, these moments of humanization are few and far between, and the work contains far more moments of portraying Shylock as a cruel and maligned character being referred to as a 'cut-throat dog' and 'misbeliever'. He is also referred to as the 'Jew' more than he is as 'Shylock', even in many stage directions.

In order to consider how the meaning and impact of the play, and more specifically this character, has changed over time, it is useful to first delve deeper into the context of production and the play's original interpretation and meaning.

The Merchant of Venice in Elizabethan England

The content of the play certainly contains **anti-Semitic** elements, reflecting Elizabethan attitudes towards Jewish people. In England, Jewish people were expelled on pain of death in 1290 and were not allowed to live in England until 1657 when the law was rescinded. This means it is unlikely Shakespeare (1564–1616) ever came into contact with any Jewish people in his lifetime. He existed in a culture that had prejudices towards those of the Jewish faith that had built up over millennia, with Jews having been accused of murdering Christian children to drink their blood, spreading the Black Death, and even having magical powers through deals with the devil – shockingly, beliefs that are still held by some people today.

It was within this context that Shakespeare created the character of Shylock. It is believed he gained inspiration from a fourteenth-century Italian text *Il Pecorone* by Giovanni Fiorentino, in which a Jewish creditor (simply referred to as 'the Jew' throughout the text) wants a pound of the Christian Gianetto's flesh to pay for a debt. Shakespeare sets the play in Venice, where historically Christians were not allowed to lend money to their brothers. However, as Jewish people were not considered 'brothers', they were legally able to act as moneylenders. People of the Jewish faith were forced to live only on a particular island in Venice that contained a cannon 'getto', or foundry, from which the modern word 'ghetto' is derived.

In the play, Shylock is portrayed stereotypically as a greedy Jew, is spat on by Christians, suffers various insults, sees his daughter run away from him and convert to Christianity (thereby abandoning her Jewish heritage), and is ultimately outsmarted and forced to convert to Christianity. Shakespeare's original title was 'The Comical History of the Merchant of Venice', and he was initially portrayed on stage as the comic figure that Shakespeare seemed to intend. However, there is still much debate as to how much Shakespeare allowed for there to be possible sympathetic interpretations of Shylock. This centres on the one brief yet humanizing speech we looked at in our extract, a section that stands in contrast amidst the other moments of clear anti-Semitism.

Additionally, the lack of stage directions by Shakespeare has meant that productions have often projected onto the character the attitudes and values of their time period. It is these changes which most obviously demonstrate how the **meaning** and **impact** of a work can change over time.

The Merchant of Venice in Nazi Germany

The Nazis employed the text to stoke anti-Jewish feeling in the build up to and during the Second World War. The focus, of course, was the character of Shylock – a character who represented all the stereotypes the Nazis were trying to portray Jews as embodying in order to justify and build support for their process of eradicating Jewish people from Europe. In a staging of the play in Berlin in 1942, it was arranged for extras to be scattered among the audience to shout and curse as soon as Shylock entered the stage, cuing the audience to be whipped into a state of hysteria and hatred. Perhaps the most infamous of these Nazi productions was the 1943 staging in the Burg theatre in Vienna.

Of this production, one critic described Shylock's entrance as follows:

> *'The pale pink face, surrounded by bright red hair and beard, with its unsteady, cunning little eyes; the greasy caftan with the yellow prayer shawl slung round, the splay-footed, shuffling walk; the foot stamping with rage; the clawlike gestures with the hands; the voice, now bawling, now muttering – all add up to a pathological image of the East European Jewish type, expressing all its inner and outer uncleanliness, emphasizing danger through humour.'*
>
> *(John Gross)*

Here we can see how Shylock is used to personify all the worst beliefs people had about Jews. Being portrayed as 'cunning' and 'greasy' and subhuman in their 'clawlike' gestures reinforced a belief that Jewish people were inferior and needed to be eradicated. This presentation of Shylock is in part due to the nature of plays as a text type – unlike a novel, play scripts are not read directly, but are performed in order to be received by an audience. This adds an extra layer of interpretation by the directors of the play who can omit certain sections, add lines and interpret characters in ways that suit their vision. The director of this particular production, Lothar Muthel, had been a member of the Nazi Party since 1933.

At this time, Jewish people were being murdered in the millions across Europe. Little did Shakespeare know it, but his play would have a part in the Holocaust 340 years after it was written. This impact of the play – turning it into hateful propaganda by magnifying the anti-Semitic elements that already existed in the script – shows how the **context of reception** and the ability for plays to be staged in particular ways can alter the meaning and magnify the impact of a work in ways not predicted by the writer.

GLOBAL ISSUES *Field of inquiry:* Beliefs, Values and Education

STEREOTYPES AND PREJUDICE

Works and texts reflect the world in which they are created, and as such they may contain stereotypes and prejudices that are then exposed to a wide audience. *The Merchant of Venice* contains the belief that Jews are conniving and money-grabbing, as was emphasized by the Nazis in their productions. For modern audiences living in a post-Holocaust world, this character of Shylock can be especially problematic as he represents Jewish stereotypes that have caused an incredible amount of suffering, damage and destruction throughout the ages. There has been much debate as to whether the play should be performed with all of its anti-Semitic moments intact, or with concessions to the changes in beliefs and values of the modern day. If performed in its original form, it can be a way of educating modern audiences of the sins of the past. However, it can also end up propagating stereotypes that would perhaps otherwise fade into history. Some have even called for the play to be banned from the stage. We have seen many other examples of works and texts that relate to this global issue of stereotypes and prejudice, and it is often a rich seam of analysis as it provides insight into the beliefs and values of the work or text's context of production.

There are many other examples of non-literary bodies of work that relate to this global issue, including advertsing campaigns, pamphlets and essays from the past that reflect prejudicial attitudes towards segments of society; these can make interesting companion pieces to *The Merchant of Venice* in an individual oral.

DISCUSSION

How are judgements made about the merits of a text? Should a text like *The Merchant of Venice* be banned for introducing prejudices of the past to new audiences despite its Shakespearean heritage? Should texts with ideas and stereotypes considered offensive today be censored? Or are they a valuable way of educating audiences of the mistakes of the past in order to avoid unknowingly repeating them?

The Merchant of Venice in modern times

It is now rare that the character is portrayed as the comic figure of its early productions, or as the figure of hate in the Nazi productions of the 1940s. The character is now portrayed sympathetically to reflect changes in attitudes and values. This is best exemplified by a 2015 production at London's Globe theatre in which an additional scene was added at the end of the play. In the original text, Shylock is largely silent as he is stripped of his possessions and told he will also be stripped of his religion. He is then not seen again on stage, and the audience is instead shown the happy outcome for the Venetian lovers. The Globe production decided to deviate from the script and show his conversion on stage, making clear its intent to primarily focus on Shylock rather than the romantic and comedic elements earlier productions brought to the fore. This moment of a character being stripped of their beliefs and heritage and having a religion forced on them against their will is a shocking moment, as described by a critic reviewing the production in the UK newspaper *The Telegraph*:

> *'Yet Pryce doesn't disappoint; and his shaking, sobbing disbelief when he's robbed of everything, including his religion, is harrowing. There's no artificial final feel-good factor here: instead we witness the vile ceremony of Shylock's enforced baptism, his eloping daughter Jessica (beautifully played by Pryce's own offspring Phoebe) sinking to her knees and keening in belated grief.'*
>
> *(Dominic Cavendish)*

You need only think back to the critic's description of the Burg theatre production in 1943 to see how the meaning and impact of the very same play has changed over time. In showing the character's suffering in such an empathetic way, the audience are invited to sympathize and share the pain of his suffering. His determination to get a pound of Antonio's flesh is seen as an act of violence he feels compelled to do due to his lifetime of suffering and abuse at the hands of Christians and his inner turmoil caused by the loss of his daughter to a Christian man. In an age when people's beliefs and traditions are largely respected, the impact of the work has shifted and the portrayal and reaction to Shylock has changed dramatically.

TOK Links

This has ramifications for the 'truth' of a text. In this case, an extra scene was added. Shakespeare's plays have had many other adaptations, including having the setting changed to outer space, the Soviet Union and ancient China. Are these adaptations still the work of the playwright? Does the play need to remain in the 'spirit' of the playwright's intention to still be true to the original? Who decides what the 'spirit' of the play is?

From a comic figure, to a hated figure, to a sympathetic figure: the meaning of *The Merchant of Venice* and more specifically the character of Shylock has changed over time, reflecting the attitudes and values of its **context of reception**. Its impact has also varied – during the Second World War the play helped encourage hatred and division, in modern times it serves as a reminder of the deplorable beliefs of the past, and throughout history it has reinforced a stereotype of Jewish people that has existed throughout the ages. As these varied portrayals of Shylock demonstrate, it is indeed true that the meaning and impact of texts can change over time, a fact further evidenced in our next text.

The Crucible by Arthur Miller (1953)

Our next example, *The Crucible*, shows how works can also have continued political relevance decades after they are written. *The Crucible*, as briefly mentioned in Section 1, is a play centred around the historical event of the Salem witch trials which took place between 1692 and 1693. In the Puritan town of Salem, over 200 people were accused of witchcraft, with 19 being found guilty and executed by hanging. One other was crushed to death during torture, and five others died in jail.

Arthur Miller

Arthur Miller (1915–2005) was one of the most famous and celebrated playwrights of the twentieth century. An outspoken and political writer, in 1956 Miller was accused of being a communist during what is known as the McCarthy era, a time at which the US government was concerned with both home-grown and Russian agents of communism attempting to bring down the capitalist and democratic foundations of the United States. His most well-known plays, *All My Sons* (1947), *Death of a Salesman* (1949), *The Crucible* (1953) and *A View from the Bridge* (1955), primarily deal with the American experience and the **American Dream**. Miller was awarded the Pulitzer Prize in 1949, had a brief marriage to Marilyn Monroe, won numerous awards, and produced a series of plays, essays and film scripts during his lifetime. He died at home in Roxbury, Connecticut, in 2005.

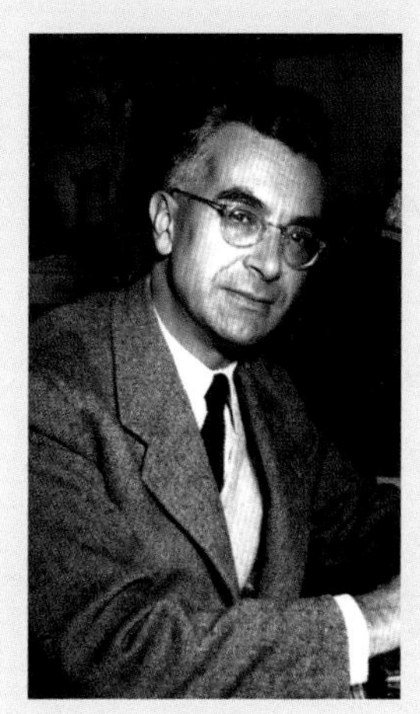

The Puritans were a protestant religious group who had strict beliefs based on a literal interpretation of the Bible. They created a theocracy (a government which gains its authority through religion) in New England, part of the modern-day United States. They believed in living simply, working hard, being thrifty, and leading a life not focused on pleasure and wealth, but on serving God. Bible passages such as Exodus 22:18, 'thou shalt not suffer a witch to live', created a quite literal belief in witches roaming the earth, tempting people into the service of the devil. Witches and witchcraft would sometimes be seen as the cause for disasters such as poor harvests, and Puritans would try to root them out of communities in order to improve their fortunes.

Miller saw parallels between this hunting for witches and the hunting for communists in the 1950s (often referred to as the 'Red Scare'), and so wrote the play as an **allegory** for the intolerance of what became known as McCarthyism – the practice of making accusations of treason without proper regard for evidence. McCarthyism was named after Senator Joseph McCarthy, a politician who was one of the main driving forces behind the Red Scare. At this time, a committee called the 'House Un-American Activities' (HUAC) would question those accused of being disloyal to America and having ties to communism. These interrogations were often public, and helped create a wave of hysteria over the perceived threat of communists to the United States.

In writing about a historical event to comment on his contemporaneous America, Miller was making clear the human capacity for repeating the same mistakes – another example of our **universal themes** related to the human condition discussed in Chapter 2.2. The play had a clear contemporary political message, despite the historical setting, and was a roaring success. It has since been revived on numerous occasions due to its continuing relevance to a range of events throughout history, as we will explore later on.

First, to get a sense of the paranoia, intolerance and need for submission that Miller revealed in Puritan society, we will look at a brief extract. Danforth, representing government authority, is questioning Proctor, who is claiming the originator of the witch accusations has made the entire thing up. He is joined in court by two other men of the village, Parris and Cheever.

DANFORTH: There lurks nowhere in your heart, nor hidden in your spirit, any desire to undermine this court?

PROCTOR, *with the faintest faltering*: Why, no, sir.

CHEEVER, *clears his throat, awakening*: I - Your Excellency.

DANFORTH: Mr. Cheever.

CHEEVER: I think it be my duty, sir - *Kindly, to PROCTOR:* You'll not deny it, John. *To DANFORTH:* When we come to take his wife, he damned the court and ripped your warrant.

PARRIS: Now you have it!

DANFORTH: He did that, Mr. Hale?

HALE, *takes a breath:* Aye, he did.

PROCTOR: It were a temper, sir. I knew not what I did.

DANFORTH, *studying him:* Mr. Proctor.

PROCTOR: Aye, sir.

DANFORTH, *straight into his eyes:* Have you ever seen the Devil?

PROCTOR: No, sir.

DANFORTH: You are in all respects a Gospel Christian?

PROCTOR: I am, sir.

PARRIS: Such a Christian that will not come to church but once in a month!

DANFORTH, *restrained - he is curious:* Not come to church?

PROCTOR: I - I have no love for Mr. Parris. It is no secret. But God I surely love.

CHEEVER: He plow on Sunday, sir.

DANFORTH: Plow on Sunday!

(Arthur Miller, The Crucible Act 3)

Though short, this extract illustrates the typical dynamic within the courtroom. Three main aspects are apparent, and each was intended to reflect the American government's hunt for communists in the 1950s.

Authority

Danforth, as judge, has ultimate authority. He uses religious language such as 'Gospel Christian' (line 16) and 'spirit' (line 1), demonstrating that his authority is derived from God. As Salem was part of a theocracy, questioning the court would mean questioning God – this would not be done lightly and prevented dissent and criticism of any decisions being made.

Danforth clearly represents the US government and, in particular, the 'House Un-American Activities' (HUAC). Whereas Danforth derives his authority from God, the HUAC derived its authority from patriotism and government power. Questioning this authority immediately conferred the suspicion of being anti-American, and prevented dissent, much as in Salem.

Those who were accused, often on flimsy evidence, were treated with intense suspicion and could do little to regain trust, much like Proctor in our extract.

Conformity

People of Salem were expected to conform to religious beliefs, and anyone acting differently was looked on with suspicion. Proctor is undermined in court for having been seen to go out and 'plow on Sunday' (line 21). Sunday was an important religious day of worship; Proctor having ploughed his field causes him to be seen as a bad Christian and biases the court against him.

In a similar way, Americans were expected to conform to the ideals of being a typical patriotic American. Those who questioned or criticized the democratic and capitalistic systems of the US were considered subversive and were rooted out much like the witches. For a country that placed such importance on freedom of speech and thought, this was seen as hypocritical by Miller.

Accusations

In the play, Salem's community is torn apart as neighbours accuse each other of witchcraft, often with ulterior motives based upon past animosities or greed. Cheever turns on Proctor by revealing his damning and tearing of the warrant, and Parris reveals Proctor only goes to church once a month. This characterizes Proctor as a bad Christian, and the ripping of the warrant shows Proctor has contempt for the court. As the court is essentially a representative from God, this is seen as Proctor having contempt for religion, damaging his credibility.

This is echoed in the 1950s. Being accused by compatriots was what caused many to end up in front of the HUAC. People would often turn on each other and sometimes make warrantless accusations to damage other people's careers. When questioned, pressure would be put on those under suspicion to accuse others as it was believed there was a web of communists trying to undermine American ideals.

It is clear, then, that Miller's play was written about a historical event that so closely mirrored contemporary events they could act as an **extended metaphor** (or **allegory**) for the Red Scare. In doing so, it was clear that there were **universal themes** to the text that transcended the specific moment – if they could apply to witchcraft in 1692 and communism in 1953, it is no surprise that they would be able to apply to future situations too.

The Crucible in modern times: politics and paranoia

Politics

Miller explained this continuing resonance in an essay printed in *The New Yorker* around the time of the film version of *The Crucible* being released in 1996. Let's read a short excerpt from the essay.

> It is only a slight exaggeration to say that, especially in Latin America, *The Crucible* starts getting produced wherever a political coup appears imminent, or a dictatorial regime has just been over-thrown. From Argentina to Chile to Greece, Czechoslovakia, China, and a dozen other places, the play seems to present the same primeval structure of human sacrifice to the furies of fanaticism and paranoia that goes on repeating itself forever as though imbedded in the brain of social man.
>
> I am not sure what *The Crucible* is telling people now, but I know that its paranoid center is still pumping out the same darkly attractive warning that it did in the fifties ... The film, by reaching the broad American audience as no play ever can, may well unearth still other connections to those buried public terrors that Salem first announced on this continent ...
>
> *(Arthur Miller)*

Miller is making clear the **universality** of his work. He sees fanaticism and paranoia as 'imbedded' (line 5) in the brains of humans, as something that is part of the human condition and needs to be fought against if we are to be civilized. He lists various places in the world where authoritarian governments have demanded this fanaticism and have prevented people from questioning or criticizing them by threat of being jailed. He pointedly remarks that the play tends to be staged just before or just after these regimes are toppled.

The play clearly has a political message that can be applied to a variety of contexts and can help have a real-world impact by making people question and stand up to fanaticism of any kind. Though the play was originally written to comment on specific events taking place around the year 1953 in the USA, its **meaning** and **impact** in new contexts of reception has changed. *The Crucible* resonates as its focus is on the human capacity for enforcing ideological beliefs, whether they be communism, socialism, capitalism, religion or a host of other things. These situations have occurred throughout the ages and throughout the world. Thanks to Miller's focus on the **universal themes** of paranoia, abuse of power, hysteria and extremism, it is still relevant and is still being staged over half a century after being written.

One such example is a staging in China, one of the countries listed by Miller in his essay. Its meaning to a modern Chinese audience is suggested in a review entitled 'Timeless *Crucible* themes familiar in China' published in *China Daily*.

www.chinadaily.com.cn/culture/2015-01/19/content_19344610.htm

Timeless *Crucible* themes familiar in China

Wang Xiaoying's staging of the Arthur Miller play opened in 2002, which was the inaugural show for the National Theater of China. The company was formed by combining China Youth Art Theater and Central Experimental Theater. Although the witch hunt of 1692 was by no means familiar to members of the Chinese public, it had been drummed home that Miller wrote it as an allegory of McCarthyism and the blacklisting of accused communists in the US.

To any experienced theatergoer in China, or anyone steeped in the culture of innuendos and suggestions, the parallels with China's own recent past would not be lost. The scenes where Salem residents, all pious believers in God, were forced to accuse fellow townsfolk of siding with the Devil are powerful reminders of how far human nature would deviate from its origin of good intentions, and how difficult it is to maintain independence of thinking in the midst of a religion–or ideology-driven mania.

(Raymond Zhou)

The 'parallels with China's own recent past' (lines 5–6) show that the play is having a continued impact and a renewed meaning that has shifted from its original Red Scare roots. The challenges of individual thinking in an 'ideology-driven' (line 8) time and place is clearly something the reviewer felt was relevant in modern China.

Paranoia

Beyond its continued political impact, the play also finds new meaning and impact whenever there is mass hysteria regarding something people fear. The play itself used witchcraft as a stand-in for the fear of communists, but in acting as a **metaphor** it can and has been applied to a variety of situations. New York is an interesting case study – each time the play has been 'revived' (restaged) in the city, audiences have found new meaning in the play's focus on mass hysteria.

1991 Production – AIDs: When the play was revived in 1991, parallels were drawn between the play and the fear of AIDs that had spread in the 1980s and 1990s. Due to misinformation and fear-mongering, many people wrongly thought the disease was exclusive to homosexuals and was contagious through simple contact. This led to discrimination and mistreatment for fear of getting the disease in much the same way the people of Salem feared interacting with the witches would lead to them being possessed.

2002 Production – Terrorism: Another example is the fear of terrorism in the aftermath of the September 11 attacks in 2001. In this situation, the 'witch hunt' was for potential terrorists, and American Muslims in particular felt that their patriotism and innocence was frequently being questioned by fellow Americans and, in some cases, the US government. Once again, this had parallels with the play, and for audiences of the time it was a chance to reflect on contemporary issues like Islamophobia and racism.

2016 Production – Immigration: A more recent production in 2016 was staged amid a fiery presidential election year, with many critics noting the parallels between the play and the political focus on immigration as an election issue. It was also a particularly divisive election, with strongly worded attacks between Democrats and Republicans, the two main political parties in the USA. This echoed the neighbour against neighbour divisions in Salem, and also the fears being stoked around immigration, particularly at the southern border of the United States.

The Crucible was always destined to be a particularly resonant play with a meaning and impact that could change over time. In being an allegory about fear and paranoia, it already had a core symbolism that was built upon **universal themes** that have existed since time immemorial. The catalyst for Miller writing the play was the Red Scare, but this historical moment was to eventually pass, and since then different eras have been able to project their contemporary examples of fear, abuse of power and mass hysteria onto the content of the play. This ties in very closely with our examples in Chapter 2.2 and the notion of universal themes that allow texts to have a continued significance through time, and to continue to speak to audiences that were not imagined in the **context of production**. In speaking to audiences, they can draw links between the themes of the text and the world in which they live, giving the text renewed contemporary relevance.

ACTIVITY 1

Imagine you are writing a letter to a theatre proposing they stage a production of Arthur Miller's *The Crucible*. What current issues would you argue make the play relevant to today? Write a letter that persuades them of its continued relevance and makes clear that staging it would have a clear impact in your context.

'A Hard Rain's Gonna Fall' by Bob Dylan (1962)

We have so far looked at literary works, but the **meaning** and **impact** of non-literary texts can change over time too. One excellent example is the song 'A Hard Rain's Gonna Fall' by Bob Dylan. This song was written in 1962 at the height of the Cold War. In order to understand how the meaning has changed, it is first important to contextualize the song. The Cold War is a term used to describe the tensions between Russia and the United States after the Second World War, driven largely by their different political systems. The United States was democratic and capitalist, whereas Russia and its Soviet Union (a union of Russia and eastern European socialist countries) was communist. Both countries pushed for their respective systems to be replicated throughout the world, leading to conflict and tension. These tensions include the Red Scare we looked at when discussing Arthur Miller's *The Crucible* earlier in the chapter. Though the tension never broke out into open conflict, there were some close calls and there was a very real and present danger of nuclear war between the two nations.

To begin, read the lyrics by following the adjacent QR code.

Given the context of the Cold War, many interpreted the song as referencing the damage of nuclear fallout.

Lines 1–7 ('Oh, where have you been' until 'mouth of a graveyard'): The song follows a question–answer pattern, with a father asking his son about what he has seen out in the world. This inter-generational aspect of the poem immediately gets the listener considering ideas of legacy and the future – the image of the next generation heading out into the world while the older generation sits back represents the world left by the old being discovered by the young. This, of course, is an example of a **universal theme**, and in this context, many young people saw the Cold War as a consequence of the previous generation's prejudices and decisions, with the younger generation being left to deal with the consequences. The adjectives used to describe the sights seen by the son are all negative, with 'misty', 'crooked', 'sad' and 'dead'. Each suggests either a sense of feeling lost or a sense of damage and destruction. To listeners of the time, these were seen as references to the aftermath of a war, with the 'graveyard' of 'ten thousand miles' making clear the loss of life such a war would cause. It is a world broken, damaged and dying due to the mistakes of the past.

Lines 12–18 ('I saw a newborn baby' until 'young children'): The image of a 'newborn baby' surrounded by 'wolves' is a clear symbol of the weak and innocent being preyed on by the corrupt and powerful. This is a reminder of those who suffer during the war – the people who had no say over it happening. The wolves could symbolize the politicians who make threats, and political manoeuvres that often lead to conflicts that make the innocent suffer. The image of men with 'hammers a-bleedin', represents the industry of man being used to create suffering – the Cold War was in many ways a technological one, and a race for bigger, better and more effective weapons, particularly nuclear bombs. The final image of the young children with 'sharp swords' shows the corruption of the young and their involvement in warfare.

Lines 44-end ('I'm a-goin' back out' until 'rain's a-gonna fall'): The final verse has images of a world after a nuclear war. The 'hard rain' was understood by many to mean the radioactive dust and rain that would poison the planet after nuclear warfare. The many people with 'empty' hands shows the humanitarian disaster that would follow as millions starve to death. References to 'black' and 'poison' connote the radioactivity spreading throughout the planet, with the 'well-hidden' executioner's face reflecting the fear of this invisible radioactivity that would kill untold millions. The ultimate ending of the song, with the son sinking in the ocean, shows the inevitable demise that would be faced by all.

'A Hard Rain's Gonna Fall' in modern times

With the Cold War a thing of the past, the lyrics of the song have taken on a new meaning. A new generation of listeners interpret the song as a warning about climate change, with the nuclear holocaust being replaced by the environmental disasters that befall the planet if action is not taken to curb fossil fuel emissions. This led to the United Nations unofficially adopting the song for their climate summit, as described in the article you can read by scanning the adjacent QR code.

ACTIVITY 2

Evidently, the meaning and impact of the song has changed over time. With this new interpretation in mind, write a commentary for the same sections of the Cold War analysis above, but this time analyse it through the lens of climate change. Example responses can be found in the back of the book.

Songs are an incredibly personal medium – I'm sure you yourself can easily create a playlist of songs that mean a lot to you. This text shows how even songs can find new meanings in different times, and in this case become a call to action to impact the world in a positive way by looking after the environment. Once again, due to the use of symbolism and the universal themes of the lyrics, the changed context of reception allows new listeners to project the issues of their time onto the text, and use it as a catalyst for thought and change.

'Swing Low, Sweet Chariot'

'Swing Low, Sweet Chariot' is an African-American Spiritual – songs created by African-Americans, usually on slave plantations, and passed on orally. Slaves at this time were forbidden from speaking their native languages and were also converted to Christianity. Due to them being denied the opportunity of learning to read and write, they would formulate the memorable and melodic songs orally on plantations, and these songs would be heard and repeated by others, spreading from area to area. The 'spiritual' designation is a consequence of the songs being primarily about Christianity and expressing religious faith. Additionally, some spirituals would describe the hardships of slavery, often through veiled figurative language, and others would have coded messages. This often means the **provenance**, or origin, of the songs is a mystery.

'Swing Low, Sweet Chariot' is widely believed to have been composed by Wallace Willis, a slave in the old Choctaw Nation area of Oklahoma during the mid-nineteenth century. He was often sent to a school to do work there, and was a popular fixture due to his singing of spirituals he composed while working. The school's headmaster, Alexander Reid, was taken by this particular song and jotted down the lyrics, passing them on to a group called the Jubilee Singers who popularized the song. A recording of this performance can be found by scanning the QR code opposite.

Context	Oklahoma, USA ~1865
Genre	Song
Audience	Subjugated African-Americans
Purpose	To entertain and to inspire hope

Swing Low, Sweet Chariot

Chorus:

Swing low, sweet chariot,
Comin' for to carry me home;
Swing low, sweet chariot,
Comin' for to carry me home.

I looked over Jordan,
And WHAT did I see,
Comin' for to carry me home,
A band of angels comin' after me,
Comin' for to carry me home.

Swing low, sweet chariot,
Comin' for to carry me home;
Swing low, sweet chariot,
Comin' for to carry me home.

If you get there before I do,
Comin' for to carry me home,
Tell all my friends I'm comin' too,
Comin' for to carry me home.

('Swing Low, Sweet Chariot')

The lyrics refer to deliverance from the material world to the afterlife, a common theme of spirituals due to the suffering and oppression experienced by slaves. However, many spirituals also included a secondary coded meaning conveying tips on how to escape; for example, 'Wade in the Water' included lyrics warning slaves to head into water when escaping to throw bloodhounds off their trail.

A fascinating interpretation of 'Swing Low, Sweet Chariot' is that it contains a coded message giving information about the 'underground railroad'. This was a metaphor referring to the network of people who would help escaped slaves head north without being captured. North, in Canada and parts of the US, slaves would be free and able to live lives as full citizens.

■ Table 2.4.2

Lyric	Surface meaning	Coded meaning
'Swing low'	Come down from heaven	Come down from the Northern states or Canada
'Sweet chariot'	Heavenly vehicle	'Underground railroad' – people who will help slaves escape
'Comin' for to carry me home'	Take me to the afterlife, to heaven	Take me to Canada or North US where I can be free
'I looked over Jordan and what did I see?'	I looked over the River Jordan of Biblical Israel	The Mississippi or Ohio rivers that blocked the journey to the North
'A band of angels'	Literal angels from heaven	Workers of the 'underground railroad'
'Comin' after me'	Coming to take me to heaven	Coming to take me to freedom

This gave the song a double meaning – not only was it an expression of Christian belief, but also a song that gave hope of escape and an opportunity to improve their lives on Earth rather than having to wait for deliverance to the afterlife. In being coded, it could be sung and spread in front of slave owners as an act of secret defiance.

'Swing Low, Sweet Chariot' during the Civil Rights Period

In the 1950s and 1960s, a series of non-violent protests were used to force the end of segregation in America (having separate schools and facilities for black and white people), to ensure voting rights, and to change racist attitudes. During this period, the song was recorded by various artists with a renewed sense of resonance for the song. The intent behind the song was no longer to be taken away from slavery to the afterlife, but as a song of resistance. The songs theme of calling to be taken to a better place also took on **new meaning** – to be taken to a better America by fighting for equal civil rights. The song's **impact** was now to inspire hope for a better future in the real world rather than the afterlife.

CONCEPT CONNECTION

TRANSFORMATION

'Swing Low Sweet Chariot' in English rugby

The meaning of this text has transformed dramatically in modern England. In the modern era, the song is an unofficial anthem for the national English rugby union team. It is frequently sung by over 80,000 fans during home games as players battle it out on the rugby pitch, a situation very far removed from its context of production. Clearly, these fans are not singing for emancipation from slavery, so what makes it such a popular song? What is its meaning understood as being by these fans? And is this transformation in meaning something that just has to be accepted, or should we always be sensitive about the roots of a texts origin? Scan the adjacent QR code to experience the song at Twickenham, England's national rugby union stadium.

In this context, its message of coming 'home' does not refer to the afterlife, but instead carries a patriotic meaning about returning to a home nation – a fitting song for supporters of a national team. The Biblical references hark back to a sense of the Christian history of England, and also give it the quality of a national anthem, much as the British national anthem makes prominent mention of God. It is a song of togetherness and pride. But does this make it okay?

Its use has certainly not been without controversy, and some accusations of cultural appropriation and cultural insensitivity have been made in the media. Headlines like 'England rugby anthem "Swing Low, Sweet Chariot" slammed by academics for ignoring slave history' and 'I used to enjoy singing "Swing Low, Sweet Chariot" – but when I found out what it meant, I felt sick' show that, for many, the original meaning of the song should live on. The image of thousands of fans in England, a country that had a pivotal role to play in the slave trade, joyfully singing a song with its origins in the suffering of a slave, is too much for some.

However, there are those who argue its meaning has changed, and that England fans do not have slavery in mind when they sing the song. Players like Dylan Hartley have also defended it, claiming, 'I don't know the history. To me "Swing Low" is the England rugby song.' Clearly, for many, the meaning has fundamentally changed as part of its new context.

ACTIVITY 3

Research this issue by reading some articles on the ongoing controversy. Afterwards, write an op-ed (like our example in Chapter 2.3) explaining your views on whether this transformation in meaning is something which should be accepted or challenged.

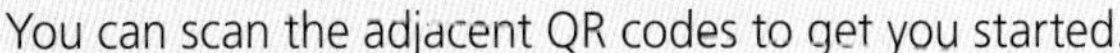

You can scan the adjacent QR codes to get you started.

'Swing Low, Sweet Chariot' is a spiritual song that has its roots in slavery, played its part in the fight for equal rights in the 1950s and 60s, and then crossed the Atlantic to become a modern-day anthem for English rugby fans. The people in each of these contexts have conferred the song with different meanings, and its impact has gone from inspiring hope for the afterlife, to inspiring hope for equal rights, to inspiring hope for winning a rugby match.

Introduction: *The Negro Motorist Green Book*

SENSITIVE CONTENT

Caution: The extract discussed in the following section includes sensitive content.

The Negro Motorist Green Book is a product of its cultural context where African-American people experienced racism and discrimination in segregation-era America. It is included to expose the themes of identity and human behaviour at the heart of this book. Furthermore, the IB recommends that your studies in Language A: Language & Literature should challenge you intellectually, personally and culturally, and expose you to sensitive and mature topics. We invite you to reflect critically on various perspectives offered while bearing in mind the IB's commitment to international-mindedness and intercultural respect.

In Chapter 1.4, you learned about American segregation and the damaging influence of the Jim Crow laws on African-American lives during the late-nineteenth and twentieth centuries. *The Negro Motorist Green Book*, first published in 1936 and written by Victor Hugo Green, is a text that was designed to help African-Americans navigate this segregation-era United States.

Despite rampant discrimination in terms of education and jobs, there was an emerging middle-class of African-Americans who could afford cars and to travel around the country. This was a significant development as the car represented the American ideal of financial success and freedom, but in the hands of African-Americans this freedom ran into conflict with the reality of racial discrimination. Travelling brought with it great dangers for their safety as many in the United States were hostile to African-Americans and did not want them in their towns or their places of work. This was most explicit in the south, where segregation was legally enforced, but even in non-segregated states they were often maligned and refused service by businesses. Driving was seen as a particular challenge to the status quo of racial inequality as it showed African-Americans were breaking free from their enforced inferior status in the United States. Consequently, when African-Americans arrived by vehicle, many white-run motels and service stations refused to serve them. Beyond this, they were also at risk of being refused petrol, food, and lodging, and many states had towns that did not allow African-Americans in the vicinity after sunset (these were known as 'sundown towns'). The combination of all these factors created a country that was unsafe for African-American motorists to freely navigate.

To remedy this, *The Negro Motorist Green Book* was a kind of survival guide; it listed hotels, restaurants, garages and various other services that were friendly to African-Americans, allowing African-American drivers to make informed decisions about where to make stops on their road-trips. It was initially published to cover the New York area, but its success led to it being expanded to cover much of the United States. The guide developed over the years it was published, and these changes reflected the shifting racial attitudes of America, as will be explored in the following section.

KEY FEATURES GUIDE BOOKS

- **Factual:** The key intent behind guide books is to convey information. They contain factual information, often in the form of listings of places and businesses with information such as phone numbers and addresses.
- **Concise:** Guide books convey information in an efficient manner, often using straightforward language and simple sentences to allow readers to quickly obtain the information they need.
- **Clear structure:** Guide books usually have clear headings and subheadings to divide information in a logical and easily navigable way. Graphological features such as text boxes and layout features such as columns are often used to help organize information.
- **Authoritative:** Guide books require the reader's trust; this can be gained through providing clear and factual information and sometimes incorporating a rhetorical introduction to the guide that persuades the reader of its utility.

The Negro Motorist Green Book in the segregation era

The meaning and impact of the text at its time of production was very clear – it was to inform and advise African-American drivers of safe services to visit on their journeys. Its impact on those who read it cannot be understated. Up until its publication, drivers sometimes carried their own toilets for fear of being denied access to bathrooms. They would also often be forced to sleep in their car or illegally in barns or outdoors as hotels and motels would not allow them to stay. The guide allowed African-American motorists peace-of-mind when planning their journeys and it undoubtedly kept many out of harm's way.

Following is the CGAP and the introduction from the 1938 edition of *The Negro Motorist Green Book*; consider how it reflects its particular context of production.

Context	New York, USA – 1938
Genre	Guide book
Audience	African-American drivers
Purpose	To inform and advise

Of particular note is the tone of the introduction. Scan the QR code adjacent and view the extract on page 53. It makes use of a personal and, at times, conversational tone. The use of rhetorical question 'perhaps you might know some?' helps create a link between the producer of the text and its receiver, with the second person pronoun 'you' creating a direct address that makes the text more personal. The personal tone reflects the sense of community and togetherness of African-Americans as they faced up to racial injustice. This interrogative makes clear that this text was considered a 'living document', one that would change and develop as time went on and new editions were printed. It was intended to contain the accumulated knowledge of African-American travellers who had hitherto relied upon word of mouth to know where to stay. This reveals Green's desire and ambition for the guide to expand and grow, thus allowing the horizons of African-American motorists to expand and grow as well.

Victor Hugo Green

Victor Hugo Green was a postal employee and travel writer from Harlem, New York, who is best known for writing *The Negro Motorist Green Book*, a travel guide for African-Americans attempting to safely drive through the United States. He was named after the French writer Victor Hugo and grew up to be a letter carrier for the United States Postal Service. This career was interrupted by being drafted into the army towards the end of the First World War in 1918. After the war, and back in the United States, he grew frustrated with the difficulties African-Americans encountered when travelling domestically, and in 1936 began publishing his travel guide with listings of services and establishments where African-Americans would be welcomed and treated fairly. His guide was a success and various editions were published up until soon after the Civil Rights period in 1966.

Green also writes that any missing African-American-friendly places should be sent in so that 'we might pass it along to the rest of your fellow motorists'. This euphemistic language uses the adjective 'fellow' to imply other African-American motorists, rather than motorists of other races. This shows a clear understanding and sense of community in the readership, an aspect that was particularly important in segregation-era America, as outsiders would not be able to truly understand the problems faced by African-Americans. Language of community helped engender a sense of belonging and shared experience that gave them hope and comfort during what could be very cruel times. Elsewhere, he writes that it is a guide that 'the Negro motorist can use and depend upon'. This designation of the 'Negro motorist' is a term that would be considered offensive today, but it was a term that was accepted by the majority of African-Americans in the 1930s.

Understatement and euphemistic language can also be seen in phrases such as 'depend upon' and 'responsible in their field'. In most contexts, depending upon advice is important, but not a matter of life or death. However, in the context of this guide, unreliable advice could lead to African-Americans being abused, arrested, or even killed, and this deeper understanding of the guide being something they could 'depend upon' would not have been lost on Green's readership. Similarly, saying that advertisements are from businesses that are 'responsible' also gains a particular connotation in this context. Green uses the term to imply that the businesses are neither racist nor discriminatory, and the target audience will have understood this when reading the introduction.

There is also a simplicity in the style that reflects the text type. A guide book such as this is used for reference and getting across information concisely. As such, the language used is straightforward and the frequent paragraph breaks ensure the introduction is easy to follow and understand. Though there is a mix of simple, compound, and complex sentences, they rarely go beyond two clauses, ensuring clarity is maintained. There are also patterns that emerge in the text, for example the final three sentences of the introduction use parallel sentence structures. Each begins with a subordinate clause that starts with 'If', and each is followed by a clear main clause that provides instruction for the reader. These clear instructions help put the reader at ease and help build their trust in the guide.

ACTIVITY 4

A letter that was printed before the listings in the guide book can be accessed through this QR code, on page 54. Using the previous commentary on the introduction as an example, write a commentary on the letter. You can find an example commentary in the back of the book.

The Negro Motorist Green Book in 1948

As the guide was frequently updated through further editions, readers looking back can trace the changes in the African-American experience through the guide. The guide had a predominant focus in early editions on safety, acting as a kind of survival guide to avoid possible aggression, discrimination, and perhaps even physical violence on journeys. Though this was still an important aspect of the guide in the late 1940s, it also started to change over time. The 1948 edition added a vacation guide – this section was less for safety, and more for pleasure. This is a clear signal that, by 1948, the emerging African-American middle class was able to afford vacations and leisure time, something previously monopolised by white Americans. It is during this time that African-American-friendly vacation towns like Idlewild thrived as they welcomed African-Americans to vacation there and to purchase property, causing it to be known as the 'Black Eden of Michigan'. You can read more about Idlewild by following the adjacent QR code.

The guide was also featuring more and more adverts, a clear sign that African-Americans were entering the 'mainstream' of America, with businesses targeting advertising at them through publications like 'The Green Book' to make a profit.

The Negro Motorist Green Book post-segregation

When the United States desegregated after the Civil Rights Act of 1964, African-Americans increasingly asserted their new-found freedoms by patronising businesses that they were previously discouraged or forbidden from using. This led to a decline in African-American centred services, and consequently a decline in fortunes for *The Negro Motorist Green Book*.

Significantly, its title changed to *Travelers' Green Book* as it attempted to broaden its appeal and reflect changing attitudes to race. The term 'negro' had increasingly been seen as having an association with slavery, segregation and discrimination – remember, this capability of words having shifting connotations and meanings is something we looked at in the introduction to this chapter. Civil rights leaders such as Malcolm X, a significant activist behind the movement, criticized the term and encouraged the use of 'black' and 'Afro-American' in its stead. The term slowly became consigned to the history books along with other terms such as 'coloured' due to their racist connotations, and they are terms that are still considered offensive today.

Despite these changes, by 1966 sales had declined so much that the final edition of the guide was published. It was a victim of changing times and was found to be increasingly obsolete by African-Americans who expected equality and fair treatment wherever they went. This is an example of wider political and social changes having a direct effect on the impact of a text, in this case driving it into redundancy.

Green Book, the film

Despite its demise, in 2018 an Oscar-winning film was named after the guide. The film was inspired by the real-life tour of an African-American classical and jazz pianist called Don Shirley and a white Italian-American called Frank Vallelonga who acted as his driver and bodyguard. The film depicts Frank's journey from someone who holds racist beliefs to someone who has a close African-American friend. It follows Shirley's tour in the Deep South of the United States, an area where segregation and racist attitudes were common. In the film, they make use of the *Green Book* to find service stations and hotels that will serve them.

An obvious question is why, over fifty years after the guide ceased to be published, was a film released with the guide as its title? The answer lies in the continued racial problems in the United States. For example, particularly with regard to driving, DWB is a colloquial term used in the modern era as an abbreviation for the 'offence' of 'Driving While Black'. It is a play on the more official term DUI (driving under the influence of alcohol) and it refers to the frequency of African-American motorists being stopped by police. This is often despite not having committed a driving violation, and can involve cars being searched and licences being checked. Stopping people based on their race is known as 'racial profiling' and is an example of discrimination that many African-Americans still experience, despite the progress made since 1964. In looking back at historical events that relate to racial discrimination, movies such as *Green Book* can prompt to the audience to reflect on the still-problematic attitudes of today.

However, the film has its critics, notably the prominent African-American director Spike Lee who stood up and left the Oscar ceremony when *Green Book* was announced as the best picture winner. The film has been faulted for focusing too much on Frank Vellonlonga, a white character, in a film about racial discrimination (something known as 'whitewashing'). It has also been accused of falling into the 'white saviour' trope, a term that describes the frequency with which the media depict white people saving or helping non-white people as a way of alleviating white society's collective guilt for the sins of the past. These 'white saviour' narratives are seen to marginalise the history of non-white people standing up for themselves. You can read a summary of the controversy by following the adjacent QR code.

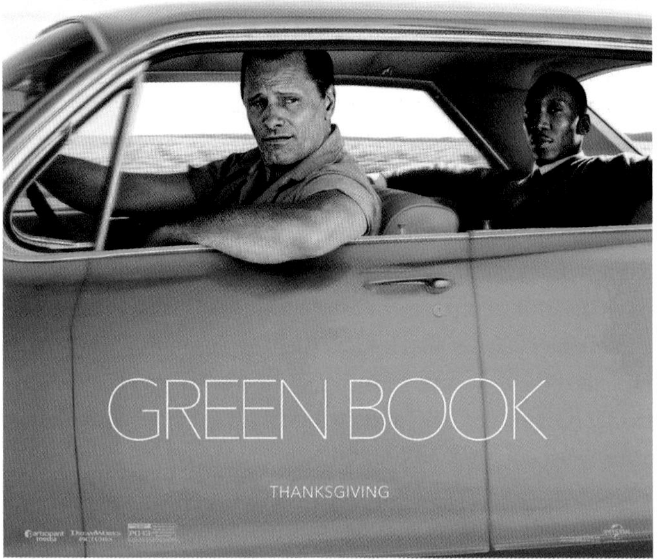

The film has, however, created a renewed interest in *The Negro Motorist Green Book* and the history of racial discrimination in the United States. In recent years, there has been an effort to preserve some of the locations listed in the guide, notably the Harlem YMCA and the AG. Gaston Motel in Birmingham. This effort to shore-up the physical history of racial discriminiation and the Civil Rights Movement is, in part, down to the impact of Victor Hugo Green's guide written all that time ago.

ACTIVITY 5

What deeper meaning can you interpret from this *Green Book* film poster? You can find an example commentary below.

One of the more striking aspects of the poster is the negative space in the top half of the poster. With sparse text, it is dominated by a blue sky, an image synonymous with hope and freedom. This reflects the uplifting intent of the film which depicts a white man overcoming his racism and building a friendship with a black man. On the blue background is simple white text stating the two lead actors and the tagline 'inspired by a true friendship'. This text not only contrasts well with the blue background, but it naturally sits well on the poster as it echoes the white clouds on the blue sky.

Just visible in the background is the setting: a wide open field. This symbolizes the road-trip taken by the characters in the movie and its flat, open aspect brings to mind the wide-open spaces of the United States. The image of a car with the wide open country behind it intertextually links the film with other American road-trip films and their sense of adventure and opportunity.

In the foreground is a blue car that complements the sky in the upper portion of the poster. Its chrome fittings bring to mind the classic era of American cars such as Cadillacs and helps the reader date the film. The two lead actors are clearly visible in the car. Viggo Mortenson's character is in a classic driving pose, with one hand on the wheel and the other resting through the open window, bringing to mind the great American tradition of road trips. His blue shirt fits in with the colour-scheme of the poster and his slicked back hair makes him look effortlessly cool. In the rear is Mahershala Ali's character. His gaze confidently meets the viewer of the poster, reflecting his confident personality in the movie. He wears a burgundy sweater over a blue shirt, dressed more formally than Mortenson's character to reflect his intelligence and talent in the film. His blue shirt beneath the sweater is similar to that of Mortenson's character, which draws a link between the two characters and hints that they will have more in common than is apparent on the surface. The title of the film rests on the doors of the car, showing the significance of the journey, and not drawing attention away from the two big-name stars who are the central focus of the poster.

Summary

The Negro Motorist Green Book is an excellent example of a text that has not only adapted over time, but has had a lasting impact nearly a century after it was first published. It traces the slow, difficult progress made by African-Americans striving for equality and their ascent into the middle class of America. Also, in serving as a record of businesses that treated African-Americans with respect and dignity at a time that it was in short supply, it has led to the historical preservation of some buildings that would otherwise have been lost to time. Thanks to a film adaptation, there has been a renewed interest in the guide and copies of it have been sold once again to a modern audience, now as a historical document rather than a practical guide.

'Keep Calm and Carry On'

Chances are, you will have seen one of these designs in some form or another adorning someone's wall, placemat, social media post ... the list goes on. Have you ever stopped to consider where this text comes from? It is, in fact, another excellent example of the **meaning** and **impact** of a text changing over time.

The text began as a propaganda poster created in the United Kingdom by the Ministry of Information on the eve of the Second World War – the various propaganda posters produced by the Ministry constitute a fascinating non-literary body of work that you may wish to explore further. As mentioned in Section 1, propaganda uses a variety of features to promote a particular political cause or point of view, meaning they are particularly interesting to analyse and have clear connections to the time and space of their production. Propaganda can also come in a variety of forms – in this case it is as a poster, but propaganda can just as easily be a speech, a movie and a radio play amongst many other text types.

Many existing posters had been focused on detailed and specific practical instructions, such as what to do in the event of a gas attack. However, the Ministry wanted posters that helped to create a more general mindset and self-belief that would help people survive the struggles of the war. The big fear of the British government was the threat of an intense bombing campaign directed at urban centres, acts that would cause extensive damage to both infrastructure and morale. These posters were envisioned as a way of providing a morale boost that would keep the country running in the face of German bombs. The poster was one of three created by the Ministry, with the two others being 'Freedom is in Peril – Defend It with All Your Might' and 'Your Courage, Your Cheerfulness, Your Resolution, Will Bring Us Victory'. The 'Keep Calm' poster was actually never used publically, whereas the other two were. 'Keep Calm' was instead kept in reserve, ready to be used in the aftermath of any intense bombing.

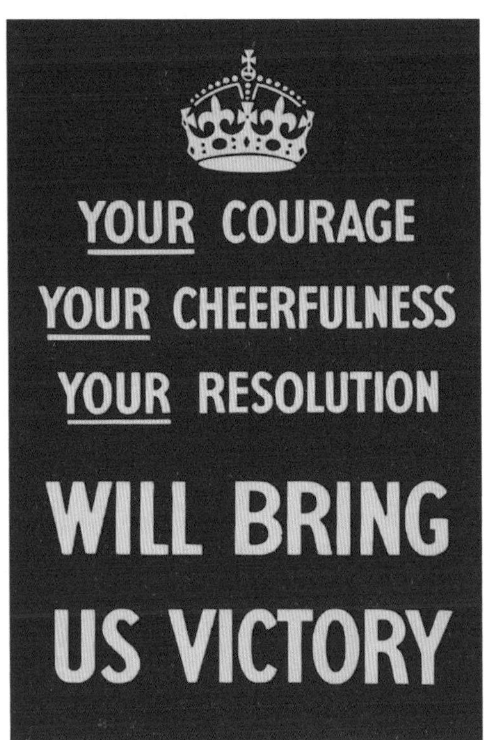

Context	Second World War – Great Britain
Genre	Propaganda poster
Audience	British public
Purpose	To persuade, advise and inspire

Having discussed the context, genre, audience and purpose, we can now focus on the other elements of the text. To be effective and eye catching, the 'Keep Calm' poster uses carefully thought through **graphological**, **typographical** and language features. There is striking use of a vivid red background colour that contrasts with the bold, capitalized white text. The conjunction 'and' is in smaller font to allow the two **imperatives** of 'keep calm' and 'carry on' to stand out, as these are the two key messages conveyed by the poster. Each word has its own line, ensuring each is given emphasis, and the simple, pared down phrasing ensures every word is essential and conveys important meaning. The alliteration of the sharp, **plosive** 'c' sounds in 'keep', 'calm' and 'carry' combined with the monosyllabism create a clear and memorable phrase that can be repeated and spread throughout the country. The graphic above the text is the Tudor Crown of King George VI (the King of England at the time), appealing to the patriotism of the British public. The King was also seen as a national symbol of togetherness, helping the public remember everyone was in this together.

Despite all these qualities, it rarely saw the light of day during the war. It was felt by some that the message could be considered condescending, as if the King was telling the public what to do regardless of their suffering. Later posters would try to persuade people rather than command them, an approach the public were more receptive to. The poster could also be seen as implying things were not calm wherever it was displayed, as it was built on the assumption of people panicking and needing to be told to relax. The content of the poster was also a little too abstract, and later posters were more specific and clear, focusing on topics such as 'Careless Talk Costs Lives'. This all meant that the poster was never officially released during war-time, so it essentially had no **impact** at the time it was produced; that was to come much later.

The rebirth of 'Keep Calm and Carry On'

Though it never quite had the impact it was intended for at its time of inception, the poster became a roaring success over half a century later. It was discovered by a couple in Leeds who had bought a box of old books in an auction. In the box, they found a 'Keep Calm' poster which they duly displayed in their bookshop. Despite it being written during war-time, the poster resonated with a modern audience. The couple began to receive messages from people asking if they could buy the poster, or if they could at least obtain a replica. As it was out of copyright, the merchandizing began, and the poster has since turned into a global icon.

Though the general sentiment of the language – stay calm when times are tough – has not changed, the situation around it has. It is now used without the high stakes of life or death bombings, but is instead used as more of a motivational poster. In an era of a very different kind of stress, the message still resonates. Instead of bombed-out Londoners, workers struggling to keep up with emails are connecting with its sentiment. Instead of families who have lost loved ones in the great battles of the Second World War, teenagers struggling with IB deadlines are finding themselves drawn to its message. It is now that the text is finally being given the chance to have an **impact** on people's lives. This has also taken the poster beyond its intended British audience. Its global appeal stems from its **universal theme** of keeping calm in the face of adversity, but also from it playing into positive British stereotypes. The crown, which used to instil patriotism into a British public suffering during wartime, now appeals to many because of the international allure of British culture and history – something referred to as **anglophilia**.

This text also has an interesting relationship with technology. Its vibrant colours designed to catch the eye in war-torn London are also typical of the modern-day palette and suit vibrant, high definition phone screens. Through sites such as the 'Keep Calm and Carry on' creator **(www.keepcalmandcarryon.com/creator)**, you can now easily generate your own version of the poster online, changing the colours, changing the iconography, and sharing it across the globe or printing it within seconds. Sites even allow you to create your own version of the poster and then order it to be printed on items like mugs, t-shirts, and phone cases. A technological shift that has taken place since the poster was first dreamed up now allows easy customization, something unimaginable in its context of production.

Inevitably, the poster has also entered the world of **memes**, being shared over social media particularly when conveying a humorous or quirky message. 'Now Panic and Freak Out' offers a humorous inversion of the poster's original meaning, and speaks of irony, self-deprecation and plays on the notion of recent generations not being as hardy as the generations who lived through two world wars. Such **pastiches** of the poster often get shared over the internet and give new life, **meaning** and impact to the original poster as it interacts with a global audience it was never intended to reach. This, of course, brings into question the idea of authorship. Though sites allow users to edit the poster, they are still imposing certain parameters and working with the original design of the poster itself. Most edits retain some of the original language of the poster, whereas others stay within the wider grammatical constructions. This in effect becomes a collaboration between the original producers of the text and the modern person editing it, a collaboration that spans nearly one hundred years and creates new texts that reflect the modern context of reception. Because of this, not only is the meaning and impact of the text changing, the text *itself* is changing too, creating new texts that retain many features of the original.

This ability of texts to be actively engaged with and changed is perhaps a sign of things to come. A text like a novel exists as it is on the page, and it remains static as you read it. A movie follows the same plot every time you watch it. But texts such as videogames allow you to actively make decisions, and some games have plots that branch off in new directions depending on the user's choices. These texts that actively respond and adapt to the reader are an area that seems set to grow and offer up new and interesting experiences as technology like AI, VR and videogames continue to develop.

GLOBAL ISSUES ***Field of inquiry:* Science, Technology and the Environment**

THE EVOLVING RELATIONSHIP BETWEEN TECHNOLOGY AND PROPAGANDA

The 'Keep Calm' campaign by the British government was war-time propaganda. Technology of the time did not allow much beyond reliable printing presses that could duplicate the original design in its thousands to be spread throughout the country, but the modern age allows for far more advanced forms of propaganda. This can be seen in the way this text is now being easily edited and spread online. Though the stakes are low with this text – an edited version being mistaken for an authentic war-time poster from the British government is unlikely to cause much trouble – the ease with which texts can be altered and disseminated is causing ever-increasing problems in modern society.

As techniques for altering texts have become more effective and accessible, 'fakes' and doctored texts have become commonplace in the modern media landscape. We are now at a stage where machine learning can help create 'deep-fake' videos of politicians saying things they never really said, that unreliable news stories can spread overnight through the internet, and incredibly realistic doctored photos can be created quickly and easily by anyone with a computer or even just a smartphone. The impact has been dramatic. It has allowed leaders around the world to decry unfavourable reports as 'fake news', allowed doctored photos and videos to spread through social media and influence millions of people, and allowed unreliable news reports to proliferate and affect how readers view current events and how they vote at the ballot box.

A wide variety of non-literary texts and literary works are related to this global issue. One of the most well-known examples is *Nineteen Eighty-Four* by George Orwell, a work that presciently warned of the dangers of propaganda when paired with technology such as mass-surveillance and fake news. Similar texts like *We* by Yevgeny Zamyatin (a text in translation) and *Brave New World* by Aldous Huxley also deal with technology being abused by those in power. As for further non-literary texts, there are many speeches, documentaries and books exploring the use of propaganda, 'fake news' and its ties with technology.

EE Links: English A – Literature category 2

Category 2 extended essays require comparing a literary work or works originally written in the language of the essay with a work or works in translation. As mentioned in our global issue, there are many works exploring propaganda and its effect on how we view the world. These are often in the dystopian fiction genre – works set in worlds where society is oppressed and controlled. Zamyatin's *We* is an early example of the genre, written in the 1920s but set in a futuristic society in which nearly every building is made of glass, thus allowing mass surveillance of the population. It inspired writers like Huxley and Orwell, and so makes an interesting comparison piece with these texts for an extended essay.

With this example, the text's core meaning of encouraging resilience in adversity has largely remained the same, but the context of reception has changed dramatically. Additionally, the advent of modern technology has allowed new meanings to be projected onto and into the text by digital alteration, a kind of pastiche that allows new meanings to be added to the text.

Conclusion

As this chapter has demonstrated, the meaning and impact of a work can change significantly over time, and these changes can sometimes be contentious. Enabling this change is, of course, **universal themes** that allow each time to project its contextual issues onto the meaning of the text. In this way, texts can often go through something of a rebirth, with past meanings being cast off to be replaced by the new. This is a fascinating consequence of the nature of texts and their relationship with the reader – they are **multivocal** and their perceived meaning often shifts with each new generation of readership.

Works cited

Cavendish, D. 'The *Merchant of Venice*, Shakespeare's Globe, review: "oak-solid".' *The Telegraph*, 1 May 2015. Web. 15 March 2019. **www.telegraph.co.uk/culture/theatre/theatre-reviews/11576773/The-Merchant-of-Venice-Shakespeares-Globe-review-oak-solid.html**.

Dylan, B. 'A Hard Rain's Gonna Fall' (lyrics). Web. 12 Oct. 2019. **www.bobdylan.com/songs/hard-rains-gonna-fall**.

Gillett, F. 'England rugby anthem Swing Low, Sweet Chariot slammed by academics for ignoring slave history.' *Evening Standard*, 9 March 2017. Web. 12 Oct. 2019. **www.standard.co.uk/news/uk/england-rugby-anthem-swing-low-sweet-chariot-slammed-by-academics-for-ignoring-slave-history-a3485826.html**.

Gross, J. 'THEATER; Shylock and Nazi Propaganda.' *The New York Times*, 4 April 1993. Web. 15 March 2019. **www.nytimes.com/1993/04/04/theater/theater-shylock-and-nazi-propaganda.html**.

Jordon, N. 'Swing Low, Sweet Chariot' sung by the Fisk Jubilee Singers (1909). *Youtube*, 23 Dec. 2012. Web. 12 Oct. 2019. **www.youtube.com/watch?v=GUvBGZnL9rE**.

Miller, A. *The Crucible*. Penguin Books, 2000.

Miller, A. 'Why I wrote "The Crucible".' *The New Yorker*, 13 Oct. 1996. Web. 15 March 2019. **www.newyorker.com/magazine/1996/10/21/why-i-wrote-the-crucible**.

Moore, J. 'I used to enjoy singing 'Swing Low, Sweet Chariot' – but when I found out what it meant, I felt sick.' *Independent*, 9 March 2017. Web. 12 Oct. 2019. **www.independent.co.uk/voices/swing-low-sweet-chariot-england-rugby-song-new-york-times-donald-trump-a7620751.html**.

Moustachio, P. 'Swing Low, Sweet Chariot – Twickenham – England v. France 2011.' *Youtube*, 27 Feb. 2011. Web. 12 Oct. 2019. **www.youtube.com/watch?v=ToJIY1PjhM8**.

Nicolaou, E. 'The Backlash To *Green Book*, Explained.' *Refinery29*, 25 Feb. 2019. Web. 13 Oct. 2019. **www.refinery29.com/en-us/2019/01/220609/green-book-movie-controversy-racism-don-shirley-family-story**.

Plett, B. 'Bob Dylan song adopted by Copenhagen climate summit.' *BBC News*, BBC, 5 Dec. 2009. Web. 12 Oct. 2019. **https://news.bbc.co.uk/2/hi/americas/8396803.stm**.

Robinson, A. '"Black Eden," The Town That Segregation Built.' *NPR*, 5 July 2012. Web. 13 Oct. 2019. **www.npr.org/2012/07/05/156089624/black-eden-the-town-that-segregation-built**.

Shakespeare, W. *The Merchant of Venice*. Wordsworth Editions, 2000.

'Swing Low, Sweet Chariot.' *Songs for Teaching*. Web. 15 March 2019. **www.songsforteaching.com/folk/swinglowsweetchariot.htm**.

Zhou, R. 'Timeless *Crucible* themes familiar in China.' *China Daily*, 19 Jan. 2015. Web. 15 March 2019. **www.chinadaily.com.cn/culture/2015-01/19/content_19344610.htm**.

2.5 How do texts reflect, represent or form a part of cultural practices?

OBJECTIVES OF CHAPTER

- To understand the meaning of the term 'cultural practice'.
- To examine the representation of cultural practice in graphic novels.
- To explore how texts can represent and reflect family and gender as cultural practice.
- To explore how texts can represent custom and tradition as cultural practice.
- To consider how texts can form cultural practice.

Now is a sensible time to revisit the notion of culture. We have previously defined it as what the inherent values, beliefs and attitudes of the time and place actually are. These are shared by a distinct group of people, and they affect how they view the world and interact with it.

Our **guiding conceptual question** wants us to focus in particular on '**cultural practices**'. This generally refers to the traditional and customary practices of a particular ethnic or other cultural group. It refers to the physical rather than the abstract, as in how people act and interact in the real world. For example, some Vajrayana Buddhists believe that after death the body is an empty vessel and that we should be generous to other creatures – a **cultural belief**. This manifests itself in sky burials, where bodies are left in specially built towers to be eaten by birds – a **cultural practice**. These cultural practices are manifestations of cultural beliefs; they are often traditional practices that have been passed down from previous generations.

Cultural practices include the following:

- religious and spiritual practices
- medical treatment practices
- forms of artistic expression
- dietary preferences, culinary practices and traditional food
- housing and construction
- childcare practices
- approaches to and systems of governance and leadership
- power relationships and gender roles
- 'everyday life' practices (including household relationships).

DISCUSSION

Can you think of any practices that are particular to your own culture? They will almost certainly have been reflected or represented in texts – see if you can research any interesting examples. Some practices may even involve texts themselves, particularly with regard to religion.

This chapter will explore a variety of texts that **reflect**, **represent**, or **form** cultural practices; we will explore texts that show the cultural importance of clothing, food, dance, gender roles, death, and, most importantly, tea.

CONCEPT CONNECTION

CREATIVITY – CULTURAL PRACTICES IN GRAPHIC NOVELS

■ *Persepolis* by Marjane Satrapi

■ *Ghosts* by Raina Telgemeier

■ *Aya of Yop City* by Marguerite Abouet and Clément Oubrerie

■ *Arrugas* by Paco Roca

■ *American Born Chinese* by Gene Luen

■ *Palestine* by Joe Sacco

All texts require creativity, imagination and artistic craft, but none more so than the graphic novel. Even from the small sample above, a range of styles is evident, each a product of its artist/writer, and each artist/writer a product of their culture and background. The use of art and imagery to express ideas and communicate requires a very different approach to prose. Art has a unique, visceral impact on readers, and a well-designed panel can communicate more than words when created by a skilled artist with an impassioned message to convey. Art has always had an ability to challenge and surprise us, and in the graphic novel format those abilities are increasingly being put to imaginative and creative use to communicate **culture** and **identity**. Over the past couple of decades, there has been a resurgence in the popularity of the graphic novel. We looked at some examples in Chapter 1.1 including the graphic novel *Maus* and its unique blend of testimonial, memoir, history and autobiography through visual storytelling. It is often within this text type that we find the most creative, artistic and imaginative ways of telling stories.

In the following few examples, we will see interesting and creative ways of reflecting and representing cultural practice. Before we look at them, let's consider why the graphic novel is such an effective vehicle for exploring these practices. Tezuka Osamu, an influential Japanese manga artist, summed it up best by saying:

> *'My experience convinces me that comics, regardless of what language they are printed in, are an important form of expression that crosses all national and cultural boundaries.'*
>
> *(Frederik Schodt 25)*

So, why are comics and graphic novels so effective at crossing national and cultural boundaries?

- **Universal visual language:** The most obvious factor is the use of predominantly visual narratives. Images are a universal language – we can all interpret a picture in a way that we cannot all interpret a Chinese character, for example, and this means that it is much easier to communicate in this form. For example, the graphic novel *The Arrival* by Shaun Tan (as explored in Chapter 1.3) takes this to its extreme and does away with comprehensible written language entirely, communicating purely through images apart from the occasional use of a made-up language to put the reader in the alienated position of an immigrant.

■ An image of a tree as it would appear in a graphic novel, and the Chinese (traditional) character for a tree – which is easier to comprehend?

- **Simple written language:** A novel requires often quite complex language to describe imagery and feelings. Visuals render the need for these long, wordy descriptions unnecessary. Instead of hundreds of words building up the image of an Indian side-alley, a graphic novel can simply put the image in a panel. What language there is – usually almost entirely dialogue – is much shorter and simpler, reducing the time and difficulty of translating the text for other markets.

- **Creative visual storytelling:** That the visuals are drawn also allows far more creativity and imagination than would be possible through mediums such as photography or film, as these would need more elaborate special effects and editing. Modern graphic novels often use very creative imagery rich in symbolism to tell stories in new and engaging ways, as we will see with some of our extracts.
- **Modern technology:** You've almost certainly seen someone reading a comic or graphic novel on their phone, and this suitability for laptops, tablets and phones has caused an explosion in the sales of graphic novels. The ability for them to be distributed, downloaded, and viewed globally has made it much easier for writers to express their culture to a global audience via the graphic novel form.

These advantages have led to many graphic novels being released that explore culture and cultural practices. Some examples not included in this section but certainly worth seeking out are *Ghosts* by Raina Telgemeier, *Persepolis* by Marjane Satrapi and *American Born Chinese* by Gene Luen Yang, all fantastic expressions of culture and identity.

Representation and Reflection

Two of the functions included in our guiding conceptual question are to '**represent**' and to '**reflect**'. When we talk of **representation**, we mean just that: to represent aspects of cultural practice. This could take the form of a written description of a cultural practice, a photograph, a drawing, or even travel writing describing the practice for tourists. These representations are usually quite explicit and literal, conveying the actual act of the cultural practice to a reader. ***Reflections*** of cultural practice are often more subtle, and may show the tertiary effects of a cultural practice and how it has a broader impact on that particular society. Our next text is a good example – it often *represents* examples of actual Indian cultural practice, such as bartering at street markets, but it also *reflects* aspects of cultural practice by deliberately using bright, vivid colours that reflect the use of colour in Indian festivals and clothing. Let's look more closely …

Pashmina, by Nidhi Chanani (2017)

Our first text is *Pashmina* by Nidhi Chanani. Chanani moved from India to the United States at the age of 4 months old, and her mixed heritage as someone of Indian descent growing up immersed in the culture of the United States was the inspiration for her graphic novel. It focuses on a girl called Priyanka, a character loosely based on the writer, growing up in America but fascinated by her mother's Indian heritage and Hindu religion. She discovers a magical pashmina (a type of shawl from Kashmir, an area between India and Pakistan) that provides her with insights into her Indian cultural background. Scan the QR code for an interview with the author and an example of the style of the panels. If you can, try and source this text from your library or bookstore so you can complete the activity.

This text uses the graphic novel form to interesting effect. When Pri is in America, the panels are all in black and white, but when Pri is in India, the panels are flooded with vibrant, visceral colour. The black and white shows that her life in the United States is lacking something, and its darker palette reflects her mood of isolation and her feeling like an outsider. However, when wearing the pashmina, she is transported to an India rich with colour, culture and presence – this vivid use of colour **reflects** the presence of colour in Indian cultural practices, from colourful saris to events like the Holi festival (sometimes known as the 'festival of colour'). This juxtaposition represents the transformative power of cultural knowledge and its ability to fill in what may be missing in someone's life and identity. The pashmina itself symbolizes a link to her Indian heritage, demonstrating that items of clothing – representations of cultural practice – can act as a bridge to another culture. This is reinforced in one particular moment of the graphic novel when she gets clothed in Indian garments for the first time and exclaims that she 'feels so ... Indian'. Her sari (a draped garment of cotton or silk), bindi (the adornment in the middle of her forehead, more often seen as a decorative red mark), and hairstyle all act as cultural artefacts and by embracing the sartorial cultural practices of India, she suddenly reconnects with her heritage. The **stative verb** 'feel' makes this very clear – she does not simply 'look' Indian, she 'feels' it. The jarring transition back to reality has all the more impact because of this return to black and white. She returns to her bland American clothing and the artist's depiction of her disappointed facial expression makes clear that adventure has awoken a new part of her, and she will not view her American life in the same way again. This would not be possible in traditional prose, and demonstrates the creative opportunities provided by the graphic novel form.

As demonstrated, this text explores notions of identity, being a third culture child, and rediscovering cultural practices that can sometimes be lost after immigration. The graphic novel's use of magical realism, with the anthropomorphized animals, transformations and magical clothing, allow fantastical elements to embellish the story and also reinforce the strong influence of mythology and religion on the Indian culture that she is rediscovering.

ACTIVITY 1

If you have access to the text, choose a spread of panels and write a commentary on how they represent or reflect cultural practice. A commentary is provided at the back of the book for pages 74 and 75 of the text for you to compare it with.

Shake a Leg by Boori Monty Pryor and Jan Ormerod (2011)

Shake A Leg by Boori Monty Pryor and Jan Ormerod is a graphic novel that revisits Aboriginal culture, something we have previously looked at in Eva Johnson's poem 'A Letter to my Mother' in Chapter 2.3. Pryor is an Indigenous Australian writer and Ormerod is a white Australian illustrator. In their text, some Australian children are buying pizza, but they are confronted with a chef that speaks Italian, but looks Aboriginal. This mixing of cultures surprises the children, who are then told about the chef's background and learn of Aboriginal cultural practices they were previously ignorant of.

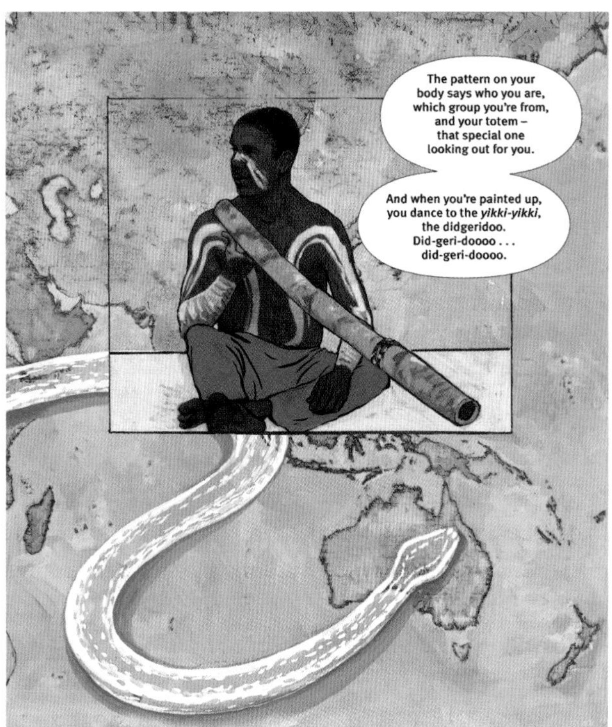

(Jan Ormerod and Boori Pryor 26)

In this text, cultural practices such as dancing and body painting are **represented** and explored through the eyes of children. This is an important issue in Australia, with various government programmes currently being put in place to enhance the general Australian population's often poor understanding of Aboriginal culture. The image of Australian children being educated about Aboriginal culture is an ideal that the writers know the Australian government is aspiring towards. The children are introduced to 'warrima' (Aboriginal dancing). They use the tomato sauce to recreate the traditional bodypaint, and then become part of the dance. This playfulness shows the openness of Aboriginal culture and their willingness to share their heritage with non-Aboriginal Australians. Our extract includes a **splash page** featuring a two-headed snake; this is a figure from Aboriginal myth and is also sometimes a totem (a kind of spirit-animal) – in the image above, it symbolically links Italy and Australia to fit the story of an Aboriginal pizza chef. An **inset panel** is used to show an Aboriginal man explaining the totemic cultural practice in more detail. The mention of 'ochre' is reinforced with the image of an earth made up of this important clay and soil – in Aboriginal culture it is used for art, for body paint and for protection from the sun. The **code switching** between the Aboriginal language and English shows the multicultural nature of Australia and also the ability for meaning to cross cultural boundaries as the children quickly comprehend the new terms.

This graphic novel's focus on non-Aboriginal Australian children learning about Aboriginal cultural practices is a powerful example of culture being shared, and cultural boundaries being transcended. This is an increasingly important function of graphic novels as they are often being used to improve cross-cultural understanding. That our two examples have been aimed at children shows that the text type can be an excellent way of ensuring future generations grow up to be global citizens.

Aya of Yop City by Marguerite Abouet and Clément Oubrerie (2012)

Our final graphic novel is actually known as a *bande dessiné*, a type of comic created for French-language readers. It is called *Aya of Yop City* and was created by Marguerite Abouet (an Ivorian writer) and Clément Oubrerie (a French illustrator). It is set in the Ivory Coast, a former French colony in Africa, and unlike our other graphic novels is aimed at an older audience. It follows a variety of characters who are all connected by the titular character Aya; Aya helps them overcome a variety of difficulties while trying to deal with her own often quite serious problems. The text explores themes such as sexuality, femininity, the blending of African and Western culture and coming of age.

Of particular interest is its appendices which provide step-by-step instructions on cultural practices such as how to wear Ivorian clothing, how to cook Ivorian food and even how to walk like an Ivorian. This mixes the text type of graphic novel with that of a kind of instruction manual, and makes very clear its intent to share and **represent** cultural practices. It shows clear step-by-step visual instructions that can help you embrace Ivorian culture. Beyond this, it even includes a step-by-step recipe to create traditional Ivorian food, much like Ha's cookbook in Chapter 1.5. This moves the text beyond simply being a reflection of cultural practices, but one that invites the reader to actively participate in them. This experiential approach to sharing cultural practices is a clever way of engaging outsiders and breaking down divisions between different cultures and cultural practices – rather than the writer jealously gatekeeping the cultural practices, the writer instead invites the reader to partake in them, helping to establish a sense of global community.

■ Summary

These extracts have given a taste of the kinds of cultural practices that are being represented, reflected, and even taught through graphic novels. Graphic novels are a unique form with a visual style that can disseminate cultural practices in a host of ways and to a variety of audiences. With such texts acting as a medium for sharing culture, they are playing an increasingly important role in helping to build global consciousness and understanding.

CHECK FOR UNDERSTANDING

Consider practices associated with your culture. In the style of *Aya of Yop City*, create a graphical guide that you think communicates these practices to outsiders in an effective way.

Gender and Family as Cultural Practice

Both our role within the world and how we interact with it are, in part, defined by our culture and its attitudes. In our interactions with other people, we are putting into practice the values held by our particular culture. A small example of this is greeting a friend: some cultures may embrace in a hug, a kiss on one cheek, a kiss on both cheeks, shake hands, bow or touch noses together. This extends beyond simple greetings to how we more broadly treat each other and what we expect of each other. This is explored in our next text by looking at a South American family and their different roles and expectations in life.

Chronicle of a Death Foretold by Gabriel Garcia Marquez

Gabriel Garcia Marquez

Gabriel Garcia Marquez (1927–2014) was a Colombian journalist and novelist. He is considered one of the most significant authors of the twentieth century, particularly within the realm of Spanish language literature. His most acclaimed novels are *One Hundred Years of Solitude* (1967), *Chronicle of a Death Foretold* (1981) and *Love in the Time of Cholera* (1985). He is notable for popularizing magic realism (fantastical elements in real-world settings, much like *The Famished Road* by Ben Okri in Chapter 2.2) and having a series of books that focused on the notion of solitude. He won the Nobel Prize for Literature in 1982 and is remembered as the most notable Latin American writer in history.

Like many of his stories, Marquez set *Chronicle of a Death Foretold* in a Colombian township to explore the culture he knew best: his own. Though the main plot revolves around the honour killing of a man who had apparently slept with a new husband's wife, the text explores a variety of other cultural practices. They are explored by portraying the lives and interactions of a raft of characters that make up the community. One such family is the Vicarios; in our extract, we learn of the family's background and how the daughters of the family were brought up to be married.

> Angela Vicario was the youngest daughter of a family of scant resources. Her father, Poncio Vicario, was a poor man's goldsmith, and he'd lost his sight from doing so much fine work in gold in order to maintain the honor of the house. Purisima del Carmen, her mother, had been a schoolteacher until she married forever. Her meek and somewhat afflicted look hid the strength of her character quite well. 'She looked like a nun,' Mercedes recalls. She devoted herself with such spirit of sacrifice to the care of her husband and the rearing of her children that at times one forgot she still existed. The two oldest daughters had married very late. In addition to the twins, they had a middle daughter who had died of nighttime fevers, and two years later they were still observing a mourning that was relaxed inside the house but rigorous on the street. The brothers were brought up to be men. The girls had been reared to get married. They knew how to do screen embroidery, sew by machine, weave bone lace, wash and iron, make artificial flowers and fancy candy, and write engagement announcements. Unlike the girls of the time, who had neglected the cult of death, the four were past mistresses in the ancient science of sitting up with the ill, comforting the dying, and enshrouding the dead. The only thing that my mother reproached them for was the custom of combing their hair before sleeping. 'Girls,' she would tell them, 'don't comb your hair at night; you'll slow down seafarers.' Except for that, she thought there were no better-reared daughters. 'They're perfect,' she was frequently heard to say. 'Any man will be happy with them because they've been raised to suffer.'
>
> *(Gabriel Garcia Marquez 30)*

The way these characters interact with each other **reflects** the attitudes of this particular culture, and some of the customs described **represent** cultural practice. Marquez particularly focuses on gender roles within the Vicario family. The way these gender roles impact people's lives in terms of their treatment, opportunities, and education constitutes a cultural practice. Marquez uses the **perfect tense** when describing the mother's career as a teacher, making clear it is a thing of the past. We find she soon 'married forever' (lines 4–5), with the post-modifying adverb 'forever' making it seem like a life sentence rather than a reason for celebration. In implying she lost her career due to marriage, we see that it is truly a defining commitment for a woman, and that they are forced to transition entirely to being child-rearers and domestic servants. She is described as 'devoted' (line 5) and the comparison to a 'nun' (line 5) implies the self-sacrifice women were expected to make in this culture. That 'at times one forgot she existed' (line 6) reinforces how invisible and taken for granted this devotion often becomes within the context of a Colombian family.

The next generation fare no better, as it is revealed that her daughters were 'reared to get married' (line 9), a description juxtaposed with the strong declarative of 'the brothers were brought up to be men' (line 9) and its implication that they would enter the world of work. The verb 'reared' is often also used with animals, and connotes a sense of training and submission for the sisters that is lacking in the phrase 'brought up' used when describing the brothers (the original Spanish text had a similar connotation). The girls are taught skills that are important in the domestic sphere, such as to 'wash and iron', but also skills in the superficial, such as to embroider and create 'artificial flowers' (lines 10–11). It is made clear at the end of the extract that the conventional idea of a perfect woman is one 'raised to suffer' (line 16) – a strong and bold statement illustrating the inferior position of women and the expectation of them to sacrifice their own pleasures and independence for the sake of others.

In **representing** and **reflecting** the cultural practices surrounding women and marriage, Garcia helps share the experience of being a woman in Colombia with the rest of the world. In showing how women are denied autonomy, he **reflects** attitudes he witnessed in Colombia when growing up, and how the reader reacts to them defines what impact a text like this has. To many, seeing a woman denied agency can be shocking, but to those with strongly religious backgrounds, these beliefs can clash. One blogger gave an interesting insight into her reading of the text, particularly regarding the character of Angela who is accused of having sex before marriage:

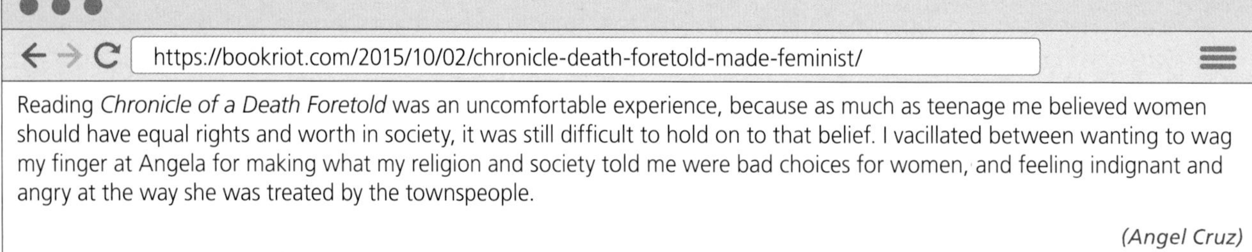

Reading *Chronicle of a Death Foretold* was an uncomfortable experience, because as much as teenage me believed women should have equal rights and worth in society, it was still difficult to hold on to that belief. I vacillated between wanting to wag my finger at Angela for making what my religion and society told me were bad choices for women, and feeling indignant and angry at the way she was treated by the townspeople.

(Angel Cruz)

This is one outcome of presenting cultural practices in texts – they are there to be examined and questioned. In taking practices out of the everyday experience and placing them into works of artistic expression such as novels, they are put in a space that invites reflection and debate.

Summary

In *Chronicle of a Death Foretold*, cultural practice is presented as it was witnessed by Marquez in order to raise a question rather than provide an answer, much as Ibsen did so in *A Doll's House*. Sometimes, in having cultural practices in texts, they are at once being reflected and questioned. Inviting the questioning of such practices can sometimes be a catalyst for change.

Custom and tradition as cultural practice

Representing traditional cultural practices that are no longer common can also be a powerful function of texts, as we will see in our next work by Wole Soyinka.

DISCUSSION

If you think back to your parents and grandparents, there are almost certainly traditions they took part in that you yourself may not. Is this an inevitable consequence of progress and globalism? How important is it that these traditions are recorded in texts? You may even want to interview elderly relatives about any traditions they used to take part in and record them yourself.

Death and the King's Horseman by Wole Soyinka (1975)

CHECK FOR UNDERSTANDING

The following text is by Wole Soyinka, a writer who was introduced in Chapter 1.5. Decide which of the following statements it true or false from memory, and then check Chapter 1.5 to see if you were correct:

- He was born in 1938.
- He is South African.
- He won the Nobel Prize for Literature.
- He spent two years in solitary confinement.
- He once escaped a country by motorcycle.

Death and the King's Horseman is about the true story of an incident that took place in Nigeria during the time of British rule. You may remember this work from Chapter 1.5, where we looked purely at the narrative structure of the play. This time, we are looking in detail at the cultural content of the play. According to Yoruba tradition, when the Yoruba King dies, his horseman must commit a ritual suicide to help the king's spirit ascend to the afterlife. If this does not happen, the king's spirit will wander the earth and bring harm to the Yoruba people. This caused a clash between European attitudes and African cultural practice, as the British prevented the ritual suicide by the horseman. When the horseman, named Elesin, fails to complete his duty, his seemingly Westernized son commits suicide in his place, affirming his cultural roots despite having been educated in England. Elesin then manages to commit suicide in his cell. Soyinka focuses on the theme of duty and culture as well as the lack of cultural understanding between the colonial powers and African people. Our extract is from the beginning of the play, soon after the Yoruba King has died. Elesin Oba, his horseman, is walking through the market embracing the honour he gains in having people know he will soon die and join his erstwhile King in the afterlife.

Scene one

A passage through a market in its closing stage. The stalls are being emptied, mats folded. A few women pass through on their way home, loaded with baskets. On a cloth-stand, bolts of cloth are taken down, display pieces folded and piled on a tray. Elesin Oba enters along a passage before the market, pursued by his drummers and praise-singers. He is a man of enormous vitality, speaks, dances and sings with that infectious enjoyment of life which accompanies all his actions.

PRAISE-SINGER: Elesin o! Elesin Oba! Howu! What tryst is this the cockerel goes to keep with such haste that he must leave his tail behind?

ELESIN *(slows down a bit, laughing)*: A tryst where the cockerel needs no adornment.

PRAISE-SINGER: O-oh, you hear that my companions? That's the way the world goes. Because the man approaches a brand-new bride he forgets the long faithful mother of his children …

ELESIN: This market is my roost. When I come among the women I am a chicken with a hundred mothers. I become a monarch whose palace is built with tenderness and beauty.

PRAISE-SINGER: They love to spoil you but beware. The hands of women also weaken the unwary.

ELESIN: This night I'll lay my head upon their lap and go to sleep. This night I'll touch feet with their feet in a dance that is no longer of this earth. But the smell of their flesh, their seat, the smell of indigo on their cloth, this is the last air I wish to breathe as I go to meet my great forebears.

PRAISE-SINGER: In their time the world was never tilted from its groove, it shall not be in yours.

ELESIN: The gods have said No.

PRAISE-SINGER: In their time the great wars came and went, the little wars came and went; the white slavers came and went, they took away the heart of our race, they bore away the mind and muscle of our race. The city fell and was rebuilt; the city fell and our people trudged through mountain and forest to find a new home but – Elesin Oba do you hear me?

ELESIN: I hear your voice Olohun-iyo.

PRAISE-SINGER: Our world was never wrenched from its true course.

ELESIN: The gods have said No.

PRAISE-SINGER: There is only one home to the life of a river-mussel; there is only one home to the life of a tortoise; there is only one shell to the soul of man; there is only one world to the spirit of our race. If that world leaves its course and smashes on boulders of the great void, whose world will give us shelter?

ELESIN: It did not in the time of my forebears, it shall not in mine.

(Wole Soyinka 7–9)

Elesin knows it is the day of his death and is proud of it, as it is an honour to die to accompany the King. He is going through the market and is celebrated by all, with the praise singers affirming his duty and his honour. On his final night on earth, no woman can deny him if he tries to sleep with her. He is walking through the market seeking a woman other than the mother of his child with whom to spend his final night. He metaphorically describes the market as his 'roost' (line 11) and the women his 'hundred mothers' (lines 11–12). This focuses on the maternal role of women in Nigerian society, not only as life givers, but nurturers. He relishes this attention and care, declaring himself to be like a monarch of a palace 'built with tenderness and beauty' (line 12). This idea of being served by the women extends to his sexual desires, and he talks of his need to 'smell their flesh, their seat' (line 15) – he wishes to luxuriate in women's bodies on his final night, taking them as if they are his right. He is warned about this distracting him from his duty by the praise-singer, who presciently declares 'the hands of women also weaken the unwary' (line 13). The praise-singer acts much as a chorus would in a Greek tragedy, foreshadowing the tragic arc of his narrative. The praise-singer reiterates the importance of this cultural practice, claiming that 'there is only one home to the life of a tortoise; there is only one shell to the soul of a man' (lines 27–28), and that if Elesin fails to complete his duty, it is believed the world could smash 'on the boulders of the great void' (line 29). The arrogance and capriciousness of Elesin is seen as unbecoming of someone about to partake in such a noble duty, and his desires of the material world cloud his spiritual purpose of ritual suicide, leading to dire consequences.

GLOBAL ISSUES ***Field of inquiry:*** **Culture, Identity and Community**

CULTURAL PRESERVATION

As we are looking at cultural practices, we are seeing works and texts that reflect how cultural beliefs are expressed in tangible ways. In this extract, we have been presented with the build-up to Elesin's ritual suicide. This aspect of Yoruba belief, that the King's chief horseman must journey with him to the afterlife, is a deliberately provocative and dramatic subject matter. Soyinka himself wished to play down the 'clash of cultures' element to the text as he felt it could be reductive and it asserts a Western perspective on viewing the practice. But this clash is still a fundamental driving force behind the narrative, and the exploration of how different belief systems can interact and come into conflict is a rich area for drama. In examining Yoruba beliefs clashing with British beliefs, Soyinka is able to explore the roots of modern Nigeria and, in effect, the roots of many other modern African countries. Through the colonial actions of European countries during the 1800s and 1900s, African beliefs were diminished and in some cases outlawed. Though the colonial era has passed, its impact on many countries' education systems, political systems, and cultural practices still lingers. A vast wealth of African cultural tradition and belief has been filtered through Western colonialism, and its legacy is a Westernization of many African countries. Soyinka examines the inflection point of this change, the moment a traditional belief and practice is stymied due to conflicting Western beliefs, in an attempt to remind modern Nigerians of their roots.

This reassertion of belief through works and texts is a powerful tool that can help begin to redress historical injustices and educate those who have lost touch with the beliefs of the past. It is apparent in *Death and the King's Horseman*, but also in many of the other extracts we have seen in this section. For instance, Chanani's *Pashmina* centred on a rediscovery of Indian cultural belief, and Johnson's 'A Letter to My Mother' contained a reassertion of Aboriginal cultural belief. The ability of texts to **reflect**, remind, and retain beliefs is a vital one, and it can help protect cultural heritage that may otherwise be lost.

This is a pertinent global issue as cultural traditions begin to fade under the conformative effects of globalism. There are many non-literary bodies of work that deal with the preservation of or reconnection with culture that could be used in your individual oral when paired with this work. You could perhaps look for a series of speeches, an advertising campaign, a series of magazine articles by the same writer or photographs by the same photographer that aim to celebrate and preserve cultures that are under threat.

■ Summary

Soyinka was passing comment on his country soon after it had entered a new era of independence. He explores the continuation of Nigeria's cultural practices and emphasizes the importance of cultural consciousness: he is reminding Nigerians of their roots and celebrating Yoruba culture. In showing the clash with Nigeria's former British colonial masters, he shows how easy it is for cultural practices to be outlawed, and shows the importance of cultural understanding.

Texts that form cultural practice

Our next texts also deal with death and the afterlife, but rather than **representing** a cultural practice, they actually **form** the practice itself. Texts that are part of cultural practice are often religious texts, for example the Jewish cultural practice of scheduled readings from the Torah that take place at synagogues throughout the world. The integration of texts into cultural practice shows the importance texts can have in a culture, as we are about to see.

Jisei – Japanese death poems

Japanese death poems were written by the Japanese literate class, mostly made up of the ruling class, samurai and monks. They were heavily tied in with the Shinto and Buddhist beliefs of Japan, particularly as Buddhism requires a focus and understanding of death. According to Buddhism, death reminds us that the material world is transitory and ephemeral, and that pleasures and worldly concerns are ultimately futile. These poems would prepare the person for death and often show a form of enlightenment or understanding about this transitory nature of existence. These are very different to the Western tradition of 'last words', which were often thought up in the moment or incidental. Contrastingly, these poems required deep rumination and sometimes even criticism and revision. In his book *Japanese Death Poems*, Yoel Hoffmann writes of a man who was so worried about his impending death, he wrote death poems from the age of fifty years onwards. He would send them for criticism by his poetry master Reizei Tameyasu; one such poem he sent read, 'For eighty years or more/ by the grace of my sovereign / and my parents, I have lived / with a tranquil heart / between the flowers and the moon.' His poetry master drily replied with 'when you reach age ninety, correct the first line' (Hoffmann 77). However, they were not always as serious. Moriya Sen'an, who died in 1838, humorously wrote 'Bury me when I die / beneath a wine barrel / in a tavern. / With luck / the cask will leak.'

KEY FEATURES JISEI – JAPANESE DEATH POEMS

- **Formal structure:** The poems were usually either written in 3 line, 17 syllable haiku form (5-7-5 syllables) or 5 line, 31 syllable tanka form (5-7-5-7-7 syllables).
- **Rumination on death:** Focus on death, usually from a Buddhist perspective, accepting and understanding that life is transitory and we live on in different forms.
- **Natural imagery:** Often be used as metaphors for death and moving on.
- **Acceptance:** Poems would show an acceptance of death, but some may reflect dark thoughts, others may be more hopeful – it would depend on the state of mind and the situation the writer found themselves in.

Below are a series of examples of death poems, some with additional context.

(a) This poem was written by a seventeenth-century Japanese woman who committed suicide. She had married an important political figure and bore him a male child, but was treated incredibly cruelly by his mother, eventually killing herself. This poem appeared in her will.

And had my days been longer	*Nagaraete*
still the darkness	*kono yo no yami wa*
would not leave this world—	*yomo hareji*
along death's path, among the hills	*shide no yamaji no*
I shall behold the moon.	*iza tsuki wo min*

(65)

(b)

There is no death; there is no life.
Indeed, the skies are cloudless
And the river waters clear.

(Taiheiki Toshimoto)

(c)

Inhale, exhale
Forward, back
Living, dying:
Arrows, let flown each to each
Meet midway and slice
The void in aimless flight
Thus I return to the source.

(Gesshu Soko)

(d)

Frost on a summer day:
all I leave behind is water
that has washed my brush.

(Shutei)

(e)

Empty-handed I entered the world
Barefoot I leave it.
My coming, my going —
Two simple happenings
That got entangled.

(Kezan Ichikyo)

Instead of **reflecting** or **representing** cultural practice, these poems actually *form* part of a cultural practice as they were a tradition performed in relation to death. Each is rich with symbolism and they contain much philosophical thought despite their brevity.

In **poem (a)**, for example, the moon symbolizes salvation in the world beyond the sufferings of the present life. There is a sense of resignation from the writer as, even if her days had been longer, she feels the 'darkness' would not have left the world, perhaps symbolic of her depression and suffering at the hands of her mother-in-law. The metaphor of a continuing path for death reflects the Buddhist belief that existence continues on after the material world, albeit in another form. Ultimately, the poem seems hopeful in looking to the future, despite being sorrowful when looking back at the past.

Poem (b) takes a more transcendental perspective. The poet is seeing beyond the human simplifications of death and life, and their inherent oppositions, instead seeing them as meaningless. To this writer, death is merely the end of the body, not the spirit. The adjectives 'clear' and 'cloudless' convey a sense of purity and clarity that the writer feels in the face of death, something approaching a sense of enlightenment.

ACTIVITY 2

Using the above commentaries of poem **(a)** and poem **(b)** to help you, analyse poems **(c)** to **(e)**. Example responses can be found in the back of the book.

TOK Links

Can texts truly express thoughts and feelings related to notions as complex as death? Or is language too imprecise and referential to capture the true essence of existence and notions such as love, life and death?

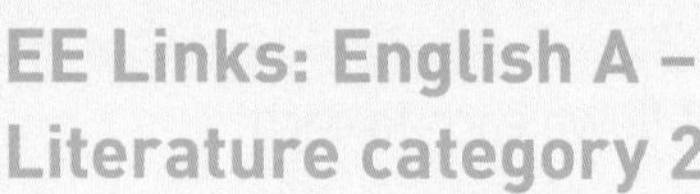

EE Links: English A – Literature category 2

Category 2 extended essays require you to compare a literary text or texts with another literary text or texts that is/are in translation. You could compare a collection of Jisei poems with English language poems or elegies related to death, exploring how each provides particular insights into their respective cultures. A possible research question could be: **To what extent do selected Jisei poems and Auden's 'Stop All the Clocks' provide insight into their respective cultures' attitudes to death?**

■ Summary

These poems are themselves a cultural practice, and provide a fascinating insight into another culture's attitude to death as well as a glimpse into the Buddhist notions of existence. Through figurative language, we learn of an accepting and understanding attitude to death, and similarities can be seen with the Yoruba attitude to death in our previous extract. Both of these examples show an attitude of facing up to mortality that can sometimes be lacking in other cultures and their cultural practices.

Depictions of cultural practice in travel writing

Our final two texts both look at cultural practice from the perspectives of outsiders. Our first is by Bill Bryson, an American who has written many successful books of travel writing and often **represents** cultural practices of the places he visits. Our second text is a **guide** for partaking in a Japanese tea ceremony, a tradition that has been practised for centuries.

Notes from a Small Island by Bill Bryson (1995)

Bill Bryson

Bill Bryson, born 1951, is an American who has spent almost his entire adult life living in Britain. He has written very successful books on travel, the English language and science. Bryson attended Drake University in Iowa, United States, before dropping out to backpack through Europe. In 1973 he visited the UK and ended up getting a job at a psychiatric hospital; it is here he met the Englishwoman who would become his future wife. After moving back to America so he could finish his degree, the couple settled in England in 1977. He has since been awarded an OBE by the Queen of England, been the chancellor of Durham University and won numerous awards for his writing.

KEY FEATURES TRAVEL WRITING

- **First person:** Travel writing is generally written from a first person perspective as it documents the personal experience of someone travelling through a particular country or place.
- **Perspective:** The reader is presented with an outsider's perspective to help convey the writer's sense of exploring a new place on their travels.
- **Chronological:** Most travel writing is chronological as it documents the progress of the writer's travels in sequence as they journey through the country or place.
- **Informative:** Most travel writers also try to provide context to the place they are visiting; this often involves including historical information and additional contextual research about the places they visit.
- **Descriptive:** In many ways, travel writing offers the reader a chance to vicariously visit the place being described. This requires creating a sense of place through descriptive language.
- **Culture:** Travel writing often tries to convey the culture of a place through describing its people and their cultural practices.
- **Entertaining:** Travel writing is written to be engaging and to capture the excitement of travel. This can be done through humour, evocative description, and detailed thoughts and feelings of the writer as they experience their travels.

As we discussed in Chapter 2.3, an outsider can often provide particular insights that an insider to a culture may fail to appreciate. A prominent example of this is *Notes from a Small Island*, a bestselling book about Britain that, despite being written by an American, ended up being voted by BBC Radio 4 listeners as the book which best represented Britain. In the book, Bryson travels the length and breadth of Britain writing a travelogue that documents the people he meets, the heritage of the places he visits, and describes the culture of the island that he now calls home. Our extract captures the typical style of the book – we have interesting vignettes and historical anecdotes followed by observations about British culture and cultural practices.

Context	United Kingdom – 1995
Genre	Travel wring
Audience	Those interested in travel, British culture
Purpose	To inform and to entertain

SO LET'S TALK about something heartening. Let's talk about John Fallows. One day in 1987 Fallows was standing at a window in a London bank waiting to be served when a would-be robber named Douglas Bath stepped in front of him, brandished a handgun and demanded money from the cashier. Outraged, Fallows told Bath to 'bugger off' to the back of the line and wait his turn, to the presumed approving nods of others in the queue. Unprepared for this turn of events, Bath meekly departed from the bank empty-handed and was arrested a short distance away.

I bring this up here to make the point that if there is one golden quality that characterizes the British it is an innate sense of good manners and you defy it at your peril. Deference and a quiet consideration for others are such a fundamental part of British life, in fact, that few conversations could even start without them. Almost any encounter with a stranger begins with the words 'I'm terribly sorry but' followed by a request of some sort – 'could you tell me the way to Brighton', 'help me find a shirt my size', 'get your steamer trunk off my foot'. And when you've fulfilled their request, they invariably offer a hesitant, apologetic smile and say sorry again, begging forgiveness for taking up your time or carelessly leaving their foot where your steamer trunk clearly needed to go. I just love that.

As if to illustrate my point, when I checked out of the Caledonian late the next morning, I arrived to find a woman ahead of me wearing a helpless look and saying to the receptionist: 'I'm terribly sorry but I can't seem to get the television in my room to work'. She had come all the way downstairs, you understand, to apologize to them for their TV not working. My heart swelled with feelings of warmth and fondness for this strange and unfathomable country.

And it is all done so instinctively, that's the other thing. I remember when I was still new to the country arriving at a railway station one day to find that just two of the dozen or so ticket windows were open. (For the benefit of foreign readers, I should explain that as a rule in Britain no matter how many windows there are in a bank, post office or rail station, only two of them will be open, except at very busy times, when just one will be open.) Both ticket windows were occupied. Now, in other countries one of two things would have happened. Either there would be a crush of customers at each window, all demanding simultaneous attention, or else there would be two slow-moving lines, each full of gloomy people convinced that the other line was moving faster.

Here in Britain, however, the waiting customers had spontaneously come up with a much more sensible and ingenious arrangement. They had formed a single line a few feet back from both windows. When either position became vacant, the customer at the head of the line would step up to it and the rest of the line would shuffle forward a space. It was a wonderfully fair and democratic approach and the remarkable thing was that no-one had commanded it or even suggested it. It just happened.

(Bill Bryson 311–312)

Here, Bryson is examining the British cultural practice of manners and of queuing. The extract begins with an anecdote regarding John Fallows. This is an effective segue into a topic as it takes an extreme and humorous example of queuing etiquette in order to make a broader point, and is a feature that is often used in travel writing. The colloquial 'bugger off' (line 4) being directed towards a man with a gun shows bravery on the part of Fallows, but also illustrates the importance of manners. Bryson's addition of 'approving nods' (lines 4–5) implies this was a shared feeling among the other people in the queue, suggesting it is an inherent part of being British; their reaction also brings to mind the 'Keep Calm and Carry On' posters we looked at in the previous chapter.

Bryson then uses contrast to emphasize his point, comparing the typical two queues you would find when there are two windows serving people as full of 'gloomy people convinced the other line was moving faster' (lines 26–27). This negative lexis is in strong contrast with words like 'ingenious' (line 29), 'democratic', 'fair' (line 31) and 'sensible' (line 28) used for the British queuing system. Its formation is described with the adverb 'spontaneously' (line 28) to suggest it is an inherent characteristic of British people and an instinctive part of their culture. As ever when dealing with stereotypes, we as readers need to be wary of broad characterizations. The cultural practice Bryson is describing reinforces a well-known stereotype that readers may have gained from other texts: the British are polite, and queuing is a national pastime. Bryson will undoubtedly have encountered poor queuing etiquette in his time in Britain, but focusing on characteristics that readers recognize can be more satisfying to the reader and more humorous to write about. This is another common feature of travel writing – as texts they are there to provide insight but also aim to explore what makes each culture unique and interesting, and this often leads to focusing on existing stereotypes, similar to the **exoticisation** we discussed when looking at *Shantaram* in Chapter 2.3.

DISCUSSION

Consider the cultural stereotypes you have of British people – how many of them have you actually seen or experienced in real life, and how many of them are purely through texts and the wider media? More often than not, most of our stereotypes are second-hand information through texts and the media – what are the dangers of this?

A Rough Guide to: the Japanese tea ceremony

In the age of cheap air travel, we no longer just experience exotic cultural practices vicariously through texts, we often experience them in person on holiday. When out of our element, we can sometimes make ignorant mistakes that can cause offence or embarrassment. Our final extract is from a series of travel guides called 'Rough Guides' that help people avoid committing such cultural faux pas. They are an accessible series of guides advising travellers on where to go and how to act in various parts of the world. This particular guide walks the reader through a traditional Japanese tea ceremony.

www.roughguides.com/article/a-rough-guide-to-the-japanese-tea-ceremony/ 

The Rough Guide to: the Japanese tea ceremony

Hushed voices, the scratch of a bamboo whisk, then a bow, a nod and a bowl of steaming *matcha* is handed around. Any delicate sounds in the room are amplified by the formality of the occasion – so quiet you can hear people holding their breath – which heightens the sense that something very important is going on. This is a tea ceremony in full swing: the ultimate in Japanese hospitality.

There's so much more to it than simply stirring a teapot; it's Zen Buddhism in a cup. Intrigued? Here's everything you need to know about 'the way of tea'.

What is it all about?

Chado or sado ('the way of tea'; sometimes also called *chanoyu,* 'hot water for tea', or *ocha,* literally just 'tea') is the ritual of preparing and serving green tea. It takes place in a room, sparsely decorated with tatami mats and a hanging scroll or flower arrangement, with up to five guests kneeling on cushions. There are countless types; a full-length formal event lasts about 4 hours and includes a meal and two servings of tea.

Rooted in Chinese Zen philosophy, the tea ceremony is a spiritual process, in which the participants remove themselves from the mundane world, seeking harmony and inner peace. It takes decades for the host to master the art of serving tea, through study of philosophy, aesthetics, art and calligraphy, as well as learning the meticulous preparations.

Everything is done for the wellbeing and enjoyment of the guests. All movements and gestures are choreographed to show respect and friendship. Beautiful ceramics with seasonal motifs are hand-picked to match the character of individual guests. Even the utensils are laid out at an angle best admired from the viewpoint of the attendees. It's important that each tea gathering is a unique experience, so the combination of objects is never used twice.

What are the dos and don'ts?

The guest is not a passive participant; everyone has a role and etiquette is an important part of the ceremony. Here are the basic rules:

1. Wear a kimono or, failing that, dress conservatively.
2. Make sure you arrive a little early.
3. Remove your shoes at the entrance and put on a pair of slippers, then wait to be invited in.
4. Avoid stepping in the middle of the tatami and use closed fists when touching the mats.
5. All guests should show their appreciation by complimenting their host on their efforts, admiring the room and the delicious tea and sweets.
6. Don't make small talk; conversation is expected to focus on the ceremony itself.
7. Finally, if you're one of several guests, don't forget to make a quarter turn of the bowl before you drink and wipe the lip of the bowl afterwards. This is mainly for hygiene reasons, to avoid drinking from the same place as the other guests.

(Ros Walford)

Reflecting the text type, this guide uses a variety of features to make the cultural practice easy to understand and follow. It is structured so that it builds the reader's knowledge up slowly and remains engaging. It begins by creating an evocative sense of place to capture the reader's interest, and then gives historical and cultural background before moving on to practical and informative instruction. It uses subheadings to delineate the sections and make it easy to follow. In being so ordered, it reflects its purpose of informing and uses the conventions of the guide text type. Each section has its own particular style of language.

The opening is there to evoke a sense of being in Japan and to capture the reader's imagination. To do so, the writer employs sensory imagery to put the reader in the position of someone at a tea ceremony. The references to 'bamboo' (line 1) and 'matcha' (line 2) both have strong connotations of Japan. The adjectives 'hushed' (line 1) and 'delicate' (line 2) emphasize the formality of the situation, and the writer describes the 'heightened' sense of something important going on. This creation of tension and excitement puts the reader in the imagined situation, making them want to read on to hear about the main event.

The following section is introduced with the subheading 'What's it all about?' (line 10), a question that is then immediately answered, an example of **hypophora** that builds your confidence in the writer and the knowledge they are passing on to you. This section has a style that has shifted to a more informative one, with fewer adjectives and a greater use of declarative sentences and parenthetical information to help build the reader's understanding. Each sentence concisely builds the reader's knowledge, providing them with the contextual background to truly appreciate a tea ceremony.

The final section is introduced with the subheading 'What are the dos and don'ts?' (line 27) At this point, the style switches to numbered information. The style becomes more imperative, as the writer provides simple commands with modal verbs such as 'should' (line 34) that make clear what you need to do in a tea ceremony. This inspires confidence and is easy to follow and remember due to its format. Its chronological ordering allows the reader to imagine every step, and by the end it is as if you have experienced a tea ceremony.

CHECK FOR UNDERSTANDING

Earlier in the chapter, you created a visual guide to a cultural practice of your own. Demonstrate your understanding of the 'guide' text type by transforming it into a style similar to the tea ceremony guide above.

Summary

Much like the appendices of *Aya of Yop City*, this text invites the reader to take part in a cultural practice. We feel a part of the culture being described, and consequently more a part of the global community than we did before we read the text. This is an important role of texts – to break down barriers and enhance intercultural understanding. As we build our intercultural understanding, we feel more like a global community rather than a range of competing cultures.

Conclusion

This chapter has explored how texts reflect, represent or form part of cultural practices. As previously stated, this is a vital role of texts as it promotes global consciousness and intercultural understanding. In sharing the rich variety of our cultures and cultural practices, we can gain an appreciation of the sheer range of cultural expressions across the globe, and often spot similarities that show there is more that binds us than divides us. These texts are all heavily tied in with **time** and **space** and show direct links between **text** and **context**.

Works cited

Abouet, M. *Aya of Yop City*. Drawn and Quarterly, 2005.

Bryson, B. *Notes from a Small Island*. Black Swan, 2015.

Chanani, N. *Pashmina*. First Second Books, 2017.

Cruz, A. 'How Chronicle of a Death Foretold made me a feminist.' Book Riot, 10 Feb. 2015. Web. 13 March 2019. **https://bookriot.com/2015/10/02/chronicle-death-foretold-made-feminist**.

Hoffmann, Y. *Japanese Death Poems: Written by Zen Monks and Haiku Poets on the Verge of Death*. Tuttle Publishing, 2018.

Ibsen, H. *A Doll'sHouse*, student edition. Methuen Drama, 2008.

Márquez, GG. *Chronicle of a Death Foretold*, reissue edition. Translated by Gregory Rabassa, Penguin Books, 2014.

Márquez, GG. *One Hundred Years of Solitude*, Penguin Books, 2007.

Márquez, GG. *Love in the Time of Cholera*. Penguin Books, 1989.

Okri, B. *The Famished Road*. Vintage Classics, 1992.

Pryor, B, Ormerod, J. *Shake a Leg*. Allen and Unwin, 2010.

Schodt, FL. 'The View from North America,' *Manga's Cultural Crossroads*. Edited by Jaqueline Berndt, Routledge, 2016.

Spiegelman, A. *The Complete Maus*. Penguin Books, 2003.

Soyinka, W. *Death and the King's Horseman*. Methuen Drama, 1998.

Tan, S. *The Arrival*. Hodder Children's Books, 2014.

Walford, R. 'A Rough Guide to: the Japanese Tea Ceremony.' *Rough Guides*, 15 May 2017. Web. 13 March 2019. **www.roughguides.com/article/a-rough-guide-to-the-japanese-tea-ceremony**.

2.6 How does language represent social distinctions and identities?

OBJECTIVES OF CHAPTER

- To understand the terms 'identity' and 'social distinctions'.
- To examine the relationship between language and identity.
- To consider the importance of accent in the media.
- To explore the differences between mother tongue and second languages.
- To consider the problematic appropriation of language originating from cultures other than our own.

The language we use can be revealing, sometimes without us even realizing. In person, the **accent** of our language can reveal where we are from and sometimes often our social class. But even the written form of language, when stripped of **paralinguistic** features like accent, can still provide insight into our identity and social distinctions. This guiding conceptual question requires us to explore how this is possible.

First, let's clarify what we mean by the terms 'social distinctions' and 'identity':

- **Identity:** In psychology, the term 'identity' is taken to mean the characteristics and idiosyncrasies that make you who you are. You have a particular way of speaking, acting and seeing the world that is unique to you. These are influenced by how you define yourself, and are often tied in with the social distinctions below.
- **Social distinctions:** Despite us all being unique, humans like to categorize, and we also like to fit within communities. This process of classifying ourselves into groups is often called social distinctions. There are a great many forms of social distinction, and we are often members of multiple social groups at the same time. Below are some of the main social distinctions we see in most societies:
    - **Social class:** Most societies contain people who have differing amounts of wealth, power, authority and esteem. This leads to differing access to educational opportunities, healthcare, culture and leisure time. These differences can be broadly grouped into the following classes: upper class, middle class and working class. Each has a strong bearing on a person's chances of success in life, and each has its own particular characteristics.
    - **Race, ethnicity and cultural background:** People are often grouped by their race, ethnicity and cultural background – of course, these particular aspects of someone are often inter-linked.
    - **Gender and sexuality:** People within different genders and sexualities often share characteristics and may be treated differently depending on which group they are in.

Each of us is at the point of intersection between these various social groupings, something known as **intersectionality**; for example, you may be a middle-class, black, Christian, hetereosexual American woman. This provides a mix of advantages and disadvantages that impact your opportunities in life.

Our primary focus is language, and each of these social distinctions has an impact on how people speak and what they say. More often than not, particular vocabulary, accents and sometimes even grammar are distinct to a particular social group. All of these are deviations from what we call **Standard English**. This is one of many **linguistic terms** that help us talk about ways of speaking language. Below are some key terms that you will need to understand.

■ Table 2.6.1

Term	Definition	Example
Accent	The pronunciation of words	The difference between an American accent and a British accent
Contraction	The process of shortening a word by **elision** and/or combining two words	would've (would have); can't (can not)
Dialect	A form of English that is specific to a particular region or social group	The Scottish use of 'bairn' to mean 'child'
Elision	The omission of a sound or syllable when speaking, sometimes combined with contraction	I'm (I am); dunno (don't know)
Ellipsis	When a word or words are omitted from a sentence for expediency, creating an informal and casual tone	You going? ('are' has been omitted)
Mother tongue	Mother tongue is generally understood to mean the language of your parents and that you are exposed to from birth	Often, people learn English as a second language and have a mother tongue of a different language
Phonetic spelling	Words written in such a way as to mimic how they sound when spoken	How lang wull yah be? ('How long will you be?' in a Scottish accent)
Received pronunciation	The standard accent of English based on how it is spoken by educated people in southern England	The Queen speaks with received pronunciation
Slang	Words and phrases regarded as very informal and often used in place of Standard English words	'Fleek' for something that is attractive or stylish
Standard English	The standard spelling, punctuation, grammar and vocabulary that is considered acceptable wherever English is spoken or understood	Use of formal English as opposed to dialect or slang

Social distinctions: social class through accent and dialect

We will begin by looking at texts that focus on social class. Our first text, *Pygmalion*, demonstrates how a person's accent and dialect can affect how they are viewed and treated by society. Our second text, an article from Britain's *The Economist*, shows how such attitudes to accent and language also exist in America, and are heavily tied in with race. Our third extract, from the *Radio Times*, calls on society to address this problem by having wider representation of accents in the media in order to prevent prejudice being attached to certain ways of talking.

Pygmalion by George Bernard Shaw (1913)

George Bernard Shaw

George Bernard Shaw (1856–1950) was an Irish playwright, **polemicist** and political activist. He grew up as part of the landed gentry of Ireland, but his father mismanaged the family's wealth, causing Shaw to grow up in a type of genteel poverty. This is something Shaw found humiliating, and it made him keenly aware of social class growing up. His mother eventually left his father and moved away, with Shaw eventually following her to London. There he lived in poverty while attempting to become a writer. However, the novels he produced were rejected by various publishers. He had more success as a journalist, particularly as a theatre critic. It is around this time that he started writing plays himself, and it is here he finally found the literary success he had been craving. His realist plays were frequently controversial, often dealing with political, social and religious issues. He had an enormous and lasting impact on British theatre, living until the age of 94 years old.

Our first text is about the British social class system. Britain is a nation with a strong history of treating people differently based on their class, an attitude which still persists today, albeit to a lesser degree. It is a stratified society, which means it is made up of distinct layers in a kind of hierarchy. At the bottom is the **working class** – traditionally people with low paying jobs in manual labour; in the middle is **middle class** – traditionally educated people who work in professions; and at the top is the **upper class** – traditionally landed gentry (people who own significant land), political leaders and aristocracy. Our first text demonstrates how these social classes had distinct **accents** and **dialects**, often affecting how people interacted with them.

Pygmalion is a comedy about love and the British class system. It is named after a Greek myth regarding a king who sculpted his idea of perfect womanhood and then fell in love with the sculpture. To answer his prayers, the goddess Venus brought the sculpture to life. This myth has parallels with the play, in which a British phonetician, Higgins, takes a lower-class flower girl and teaches her to speak and act like a higher-class woman. Higgins is essentially creating his image of perfect womanhood through education instead of sculpture. He teaches her to speak in a style that is known as **received pronunciation**, a particular accent that uses **Standard English** rather than a regional **dialect**. However, unlike the myth that inspired it, Higgins immediately loses interest in her once she has become his image of what a woman should be. The play reflects England's historically rigid class-based society, with a person's accent and vocabulary being the most obvious signifier of social status. This social status would have a dramatic impact on a person's opportunities in life and how they were treated by society.

For our first extract from this play, in Act 1, we will focus on how Eliza (the flower girl) has her very particular style of language represented in the script.

London at 11.15pm … Pedestrians running for shelter into the portico of St Paul's church (not Wren's cathedral but Inigo Jones's church in Covent Garden vegetable market).

[FREDDY comes into collision with a flower girl who is hurrying in for shelter, knocking her basket out of her hands. A blinding flash of lightning, followed instantly by a rattling peal of thunder, orchestrates the incident].

THE FLOWER GIRL:	Nah then, Freddy: look wh' y' gowin, deah.
FREDDY:	Sorry *[he rushes off].*
THE FLOWER GIRL:	*[picking up her scattered flowers and replacing them in the basket]:* Theres menners f' yer! Te-oo banches o voylets trod into the mad. ----*[She sits down on the plinth of the column, sorting her flowers …]*
THE MOTHER:	How do you know that my son's name is Freddy, pray?
THE FLOWER GIRL:	Ow, eez, ye-ooa san, is e? Wal, fewd dan y' d-ooty bawmz a mather should, eed now bettern to spawl a pore gel's flahrzn than ran awy athaht pyin. Will ye-oo py me f'them? *[Here, with apologies, this desperate attempt to represent her dialect without a phonetic alphabet must be abandoned as unintelligible outside London] …*

(George Bernard Shaw, Act 1 9–11)

In this scene, the audience is introduced to Eliza and her cockney accent and dialect (the type of English spoken by many working-class Londoners). Cockneys are known for being quick-witted, tough and having a good sense of humour, as well as for their very distinctive accent. Shaw uses a stage direction to apologize for his phonetic spelling of her accent, saying that he only uses it to illustrate her manner of speaking at the beginning and will abandon if for the rest of the script as it would otherwise be 'unintelligible outside London'. Each line of hers in this short extract, both in style and content, reveals how cockneys were viewed by society.

ACTIVITY 1

Eliza is speaking in a very particular dialect called 'cockney' – you may recognize it from films like *Mary Poppins*. You can hear the actor Michael Caine discuss his cockney accent by following the adjacent QR code. Shaw has used phonetic spelling to convey how she pronounces words – see if you can write out Eliza's spoken dialogue in Standard English. Once you are done, compare it to the 'translation' in the back of the book. Do you have an accent of your own? If so, you could also attempt rewriting her lines phonetically in your own accent.

Eliza's first line in the play, 'Nah then, Freddy: look wh' y' gowin, deah' (line 6), means 'Now then Freddy: look where you are going, my dear' in Standard English. The phonetic spelling, for example, 'nah' to mean 'now', captures the nasal cockney accent and immediately identifies her as a working-class Londoner. A higher-class man has bumped into her, and she reacts with the plucky and slightly cheeky attitude that was seen as being typical of working-class Londoners. She is immediately confrontational with Freddy, using an **imperative** to admonish him despite his higher social standing. Being so bold and familiar with a stranger would have been considered improper by the upper classes, but Eliza's particular regional social class has a very different manner, as demonstrated by her imperative use of language and her familiar use of the term 'dear' when speaking to a stranger.

Her next line means 'There's manners for you! Two bunches of violets trodden into the mud'.

In criticizing his manners, she is implying that he should have known better, particularly as a member of a higher class. That he dismissively bumped into her and did not stop to help shows that lower-class people were often seen as invisible by the upper classes – had it been a middle or upper class woman, he would almost certainly have stopped to apologize more formally and helped pick up the flowers.

We are then again shown the boldness typical of cockneys as Eliza says 'Oh, he's your son, is he? Well, if you had done your duty by him as a mother should, he'd know better than to spoil a poor girl's flowers then to run away without paying. Will you pay me for them?' (line 14).

Eliza's speech here is in stark **juxtaposition** with Freddy's mother's speech. Her formal question is met with a personal attack as Eliza questions her abilities as a mother. Again, her accent and the content of her words show characteristics typical of her regional social class, and the contrast with the mother's use of Standard English makes clear that accent and dialect are key to revealing social class in British society.

In our next extract, we will look at the importance of accent and how the way Eliza speaks is used by middle-class Higgins to define her as a person.

THE NOTE TAKER: Simply phonetics. The science of speech. That's my profession; also my hobby. Happy is the man who can make a living by his hobby! You can spot an Irishman or a Yorkshireman by his brogue. I can place any man within six miles. I can place him within two miles in London. Sometimes within two streets.

THE FLOWER GIRL: Ought to be ashamed of himself, unmanly coward!

THE GENTLEMAN: But is there a living in that?

THE NOTE TAKER: Oh yes. Quite a fat one. This is an age of upstarts. Men begin in Kentish Town with 80 pounds a year, and end in Park Lane with a hundred thousand. They want to drop Kentish Town; but they give themselves away every time they open their mouths. Now I can teach them—

THE FLOWER GIRL: Let him mind his own business and leave a poor girl—

THE NOTE TAKER *[explosively]*: Woman: cease this detestable boohooing instantly; or else seek the shelter of some other place or worship.

THE FLOWER GIRL *[with feeble defiance]*: I've a right to be here if I like, same as you.

THE NOTE TAKER: A woman who utters such depressing and disgusting sounds has no right to be anywhere – no right to live. Remember that you are a human being with a soul and the divine gift of articulate speech: that your native language is the language of Shakespeare and Milton and The Bible: and don't sit there crooning like a bilious pigeon.

THE FLOWER GIRL *[quite overwhelmed, looking up at him in mingled wonder and deprecation without daring to raise her head]*: Ah-ah-ah-ow-ow-ow-oo!

THE NOTE TAKER *[whipping out his book]*: Heavens! what a sound! *[He writes; then holds out the book and reads, reproducing her vowels exactly]* Ah-ah-ah-ow-ow-ow-oo!

THE FLOWER GIRL *[tickled by the performance, and laughing in spite of herself]*: Garn!

THE NOTE TAKER: You see this creature with her kerbstone English: the English that will keep her in the gutter to the end of her days. Well, sir, in three months I could pass that girl off as a duchess at an ambassador's garden party. I could even get her a place as lady's maid or shop assistant, which requires better English.

THE FLOWER GIRL: What's that you say?

THE NOTE TAKER: Yes, you squashed cabbage leaf, you disgrace to the noble architecture of these columns, you incarnate insult to the English language: I could pass you off as the Queen of Sheba.

(George Bernard Shaw 17–18)

Here, Shaw makes clear the distinctive qualities of British accents. Britain is notorious for its variety of accents; despite being a relatively small country, there exist a vast array of **accents** and **dialects** that have sometimes developed only miles apart from each other. This is often used in a prejudicial way, with stereotypes developing such as northern English accents suggesting a lack of education, and cockney accents suggesting criminality. In the play, the middle-class character Higgins (referred to as the 'note taker' in our extract) can geographically pinpoint where a person was brought up from the way they speak in very specific detail, something of a party trick. Shaw is satirizing the British obsession with accents by presenting a character that has this superhuman ability to locate someone's origin and then judge them by it.

This note taker's prejudice is shown in his describing of his time as being one of 'upstarts' (line 7). He is referring to improving social mobility, which means an improving ability to climb the social ladder from working class to middle class. The particular use of 'upstart' has a negative connotation, as if the person does not necessarily belong in their new, higher position. The example given is of moving from 'Kentish Town' (line 7), a lower-class area of London, to 'Park Lane' (line 8), an upper-class area, showing that working-class people are starting to find financial success. However, he claims that 'every time they open their mouths' (lines 9–10) their humble origins are revealed. A clear snobbery is shown; Higgins believes that the way people speak defines them, and that even if they have managed to attain the typical economic success of a higher-class person, they are still lower class because of the way they speak. Essentially, they need to speak Standard English with a received pronunciation accent in order to be truly accepted into high society, something shown later in the play with Eliza's new manner of speaking allowing her a social ascent.

Eliza's cockney accent leads to quite vicious criticism of her as a person. The description of her 'kerbstone English' (line 26) is a particularly revealing characterization. It suggests she belongs on the kerb next the gutter, a symbolically low place often occupied by the homeless and by poverty-stricken people selling items or begging in the street. Higgins is saying that her particular type of English shows how far down the social scale she is. Her way of speaking is contrasted with that of Shakespeare, Milton and the Bible, all examples of high culture and importance; it is as if she is defiling a language that is capable of such beauty. Because of this, she is dehumanized as a 'bilious pigeon' (lines 18–19) implying her manner of speaking is subhuman. Though humorous in its hyperbole, this reveals a very real snobbery to accent and dialect in British society. As if to illustrate his point, she responds in guttural interjections as she attempts to express frustration and annoyance, 'Ah-ah-ah-ow-ow-ow-oo!' (line 21) His writing down in the notebook of these sounds, as if she is an animal being studied, further illustrates this divide in class and the lack of respect poor people receive. Higgins then says that better English is needed to be a 'lady's maid' or a 'shop assistant' (lines 28–29).

The playwright is making clear to the audience that language defines a person's social standing, and that even jobs may be denied you if you do not speak in the correct way. Shaw is satirizing this aspect of British society to criticize it; he shows an exaggerated and humorous example of someone being judged by the way they speak to show the ridiculousness of it. It is obviously unfair that people are judged by superficial signifiers of class rather than on the content of their character. Shaw was quite pragmatic about this issue. He was well aware that people often have to adapt their manner of speaking to fit in, even writing in the preface to the play that he hopes it acts to the 'encouragement of people troubled with accents that cut them off from all high employment'. In one of his many essays, Shaw criticized the English language and its unsuitable alphabet, suggesting it is inherently difficult for English to be spoken consistently and easily, and that this creates the various regional dialects and accents that are used to fuel divides in social class.

To explore this issue further, we will look at two recent articles focused on the issue of accent and dialect. After reading both, you will get an opportunity to share your own thoughts on this issue.

'Black voices, white voices: the cost of accents' *The Economist* (2018)

The following article from *The Economist* primarily focuses on America, showing that the issues in *Pygmalion* are not exclusively British. It shows that accent is not only used to identify social class, but also race, and that this can lead to similar prejudices and mistreatment.

Black voices, white voices: the cost of accents

Sounding black has a profound impact on Americans' lives

BY COINCIDENCE, two big new films feature race, voice and the telephone in America. In Spike Lee's *BlacKkKlansman*, based on a true story, a black policeman, successfully putting on his whitest-sounding voice, convinces a Ku Klux Klansman he is a supporter. (When the time comes to meet the group in person, he enlists a white partner.) And in Boots Riley's *Sorry to Bother You*, the down-on-his-luck young black protagonist, Cassius Green (Lakeith Stanfield), takes a job in telemarketing. A wise old black colleague (played by Danny Glover) tells him: 'You wanna make some money here? Use your white voice.' And as if flipping a switch, Mr Glover's character demonstrates it. Cassius learns his own white voice (played by David Cross, a white comedian), and soon he is on a rocket-ride to success.

Sorry to Bother You is an absurd magical-realist romp. The truth of race and voice in America is not. The second half of the film is more about free-for-all capitalism than it is about race. But the thread that links them is that sounding black is costly.

Americans know instinctively that 'Cassius Green' is more likely to be black than white, and many studies have shown that applicants with typically black names get fewer responses from potential employers than otherwise identical ones with white names. But voices offer clues to race, too, through timbre and accent. In 1999 John Baugh, a black professor at Washington University in St Louis, who grew up in Philadelphia and Los Angeles and has several accents at his command, rang round estate agents and found that they were less likely to offer him properties in white or Hispanic neighbourhoods when he used his black voice. When he used his white voice, he was mostly offered white neighbourhoods and when he used his Hispanic voice he was mostly offered Hispanic ones.

Two decades on, Kelly Wright, a graduate student at the University of Michigan, carried out a similar study. Ms Wright is the daughter of a German mother and an African-American-Cherokee father, was raised in Knoxville, Tennessee, and has a native command of black, standard American and southern white accents. She made recordings of all three accents, and had a group of 340 subjects rate the person they heard. Speaking in her black accent, she was judged to be more 'difficult' and 'poor' than when she used the other two. The white accent was considered the most 'pleasant', 'educated', 'attractive', 'confident', 'trustworthy' and 'rich'. The southern accent scored between the two on most of the rankings. Sounding southern and white costs you a bit; sounding black costs a lot.

Ms Wright is now updating Mr Baugh's study, calling property managers to find out whether they respond with offers, enticing information or special deals. Overt discrimination – 'you can't see the place' – remains rare, she says; subtle steering towards this or that kind of home is commoner.

The British discriminate on the basis of class and region more than race. British newspapers often report on studies of which accents sound the most pleasant or intelligent (Received Pronounciation, south-eastern and posh without being grand), which the most annoying or ill-educated (Birmingham, Liverpool and Manchester). Ambitious people from outside the south-east are told to 'lose their accents' (speak RP, in other words) if they want to do well.

The consequences of voice discrimination are profound. Consider those studies of estate agents. A house in a good area is a ticket to a good school, which allows your children to mix with the right sort of people and thus acquire the right accent so that the virtuous cycle continues. All of this, of course, works the other way around, too.

Society can approach this problem in two ways. One is to expect everyone to learn the most mainstream, least noticeable accent. Black Americans who sound like Barack Obama can expect to be condescendingly called 'articulate', but at least they will face less discrimination. Not everyone, however, has a white parent from whom to learn that accent, and adults can't easily change the way they speak. An alternative is for people to stop judging each other on the basis of their voices. People can be inarticulate in standard accents, or eloquent in looked-down-upon minority ones. Accent prejudice isn't just wrong; it's irrational.

(Johnson)

This article makes some interesting points regarding accent, and echoes the sentiment of Higgins in our *Pygmalion* extract: your accent will be used to define you, whether it is fair to or not. It does so through referencing experts and studies, frequent use of declarative sentences, and a powerful concluding sentence that asserts accent discrimination is 'irrational' (line 41). Depsite this irrationality, it remains a global phenomenon, with language and accent being used to define social distinctions and identities in countries all around the world.

DISCUSSION

Can you think of examples of discrimination through dialect or accent in your own context?

Consider your own accent and dialect – what advantages and disadvantages does it provide you with in the country you reside in? How does this change when you travel abroad?

CONCEPT CONNECTION

REPRESENTATION

Representing accents in the media

Representation has become increasingly important in the media and in literature. It began in the 1800s with the development of realism as a genre – suddenly, rather than portraying the courts of Kings and Queens, novels and plays were being set in the houses and streets of middle- and working-class people. This trend has continued to the modern day – in everything from films to TV shows to books, a much wider array of races, social classes, sexualities and ethnicities are being represented in a positive way. This is a powerful tool – in being represented in texts, people can feel accepted in a society and at peace with who they are. Popular shows like *Modern Family* depict a variety of races, ethnicities, sexual orientations, social classes and gender orientations to reflect how people are in the real world. Increasingly, a character being gay is seen as incidental rather than a major plot point, and this normalizes issues like homosexuality in a way that shows tremendous progress from the prejudices of the past. Thanks to this, people feel less of a pressure to conform to some sort of narrow 'ideal' portrayed in the media, and a much broader variety of people can celebrate their individuality and distinctiveness.

Our next op-ed extract deals with this concept and calls on further inroads to be made in terms of representing a variety of accents in TV news.

www.radiotimes.com/news/tv/2018-01-09/there-needs-to-be-a-more-diverse-range-of-voices-reading-the-news/

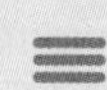

There needs to be a more diverse range of voices reading the news

British television executives may think there is a rich spread of voices on the small screen, but in fact the extraordinarily varied historic dialects of our language are effectively censored. The few times you do hear them it's for light entertainment – usually poking fun. The only exception is when a disaster occurs and news reporters seeks bystanders to react – then we do get to hear how the people of Britain really speak countrywide.

Why? The answer is obvious: our great national taboo, social class. The working-class voice is excluded from British television. Surveys report that Britons don't like the accents of the industrial cities, such as Birmingham. They reportedly feel more kindly towards 'quaint' rural voices, but with the correlative stereotypes that rural speakers sound thick and urban speakers sound criminal.

[…]

There's nothing wrong with Standard English, of course. It's highly useful the world over, and I'm writing in it now. But it's not the only dialect, and it's not the one most speakers use. If you speak Birmingham dialect with a Birmingham accent, you are, by definition, a working-class Brummie rather than an earl. So saying you don't like Birmingham accents really means you don't like Birmingham working-class people. It says nothing about your aesthetic sensibilities and everything about your social conditioning. If regional dialect speakers are excluded from television – as they currently are – then that is the same thing as excluding working-class people. Which is to say, excluding most of the population of Britain.

(Laura Wright)

CHECK FOR UNDERSTANDING

See how many features of an op-ed you can write down from memory.

Next, note down all the rhetorical techniques you can spot in the previous extract – you will be putting some of them to use in our next activity.

The previous op-ed makes a compelling argument regarding accent. The use of the modal verb 'needs' (line 1) creates an assertive tone that helps convince the reader that more diversity in the media is necessary. Effective use of **hypophora** in line 6 provides clear answers to questions the reader is prompted to consider, and the final paragraph uses an emotive argument that makes clear prejudice towards accents is prejudice towards people.

Evidently, there is still a problem with representation of accent, particularly in areas of prestige such as TV news. This is again down to language and the accent with which it is spoken being used to apply social distinctions, and those social distinctions often having stereotypes and prejudices attached to them.

ACTIVITY 2

To explore this concept, there are two activities to complete.

1 Rewrite the second *Pygmalion* extract, providing Eliza (the flower girl) an opportunity to assert her individuality and react against the pressure to conform being put on her by Higgins (the note taker).
2 Using your notes from the op-ed key features box in Chapter 2.3 to help you, write an op-ed about your opinions on the importance of representing a variety of dialects in the media – if possible, link it to your own context.

Identity: race, ethnicity and cultural background

Our next texts are focused on race, ethnicity and cultural background. We will begin by focusing on the idea of language and its links to ethnicity and cultural background.

Mother tongue

You are studying this course in English, a language considered the **lingua franca** of the world – a global language that is the standard common language to be used between speakers whose native languages are different. If you are in a country where the official language is not English, then there is a good chance you are bilingual or perhaps even multilingual. In that case, your identity may be complicated by your many languages, and you may find you express yourself better in one more than the other. The following poems explore this notion of identity being affected by the language we speak.

'Speak White' by Michèle Lalonde (1968)

Michèle Lalonde

Michèle Lalonde (born 1937) is a French-Canadian poet, playwright and essayist. She was born in Montréal and gained a degree in philosophy from Montréal University. She is best known for her strong political views on Québec, best illustrated in her poem 'Speak White'. She has written two plays and several collections of poetry, and in 1984 became the president of the International Federation of French-language Writers.

'Speak White' is a poem about the inferior cultural, economic and social conditions French Canadians were living with in comparison to English-speaking Canadians. Québec is the second-most populous province of Canada, and the majority of people there speak French as their first language. In order to succeed, it was often felt you needed to speak English, and there was a worry that French was going to eventually be displaced. This echoes Eliza in *Pygmalion*, but this time it is the actual language itself rather than accent and dialect being used to judge people by. Québec has historically felt poorly treated by the Canadian government, and there have been attempts to become independent. During the 1970s, there was political tension in the region as the *Front de Libération du Québec* (a paramilitary group that wanted Québec's separation from Canada) kidnapped a British diplomat and kidnapped and murdered the Vice Minister of Québec. In the wake of this, the government arrested hundreds of people they suspected of separatism. In support of these political prisoners and the French heritage of Québec, a night of poetry was held. The most famous of these poems is 'Speak White' by Michèle Lalonde, the original performance of which you can watch by following the adjacent QR code (with English subtitles).

'Speak white' was a term used by American slave owners to force their slaves to speak in English rather than their native languages. This prevented them from secretly plotting escapes and helped erase their heritage and memories of their home countries, helping ensure they remained under control. This was also a phrase sometimes used by English-speaking Canadians towards French-speaking Canadians, expecting them to communicate in English in order to get jobs or financial support. The term, then, has resonance and impact due to its history of oppression, colonialism and imperialism.

The poem was originally performed mostly in French, with the sections in italics being spoken in English. Below is the opening section of the poem. The sections (a), (b), (c) and (d) will be analysed – (a) and (b) will be completed for you, and you will have to analyse sections (c) and (d) yourself.

Speak White

Speak white
It sounds so good when you
Speak of Paradise Lost
And of the gracious and anonymous profile that trembles
In Shakespeare's sonnets

(a) We're an uncultured stammering race
But we are not deaf to the genius of a language
Speak with the accent of Milton and Byron and Shelley and Keats
Speak white
And forgive us our only answer

Being the raucous songs of our ancestors
And the sorrows of Nelligan
Speak white
(b) Talk about this and that
Tell us about Magna Carta

Or the Lincoln Memorial
The grey charm of the Thames
The pink waters of the Potomac
Tell us about your traditions
As a people we don't really shine

But we're quite capable of appreciating
All the significance of crumpets
Or the Boston Tea Party
But when you *really speak white*
When you *get down to brass tacks*

(c) To talk about gracious *living*
And speak of standing in life
And the Great Society
A bit stronger then, *speak white*
Raise your foremen's voices

We're a bit hard of hearing
We live too close to the machines
And we only hear the sound of our breathing over the tools.
Speak white and loud
So that we can hear you

From St-Henri to St-Domingue
What an admirable tongue
For hiring
Giving orders

Setting the time for working yourself to death
And for the pause that refreshes
And invigorates the dollar
(d) *Speak white*
Tell us that God is a great big shot
And that we're paid to trust him
Speak white
Talk to us about *production profits* and percentages
Speak white
It's a rich language
For buying
But for selling
But for selling your soul
But for selling out

(Michèle Lalonde)

With section **(a)**, the poem begins in sarcastic fashion, ironically describing French speakers as the narrator feels they are viewed by English-speaking Canadians, an 'uncultured stammering race' (line 6). The use of the plural first person pronoun 'we' puts the narrator in the position of representing all French-speaking Canadians, and the sarcastic apology for 'stammering' when speaking in English sets up the poem to be a reassertion of their fluent and native-tongue: French. The narrator then makes clear that they do appreciate the genius of a series of prominent English language literary figures such as 'Milton' (line 8). However, this language and culture is forced upon them with the imperative 'speak white' (line 9). This command to assert cultural dominance is met with an answer of the 'raucous songs of our ancestors / and the sorrows of Nelligan' (lines 11–12). This is a reference to French-Canadian culture – they do not have the depth of history English has with Milton, Byron, Shelley and Keats, but instead they have French folk songs and the works of French-Canadian Émile Nelligan, a poet born in Québec. In showing the parallel culture of Francophone Canadians, they make clear that they have their own cultural background that does not need to be replaced with the famous English-language playwrights and poets – these songs and poems are part of their identity.

Section **(b)** focuses on the cultural imperialism of the English language, in particular of British and American culture being forced on French Canadians. The verbs 'talk' (line 14) and 'tell' (line 15) suggest they are constantly spoken down to about English-language culture, with the listing of cultural places like the American Lincoln Memorial and cultural documents like the British Magna Carta being relentlessly forced upon them as if they are their own. Amid this relentless listing of English-language culture, the narrator claims 'as a people we don't really shine' (line 20), a self-deprecating claim suggesting they cannot compete with the culture and history of these two countries, but they are capable of 'appreciating' it. Again, a sense of French-Canadian culture being under siege by English-language culture is created, making the people unsure of themselves and creating a lack of cultural confidence and assertiveness.

ACTIVITY 3

Using the examples above to help you, analyse parts **(c)** and **(d)** of the poem, then compare your responses to those in the back of the book.

GLOBAL ISSUES *Field of Inquiry:* **Politics, Power and Justice**

LANGUAGE AND POWER

This is a powerful poem exploring how language is tied in with power. English has spread throughout the world largely on the back of the British Empire and, more recently, American economic success (this will be explored in more detail in Chapter 3.2). Because of the global reach of American companies, the language of business is English, and this has had a profound impact on countries around the world. In Québec there has been political and economic pressure to speak English in order to share in the wealth of global business, and the poem makes clear this is a kind of colonialism. English is the language of the 'foremen' (line 30), of those in power, and Canadian French is the language of the workers, of those without power. In order to gain a position of power, English is seen as a prerequisite, and in order to make political change, English is needed to communicate with the Canadian government. These close ties between English and politics, English and power, and English and attempts at getting justice, is problematic. To conduct business globally, countries often have their native language sidelined, and this can lead to English words seeping into common usage – even 'global' and 'business' have been adopted into the French language, for example. International schools are another example of this – throughout the world there are students being educated entirely in English despite being in countries where this is not the official language. In doing so, English language culture like Shakespeare and Milton begins to displace the culture of the native language, an issue addressed in section (a) of 'Speak White'. In the global economy, these English-educated students often go on to have positions of financial success and power, helping solidify English as the language of the elite. You may see this in your own context if it is a largely non-English speaking country – is speaking English common among the wealthy but not the poor? Does this create division in society? Is this if a form of colonialism? Are you yourself part of the problem?

TOK Links

Read the article linked in the adjacent QR code. If language affects which culture you access, and culture influences knowledge, is the spread of English fundamentally changing the reality of the world we inhabit? Should we be viewing the world through the lens of our own culture and language, rather than one that has been spread through colonialism and linguistic imperialism?

'Bilingual Sestina' by Julia Alvarez (1995)

Our next poem is about language and its impact on **identity**, but this time on a much more personal scale. 'Bilingual Sestina' focuses on Alvarez's experience of growing up between two cultures and languages. It explores a person who is trapped between the past and the present, the Spanish and the English, the Dominican and the American. It occasionally **code switches** between English and Spanish to represent this mixed heritage and identity.

Julia Alvarez

Julia Alvarez (born 1950) is a Dominican-American poet, novelist and essayist. She was born in New York but spent the first ten years of her life growing up in the Dominican Republic, where Spanish is widely spoken. While there, her father became involved in a failed coup and consequently needed to flee to the United States with his family. This experience of trying to assimilate into what was a new culture that did not use her native language had a big impact on her growing up. She became introverted and sought refuge in books. She grew up to focus on teaching and writing, and has since become one of the most successful Latina writers of the current day. Her writing predominantly focuses on cultural expectations of women, stereotypes and identity.

The form of the poem is a **sestina**, a complicated form that is explained in the key features box.

KEY FEATURES SESTINA

- **Six stanzas of six lines:** The poem has a very clear form, the most obvious of which is the consistent stanza length.
- **Line endings:** The same six words are at the ends of the lines in each stanza. They are in a different order for each of the six stanzas following a complex pattern:

STANZA	I	... new order ...	STANZA II	III	IV	V	VI
end-word	1	2nd	6	3	5	4	2
	2	4th	1	6	3	5	4
	3	6th	5	4	2	1	6
	4	5th	2	1	6	3	5
	5	3rd	4	2	1	6	3
	6	1st	3	5	4	2	1

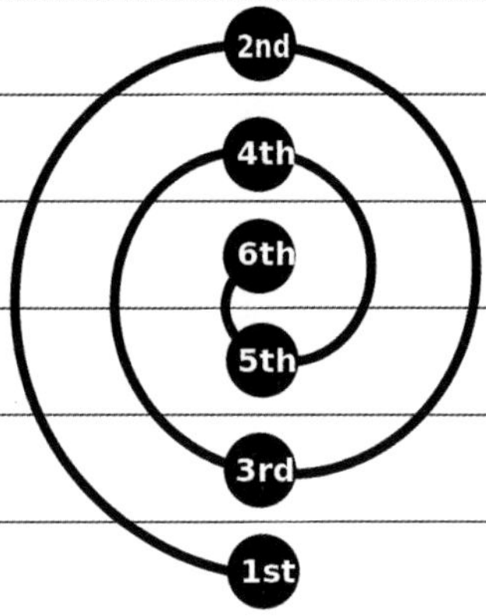

- **3 line 'envoi':** The poem ends in a special type of **tercet** (three line rhyming stanza) called an envoi. An envoi is a short stanza concluding a ballad, essentially the closing remarks to a poem that often address the reader or listener of the poem. In the sestina form, the six repeating end-line words should be used in the envoi.
- **Poem of complaint:** Historically, the poem's contents have been focused on a complaint of some sort, often about trouble caused by loving someone.

Bilingual Sestina

Some things I have to say aren't getting said
in this snowy, blonde, blue-eyed, gum chewing English,
dawn's early light sifting through the *persianas* closed
the night before by dark-skinned girls whose words
evoke *cama, aposento, suenos* in *nombres*
from that first word I can't translate from Spanish.

Gladys, Rosario, Altagracia–the sounds of Spanish
wash over me like warm island waters as I say
your soothing names: a child again learning the *nombres*
of things you point to in the world before English
turned *sol, tierra, cielo, luna* to vocabulary words–
sun, earth, sky, moon–language closed

like the touch-sensitive *morivivir.* whose leaves closed
when we kids poked them, astonished. Even Spanish
failed us when we realized how frail a word
is when faced with the thing it names. How saying
its name won't always summon up in Spanish or English
the full blown genii from the bottled *nombre.*

Gladys, I summon you back with your given *nombre*
to open up again the house of slatted windows closed
since childhood, where palabras left behind for English
stand dusty and awkward in neglected Spanish.
Rosario, muse of el patio, sing in me and through me say
that world again, begin first with those first words

you put in my mouth as you pointed to the world–
not Adam, not God, but a country girl numbering
the stars, the blades of grass, warming the sun by saying
el sol as the dawn's light fell through the closed
persianas from the gardens where you sang in Spanish,
Esta son las mananitas, and listening, in bed, no English

yet in my head to confuse me with translations, no English
doubling the world with synonyms, no dizzying array of words,
–the world was simple and intact in Spanish
awash with *colores, luz, suenos*, as if the *nombres*
were the outer skin of things, as if words were so close
to the world one left a mist of breath on things by saying

their names, an intimacy I now yearn for in English–
words so close to what I meant that I almost hear my Spanish
blood beating, beating inside what I say *en ingles.*

(Julia Alvarez)

ACTIVITY 4

Read the questions below and write down your thoughts and responses to them. Then read the subsequent commentary.

1 Why might Alvarez have used the sestina form?

2 How does Alvarez show that she has a closer bond to the Spanish language?

3 What is the significance of the envoi?

The use of the sestina form is artificial and complex, mimicking the artifice of language and the complexity of dealing with bilingualism. In having to maintain the rules of the sestina throughout, the use of language becomes unnatural and considered, in much the same way Alvarez feels when using English. The six words that are repeated throughout are 'said', 'English', 'closed', 'words', 'nombres' (names) and 'Spanish'. These are clearly central to the poem, and the notion of words being 'closed' ties in with the lines 'how frail a word / is when faced with the thing it names' (lines 15–16). The limitations of language are being explored by describing the frailty and inability of words to capture the quiddity or true essence of what it is referring to. This ties in with the narrator's experience – in speaking English, she feels she cannot capture her true feelings, and even in Spanish, the words sometimes seem hollow compared to the true experience of the world.

Despite this qualification, she does express a closer bond to the Spanish language. English is described as a 'snowy, blonde, blue-eyed, gum chewing' (line 2) language. This is a stereotypical American white person, and in personifying the language as such she implies that it cannot fully capture the experience of a Dominican and their different cultural background. The sounds of Spanish instead 'wash over me like warm island waters' (line 8). This natural imagery of this simile suggests the language is more natural and comforting to her, and the reference to an island links back to her past in the island nation of the Dominican Republic. In the second stanza, the words 'sol, tierra, cielo, luna' (line 11) are words that she learned by having someone 'point to' (line 10) them – she learned these words through experiencing them in the real world, giving them a much stronger attachment to experience. Contrastingly, the English equivalents of 'sun, earth, sky, moon' (line 12) are mere 'vocabulary' words, words learned in abstract and away from true experience, they are examples of 'language closed' (line 12) from her past experiences and history.

The envoi shows her desire for the English to be as central to her identity as the Spanish. She yearns for an 'intimacy' (line 37) with the English language, for it to be as fundamental to her identity, and for the words to have inside them her metaphorical 'blood beating' (line 39). This image of her blood, her essence, being inside the words shows the importance of language to experience and identity, and the power of a mother tongue compared to one learned as a secondary language. Ending the poem with 'en ingles' shows that, for her, the process of the English language being part of her identity has not quite happened for her yet, and perhaps it never will.

DISCUSSION

This poem powerfully shows the link between language and identity, and that the world we experience is often done so through language. In being bilingual, the narrator has two separate experiences of the world, yet the mother tongue is the one that is more evocative and closely tied to experience. If you yourself are bilingual, this poem may resonate with you. Which language for you is the most closely tied to how you experience the world?

'Mother to Son' by Langston Hughes (1922)

The next poem, 'Mother to Son' by Langston Hughes, focuses on language and how it can represent racial identity. 'Mother to Son' is a poem that shares the African American experience, and uses the language of black America at a time when it was rarely seen in print. The formal term for black America's particular way of speaking is **African American Vernacular English (AAVE)**. This style of speaking has developed over time and has its own grammatical rules and uses words that often deviate from Standard English. The adjacent QR link provides more insight into the complex rules of AAVE.

Langston Hughes

Langston Hughes (1902–1967) was an American poet, novelist, social activist, playwright and columnist. As with many Americans growing up in segregation-era America, race was a common theme of his writing. He focused on revealing the experiences, attitudes and language of black America to a wider audience. He had an influence on Martin Luther King and the Civil Rights Movement, and his poetry regarding dreams focused on the struggle of African-Americans and their need for escape from institutionalized racism.

The poem itself is a dramatic monologue of a mother talking to her son, symbolic of the older generation of African-Americans giving advice to the newer generation of African-Americans that were going to need to continue the struggle for acceptance and equality.

Mother to Son

Well, son, I'll tell you:
Life for me ain't been no crystal stair.
It's had tacks in it,
And splinters,
And boards torn up,
And places with no carpet on the floor—
Bare.
But all the time
I'se been a-climbin' on,
And reachin' landin's,
And turnin' corners,
And sometimes goin' in the dark
Where there ain't been no light.
So boy, don't you turn back.

Don't you set down on the steps
'Cause you finds it's kinder hard.
Don't you fall now—
For I'se still goin', honey,
I'se still climbin',
And life for me ain't been no crystal stair.

(Langston Hughes)

In this poem, AAVE is used to reflect how some African Americans speak. Using this **dialect** in a poem at a time of segregation was an act of defiance and confidence by Hughes, asserting black America's identity through language rather than conforming to white America's style of communication. One prominent example of AAVE can be seen in the use of double negative in 'life for me ain't been no crystal stair' (line 2). The use of a double negative for emphasis (even though the conventional rules of grammar dictate that his phrase means life *has* been a crystal stair) portrays an African-American woman speaking authentically, giving the poem added impact. The metaphor of a crystal stair works on two levels: the staircase itself represents progress for African-Americans like herself, an ascent that has been a battle; additionally the adjective 'crystal' suggests luxury, and this being denied implies the narrator's life has been one of poverty. This climb of progress has had many obstacles: 'tacks', 'splinters', 'boards torn up' and 'no carpet' (lines 3–6). These metaphorical obstacles represent the social and political obstacles put in place by white America to keep African-Americans in a position of subservience. They could represent segregation, denial of voting rights, limited educational opportunities, and limited workplace opportunities among a host of other problems.

Further use of AAVE is contraction and elision such as 'I'se' (line 9), 'turnin'' (line 11), 'goin'' (line 12) and ''cause' (line 16). Their usage creates a distinct voice for the character, a sense of authentic monologue that makes the reader feel as if they are being genuinely and directly spoken to, heightening the emotive impact of the struggles she describes. The **extended metaphor** of climbing and searching continues as the narrator describes searching in the 'dark' (line 12), with darkness representing how hard it is to find equality, as well as having to face up to the fear and evil it has connotations of. The sense of hardship is reinforced in 'Cause you finds it's kinder hard' (line 16). Here we can see another characteristic of AAVE, the ellipsis in omitting 'will'. The line is advice from a member of the older generation to the younger, passing on knowledge as the new generation continues the metaphorical climb and search for the light of justice and equality.

The representation of an African-American speaking in a natural, AAVE style was a bold statement by Hughes, embracing African-American identity through language and not conforming to **Standard English**. This was a choice he had the luxury to make as he had been provided with a good education and a strong grounding in Standard English, something the majority of African-Americans of the time were denied. This representation of an authentic voice in a work showed a belief that African-American culture could exist in the arts and should embrace its distinctiveness rather than adapt to fit in. The central metaphor extended throughout the poem made clear that this struggle needed to continue into the future until acceptance and equality was finally theirs.

Our next text looks at how AAVE has become far more commonplace since the time of Langston Hughes, and how its use by non-African-Americans can be seen as appropriating an identity that is not necessarily theirs to take. In reading this article, you may find that you yourself have been using words that have their origin in African-American culture without even realizing.

www.theguardian.com/commentisfree/2015/jan/14/white-people-declared-bae-over-black-people-can-use-it

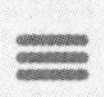

Now that white people have declared 'bae' over, black people can use it in peace

While 'bae' only made its way to mainstream parlance in the last few years, it is a word that most black folk have been intimately familiar with for decades. Its etymology was unclear, but its meanings and nuances are deeply understood in context. 'What's up, bae?' 'That's my bae', etc. have been ways of staking claim and announcing intimacy between oneself and one's (sometimes prospective) lover. Bae is also used as a term of endearment and affection for someone with whom there is no romantic involvement or interest (not unlike 'honey' or 'sweetheart' is used in Southern dialogue), as in 'Hey bae, can you pass me that plate?'

And then Pharrell put it in a song, Miley Cyrus did a cameo, and it gained the attention of mainstream media. Suddenly there were articles attempting to define the word 'bae', otherwise reputable businesses began implementing 'bae' in their social media ad campaigns, and everybody and they mama started using it. At which point it was declared overused by organs of upper-class white folk media like *Time* magazine.

Fair enough: white people's adoption of the term distorted it to the point of misuse and meaninglessness. What was once a word born of the beautifully eclectic black Southern laziness of the tongue and a shortened version of baby, became a catchall term for anything from inanimate objects to food. The reference to affection was consistent but bae was used to describe everything from one's (desired or actual) significant other to pancakes. 'That's bae', a student swooned, glancing at a picture of J Cole during a discussion of black masculinity last summer in class. 'These cupcakes are bae', I read in a Facebook post attached to a picture of a delicious-looking dessert not many months later. And just like that, the shelf life of bae in the public imagination expired and the gatekeepers of mainstream language decided that it must be banned.

Cultural appropriation at its best, steals, reduces, overuses and then disposes of words like so much bathwater. The linguist Jane H Hill defines language appropriation as 'a type of complex cultural borrowing that involves a dominant group's "theft" of aspects of a target group's language.' Hill claims that the 'theft' adds value to white identity while further marginalizing nondominant groups. This cultural 'borrowing' of black language and phraseology happens regularly, allowing non-black folk to 'try on' black culture through the use of African American English vernacular and slang without having to 'put on' the cultural consequences of actually being black in a culture conditioned to devalue and dismiss it.

As Hill claims, language appropriation is further problematic because it gives dominant groups control over the language. Dominant groups get to decide, for example, when and if certain words are worth appropriation, when and how the words should be used, and then when the word becomes cliché, overused and therefore passé. And often in the process, as happened with 'bae', the dominant group ends up changing the meaning or pronunciation of words entirely.

The good news is that black language is resilient and black folk are creative. So even when the dominant culture tries to dispose of the terms it wears out, other words and phrases will emerge. We already know some of them. Already you can see terms grounded in communities ('bye Felicia'), disguised in pronunciation ('ratchet'), or invented from imagination ('on fleek') slipping into mainstream and popular culture lexicons (again). There, they will be mass produced for financial gain (again), and eventually disposed of (again).

So, what happens when mainstream culture decides to dispose of a word stolen from black language and then used to the point of saturation in popular culture? Nothing. The word may lose its novelty so that those who appropriated it stop saying or using it, but the word won't disappear or lose its utility in the black community. We will go on saying bae. We will say it to our lovers in casual moments at home, and to our children to be endearing. We will say it in the grocery store, at the movie theatre and across church pews on Sunday mornings as a substitute for names. We will say it to each other – as we have always done – lovingly, reverently and mindfully. And with any luck, the word will settle back into its original meaning, sans the unsolicited remix of dominant white culture.

(Robin Boylorn)

This opinion article raises some interesting issues regarding language and identity. Words such as 'fleek', 'hella', 'throw shade' and 'slay' have their origins in AAVE, but have entered common usage through the internet and popular culture. As language is so closely tied to identity, some feel that in using such words, this identity is being appropriated by those to whom it does not belong.

AAVE has developed through the experience of African-Americans, something which cannot be shared by those who are not part of that culture and share that identity. This raises questions about such terms being adopted by others – are they just words, or are they something more? Is their use a celebration of African-American culture or another example of something being taken from a group that has historically suffered persecution and deprivation? Can people outside the African-American community decide whether it is okay to use these words or not?

ACTIVITY 5

Follow the QR codes opposite.

- **Source 1:** Consider how this performance poem conveys an African-American perspective on AAVE usage. This link may contact explicit language (top QR code).
- **Source 2:** Consider how the following article offers a defence of cultural appropriation (middle QR code).
- **Source 3:** Consider the following article arguing against cultural appropriation (bottom QR code).

This issue is not restricted to just African-American culture. Research this issue in more detail and write a persuasive speech explaining your considered views on the issue. Use the key features of persuasive speeches box in Chapter 1.4 to help you.

Conclusion

In this chapter we have seen how closely our identities are tied to the language we use, and how this can often be used to categorize us and even judge us. We have also seen how using the language of another group is problematic, and the ability of language to be shared through mediums such as the internet and memes is exposing us to forms of language that we otherwise may not come into contact with. Language is fundamental to how we experience and interact with the world, and thus ties directly in with our identities and positions in society.

Works cited

'African-American Vernacular English.' *Wikipedia*. Web. 13 Oct. 2019. **https://en.wikipedia.org/wiki/African-American_Vernacular_English**.

Alvarez, J. 'Bilingual Sestina.' Web. 13 March 2019. **http://intersession2005.tripod.com/Sestina.html**.

Anyangwe, E. 'There is no such thing as "harmless" cultural appropriation, and we must call it out if we hope to fight systemic oppresssion.' *Independent*, 1 May 2018. Web. 13 Oct. 2019. **www.independent.co.uk/voices/cultural-appropriation-prom-dress-chinese-keziah-daum-a8331326.html**.

Boylorn, R. 'Now that white people have declared "bae" over, black people can use it in peace.' *The Guardian*, 14 Jan. 2015. Web. 13 March 2019. **www.theguardian.com/commentisfree/2015/jan/14/white-people-declared-bae-over-black-people-can-use-it**.

Hughes, L. 'Mother to Son.' *Poetry Foundation*. Web. 13 March 2019. **www.poetryfoundation.org/poems/47559/mother-to-son**.

Johnson. 'Black voices, white voices: the cost of accents.' *The Economist*, 2 Aug. 2018. Web. 13 March 2019. **https://www.economist.com/books-and-arts/2018/08/02/black-voices-white-voices-the-cost-of-accents**.

Lalonde, M. 'Speak White.' Translated by Albert Herring, *everything2*, 24 Dec. 2001. Web. 13 March 2019. **www.everything2.com/index.pl?node_id=738881**.

Malik, K. 'In Defense of Cultural Appropriation.' *The New York Times*, 14 June 2017. Web. 13 Oct. 2019. **www.nytimes.com/2017/06/14/opinion/in-defense-of-cultural-appropriation.html**.

Phillipson, R. 'Linguistic imperialism alive and kicking.' *The Guardian*, 13 March 2012. Web. 13 Oct. 2019. **www.theguardian.com/education/2012/mar/13/linguistic-imperialism-english-language-teaching**.

Shaw, GB. *Pygmalion*. Penguin Classics, 2003.

'Speak White' read by Michele Lalonde. *Youtube*, 31 Oct.2016. Web. 13 Oct. 2019. **www.youtube.com/watch?v=Yx1-N6AFucw**.

Stevenson, R. (dir.) *Mary Poppins*. Walt Disney Studios HE, 1964.

'Sestina.' *Wikipedia, The Free Encyclopedia*, 4 Nov. 2018. Web. 13 March 2019. **https://en.wikipedia.org/w/index.php?title=Sestina&oldid=867219363**.

'Taylor Steele – "AAVE" (WoWPS 2016).' *Youtube*, 3 April 2016. Web. 13 Oct. 2019. **www.youtube.com/watch?v=xFgoiJ6udq8**.

Wright, Dr L. 'There needs to be a more diverse range of voices reading the news.' *Radio Times*, 9 Jan. 2018. Web. 13 March 2019. **www.radiotimes.com/news/tv/2018-01-09/there-needs-to-be-a-more-diverse-range-of-voices-reading-the-news**.

Intertextuality: connecting texts

How do texts adhere to and deviate from conventions associated with genre or text type?

OBJECTIVES OF CHAPTER

- To understand how to define the term 'genre'.
- To be able to recognize different generic conventions.
- To provide an overview of how and why generic conventions have evolved over time.
- To understand the reasons why writers may deliberately adhere to and deviate from generic and text-type conventions.
- To demonstrate ways to apply course concepts to specific works of literature and non-literary texts.
- To demonstrate ways to understand specific works of literature and non-literary texts in the context of global issues.

What does 'intertextuality' mean?

Intertexte in Latin means 'interwoven' and this is an apt way of defining the term 'intertextuality'.

To apply intertextuality to a non-literary text or a literary work essentially means to not view the text/work in isolation, but instead to view how it is connected to (or interwoven with) other works/texts. Intertextuality also includes an exploration of how the reader, bringing with them their life experience and exposure to various works and texts, can shape the meaning of a text/work and as a result interpret a text or work in a variety of ways.

This section will explore this approach in detail, examining how writers deliberately create connections, how these connections can organically occur and how readers themselves can create these connections.

How do we define genre and text type?

Before we begin to explore the ways in which texts and works adhere to and deviate from conventions associated with genre or text type, it is important to first think about how it is that we define genre and text type.

Throughout Sections 1 and 2 of this book, you have analysed the conventions of a wide array of text types and should now be familiar with their conventions. However, after reading Chapter 1.2, for example, you may be wondering *how* text types as diverse as a poem and an advisory text could possibly all be grouped together or be seen as being similar.

This is where it becomes important to explore what the word 'genre' could potentially mean. Some **synonyms** of the word include: category, set, grouping, style, variety. Essentially, when we place a literary work or a non-literary text into a genre, we are placing them into a specific classification. This means that we would expect the texts and works in this classification to share commonalities in form, content and style; for example, in their use of specific literary features, in their thematic focus or in their contextual concerns.

If we are to see genre as a way of categorizing or classifying works and texts, then how is it that we define these categories or classifications? The next part of this chapter will outline some of the ways in which we can identify the genre to which a text or work may belong, as well as exploring how some genres have been created.

Generic conventions: fiction and non-fiction

One of the key ways in which we classify works and texts is as **fiction** and **non-fiction**. Works and texts that are categorized as **fiction** are seen as not being true or factual, but instead created from the imagination of the writer. Literary works and non-fiction texts that are categorized as non-fiction are seen as being factual and true, and it is assumed that the writer has based the content on events exactly as they occurred in real life.

The following texts and works are both based on the real-life historical event of the British military-led removal of King Thibaw of Myanmar (formerly known as Burma) from his throne in 1885. The extract below is an online encyclopaedia entry from the oldest English-language encyclopaedia still in production. It is now published exclusively online, having its last print edition in 2010. This source details the facts of King Thibaw's dethroning and would be considered a piece of **non-fiction**. The second extract is a **prose** extract from *The Glass Palace* by Indian writer Amitav Ghosh. It describes the same event as the encyclopaedia, however this piece of prose would be considered **fiction**.

Britannica Online Encyclopaedia entry about King Thibaw of Myanmar

Thibaw, also spelled **Theebaw**, (born 1858, Mandalay, Burma—died Dec. 19, 1916, Ratnagiri Fort, India), last king of Burma, whose short reign (1878–85) ended with the occupation of Upper Burma by the British.

Thibaw was a younger son of King Mindon (reigned 1853–78) and studied (1875–77) in a Buddhist monastery. As king he was strongly influenced by his wife, Supayalat, and her mother, and his accession to the throne was accompanied by much violence and civil strife.

In an attempt to enlist the aid of the French against the British, who had annexed Lower Burma during his father's reign, Thibaw's government sent a mission to Paris in 1883. Two years later a commercial treaty was concluded, and a French representative arrived in Mandalay. Rumours circulated that Thibaw's government had granted the French economic concessions in exchange for a political alliance, and British officials in Rangoon, Calcutta, and London began demanding immediate annexation of Upper Burma.

An occasion for intervention was furnished by the case of the British-owned Bombay-Burmah Trading Corporation, which extracted teak from the Ningyan forest in Upper Burma. When Thibaw charged it with cheating the government, demanding a fine of £100,000, the Indian viceroy, Lord Dufferin, sent an ultimatum to Mandalay in October 1885 demanding a reconsideration of the case. Thibaw ignored the ultimatum, and on Nov. 14, 1885, the British invaded Upper Burma, capturing Mandalay two weeks later. Thibaw was deposed and Upper Burma incorporated into the province of British Burma. Thibaw was exiled to India, where he remained until his death.

(Thibaw, King of Myanmar)

The Glass Palace by Amitav Ghosh (2001)

The King walked out of the pavilion, flanked by Queen Supayalat and her mother. Halfway down the meandering path the Queen turned to look back. The Princesses were following a few paces behind with the maids. The girls were carrying their belongings in an assortment of boxes and bundles. Some had flowers in their hair, some were dressed in their brightest clothes. Dolly was walking beside Evelyn, who had Second Princess on her hip. The two girls were giggling, oblivious, as though they were on their way to a festival.

The procession passed slowly through the long corridors of the palace, and across the mirrored walls of the Hall of Audience, past the shouldered guns of the guard of honour and the snapped-off salutes of the English officers.

Two carriages were waiting by the east gate. They were bullock-carts, *yethas*, the commonest vehicles on Mandalay's streets. The first of the carts had been fitted out with a ceremonial canopy. Just as he was about to step in, the King noticed that his canopy had seven tiers, the number allotted to a nobleman, not the nine due to a king.

(Amitav Ghosh 43)

Amitav Ghosh

Amitav Ghosh was born in Kolkata (the capital of the Indian state of West Bengal) in 1956. He is best known for his works of historical fiction, most notably *The Ibis Trilogy,* for which he has received numerous literary awards and honours such as one of India's highest – the Sahitya Akademi Award. His writing primarily focuses on the inter-connected colonial histories of south Asia, south-east Asia and east Asia. He withdrew *The Glass Palace* from the Commonwealth Writers Competition in 2001 citing objections to the award only being open to works written in the English language. He now lives in New York and has worked in various roles in academia, including in institutions such as City University of New York and Harvard.

In Section 1 of this coursebook you will have become familiar with the text conventions of both prose and encyclopaedia entries (Chapters 1.1 and 1.2). Read the table below which outlines some of the conventions used in each extract, and how these conventions are used to communicate clearly to the reader why and how the source is non-fiction or fiction.

■ Table 3.1.1

Prose non-fiction: online encyclopaedia entry	**Prose fiction: *The Glass Palace***
The article title uses precise and concise **nouns** which helps the reader understand the exact and specific topic that the article will cover – this is useful for its informative and factual purpose as readers can easily locate this article on an online search engine just by using these key **nouns**.	The use of descriptive **verbs** and **adverbs** doesn't just tell the reader how the characters moved, but helps the reader imagine how they felt while moving; this has obviously been invented by the writer as he was not there when this event happened.
The text is organized logically and is very easy to follow and understand. For example, an overview of the key events of King Thibaw's life is provided in the introductory first paragraph. This information is expanded upon chronologically throughout the article. The precise and logical structure of the article helps to create a factual tone as the reader is not distracted by superfluous information.	The extract is told from a **third-person perspective** and focuses upon different characters at different times throughout the extract. This creates distance between the reader and the events, making it clear that these events are being re-told not from someone's actual memory of them happening, but from the writer's imagination.
The use of **hyperlinks** mean that the reader can find out more facts about this event if they need or want to and helps the reader trust the text as they can verify the facts given by clicking on the link.	The extract does not contain any **photographs** of the events described or **typography** to indicate direct quotation, which makes it clear to the reader that the events, and the feelings of the characters, as described are not based on a factual source.
There is no usage of **personal opinion**, **bias** or **emotive language** which helps to keep the text factual in tone as opposed to descriptive.	The extract makes use of many literary features such as **sensory language**, **figurative language** and **irony**, 'The two girls were giggling, oblivious, as though they were on their way to a festival'. This contributes to the descriptive nature of the extract and is designed to evoke an emotional response in the reader – perhaps one of sympathy for King Thibaw and his family.

DISCUSSION

It is clear from the table how each extract can be classified as non-fiction and fiction respectively. However, as a piece of fictional prose based on historical fact, *The Glass Palace* could potentially be seen as resisting a straightforward classification as 'fiction' or 'non-fiction'. Imagine that you are a librarian trying to decide where to place the book. Why should the book be placed in the fiction part of the library? Why should the book be placed in the non-fiction part of the library? See the Concept Connection box below for some responses to these questions.

CONCEPT CONNECTION

PERSPECTIVE AND TRANSFORMATION

There are good reasons to justify each perspective. For example, you could suggest that even though the author of *The Glass Palace* has fabricated the thoughts and feelings of his characters, the characters themselves and the events depicted are actual historical events which would justify the perspective that the novel should be placed in the non-fiction section of the library. However, you could also suggest that there are many other characters and events in the novel that are purely fabricated from the author's imagination, justifying the perspective that the novel should be placed in the fiction section of the library.

There are many examples of fictional prose based on historical fact. You could read any of the titles listed below and explore how the factual information of a historical event has been transformed into a work of fictional literature, and consider from whose perspective it is written. You could do this formally by creating a table, like the one modelled above, or discuss in groups.

- *Wolf Hall* and *Bring up the Bodies* by English writer Hilary Mantel are two fictional novels written from the perspective of Thomas Cromwell who was a powerful and leading figure in the court of King Henry VIII of England.
- *Homegoing* is a fictional novel by Ghanian-American writer Yaa Gyasi which charts the descendants of an Asante woman named Maame over the course of several hundreds of years.
- *Lincoln in the Bardo* by American writer George Saunders is a fictional experimental novel which focuses upon the premature death of William Lincoln, who was the son of former President of the United States Abraham Lincoln.

TOK Links

When reading the encyclopaedia extract it is clear that the conventions and content of the text lend it to being easily classified as an example of non-fiction. However, *The Glass Palace* is harder to classify as although it uses the conventions of a work of fictional prose, the events it describes did, largely, actually happen in real life.

Although we cannot know for certain the anguish and humiliation that King Thibaw felt as he and his family were unceremoniously exiled from their palace and country, we as human beings with a sense of pathos can probably surmise that this would be exactly how they *would* have felt at this moment. We could also presume, from our own life experience as having been children or knowing children of a similar age, that the ironic and innocent reaction of King Thibaw's children to this event 'as though they were on their way to a festival' as probably being entirely accurate given the likelihood of the children not realizing the gravity of the situation and because they were maybe even told that they actually were going on a holiday and not into permanent exile.

With this in mind, what are the boundaries between a fiction and non-fiction text and how are these boundaries determined?

Needless to say, it can often be difficult to neatly place texts into different and distinct genres. However, many of the classical writers who wrote during the time of Ancient Greece (roughly between 800BCE and 600AD) saw genre as static and wrote literature that maintained rigid adherence to rules pertaining to genre. The philosopher and scientist Aristotle, went even further to codify these rules writing an essay called 'Poetics' in around 335BC that is regarded today as the earliest surviving work focused on Western literary and dramatic theory. In this essay, Aristotle defined various genres of writing such as comedy, tragedy and epic poetry. It is also from this source, for instance, that it is claimed (probably inaccurately) that the idea of the classical 'unities' of time, place and action developed.

This is important as many writers have used these conventions ever since as a blueprint to guide the conventions used in their own texts and works. In this next part, we will explore the features of tragedy as defined by Aristotle and see how these features have been used by writers to create their own works.

CHECK FOR UNDERSTANDING

Earlier in this book, in Chapters 1.4 and 1.5, you learned about some of the influences that Aristotle has had on the language, form and structure of various works and texts. See if you can list any of these influences before reading the next section.

Generic conventions: classical interpretations

The Greek philosophical writings during the time of Ancient Greece were highly influential on the Ancient Romans who, through the expansion of their empire, carried these ideas throughout much of Europe. For this reason, classical Greek philosophy is seen as being integral to the formation of Western civilization and culture. For example, the English word for 'logic' meaning 'reason' comes from the Ancient Greek philosophical term '*logoi*' which relates to the order and reason given by the divine and the cosmos. Another example would be the political system of 'democracy' or 'direct representation and participation' (which is the political system used in many Western nations today), which was first documented as being used in Athens during this period.

GLOBAL ISSUES ***Field of Inquiry:*** **Politics, Power and Justice**

GLOBAL JUSTICE SYSTEMS

If you would like to read further about this topic Malcolm Heath created an up-to-date and lucid translation of Aristotle's *Poetics* in 1997 – this is a useful read if you would like a challenge and if you would like to extend your knowledge of classical forms of writing. Plato was another eminent Greek philosopher from this time and his most famous work is *The Republic*. Benjamin Jowett translated the text into English in the late 1800s and his version is still widely used today, though there is a more up-to-date version created by Desmond Lee from 2007. *The Republic* discusses what may be the ideal construction of society and explores issues to do with public policy and the justice system. An extract from this work, along with a more modern non-literary text such as a news report or opinion article, would make an ideal springboard from which to explore the global issue of justice systems around the world.

Look at the key features box below which outlines some of key features of tragedy in drama as stated by Aristotle.

KEY FEATURES **TRAGEDY IN DRAMA**

- **Imitation** (or *mimesis)* – the play should imitate life not as how it exactly is but how it could be, yet the play should be serious in its intention.
- The main character (the protagonist) should be **a tragic hero** – this character is neither wholly good or bad, and they should start a path to their own downfall via a fatal flaw (*hamartia*) in their character.

- The **structure of the play** should be focused upon and driven by **action** – the play should have a clear beginning, middle and end and should have a singular theme that clearly unites the whole play drawing it to a clear conclusion *(dénouement)*.
- The **audience response** should be one based primarily on '**fear and pity**' – the audience should be able to identify with the protagonist and understand the implications of their fate *(pathos)*. The emotion that the audience should be left with is one of release and relief (*catharsis)* where the audience feels they have been emotionally and spiritually cleansed through their viewing of the play.
- Certain **dramatic events** should be included for **emotional impact** – for example, a 'reversal' (*peripeteia)* where an event which is the opposite of what the protagonist thought would happen occurs, or a sudden realization or recognition (*anagnorisis*) where a character realizes the truth of a situation, event or another character.

Aristotle

Aristotle was a philosopher and scientist who lived during the time of Ancient Greece. Aristotle is seen as an eminent figure of this time and wrote about a huge variety and diversity of topics including physics, literature, politics, geology and psychology to name a few examples.

To see the impact of Aristotle's definition of tragedy on how writers craft their works, we will read an extract from William Shakespeare's tragic play *Macbeth* which was written centuries after Aristotle's 'Poetics'.

In this speech, Macbeth is weighing up the pros and cons of killing the King Duncan of Scotland. Duncan has just rewarded Macbeth with a new royal title (making him closer in line to ascending to the position of king) due to his bravery in a recent battle and he is staying overnight as a guest at Macbeth's castle. It is useful to know that Shakespeare wrote this play shortly after the 'Gunpowder Plot' was foiled in England (1605). This plot was an attempt to blow up the Houses of Parliament and assassinate the Protestant King of England and Scotland (James I and VI, respectively) by a group of Catholic men who wanted greater religious freedom. Much of the play *Macbeth* was influenced by these events, and the play can be seen as a warning to those who seek to disrupt the 'natural order' and 'divine rights' of kingship; ideologies that were deeply ingrained in society during this time.

MACBETH: If it were done when 'tis done, then 'twere well
It were done quickly: if the assassination
Could trammel up the consequence, and catch
With his surcease success; that but this blow
Might be the be-all and the end-all here,
But here, upon this bank and shoal of time,
We'd jump the life to come. But in these cases
We still have judgment here; that we but teach
Bloody instructions, which, being taught, return
To plague the inventor: this even-handed justice
Commends the ingredients of our poison'd chalice
To our own lips. He's here in double trust;
First, as I am his kinsman and his subject,

Strong both against the deed; then, as his host,
Who should against his murderer shut the door,
Not bear the knife myself. Besides, this Duncan
Hath borne his faculties so meek, hath been

So clear in his great office, that his virtues
Will plead like angels, trumpet-tongued, against
The deep damnation of his taking-off;
And pity, like a naked new-born babe,
Striding the blast, or heaven's cherubim, horsed
Upon the sightless couriers of the air,
Shall blow the horrid deed in every eye,
That tears shall drown the wind. I have no spur
To prick the sides of my intent, but only
Vaulting ambition, which o'erleaps itself
And falls on the other.

(William Shakespeare, Macbeth Act 1 Scene 7, 19)

In this speech we can see that Macbeth is conflicted. He is aware of the reasons why killing King Duncan is morally wrong and how the act could lead to disastrous consequences. However, he also recognizes the power of 'vaulting ambition' (line 27) which has led others into peril in their pursuit of power 'which o'erleaps itself and falls on the other' (lines 27–28). Later in the play, Macbeth will disregard these concerns and still commit the act of murdering King Duncan. This fits with Aristotelian features of tragedy as Macbeth is characterized here as a 'tragic hero' – he clearly knows right from wrong, and he recognizes the danger that lies in following through on ambitious motivations, but he still does evil and commits murder purely to satisfy his own lust for power.

The audience response here may be one of pity and fear, again linking back to the Aristotelian features of tragedy. As the speech unfolds, the audience may be lured into a false sense that Macbeth will not commit the murder and the reasons that he gives for not committing the murder, for example, 'I am his kinsman and his subject' (line 13), are reasons that an audience would understand (or *empathize* with). Similarly, the play could be seen as imitating life in the sense that most people will have, at some point, found themselves in a situation where they were unable to make a decision but were fully aware that the decision they made could have serious consequences; for example, choosing where to go to college or university, choosing whether to take a job or even the decision to enter into a relationship. Later, when Macbeth does murder King Duncan and when all of the barbaric consequences of this decision are played out in front of the audience, they will pity Macbeth for having had the potential to save himself from destruction but will also fear the very relatable situation of making a poor or ill-judged decision with life-changing consequences.

The key themes of ambition, fate and violence that unite the action of Macbeth are also clearly in evidence in this speech and are another example of Shakespeare's adherence to the Aristotelian conventions of tragedy. As previously explained, Macbeth is fully aware that it is only ambition that is motivating him to kill King Duncan but earlier in the speech he also refers to 'Bloody instructions, which, being taught, return to plague the inventor' (lines 9–10). Through this metaphor, the audience can see a clear recognition from Macbeth of the idea of fate – that if you commit 'bloody' or violent actions then it is likely that these violent actions will be fated to come back later in your life to be acted upon you by someone, or something, else. As the play unfolds the action of the play is driven by this idea, and each time Macbeth commits a violent action on account of his ambitious lust for power then later in the play, at some point, a violent action is brought upon Macbeth and those close to him.

It should be obvious from this analysis of the extract that the play *Macbeth* could be seen as an **archetype** of Aristotelian tragedy. Are there any other works or texts, of any type or era, that you have read and that you could argue have been clearly influenced by the theories of Aristotle?

EE Links: Language A – category 1

In this section we have explored the ways in which the play *Macbeth* does adhere to the generic conventions of Aristotelian tragedy and how Macbeth as a character could be considered the archetype of an Aristotelian 'tragic hero'. However, there are many ways in which the play subverts these conventions. For example, the play does not strictly follow a clear and logical structure with many different locations, temporal settings and a huge (and potentially confusing) cast of characters. The play also doesn't end with a clear conclusion, even after Macbeth has been executed. We are unsure if, after all of the bloodshed and personal losses, Scotland can return to the way it was prior to Duncan's reign or if this pattern of violence will continue. There is also an argument to suggest that the play does not focus long enough on Macbeth's virtues to engender a response of pity from the audience – especially when considering some of the heinous acts he commits throughout the play such as the slaughter of innocent and defenceless women and children. Some audiences may find it difficult to find any sympathy or understanding for the character of Macbeth and may instead simply be repulsed by him by the end of the play.

With this in mind, to what extent could *Macbeth* be considered a tragic play? And to what extent could Macbeth be considered a tragic hero?

TOK Links

One of the key features of Aristotelian tragedy is the imitation of real life, and when reading the speech from *Macbeth* you may be able to equate its events, themes and emotions to those of a similar real-life situation. However, how far can fiction, as a literary construct in a completely fabricated world, ever truly imitate real life?

In our analysis of Aristotle and *Macbeth*, we explored how classical writers have helped to create some of the notions of genre that we still have today – especially in regard to broader genres such as **tragedy** and **comedy**. However, there are many other ways of classifying texts and works that you may also be familiar with.

This may include genres such as **science fiction, romance, horror, historical** or **crime** (to name just a few examples). But, how does a reader identify whether a text or work belongs to such a specific category of writing?

Some of the conventions that a reader may look to for guidance are the following:

- **plot**
- **characters**
- **setting**
- overall **structure** of a work or text
- use of **colour**
- use of **language** and **structural features**, such as **punctuation**, **sentence length**, **tone** and **descriptive techniques**.

For example, if a reader was reading a **science-fiction** novel, they may expect **characters** such as researchers and scientists to feature prominently, and they may expect the novel to be **set** in outer-space or a laboratory. If a reader was reading a **romance** novel, they might expect the **plot** to focus on a turbulent or unexpected romantic relationship, and may also expect the **colour** red (which is often used to connote passion) to be used symbolically throughout. Similarly, a reader of a **horror** novel may expect **cliffhangers** and lots of **tension** building throughout the novel, along with features such as **short sentences** and **ellipses** to create **suspense**.

Generic conventions: gothic fiction

The next part of this section will focus in detail on a specific genre of writing: **gothic fiction**.

Horace Walpole's *The Castle of Otranto* (1764) is considered to be the first example of 'gothic fiction' and established many of the **literary tropes** that we now connect with the genre. Gothic fiction shares many **commonalities** with **Romanticism** – the features of which are detailed in Chapter 1.2. Gothic fiction was written mostly in western Europe during the 1800s and can be seen, like Romanticism, as a reaction to huge advances being made in science, technology and industry at the time.

KEY FEATURES GOTHIC FICTION

The key ingredients of gothic fiction are listed below:

- **Plot:** The plot of many gothic fiction works and texts focus on science experiments and new technology which is 'out of control', fear of the capability of human beings to commit evil and the supernatural wreaking vengeance on humans. Romance (which often ends badly) is also a key feature of many gothic fiction works and texts. In addition, **inexplicable and unexplainable events** are often a key part of a gothic fiction plot.
- **Characters:** There a few different types of characters that a reader would expect to find in a gothic novel. A **male authoritative figure** or **tyrant** who terrorises a **female 'in distress'** who is then saved by a **male hero figure** often feature, reflective of **patriarchal** systems of power at the time when gothic fiction was first created. Scientists, inventors and writers tend to be included as the male 'hero' figure. **Supernatural characters** such as **vampires, ghouls, re-animated corpses** and **werewolves** are also often featured.
- **Settings:** Gothic fiction novels are often set in isolated places, places that are dark and unwelcoming, that may be haunted or have been abandoned. Ancient dwellings such as castles, churches and manors often feature. Science laboratories, hospitals and morgues are also frequently included by gothic writers. Additionally, **pathetic fallacy** is often utilized by gothic writers who often include thunderstorms, rain, clouds, mist, fog, extreme cold and other adverse weather patterns in their texts and works.
- **Structure:** Gothic writers often utilize **foreshadowing** in their works and texts; often there will be some kind of **prophecy** or **omen** that gives clues to the reader (and/or characters) of what may happen later in the novel. **Cliffhangers** will be used frequently, perhaps at the end of chapters and parts, in order to build **suspense**. Gothic fiction novels often end in a way that is bad for the characters involved.
- **Colour:** The palette of colours used by gothic writers is often limited to dull colours such as black, white, grey and shades of these. Flashes of other, brighter colours may be used by a writer for symbolic purposes or to shock, for example, red for blood and passion or yellow to denote sickness and frailty.
- **Literary features:** Gothic fiction will often include many examples of **sensory language** which reduces the distance between the reader and the text, and will make them feel much closer to the events being described. Heightened emotion is also a key feature of gothic fiction with writers often including emotive language to convey this. **Religious iconography** is also often included; used in gothic works and texts as a way of combating evil and supernatural forces. An **atmosphere** of suspense and tension is integral to gothic fiction and as such **short sentences**, ellipses, **exclamation marks** and **one-sentence paragraphs** are often used by writers to create this.

The extract below is from the novel *Wuthering Heights* by Emily Brontë (1847). The novel can be seen as belonging to the **gothic fiction** genre. The novel is set in rural Yorkshire, which is in the north of England. The plot focuses predominantly on a complicated love triangle between three characters: Heathcliff, Catherine and Edgar. In this extract, many years after the death of both Catherine and Edgar, the narrator, Lockwood (who is a visitor from the south of England), is renting Catherine and Edgar's former home, Thrushcross Grange, for some peace and recuperation. In the night, Lockwood has a nightmare where he sees the ghostly figure of Catherine trying to enter the bedroom window.

The extract has been numbered to explain where and how the features of gothic writing have been used by Brontë.

This time, I remembered I was lying in the oak closet, and **(1)I heard distinctly the gusty wind, and the driving of the snow;** I heard, also, the fir bough repeat its teasing sound, and ascribed it to the right cause: but it annoyed me so much, that I resolved to silence it, if possible; and, I thought, I rose and endeavoured to unhasp the casement. The hook was soldered into the staple: a circumstance observed by me when awake, but forgotten. 'I must stop it, nevertheless!' I muttered, knocking my knuckles through the glass, and stretching an arm out to seize the importunate branch; **(2)instead of which, my fingers closed on the fingers of a little, ice-cold hand! The intense horror of nightmare came over me:** I tried to draw back my arm, but the hand clung to it, and **(3)a most melancholy voice sobbed, 'Let me in—let me in!'** 'Who are you?' I asked, struggling, meanwhile, to disengage myself. **(4)'Catherine Linton,' it replied, shiveringly (why did I think of Linton? I had read Earnshaw twenty times for Linton) 'I'm come home: I'd lost my way on the moor!'** As it spoke, I discerned, obscurely, a child's face looking through the window. **(5)Terror made me cruel; and, finding it useless to attempt shaking the creature off, I pulled its wrist on to the broken pane, and rubbed it to and fro till the blood ran down and soaked the bedclothes**: still it wailed, 'Let me in!' and maintained its tenacious gripe, almost maddening me with fear.

(Emily Brontë 21–22)

1 **Pathetic fallacy** is used here to establish the inhospitable and wild weather of the Yorkshire moors where the novel is set – establishing key ideas about the theme of **isolation** and creating an **atmosphere of tension** from the beginning. This volatile weather also **foreshadows** the passionate love story that will unfold throughout the novel.

2 **Sensory language** is used to describe the cold touch of the apparition's arm – the appearance of which is in itself a **supernatural and inexplicable occurrence** which the reader would be shocked by. It is also important to note that the writer highlights here that the narrator is having a 'nightmare' which are often used by gothic writers as **omens** to suggest to the reader events that may happen in the real world later in the novel. The use of the **exclamation mark** also helps to not only convey the shock of the narrator but also provoke it within the reader.

3 Instead of the apparition being merely sad, or merely crying, the writer has chosen **emphatic adjectives and verbs** to heighten the emotion of the apparition, making it appear **overwrought** in its despair.

4 It is established here that the apparition is supposedly Catherine Linton who the narrator, and the reader, know has been dead for many years. As well as creating an **atmosphere of mystery**, this also utilizes the gothic character **trope** of the **woman in distress** as the reader imagines a young female, in between life and death, condemned to wander the Yorkshire moors on her own in abysmal weather, desperate to seek shelter.

5 The **graphic violence** described here would disturb the reader, as it does even the narrator, and the use of **polysyndetic listing** to elongate and build up the brutal actions of the narrator

would help to increase the **tension** in this part of the extract. The mention of 'blood' here introduces a flash of red into the dark palette of **colours** used by the writer so far – here, we can surmise that the use of red could be signalling danger.

Emily Brontë

Emily Brontë is an English author who was born in 1818. She is the sister of fellow novelists Charlotte Brontë and Anne Brontë. She was a recluse and preferred a solitary life. She only wrote one novel, *Wuthering Heights*, which although now considered a classic of English literature was criticized at the time for its perceived immorality on account of the unbridled passion and sexual desire implicitly referred to throughout. She died shortly after the publication of the novel.

Now, let's read an extract from the poem 'Porphyria's Lover' by Robert Browning (1836) which could be seen as another example of **gothic fiction**. The poem is told from the perspective of a speaker who is having a seemingly illicit relationship with a woman called Porphyria, who we can also assume is from a higher social class than the speaker himself. In the poem, Porphyria leaves a social engagement to join the speaker of the poem, which has an unexpected and dark consequence.

Porphyria's Lover

The rain set early in to-night,
    The sullen wind was soon awake,
It tore the elm-tops down for spite,
    And did its worst to vex the lake:
    I listened with heart fit to break.
When glided in Porphyria; straight
    She shut the cold out and the storm,
And kneeled and made the cheerless grate
    Blaze up, and all the cottage warm;
    Which done, she rose, and from her form
Withdrew the dripping cloak and shawl,
    And laid her soiled gloves by, untied
Her hat and let the damp hair fall,
    And, last, she sat down by my side
    And called me. When no voice replied,
She put my arm about her waist,
    And made her smooth white shoulder bare,
And all her yellow hair displaced,
    And, stooping, made my cheek lie there,
    And spread, o'er all, her yellow hair,
Murmuring how she loved me — she
    Too weak, for all her heart's endeavour,
To set its struggling passion free
    From pride, and vainer ties dissever,
    And give herself to me for ever.
But passion sometimes would prevail,

Nor could to-night's gay feast restrain
A sudden thought of one so pale
For love of her, and all in vain:
So, she was come through wind and rain.
Be sure I looked up at her eyes
Happy and proud; at last I knew
Porphyria worshipped me; surprise
Made my heart swell, and still it grew
While I debated what to do.
That moment she was mine, mine, fair,
Perfectly pure and good: I found
A thing to do, and all her hair
In one long yellow string I wound
Three times her little throat around,
And strangled her.

(Robert Browning)

Robert Browning

Robert Browning is an English poet who was born in 1812. He is known for his use of the dramatic monologue, the form in which he wrote many of his famous poems such as 'My Last Duchess' and 'The Laboratory'. He was an adherent of the Romantic movement of literature (which you can read about in Chapter 1.2) and wrote poems that focused predominantly on corresponding ideas and themes, such as the beauty of the natural world, on the capacity of love to cause both good and evil and on universal human experiences, such as betrayal and death.

ACTIVITY 1

1 Using the notes on *Wuthering Heights* as a model, go through 'Porphyria's Lover' and annotate the features of the gothic fiction genre that you can see within the text.

2 Think individually or discuss in a pair/group answers to the following questions:

(a) In the contextual information for this source it explained that we could assume that the speaker of the poem and Porphyria are from different social classes – where in the poem is this revealed?

(b) Gothic fiction often explores and harnesses the fears of its reader(s) for literary effect – what do you think the speaker is fearful of? Does this reflect any larger societal fears that existed in 1800s England?

(c) How are the speaker of the poem and Porphyria characterized? Does this characterization change as the poem develops?

3 Write an explanation of how the writer's use of literary tradition or conventions creates meaning through a comparison of the extract from *Wuthering Heights* by Emily Brontë and 'Porphyria's Lover' by Robert Browning. After you have written your own explanation, you can read an example of one at the end of the book.

SENSITIVE CONTENT

Caution: this article through the QR code includes sensitive content, dehumanizing language and visuals and expletives.

The images show vulnerable women in extremely distressing circumstances but have been chosen to illustrate the themes of identity and human behaviour at the heart of this book. Furthermore, the IB recommends that your studies in Language A: Language and Literature should challenge you intellectually, personally and culturally, and expose you to sensitive and mature topics. We invite you to reflect critically on various perspectives offered while bearing in mind the IB's commitment to international-mindedness and intercultural respect.

GLOBAL ISSUES *Field of Inquiry:* Politics, Power and Justice

DOMESTIC VIOLENCE

Robert Browning describes how the speaker of the poem strangled his lover, Porphyria, to preserve a moment of absolute submission from her – essentially to perpetuate for eternity a sense of power and ownership over her. This would now be categorized, in most parts of the world, as not only an act of murder but also as an act of domestic violence. At the time that the poem was written, how likely was it that Porphyria's lover would be brought to justice for this act?

Using the poem as a springboard, research non-literary texts that address the issue of domestic violence. You could find, for example, informative articles, academic journals or personal accounts that are focused on this issue. Choose a text from a series of the above and examine the ways in which domestic violence is presented through the content and form of the text you have chosen. Do you feel that attitudes towards this issue have changed since 'Porphyria's Lover' was written? How likely is it now that the victims of domestic violence receive justice for the crimes committed against them and how does this vary around the world?

Scan the QR code in the margin to see a body of work in the form of several appeal posters from Lebanese non-profit, non-governmental organization (NGO) KAFA (Enough) Violence and Exploitation. This NGO seeks to end all forms of discrimination against women within Lebanese society. Read on to find out the key features of appeal posters and for a model analysis of the appeal posters from this body of work.

Appeal posters need to convey a strong, simple message to their readers and encourage them to take action. To help with this, the following features are often used.

KEY FEATURES APPEAL POSTERS

- A limited **colour palette** – bold, striking (usually primary) colours can be used to immediately hold the attention of the reader. Muted colours can also be used in order to connote the seriousness of the topic of the poster and to not distract the reader from its key message.
- The **layout** of most appeal posters will be sparse, usually with one large, key image dominating the majority of the poster and a limited quantity of text.
- The **text** included in appeal posters will often take the form of a series of short sentences designed to convey **key information** about the appeal as directly as possible to the reader. Slogans and memorable phrases will often be used as a way of encapsulating in a shortened form what may be larger, complex ideas about a topic for the reader. Second person pronouns and imperatives will often be used to direct the reader to take some form of action linked with the topic of the appeal poster.

- The **typography** used in appeal posters will often take the form of bold, all uppercase, non-cursive font in a bold, striking colour.
- **Imagery** in the form of **signs and symbols** will often be used in appeal posters to convey implicit ideas about the topic to the reader
- Appeal posters often use **shock tactics** in order to gain the attention of the reader and provoke them into taking action – this can be in the form of an image or text.
- The **logo** of the organization that produced the appeal poster will often appear somewhere on the appeal poster, along with details about where and how the reader can access more information about the topic or the call to action.

In order to analyse the appeal posters through the lens of the global issue of domestic violence, we will use step 1 (genre, audience and purpose), step 3 (typographical and graphological features) and step 5 (visual image and layout) of the non-literary text reading strategy as delineated in Chapter 1.1. You may wish to re-read this in order to understand this commentary.

The appeal posters you looked at via the QR code on the previous page are all focused on the **global issue of domestic violence**. All three posters featured are trying to **convey the message** that the **emotional and verbal abuse of a partner** can be **just as damaging as the physical abuse of a partner**. The appeal posters also provide readers with a helpline where the victims of this type of domestic violence can seek help.

All three appeal posters utilize **shock tactics** in the form of a **large, central image** of an otherwise stereotypically attractive woman with visible and graphic injuries to either her face or neck. These images would be immediately striking to a reader perhaps not used to seeing images of woman such as this displayed in public – as a society we are much more used to seeing polished, airbrushed depictions of women displayed in public. This is used, perhaps, to suggest the idea that even though the **damage of verbal/emotional abuse** is less obvious (and perhaps easier to hide) than that of physical abuse it is still just as damaging and should be as publicly condemned. The use of the graphic injuries in the **images** immediately **conveys the seriousness of the topic** and indicates to the reader how harmful the effects of **emotional/verbal abuse of a partner** are.

The text used in the appeal posters also use **shock tactics** – each poster contains the use of a derogatory, sexual slur such as 'whore', 'slut' or 'bitch' next to the use of an audio wave **image**, clearly **connoting to the reader** that this is the kind of language that the women in the posters are used hearing. Again, this kind of language would generally not be tolerated within society and it may **shock a reader** to see this displayed so publicly. The organization that created the posters, KAFA Violence and Exploitation, has perhaps used this to **convey a parallel message** to that of the **central image** – that even though the damage of verbal/emotional abuse of a partner is less obvious (and perhaps easier to hide) than that of the **physical abuse of a partner** it is still just as damaging and should be as publicly condemned. This larger idea has been **condensed into three short, easy-to-remember sentences** that are also included on the poster.

The **purpose** of an appeal poster is to convey a **simple, strong message** to its reader and to encourage them to take action against **domestic violence**. These posters have included both a helpline and a website link, along with the **organization's logo**, in order to clearly direct readers to where they can access help/information about domestic violence which may also **encourage them to take action.**

CAS Links

If you are concerned by the issue of domestic violence, research your local area to see if there are any organizations that are focused on this issue. You could potentially help these organizations in the form of fundraising, volunteering or advocacy. This could make a potentially very worthwhile service opportunity.

Throughout the last three sections we have discussed how we can categorize texts and works into various genres. The next section will discuss the reasons why or why not a writer would choose to adhere to or deviate from conventions associated with genre or text type.

Conventions associated with genre or text type

The system of separating works and texts into different genre classifications can be contentious and can engender a variety of opinions. Read the two quotes below that provide two alternative perspectives about this process:

> *'"Genre", if it means anything at all, is a restrictive commercial requirement. "Westerns" must be set in the Old West. "Mysteries" must have a detective solving a crime, usually murder. "Nurse Novels" must have a nurse. And so forth.'*
>
> *Norman Spinrad*

> *'Can one identify a work of art, of whatever sort, but especially a work of discursive art, if it does not bear the mark of a genre, if it does not signal or mention it or make it remarkable in any way?'*
>
> *Jacques Derrida*

From the Jacques Derrida quote, you could interpret that he is commenting on a positive aspect of the generic classification process where writers are able to communicate clearly to a reader how their text or work can be differentiated from another. This could be considered useful in a utilitarian and commercial sense as readers will be able to easily identify texts and works that best fit their needs. However, from the Norman Spinrad quote, you could interpret that he is commenting on a negative aspect of the generic classification process where writers can feel restrained in the writing process as they feel that they must include certain text conventions to adhere to a specific genre or must even write entirely in a specific genre, again maybe for utilitarian and commercial reasons.

ACTIVITY 2

1 Read the listed scenarios below and imagine that you are the person described in each one. Either thinking individually, or discussing in a pair or a larger group, explore the decision that you could make to resolve each scenario.

(a) You are the editor of a successful print newspaper which, according to market research, is used by the majority of its readers as their primary source of news. An event of huge and significant national importance has just taken place, but your next edition of the paper was supposed to introduce a much prepared and developed fresh and different layout on its front page. It's crucial that the details of this event are conveyed in a way that is clear and direct, and you are worried that deviating from your usual front page layout would hinder this. What would you do?

(b) You are the editor-in-chief of a long-running print fashion magazine that is experiencing gradually declining sales. Your market research has shown that the commercially crucial younger **demographic** of readers sees the magazine as old-fashioned and would like the magazine to cover issues usually seen as taboo or inappropriate by your older board members and existing readership. They would also be more likely to subscribe to an online version of the magazine than purchase a print copy. Doing either of these suggestions would risk alienating your board members and existing readership, as well as potentially resulting in job losses if the magazine was to shift to an online publication. What would you do?

(c) You are a commercially successful author of a series of romance novels. You use the same conventions in each of your novels, your readers know what to expect and this is a key reason why readers keep on buying your novels. However, you are feeling bored and uninspired – when you were studying creative writing you loved mixing genres and experimenting with conventions. You are planning to introduce some elements of a different genre and change some of your usual conventions in your new novel, but your publisher and editor are concerned that this will harm your chances of the novel performing well commercially. What would you do?

From your thoughts and/or discussions you should now have some ideas about why or why not a writer may adhere or deviate from conventions associated with genre or text type. The next two parts of this chapter will explore these ideas in more detail and will link back to these scenarios.

Why do texts adhere to conventions associated with genre or text type?

Writers may adhere to conventions associated with genre and text type for a variety of reasons. Some of these reasons may be because:

- their life experience, values and exposure to different texts may impact their ability or desire to deviate from conventions belonging to a specific genre or text type
- they may feel as though their perspective and creativity is best conveyed through a specific genre or text type
- for some text types, such as news articles or instructional guides, it may be important to adhere to conventions in order to convey important information clearly and effectively
- it may be beneficial commercially to have your work or text clearly belong to a genre or text type.

In previous sections of this chapter, we have looked at how literary works have adhered to generic conventions and have explored some of the reasons why they may adhere also. For example, Shakespeare's use of classical conventions of Aristotelian tragedy helped make the play *Macbeth*, and its protagonist, relatable to his audience making clear the warning against meddling with the 'natural order' that lies at the heart of the play, and Brontë's use of gothic fiction conventions helped to evoke horror in the reader by placing them horrifyingly close to the brutal description of Lockwood's violent defence against the ghostly nightmare of Catherine Linton.

Linking back to the thoughts and/or discussion that you had in response to the activity, we will explore the idea that adhering to conventions associated with genre and text type could be important when conveying important information clearly and effectively in non-literary texts, and how it could also be beneficial commercially.

Read these key features of newspaper front pages.

KEY FEATURES NEWSPAPER FRONT PAGES

- Newspapers can be separated into three categories – **compact**, **tabloid** and **broadsheet**.
- **Tabloid** and **broadsheet** were the original terms used to describe the size of a newspaper (**broadsheet** being larger which you have to fold to read and **tabloid** being half this size), and traditionally these terms were also linked to the **tone** and **content** of the paper.
- **Broadsheet** newspapers are usually more serious in **tone** and **content** and tend to avoid **sensational** stories. **Tabloids** are usually lighter in **tone** and **content** and tend to be more likely to feature **sensational** stories.
- However, some newspapers have opted in recent times to change the size of their newspapers to help increase their readability (for example, UK-based newspapers such as *The Times* or *The Guardian*). These newspapers are called **compact** newspapers as they are the same size as a **tabloid** newspaper, but like a **broadsheet** they are usually more serious in **tone** and **content** and tend to avoid **sensational** stories.
- **Tabloids**, **broadsheets** and **compacts** can all contain **bias**.

- The layout of **tabloid** newspaper front covers are likely to feature large **images** and a low amount of **text**. Large **typography** is usually used for their **headlines** and **subheadings**. They will be more likely to use **language features** such as **metaphors**, **similes**, **hyperbole**, **puns** and **loaded language**.
- The **layout** of **broadsheet** and **compact** newspaper front covers are likely to feature smaller **images** and much more **text**. Medium-sized **typography** is usually used for their **headlines** and **subheadings**. They will be more likely to avoid **figurative** and **descriptive language** and will usually use **higher register**, **direct language**.

Here is a front page from the British print newspaper *The Daily Mail*. This front page was designed by The Daily Mail in 2015 to commemorate the death of Winston Churchill who was the prime minister of the United Kingdom throughout the period of the Second World War. Churchill is regarded as a hugely important and iconic figure in British history, and he was much lauded for his military and diplomatic prowess throughout his time as leader of the United Kingdom.

Page 1
Daily Mail
SPECIAL TRIBUTE EDITION
NO. 21,381 FOR QUEEN AND COMMONWEALTH MONDAY, JANUARY 25, 1965 PRICE 3D
THE GREATEST ENGLISHMAN
When Churchill died yesterday, the years fell away and he looked again as he did during the war
by VINCENT MULCHRONE
National inspiration: Winston Churchill in Downing Street in 1943, leading Britain to victory
TURN TO NEXT PAGE

■ Front page of the print edition of *The Daily Mail* (2015)

Here is another front page from *The Daily Mail*. This front page was published in 2013 and reports on the death of Nelson Mandela who was the president of South Africa between 1994 and 1999. Before he became president, Nelson Mandela spent 27 years in prison as a political prisoner due to his activities against apartheid in South Africa (a system of racial segregation that privileged the white population of the country). Nelson Mandela is seen as a hugely important and iconic figure in the history of South Africa.

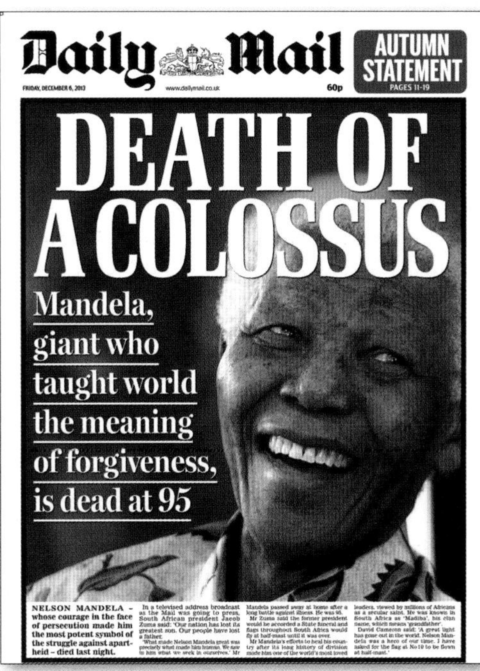
Daily Mail
AUTUMN STATEMENT PAGES 11-19
FRIDAY, DECEMBER 6, 2013 www.dailymail.co.uk 60p
DEATH OF A COLOSSUS
Mandela, giant who taught world the meaning of forgiveness, is dead at 95
NELSON MANDELA – whose courage in the face of persecution made him the most potent symbol of the struggle against apartheid – died last night.

■ Front page of the print edition of *The Daily Mail* (2013)

It should be clear from the key features of newspaper front pages box that both of these front pages are examples of tabloid newspapers. It should also be clear that the two newspaper front pages are strikingly similar in their use of text conventions despite focusing on two very different subjects. Some of these similarities are detailed in the box below.

■ Table 3.1.2

Feature	How is the feature used in both newspaper front pages?
Layout and typography	Both newspaper front covers are dominated by large images of the subject of the front page report. The headline and subheadings are also large. There is only a small amount of written text, giving more detail to the cover story, placed at the bottom of the page.
Language features	Both of the newspaper front pages use sensational language in their headlines. The front page about the death of Winston Churchill, for example, uses the superlative 'greatest' when describing him and the front page about Nelson Mandela's death describes him metaphorically as a 'colossus'. The subheadings of both are also reverential in tone, alluding to the past events that made both of them so significant and iconic. For example, Churchill's front page refers to 'the war' which the reader would know to understand as the Second World War, in which Churchill led Great Britain and her allies to victory. Mandela's front page meanwhile refers to 'forgiveness' which the reader would know as an allusion to South Africa's remarkably peaceful shift to democracy that Mandela was instrumental in leading.

It is clear that *The Daily Mail* keeps the conventions of its print front pages the same deliberately, but what benefits does this bring to both the writer and the reader? Think back to the thoughts and/or discussions that you made in response to the first scenario in the previous activity. What did you decide? If you decided to keep the newspaper front page the same then there are a variety of good reasons for this decision. For example, the purpose of newspaper reportage is to impart information. To do this effectively, a text needs to use a clear and logical format. *The Daily Mail* front pages are clear and logical in their structure and a reader is able to easily navigate the text in order to find the relevant information. For example, the layout and typography of the headline and the image makes the key message immediately clear to the reader what the important information being imparted is. Coupled with that, readers tend to stay loyal to a publication because they like it. If a reader is used to receiving information in a particular way and then this suddenly changes to a way that they find confusing or that they simply don't like, then they won't stay loyal for very long, and will begin to purchase a different publication. This is similar logic pertaining to the consistent use of language features across both publications, as readers will often buy news publications where the tone and style of reportage aligns with their own values and attitudes. For example, readers of *The Daily Mail* may expect a sensationalized tone of reverence in their chosen publication's report upon the news of an influential political figure's death, and if this were to change, again, they may be likely to switch to another publication. Essentially, adherence to text conventions for newspaper publications can be essential in the process of imparting information clearly and in retaining a loyal customer base.

However, you may have decided that it would be best to change the format of the newspaper front page – if you did, then there are also a variety of very good reasons for this, which will be discussed in the next section.

Why do texts deviate from conventions associated with genre or text type?

We have explored throughout this chapter how we can group works and texts together into different genres and text types, and we have also explored the reasons why and how a writer may deliberately adhere to the conventions associated with genre and text type. Thinking about all of this exploration, how far do you agree with this quote by novelist Gaynor Arnold?

> *'Genre goes along with our wish to read what we already know that appeals to us. But that's the danger. We could spend all our lives reading within the narrow confines of the genre we know (and think we love) and never set a readerly foot outside it. Genre encourages us to have the same reading experience each time.'*
>
> *(Gaynor Arnold)*

Though there are reasons why a writer may adhere to generic and text type conventions there are many reasons why some writers deliberately deviate from these. Some of these reasons may be because:

- their life experience, values and exposure to different texts has led them to question or challenge the conventions used in some genres or text types
- they may feel that their perspective and creativity is restricted by the conventions associated with text type and genre
- over time genre and text types may need to change to reflect changes in society and culture
- it may be beneficial commercially to introduce readers to an updated version of a genre or text type, or to an entirely new genre or text type.

We will explore the commercial and functional benefit of deviating from these conventions.

The next text is the homepage of the *Times Live* online news website. *Times Live* was a South African daily tabloid print newspaper that moved to a digital only format in 2018. The **online news** homepage we will consider is dominated by the story of Nelson Mandela's death (which was also the focus of the 2013 *Daily Mail* front page).

KEY FEATURES ONLINE NEWS WEBSITES

- A **website header** will usually be at the top of the page detailing the name of the news publication and maybe some other **content** such as weather conditions where the publication is based, or a **search box** that can be used by readers to search for specific news stories.
- There will usually be a series of **subheadings** underneath the header that are **clickable links** to take readers to specific areas of the website, for example, 'lifestyle', 'education', 'sport' and 'business'.
- There will sometimes be a '**live feed**' delivering real-time breaking news stories, or updates about an existing significant news story, either underneath the **subheadings** or in a box near the top of the page.
- Whatever the publication has decided is the 'most important' news story will be at the top of the page with a large **clickable headline**, a large corresponding **image** and more **text** than the rest of the stories. If it is a particularly important story there may be links around or underneath the story that can take a reader to contextual information like a timeline of events, to an **opinion article** about the story, or to informative videos about the story.
- Underneath the top story, there will be a list of other stories that can be ordered in importance or in popularity (the number of readers clicking to read the story). These other stories will have smaller **clickable headlines**, smaller **images** and less **text** (sometimes only one sentence long).
- Online news sources often derive most of their income through advertising and so **advertising banners** will often be found on online news websites.
- **Language techniques** used on **news websites** can include **elliptical sentences** in **clickable headlines** that contain only the important **keywords** (that can later be easily searched by online search engines or the website's own search tool). As newspapers often rely on advertising revenue to make money they need to be able to show how many readers are clicking onto their news stories. As a result, **online news websites** will use **hyperbole** and **sensational language** to encourage readers to click on a story – giving rise to the **neologism 'clickbait'**.
- The **colours** used on online news websites will match the **colour** scheme of the publication's branding and often these colours will be bold and striking, such as red, black, white and yellow.
- **Typography** will be **non-cursive script** to ensure that the text is clear and easy to read.

Scan the QR code opposite to view a collation of newspaper front pages and online news homepages concerning the death of Nelson Mandela. In particular, look closely at the *Times Live* page (around two-thirds of the way down the page) and compare this to the conventions used in the *Daily Mail* front page.

The conventions of print and online news are clearly very different. As time has passed, as technology has advanced, and as more people tend to read the news online, the way in which texts communicate the news have also had to evolve and transform to meet the changing needs of their readers.

Think about the last time that you read a print newspaper. Maybe you read one every morning over breakfast, during your commute to/from school or work, during your lunch hour or even in the evening. Or, maybe you only read one at weekends when you are less likely to be reading it for up-to-date news and are more likely to be reading its feature articles, opinion editorials and magazine supplements. Maybe you can't even remember the last time that you read a print newspaper – and you wouldn't be alone!

CONCEPT CONNECTION

COMMUNICATION

Increasing numbers of people are now reading the news almost exclusively online, and ever more increasing numbers of people are accessing the news directly from social media websites such as Facebook or video platforms like YouTube. This is why online news websites will often only feature keywords (that can later be searched via online search engines or the websites own search tool) in their headlines and subheadings, which is very different from *The Daily Mail* print news front pages. This is why online news websites will often also feature interactive elements to their news stories such as videos and timelines that can easily be uploaded to a social media platform or a video platform. The amount of 'clicks' a news story gets (from readers clicking on the headline to read the story) can also impact where it is placed on the online news website, with more popular stories (stories that have been clicked the most times) being placed higher on the page so that readers can easily find and access them.

It is also worth noting that the greater connectivity and communication across the world as a result of advancing technology has also meant that many print newspapers are often fighting a losing battle when trying to stay relevant. By the time a news story has become public, has been researched, written about and printed it will most likely already have faded from public attention which may already have moved onto a brand new story. Online news websites are obviously much better placed to combat this as they will often have news and editorial teams all around the world in different timezones, reporting, editing and publishing news as and when it happens. It is much less time consuming to write and publish an online news story than a printed one meaning the news on online websites has the capability to be much more reactive and up-to-date. The 'live feed' feature that you can see is a common feature across most online news websites meaning that even before a full story is written about a piece of news, the key information as it is known can be communicated immediately to the reader.

There are some people who have the perspective that constant and easy access to up-to-date news can be hugely beneficial to readers. For example, if a national disaster occurs then people can be kept safe far more easily than ever before as they will know just from a few clicks on their device immediately what to do and where to go, or not go. Online news has also given a voice to many people around the world who are silenced by repressive Governments or rulers who have state-control of official media outlets – people in these countries can use their devices to send first-hand reports of abuses of power direct to online media outlets who don't even need to be in the same country as the writer in order to publish these reports. These benefits can even be as simple as people being able to be more prepared when going into a business meeting, as they can be armed with the most up-to-date information regarding any news in the global financial markets that may be pertinent to decisions made in that meeting.

However, there are many people who believe that the transformation of print news to online news is a negative one. For example, due to the 'clickable' and 'searchable' nature of many online news reports, there is an argument that readers can fall into an 'echo chamber' of only accessing news that supports and re-affirms their own perspectives and ideas, which is problematic when considering that toleration and acceptance of opposing viewpoints is integral to a well-functioning society. The practice of online news websites pushing stories higher up on the page dependent on their popularity is also seen as negative by some people who purport that news stories that are of public importance can become 'buried' under news stories that are perhaps more sensational in nature, but perhaps not as significant. The perceived declining quality of journalism in online news is also seen as an issue by some who argue that as reporters and editors have to write and publish new stories at such a fast rate to stay relevant and ahead of competitors, the research and time that should go into a good quality piece of news is being compromised.

GLOBAL ISSUES ***Field of Inquiry:* Science, Technology and the Environment**

THE IMPACT OF TECHNOLOGY ON THE MEDIA

Times Live has now moved to an entirely digital format and no longer has a print publication. Think back to the discussion that you had in response to the second scenario in the previous activity. Why might the publication have made that decision? Thinking about some of the points raised above, do you think that this is a decision that many news publishers will have to make?

The decision to move a news publication from a print edition to a digital edition (and drastically change the conventions of the text type) can be contentious but necessary. Individually, research this topic online and read a series of online news and opinion articles about this. You could use any non-literary text that you find from this series, along with an extract from a literary work such as *Nineteen Eighty-Four* by George Orwell or *Brave New World* by Aldous Huxley (novels that both contain an exploration of the use of mass media in a dystopian society) to discuss the global issue of the impact of technology on the media.

Please read the commentary below that analyses the features of the aforementioned *Times Live* news website through the lens of this specific global issue.

In order to analyse the *Times Live* website through the lens of the **global issue of the impact of technology on the media**, we will use step 2 (**structure and style**) and step 3 (**typographical and graphological features**) of the non-literary text reading strategy as delineated in Chapter 1.1. You may wish to re-read this in order to understand this commentary. It would also be useful for you to re-read the key features of online websites box from earlier in this chapter in order to understand what the key **structural, stylistic, typographical and graphological features** of online news websites are.

The *Times Live* source utilizes many of the common structural and stylistic features found on online news websites. However, when analysing the writers' choice to use these features through the lens of the **global issue of the impact of technology on media**, there are some interesting points that could be made. For example, unlike the coverage of Mandela's death as seen on the front cover of *The Daily Mail*, which could be viewed as conveying a tone of **reverence**, the **tone and style** of the coverage of the *Times Live* website arguably veers into the **sensational**. Some of **key structural features of an online news website**, such as the **clickable headlines** under the **main headline** and **image**, use Mandela's death as a vehicle through which to explore stories about his private life, the intense reaction from the public towards his death and the need to put social discord in South Africa to one side in light of his death. As discussed previously, the need for online news websites to generate advertising revenue in order to survive as a business has made the need for readers to 'click' onto online news stories paramount as this is usually the way in which advertisers judge the value of advertising on the news website. As such, it could be argued that the **sensational style** of the online news website (a clear deviation from its print counterpart) is an example of the **impact that technology has had on the media** – perhaps a negative one.

Similarly, some of the other **key structural features of an online news website** such as the **live feed**, the **main headline**, the **other clickable headlines**, **links to opinion articles** and the **video links** are all focused on the one story – that of Nelson Mandela's death. While this news story was, of course, of huge global importance, it could be inferred that this focus on just the one news story devalues all other news stories taking place that day and marks them as irrelevant. However, the front cover of *The Daily Mail* print newspaper similarly devotes itself entirely to the subject of Nelson Mandela's death. Like *Times Live*, *The Daily Mail* also needs to attract customers to pay for the newspaper as well as advertisers – thus, the temptation to only cover, or give an unequal prominence to, news stories that are deemed to be the most 'popular' with readers is also present here and arguably always has been even before the advent of online news, perhaps evidence of how **technology has not had the negative impact upon the media** as previously suggested.

It could also be argued, through the analysis of **typographical and graphological features** within the *Times Live* website, that the **impact of technology on the media** could be of benefit to readers. In a clear deviation from the **typographical and graphological features** of the front cover of print newspapers, there is no **singular, large, central image** of Mandela taking prominence on the page, instead a **variety of images** depicting different stages of Mandela's career and life are used to lead the reader to links to stories that explore a variety of facets of Mandela's life. This offers the reader a more nuanced understanding of Mandela and his impact upon politics and history than that of the print newspaper which is unable to offer this due to its non-interactive medium. The **typography** used for the **clickable headlines** for these stories is of the same size and font style of that used for the 'main' headline, and all of these headlines are also in **bold**. This implies to the reader, unlike the print newspaper, that it is not just the bare facts and details of the death of Mandela that is the main news story. Instead, it is implied that it is all of the other parts of his life that have had a lasting impact on the society that are also a part of the 'main' story of Mandela's death. Again, the ability of an online news website to offer this multi-faceted narrative of one singular news story could be a positive that is gained for the reader from the **impact of technology on the media**.

DISCUSSION

What could be debated here is that the media is not so much affected by technology per se, but is more affected by economics. How far do you feel the need for media organizations to make a profit affects the quality of their journalism? How far do you trust the news that you access through platforms that are run for profit? Do you think that it is possible for news outlets to be free from the influence of economics?

Works cited

Aristotle, *Poetics*, Penguin Classics, 1997

Arnold, G. 'The genre debate: We don't think of Dickens as a historical novelist.' *The Guardian*, 17 April 2014. Web. 29 Jan. 2019. **www.theguardian.com/books/booksblog/2014/apr/17/genre-debate-dickens-not-historical-fiction**.

Brontë, E. *Wuthering Heights*. Wordsworth Editions Ltd, 1997.

Browning, R. 'Porphyria's Lover.' *New Oxford Student Texts*, Oxford University Press, 2011.

Ghosh, A. *The Glass Palace*. Ravi Dayal, Penguin India, 1997.

Green, D. 'Here's What Domestic Violence Ads Look Like In The Middle East.' *Business Insider*, 26 March 2013. Web. 13 Oct. 2019. **www.businessinsider.com/lebanese-anti-domestic-violence-ads-2013-3**.

Gyasi, Y. *Homegoing*. Vintage, 2017.

Huxley, A. *Brave New World*. Harper Perennial, 2006.

'Jacques Derrida: "The Law of Genre".' *Dissertation Sensation*, 28 Feb. 2013. Web. 29 Jan. 2019. **https://dissertationsensation.wordpress.com/2013/02/28/jacques-derrida-the-law-of-genre**.

'Norman Spinrad – Quotes.' *Good Reads*. Web. 29 Jan. 2019. **www.goodreads.com/quotes/432577-cat-rambo-where-do-you-think-the-perennial-debate-between**.

Mantel, H. *Bring up the Bodies*. Picador, 2013.

Mantel, H. *Wolf Hall*. Picador, 2010.

'Nelson Mandela's death: the newspaper front pages – in pictures.' *The Guardian*, 6 Dec. 2013. Web. 13 Oct. 2019. **www.theguardian.com/media/gallery/2013/dec/06/newspapers-national-newspapers**.

Orwell, G. *Nineteen Eighty-Four.* Houghton Mifflin Harcourt, 2017.

Plato, *The Republic*, Vintage Classics, 1991

Saunders, G. *Lincoln in the Bardo*. Random House, 2017.

Shakespeare, W. *Macbeth*. Edited by Roma Gill, Oxford School Shakespeare, Oxford University Press, 2009.

'Thibaw, King of Myanmar.' *Britannica Online Encyclopaedia*, Web. 29 Jan. 2019. **www.britannica.com/biography/Thibaw.**

Walpole, H. *The Castle of Otranto*. William Bathoe, 1764.

How do conventions evolve over time?

OBJECTIVES OF CHAPTER

- To understand how writers can modify the expected conventions of a text or work in response to changes in societal values and concerns.
- To recognize how readers and writers can question and change the use of traditional literary and non-literary conventions in order to discuss significant issues within society.
- To provide an overview of how, as the use of the English language changes over time, the conventions of the language can also change.
- To demonstrate ways to apply course concepts to specific works of literature and non-literary texts.
- To demonstrate ways to understand specific works of literature and non-literary texts in the context of global issues.

In Chapter 3.1 we explored how we can define the conventions that belong to a particular genre or text type and why it is that writers may adhere and deviate from these conventions. In this chapter, we will be exploring how and why these conventions can change over time. To do this, we will be exploring, in detail, each of the objectives listed at the beginning of this chapter.

In addition, throughout Chapter 2.1, you will have explored how we can define culture and the impact that a person's culture can have upon how they receive a text or work. In this next part, we will discuss the impact that culture can also have on the production of texts and works.

How and why writers modify the expected conventions of a text

In this section we will explore how and why writers modify the expected conventions of a text or work in response to changes in societal values and concerns.

All varieties of writing, whether they are fiction or non-fiction, prose or poetry, advertisements or news reports, can be seen as a product of the environment in which they were produced. Writing can be affected by, just to mention a few examples, the political climate during the time period in which it is being written, by major events that are happening locally, nationally or globally at the time of writing, and/or by trends within society such as the popularity of a certain kind of music or aesthetic during the writing process. As all of these factors shift and change throughout time, so does the writing that reflects them.

CONCEPT CONNECTION

CULTURE

If you were to research events of global significance that occurred in the years 2001 or 2002 you may note down the September 11 attacks (which took place in the USA in 2001) as being a key political/historical event from that time. Then, if you were to research significant cultural events from the same time period you may note down that the highest grossing film at the US Box Office during 2002 was the film *Spider-Man* directed by Sam Raimi. The film tells the 'origin' story of the eponymous *Marvel Comics* character and is set in New York City. Part of its success could be attributed to the resonance it had with Americans at this highly emotional time through its characterization of *Spider-Man* as a hero of New York who strives to save the city from crime and a variety of 'evil' influences, (many of the battle scenes were set among the key landmarks of the New York city skyline); along with its depiction of *Spider-Man* struggling and then succeeding in bearing the weight of the responsibility that he felt came with his superhuman powers and the sacrifices that he had to make for the greater good of the city and its people. This more nuanced, serious, and character-driven approach to a 'superhero' film was a change in convention from previous incarnations of the genre that had focused primarily on more sensational action-driven narratives. Can you think of any other cultural products that have been created as a direct result of, or have clearly been influenced by, an event of global significance?

To further the relationship between culture and texts/works, we will analyse two magazine front covers. They are both magazine front covers from the print publication *Cosmopolitan*. *Cosmopolitan* is an international lifestyle magazine intended for a female readership which is published in 35 different languages and in 110 countries around the world. The magazine originated in the USA in 1886 as a family magazine, before becoming a literary magazine, and then a fashion and lifestyle magazine in 1965. The magazine has traditionally focused on content such as fashion, celebrities, horoscopes, beauty, relationships and health. Despite the challenges to the print media industry as explored in the previous chapter, *Cosmopolitan* still has over three million subscribers to its print edition, even though it does have an online version of the magazine and is also increasingly viewed through various social media platforms.

KEY FEATURES MAGAZINE FRONT COVERS

- It is important to remember that aside from sales of the actual magazine itself, advertising is a huge source of revenue for the magazine industry. The front cover of a magazine is ultimately its advertisement to the public and so is crucial to its commercial success and therefore its potential to attract companies to advertise in its publication. This is important to consider when analysing the features of a magazine front cover.
- **Masthead:** the name of the magazine (usually at the top of the page).
- **Tagline:** memorable phrase that readers may apply to magazine.
- **Headline:** text that reveals the main article (usually in large font or a different font to stand out).
- **Main image:** a large visual image, often a photograph, that promotes the main article in the magazine. Often this will be the central feature of the cover.
- **Subtitle:** text that advertises the other big stories (usually denoted through larger font than the cover lines).
- **Cover lines:** text that reveals the other stories.
- **Pull quote:** a quotation from the main article – words are surrounded with quotations marks.
- **Buzz words:** words that promise there is even more in the magazine ('plus …', 'and …', 'exclusive …').
- **Strapline:** a narrow strip of text at the bottom of the cover.
- **Puff:** an incentive to buy the magazine, usually put in a different shaped 'box' or 'balloon' to stand out.

The QR codes in this part of the chapter will introduce you to a series of *Cosmopolitan* magazine front covers, together these can constitute a body of work.

Scan the QR code on the previous page to view the *Huffington Post* article 'Six Decades of Cosmo'. In particular, look at the cover from April 1990 featuring supermodel Christy Turlington. Then, scan the second QR code to view the article from *Cosmopolitan* featuring their October 2018 cover, with plus-size model Tess Holliday on the front. After reading the two *Cosmopolitan* magazine front covers, read the table below that highlights the key differences in the conventions used in each magazine front cover.

■ Table 3.2.1

Feature	*Cosmopolitan* 1990	*Cosmopolitan* 2018
Masthead	The masthead is capitalized in a print font, which is coloured white, and isn't large enough to fill the entire of the top of the magazine from left to right.	The masthead is capitalized in a print font, which is coloured a soft pink, and fills the entire of the top of the magazine front left to right. The masthead seems bolder and more assertive, definitely less stereotypically 'soft' and 'feminine' in its aesthetic.
Colours	The main colour used for the background and the dress of the cover model, is a soft purple/lilac. The text is all the same colour – white.	The main colour used for the background is a steely, cold blue varying in shade. The cover model is wearing a swimming costume that is a dark, emerald green. The text varies between bold black and white, and a softer pink. Like with the masthead, these colours are less stereotypically 'feminine' when compared to the colours used in the 1990 front cover.
Layout	The layout of the magazine is fairly minimal, with only the masthead at the top of the page, the main visual image of the model featured in the middle with eight cover line stories featured around her, all in the same font and text colour. When looking at the front cover, there seems to be a lot of blank space only occupied by the background colour.	The layout of the magazine front cover is very 'busy' with the masthead at the top, the main visual image of the model in the middle, and the cover lines featured around the model taking up almost every available space on the page. This mirrors the change in pace of many women's lives in the modern era which are as full and frenetic as their male counterparts.
Main visual image	The main visual image on the front cover is of supermodel Christy Turlington. The model is slim and tanned, and is wearing a strapless purple satin dress which while being short, isn't too revealing. Her hair and make-up, while being clearly styled in a way that was fashionable at the time, are 'natural' in their style and colour palette.	The main visual image on the front cover is of plus-size model Tess Holliday. The model has paler skin covered in a variety of tattoos and is larger in size than a typical fashion model. She is wearing an emerald green vintage style swimsuit that is quite revealing. Her hair and make-up are similar to the 1990 front cover, naturally styled but more in a vintage 1950s aesthetic fashion. It is clear that the stereotypical notion of a 'desirable' and 'beautiful' cover girl is being subverted here through the inclusion of an atypical model.
Cover lines	The cover lines on the 1990 front cover frequently refer to marriage, with words belonging to its **semantic field** appearing many times; 'married', 'wives', 'husband'. This perhaps connotes that the intended reader would also be a married woman, or a woman actively looking to be married. The topics covered are stereotypically feminine and focused on issues within relationships – 'What Makes a Man Want to Marry', or mainstream entertainment and culture, for example, an interview with an A-list Hollywood actress and the release of a new romance novel.	Even though this magazine cover has fewer cover lines than the one from 1990, their typography is much larger and there are subheadings provided that give more details about the topics being covered. The topics are still female-centred but in, perhaps, a less stereotypical way. For example, one cover line details a husband's viewpoint of his wife's affair and one cover line is about a survivor of sexual assault. There is also the inclusion of profanity in the cover line, 'Tess Holliday Wants the Haters to Kiss her Ass'. This implies that perhaps the readership of *Cosmopolitan* is more interested in reading detailed, serious features than before and also does not shy away from strong opinions like those of Tess Holliday.
Language features	The front cover utilizes the type of language features that we would expect to find on a magazine front cover such as elliptical sentences 'Battered wives. Why they stay', alliteration in 'What Makes a Man Want to Marry' and tricolons in 'Tall, Blonde and Terrific'. The language never directly addresses the reader, referring ambiguously to 'a man' and 'women' throughout. As mentioned previously, most of the language belongs to the semantic field of marriage or heterosexual relationships between men and women.	The front cover also utilizes the type of language features that we would expect to find on a magazine front cover such as rhetorical questions in, 'Is Success an Illness?' and intensifiers in 'Total Chic' and 'The UK's Most Eligible Man'. The front cover, like its 1990 counterpart, also doesn't ever directly address the reader. This front cover only once refers to marriage, and it is ambiguous whether this is a same-sex or heterosexual marriage.

CONCEPT CONNECTION

REPRESENTATION

How far that the texts we read represent the truth of our human experience has long been a contentious topic, and none more so than in the beauty industry and the mass media connected to it. Once you have read the two magazine front covers and read the above features table, it is clear that there has been a deviation from the conventions that used to be used by *Cosmopolitan* to represent women on their magazine front covers, and a shift in the topics that they feel women would like to read about. But, why is this?

The lives of women, and the things that they desire and expect from life, have drastically changed in many parts of the world across time. For example, in 1990, in both the UK and USA, marital rape still hadn't been criminalized, and laws pertaining to statutory maternity leave for all working women were still not fully in place. In 1990, the USA still hadn't had a female speaker in the House of Representatives, and in both the UK and USA women were still barred from serving in any combat role within the military. However, by 2018 all of this had changed, with marital rape criminalized in both countries and statutory maternity leave being required by law for all working women in both countries. By 2018, all combat roles in the UK and USA military were open to women, and in 2007 Nancy Pelosi became the first woman to take up the position of Speaker of the US House of Representatives. This great change in the rights of women across time is perhaps best summed up in Nancy Pelosi's speech to the opening of the 110th US Congress:

> *'For our daughters and granddaughters, today, we have broken the marble ceiling. For our daughters and our granddaughters, the sky is the limit, anything is possible for them.'*
>
> *(Nancy Pelosi)*

ACTIVITY 1

As the way that society views and treats women changes, then it is hardly surprising that the way in which they are represented in mass media will also change. When looking at the two front covers of *Cosmopolitan* magazine from the QR codes, how do you think the visual and language conventions used in the 2018 cover show a deviation from those used in the 1990 front cover to show this shift in culture and representation? Read the example response below.

The main visual image used in the 2018 *Cosmopolitan* print magazine front cover depicts a large photograph of the model Tess Holliday. Tess Holliday is a 'plus-size' model meaning that she is larger in dress size than that of usual fashion models. She is wearing an emerald green swimsuit that is vintage in style, and her make-up and hair is also styled in this fashion. She has on display her many tattoos. There has been a backlash against stereotypical representations of women in the mass media, especially in fashion and advertising, in contemporary society and the use of Tess Holliday as an atypical fashion model could be seen as an attempt by *Cosmopolitan* to meet the needs of its young, socially aware, female readership who may be aware of, and involved in, this discussion about the representation of women in the mass media. The vintage style of Tess Holliday is an allusion to fashion models from the 1950s, who although larger in size than models commonly used today, were still considered beautiful. This allusion connotes to the key idea contained in the use of the main image that even if a woman does not conform to stereotypical notions of beauty she can still be considered beautiful. This is a message that the readership of the magazine may wish to see on the front cover of the magazine and thus help to sell it.

Revisit the 'Six Decades of Cosmo' article via the QR code and look at the covers from March 1987 and September 2013. Use the model above to write a commentary of how you think the visual and language features used in them show a shift in culture and the representation of women in the mass media.

ACTIVITY 2

The above response focuses on how *Cosmopolitan* uses magazine cover conventions in order to meet the needs of a female readership that is now far more likely to question the way in which they are represented in the media due to the greater opportunities and rights being afforded to women in many contemporary societies. However, it is clear from the first cover example that women didn't always feel that they had the voice to question this representation, or simply didn't feel the need to. Also, despite some positive changes in the representation of women in the media there is still, in some people's opinion, a lot of progress to be made in order to create a diverse, equal and accurate representation of women in the mass media. For example, there is still discussion ongoing about how few women of colour are used for the main image of fashion magazines compared to their white counterparts and there is still concern about the main focus of many fashion magazines still being on how to make women as sexually attractive to men as possible.

Go online and see if you can find the front covers for this month's leading fashion magazines such as *Vogue, Elle, Cosmopolitan* and *Harper's Bazaar.* How truly representative do you think the models depicted on this array of front covers are? In your opinion, how could these be changed to be more representative? Write down a summary of your ideas.

From your analysis of the *Cosmopolitan* covers you should be able to see how and why *Cosmopolitan* changed the conventions used in its print magazine front covers in order to respond to a societal shift in the way women are depicted, and expect to be depicted, in the magazines that they read. In the next part, we will look at how and why literary works can also respond to shifts in the concerns of society.

The next text is an extract from the novel *Frankenstein* by Mary Shelley (1818). The novel focuses on the scientist Victor Frankenstein and the scientific experiments that he conducts with the intention of reanimating a human corpse. In the extract, Frankenstein has succeeded in his scientific attempts, but the end result is not what he anticipated. The novel can be seen as containing elements of the **gothic fiction** genre (see previous chapter) and **Romanticism** (see Chapter 1.2). The novel can also be seen as an early example of the **science fiction** genre, key features of which are listed below.

KEY FEATURES SCIENCE FICTION

- Science fiction can trace its origins back to the tenth century, with some people seeing the first examples of science fiction in the compilation of tales and folk stories in *One Thousand and One Nights* or as it's commonly known, *Arabian Nights*.
- The modern concept of a science fiction novel was developed throughout the eighteenth century and the novel *Frankenstein* is seen as being one of the first, if not the first, example of this.
- Science fiction shares **commonalities** with **gothic fiction, Romanticism** and **dystopian fiction** (which can be seen as a science fiction **subgenre**) and resists a straightforward definition as it is a blend of various genres and styles.
- Science fiction is a genre that can be applied to non-literary texts such as films and television programmes, but in this section we will focus on how the genre applies to science fiction literary works. Some of the key ingredients of science fiction works are listed below:
  - **Plot:** The **plot** of many science fiction novels focus on scientific experimentation, advancements in technology and the lives of people living in societies and worlds much more scientifically advanced or different from our own. This focus on the future and what may happen to society as science and technology advances has led to science fiction also being called '**speculative fiction**'.
  - **Characters:** The type of **characters** that a reader would expect to find in a science fiction novel would include scientists and researchers, and the

subjects of their experimentations and research. This could include supernatural creatures (like the reanimated corpse seen in *Frankenstein*), or animals that possess special scientifically advanced skills, or robots and other forms of artificial life. Extra-terrestrial life from outside our own planet or from a fictional planet are also often used as characters in science fiction novels.

- **Settings:** Science fiction novels are often set in centres of scientific and technological research such as laboratories and universities. As mentioned in the information on 'plot', science fiction novels can also be set in societies and worlds much more scientifically advanced or different from our own, for example, outer-space or very far into the future. A lot of modern science fiction is set in a **post-apocalyptic** world where civilization as we know it has been destroyed by a scientific or technological accident or advancement.
- **Structure:** There is no distinct overall structural form used in science fiction, but writers will often use **flashbacks**, **leaps in narrative time-frames**, **cliffhangers** and the **gradual unfolding** of the consequences of a scientific experiment or technological advancement to keep the reader guessing what may happen next.
- **Colour:** The colours used in science fiction can vary between the dark and dull colours that we normally associate with **gothic fiction** to depict a world that has been negatively affected by, or currently is being affected by, scientific experiments and technological advancements. Or, writers can use bright and bold colours such as electric and neon colours to connote an other-worldliness that we associate with outer-space and technologically advanced societies.
- **Literary features:** Like gothic fiction, science fiction will often include many examples of sensory language which reduces the distance between the reader and the text and will make them feel much closer to the events being described. This is important when describing events that may seem inexplicable or unbelievable to a reader. Science fiction often aims to inspire a sense of wonder and awe in the reader and so will be highly descriptive using elaborate **metaphors**, **similes**, **personification** and other forms of **figurative language**. A **semantic field** of scientific and technological **jargon** will also often be used, and in some cases, brand new words will be invented by the writer to give language to people, events and things that may not currently exist. Also like gothic fiction, an **atmosphere** of suspense and tension is integral and as such **short sentences**, **ellipses**, **exclamation marks** and **one-sentence paragraphs** are often used by writers to create this.

Further reading

- Some examples of science fiction works that are seen as important in the development of the genre are listed below:
  - *The War of the Worlds* and *The Time Machine* both by HG Wells
  - *Do Androids Dream of Electric Sheep?* by Philip K Dick
  - *Neuromancer* by William Gibson
  - *The Hitchhiker's Guide to the Galaxy* by Douglas Adams.

Read the extract from *Frankenstein* below. It has been numbered to explain where and how the features of science fiction writing have been used by Shelley.

How can I describe my emotions at this catastrophe, or how describe the wretch whom with such infinite pains and care I had endeavoured to form? His limbs were in proportion, and I had selected his features as beautiful. Beautiful? Great God! His yellow skin scarcely covered the work of muscles and arteries beneath; his hair was a lustrous black, and flowing; his teeth of pearly whiteness; but these features only formed a more horrid contrast with his watery eyes, that seemed almost of the same colour as the dun-white sockets in which they were set, his shrivelled complexion and straight black lips.

(1) I had worked hard for nearly two years, for the sole purpose of infusing life into an inanimate body. For this I had deprived myself of rest and health. I had finished, the beauty of the dream vanished, and breathless horror and disgust filled my heart. Unable to endure the aspect of the being I had created, I rushed out of the room and continued a long time traversing my bedchamber, unable to compose my mind to sleep.

(Mary Shelley 43)

(1) The main **plot** point of the extract is focused on the science experiments of the protagonist pertaining to his attempts to re-animate a human corpse. The idea of a scientist attempting to carry out such a dark, and morally dubious, science experiment clearly links to the main **plot** focus of many science fiction novels that **speculate** about the capability for science and technology to be used for nefarious purposes.

Mary Shelley

Mary Shelley was a writer from the UK who was born in 1797. She was the daughter of the philosopher and feminist Mary Wollstonecraft, and was married to the Romantic poet Percy Bysshe Shelley. Shelley wrote novels, essays, dramas and travelogues but is perhaps best known for her novel *Frankenstein* which contains gothic and Romantic elements, as well as often being regarded as one of the first examples of a science-fiction novel. There has been renewed interest in her larger body of work in recent times, especially from feminist literary critics who see many feminist themes in her writings, such as implicit questions about the role of women in society, anxieties surrounding motherhood and repressed female sexuality.

ACTIVITY 3

Use the key features of science fiction box to label the conventions of science fiction where you can see them being used in the extract on the previous page. A model of how to label the extract in this way has been demonstrated in the previous chapter of this section, and there is a further example demonstrated below the extract.

GLOBAL ISSUES *Field of Inquiry:* Science, Technology and the Environment

THE IMPACT OF SCIENCE AND TECHNOLOGY ON THE NATURAL WORLD

Society in nineteenth-century Britain and western Europe (where *Frankenstein* was written and is set) was largely conservative and Christian; believing that only God had the power and right to create and take life. However, during the time the novel was written, there was much public debate and controversy about the possibility of 'raising the dead' – in part due to the experiments of Luigi Galvani, who in the late-eighteenth century used electric currents to 're-animate' animals. In *Frankenstein,* we see Victor Frankenstein 're-animate' a human corpse, but inadvertently create a monster that he is disgusted by: 'How can I describe my emotions at this catastrophe, or how describe the wretch whom with such infinite pains and care I had endeavoured to form?' The use of hyperbolic metaphors ('this catastrophe', 'the wretch') and the rhetorical question helps convey the despair that Frankenstein feels when he sees what he has created. This links to Christian fears at the time the work was written about the 'unholy' consequences of human beings 'playing God' and interfering in the 'natural' processes of life. It is clear when reading the extract from *Frankenstein* above that Shelley was using the conventions of the science fiction genre to respond to and mirror the concerns felt by many towards science and technology.

There will be further discussion of this Global Issue in a commentary on Cormac McCarthy's 'The Road' further on in this chapter.

Now let's read an extract from what could be considered a more contemporary science fiction work that also focuses upon the concerns of society towards science and technology. Below is an extract from the novel *The Road* by Cormac McCarthy (2006). The novel describes a post-apocalyptic America where most of human life and the landscape have been destroyed by an unspecified event. In the novel a father and son are travelling to an (also) unspecified location south, hoping to find better conditions in which they can survive.

> With the first gray light he rose and left the boy sleeping and walked out to the road and squatted and studied the country to the south. Barren, silent, godless. He thought the month was October but he wasn't sure. He hadn't kept a calendar for years. They were moving south. There'd be no surviving another winter here.
>
> When it was light enough to use the binoculars he glassed the valley below. Everything paling away into the murk. The soft ash blowing in loose swirls over the blacktop. He studied what he could see. The segments of road down there among the dead trees. Looking for anything of color. Any movement. Any trace of standing smoke. He lowered the glasses and pulled down the cotton mask from his face and wiped his nose on the back of his wrist and then glassed the country again. Then he just sat there holding the binoculars and watching the ashen daylight congeal over the land. He knew only that the child was his warrant. He said: If he is not the word of God, God never spoke.
>
> *(Cormac McCarthy 4–5)*

Cormac McCarthy

Cormac McCarthy is an American writer who was born in 1933. McCarthy writes novels that belong to a variety of genres such as western, post-apocalyptic and southern gothic. He is known for his sparse style of literature where he often dispenses with conventional usage of punctuation and tends to write with few literary flourishes such as the excessive use of figurative language. Many of his novels have been turned into successful films such as *No Country for Old Men* and *The Road*.

Instead of focusing the plot of the novel on the consequences of the dubious scientific experiments of one physician which then has very personal implications, McCarthy focuses upon the consequences of a scientific experiment that has had terrible consequences for everybody in the natural world. It is clear from reading the extract that some kind of terrible event has destroyed both human life and the landscape. It is unclear what this event was, but from the striking description of the natural landscape as being smoky and devoid of both colour and life you could easily surmize that some kind of environmental disaster has befallen the land. This work was written in 2006 when society was becoming gradually more aware of, and concerned about, the consequences of environmental issues such as pollution, resource shortages and extreme changes in weather patterns. You could read this work as an attempt from McCarthy to alter some of the conventions of the science fiction genre, transforming the conventions into those belonging to speculative fiction, to explore societal anxieties about the changes to the natural world being wrought by developments in science and technology. As mentioned before, Shelley makes the story of *Frankenstein* a personal one – it is essentially the story of the personal tragedy of Victor Frankenstein which helps to convey a clear warning to the reader about the dangers that can occur when science and technology are misused. However, the ambiguity in setting and in who the characters are in *The Road* helps to makes this work universal, mirroring the universal nature of the issue being discussed in the novel which is far more apt if you were to read this work as a warning against the potentially catastrophic results of environmental damage on the global population and the natural world.

It is clear when reading the extract from *The Road* that McCarthy is using the conventions of the speculative fiction genre (a subsidiary of the science fiction genre) to respond to and to mirror the concerns felt by many today towards science, technology and its impact on the natural world around us.

TOK Links

When reading *Frankenstein* and *The Road* it is clear that through the utilization of genre conventions, both works are able to discuss and explore issues pertinent to the society and culture in which they were written. However, though both works could be seen as belonging to the science fiction genre and though both works explore anxieties surrounding the development of science and technology they were written hundreds of years apart; they both focus on very different aspects of science, technology and the natural world and they utilize the conventions of science fiction very differently.

With that in mind, is the study of texts better approached by means of a temporal perspective, grouping texts according to when they were written, or by means of a thematic approach, grouping them according to the theme or concern they share?

In the last part of this chapter, we have explored how and why texts and works can modify their use of conventions in response to changes in societal values and concerns. In the next part of this chapter we will explore how readers and writers can interpret and change traditional literary and non-literary conventions, changing the way in which they are received and reproduced. We will also analyse how the use of the English language has changed over time and, as a result, its conventions.

How can readers and writers interpret and change traditional literary and non-literary conventions to discuss significant issues?

In this section we will explore how readers and writers can question and change the use of traditional literary and non-literary conventions in order to discuss significant issues within society.

When you think about the works and texts that you have explored throughout your studies in English Language and Literature, where were these texts and works from – geographically, culturally, temporally? In the literary works you have studied, what characters or settings do you feel were used most frequently? In the non-literary texts, from whose perspective did you often read? Who or what was the subject matter of these texts? How relatable have you found the texts and works that you have studied to be? Were the characters and settings recognizable to you? Was the subject matter something that you had experienced or were likely to experience?

In your responses to the above questions, you have begun to explore the issues central to the debate about how diverse the books that we read and study are and should be. Some people feel that, currently, the majority of books that are published, discussed in the media and/or studied in academic institutions only represent a minority of readers in terms of ethnicity, culture, gender and social background. As a result, some writers are changing the traditional conventions of the works and texts that they create in order to be more diverse.

The next text is an excerpt from Nigerian author Chimamanda Ngozie Adichie's longer TED talk about diversity in English language works and texts, which you can watch online on the TED website via the QR code opposite.

You have already analysed informative texts in Chapters 1.2 and 1.4, persuasive texts in Chapters 1.2 and 1.4 and speeches in Chapter 1.4 and so you may want to use the notes that you made in those chapters to help you to understand this lecture.

I'm a storyteller. And I would like to tell you a few personal stories about what I like to call 'the danger of the single story'. I grew up on a university campus in eastern Nigeria. My mother says that I started reading at the age of two, although I think four is probably close to the truth. So I was an early reader, and what I read were British and American children's books.

I was also an early writer, and when I began to write, at about the age of seven, stories in pencil with crayon illustrations that my poor mother was obligated to read, I wrote exactly the kinds of stories I was reading: All my characters were white and blue-eyed, they played in the snow, they ate apples, and they talked a lot about the weather, how lovely it was that the sun had come out. Now, this despite the fact that I lived in Nigeria. I had never been outside Nigeria. We didn't have snow, we ate mangoes, and we never talked about the weather, because there was no need to.

My characters also drank a lot of ginger beer because the characters in the British books I read drank ginger beer. Never mind that I had no idea what ginger beer was. And for many years afterwards, I would have a desperate desire to taste ginger beer. But that is another story. What this demonstrates, I think, is how impressionable and vulnerable we are in the face of a story, particularly as children. Because all I had read were books in which characters were foreign, I had become convinced that books by their very nature had to have foreigners in them and had to be about things with which I could not personally identify.

Now, things changed when I discovered African books. There weren't many of them available, and they weren't quite as easy to find as the foreign books. But because of writers like Chinua Achebe and Camara Laye, I went through a mental shift in my perception of literature. I realized that people like me, girls with skin the color of chocolate, whose kinky hair could not form ponytails, could also exist in literature.

I started to write about things I recognized. Now, I loved those American and British books I read. They stirred my imagination. They opened up new worlds for me. But the unintended consequence was that I did not know that people like me could exist in literature. So what the discovery of African writers did for me was this: It saved me from having a single story of what books are.

(Chimamanda Ngozie Adichie)

Chimamanda Ngozie Adichie

Chimamanda Ngozie Adichie is a novelist who was born in Nigeria in 1977. She moved to America for her university studies in 1996. Much of her writing is set in Nigeria and includes Nigerian narrators, protagonists and characters. Thematically, much of her writing focuses on relationships, cultural identity and feminist issues. She is perhaps best known for her novels *Purple Hibiscus*, *Half of a Yellow Sun* and *Americanah*. Adichie is also known for her contributions to TED talks such as her lecture on 'We Should All Be Feminists'. Her above lecture is one of the top-ten most viewed TED talks of all time.

EE Links: English A - Language category 3

TED lectures are a relatively new and innovative text type that can be used by speakers to explore issues that they feel are of significance within society. You could use this text type for a category 3 extended essay which could analyse a variety of the most-watched TED lectures in order to answer this research question: **How do TED lectures use language, structure and prosodic/phonological features in order to convey their message effectively to their intended audience?**

CONCEPT CONNECTION

IDENTITY AND REPRESENTATION

It is clear from Adichie's TED talk that her lack of exposure to works and texts that represented her own identity and culture meant that she then struggled to articulate that culture and identity herself in her own writing. It was only when she was exposed to the writings of authors who authentically represented her own identity and experiences that she was then able to express them herself. Through creating her own works of literature containing characters and language that represented her own identity and experiences, Adichie has deviated from the traditional conventions of the literature that she grew up recognising into a set of conventions that better fits the messages and ideas that she wants to convey to her reader.

Is Adichie's experience one to which you can relate? Whether you can or cannot will depend entirely on your own identity; for example, the gender that you identify with, the ethnicity that you feel like you belong to, the sexual orientation that you feel represents you, the religion that you believe in and the nation, or nations, that you were born and/or grew up in. It would also depend on how rigidly the curricula that you were taught in school, or the facilitators of your education, adhered to 'classic' or 'canonical' reading lists that tend to be dominated by Western writers who also tend to be white and male. If you grew up, for example, as a female in an economically and socially deprived area but only ever read and studied works and texts that were set in a more prosperous area, written by and about men who come from wealthy backgrounds, then this may affect the way that you view your own identity, perhaps as something other and inferior. How useful would these works be in constructing and representing your own identity and experiences in the texts and works that you create? The variety of answers that this debate engenders are important and relevant and will be discussed further in Chapter 3.3 of this section, when we ask how valid the notion of a classic work is.

In her TED lecture, Adichie clearly questions the conventions of the works and texts that she was exposed to when she was younger and makes a powerful argument against a 'single story' of one nation and its citizens. If you would like to understand how Adichie used language and structural features effectively to do this then read the commentary analysing her TED lecture in the end of book commentaries. If you would like to read the rest of the transcript of the lecture (which will be useful for understanding the end of book commentary analysing the speech and for the concluding activity) then scan the QR code opposite and click on the 'transcript' tab under the video of the speech.

CHECK FOR UNDERSTANDING

Once you have read the end of book commentary analysing Adichie's TED lecture use the information in Chapters 1.4 and 1.5 about speeches to see if you can spot anymore language and structural features that Adichie has used in her lecture.

Next, we shall explore how a particular writer has changed, and experimented with the more traditional conventions of poetry, in order to represent his own identity more authentically.

The following poem is called 'Parade's End' by the writer Daljit Nagra (2007). In this poem, Nagra describes a British-Indian family who have moved from the south of England to a part of northern

England called Yorkshire. The family own a shop in an economically deprived area and are the targets of racism and violence.

You have already studied the key features of poetry in Chapter 1.2 and so you should use the notes that you made there to help you understand and analyse this poem. In the table below there are listed two definitions of language features that you will need to know in order to understand the poem.

■ Table 3.2.2

Language Feature	Definition
Colloquial language (or **colloquialisms**)	Words that are informal and 'everyday', words that you might use when speaking with friends or in another informal environment. For example, 'mates' instead of the more formal 'friends', or 'kids' instead of the more formal 'children'.
Dialectical language (or **dialect**)	In linguistics, dialect refers to words that belong to a specific geographical region or social group. For example, in Australia people may refer to the 'afternoon' as the 'arvo' or in Scotland some people may refer to a 'baby' as a 'bairn'.

Parade's End

Dad parked our Granada, champagne-gold
by our superstore on Blackstock Road,
my brother's eyes scanning the men
who scraped the pavement frost to the dole,
one 'got on his bike' over the hill
or the few who warmed us a thumbs up
for the polished recovery of our re-sprayed car.

Council mums at our meat display
nestled against a pane with white trays
swilling kidneys, liver and a sandy block
of corned beef, loud enough about the way
darkies from down south *Come op ta*
Yorksha, mekkin claaims in aut theh can
befoh buggerin off in theh flash caahs!

At nine, we left the emptied till open,
clicked the dials of the safe. Bolted
two metal bars across the back door
(with a new lock). Spread trolleys
at ends of darkened aisles. Then we pressed
the code for the caged alarm and rushed
the precinct to check it was throbbing red.

Thundering down the graffiti of shutters
against the valley of high rise flats.
Ready for the getaway to our cul-de-sac'd
semi-detached, until we stood stock-still:
watching the car-skin pucker, bubbling smarts
of acid. In the unstoppable pub roar
From the John O'Gaut across the forecourt,

We returned up to the shop, lifted a shutter,
queued at the sink, walked down again.
Three of us, each carrying pans of cold water.
Then we swept away the bonnet-leaves
from gold to the brown of our former colour.

(Daljit Nagra)

Daljit Nagra

Daljit Nagra is a British writer who was born in 1966. His parents emigrated from India to Great Britain in the late 1950s. Nagra often writes about the experience of Indians who have emigrated to Britain and the experience of British people who have Indian heritage. He is perhaps best known for his collection of poems, *Look We Have Coming to Dover!*

How many of the words in the poem did you struggle to understand? For example, there is a section of the poem which is written phonetically in the Yorkshire dialect that you may have struggled with:

Come op ta
Yorksha, mekkin claaims in aut theh can
befoh buggerin off in theh flash caahs!

(Daljit Nagra)

This roughly translates as, 'Come up to Yorkshire, making claims on anything they can before buggering off in their flash cars.' As well as the use of this dialect, there are also some other British colloquial words and terms used such as 'dole' (line 4), 'got on his bike' (line 5). The use of this language is perhaps unusual in more classic and canonical examples of poetry that tend to refrain from using this kind of English. However, as a writer who is from and grew up in this particular area, Nagra has used this language to ensure that the voice of the speakers within his poem sound authentic, while also giving a voice and representation to an alternative perspective on growing up in England that some readers of literature may not have otherwise considered.

The speaker of the poem and his family have had economic success in their migration from India to England, and from the south of England to the north of England. The colour imagery of their car being 'champagne gold' (line 1) and the allusion to the 'cul-de-sac' (a closed-off residential street; line 24) that they live in both connote to the wealth that the speaker's family have, which also contrasts with the poverty of the area that their shop is located in 'valley of high-rise flats' (line 23) and 'scraped the pavement frost to the dole' (line 4). This contrast may be considered unusual as a stereotypical representation of recently arrived migrants to the West usually depict these people as poor, and certainly poorer than their Western-native counterparts, and living a life of struggle and hardship. Again, Nagra has subverted the traditional representation of the newly arrived immigrant experience to give voice to an alternative experience and identity that is accurate for some.

In the final stanza, a violent act is committed towards the family by local people who are clearly resentful of the success of the speaker's family. Their luxury car is set alight (not for the first time) and the speaker describes how he and his family 'stood stock-still: watching the car-skin pucker, bubbling smarts of acid' (lines 25–27). The use of plosives in the verbs 'pucker' and 'bubbling' to describe how the golden paint on their car melted away helps to convey the anger and resentment that the local people feel towards the speaker and his family which is rooted in fear of the unfamiliar, racism and ignorance. Again, Nagra gives voice to something that many people of colour, especially newly arrived migrants, have experienced in their lives. This may not be the type of experience that many classic or canonical poems explore, but it is an experience with which many people can identify and thus has value and importance.

GLOBAL ISSUES ***Field of Inquiry:* Beliefs, Values and Education**

PREJUDICE

Nagra's poem also explores, through the deviation from some of the more classic conventions of poetry and Standard English, how the speaker of the poem and their family have become the targets of violence and racism in the Yorkshire town where the poem is set. This poem could be used to discuss the global issue of prejudice (also within the beliefs, values and education field of inquiry) along with another non-literary text focused on this issue. An example could be this online interview, see QR code alongside, which may contain controversial content, with Milo Yiannopoulos who was a former editor of the far-right *Breitbart News* and who is a political commentator, writer and speaker. Read the key features of interviews box, the activity and the commentary below to see how the writer has deviated from some of the usual conventions of interviews in order to explore the global issue of prejudice within the interview.

KEY FEATURES INTERVIEWS

- Interviews can either take a traditional question and answer format or can be narrative in style where the interviewees responses are embedded within the interviewers narration of the interview. The balance of content between the interviewer and interviewee will usually be evenly split, usually a deliberate decision by the interviewer to keep the interview focused on the topics and themes that they wish to be discussed.
- The formality of an interview will depend upon the subject of the interview, the interviewer and the publication in which the interview appears.
- Even a formal interview will usually include examples of spoken discourse to ensure that the conversation between the interviewer and interviewee and/or the interviewees responses seem natural – this can include features such as elliptical syntax, colloquial language, idioms, humour, contractions and dialectical language. However, taboo language/derogatory language that could offend is often omitted by publishers for reasons pertaining to taste and sensitivity.
- Interviews will usually include direct quotes from the interviewee. One of these quotes will often be used as the title of the article.
- There will usually be a clear introduction and conclusion to the interview.
- The interview will usually be focused on an overarching theme or series of themes to ensure that there is a coherent structure.

ACTIVITY 4

Write down your thoughts in response to these activity questions and consider how the writer has deviated from some of the traditional conventions of interviews in order to explore ideas about **the global issue of prejudice** in the interview. When you are finished, read the commentary under the activity box to see a model response to these questions.

In order to analyse this interview website through the lens of the **global issue of prejudice**, we will use step 1 (**genre, audience and purpose**), step 2 (**structure and style**) and step 6 (**reader response to ideas, message and/or purpose**) of the non-literary text reading strategy as delineated in Chapter 1.1. You may wish to re-read this in order to understand the text and the end of book commentary.

1 How is the interview structured in terms of the balance of content between the interviewer and interviewee? What effect does this have?
2 Can you spot any features of spoken discourse? Why do you think the writer of the interview has decided to include these, and some of the more taboo/derogatory language and comments used by the interviewee?
3 The subject of the interviewee, Milo Yiannopoulos, is a controversial public figure who espouses viewpoints that many in society deem unacceptable. What could be some of the reasons that *The Nation* has decided to give him a platform through this interview?
4 What overarching theme/themes can you see in the interview, are these discussed in a logical/coherent format?
What linguistic and structural choices are used by the writer to highlight these?
5 How is the global issue of prejudice explored differently here when compared to Nagra's poem?

The balance of content between the interviewer and the interviewee (Milo Yiannopoulos) is heavily skewed towards the interviewee. The interviewer has taken the deliberate decision to deviate from conventions and give Yiannopoulos a lot of time to respond to his short prompts/questions to perhaps add authenticity to the interview. This helps to remind readers that Yiannopoulos' interview responses are a true representation of Yiannopoulos' thoughts and beliefs which could be seen as being prejudiced. This perhaps manipulates the reader into viewing Yiannopoulos as a prejudiced person.

The interview is structured in a traditional question and answer format which should help to create a formal tone. The subject of the interview and the topics discussed are of a serious nature which would make a formal tone of the interview appropriate. However, the examples of spoken discourse evident within the interview, for example humour – 'Maybe, but that wouldn't be the top of your list, because you might actually want to see a good movie once in a while', colloquial language – 'This stuff isn't just over there now. It's here, too, and we welcomed it in' and idioms, 'They want to visit the sins of the fathers on the sons' make the interview feel more light hearted in tone which is unusual considering the serious topics that are being discussed. These features may have deliberately been included to signpost to the reader that Yiannopoulos does not take the potential impact of his prejudiced views seriously – instead he views them (and speaks about them) in a light-hearted way.

The Nation may have decided to give Yiannopoulos this platform to speak his beliefs (and, in a deviation from conventions, have included clear examples of taboo/derogatory language/comments) for ideological reasons – they may believe that it is important for the public to know what Yiannopoulos' views are, even if they are prejudiced, so that they can make an informed decision about whether they agree with them or not. It may even have been a deliberate decision made *The Nation* to try to suggest to the reader that Yiannopoulos' views are prejudiced.
The writer signposts to the reader that the interview responses are a true representation of Yiannopoulos' thoughts and beliefs and within the interview Yiannopoulos states opinions that could be considered prejudiced, especially against Muslims and women. It could be the case that *The Nation* wanted to make it clear to the reader through Yiannopoulos' own words that, despite his denials, Yiannopoulos is a prejudiced person.

The overall themes of the interview are focused upon those of culture, politics and societal issues but the order in which they are discussed by Yiannopoulos are not in any cogent or logical structure. Usually, an interviewer would help to steer the interviewee towards certain issues and topics but, in a deviation from conventions, the interviewer largely allows Yiannopoulos to tangentially discuss his ideas as he wishes. This creates the impression that Yiannopoulos is incapable of discussing these issues in an articulate way which helps to perhaps demean him and his prejudiced views in the eyes of the reader.

Yiannopoulos, the subject of the interview, could be seen as someone who espouses prejudiced views, 'single men in their 30s are fine. Single women in their 30s are a mess' and 'Whether that is from mass immigration from backward cultures into rich nations, whether it is, in my case, I care more about Islam. I don't want it here', which is different from the speaker in Nagra's poem who is the victim of prejudiced views.

However, it could be argued that both the poem and the interview are designed to explore prejudice as a negative part of society. Both the poem and the interview deviate from conventions associated with their text type or genre in order to, respectively, explore the effects of prejudice on someone who experiences it on a daily basis and in the interview through the writer's decision to allow Yiannopoulos to shock the reader through giving him the platform to express his prejudiced views unimpeded.

How the use and conventions of the English language have changed over time

In Chapter 1.3 you explored how advancements in technology and its increasing use in our daily lives has affected the English language, leading to the creation of new forms of language such as **textspeak**, **emoticons** and **emojis**. In the next part of this chapter, we will explore how British colonialism, global trade and the passing of time have modified some conventions of the English language, and the way that it is used in some parts of the world.

In the previous part of this chapter you explored how Daljit Nagra used **colloquialisms** and **dialect** in his poetry to convey the characteristics and identity of the area of Yorkshire that the poem was set in. You can separate the way that we describe the usage of the English language into two broad terms – **Standard English** and **non-Standard English**. Standard English refers to the type of formal English that you would use in an academic essay or when writing a letter of application for a job. This type of English is the English that you will have learnt about in school that adheres to rules about spelling, grammar and punctuation. Non-Standard English is any form of English that does not adhere to these rules and includes the usage of **colloquialisms** and **dialectical language**. There are some people who see non-Standard English as 'wrong' and 'incorrect' and who believe that it shouldn't be used in any context. However, there are many writers who come from places where dialectical English is the type of English that they are most familiar with, or who are writing about places where non-Standard English is more likely to be used or about people who are more likely to use it. As a result, many of these writers (like Daljit Nagra) are using this type of non-Standard English in their works and texts to lend authenticity to their writing.

As well as dialectical and colloquial language, there are other examples of non-standard forms of the English language whose conventions have formed through the influence of British colonialism and global trade. In the next part of this chapter we will explore the idea of **linguistic imperialism** and the meaning of the terms **lingua franca**, **Creole** and **pidgin**.

THE BRITISH EMPIRE AND THE ENGLISH LANGUAGE

- From the late-sixteenth century into the twentieth century, Great Britain took possession of a large number of countries around the world which included the modern-day nations of the United States of America, India, Guyana, Jamaica, Fiji, Kenya and many more. The British Empire was the largest in known history and at the peak of its power in 1913 was directly or indirectly ruling 23 per cent of the world's population.
- After the conclusion of the Second World War, Great Britain worked towards a policy of 'decolonization' where many countries achieved or were granted independence. Many see the real end of the British Empire as only taking place in 1997 when Britain handed control of Hong Kong to China. There are many ex-British Empire countries who are independent but have opted to become a part of the 'Commonwealth of Nations' which are united under the monarchy of the United Kingdom.
- The colonial governments of many of the countries that were colonized by Great Britain enforced the compulsory use of the English language in educational institutions, the legal system and other public offices in order to control the native population of those countries. This imposition of one language upon the speakers of another language is called **'linguistic imperialism'**.
- Arguably as a result of this practice, English is the world's most learned second language and is the official, or one of the official, languages of over 60 different countries. It is recognized as a global **lingua franca** meaning that if two people do not speak the same language as each other, they are likely to use English as a way of communicating with one another. For example, in the United Nations where there are native speakers of many different languages, English is often used as the language in which to conduct discussions and negotiations as most delegates will at least know and understand it as a second language.
- Another impact of the British Empire upon the evolution of the English language is the creation of **pidgin** and **Creole** forms of the language in places that were colonized. As global trade took place between these countries, there was a need for officials, traders and consumers to communicate with one another. A **pidgin** language is a language that is created in this process and is a mixture between two or more languages. Pidgin is a language that is exclusively oral, with no native speakers and which does not adhere to conventions of **orthography** or **grammar**. However, as time passes these pidgin languages can become the first language of descendants of the speakers of the original pidgin language and become a stable language that has conventions regarding **orthography** and **grammar**. These languages are called **Creole** languages.
- English-based Creole variants are now a national language or most-spoken first language of many ex-British Empire colonies. **Jamaican Patois**, **Guyanese Creole** and **Tok Pisin** (from Papua New Guinea) are all examples of this.

Further reading

Like **dialectical** and **colloquial** language, there are some writers who believe that their ideas are best expressed and are more authentic when they write using an English-based pidgin or Creole language. Some of these writers are listed below:

- Amitav Ghosh – we explored an extract from Ghosh's novel *The Glass Palace* in Chapter 3.1. He has also written a trilogy of books called *Ibis* which explore the opium trade in the nineteenth century, and includes characters who converse in English-based **pidgin** languages.
- Marlon James – in *A Brief History of Seven Killings* James often uses **Jamaican Patois** in the dialogue between various characters.
- John Agard – a poet, playwright and children's writer who often uses **Guyanese Creole** in his writing, for example, in the poems 'Checkin' Out Me History' and 'Half Caste'.
- Cheryl Lu-Lien Tan – in *Sarong Party Girls* Tan writes entirely in **Singlish** which is a **pidgin** form of English mixed with different languages spoken in Singapore, such as Putonghua, Cantonese, Hokkien, Malay and Tamil.

Like **dialectical** and **colloquial** English, the acceptability in the use of English-based **pidgin** and **Creole** languages is a contentious issue for some people. However, in 2017 BBC News decided to launch a digital platform for readers in West and Central Africa that would be written entirely in pidgin. Pidgin is the name given to an English-based Creole language which is spoken as a first language by an estimated three to five million people and by an estimated 75 million in Nigeria alone. Visit the website via the QR code in the margin. You may want to use the notes that you made in the previous chapter about online news websites to help you analyse and understand this source.

CONCEPT CONNECTION

COMMUNICATION AND TRANSFORMATION

If you are not already a speaker of pidgin, can you understand the text on the homepage? The likely answer to this question is 'yes' as the transformation of Standard English into pidgin is more of a modification than a wholesale rewrite of the language. Many of the keywords within the sentences such as nouns, verbs and adjectives (words such as 'activist', 'escape', 'new', for example) are the same as Standard English and so the key message is still easily communicated even to someone who doesn't speak pidgin fluently or natively. Despite using a different, sometimes elliptical, syntax ('dey beg for war', for example) and phonetic versions of Standard English words ('don', 'di', 'dey') it is easy to see how the language of Nigerian Pidgin has evolved from Standard English through the lingua franca process described in the above information box.

Earlier, we discussed the debate surrounding the responsibility of educators and curricula writers to include works and texts that represent a variety of readers instead of a small minority. We could extend this debate to ask the question about how much of a responsibility do media outlets have to communicate information in a way that is most accessible to those reading it. The transformation in language that you can see in this text may make some people feel uneasy as they may feel that it compromises the integrity and importance of Standard English too much. They may argue that media outlets using a pidgin language could signpost to readers that they do not need to use Standard English at all, and that it may lead to a deterioration in the quality of English used in the place where this change in medium of communication occurs. Others would see that the transformation is necessary to avoid linguistic imperialism and to ensure that a wide variety of people are able to access important information and news, instead of a small minority.

ACTIVITY 5

Imagine that you come from, or live in, a country where English is spoken as an official language but the majority of the population's first language and most widely spoken language is an English-based Creole language. Think about the reasons why this language should become an official language and why it should be used in official settings. Then think about the arguments against this idea. Spend ten minutes coming up with these ideas – being able to see a singular issue from multiple viewpoints clearly connects to the key concept of perspective. Some ideas for this task are provided below.

■ Table 3.2.3

Reasons for the English-based Creole language becoming an official language	Reasons against the English-based Creole language becoming an official language
As the majority of the population understand the English-based Creole better than Standard English it would be fairer if the Court of Law was conducted in this language as currently people are at a disadvantage if they have to argue their case through an interpreter or in a language that they are unfamiliar with.	Making the English-based Creole an official language would be disastrous for the economy. Businesses would be reluctant to base themselves in a country where institutions important to business like the Court of Law and other public offices were conducted in a language that is understood by very few people globally. It would also be difficult to attract talented workers to come to the country if they knew that their work contracts, their tax returns and other important bureaucratic processes were in a little used language that barely anyone outside of the country can understand.

GLOBAL ISSUES ***Field of Inquiry:* Culture, Identity and Community**

THE ACCEPTABILITY OF NON-STANDARD ENGLISH

Some examples of noted writers who use **colloquial** and **dialectical language** in their writing are listed below:

- Ken Loach – a film director from the UK, often uses regional dialects in his films. For example, his film *Sweet Sixteen* is written entirely in Scottish dialect, particularly that belonging to Glasgow and the surrounding areas.
- Willy Russell – playwright who wrote *Educating Rita*, *Blood Brothers* and *Our Day Out* includes many characters who speak using a dialect native to the city of Liverpool in north-west England called 'Scouse'.
- Simon Armitage – poet who wrote a collection of poems called *The Not Dead* based on testimonies from ex-soldiers. Many of these poems include examples of colloquial and dialectical language from various regions of the United Kingdom.
- Anna Burns – author of *Milkman*, which is written entirely in Northern Irish dialect.
- Donald Glover – a musician, actor and writer from the USA, created the critically and commercially successful television sitcom *Atlanta* whose characters often speak in African-American Vernacular English (also known as AAVE).

The acceptability of **non-Standard English** is a contentious issue in many countries around the world. You could use an extract from one of the literary works listed above and use a non-literary text (perhaps from a writer who writes a series of texts about the confluence of language and culture), such as 'Why did Singapore writers festival bar a Singlish novel on girls looking for white western husbands?', (Muhammad Cohen, SCMP) that is focused on this topic, to explore the global issue of the acceptability of non-Standard English. You can access this article and two others by Cohen through these QR codes alongside. This series of articles by Muhammad Cohen can constitute a body of work.

Now that you have finished this chapter, let's review the key ideas in it and practise the several skills that it introduced. You may want to look back at the key features of gothic fiction box in the previous chapter (page 385) before reading the next extract.

The next text is an extract from *My Sister, The Serial Killer* by Oyinkan Braithwaite (2017). The novel tells the story of a woman whose sister continually murders her boyfriends and always enlists her sister's assistance when trying to cover up these murders.

Femi's family sent a cleaner to this home, to ready it to be put on the market – to move on, I guess. But the cleaner discovered a bloody napkin down the back of the sofa. It's all there on Snapchat, for the world to see that whatever happened to Femi, it did not happen of his own volition. The family is asking again for answers.

Ayoola tells me she may have sat there. She may have put the napkin on the seat to keep from staining the sofa. She may have forgotten about it …

'It's fine, if they ask me I'll just tell them he had a nosebleed.' She is sitting in front of her dressing table tending to her dreadlocks and I am standing behind her, clenching and unclenching my fists.

'Ayoola, if you go to jail–'

'Only the guilty go to jail.'

'First of all, that's not true. Second of all, you *killed* a man.'

'*Defending* myself; the judge will understand that, right?' She pats her cheeks with blusher. Ayoola lives in a world where things must always go her way. It's a law as certain as the law of gravity.

I leave her to her makeup and sit at the top of the staircase, my forehead resting on the wall. My head feels as though there is a storm brewing inside it. The wall should be cool, but it is a hot day, so there is no comfort to be had there.

When I'm anxious, I confide in Muhtar – but he is in the hospital, and there is no one to share my fears with here. I imagine for the millionth time how it would go if I were to tell my mother the truth:

'Ma …'

'Hmmmm.'

'I want to talk to you about Ayoola.'

'Are you people fighting again?'

'No, ma. I … there was an incident with erm Femi.'

'The boy who is missing?'

'Well, he isn't missing. He is dead.'

'Hey!!! Jésù şàánú fún wa o!'

'Yes … erm … but you see … Ayoola was the one who killed him.'

'What is wrong with you? Why are you blaming your sister?'

'She called me. I saw him … I saw his body, I saw the blood.'

'Shut up! Does this look like something you should be joking about?'

'Mum … I just …'

'I said shut up. Ayoola is a beautiful child with a wonderful temperament … Is that it? Is it jealousy that is making you say these horrible things?'

(Oyinkan Braithwaite)

ACTIVITY 6

1 It has been suggested that this work could be categorized as a modern example of the gothic fiction genre (see Chapter 3.1, page 385). In what ways does the work modify the conventions associated with these genre classifications? Why do you think the writer has done this and how does it link to changes that have occurred in society since the first gothic fiction works were published?

2 In what ways does the work question stereotypical depictions of life in Nigeria?

3 Are there any uses of non-Standard English in the work? If so, how and why is it used?

When you have finished, compare your responses with those at the back of the book.

Oyinkan Braithwaite

Oyinkan Braithwaite is a Nigerian author who was born in 1988 – she grew up living between Nigeria and the UK. Her story *The Driver* was nominated for the Commonwealth Short Story Prize in 2016. If you would like to read more about Braithwaite then use the QR code to read this interview with her from *The Guardian*.

Works cited

Adams, D. *The Hitchhiker's Guide to the Galaxy*. Del Rey, 1995.

Adichie, CN. *Americanah*. Anchor, 2014

Adichie, CN. *Half of a Yellow Sun*. Anchor, 2007

Adichie, CN. *Purple Hibiscus*. Algonquin Books, 2012

Adichie, CN. 'The danger of a single story.' *TEDGlobal*, 2009. Web. 13 Oct. 2019. **www.ted.com/talks/chimamanda_adichie_the_danger_of_a_single_story**.

Adichie, CN. 'We Should All Be Feminists.' TEDGlobal, 2012. Web. 28th October 2019 **https://www.ted.com/talks/chimamanda_ngozi_adichie_we_should_all_be_feminists?language=en**.

Agard, J. *'Half-Caste', Half-Caste and Other Poems*. Hodder Children's Books, 2005.

Armitage, S. *The Not Dead*. Pomona Press, 2008.

BBC News Pidgin. Web. 17 Feb. 2019. **www.bbc.com/pidgin**.

Braithwaite, O. *My Sister, The Serial Killer*. Doubleday, 2018.

Burns, A. *Milkman*. Graywolf Press, 2018.

Cohen, M. 'Why did Singapore writers festival bar a Singlish novel on girls looking for white western husbands?' *This Week in Asia*, *South China Morning Post*, 7 Nov. 2016. Web. 1 Sept. 2019. **www.scmp.com/week-asia/society/article/2043139/why-did-singapore-writers-festival-bar-singlish-novel-girls**.

Cohen, M. 'Hijab-wearing stand-up comic fights Islamic extremism in Indonesia using laughter as her weapon.' *South China Morning Post*, 15 Feb. 2018. Web. 1 Sept. 2019. **www.scmp.com/culture/arts-entertainment/article/2133375/hijab-wearing-stand-comic-fights-islamic-extremism**.

Cohen, M. 'I never escaped the violence: Fatima Bhutto on her new novel *The Runaways*.' *This Week in Asia, South China Morning Post*, 25 Nov. 2018. Web. 1 Sept. 2019. **www.scmp.com/week-asia/people/article/2174085/i-never-escaped-violence-fatima-bhutto-her-new-novel-runaways**.

Dick, PK. *Do Androids Dream of Electric Sheep?* Del Rey, 1996.

Ghosh, A. *The Glass Palace*. Ravi Dayal, Penguin India, 1997.

Gibson, W. *Neuromancer*. Penguin Classics, 2016.

Glover, D. *Atlanta*. Distributed by FX, 2016.

Guttenplan, DD. 'An Interview with the Most Hated Man on the Internet.' *The Nation*, 16 Oct. 2016. Web. 1 Sept. 2019. **https://www.thenation.com/article/an-interview-with-the-most-hated-man-on-the-internet**.

Harvey-Jenner, C. 'This blogger pointed out the double standard of criticising Tess Holliday's *Cosmopolitan* cover.' *Cosmopolitan*, 5 Sept. 2018. Web. 13 Oct. 2019. **www.cosmopolitan.com/uk/body/a22993945/stephanie-yeboah-double-standard-tess-holliday-cosmopolitancover-criticism**.

James, M. *A Brief History of Seven Killings: A Novel*. Riverhead Books, 2015

Lea, R. 'Oyinkan Braithwaite's serial-killer thriller: would you help your murderer sister?' *The Guardian*, 15 Jan. 2019. Web. 13 Oct. 2019. **www.theguardian.com/books/2019/jan/15/oyinkan-braithwaite-thriller-nigerian-author-comic-debut-novel-my-sister-the-serial-killer**.

Loach, K. *Sweet Sixteen*. Icon Film Distribution, 2002.

McCarthy, C. *The Road*. Picador, Pan MacMillan, 2009.

Nagra, D. 'Parade's End,' *Look We Have Coming to Dover!* Faber and Faber, 2007.

Raimi S. *Spider-Man*, Columbia Pictures, 2002

Russell, W. *Blood Brothers*. Methuen Drama, 2009.

Russell, W. *Educating Rita*. Methuen Drama, 2013.

Russell, W. *Our Day Out*. Methuen Drama, 2013.

Shelley, M. *Frankenstein*. Norton Critical Editions, W.W. Norton & Company, 2012.

'Six Decades Of Cosmo Covers Show How "Sexy" Has (And Hasn't) Changed.' *Huffington Post*, 7 Dec. 2017. Web. 13 Oct. 2019. **www.huffpost.com/entry/cosmo-covers-sexy_n_3745959**.

'Speaker of the House Pelosi makes history.' *Associated Press*, NBC News Online, 4 Jan. 2007. Web. 17 Feb. 2019. **www.nbcnews.com/id/16449288/ns/politics/t/speaker-house-pelosi-makes-history**.

Tan, CLL. *Sarong Party Girls: A Novel*. William Morrow Paperbacks, 2017.

Wells, HG. *The Time Machine*. Prestwick House Inc, 2006.

Wells, HG. *The War of the Worlds*. Dover Publications, 1997.

3.3 How valid is the notion of a 'classic' work?

OBJECTIVES OF CHAPTER

- To understand how a work can become defined as a 'classic'.
- To provide an overview of the varied opinions that exist pertaining to the notion of a 'classic' work.
- To demonstrate how some writers subvert the notion of a 'classic' work.
- To demonstrate ways to apply course concepts to specific works of literature and non-literary texts.
- To demonstrate ways to understand specific works of literature and non-literary texts in the context of global issues.

In the previous chapter, through our exploration of Adichie's TED talk 'The Danger of a Single Story', we began to explore aspects of the debate that surrounds the validity of notions about 'classic' works. We will begin this chapter by outlining how works can become defined as a 'classic' in the first place, before moving on to explore the variety of perspectives that exist towards this notion. We will conclude this chapter by analysing two very different works that would both be considered 'classic'.

How do we define a 'classic' work?

The notion of a 'classic' work is one that is fraught with contention and ambiguity. Who decides which works can be considered a 'classic'? How are these people chosen and do these people represent the viewpoint of a large variety of people or just a few? Can we ever really know at the time of publishing whether a work can be considered a 'classic' or can we only know when they have stood the test of time?

Below are some quotes from a variety of writers and academics attempting to define what we mean by the term 'a classic work'.

> *'A classic is a book that has never finished saying what it has to say.'*
>
> *Italo Cavino*

> *'A classic is something that everybody wants to have read and nobody wants to read.'*
>
> *Mark Twain*

> *'The classics are important not because they are old but because they are always being renewed.'*
>
> *Michael Dirda*

> *'Classics aren't books that are read for pleasure. Classics are books that are imposed on unwilling students, books that are subjected to analyzes of "levels of significance" and other blatt, books that are dead.'*
>
> *Alexei Panshin*

As you can see from these responses, there is a clear disparity in perspectives towards the concept of 'a classic work'. Where Cavino sees 'classics' as being integral to the significance bestowed upon literature for its capacity to provoke discussion about important issues across time, Twain sees 'classics' as works that are merely read for social status and cultural capital, and not for pleasure.

Where Dirda sees 'classics' as being important in their ability to influence other writers to create newer, more relevant, but just as significant versions of the original 'classic work', Panshin sees 'classics' as works that have zero relevance for most readers and that are generally 'imposed' on readers against their will.

Generally, works could be considered a 'classic' when they are noted as being significant and/or laudable through their inclusion in the following:

- lists compiled by literary academics and critics
- literary prize long and short-lists
- the reading lists of examination qualifications and academic institutions
- a significant number of reviews, blogs and/or public discourse.

However, opinions about and towards the people who create these award lists, reading lists and other forms of mass media (and what works are included in them) are also varied. The next part of this section will explore the variety of perspectives that exist regarding this issue.

What are the variety of perspectives regarding the notion of a 'classic work'?

There are some people who view the notion of a 'classic' work as one that brings great benefit to writers and readers and there are some who view this notion as one that can be negative and damaging for both readers and writers. An overview of some common opinions relating to these opposing perspectives are listed below:

Some of the benefits of a work being considered a 'classic' could include:

- the public recognition of the value of a work can lead to positive social change
- the inclusion of works in prize lists and reading lists can bring visibility to voices in literature that have previously been invisible or not recognized
- when groups of people have all read or been encouraged to read a work this can lead to unity in the form of a shared point of reference.

Some of the disadvantages of the concept of 'classic' works are:

- a perceived lack of diversity in its interpretation
- the value of other, less typically 'classic', works can be devalued
- the exposure to literature by entire groups of people can be narrowed when this concept is strictly adhered to.

To begin exploring this issue, we will read an opinion article by Julian Barnes for the *London Review of Books* (a UK journal of literary discussion which is published fortnightly) where he explains his viewpoint on the judges who decide who should win the Booker Prize for Fiction. This is a literary prize that is awarded to books that are published in the English language in the UK. Recipients of the award have included submissions from a variety of nations including India, Nigeria, New Zealand, USA, Australia, South Africa and the UK. The impact of winning the Booker Prize is termed the 'Booker Effect' and is described by a blog entry on the prize's own website in this way.

https://thebookerprizes.com/news/2012/11/13/man-booker-effect

The Man Booker Effect

Despite both the column inches it generates and the amount of chatter and comment it enjoys, the Man Booker Prize's remit is really very simple: the judges' task is to pick the best novel of the year written by a British, Commonwealth or Republic of Ireland citizen. No more than that: pretty straightforward really. The prize has nothing to do with sales. At least in theory. In reality, such is its prestige and old-fashioned clout, that to win is to become a best-seller.

Hilary Mantel is no exception, though she makes a particularly interesting case study. In 2009 she was a well known, widely admired, prize winning and relatively commercial novelist – and then she won the Man Booker with *Wolf Hall*. The effect can be judged in numbers: up to announcement of the longlist she had sold in hardback a very respectable 13,129 copies (sales for hardback literary fiction tend to be deep in the lower atmosphere rather than stratospheric) and in the next six weeks up to the announcement of the shortlist she almost doubled that figure, selling another 11,000 or so. In the six weeks between the shortlist announcement and the picking of the winner she really flew, selling another 42,217 books. As the winner though she entered another league. Her sales currently stand at some 225,000 copies – that is in hardback alone without the numbers for paperbacks and ebooks.

(Leah)

KEY FEATURES OPINION ARTICLES

- **Register and tone:** The vocabulary, sentence structure(s) and grammar used by the writer should be in Standard English. However, the tone and register of the essay will usually be more conversational (for example, through the use of figurative language, rhetorical questions and direct address) depending upon the context of production and the purpose. For example, if the article is discussing a very serious topic, it may be in bad taste to use a conversational tone or register.
- Opinion articles will usually start with an opening thesis paragraph which will make clear to the reader the focus of the article and the line of reasoning that it wishes to prove or disprove. The paragraphs that follow will usually use topic sentences to delineate what area of the topic will be explored within the paragraphs. Discourse markers such as 'however', 'although' and 'nevertheless' will be used by the writer to ensure fluidity and cohesion throughout the essay. A clear conclusion will be used to synthesize the key arguments for the reader at the end of the article.
- **Active voice:** Writers will usually use the active voice within their articles to avoid vagueness and to ensure that their discussion of the topic seems current and dynamic.
- **Language techniques:** A variety of language techniques can be utilized by the writer of an essay, dependent upon the context of production and the purpose of the essay. A less formal article may utilize figurative language such as metaphors and similes, rhetorical questions, as well as personal opinion, anecdotes, **sarcasm** and irony. A more formal article is more likely to use facts and statistics, direct speech and expert opinions in order to sound more credible.

When literary editors pen those overnight pieces on the Booker short-list and lament the omissions – where was McEwan? Where was Boyd? Where was Amis? And the other Amis? – they are examining the candidates (not all of whom they can possibly have read) rather than the judges. If I were Mr Ron Pollard of Ladbrokes (whose odds have got a great deal meaner since the days when some of us cleaned up on Salman Rushdie at 14-1), I would give only cursory attention to the books on the short-list: instead I would study the psychology and qualifications of the judges. And it does take all sorts. Three years ago, when I was short-listed for my novel *Flaubert's Parrot*, I was introduced after the ceremony to one of the judges, who said to me: 'I hadn't even heard of this fellow Flaubert before I read your book. But afterwards I sent out for all his novels in paperback.' This comment provoked mixed feelings. Still, perhaps there are judges of the Turner Prize who have never heard of – let alone seen a painting by – Ingres.

So how did the judges do this year? Well, let us begin by congratulating them: for having chosen a serious book by a serious novelist; for behaving, mostly, with propriety; and for having turned up to the dinner. These seem pale compliments? They aren't in Booker terms. Previously, some notably minor and incompetent novels have gained the prize; judges, inflated by their brief celebrity, have competed like kiss-and-tell memoirists to spill all to the radio and newspapers; while two years ago one of the judges didn't even make it to the judicial retiring-room.

(Julian Barnes)

Julian Barnes

Julian Barnes is a British writer who was born in 1946. When he wrote the above article, Barnes had been nominated for the Booker Prize once and would be nominated a further two times before winning the prize for his novel *A Sense of an Ending* in 2011. Barnes writes prose, short stories and essays and also publishes crime fiction under the pseudonym Dan Kavanagh.

CHECK FOR UNDERSTANDING

Read the concept connection of perspective box below. Using the key features of opinion articles box, list the different techniques that Julian Barnes uses in his opinion article to convince the reader that the Booker Prize isn't worth taking seriously.

CONCEPT CONNECTION

PERSPECTIVE

In order to analyse how Barnes conveys his perspective about the Booker Prize to the reader through various features of his opinion article, we will use step 4 (other features of text type) and step 6 (reader response to ideas, message and/or purpose) of the non-literary text reading strategy as delineated in Chapter 1.1. You may wish to re-read this in order to understand this commentary.

In his article, Barnes offers a perspective to the reader that the Booker Prize isn't worth taking seriously and that it is inherently flawed as a process of judging the literary worth of works. Barnes explains that, in his opinion, instead of popular discourse surrounding the competition focusing upon the books themselves more attention should be focused upon the judges. Barnes explains how, through irony and the use of an anecdote, one of the judges who judged his Booker Prize nominated submission of the novel *Flaubert's Parrot* had never read anything by Gustave Flaubert (a French novelist who the protagonist of Barnes' novel obsesses over). Barnes, sarcastic in tone, implicitly suggests that perhaps the prize's judges aren't well read enough to be able to judge a literary competition: 'Still, perhaps there are judges of the Turner Prize who have never heard of – let alone seen a painting by – Ingres'. He also, using a rhetorical question, suggests that some judges are incapable of recognizing a work that is 'serious' enough for the competition and so resort to bestowing the prize upon works that Barnes deems 'minor and incompetent'. He also suggests, using figurative language, that some judges aren't as discreet as they should be during the process – 'judges, inflated by their brief celebrity, have competed like kiss-and-tell memoirists to spill all to the radio and newspapers' and that some haven't even turned up when they should do to judge the competition. This connotes the idea that, in Barnes' perspective, that as some judges aren't taking the competition seriously then, ultimately, neither should writers or readers.

Despite Barnes' reservations about the prize, it is clear from the information provided earlier about the 'Booker Effect' that the prize does have important consequences especially concerning the commercial sales of works (which in itself suggests that many readers don't share the same perspective of the prize as Barnes). It is also worth noting that, often, works that win the Booker Prize go on to be included in academic reading lists and can go on to be considered 'classic' works in literary circles and discussion. Barnes' perspective may be one that you agree with; however, the Booker Prize has existed since 1969 and, due perhaps to its cultural and commercial significance, shows no sign of discontinuing. If this is the case then how can the cultural and commercial impact of the prize be harnessed by writers positively?

The source below provides an alternative perspective on the Booker Prize. The source is an opinion article written by columnist Rhiannon Lucy Cosslett for *The Guardian Online* about the winner of the 2018 Booker Prize, *Milkman* by Anna Burns.

SENSITIVE CONTENT

Caution: the following extract includes mild expletives.

We have chosen to allow you to view the words of this extract as they originally appear, so you can consider for yourself the effects of how these words are used. This is central to understanding the themes of identity and human behaviour at the heart of this book. Furthermore, the IB recommends that your studies in Language A: Language & Literature should challenge you intellectually, personally and culturally, and expose you to sensitive and mature topics. We invite you to reflect critically on the various perspectives offered while bearing in mind the IB's commitment to international-mindedness and intercultural respect.

www.theguardian.com/commentisfree/2018/oct/22/anna-burns-man-booker-prize-food-banks

Anna Burns's Man Booker prize is more than a fairytale – it's a lesson

This win, for an author who was in pain and reliant on food banks, is a reminder that great art can come from anywhere

'I've got 30 days to declare a change in circumstance and this is one hell of a change,' said the writer Anna Burns during a news interview about winning the Man Booker prize for *Milkman*. The novel is about a teenage girl living in an unnamed Northern Irish city during the Troubles, who is being pursued by an older paramilitary dubbed the Milkman – and Burns managed to write it in chronic pain, while on benefits. The £50,000 prize would help to clear her debts, she said. In the acknowledgements, she thanked her local food bank, housing charity and the Department for Work and Pensions, as well as other governmental and non-governmental bodies set up to help people in poverty. If there were to be a Booker winner to blow Julian Barnes's description of the Booker as 'posh bingo' out of the water, this is it.

Burns's win will give hope to other poor artists, especially those struggling and skint, with no connections, who went to crap schools or are suffering rubbish circumstances – stuck with 'shit life syndrome' in other words. What a symbol of the times we live in, that a woman who was forced to rely on food banks to survive has won the most prestigious literary prize in the country.

We hear so much about the cultural sector being dominated by upper-middle class tastemakers, some of them horrendous snobs, many of whom know each other. And there is truth to this: it is a tiny bubble. But Burns shows you can be radically different and still burst the bubble open.

The author gives hope to her left-behind community, too. 'She was not born with a silver spoon in her mouth and had no advantages bestowed upon her. This honestly is brilliant, it's just so great for people from north Belfast, in a place that lacks hope, to see one of our own do so well,' said fellow writer Lyra McKee, who went to the same school. Her win is timely for all sorts of reasons – the #MeToo movement, Brexit reviving the prospect of a hard border in Northern Ireland – but what I find most moving is buried in those words: the notion that things like this don't normally happen to 'people like us'. It's true, they don't.

Perhaps this is why the reception to the news in some quarters has been bizarre. *Milkman* has been branded a difficult book. It isn't. It's written how many people speak. To a normal reader, from a normal background, it reads like a girl from school trotting alongside you down the road, telling you a story. Often, there is an implication that people who are disadvantaged can't cope with literary fiction. *Milkman* turns this on its head: if you went to public school, didn't grow up in a working-class community and only read a certain type of novel, then yes, you might find it difficult – opaque, even. 'I couldn't put it down and I was brought up on a council estate. That may be the point' wrote one reader to this newspaper.

(Lucy Cosslett)

CHECK FOR UNDERSTANDING

Read the concept connection of perspective box below. Using the Key key features of opinion articles box, list the different techniques that Rhiannon Cosslett uses in her opinion article to convince the reader of how valuable being awarded the Booker Prize can be.

CONCEPT CONNECTION

PERSPECTIVE

In order to analyse how Cosslett conveys her contrasting perspective about the Booker Prize to the reader through various features of her opinion article, we will use step 4 (other features of text type) and step 6 (reader response to ideas, message and/ or purpose) of the non-literary text reading strategy as delineated in Chapter 1.1. You may wish to re-read this in order to understand this commentary.

In this opinion article, it is clear to see that Cosslett's perspective of the Booker Prize is radically different when compared to Barnes' and she explicitly alludes to this in the sentence, 'If there were to be a Booker winner to blow Julian Barnes's description of the Booker as "posh bingo" out of the water, this is it.' Cosslett opens her article with direct speech from the winner of 2018's Booker Prize, Anna Burns – 'I've got 30 days to declare a change in circumstance and this is one hell of a change', and then goes on to explain how Burns will use the money to simply 'clear her debts'. This is perhaps ironic, as the stereotypical assumption by a reader may be that most professional authors (especially winners of a prestigious literary prize) would be wealthy enough to be able to use the money to perhaps fund a more extravagant purchase. Cosslett does this purposefully to convey her perspective of the value of the Booker Prize – that it has a real-world impact upon authors and isn't merely a meaningless accolade.

Cosslett metaphorically refers to how, by receiving the award, Burns has been able to 'burst the bubble open' – with 'the bubble' referring to literary circles that are often 'dominated by upper-middle class tastemakers, some of them horrendous snobs, many of whom know each other'. This implies that, in Cosslett's opinion, Burns' win is significant and has value as it shows that the prize is able to open doors and give opportunities to writers from a variety of backgrounds and not just those from the most privileged in society. She extends this further by using the active voice to explain how relevant and timely Burns' win is, '*Milkman* has been branded a difficult book. It isn't. It's written how many people speak. To a normal reader, from a normal background, it reads like a girl from school trotting alongside you down the road, telling you a story.' In this part of the article, Cosslett explains to the reader how, in her opinion, the Booker Prize has been able to legitimize and bestow importance upon a voice rarely heralded in 'serious' literature – a young, working-class girl.

GLOBAL ISSUES *Field of inquiry:* Politics, Power and Justice

LITERARY WORKS AND NON-LITERARY TEXTS AS AGENTS OF SOCIAL CHANGE

Both of these articles convey the perspective of their writer towards the value and significance of a literary prize. Though it would be easy to dismiss this debate as inconsequential in the grand scheme of things, as explored in Section 2 and in Chapter 3.2 it is important to note that literary works are often integral in the formation of culture. Literary works often have the capability to shape and challenge perceptions through art. Therefore, works that are awarded literary prizes, and that thus become more widely read, can have the power to provoke discussion and be an agent of social change.

Research online award-winning works that have been integral in challenging social norms and provoking discussion and see if you can find evidence of their impact in the form of non-literary texts such as articles and speeches. An example of this would be John Steinbeck's 1939 novel *The Grapes of Wrath*, which details the plight of the poor, especially the rural poor, during the time of the Great Depression in America. The novel provoked a huge public response and after the first lady of America at the time, Eleanor Roosevelt, read the novel she called for a legislative response that resulted in significant reforms to US labour laws. You can read more about the novel's social impact by scanning the QR code opposite.

As detailed earlier in this section, the inclusion of works in the reading lists for examination qualifications and academic institutions can also lead to works being considered 'classic'. However, there are a variety of perspectives that exist pertaining to what works should be included in these reading lists. As explored in the previous chapter, there has been contemporary discussion about the responsibility of educators, and those working in the education sector, to construct reading lists that represent a variety of readers and their experiences instead of a minority. Below are two opinion articles that explore opposing perspectives towards this issue. The first is an opinion article by Anjali Enjeti for the online publication of *Al Jazeera* which explains her opinion about reading lists for students in high schools in America. The second is an opinion article by Katy Waldman for the online magazine *Slate* which explains her opinion towards calls from literature students at an American university (Yale) to change the 'canonical' requirements within their reading lists.

www.aljazeera.com/indepth/opinion/time-diversify-decolonise-schools-reading-lists-180318100326982.html

It's time to diversify and decolonise our schools' reading lists

Unfortunately, when it comes to reading lists for language arts' curricula, very little has changed. My own high school and middle school children have reading lists almost identical to the lists from my English classes in the 1980s and 90s.

For some people, *Huck Finn* and *To Kill a Mockingbird* are beloved classics. But nostalgia is not a good reason to keep them on literature syllabi. What we teach students about people from marginalised communities should be authentic; and to be authentic, it should come from marginalised authors and the richly drawn characters they create. Indigenous, black and brown characters shouldn't simply serve as targets of white violence or lessons for white morality. They should play central roles in their own stories, with a full range of emotions and personalities, absent what Toni Morrison has called the 'white gaze', the presumption that people of colour's lives 'have no meaning, no depth', beyond white people's imagination or interpretation of them.

Thankfully, literature is not rocket science. We don't need and have never needed texts that incorporate racist tropes. Authors of myriad racial, ethnic and cultural backgrounds have been writing about their own communities as far back in time as white authors. If Zora Neale Hurston's *Their Eyes Were Watching God*, or Octavia Butler's *Kindred* replaces *The Adventures of Huckleberry Finn* or *To Kill a Mockingbird,* students, particularly white students, will not only be reading more rigorous, realistic and layered books about the black community, they will understand bigotry at a deeper, systemic level. The same argument can be made for replacing EM Forester's *A Passage to India*, (yet another book about a brown man being accused of raping a white woman) with Salman Rushdie's *Midnight's Children*, dumping John Steinbeck's *The Pearl* in favour of Ana Castillo's The *Mixquiahuala Letters*, and replacing Scott O'Dell's Island of the Blue Dolphins with Kristiana Kahakauwila's *This is Paradise*.

We don't need nor have we ever needed to teach books written by white authors that capitalize on inaccurate stereotypes and vulgar and barbaric tropes about marginalised communities. What's more, we can also teach books about marginalised communities that celebrate joy and love, health and success. Indigenous, black and brown stories don't need to always be about suffering to teach valuable lessons about sociopolitical issues.

In the meantime, it's high time educators realized that our policies about racism in school texts must go far above and beyond a conversation about racial slurs. Indigenous and students of colour deserve to have the same privilege in education that white students have always had – the opportunity to examine and imagine the full extent of their humanity in literature. If people can evolve to become more inclusive and less harmful, shouldn't the predominantly white literary canon evolve, too?

(Anjali Enjeti)

https://slate.com/human-interest/2016/05/yale-students-want-to-remake-the-english-major-requirements-but-there-s-no-escaping-white-male-poets-in-the-canon.html

The Canon Is Sexist, Racist, Colonialist, and Totally Gross. Yes, You Have to Read It Anyway

If you want to become well-versed in English literature, you're going to have to hold your nose and read a lot of white male poets. Like, a lot. More than eight.

The canon is what it is, and anyone who wishes to understand how it continues to flow forward needs to learn to swim around in it. There is a clear line to Terrance Hayes (and Frank and Claire Underwood, and Lyon Dynasty) from Shakespeare. There is a direct path to Adrienne Rich (and Katniss Everdeen, and Lyra Belacqua) from Milton. (Rich basically says as much in Diving into the Wreck.) These guys are the heavies, the chord progressions upon which the rest of us continue to improvise, and we'd be somewhere else entirely without them.

You've written that 'it is possible to graduate with a degree in English language and literature by exclusively reading the works of (mostly wealthy) white men.' It is possible to graduate a lot of ways, and every English major is responsible for taking advantage of the bounty of courses the department offers to attain a full and deep education. What is not possible is to reckon with the racist, sexist, colonist poets who comprize the canon – and to transcend their failures – via a 'see no evil, hear no evil' policy.

I want to gently push back, too, against the idea that the major English poets have nothing to say to students who aren't straight, male, and white. For all the ways in which their particular identities shaped their work, these writers tried to represent the entire human condition, not just their clan. A great artist possesses both empathy and imagination: Many of Shakespeare's female characters are as complexly nuanced as any in circulation today, *Othello* takes on racial prejudice directly, and *Twelfth Night* contains enough gender-bending identity shenanigans to fuel multiple drag shows and occupy legions of queer scholars. The 'stay in your lane' mentality that seems to undergird so much progressive discourse – only polyamorous green people really 'get' the 'polyamorous green experience', and therefore only polyamorous greens should read and write about polyamorous greens, say – ignores our common humanity.

But even if you disagree, there's no getting around the facts. Although you've written that the English department 'actively contributes to the erasure of history', what it really does is accurately reflect the tainted history we have – one in which straight white cis-men dominated art-making for centuries – rather than the woke history we want and fantasize about. There are few (arguably no) female poets writing in Chaucer's time who rival Chaucer in wit, transgressiveness, texture, or psychological insight. The lack of equal opportunity was a tremendous injustice stemming from oppressive social norms, but we can't reverse it by willing brilliant female wordsmiths into the past. Same goes for people of color in Wordsworth's day, or openly queer people in Pope's, or …

Here is what I am *not* saying. I am *not* saying that Yale shouldn't offer a rich panoply of courses on female writers, queer writers, writers with disabilities, and writers of color. And it does! In addition to featuring names like Elizabeth Bishop and Ralph Ellison in its survey classes, the course catalog presents such titles as 'Women Writers from the Restoration to Romanticism', 'Race and Gender in American Literature', 'American Artists and the African American Book', 'The Spectacle of Disability', 'Asian American Literature', 'Chaucer and Discourses of Dissent', 'Postcolonial World Literature: 1945–present', 'Black Literature and U.S. Liberalism' … and I'm not even counting the cross listings with the comparative literature; American studies; and women's, gender, and sexuality studies departments.

Moreover, I am *not* arguing that it is acceptable for an English major to graduate from college having only read white male authors or even 70 percent white male authors. But you cannot profess to be a student of English literature if you have not lingered in the slipstreams of certain foundational figures, who also happen to be (alas) both white and male: In addition to the majors listed above, Jonson, Shelley, Keats, Pound, Auden, and Frost. This is frustrating, unfair, and 100 percent nonnegotiable. (But hey, try to have some fun reading Frost? You could do so much worse!)

The canon of English literature is sexist. It is racist. It is colonialist, ableist, transphobic, and totally gross. You must read it anyway.

(Katy Waldman)

Readers bring their own perspectives when reading works, and the opinions delineated in the above articles help to demonstrate this. Enjeti believes that in order to authentically challenge and discuss stereotypes about marginalised groups in a high-school classroom, you must use works by authors who have been negatively affected by these stereotypes to do so. Within canonical works that are widely taught, specifically *To Kill a Mockingbird* by Harper Lee, Enjeti perceives the inclusion of harmful racial stereotypes within the novel and this influences her perspective towards the inclusion of such works in high school reading lists. Waldman also recognises that many of the works included in the 'canon', and thus the reading lists of many academic institutions, do contain harmful stereotypes and depictions of marginalised groups but feels that in order to understand the progression of Literature over time readers must read these 'classic' works as a starting point. She also has the perspective that even though a writer may not be from a marginalised community, this doesn't stop a writer from conveying a message that is relevant and profound to a reader from a marginalised community and therefore shouldn't be dismissed automatically.

DISCUSSION

In order to fully understand the perspectives that you bring to this debate, think about what you would include in an ideal reading list for your fellow IB students. You can include any writer or work that you wish, but you must be able to justify its inclusion. For ideas, use the QR code to read about other writers' ideal reading lists.

Once you have decided who and what you would include in your ideal reading list discuss your ideas with your peers.

TOK Links

Throughout this section we have discussed how a work can become to be considered a 'classic' and the variety of perspectives pertaining to this process. As discussed previously, this grouping of some works as 'classic' or as being a part of the English literary 'canon' can be contentious and there are a wide variety of opinions regarding who or what should be included in this classification.

However, why do we feel the need to categorize works in this way in the first place? How are judgements made about the merit of a work? What makes a work better than others?

EE Links: English A – Language category 3

Throughout this section of the chapter we have analysed how opinion articles can be used to effectively convey the perspective of a writer towards a topic of their choice. **How far do you think, however, the conventions used by opinion article writers change depending on the publication in which the opinion article is published? Do you think that the language and tone of opinion articles has changed over time?** Either of these areas would make an ideal focus for a category 3 extended essay.

In the next part of this chapter we will consider all of the perspectives that we have explored so far to analyse and compare two very different works that are regarded as 'classics'.

Considering Joseph Conrad's *Heart of Darkness* and Chinua Achebe's *Things Fall Apart*

Joseph Conrad's novel *Heart of Darkness* was written in 1899 and begins in London before mostly taking place in what was then known as the Congo Free State (modern-day Democratic Republic of Congo). To initially take an immanent approach to the work, little context will be given here at this point. However, you should know that the work is told from the perspective of narrator Charles Marlow who is telling his fellow sailors on a boat in London about his time as a captain of a steamboat for a colonial European ivory company operating in the Congo Free State. In this extract, Marlow is at his company's work station and has wandered into an area close to a railway line that is being built by forced labourers who are from the Congo Free State.

In Chapter 1.1 you explored the conventions of literary prose. Use the notes that you made in that chapter to help you understand this extract.

Black shapes crouched, lay, sat between the trees, leaning against the trunks, clinging to the earth, half coming out, half effaced within the dim light, in all the attitudes of pain, abandonment, and despair. Another mine on the cliff went off, followed by a slight shudder of the soil under my feet. The work was going on. The work! And this was the place where some of the helpers had withdrawn to die.

'They were dying slowly – it was very clear. They were not enemies, they were not criminals, they were nothing earthly now – nothing but black shadows of disease and starvation, lying confusedly in the greenish gloom. Brought from all the recesses of the coast in all the legality of time contracts, lost in uncongenial surroundings, fed on unfamiliar food, they sickened, became inefficient, and were then allowed to crawl away and rest. These moribund shapes were free as air – and nearly as thin. I began to distinguish the gleam of eyes under the trees. Then, glancing down, I saw a face near my hand. The black bones reclined at full length with one shoulder against the tree, and slowly the eyelids rose and the sunken eyes looked up at me, enormous and vacant, a kind of blind, white flicker in the depths of the orbs, which died out slowly.'

(Joseph Conrad 44–45)

Joseph Conrad

Joseph Conrad was a Polish-British writer born in 1857. Conrad didn't speak English fluently until he was in his twenties, but is considered today as one of the most important writers in English literature. Many of his works have a nautical theme mirroring his long career at sea, and he is known for blending both romantic and modernist styles of literature in his works. He is best known for his novels *Lord Jim*, *Nostromo* and *The Secret Agent*.

ACTIVITY 1

Read the questions below and write down your thoughts in response to them. A full commentary on the extract is provided in the global issues box for you to check your understanding.

1. In the extract, Conrad describes the workers through the perspective of the narrator Marlow, how are they depicted? Why do you think Conrad did this?
2. What is your emotional response to the extract as a reader? Do you think Conrad is making a wider point by deliberately trying to evoke this emotional response?
3. Harold Bloom (eminent American literary critic) has written that '*Heart of Darkness* has been analysed more than any other work of literature that is studied in universities and colleges'. Why do you think this is? Why might this work be considered a 'classic'?

GLOBAL ISSUES *Field of inquiry:* Beliefs, Values and Education

COLONIZATION

This extract from *Heart of Darkness* is written deliberately to disturb and unsettle the reader. Conrad utilizes animalistic and graphic imagery when describing 'the helpers' who are presumably building the nearby railway, 'Black shapes crouched, lay, sat between the trees, leaning against the trunks, clinging to the earth' and 'They were dying slowly – it was very clear. They were not enemies, they were not criminals, they were nothing earthly now, – nothing but black shadows of disease and starvation, lying confusedly in the greenish gloom'. The use of the verb 'clinging' and the adverb in 'dying slowly' connotes how the Congolese 'helpers' have been completely dehumanizsed and left to die, without compassion, like how an animal would be treated – not a human being. This, along with the lexical set of body parts that are used 'face', 'bones', 'eyelids', 'eyes', reduces the Congolese and renders them as devoid of identity and character – mirroring the viewpoint of the colonial Europeans. This grotesque description of the sickness and death taking place at Marlow's company workstation is supposed to raise questions about the ethics of European colonization and trading – readers are supposed to wonder whether these consequences of such expansion and trade are acceptable. Questioning what would have been widely accepted values and beliefs about the 'right' and the 'duty' of Europeans to colonize countries, like those in Africa, would have been highly unusual at the time. As well as in terms of the quality of the written prose, as a unique and bold critique of colonization (especially so when considering the historical context in which it was written), it is perhaps easy to see why *Heart of Darkness* is considered worthy of study, discussion and being regarded as a 'classic'.

However, in contemporary literary discourse, some writers have questioned the representation of the Congolese throughout the work and have also criticized Conrad for perpetuating stereotypes about Africa, and Africans, in the work. In 1975, Nigerian writer Chinua Achebe delivered a lecture to the University of Massachusetts Amherst titled, 'An Image of Africa: Racism in Conrad's *Heart of Darkness*'. Read an excerpt from this lecture on the next page. If you would like to read the whole lecture, then use the QR code opposite.

●●●

https://genius.com/Chinua-achebe-an-image-of-africa-racism-in-conrads-heart-of-darkness-excerpt-annotated

An Image of Africa: Racism in Conrad's Heart of Darkness

Joseph Conrad was a thoroughgoing racist. That this simple truth is glossed over in criticisms of his work is due to the fact that white racism against Africa is such a normal way of thinking that its manifestations go completely unremarked. Students of *Heart of Darkness* will often tell you that Conrad is concerned not so much with Africa as with the deterioration of one European mind caused by solitude and sickness. They will point out to you that Conrad is, if anything, less charitable to the Europeans in the story than he is to the natives, that the point of the story is to ridicule Europe's civilizing mission in Africa. A Conrad student informed me in Scotland that Africa is merely a setting for the disintegration of the mind of Mr Kurtz. Which is partly the point. Africa as setting and backdrop which eliminates the African as human factor. Africa as a metaphysical battlefield devoid of all recognizable humanity, into which the wandering European enters at his peril. Can nobody see the preposterous and perverse arrogance in thus reducing Africa to the role of props for the break-up of one petty European mind? But that is not even the point. The real question is the dehumanization of Africa and Africans which this age-long attitude has fostered and continues to foster in the world. And the question is whether a novel which celebrates this dehumanization, which depersonalizes a portion of the human race, can be called a great work of art. My answer is: No, it cannot. I do not doubt Conrad's great talents. Even *Heart of Darkness* has its memorably good passages and moments: 'The reaches opened before us and closed behind, as if the forest had stepped leisurely across tile water to bar the way for our return.' Its exploration of the minds of the European characters is often penetrating and full of insight. But all that has been more than fully discussed in the last fifty years. His obvious racism has, however, not been addressed. And it is high time it was!

(Chinua Achebe)

Chinua Achebe

Chinua Achebe is a Nigerian novelist, poet, essayist and academic who was born in 1930 and who died in 2013. Achebe was a part of the Igbo people and their traditions, culture and history heavily influenced his writing style. He is best known perhaps for his novel *Things Fall Apart* (1958) which was considered a milestone for modern African literature when it was published and is still considered by many writers, especially Nigerian and African writers, as hugely influential.

ACTIVITY 2

Read the questions below and write down your thoughts in response to them. A full commentary on the extract is provided below the questions for you to check your understanding.

1 In what way can you link the perspective of Achebe to the perspective of Anjali Enjeti in the article 'It's time to diversify and decolonise our schools' reading lists' on page 428?

2 What ideas about the notion of a 'classic' work does Achebe express towards the end of the text?

Achebe explains how he feels that the representation of the Congolese and of Africa in *Heart of Darkness* is one that is steeped in racist stereotypes – 'Africa as setting and backdrop which eliminates the African as human factor. Africa as a metaphysical battlefield devoid of all recognizable humanity, into which the wandering European enters at his peril' (lines 7–8). Achebe questions the use of African people, and of Africa, as a mere literary tool and regards it as reductive and degrading – 'Can nobody see the preposterous and perverse arrogance in thus reducing Africa to the role of props for the break-up of one petty European mind?' (Lines 8–9). This links with the viewpoint of Enjeti who opined, 'Indigenous, black and brown characters shouldn't simply serve as targets of white violence or lessons for white morality' (lines 5–6). It is clear when reading the end of the extract that Achebe believes that Conrad's work is of great literary quality and so its categorization as a 'great work of art' can be understood. However, it is also clear that Achebe believes that 'classic' works should over time, as cultural norms and values change, be questioned in regards to their intentions and representations – 'Its exploration of the minds of the European characters is often penetrating and full of insight. But all that has been more than fully discussed in the last fifty years. His obvious racism has, however, not been addressed. And it is high time it was!' (lines 14–16).

It is also clear that Achebe believes that the label of a 'classic' work should only be attributed to works that are morally deserving of the title in terms of their representation of marginalized groups – 'The real question is the dehumanization of Africa and Africans which this age-long attitude has fostered and continues to foster in the world. And the question is whether a novel which celebrates this dehumanization, which depersonalizes a portion of the human race, can be called a great work of art. My answer is: No, it cannot' (lines 10–13). This links again with Enjeti's perspective that as the voices of people of colour have become more visible in mainstream literature, then the literary 'canon' needs to evolve to include these voices – 'Indigenous and students of colour deserve to have the same privilege in education that white students have always had – the opportunity to examine and imagine the full extent of their humanity in literature. If people can evolve to become more inclusive and less harmful, shouldn't the predominantly white literary canon evolve, too?' (lines 22–24).

Achebe's own novels have been praised for their representation of African culture that subverts misconceptions and stereotypes. His novel *Things Fall Apart* presents pre-Western

Igbo culture as having its own structures, values and meaningful traditions, similar to the way in which Western writers depict their own cultures. The literary complexity with which the African characters and their lives are presented was a first in English literary tradition, and for this, and many other, reasons the novel is considered today a 'classic'. The novel has been the subject of much literary academic focus, is often included in lists of literary accolades, and is widely taught across Africa and the rest of the world.

In this extract, from Chapter 2 of *Things Fall Apart*, the reader is provided with a character profile of Okonkwo who is the protagonist within the novel.

Okonkwo ruled his household with a heavy hand. His wives, especially the youngest, lived in perpetual fear of his fiery temper, and so did his little children. Perhaps down in his heart Okonkwo was not a cruel man. But his whole life was dominated by fear, the fear of failure and of weakness. It was deeper and more intimate than the fear of evil and capricious gods and of magic, the fear of the forest, and of the forces of nature, malevolent, red in tooth and claw. Okonkwo's fear was greater than these. It was not external but lay deep within himself. It was the fear of himself, lest he should be found to resemble his father. Even as a little boy he had resented his father's failure and weakness, and even now he still remembered how he had suffered when a playmate had told him that his father was agbala. That was how Okonkwo first came to know that agbala was not only another name for a woman, it could also mean a man who had taken no title. And so Okonkwo was ruled by one passion – to hate everything that his father Unoka had loved. One of those things was gentleness and another was idleness.

(Chinua Achebe 12–13)

ACTIVITY 3

Read the questions below and write down your thoughts in response to them. A full commentary on the extract is provided below the questions for you to check your understanding.

1 What does the reader learn about Okonkwo in this extract? How is Okonkwo presented as a complex character?

2 What is significant about the style of prose used in the extract and what are the reasons why this work may be considered a 'classic'? (Refer to the notes that you made in Chapter 1.1 about the stylistic features of prose to help you here.)

3 How is the representation of Okonkwo in this extract different to the representation of the Congolese in Conrad's *Heart of Darkness*? In what ways can you link the significance of this representation to the perspectives in 'Anna Burns's Man Booker prize is more than a fairytale – it's a lesson' by Cosslett on page 426–427 and Waldman in 'The Canon Is Sexist, Racist, Colonialist, and Totally Gross. Yes, You Have to Read It Anyway' on page 429?

In the extract, we learn that Okonkwo is a complex character whose behaviours are informed by his past experiences. Okonkwo is characterized by Achebe as a fierce man, 'Okonkwo ruled his household with a heavy hand. His wives, especially the youngest, lived in perpetual fear of his fiery temper, and so did his little children' (lines 1–2). However, it is made clear that this is because 'his whole life was dominated by fear, the fear of failure and of weakness' (line 3). It seems that when Okonkwo was growing up, he grew to 'resent' his father and the taunts he received from his playmates because of his father's behaviour, 'he still remembered how he had suffered when a playmate had told him that his father was agbala. That was how Okonkwo first came to know that agbala was not only another name for a woman, it could also mean a man who had taken no title' (lines 7–10). It would seem that Okonkwo's whole attitude and philosophy towards life has been informed by a psychological impulse to be as different from his father as possible, and that it is the fear of resembling him that has led to the fierce and stoic man that he has become.

When reading the complexity of the prose and its atypical representation of a pre-Western African character it is clear that the extract is worthy of its status as a 'classic' literary work. The fact that this work is considered a 'classic', and the fact that it is still widely discussed and analysed in literary circles and taught to students across the world, is perhaps supportive of Cosslett's perspective that the 'classic' work tag can give prominence to alternative representations of marginalized groups – 'We hear so much about the cultural sector being dominated by upper-middle class tastemakers, some of them horrendous snobs, many of whom know each other. And there is truth to this: it is a tiny bubble. But Burns shows you can be radically different and still burst the bubble open' (lines 12–14). In addition to this, when contrasting the representation of Okonkwo to the representation of the Congolese in Conrad's *Heart of Darkness* it is clear that they are the antithesis of each other, that there has been a clear progression in the literary representation of Africa and Africans across the time period when each work was written. This perhaps supports Waldman's view that the notion of 'classic' works and the 'canon' is still valid as without the study of Conrad's 'classic' novel, it would be harder to appreciate the significance of Achebe's.

EE Links: English A – Literature category 1

Some of the issues discussed in the case study of *Heart of Darkness* and *Things Fall Apart* are complex. If you are interested in researching these issues further, they can make ideal prompts for your extended essay:

- **To what extent can Joseph Conrad's *Heart of Darkness* be considered a critique of European colonization in Africa?**
- **To what extent can Joseph Conrad's *Heart of Darkness* be regarded as using stereotypes in his representation of Africa and Africans?**

Now that you have finished this chapter, let's review the key ideas in it and practise the several skills that it has introduced. Read the source below before attempting to respond to the activities. When you have finished, you can read the commentary underneath the activity box. You may want to review the notes that you made in Chapter 1.5 when deconstructing adverts to help you to respond to the questions here.

The next source is an article from *The Telegraph* which explains one writer's viewpoint towards why the Coca-Cola adverts featuring the Christmas truck could be considered 'classic'. The article is available to view via the QR code or search for 'The Telegraph "20 years of the Coca-Cola Christmas truck"'.

ACTIVITY 4

Throughout this chapter we have applied ideas about what constitutes a 'classic' to literary works, however for this activity you will need to apply these ideas to the non-literary text above. For this activity, review the information earlier in the chapter that delineated how and why texts and works come to be considered 'classic' along with some of the arguments for and against this notion that have been delineated throughout the chapter.

You may also want to re-read the key features of opinion articles box which appears at the beginning of this chapter and some of the commentaries analysing opinion articles that appear throughout this chapter to help you with this activity. Also, for the first activity you may wish to use step 4 (other features of text type) and step 6 (reader response to ideas, message and/or purpose) of the non-literary text reading strategy as delineated in Chapter 1.1. For the second activity you may wish to use step 3 (typographical and graphological features) and step 5 (visual image and layout) of the same non-literary text reading strategy to help you answer the question.

This opinion article analyses a series of Coca-Cola adverts and together, these adverts can constitute a body of work. Please see below this activity box for a commentary responding to the following questions.

1 How does the writer of the article justify the Coca-Cola Christmas Truck advert's 'classic' status? How does an analysis of the article support this view?

2 Why might a reader disagree with categorising the Coca-Cola advert as a 'classic' advert?

1 The writer of '20 Years of the Coca-Cola Christmas Truck' justifies the categorization of Coca-Cola's Christmas Truck advert as 'classic' in a variety of ways. For example, she draws attention frequently to how long Coca-Cola has been producing similar styles of Christmas adverts – 'This year marks twenty years of the iconic Coca-Cola "Holidays are Coming" Christmas adverts featuring the trucks.' This implies that, in the view of the writer, the adverts are steeped in 'tradition' and 'heritage' and as a result are of cultural significance. She furthers this idea by drawing attention to their popularity and award-winning status – 'Voted Britain's favourite Christmas advert of all time back in 2014'. This connotes to the value that the general public attributes to them and how high mass opinion judges their quality to be. The writer uses a positive lexis when discussing the effect of the adverts upon the reader and also uses a semantic field of celebration and joy – 'one thing we can always guarantee will put us in the festive spirit', 'In recent years, Coca-Cola have re-imagined the classic advert and sent its famous trucks around the country to spread festive cheer' and 'It really was a dream come true to get behind the wheel of one of the most iconic trucks in the world and I couldn't stop smiling.' This conveys to the reader that, in the opinion of the writer, the fact that the adverts invoke such strong emotion within the mass public is a sign of their iconic and classic status in popular culture.

2 An analysis of the Coca-Cola print advert, 2017 would support the opinion offered to the reader by '20 Years of the Coca-Cola Christmas Truck'. For example, the writer has deliberately included the symbol of the Coca-Cola Christmas truck in the advert as this has been their symbolic representation of Christmas spirit since 1995. By repeating this symbol year after year, the reader will immediately recognize it and connote the idea of Christmas to it; it then becomes a 'traditional' and 'classic' symbol of Christmas. The writer of the advert also deliberately uses the slogan 'holidays are coming' in the advert as this is the slogan that was first used in conjunction with the first 'holiday truck' advert in 1995. By repeating this slogan, the reader becomes accustomed to associating 'holidays' with the Coca-Cola Christmas truck and begins to see the truck as a metaphor for Christmas. This leads to, as delineated in '20 Years of the Coca-Cola Christmas Truck' the feeling that 'it only really feels like Christmas when you see the Coca-Cola Christmas truck on TV'. The fact that this image and slogan are so intrinsically associated with the holiday would suggest a justification for its status as a 'classic' advert.

However, there could be a justification in a reader disagreeing with the categorization of the Coca-Cola print advert, 2017 as a 'classic' advert. There has been a societal shift in perception towards the Coca-Cola brand in recent times with some pointing out that Coca-Cola is a form of 'junk food' which negatively affects a person's health. There have also been various well-publicized scandals concerning the human rights record of the company, especially in the less-developed parts of the world that produce Coca-Cola. In addition, more and more people in society are questioning the commodification of a festive holiday that is supposed to be about immaterial joy and may point to Coca-Cola's role in the materialistic aspect of contemporary celebrations of Christmas. With all of these points in mind, a reader may understand that the Coca-Cola Christmas Truck advert may have been seen as a 'classic' advert in the past, however may question whether it should continue to be regarded as so with such shifts in societal perception towards the brand.

Works cited

Achebe, C. 'An Image of Africa: Racism in Conrad's "Heart of Darkness".' Web. 24 Feb. 2019. **https://polonistyka.amu.edu.pl/__data/assets/pdf_file/0007/259954/Chinua-Achebe,-An-Image-of-Africa.-Racism-in-Conrads-Heart-of-Darkness.pdf**.

Achebe, C. *Things Fall Apart*. Penguin Books, 1994.

Alexander, S. '20 Years of the Coca-Cola Christmas Truck.' *The Telegraph*, 21 Dec. 2015. Web. 10 March 2019. **www.telegraph.co.uk/goodlife/living/20-years-of-the-coca-cola-christmas-truck**.

'Alexei Panshin – Quotes.' Good Reads. Web. 23 Feb. 2019. **www.goodreads.com/quotes/538599-classics-aren-t-books-that-are-read-for-pleasure-classics-are**.

Barnes, J. 'Diary.' London Review of Books, Vol. 9: No. 20, 12 Nov. 1987, page 21.

Cosslett, RL. 'Anna Burns's Man Booker prize is more than a fairytale – it's a lesson.' *The Guardian*, 22 Oct. 2018. Web. 23 Feb. 2019. **www.theguardian.com/commentisfree/2018/oct/22/anna-burns-man-booker-prize-food-banks**.

Conrad, J. *Heart of Darkness*. Dover Publications, 1990.

Dirda, M. 'Why Read the Classics?' One-Minute Book Reviews, 27 April 2008. Web. 23 Feb. 2019. **https://oneminutebookreviews.wordpress.com/2008/04/27/why-read-the-classics-quote-of-the-day-michael-dirda**.

Enjeti, A. 'It's time to diversify and decolonise our schools' reading lists.' *Al Jazeera*, 18 March 2018. Web. 23 Feb. 2019. **www.aljazeera.com/indepth/opinion/time-diversify-decolonise-schools-reading-lists-180318100326982.html**.

'Italo Cavino – Quotes.' Good Reads. Web. 23 Feb. 2019. **www.goodreads.com/quotes/23666-aclassic-is-a-book-that-has-never-finished-saying**.

Jordison, S. 'Heart of Darkness by Joseph Conrad – a trip into inner space.' *The Guardian*, 29 July 2015. Web. 24 Feb. 2019. **www.theguardian.com/books/booksblog/2015/jul/29/journeys-in-literature-heart-of-darkness-by-joseph-conrad**.

Leah. 'The Man Booker Effect.' *The Man Booker Prize*, 13 Nov. 2012. Web. 23 Feb. 2019. **https://themanbookerprize.com/news/2012/11/13/man-booker-effect**.

'Mark Twain – Quotes.' Good Reads. Web. 23 Feb. 2019. **www.goodreads.com/quotes/1035168-a-classic-is-something-that-everybody-wants-to-have-read**.

'"Open the doors and let these books in" – what would a truly diverse reading list look like?' *The Guardian*, 11 Nov. 2017. Web. 23 Feb. 2019. **www.theguardian.com/books/2017/nov/11/black-and-minority-ethnic-books-authors-on-decolonising-the-canon-university-english-literature-syllabus**.

Schleeter, R. 'The Grapes of Wrath.' *National Geographic*, 7 April 2014. Web. 23 Feb. 2019. **www.nationalgeographic.org/news/grapes-wrath**.

Steinbeck, J. *Grapes of Wrath*. Penguin Classics, 2006.

Waldman, K. 'The Canon Is Sexist, Racist, Colonialist, and Totally Gross. Yes, You Have to Read It Anyway.' *Slate*, 24 May 2016. Web. 23 Feb. 2019. **https://slate.com/humaninterest/2016/05/yale-students-want-to-remake-the-english-major-requirements-but-there-s-no-escaping-white-male-poets-in-the-canon.html**.

3.4 How can texts offer multiple perspectives of a single issue, topic or theme?

OBJECTIVES OF CHAPTER

- To understand the meaning of the term 'multivocality'.
- To provide an overview of different forms of literary criticism.
- To provide an overview of the different perspectives a reader can bring to a text or work – reader-response theory.
- To demonstrate an application of different models of interpretational theory to texts and works.
- To demonstrate ways to apply course concepts to specific works of literature and non-literary texts.
- To demonstrate ways to understand specific works of literature and non-literary texts in the context of global issues.

In Section 2 you explored the impact that a reader and writer's context can have on the production and reception of a text or work. This may have been at odds with what you learnt in Section 1 which took a more 'immanent' approach to texts and works, where texts and works were explored purely as products of authorial intention or as isolated entities whose meaning can only be interpreted through close reading of the text or work itself. This tension between how the author intended a text or work to be received, and how it is actually received by a reader means that texts and works are often 'multivocal' and, as such, can offer a variety of perspectives to the reader of a single issue, topic or theme.

A combination of the words 'multi' and 'vocal' (meaning 'many' and 'voice' in Latin), when a text or work is 'multivocal' it can be read as having 'many voices'. As explained in Chapter 2.1, there will be a 'dominant reading' of the text or work (a reading that the writer intended the reader of the text or work to receive); however, when we apply the concept of 'multivocality' to a text or work we are accepting that there may be other ways in which a text or work is received – not just the one intended by the writer. In Chapter 2.1, you will have explored how the context of a reader or writer can shape these 'voices', for example, an advert that may have been socially acceptable in the 1900s may now be seen as unacceptable as values and attitudes within society have shifted.

In this chapter, we will learn about 'reader-response theory' which extends this idea, suggesting that it is not only the context of a reader that determines their response to a text but many other factors. We will explore the different facets of literary criticism before applying some of its connected theories to a variety of texts and works. It is worth noting that although these models of interpretation were originally intended for literary works, it is now largely seen as valid to also apply them to non-literary texts.

What is literary criticism?

Literary criticism is the study and analysis of texts and works, often through the lens of a specific literary theory. These literary theories often advocate for the interpretation of a text or work to be conducted in a specific way.

For example, many of the earliest forms of literary criticism focused primarily on authorial intention as a method by which to interpret texts and works. **Authorial intentionalism** and **biographical criticism** are interlinked theories of literary criticism that focus on interpreting texts and works via the meaning intended by the writer. These theories consider the understanding of the writer's intention as they wrote the text or work and their biographical history as the key to unlocking the meaning of the text or work. This method of understanding a text or work was particularly popular during the Renaissance period in Europe. Although not now usually considered as the only way of interpreting texts or works, it is still a valid framework that can be used to understand a perspective offered by a text or work. If you would like to read more about why authorial intentionalism and biographical criticism can still be a useful way to understand the meaning conveyed in texts and works, scan the QR code opposite to access the *New York Times* article 'Should an Author's Intentions Matter?'

In Chapter 2.1, you also explored a variety of texts and works and considered the effect that they could elicit from a reader upon close reading. This process of studying a text or work in isolation and excluding authorial intention and reader context in favour of simply closely reading the text is called **New Criticism**. This process does not wholly disregard the importance of context to a text or work, but simply does not consider it to be the main focus of literary study. This way of analysing and studying texts and works was especially popular in academic institutions throughout the middle of the twentieth century. However, it has now fallen largely out of favour as academic institutions have moved towards frameworks and theories that view the interpretation of texts and works as a personal and individual process. The New Criticism model is still a method that you can use to interpret a text or work and is simply just one way of understanding a perspective offered by a text or work. If you would like to read more about the benefits of using the New Criticism model to interpret a work or text then scan the QR code opposite to access the *Public Discourse* article 'It's Time to Return to the New Critics'.

How far a writer affects the communication between their text or work and its reader through their stylistic and structural choices is linked to the theory of authorial intentionalism. However, whether the perspective that the author intended to offer to the reader correlates to the one actually received by the reader is linked to the theory of New Criticism.

Scan the adjacent QR code and then read the New Criticism interpretation of the text which analyses its presentation of the theme of globalization. Because this approach to interpretation exalts a close-reading of the structural and stylistic techniques used in the text, without consideration of its context, you will not be provided with contextual information about the text yet.

New Criticism interpretation

This advertisement ultimately conveys a pro-globalization message to the reader of the text. By utilizing the asyndetic listing of an array of recognizable foreign cultural products that its UK readers will recognize and are presumed to enjoy ('American movie', 'Belgian striker', 'Dutch beer'), the advert frames the shared and intertwined culture of the UK and its global neighbours in a positive way. The advert starts and ends with a declarative ('We are not an island' and 'We are part of something far, far bigger') which helps to create an authoritative tone, encouraging the reader to agree with the message being conveyed. The bold and simple colour scheme of red, white and black is a subtle subversion of the UK national colours of red, white and blue, helping to symbolize its pro-globalization message of the efficacy and power of cultures coming together.

ACTIVITY 1

This advert was part of a larger 'Together we thrive' advertising campaign that was launched by the banking corporation HSBC with the intention of celebrating diversity and multiculturalism in the UK – in keeping with its values and status as a global bank. It is important to note that this particular advertising campaign was launched in the UK at the beginning of 2019 when the negotiations for the UK to leave the European Union were ongoing and subject to much public, and impassioned, debate. HSBC's response to Brexit (as this process has been named in the mass media) has largely been a negative one; the bank has published research suggesting the value of UK currency could decline by 20 per cent if the UK was to leave the European Union, and they have since moved seven of their offices from London to Paris in the wake of the UK referendum that put the Brexit process into motion.

In light of this information, can you see another perspective that is offered by the text on the theme of globalization? Write your own interpretation of the text, applying the authorial intentionalism model. Read the commentary underneath here once you have written your own.

In Section 2 you will have also have been exposed to (and will have analysed) a series of HSBC adverts. Together, these adverts can constitute a body of work.

Authorial intentionalism interpretation

This advertisement conveys an anti-Brexit message to its UK audience, presenting the perspective that 'Brexit' will be harmful to globalization. As a global bank, HSBC will be wary of the Brexit process as it could have a negative impact upon its banking operations in the UK. This anti-Brexit message is conveyed through the use of an antithesis, commonly used for rhetorical effect, in the statement 'We are not an island' which is closely followed by 'We are a ...' which includes all of the positive ways in which the UK could be considered as far more globally and internationally connected than the original phrase would suggest. This message subverts the notions presented by many pro-Brexit leaders who have justified the process of Brexit as a way of protecting the UK from the supposedly 'harmful' effects of globalization. By presenting the positive impact of globalization upon the UK, HSBC effectively manages to implicitly convey its anti-Brexit perspective to the reader.

Summary

When reading both interpretations, there are obvious similarities between the two. Both of the models suggest an interpretation that the perspective of globalization communicated by the advert is one of its positive effects upon the UK. However, the New Criticism model does not consider the reasons as to why a bank would want to convey such an ideologically loaded perspective, whereas the authorial intentionalism model does. This perhaps suggests that the New Criticism model of interpretation could lead to a narrower and more constrained interpretation when compared to that of the authorial intentionalism model.

Interestingly though, if not more confusingly, since the advert launched and then went on to generate a lot of criticism and debate, HSBC has explicitly stated that the advert is not a comment on the Brexit process at all and was merely designed to celebrate 'the importance of being open and connected to the world'. If you would like to read more about the discussion generated by this advert, then scan the QR codes opposite.

One of the key criticisms of the authorial intentionalism model of interpretation is based on the idea that we as readers often have very little awareness and concrete knowledge of what the writer intended to communicate when they created the text or work, which could make this a flawed model of interpretation from the very beginning. This view is often termed 'intentional fallacy' and you can read more about this by scanning the QR code opposite.

Also, there is a chance that the writer themselves were not even aware of the subconscious intentions they also had when creating the text or work (this is part of the Psychoanalytic theory of interpretation that we will explore later in the chapter). This could mean that HSBC *did* just intend the text to be read as simply pro-globalization without any specific links to the Brexit process, or perhaps the creators of the advert were subconsciously anti-Brexit themselves and so included an anti-Brexit message within the advert without even realizing it!

This is just one example of how the application of models of interpretation can lead to texts and works becoming 'multivocal'. In the next part of the chapter we will take this idea even further when we consider how the reader themselves can impact the perspectives offered by a text.

TOK Links

In this part of the chapter we have considered the impact that a writer, and the structural and stylistic choices that they make, can have on the ability of a text or work to communicate a specific perspective to a reader. We have not yet considered how the readers themselves can interact with a text or work to generate their own interpretation.

In light of this, how limiting is an interpretation of a text or work that doesn't consider the reader's response? How important is reader-response when constructing knowledge of a text or work?

What is reader-response theory?

Reader-response theory is a form of literary criticism that emerged and became prominent in academic institutions in the latter half of the twentieth century. This theory focused on the reader as an active agent in the interpretation of texts and focuses upon the individual and personal criticism that each reader can bring to a text or work. It would be impossible to list and categorize all of the different ways in which a reader can respond to, interpret and criticize a text or work, but there are some forms of reader-response theory which are particularly prominent. Some of these are listed in the table below.

CONCEPT CONNECTION

CREATIVITY

Before we begin to explore this variety of reader-response theory frameworks, it is perhaps pertinent to consider *why* it is important for us to consider the different responses that a reader can bring to a text and/or work. When we consider the personal interpretation that we as a reader bring to texts and works, an interpretation that will be shaped by our own context, we are bridging the gap between the reality of our lives and the fabricated reality that exists in the texts and works that we read. We are fully realizing the potential that art has as a way of understanding ourselves and our own context. When we consider the categories of reader-response theory that can be used as a method of understanding a text or work, we are potentially considering how a text or work can be perceived in a way that may challenge our own viewpoint. By considering alternative perspectives in this way, we are also realizing the potential that art has to challenge our own preconceptions and to change our stance on important global issues that affect all readers.

CAS Links

Once you have read all of the different forms of reader-response criticism below, think about all of the different forms of creative art that you could apply them to. Next time you're at an art gallery, the theatre, watching a film or even listening to a song, try to see if you can apply them in order to understand the variety of responses that creative art can engender within an audience.

You could create a group in the educational institution that you attend to give a cross-section of people the opportunity to discuss all of these different forms of creative art and their perspectives of them. This could take the form of a book club, an art appreciation society or a film review club just as a few examples. To make this even more worthwhile, you could try and set this group up in an educational institution that serves a disadvantaged cohort of students.

■ Table 3.4.1

Feminist reader-response	Feminist critics of texts and works would focus on how 'literature (and other cultural productions) reinforces or undermines the economic, political, social and psychological oppression of women'. A feminist reader-response would be concerned with, for example, how female characters (if there are any) are presented in a text or work, whether the text or work has been written by a man or woman and how evident (and how positively presented) patriarchal systems of power are in the work or text.
Marxist reader-response	Marxist critics of texts focus on texts and works through their perspective that, 'our socioeconomic system is the ultimate source of our experience'. A Marxist reader-response would be concerned with, for example, how class differences are presented in the text or work, how positively the capitalist system is presented in the text or work, and would also question who in society (in terms of socioeconomic background) the text or work benefits.
Psychoanalytical reader-response	A psychoanalytical response to a work or text would involve the reader interpreting a text or work by analysing the psychology of the characters and/or even the author of the text or work. A psychoanalytical reader may apply psychological frameworks from noted psychology theorists such as Sigmund Freud and Carl Jung to texts and works to, for example, explain and interpret the behaviour of characters, the key message being conveyed by the writer or even the alternative subconscious message being conveyed by that same writer.
Archetypal reader-response	An archetypal critic of works and texts would apply the theory created by the aforementioned Carl Jung that espoused that all humans have a collective experience of repeated symbols and motifs in life and the use of these in texts and works informs and creates a reader's response to them. Some of these repeated symbols and motifs include character archetypes such as the father figure, the mother, the innocent maiden, and the hero. They can also include images such as an apple to connote temptation and a snake to connote evil which are linked to systems of belief that are created through religion.
Post-colonial reader-response	A post-colonial critic of texts and works would analyse texts and works that focus on places that were once colonized or that are written by writers who come from, and write about, countries that were once colonized. These readers would be concerned with how texts and works present the colonized and the colonizers, and would be concerned with how the relationship between the colonizer and colonized is presented. Another area of interest would be how the place itself is presented to the reader and who the writer of the text or work is, and what their intentions are in their presentation of the place where the work or text is set. In the previous chapter, Chinua Achebe provided a post-colonial reader-response to Joseph Conrad's *Heart of Darkness* in his lecture to the University of Massachusetts Amherst about the work. His own work, *Things Fall Apart*, could be considered a post-colonial re-write of *Heart of Darkness*, linked to his post-colonial reading of the work.

In the next part of this chapter we will apply some of these theories to different texts in order to understand the multiple perspectives of issues, topics and themes that they can offer to the reader.

CONCEPT CONNECTION

TRANSFORMATION

As the IB Language and Literature guide states, 'the act of reading is potentially transformative in itself, both for the text and the reader. Different readers may transform a text with their personal interpretation. The text can also have an impact on the reader which potentially might lead to action and to the transformation of reality.' As we go through the application of these theories to works and texts and consider the perspectives that they offer to the reader as a result of this act of interpretation, you may want to consider how evident these ideas about transformation are.

As detailed in Chapter 2.1, the first response that you will have to a text or work as a reader will be your own, personal response which will be informed by your own context of reception. This context of reception may be informed by your beliefs and values which may correlate with the beliefs and values of some of the reader-response theories listed above. If this is not the case, or if your own context of reception is too broad and complex (very likely) to fit neatly into one of the categories, then where do you start in attempting to apply them? Sometimes, texts and works focus on issues, topics and themes that lend themselves more neatly to some reader-response theories then others.

For example, scan the adjacent QR code to see a photo of the model Emily Ratajkowski taken by the photographer Michael Avedon for fashion magazine *Harper's Bazaar*. In the photograph,

Ratajkowski is posing in lingerie and has body hair visibly shown. You may want to go back to Chapter 1.1 to re-read about the features of photographs in order to fully understand this text.

DISCUSSION

Think about which reader-response theory you would most likely apply to the photograph of Emily Ratajkowski in order to understand the variety of perspectives that it can offer to the reader. Think about the presentation of Ratajkowski and the topic/themes that it explores to help you with this. Once you have done this, discuss your ideas with a peer and then read the concept connection box below.

CONCEPT CONNECTION

PERSPECTIVE AND REPRESENTATION

It is clear that the director of the photograph is attempting to challenge traditional representations of women in fashion magazines while advertising the clothes and accessories that the model is wearing. For this reason, it would perhaps be most obviously appropriate to analyse the photograph through the lens of the feminist critical perspective and the Marxist critical perspective.

Feminist critical perspective: it could be suggested that the director of the photograph is clearly subverting stereotypical representations of women in fashion magazines. The photograph depicts Ratajkowski (a model who could be considered stereotypically attractive) wearing lingerie. Her make-up and hair, along with the black and white filter applied to the photograph, is reminiscent of provocative photographs taken in the past of models (such as Brigitte Bardot) who used to pose for fashion magazines. However, Ratajkowski has on clear display visible body hair which is not usually seen in traditional fashion photographs. The juxtaposition between these elements of the photograph clearly convey to the reader that the director of the photograph feels that visible body hair on a woman should be seen as just as attractive as the other, more-styled parts of a woman's body. The fact that Ratajkowski is staring directly at the reader challenges the concept of the 'male-gaze' is it feels to the reader as though Ratajkowski is comfortable with, and empowered by, being depicted in this way and does not care whether the reader finds this depiction sexually attractive or not. This ownership of the photograph makes the model an active participant in the meaning that the photograph conveys which is a subversion of the passive role that female models usually take in fashion photographs.

Marxist critical perspective: it could be suggested that the director of the photograph intentionally exploits female insecurities regarding beauty, and ideas belonging to the social movement of modern female empowerment, in order to sell designer clothes and accessories. Although the depiction of the model, Ratajkowski, could be seen as radically feminist in its subversion of stereotypical notions of feminine beauty it still needs to be noted that the photograph could be primarily designed to sell clothes and accessories. This could be seen in the caption accompanying the photograph which says 'Inamorata bralette; Chanel pants; Chanel Fine Jewelry earrings' The naming of the luxury, designer brands in conjunction with the highly-stylised photograph could firstly convey to the reader that in order to look more like the model (who is stereotypically attractive) they must buy these products from these specific brands. It could also be suggested that within society today women are feeling more empowered than ever before and that as a result they purposefully may seek out brands that are associated with the values of modern-day feminism. To this end, the director of the photograph may have intentionally included the depiction of the model having visible body hair in order to gain the attention of this specific market to then meet its capitalist aim of selling them designer clothes and accessories.

DISCUSSION

Now that you have read the commentaries of, and applied a feminist and Marxist critical reading to, the photograph you could discuss with a peer if any of the other critical perspectives explored in this chapter could be applied to the photograph.

GLOBAL ISSUES *Field of inquiry:* Politics, Power and Justice

CONFIRMATION BIAS IN THE MEDIA

How easy was the task of applying each critical perspective in isolation to the text? Was it difficult to interpret the photograph using just one theory at a time?

Although the feminist and Marxist readings when read together present two different perspectives of the photograph, if you were to apply these in isolation how much would that narrow the interpretation? Is there a danger when applying reader-response theories, that readers will only apply the theories that correlate with their own values and validate their own beliefs? How dangerous can the narrow reading and interpretation of a text or work be?

Research online examples of when a specific interpretation of a text or work has been damaging to people and/or society. Read the text below for an infamous example of this issue.

An infamous example of when a specific interpretation of a text or work has been damaging to people and/or society was the allegation by some media outlets and some US politicians that the hard-rock group Marilyn Manson were to blame for inciting the perpetrators of the Columbine High School massacre (a US school shooting that occurred in 1999 that resulted in the deaths of twelve students, one teacher and the two perpetrators who were also students at the school) to commit the shootings. Senator Jeff Sessions (at the time Chairman of the Senate Judiciary Committee Subcommittee on Youth Violence) testified before the senate in the aftermath of the incident that:

> *'In music, there is Marilyn Manson, an individual who chooses the name of a mass murderer as part of his name. The lyrics of his music are consistent with his choice of name. They are violent and nihilistic, and there are groups all over the world who do this, some German groups and others. I guess what I am saying is, a person already troubled in this modern high-tech world can be in their car and hear the music, they can be in their room and see the video, they can go into the chat rooms and act out these video games and even take it to real life.'*
>
> *(Jeff Sessions)*

This interpretation of Manson's lyrics are archetypal in nature, focusing on the universal symbols of death and violence that they contain. However, this is not the only interpretation of Manson's lyrics, with the eponymous lead singer of the band himself pointing out that an alternative interpretations of their song lyrics (using the authorial intentionalism theory) would suggest that they decry violence instead of propagating it. It has been suggested that some politicians used this single interpretation of the band's lyrics as a scapegoat tactic to avoid focusing on other, underlying causes of youth nihilism and violence, a focus that may have been beneficial in the prevention of future school shooting tragedies. To read more about this incident, and the debate that it generated, scan the QR codes opposite.

In the next part of this chapter we will consider all of the literary theories that we have explored so far to analyse and compare the multivocal perspectives presented by a literary work and a non-literary text.

'People and Service' print advert by Cathay Pacific

We will begin by reading a print advert by the Hong Kong based airline company Cathay Pacific, scan the QR code in the margin to see the advert. This print advert was part of the 'People and Service' advertising campaign by Cathay Pacific which aimed to promote the quality of its customer service as a means to attract customers. In Chapter 1.5 you explored the key features of advertisements. Use the notes that you made in this chapter to help you analyse this text.

ACTIVITY 2

After you have read the text, apply a New Criticism approach to interpreting it. Think about how the writer uses structural and stylistic techniques to promote the quality of its customer service to the reader. Once you have written your own interpretation, read the one below.

New Criticism reading

The writer uses various structural and stylistic choices in the advert to promote the quality of its customer service to the reader. For example, the layout of the text features a large visual image of a smartly dressed member of the Cathay Pacific cabin crew which dominates the majority of the page. The attire of the member of the cabin crew is modest, stylish and practical – the colours used correlate with the colours of the brand and are not garish or obtrusive – the whole image connotes professionalism. This image helps to attract customers as it conveys the idea that when you buy a seat on a Cathay Pacific flight, you can expect a professional level of service from their cabin crew. The text is multimodal and the written text conveys a parallel message to that of the visual image, the largest text on the page is a direct quote from the member of cabin crew pictured and states 'I just like to listen more than talk'. The action of 'listening' to the customer (a passive action) as opposed to 'talking' to the customer (an active action) are directly contrasted within the sentence. This implies professionalism and a high quality of customer service as the member of cabin crew is directly stating that they enjoy putting the customer's needs and actions at the centre of their work, as opposed to their own.

GLOBAL ISSUES ***Field of inquiry:* Culture, Identity and Community**

CULTURAL STEREOTYPES

As discussed earlier in this chapter, though the New Criticism model is a useful way of analysing texts and works to gain a preliminary interpretation of them, it can sometimes lead to a narrow or superficial understanding of a text or work.

When you first read this advert, what was your immediate reaction to it? Did the advert seem problematic in any way to you, especially in its representation of East Asian culture and gender stereotypes? Depending on your own context of reception the text may or may not have been problematic to you as a reader, but perhaps by questioning the intentions of the writer (and thereby constructing an authorial intentionalism response to the advert) you will be able to understand how and why the advert was considered controversial at the time of its publication.

ACTIVITY 3

Read the questions below and write down your thoughts in response to them. A full commentary on the extract is provided below the questions for you to check your understanding.

1 Why do you think the author of the text chose to use a female member of the cabin crew as opposed to a male member? What assumptions is the writer making about their targeted audience?

2 Why do you think the author of the text chose to depict the cabin crew member as averting her gaze from the camera?

3 When considering the multimodal elements of the advert, the written text and the visual image, are there any stereotypes about East Asian culture (Cathay Pacific is a Hong Kong based company) that are being utilized to attract the UK audience towards which it is targeted?

The author of the text has deliberately chosen to use a young and traditionally attractive female member of Cathay Pacific's cabin crew in the advert as they are making assumptions about their target audience. You could argue that the author is intentionally targeting a male, heterosexual audience by utilizing this member of its cabin crew to represent its brand in the assumption that this particular demographic of customer would be attracted to use Cathay Pacific's services, presuming that all of their cabin crew would look and act similarly to the crew member depicted in the advert. The writer of the text has deliberately depicted the member of the cabin crew as averting her gaze from the camera to convey docility and submission. Again, this is the writer assuming that its targeted audience would be persuaded to fly with Cathay Pacific on the presumption that its cabin crew are willing to passively submit to the demands of their customers without any question. These representations are problematic when considering the context of production and reception. The writer is clearly, and intentionally, harnessing inaccurate and harmful stereotypes about the beauty, passivity and subservience of East Asian women in order to attract UK customers (who will be familiar with these stereotypes) to fly with Cathay Pacific. The written text details how the cabin crew member depicted, Karina Yau, 'went from fashion model to flight attendant' which, when read in conjunction with the visual image, conveys the idea that she hasn't been hired by the company because of her skills as a member of cabin crew, but only as a cultural object to be admired by customers of the flight company.

Summary

The above commentary details how the writer of this advert may have intentionally used stereotypes about East Asian people and their culture in order to attract its UK customers to purchase Cathay Pacific flights. However, when applying the various reader-response theories detailed earlier in the chapter we, as a reader, can broaden our interpretation of this issue and see other perspectives pertaining to it. Read the table below which applies each of the reader-response theories to the text and think about how it aids your understanding of how texts and works can depict cultures in a narrow way to suit the purpose of the writer and the needs of its intended audience.

■ Table 3.4.2

Feminist reader-response	The main image depicts the member of cabin crew through the exploitation of preconceived and stereotypical notions within society about the female biologically-determined caregiver role. Not only has the writer chosen a female member of cabin crew for this advert, but they have depicted her clearly as someone who, through her facial expression, modest attire and body language, is submissive and anxious to please. The reader is encouraged to want to fly with Cathay Pacific as they will presume that they will be 'looked after' by a cabin crew member who is well equipped to do this job as she is not only female, but also because she is stereotypically feminine and caring in her approach to her work. This representation also plays on racist stereotypes about how East Asian women are more passive than their Western counterparts which makes Cathay Pacific an attractive flight option for its Western audience, as they will assume that the cabin crew will be more willing to fulfil their needs than the cabin crew of a European airline.
Marxist reader-response	The commodification of East Asian culture is a conduit through which Cathay Pacific attempts to sell its product in this advert to a Western reader who would be familiar with such a capitalist use of culture. The depiction of the cabin crew member as both exotic and tranquil is conveyed through the parallel usage of the visual image and the text. The cabin crew member is wearing traditionally auspicious colours in East Asian culture, red and gold, and her attire is styled in the fashion of a 'cheongsam' which is a traditional East Asian style of dress. The **phonology** of much of the text utilizes soft sibilance and assonance, 'Karina went from fashion model to flight attendant – and still doesn't think that life has had any real ups and downs' which connotes a serene tranquillity stereotypically associated with East Asian culture. This conveys that the airline's unique selling proposition is the culture of its staff. The stereotypical presentation of a person's culture for capitalist gains is damaging as it devalues the non-monetary worth of a person's culture.
Psychoanalytical reader-response	The advert plays into concepts of the 'male gaze' and the psychological compulsion of men to control women in order to attract its intended audience of Western men to purchase Cathay Pacific flights. The cabin crew member averts her gaze from the camera and so doesn't address the reader directly. This positions the reader as a voyeur and creates distance between the reader and the text which could make them more comfortable in the process of objectifying the woman as an exotic and foreign 'other'. By inviting the reader to objectify the cabin crew member in this way, the writer of the text is implying that this will be an experience that the reader can have on the actual flight, which may attract its target audience to buy flights with Cathay Pacific. The written text also uses a declarative to instruct the reader to 'recommend a favourite book' to the cabin crew member which implies that she is incapable of choosing her own books to read and is eager to be instructed in how to do this by the reader. This depiction plays into Freudian theories about the psychological drive of men to control women (due partially to their envy of their ability to become pregnant and bear children) and may encourage them to buy flights from Cathay Pacific in the knowledge that their staff will conform to behaviours that will make them comfortable as opposed to threaten them. This is a further extension of inaccurate stereotypes concerning the Western man's preference for East Asian women who are more likely to adopt these behaviours than their Western counterparts.
Archetypal reader-response	The Jungian archetypal symbols of 'the mother' who is caring and nurturing and 'the maiden' who is naive and innocent are both evident in this advert. The depiction of the member of the cabin crew being simultaneously nurturing and innocent is likely to appeal to a Western reader, who the writer also assumes is male, as this re-affirms preconceived notions about race and gender which are explored in the Feminist and the Psychoanalytical reader-responses. By re-affirming these belief systems about race and gender, the Western reader is encouraged to buy flights from Cathay pacific as they will also be buying into the mythology that surrounds East Asian culture and East Asian women in particular.
Post-colonial reader-response	The presentation of the cabin crew member (who is from the once colonized region of Hong Kong) as submissive to the needs and desires of her white, Western customer base is a contemporary manifestation of the relationship between the colonizer and the colonized. Cathay Pacific is deliberately presenting this relationship in this anachronistic way to encourage a Western audience to buy flights with the company as they will feel comfortable and familiar with the racially based power dynamic between themselves and their East Asian cabin crew member.

By applying the various reader-response theories to the text, it should be clear to you how through their application, texts can offer multiple perspectives of a single issue, theme or topic – this one being how texts and works can depict cultures in a narrow way to suit the purpose of the writer and the needs of its intended audience.

If you would like to read more about the debate surrounding the problematic depiction of culture in this advertisement then scan the QR codes opposite.

EE Links: English A – Language category 3

The stereotypical depiction of culture and people in literature and the mass media is widespread and can be controversial. You could explore this issue further through the following suggested extended essay research question:

- **To what extent do contemporary airline adverts** [these could be anywhere as long as they are in English] **still use stereotypical representations of gender to sell their products?**

Now that you have finished this chapter, let's review the key ideas in it and practise the several skills that it introduced.

Tess of the d'Urbervilles by Thomas Hardy (full title, *Tess of the d'Urbervilles: A Pure Woman Faithfully Presented*) was written in 1891. The novel centres on the story of Tess Durbeyfield who is the daughter of a poor agricultural family from rural England. In the novel, Tess is forced to take up a position of employment at the d'Urberville mansion (under the illusion that she is distantly related to the wealthy family that own it) because of her family's near destitution. She is reluctant to take up the position of employment as it means that she has constant exposure to Alec d'Urberville. Alec is the son of the wealthy widower Mrs d'Urberville, who owns the mansion, and he repeatedly makes unwanted sexual advances towards Tess. In this extract, Alec has 'rescued' Tess from an unprovoked altercation with Alec's spurned previous lover. He promises to take her home in his carriage but instead rides deep into the forest (into an area called 'The Chase') where he declares them lost and gets out of the carriage to find a way out. Tess falls asleep and it is implicitly suggested by Hardy that Alec rapes Tess as she sleeps.

In Chapter 1.1 you explored the conventions of literary prose. Use the notes that you made in that chapter to help you understand this extract.

SENSITIVE CONTENT

Caution: this extract includes sensitive content.

The author (Thomas Hardy) includes the suggestion of rape in the following extract. We have chosen this extract so you can consider for yourself the way Thomas Hardy wishes to portray this crime. It is central to understanding the themes of identity and human behaviour in this extract. Furthermore, the IB recommends that your studies in Language A: Literature should challenge you intellectually, personally and culturally, and expose you to sensitive and mature topics. We invite you to reflect critically on various perspectives offered while bearing in mind the IB's commitment to international-mindedness and intercultural respect.

In the meantime Alec d'Urberville had pushed on up the slope to clear his genuine doubt as to the quarter of The Chase they were in. He had, in fact, ridden quite at random for over an hour, taking any turning that came to hand in order to prolong companionship with her, and giving far more attention to Tess's moonlit person than to any wayside object. A little rest for the jaded animal being desirable, he did not hasten his search for landmarks. A clamber over the hill into the adjoining vale brought him to the fence of a highway whose contours he recognized, which settled the question of their whereabouts. D'Urberville thereupon turned back; but by this time the moon had quite gone down, and partly on account of the fog The Chase was wrapped in thick darkness, although morning was not far off. He was obliged to advance with outstretched hands to avoid contact with the boughs, and discovered that to hit the exact spot from which he had started was at first entirely beyond him. Roaming up and down, round and round, he at length heard a slight movement of the horse close at hand; and the sleeve of his overcoat unexpectedly caught his foot.

'Tess!' said d'Urberville.

There was no answer. The obscurity was now so great that he could see absolutely nothing but a pale nebulousness at his feet, which represented the white muslin figure he had left upon the dead leaves. Everything else was blackness alike. D'Urberville stooped; and heard a gentle regular breathing. He knelt and bent lower, till her breath warmed his face, and in a moment his cheek was in contact with hers. She was sleeping soundly, and upon her eyelashes there lingered tears.

Darkness and silence ruled everywhere around. Above them rose the primeval yews and oaks of The Chase, in which there poised gentle roosting birds in their last nap; and about them stole the hopping rabbits and hares. But, might some say, where was Tess's guardian angel? Where was the providence of her simple faith? Perhaps, like that other god of whom the ironical Tishbite spoke, he was talking, or he was pursuing, or he was in a journey, or he was sleeping and not to be awaked.

Why it was that upon this beautiful feminine tissue, sensitive as gossamer, and practically blank as snow as yet, there should have been traced such a coarse pattern as it was doomed to receive; why so often the coarse appropriates the finer thus, the wrong man the woman, the wrong woman the man, many thousand years of analytical philosophy have failed to explain to our sense of order. One may, indeed, admit the possibility of a retribution lurking in the present catastrophe. Doubtless some of Tess d'Urberville's mailed ancestors rollicking home from a fray had dealt the same measure even more ruthlessly towards peasant girls of their time. But though to visit the sins of the fathers upon the children may be a morality good enough for divinities, it is scorned by average human nature; and it therefore does not mend the matter.

(Thomas Hardy 71–72)

Thomas Hardy

Thomas Hardy was an English writer born in 1840. His writings were influenced by the Romantic style of literature, and he was a critic of Victorian social mores and values. He was especially critical of what he saw as the decline of rural England and set most of his writings in the former Anglo-Saxon Kingdom of 'Wessex' in the south of England. He is considered a Victorian 'realist' and much of his writing focuses on characters who suffer tragedy and unhappiness due to Victorian societal constraints on relationships, religion, education and class. He is perhaps best known for his novels *Far From the Madding Crowd*, *Jude the Obscure* and *Tess of the d'Urbervilles*.

ACTIVITY 4

Read the questions below and write down your thoughts in response to them. A full commentary on the extract is provided at the end of the book for you to check your understanding.

1 The focal event of this extract is the implied rape of Tess Durbeyfield by Alec d'Urberville. What stylistic and structural choices does the writer intentionally use to convey this event? Think back to the notes that you made about Victorian era societies in Chapter 2.1 to help you with this.

2 When Thomas Hardy was 16 he witnessed the execution of a woman called Elizabeth Martha Brown, who was hanged for murdering her violent and abusive husband. The event was said to have profoundly affected him and was the inspiration for his construction of the character of Tess in *Tess of the d'Urbervilles*. How does this information aid your understanding of the extract?

3 The novel itself can be seen as a form of social criticism, especially of Victorian-era sexual morals and class hierarchy. Apply three of the reader-response theories that you have learnt about in this chapter to explore different perspectives of this topic as conveyed in the novel.

Works cited

Achebe, C. 'An Image of Africa: Racism in Conrad's "Heart of Darkness".' Web. 24 Feb. 2019. **https://polonistyka.amu.edu.pl/__data/assets/pdf_file/0007/259954/Chinua-Achebe,-An-Image-of-Africa.-Racism-in-Conrads-Heart-of-Darkness.pdf**.

Cherkis, J. 'Sen. Jeff Sessions blamed culture, not guns, for Columbine Massacre.' *Huffington Post*, 2 March 2017. Web. 2 March 2019. **www.huffingtonpost.com/entry/jeff-sessions-guns-columbine_us_5894d54de4b0c1284f25dd10**.

Hardy, T. *Tess of the d'Urbervilles*. Penguin Classics, 2003.

Heller, Z, Kirsch, A. 'Should an author's intentions matter?' *The New York Times*, 10 March 2015. Web. 2 March 2019. **www.nytimes.com/2015/03/15/books/review/should-an-authors-intentions-matter.html**.

'HSBC criticized over new "anti-Brexit advert campaign".' *Sky News*, 7 Jan. 2019. Web. 2 March 2019. **https://news.sky.com/story/hsbc-criticised-over-new-anti-brexit-advert-campaign-11601374**.

Manson, M. 'Columbine: Whose Fault Is It?' *The Rolling Stone*, 24 June 1999. Web. 2 March 2019. **www.rollingstone.com/culture/culture-news/columbine-whose-fault-is-it-232759**.

Mattix, M. 'It's time to return to the New Critics.' *Public Discourse*, 17 Dec. 2013. Web. 2 March 2019. www.thepublicdiscourse.com/2013/12/11032.

Minter, A. 'Cathay Pacific's sexual harassment problem.' *The Straits Times*, 7 May 2014. Web. 2 March 2019. www.straitstimes.com/opinion/cathay-pacifics-sexual-harassment-problem.

Ratajkowski, E. 'Emily Ratajkowski Explores What It Means to Be Hyper Feminine.' *Harper's Bazaar*, 8 Aug. 2019. Web. 1 Sept. 2019. https://www.harpersbazaar.com/culture/features/a28577727/emily-ratajkowski-sexuality-essay.

Sharp, G. 'Selling Feminine Passivity in a Cathay Airlines Ad.' *Sociological Images*, The Society Pages, 17 Feb. 2011. Web. 2 March 2019. https://thesocietypages.org/socimages/2011/02/17/selling-feminine-passivity-in-a-cathay-airlines-ad.

Shepherd, R. 'On the Intentional Fallacy' *Poetry Foundation*. Web. 2 March 2019. www.poetryfoundation.org/harriet/2008/03/on-the-intentional-fallacy.

Watson, I. 'HSBC continues its "Together we Thrive" pledge with "We are not an Island" campaign.' *The Drum*, 3 Jan. 2019. Web. 2 March 2019. www.thedrum.com/news/2019/01/03/hsbc-continues-its-together-we-thrive-pledge-with-we-are-not-island-campaign.

Watson, I. 'HSBC says "We are not an Island"campaign isn't about Brexit amid Twitter criticism.' *The Drum*, 7 Jan. 2019. Web. 2 March 2019. www.thedrum.com/news/2019/01/07/hsbc-says-we-are-not-island-campaign-isnt-about-brexit-amid-twitter-criticism.

3.5 In what ways can diverse texts share points of similarity?

OBJECTIVES OF CHAPTER

- To provide an overview of the ways in which texts and works can be diverse.
- To provide an overview of the ways in which texts and works can share points of similarity.
- To demonstrate how this similarity can be manifested in texts and works and what it can add to the experience of the reader.
- To demonstrate ways to apply course concepts to specific works of literature and non-literary texts.
- To demonstrate ways to understand specific works of literature and non-literary texts in the context of global issues.

In the previous chapter we explored how a single text and work could provide a reader with multiple perspectives on a single issue, theme or topic. In this chapter we will be exploring how multiple, and diverse, texts and works can share points of similarity in their treatment of an issue, theme or topic.

First, we will consider the ways in which texts and works can be considered diverse, before exploring the ways in which these same texts and works could be seen as similar. We will then apply these ideas to a case study of a specific set of texts and works.

What is diversity in texts and works?

The word diversity comes from the Latin word *diversitas* meaning 'different'. When we use the word 'diversity' in relation to a group of texts and/or works, we are implying that there is something about them which differentiates them from each other. For example, texts and works can deviate and be differentiated from each other in the following ways:

- by the conventions of the text type or genre to which they belong
- by the attitudes, values, life experience and intentions of the writer
- by their intended effect upon the reader
- by their content and subject matter
- by considering the time period and context in which the text or work was produced
- by their use of visual, structural, literary and language techniques.

We will start by exploring two works and the ways in which they could be considered to differentiate from each other. In Sections 1 and 2, you analysed the conventions of autobiographical works so you can use the notes that you made there to help you read the first text. In that chapter, you will also have learnt about the Holocaust through your exploration of the graphic novel *Maus*. You may want to look again at that section which will help you understand the historical context of the following works. You also explored the conventions of personal diaries in Chapter 2.1, so you can use the notes that you made there to help you understand the second extract.

In the first extract below, from *If This is a Man* by Primo Levi (1979), Levi is describing the morning of his forcible transportation to Auschwitz concentration camp which happened in 1943.

Dawn came on us like a betrayer; it seemed as though the new sun rose as an ally of our enemies to assist in our destruction. The different emotions that overcame us, of resignation, of futile rebellion, of religious abandon, of fear, of despair, now joined together after a sleepless night in a collective, uncontrolled panic. The time for meditation, the time for decision was over, and all reason dissolved into a tumult, across which flashed the happy memories of our homes, still so near in time and space, as painful as the thrusts of a sword.

Many things were then said and done among us; but of these it is better that there remain no memory.

(Primo Levi 22)

Primo Levi

Primo Levi was an Italian writer and chemist who was born in 1919. He was a Holocaust survivor and is perhaps best known for *If This is a Man*, which is a testimony of the year that he spent as a prisoner in the Auschwitz concentration camp. Levi spent much of his life bearing witness to the horrors of the Holocaust and much of his poetry, memoirs and essays focus on its events and intricacies. Levi died in 1987 from a fall from a third-floor landing in his apartment block, which was ruled a suicide at the time, but which has since been questioned by his friends and associates.

In the second extract below, from *The Diary of a Young Girl*, Anne Frank, in 1942, is describing how she feels about the information that she has heard about Nazi concentration and extermination camps.

October 9th 1942: Today I have nothing but dismal and depressing news to report. Our many Jewish friends and acquaintances are being taken away in droves. The Gestapo is treating them very roughly and transporting them in cattle cars to Westerbork, the big camp in Drenthe to which they're sending all the Jews. Miep told us about someone who'd managed to escape from there. It must be terrible in Westerbork. The people get almost nothing to eat, much less to drink, as water is available only one hour a day, and there's only one toilet and sink for several thousand people. Men and women sleep in the same room, and women and children often have their heads shaved. Escape is almost impossible; many people look Jewish, and they're branded by their shorn heads. If it's that bad in Holland, what must it be like in those faraway and uncivilized places where the Germans are sending them? We assume that most of them are being murdered. The English radio says they're being gassed. Perhaps that's the quickest way to die. I feel terrible. Miep's accounts of these horrors are so heartrending … Fine specimens of humanity, those Germans, and to think I'm actually one of them! No, that's not true, Hitler took away our nationality long ago. And besides, there are no greater enemies on earth than the Germans and Jews.

(Anne Frank 53–54)

Anne Frank

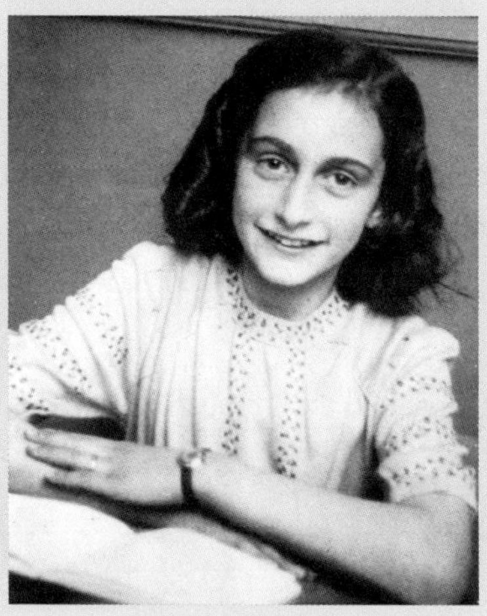

Anne Frank was born in Germany in 1929, but spent most of her life in Amsterdam in the Netherlands. When the Nazi regime occupied the Netherlands, she and her family went into hiding as persecutions upon Jewish people in the country increased. In *The Diary of a Young Girl* she details her life in hiding. In 1944, she and her family were discovered and were sent to various concentration camps. Frank died at Bergen-Belsen concentration camp in 1944. Frank's father, Otto, survived his time at Auschwitz-Birkenau, and when he returned to Amsterdam he was given Frank's diaries which had been salvaged by his former secretary, Miep Gies. These diaries were later published as *The Diary of a Young Girl*.

CONCEPT CONNECTION

COMMUNICATION

When reading both sources it is clear to see that even though both works are focused on the same historical event each writer has facilitated the act of communication between the work and the reader differently through their choice of style and structure. It is also important to note that both writers' act of communication can be differentiated through their context of production and perspective. Read the table below which details the diversity that exists between the two works.

TOK Links

How can our understanding of the universal topics, themes and issues that affect humanity be enhanced by the comparative study of diverse artforms that explore them?

■ Table 3.5.1

	***If This is a Man* by Primo Levi**	***The Diary of a Young Girl* by Anne Frank**
Perspective	The source is told from the perspective of a 24-year-old Italian man who survived the events of the Holocaust and who is recounting these events retrospectively. Levi experienced the Holocaust first-hand, and after having survived it, was able to bear witness to its horrors.	The source is told from the perspective of a 13-year-old Dutch/German girl who did not survive the events of the Holocaust. Her diary describes the events leading to her removal to a concentration camp, and her thoughts and feelings throughout this process, as they occurred. Frank did not survive the Holocaust and at the time of writing did not have first-hand knowledge of the concentration camps to which she would eventually be taken.
Context	Levi was a highly-educated person who wrote the work primarily for the purpose of educating the public about the harrowing reality of the events of the Holocaust. He was profoundly affected by his own personal experience and was able to articulate this experience deliberately through his choices in structure and style.	Frank was very young when she wrote her diary. She was also isolated from the rest of society at the time of writing as she was in hiding. She did not intend her diaries to be read by the public, and they were intended to be more of an outlet for her thoughts and feelings in an incredibly restricted environment. As a result, she probably didn't make intentional choices in her use of structure and style.

	If This is a Man by Primo Levi	*The Diary of a Young Girl* by Anne Frank
Structure	Levi utilizes long sentences, often containing consecutive parallel clauses to convey the distance that has lapsed between the event being described and his time recounting it – 'The different emotions that overcame us, of resignation, of futile rebellion, of religious abandon, of fear, of despair, now joined together after a sleepless night in a collective, uncontrolled panic.' His choice in structure is clearly considered and intentional – he has been able to dwell upon the exact details of the event and his thoughts and feelings in relation to it, thus equating to the detail he is able to include in each sentence.	Frank utilizes short, often fragmentary, sentences that connote immediacy and urgency – 'The English radio says they're being gassed. Perhaps that's the quickest way to die. I feel terrible.' This shows that Frank is writing her thoughts as they occur, she is not considering grammatical accuracy or communicative efficacy in her writing, also connoting that she does not expect this writing to be read by anyone but herself.
Stylistic choices	Levi utilizes much figurative language throughout the source, for example metaphors and personification – 'The time for meditation, the time for decision was over, and all reason dissolved into a tumult, across which flashed the happy memories of our homes, still so near in time and space, as painful as the thrusts of a sword.' The complexity of the description mirrors the complexity of emotions that he, and his fellow prisoners, felt before they were taken to Auschwitz. Levi has had time to think about this multitude of thoughts and feelings and thus has been able to convey them in a style that is most fitting. The choice helps to create empathy within the reader – through the utilization of these techniques the reader is able to fully comprehend an experience that, fortunately, for most people would be incomprehensible. This helps to fulfil the authorial intention of the work acting as a medium through which to convey the horrors of the Holocaust.	Frank writes in a clear and factual style, almost devoid of any descriptive techniques, which recounts the information that she has received and her thoughts and feelings in response to it – 'Today I have nothing but dismal and depressing news to report. Our many Jewish friends and acquaintances are being taken away in droves. The Gestapo is treating them very roughly and transporting them in cattle cars to Westerbork, the big camp in Drenthe to which they're sending all the Jews.' Again, it is clear that Frank used this diary as a way of expressing and synthesizing her own emotions in relation to the news that she was hearing about the Holocaust and was not considering the literary experience of any reader other than herself.

It is clear that these extracts could be considered diverse works in a variety of ways. However, how could these two works be considered similar? Even though the works can clearly be differentiated from each other, both works are significant in their act of communicating the writer's experience of the same event – the Holocaust.

CONCEPT CONNECTION

PERSPECTIVE AND CREATIVITY

You may be wondering why we have just spent a large portion of this section highlighting the differences between the two works. The answer to this question lies in the value of the interpretations that can be gained in the act of comparing and contrasting texts and works – an area that will be explored more fully in the next chapter. When analysing and exploring texts and works that are focused on the same issue, topic or theme, it is important to consider their diversity when constructing your own response to them as a reader. For example, how reductive is it for a reader to only consider one form of art in their exploration of an issue, topic or theme? Even though Levi's work is perhaps more literary and intentional in its creative form than Frank's, does that make Frank's less valuable to the reader? Art has the power to convey multiple perspectives of a single issue, topic or theme to a reader and only by considering a variety of artistic interpretations in response to this issue, topic or theme, and being able to appreciate their differences, are you able to construct a fully rounded and informed perspective.

Think about a time when your exposure to a variety of art (a piece of literature, a painting, a photography exhibition, for example) changed your perspective towards an issue, topic or theme. Or, a time that it challenged you to see an issue, topic or theme from a different perspective. A good example of this could be a consideration of Bao Ninh's *The Sorrow of War*, Michael Herr's *Dispatches* and the 'Napalm Girl' photo by Nick Ut (discussed in Chapter 1.1) in relation to perspectives about the events of the Vietnam War.

How can diverse texts and works share points of similarity?

ACTIVITY 1

Listed below are a variety of ways in which texts and works can be seen as being similar.

- They may share a similarity in text type or conventions used.
- They may share a similar perspective of a single issue, topic or theme.
- They may share a similarity in their intended effect upon the reader.
- They may share a similarity in focus upon a single issue, topic or theme.
- They may be similar in terms of the time period or context in which they were produced.
- They may use similar visual, structural, literary and language techniques.

1 After reading this list, in what ways can you see Primo Levi and Anne Frank's texts as being similar? Create a table, like one used earlier in the chapter, to highlight their diverse aspects, detailing the works' similarities in their perspective, context, structure and style. Read the end of book commentary which contains a completed table in response to this question.

2 What does an understanding of the works' similarities add to your response as a reader to the two works? Write down your thoughts in response to this question and then read the full commentary in the global issues box below.

GLOBAL ISSUES ***Field of Inquiry:* Politics, Power and Justice**

EXTREME POLITICAL IDEOLOGIES

An understanding of the similarities that exist between the two works helps a reader to understand their importance as testaments to one of the most significant historical events of the last century. When read in isolation, or when read as two entirely different works, they help to convey just one perspective of what it was like to be Jewish and living under the persecution of the Nazi regime. However, when read together, and seen as similar voices laying bare the truth of extreme political ideologies, they are powerful reminders of how these kinds of regimes can affect everyone regardless of age, gender or nationality. The universal aspects of their voices in terms of their fear but most importantly their strength in the face of adversity, helps the reader understand that there is a power in speaking the truth of an event such as this, and hopefully realize the importance of preserving the unified voices that exist relating to events such as these. By considering the similarities between the two accounts, readers should also be able to be moved emotionally by the wide-ranging consequences of a political system such as the Nazi regime and hopefully be able to take action to ensure that these kinds of systems do not gain such a huge amount of power ever again.

EE Links: English A – Literature category 2

If you are interested in this topic, here are a couple of questions that you could consider for your extended essay. Both questions refer to Art Spiegelman's *Maus* which you looked at in Chapter 1.1.

- **How does Anne Frank's *The Diary of a Young Girl* and Art Spiegelman's graphic novel *Maus* explore the theme of survival through their use of structure and style?**
- **To what extent does Primo Levi's *If This is a Man* and Art Spiegelman's *Maus* convey the dehumanizing effects of war through their use of literary conventions?**

The next two works could also be considered diverse, while sharing points of similarity. Read the two sources and use the skills that you have just learnt about identifying diversity and similarities in texts and works in order to respond to the activity questions that follow them.

The first extract is from George Orwell's novel *Burmese Days* (1934). The novel tells the story of Flory who is a British timber merchant in British ruled colonial-era Myanmar (or Burma as it was known then). The novel is written as a critique of the European colonial system of power and its ability to dehumanize the colonized and the colonizer. The extract below is taken from the end of the novel when after being publicly humiliated and seeing no hope in continuing his life, Flory commits suicide.

SENSITIVE CONTENT

Caution: this extract includes sensitive content and violence.

'Flo! Come here, Flo!'

She heard him and came obediently, and then stopped short at the bedroom door. She seemed to have grasped now that there was something wrong. She backed a little and stood looking timorously up at him, unwilling to enter the bedroom.

'Come in here!'

She wagged her tail, but did not move.

'Come on, Flo! Good old Flo! Come on!'

Flo was suddenly stricken with terror. She whined, her tail went down, and she shrank back. 'Come here, blast you!' he cried, and he took her by the collar and flung her into the room, shutting the door behind her. He went to the table for the pistol.

'No come here! Do as you're told!'

She crouched down and whined for forgiveness. It hurt him to hear it. 'Come on, old girl! Dear old Flo! Master wouldn't hurt you. Come here!' She crawled very slowly towards his feet, flat on her belly, whining, her head down as though afraid to look at him. When she was a yard away he fired, blowing her skull to fragments.

Her shattered brain looked like red velvet. Was that what he would look like? The heart, then, not the head. He could hear the servants running out of their quarters and shouting – they must have heard the sound of the shot. He hurriedly tore open his coat and pressed the muzzle of the pistol against his shirt. A tiny lizard, translucent like a creature of gelatine, was stalking a white moth along the edge of the table. Flory pulled the trigger with his thumb.

(George Orwell 292–293)

George Orwell

George Orwell was an English writer in the 1920s and 1930s whose non-fiction and fiction often focused on the flaws of society and attempted to elicit a response of shock, anger and at times fear in the reader. Rather than using his real name on his books, Eric Arthur Blair, he opted for a pseudonym, George Orwell. He had won a scholarship for Eton College, the most prestigious private (fee-paying) boys' school in England, and was from a respectable middle-class background. Orwell had first-hand experience of the British colonial system of power having served as a part of the Indian Imperial Police in Burma (as it was known then) for five years. He ended his time in Burma disillusioned by the system of British colonial power.

The next work is a poem by Irish writer WB Yeats. 'Sixteen Dead Men' (1920) was written in the context of Irish Republicans' push for the independence of the Republic of Ireland from British rule. The poem is Yeats' angry response to those who called for Ireland's revolutionaries to cease their fight for Ireland's independence due to the outbreak of the First World War. Yeats uses the sixteen men who were convicted and executed for leading the Easter Uprising (a significant armed insurrection against British rule in Ireland) as a metaphor for British brutality in the poem.

Sixteen Dead Men

O but we talked at large before
The sixteen men were shot,
But who can talk of give and take,
What should be and what not
While those dead men are loitering there
To stir the boiling pot?
You say that we should still the land
Till Germany's overcome;
But who is there to argue that
Now Pearse is deaf and dumb?
And is their logic to outweigh
MacDonagh's bony thumb?
How could you dream they'd listen
That have an ear alone
For those new comrades they have found,
Lord Edward and Wolfe Tone,
Or meddle with our give and take
That converse bone to bone?

(WB Yeats)

WB Yeats

WB Yeats was an Irish poet born in 1865. He was an Irish Nationalist who frequently included symbols of Irish culture and history in his works. He was awarded the Nobel Prize for Literature in 1927 for the body of poetry that he had created throughout his life – it was seen as a significant moment for Irish literature coming so soon after the independence of Ireland from British rule in 1922.

ACTIVITY 2

Once you have answered these questions, you can read a full commentary of the two works at the end of the book.

1 How could the two works be seen as diverse?

2 What are the similarities that exist between the two works? How does an understanding of these similarities add depth to our understanding of the meaning that they convey?

In the next part of this chapter we will explore the ways in which diverse texts and works can be seen as similar.

So far, we have explored how readers can create connections between works and texts so that they can be read as sharing points of similarity. In the next part of this chapter, we will explore how writers can deliberately ensure that their writings share points of similarity with other texts and/or works, but often for a different purpose or to convey a different message to the reader.

Allusion, parody and pastiche

Have you ever been in trouble for copying somebody else's work? If you have, then you might find this next part of the chapter a little confusing. This next part will explain the ways in which a writer can intentionally borrow parts of another writer's text or work for a specific effect. However, it is worth noting that when writers do this they are doing it in full knowledge that the reader will recognize the part of the other writer's text or work that has been borrowed. Also, the reason the writer has done this can be to make a significant and serious comment on an issue, topic or theme – and not just because they ran out of time to complete their homework!

The table below outlines the definition of allusion, parody and pastiche which are all techniques that a writer can use when intentionally making their text or work similar to another writer's.

■ Table 3.5.2

Allusion	In works or texts, an allusion is a direct or indirect reference to a person, thing, event or idea that exists outside of the work or text. These references are usually to something that is of cultural or historical significance. For example, if you have ever used the snake emoji in a conversation on social media to symbolize someone's behaviour as deceptive then you are actually using a biblical allusion. The snake image as a symbol of suspicion or evil alludes to the story of Adam and Eve where Eve was tempted into eating a forbidden apple by a snake, who was actually the devil (this bible story will be analysed further in the next chapter).
Parody	A parody is when one text or work imitates another in terms of its style and/or structure. This is usually to provoke a specific response within the reader, for example to make them laugh or to question a belief or an idea. An example of a parody will be analysed in the next part of this chapter.
Pastiche	A pastiche is when one text or work imitates another in terms of its style or structure – but to celebrate or honour the other work or text as opposed to mocking it (like a parody). An example of a pastiche will be analysed in the next part of this chapter.

Case study: how do allusions, parodies and pastiches work?

In the next part of this chapter we will analyse a set of texts that all share points of similarity in their use of **allusion**, **parody** or **pastiche**; however, all of these texts have very different contexts of production and were constructed to engender a diverse reader-response.

The next two texts are examples of propaganda, which is a category of texts and works that are designed to manipulate the opinions and behaviours of the reader usually to further a political ideology or agenda.

KEY FEATURES PROPAGANDA POSTERS

- Propaganda usually utilizes limited information and text – this **simplifies and reduces** what is usually an issue fraught with complexity to a key, simple message that the writer wants to convey to the reader.
- Misleading and manipulative information is usually used to **create bias**. This can be through, for example, the deceptive use of statistics, ambiguous language and unsubstantiated opinions.
- **Symbols** are often used to connote important concepts and ideas that are integral to the writer's message, for example, a public figure who represents certain ideals within society, an anchor to represent security, a flag to connote nationalism and patriotism or a rat to represent infection and disease.
- **Emotive language** is often used to manipulate the reader into feeling a specific way after reading the text or work, for example, fear, anger or pride.

- **Direct address** is used to speak directly to the reader in order to make the text or work more persuasive.
- **Stereotypes** and **scapegoating** are often used as a way of creating an 'us' and 'them' mentality within the reader – this is usually to encourage the reader to blame someone other than the producer of the text or work for an ill within society.
- **Imperatives** (a direct instruction to the reader) are usually utilized to incite the reader to take a specific action once they have read the text or work.

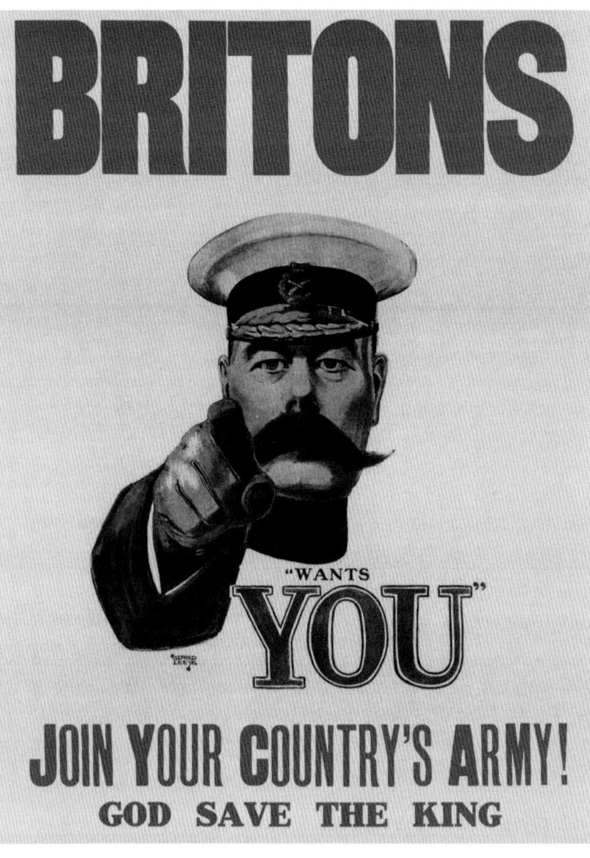

■ 'Lord Kitchener Wants YOU' army recruitment poster, Alfred Leete, 1914

■ 'I Want YOU' army recruitment poster, James Montgomery Flagg, 1916

The person depicted on the front of the poster above is Lord Kitchener who was the Secretary of State for War in the UK from 1914 until his death in 1916. He was the first currently serving soldier to hold the post of Secretary of State for War and was appointed during the outbreak of the First World War across Europe. Lord Kitchener was well known throughout the UK as he had had a long and highly publicized military career. The UK had relied on volunteer military recruitments for its wars throughout most of the 1800s, but unlike most of his contemporaries who expected a brief war, Kitchener foresaw that the war would last at least three years and predicted that the army would need huge numbers of soldiers to be recruited. The poster first appeared as a full page cover in September 1914's *London Opinion* magazine before being printed in postcard form and as full size posters to be displayed in public areas around the UK.

The poster above was also used to encourage citizens to join the army during the First World War period but was used in the USA and only from 1916. The poster was first published as the front cover of *Leslie's Week* magazine for its July 1916 issue. The USA did not officially declare war on Germany and become an active party in the First World War until 1917, but it was clear to the public by 1916 that US involvement in the war was becoming increasingly likely.

CONCEPT CONNECTION

COMMUNICATION

Even though both posters are diverse in the sense that they were created at different times, by different people, in a different national context, there are enough similarities between them to make it clear that the US poster is an allusion to the British one. Just from a superficial reading of both texts it is clear that the writer intentionally borrowed the key elements of the first poster and changed them subtly to suit its different context of production. Ultimately, both of the texts are attempting to manipulate the reader into doing the same thing – joining their nation's army. They are unified by the message that they are communicating to the reader, but also in the methods that they are using to do this act of communication. Both sources could be considered to be examples of propaganda.

For example, the symbol of Lord Kitchener (a nationally recognized image connected with nationalism, masculinity and fighting prowess) pointing at the reader directing them to enlist. The US poster uses exactly the same visual image, except it contains the symbol of 'Uncle Sam', used commonly as the personification of the USA and its values, pointing at the reader. Both of the sources communicate their message simply using very little written text. The text in both sources is also interesting – 'Britons! Lord Kitchener wants you. Join your country's army! God save the King' and the simply stated – 'I want you for US Army. Nearest recruiting station.' Both utilize direct address using the pronoun 'you' repeatedly and both use imperatives, a direct command for that reader to go and enlist into the army. The use of the nationalistic symbols as well as the direct address and imperatives have an emotionally manipulative effect upon the reader as they are led to believe that it is the nation itself, and all that it stands for, that needs them to enlist into the army.

The bias within both sources is inherent in the fact that neither give full or specific information about what it is that the civilians would be signing up for upon joining the army. For example, Lord Kitchener himself was fully aware that the war was not going to be the short, emphatic victory that most people in the UK believed it would be and he knew that if his predictions were correct, huge numbers of soldiers would die in the process of the war. However, this information is nowhere to be seen on the poster and if this information was communicated to the reader it is highly unlikely that people would have enlisted in the numbers that they did. Similarly, the obscenely high death toll of soldiers fighting in the First World War was widely known by the time the US poster was published, but again, this information is deliberately not communicated to the reader.

GLOBAL ISSUES *Field of inquiry:* Beliefs, Values and Education

THE MANIPULATION OF LANGUAGE

The power of **allusions** in texts and works rely on the intended readers having shared reference points, usually in the form of beliefs and values that are often instilled in us through both formal and informal education. For example, the reason that many Western politicians use Western classical allusions in their speeches – quotes from classical philosophers or figures in literature – to add gravitas or importance to their message is because they assume their audience will recognize these references. They assume that even if the audience does not recognize the reference in its entirety, they will at least recognize the name of the person who first made the reference, as they assume that they will have probably learnt about these people in their formal education or through their consumption of Western culture. This is why the writers of **propaganda** often use allusions through symbols in their act of communication as it can be a very effective way of manipulating a reader. For example, if the creator of a piece of propaganda wants a reader to attach morality to their message then they just need to include a religious reference that is appropriate to their target demographic. If they want to lend credibility to a message, they just need to include a visual image depicting someone who, within the collective consciousness of its intended audience, connotes values pertaining to honesty and integrity.

It is important that you, as a reader, are educated to be able to spot **propaganda** within the mass media as its usage can have significant consequences. For example, just think about all of the soldiers who enlisted to take part in the First World War as a result of wartime propaganda, of which these posters are just two examples – soldiers who may not have known fully the reality of the horror which they were to experience.

Opposite are QR codes which will take you to some contemporary examples of mass media that could be categorized as examples of propaganda. These are written forms of propaganda, as opposed to posters, but see if you can spot some of the elements of propaganda delineated within this chapter in the writing.

TOK Links

How does the use of propaganda in mass media affect the way that we perceive information?

The next two texts can be seen as examples of **parody** and **pastiche**. Read the two sources and the contextual information before reading the commentary about them below.

The poster below was created in the USA in 1971 by 'The Committee to Help Unsell the War'. This 'Committee' was created by Ira Nerken, a political science student at Yale, who, along with a group of academics and advertising professionals, decided to organize a collective group of marketing and advertising experts who would help to 'unsell' the Vietnam War to the general US population. The USA had been involved in the war in Vietnam from the 1950s and due to

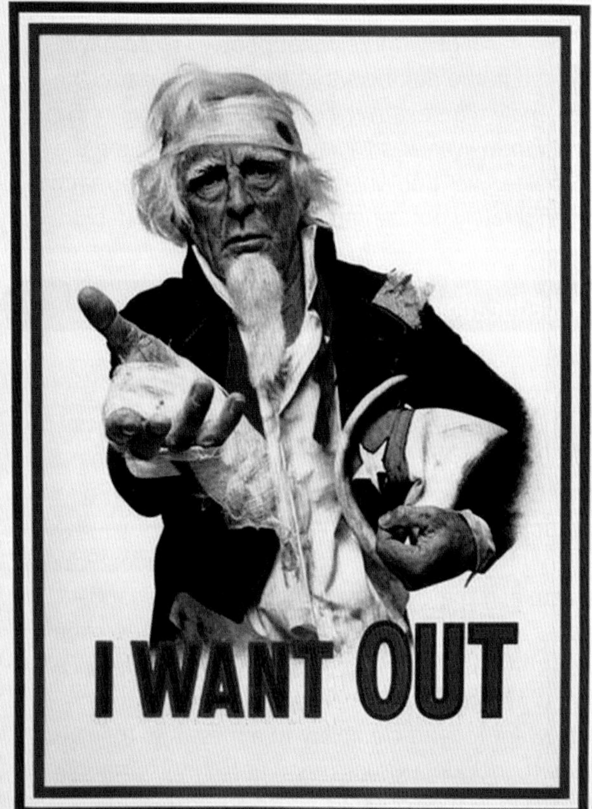

■ 'I Want Out' poster by Larry Dunst, John Daniel, Murray Smith and Steve Horn, USA, 1971

compulsory army conscription, huge casualties, military losses, and a general lack of belief in the reasons for US involvement, the war was becoming increasingly unpopular with US citizens throughout the 1960s and 1970s. It was revealed, in 1969, that the US Government's Defense Department had spent an extraordinarily large sum of money on 'selling' the Vietnam War to the US population throughout the US's period of involvement in it. This prompted Nerken to create the 'Unsell the War' committee in an attempt to redress this, and the poster above was created as a part of the committee's efforts. If you would like to read more about this then scan the QR code opposite.

Scan the adjacent QR code to see posters created by the British Army in 2019 as part of a recruitment drive targeting young people in the UK aged 18–25.

Both of the writers of these posters have creatively re-imagined the first two war posters we analysed to create an original text that fits the needs of their intended purpose and reader.

The 'I want out' poster is clearly a **parody** of the US army recruitment poster and its writer deliberately utilizes an altered version of its visual images and written text to convey an alternative message to the one originally communicated. It is clearly constructed to communicate an anti-war message which is the exact opposite of the message conveyed in the US army recruitment poster. It utilizes the same visual image of Uncle Sam but instead of him being depicted as strong-willed and smartly dressed, he is depicted as injured, frail, falling apart and desperate for assistance – almost begging. This is a **subversion** of the use of Uncle Sam as a personification of US beliefs and values and his utilization as a tool to help recruit US citizens to a militaristic cause. He is instead creatively re-imagined as a symbol of the negative US experience of the Vietnam War – his status as a universal symbol of the USA helps to connote the idea that this experience is also universal within most US citizens. It **connotes** that this anti-war sentiment is almost akin to a national trait. Again, instead of the text reading 'I want you', this has been subverted to read, 'I want out'. Instead of directing the US public to support a war, the language has been changed to encourage them to think about supporting efforts to leave a war. Through its creative re-imagining of an iconic piece of **propaganda**, the writer is able to parody the original pro-war message to point out the flaws of continuing the US involvement in the Vietnam War while also highlighting the issue of propaganda being used to convince the US public to support the war in the first place.

The millennials poster is a **pastiche** of the British army poster in the way that it has creatively re-imagined many of the elements to celebrate and replicate its original purpose. The writer has deliberately used the same **graphology** in terms of its colour, layout, visual image and typography to ensure that it is instantly recognizable as clearly **alluding** to the wartime poster. Even though a contemporary audience may be uneasy about the nefarious propaganda elements of the original poster, it is still iconic within the collective consciousness of British people and still is regarded as an incredibly effective example of visual design. The writer of the millennials poster celebrates this efficacy in design by replicating parts of it; however, they re-imagine other parts of it to make its message more positive and suitable for its context, purpose and audience. For example, instead of using an image of a white, male, military figure, the writer has included an image of a female soldier who is also a person of colour. This helps to **convey** the idea that being a part of the army is open to all British citizens regardless of gender and race – a message that would be important for a diverse, young, socially aware reader.

The millennials poster also contains much more written information than the wartime poster and uses a subtler form of **persuasion** than that of the short, sharp, imperatives used in the original. By referring to 'Me me me millennials' and the army's need for their 'self belief' the army is alluding to an inaccurate and harmful stereotype within contemporary society that the demographic the advert is attempting to target is narcissistic and self-centred. By ironically converting what could be seen as an insult into a positive characteristic, the poster is conveying the message that if the target audience is feeling undervalued within society then they will find purpose and appreciation by joining the British army. By replicating some aspects of the original poster while modernizing some of its other aspects, the writer effectively creates a pastiche that celebrates the original Kitchener poster's creativity in design while ensuring its message is more appropriate to the young and socially aware reader it is targeting.

CAS Links

Are there any forms of mass media from the past that you particularly like the design or style of? If so, use elements of that style or design to help you create a pastiche of it. This is something that you could apply to your IB study of group six subjects in the Arts. You could also use these skills to create promotional materials for the service and activity projects that are taking place around your educational institution. For example, you could create pastiche posters for an upcoming theatre production or sporting event. You could even offer to create pastiche promotional materials for a local charitable organization. All of these tasks could be a great way of applying your creative skills to a service activity.

Now that you have finished this chapter, let's review the key ideas in it and practise the several skills that it introduced.

Read the sources below and their contextual information and then respond to the questions. When you have finished, you can read the notes at the end of the book.

■ *Firestarter* print advert, USA, 1984,

■ *Stranger Things* online advert, USA, 2017

The poster to the left (on the previous page) is advertising the film version of the Stephen King novel *Firestarter*. In the film/novel, the protagonist, Charlie, is a young girl who has 'pyrokinesis' – the ability to create fire with her mind. Throughout the film/novel, Charlie is on the run with her father from government officials who would like to capture Charlie and use her as a weapon. In the shot depicted on the film poster, Charlie has just created a raging fire in order to burn down the government facility where it was intended for her to be kept as a prisoner and her power used as a weapon at the government's will.

The poster to the right (on the previous page) is an advert promoting the Netflix television series *Stranger Things*. The series is heavily influenced by 1980s US popular culture and the series centres, in part, on the story of a young girl, Eleven, who has 'psychokinetic' abilities – the ability to move things with her mind. Eleven, who is depicted in the main visual image of the poster, is in hiding from the science laboratory where she has been kept for most of her life and where she has been used in sinister science experiments.

This painting depicts the story of Elijah from the Old Testament of the Christian Bible. Elijah is a religious figure who features in some form in many of the world's major religions. In the Book of Kings in the Old Testament of the Christian Bible, Elijah is a prophet who God performs many miracles through. This includes the bringing down of fire from the sky as a protestation against the worship of 'false idols' and his entering into Heaven alive on a chariot of fire. If you would like to read more about the story of Elijah then scan the QR code opposite.

■ Painting of *Elijah Taken up in a Chariot of Fire* by Giuseppe Angeli, Italy, 1740–1755

ACTIVITY 3

1 Do you think the *Stranger Things* poster is a pastiche or a parody? What does the use of pastiche or parody add to your understanding of the text?

2 **Extension activity:** Does the Angeli painting and the *Firestarter* poster allude to each other in any way? What can this add to your understanding of the *Firestarter* poster?

When you have finished, compare your responses with those at the back of the book.

Works cited

'Elijah, Hebrew Prophet.' *Encyclopedia Britannica*. Web. 8 March 2019. **www.britannica.com/biography/Elijah-Hebrew-prophet**.

'Elijah Taken up in a Chariot of Fire' Giuseppe Angeli, National Gallery of Art, Web, accessed 8 March 2019, **https://www.nga.gov/collection/art-object-page.41685.html**.

Ellicott, C, Glanfield, E, Robinson, M, Wright, S. 'Fury after PM warns of 'swarm': As police seize stowaway migrants across South, Cameron is attacked for 'likening them to insects.' *The Daily Mail*, 30 July 2015. Web. 8 March 2019. **www.dailymail.co.uk/news/article-3180063/British-police-stop-lorry-M20-just-15-miles-Folkestone-arrest-12-migrants-patrols-stepped-sides-Channel-days-migrantsstorming-tunnel.html**.

Firestarter, film poster, Web, accessed 8 March 2019, **https://tvtropes.org/pmwiki/pmwiki.php/Literature/Firestarter**.

Frank, A. *The Diary of a Young Girl*. (extracts) *Alpha History*, Web. 7 March 2019. **https://alphahistory.com/holocaust/anne-frank-diary-1942-44**.

'I want out', Web, accessed 8 March 2019, **https://collections.vam.ac.uk/item/O75555/i-want-outposter-daniel-john/**.

'I want you for US army', Web, accesses 8 March 2019, **http://time.com/4725856/uncle-sam-posterhistory/**.

King, S. *Firestarter*. Pocket Books, 2016.

Levi, P. *If This is a Man/The Truce*. Abacus, Little, Brown Book Group, 2003.

'Lord Kitchener Wants You', Web, accessed 8 March 2019, **https://en.wikipedia.org/wiki/Lord_Kitchener_Wants_You**.

Mohdin, A. 'UK army recruitment ads target "snowflake" millennials.' *The Guardian*, 3 Jan 2019. Web. 8 March 2019. **www.theguardian.com/uk-news/2019/jan/03/uk-army-recruitment-ads-target-snowflake-millennials**.

Orwell, G. *Burmese Days*. Penguin Modern Classics, 2010.

Pollak, JB. 'Donald Trump Tackles Murder, Expropriation of White Farmers in South Africa.' *Breitbart*, 22 Aug. 2018. Web. 8 March 2019. **www.breitbart.com/politics/2018/08/22/donald-trumptackles-murder-expropriation-of-white-farmers-in-south-africa**.

Stranger Things. Netflix, 2016.

'Text of George Bush's speech.' The Guardian, 21 Sept. 2001. Web. 8 March 2019. **www.theguardian.com/world/2001/sep/21/Sept.11.usa13**.

'The Committee to Help Unsell the War.' Social Design Notes, 31 Jan. 2003. Web. 8 March 2019. **https://backspace.com/notes/2003/01/the-committee-to-help-unsell-the-war.php**.

Yeats, WB. 'Sixteen Dead Men.' *Poetry Foundation*. Web. 10 March 2019. **www.poetryfoundation.org/poems/57314/sixteen-dead-men**.

3.6 In what ways can comparison and interpretation be transformative?

OBJECTIVES OF CHAPTER

- To explain how comparing texts and works can transform the reader's perspective of an issue, topic or theme.
- To provide an overview of how the meaning of a work of text can be transformed by a reader's response to it.
- To demonstrate how a writer can deliberately transform a text or work through the act of translation.
- To provide an opportunity to apply some the skills learnt throughout this section to a variety of texts and works.
- To demonstrate ways to apply course concepts to specific works of literature and non-literary texts.
- To demonstrate ways to understand specific works of literature and non-literary texts in the context of global issues.

Derived from the Latin words *trans* and *forma* meaning 'across' and 'form', the word 'transform' means essentially to 'change form'. 'Transformation' is one of the seven key concepts that are central to your studies in IB English Language and Literature, and this chapter will focus on what this concept means when applied to texts and works.

As defined in the IB guide to this course, texts and works can 'transform' or be 'transformative' when, for example:

- they cause a reader (or group of readers) to **change their previous perspective** of an issue, topic or theme
- they **provoke discussion or action** within a mass audience
- their text type and conventions are **altered** for a **new purpose**
- they **change language** and become a text or work 'in translation'.

This chapter will be structured around the exploration of each of these examples through an analysis of a variety of texts and works. As this is the final chapter in this section, we will also be applying the skills that we have learnt throughout this section in the interpretation of the texts and works in this chapter.

How can comparison cause a reader to change their previous perspective of an issue, topic or theme?

As explored in the previous chapter, when a reader constructs their perspective of a single issue, topic or theme through the texts and works that they are exposed to, it is important that those texts and works are **diverse**. The importance of this can be demonstrated in the analysis of the following works and texts.

The first extract is from William Leonard Laurence's Pulitzer-Prize-winning account of the dropping of an atomic bomb on Nagasaki, Japan towards the end of the Second World War in 1945. The European arena of the Second World War had concluded in 1945 upon Germany's surrender to the Allied forces. However, Imperial Japan made it clear that they had no intention of surrendering which meant that the Allied forces anticipated they would have to pursue a land invasion of Japan which would inevitably lead to a huge number of military and civilian casualties, as well as involving huge sums of expenditure. To this end, a decision was made by the USA, with the consent of the UK, to drop an atomic bomb on Japan if they did not accept one final request to surrender. After Japan's refusal to surrender after this final ultimatum, an atomic bomb was dropped on the Japanese city of Hiroshima on 6 August 1945 with devastating consequences. After a further refusal from Imperial Japan to surrender, another atomic bomb was dropped on the Japanese city of Nagasaki with yet more devastating consequences. Imperial Japan surrendered shortly after this second bomb. If you would like to read more about this hugely significant historical event, scan the QR code opposite.

Scan the QR code to read the opening six paragraphs of *Atomic Bombing of Nagasaki Told By Flight Member* published in September 1945 (you can read it in full, of course, but the following commentary focuses on those opening paragraphs). All 11 articles of Laurence's winning work are available to read on this Pulitzer page if you would like to explore further.

William Leonard Laurence

William Leonard Laurence was a Lithuanian-American journalist who was born in 1888. He is perhaps best known for his work as a science writer for the *New York Times* and he was the official historian for the 'Manhattan Project' which was the name of the research and development team (led by the USA with support from Canada and the UK) that worked to create the atomic bombs that were eventually dropped on Hiroshima and Nagasaki. He was the only journalist to witness the dropping of the atomic bomb on Nagasaki, and he won a Pulitzer Prize for his reportage on this event – reportage that is partially detailed in the above extract. If you would like to read the rest of his reportage on this topic and event, scan the QR code.

CONCEPT CONNECTION

PERSPECTIVE

When reading the extract it is clear that the perspective of the writer towards the atomic bomb is one of awe and wonder. The writer metaphorically describes the bomb as 'a thing of beauty' connoting his perspective that the bomb is something to admire. This is extended in the writer's use of scientific jargon and hyperbole that he uses when describing the process of developing the bomb and the final stages of preparing for its use – 'In its design went millions of man-hours of what is without doubt the most concentrated intellectual effort in history' and 'But our lead plane is on its way with another atomic bomb, the second in three days, concentrating in its active substance an explosive energy equivalent to 20,000 and, under favorable conditions, 40,000 tons of TNT.' It is notable that the writer barely mentions the use of the bomb on the Japanese city of Hiroshima, which occurred only days earlier, and the horrific consequences that it had. Read together, this use of jargon and hyperbole helps to convey the writer's perspective that the bomb is a scientific marvel, and that when appraising the bomb this should be the main focus and not the human cost of its usage.

The fact that Laurence was awarded the Pulitzer Prize for this reportage implies that there were many readers who either agreed with this perspective or at the very least appreciated the quality of the writing through which he conveyed this perspective.

It is worth noting that at this time the horror of Japanese war crimes such as those that occurred in the Nanjing massacre, the treatment of prisoners of war in (what was then known as) Burma, the use of human shields in the Battle of Okinawa and the forced sexual slavery of women across Japanese occupied lands, were at the forefront of many people's minds – which may provide an understanding of why the perspective of Laurence was so lauded at the time.

As a contemporary reader you may find the extract to be an uncomfortable read. We now know, with hindsight, the unimaginable and tremendous amount of death and suffering caused by the use of the atomic bombs on Hiroshima and Nagasaki. Knowing this, it may seem that Laurence's perspective of the bombs as being impressive, extraordinary and awesome, is in bad taste. It is possible that the passage of time can transform a reader's interpretation of a text.

The next two extracts are examples of texts that clearly provide a **diverse perspective** of the atomic bombing of Hiroshima and Nagasaki to the one offered to the reader in Lawrence's article.

■ Photograph of Hiroshima bomb aftermath

CHECK FOR UNDERSTANDING

In Chapter 1.1 you analysed an example of photojournalism. The text above could also be regarded as an example of photojournalism. Check your understanding of this text type by re-reading the information in Chapter 1.1 and filling in the table below which uses step 1 (genre, audience and purpose) and step 4 (other features of text type) of the non-literary analysis strategy that you were introduced to in the same section and chapter. You should focus on how the photograph effectively conveys the scope of the devastation of the atomic bomb on Hiroshima to the reader.

Once you have done this, read the end of book commentaries for an example of a table that has been filled out for you.

Genre	
Audience	
Purpose	
Other features of text type	

The next extract from *Hiroshima* takes the form of a **personal diary**, the conventions of which you learnt about in Chapter 2.1. Use the notes that you made in that chapter to help you understand this text.

The morning again, was hot. Father Kleinsorge went to fetch water for the wounded in a bottle and a teapot he had borrowed. He had heard that it was possible to get fresh tap water outside Asano Park. Going through the rock gardens, he had to climb over and crawl under the trunks of fallen pine trees; he found he was weak. There were many dead in the gardens. At a beautiful moon bridge, he passed a naked, living woman who seemed to have been burned from head to toe and was red all over. Near the entrance to the park, an Army doctor was working, but the only medicine he had was iodine, which he painted over cuts, bruises, slimy burns, every-thing—and by now everything that he painted had pus on it. Outside the gate of the park, Father Kleinsorge found a faucet that still worked— part of the plumbing of a vanished house—and he filled his vessels and returned. When he had given the wounded the water, he made a second trip. This time, the woman by the bridge was dead. On his way back with the water, he got lost on a detour around a fallen tree, and as he looked for his way through the woods, he heard a voice ask from the underbrush, 'Have you anything to drink?' He saw a uniform. Thinking there was just one soldier, he approached with the water. When he had penetrated the bushes, he saw there were about twenty men, and they were all in exactly the same nightmarish state: their faces were wholly burned, their eyesockets were hollow, the fluid from their melted eyes had run down their cheeks. (They must have had their faces upturned when the bomb went off; perhaps they were anti-aircraft personnel) Their mouths were mere swollen, pus-covered wounds, which they could not bear to stretch enough to admit the spout of the teapot. So Father Kleinsorge got a large piece of grass and drew out the stem so as to make a straw, and gave them all water to drink that way.

(John Hersey 55–56)

John Hersey

John Hersey was an American writer and journalist who was born in 1914. He won the Pulitzer Prize for his work, *A Bell for Adano* but he is perhaps best known for *Hiroshima* which was his account of the aftermath of the Hiroshima bomb, an extract from which is detailed in the source above. *Hiroshima* was first published in 1946 as an article that comprized almost the entirety of the publication in which it was published, *The New Yorker.* It was later adapted into a novel which has never been out of print since its publication. The text tells the true story of six different people's accounts of the aftermath of the Hiroshima bomb and alternates between these perspectives throughout the course of the text.

ACTIVITY 1

Read the questions below and write down your thoughts in response to them. There is a full commentary of the two texts provided in the concept connection box below these questions.

1. Review the notes that you made about diversity in texts and works from Chapter 3.5. How do the photograph and the diary entry differ from Laurence's perspective? How could a comparison of the photograph and the diary entry to the account written by Laurence transform a reader's perspective towards the atomic bombing of Hiroshima and Nagasaki?
2. Remind yourself of conventions of fiction and non-fiction texts and works as detailed in Chapter 3.1. Hersey's extract is one of earliest examples of 'New Journalism', where writers adopted the prose style of fiction in order to create non-fiction texts. How does the blending of fiction and non-fiction conventions impact your response as a reader to this text?
3. Refresh your memory of the debate surrounding the validity of the notion of a 'classic' text or work from Chapter 3.3. As aforementioned, Laurence's account received a Pulitzer Prize for its reportage on the dropping of the atomic bomb on Nagasaki and was seen as a 'classic' piece of journalism. How far could a reading of the photograph and Hersey's account challenge its award-winning and 'classic' status?

CONCEPT CONNECTION

PERSPECTIVE AND TRANSFORMATION

Although all the texts share a similarity by way of their **shared focus** on the events of the atomic bombing of Hiroshima and Nagasaki, they **diversify** in the **perspective** that they offer to the reader towards this event. The photograph shows the aftermath of the Hiroshima bomb and it is characterized by its destruction and desolation; depicting Hiroshima as completely devoid of life and there is barely any remnant left of the society that once inhabited it. The haunting, crumbling skeleton of a building depicted likely provokes the reader into thoughts about how if the bomb could have such a devastating effect upon a building, what were the effects upon a human?

That question is answered by a reading of Hersey's account which, in graphic detail, conveys to the reader the specific consequences that an atomic bomb has on a human – 'here were about twenty men, and they were all in exactly the same nightmarish state: their faces were wholly burned, their eyesockets were hollow, the fluid from their melted eyes had run down their cheeks.' Both of these texts, then, are unified in the perspective that they offer to the reader, which is of the incomprehensible horror of the atomic bombs. This challenges the perspective of Laurence who barely comments upon or refers to the impact that the bombs had upon the citizens of Hiroshima and Nagasaki. When comparing the sources, the reader's response is potentially transformed – the reader may question the morality and ethical reasoning behind the writer's decision to describe the bomb in such hallowed terms when it is clear that the bomb's impact upon humans was so terrible.

The blending of **fiction and non-fiction conventions** utilized in Hersey's account aids the transformative effects of the text. The writer uses a factual tone, common in non-fiction texts, when chronologically recounting the events of Father Kleinsorge's morning. This unemotive and distant narrative voice is juxtaposed with the graphic, evocative vocabulary, more common in fictional works, that the writer uses when describing the injuries to the people affected by the atomic bomb – 'slimy', 'burned', 'red', 'pus covered'. This juxtaposition is shocking to the reader, as they may not expect such grotesque injuries to be described in such detail in such a detached tone. By combining a factual register with literary flourishes of description, the writer is able to lend credibility to his reporting of the event while also allowing the reader to be immersed in the full horror of it. A reader of Laurence's text, who may have agreed with the perspective that it offered towards the atomic bomb, would be challenged to not transform their viewpoint after reading Hersey's account. Not only does the writer humanize the effects of the atomic bomb, he also challenges pre-conceived societal notions of Japanese culpability for the effects of the bomb, as he makes clear the wide ranging and terrible effects of the bomb upon innocent citizens who are probably not too unlike the reader.

In 2005, journalists Amy and David Goodman wrote an opinion piece where they argued, 'Mr. Laurence won a Pulitzer Prize for his reporting on the atomic bomb, and his faithful parroting of the government line was crucial in launching a half-century of silence about the deadly lingering effects of the bomb. It is time for the Pulitzer board to strip Hiroshima's apologist and his newspaper of this undeserved prize.' With the awarding of such a prestigious literary prize comes the status of a text and work becoming a 'classic'. Texts such as those in the photograph and diary entry could transform opinion towards a text such as Laurence's account being regarded in this way. As delineated in Chapter 3.3, there is an argument to suggest that as society's values and beliefs transform, so should our classification of what constitutes a 'classic' text or work. Perceptions towards the atomic bombing of Hiroshima and Nagasaki, and how morally just an action it was, have transformed during the time that has elapsed since the event occurred. Whether or not you agree with the decision to drop the bombs, it is perhaps undeniable that a text describing a bomb that had such a well-documented (through texts such as the photograph and diary entry) horrendous effect upon so many people as 'a thing of beauty' is perhaps questionable and could perhaps justify a re-classification of the text.

If you would like to read more about Amy and David Goodman's opinion piece advocating for 'Atomic Bombing of Nagasaki told by Flight Member' to be stripped of its Pulitzer Prize, scan the QR code opposite.

GLOBAL ISSUES ***Field of inquiry:* Politics, Power and Justice**

THE REPORTING OF SIGNIFICANT HISTORICAL EVENTS

The three sources that we have explored as part of this chapter so far are focused on an event of huge global and historical significance. In the aftermath of events such as these, the way in which the event is written about in texts and works can define the way that it is remembered. Sometimes, the way in which an event is presented to the public in the form of texts and works can determine if the people who are most affected by it ever receive justice for the suffering they may have endured as a result of the event. Research online instances in history where this may have happened. See below for an example of one of these instances.

An infamous example of the impact that reportage can have on the delivery of justice can be seen in the aftermath of the Hillsborough Disaster that took place in the UK in 1989. The Hillsborough Disaster resulted in the deaths of 96 people who had gone to Hillsborough Stadium in Sheffield (the north of England) to watch the FA Cup Final between Liverpool Football Club and Nottingham Forest Football Club. The victims were killed in a human crush through catastrophic crowd control mismanagement. An inexperienced team from South Yorkshire Police (who were in charge of crowd control) opened a gate to the stadium which led to a huge influx of people into an already overcrowded standing part of the stadium. In the aftermath of the disaster, the police fed false information to the press blaming (the predominantly Liverpool) fans for causing the disaster through hooliganism and drunken behaviour. This led to a particularly damaging story by tabloid newspaper *The Sun* that you can read more about by scanning the QR codes opposite. The reportage of the disaster contributed, in part, to the public view that the deaths of the victims were accidental and not the avoidable result of incompetence and ineptitude. It wasn't until 2016 that it was ruled in court that the deaths of the victims were unlawful and the families of the victims are still in the process of acquiring justice for their loved ones.

EE Links: English A – Literature category 1 and category 3

If you are interested in this topic a category 1 extended essay question could be: **How far does the style and structural choices made by John Hersey in 'Hiroshima' challenge perceptions about the morality of the use of the atomic bomb on Japan in 1945?**

A category 3 extended essay question could be: **How far did the stylistic choices of photographs taken in the aftermath of the atomic bombing of Japan in 1945 by photojournalists affect and challenge perceptions about the morality of their use?**

TOK Links

What kind of transformation does your knowledge about a text undergo when it is compared and contrasted with other texts?

In our analysis of the first extract by William Laurence, we alluded to the idea that the **passage of time** can transform the way that a reader, or a group of readers, perceive texts and works. The next two sources will explore this idea further.

The first source is an extract from the Christian Bible's Book of Genesis, which is the first part of the Old Testament. In this part of the Bible, God creates the world in six days (designating the seventh day for rest) and creates the first humans, Adam and Eve, and the utopia where they live – the Garden of Eden. He instructs them to remain unclothed as he created them and to not eat fruit from the Tree of Knowledge which was in the Garden of Eden. However, a cunning snake (who has been interpreted as a variety of metaphors, for example, as the manifestation of humankind's sins or alternatively as Satan) tempts Eve into eating an apple from the Tree of Knowledge and she in turn persuades Adam to also eat fruit from the Tree. When God finds out he banishes Adam and Eve from the Garden of Eden and this is seen by Christians as the Fall of Mankind.

Now the serpent was more crafty than any of the wild animals the Lord God had made. He said to the woman, 'Did God really say, "You must not eat from any tree in the garden"?'

The woman said to the serpent, 'We may eat fruit from the trees in the garden, but God did say, "You must not eat fruit from the tree that is in the middle of the garden, and you must not touch it, or you will die."'

'You will not certainly die', the serpent said to the woman. 'For God knows that when you eat from it your eyes will be opened, and you will be like God, knowing good and evil.'

When the woman saw that the fruit of the tree was good for food and pleasing to the eye, and also desirable for gaining wisdom, she took some and ate it. She also gave some to her husband, who was with her, and he ate it. Then the eyes of both of them were opened, and they realized they were naked; so they sewed fig leaves together and made coverings for themselves.

Then the man and his wife heard the sound of the Lord God as he was walking in the garden in the cool of the day, and they hid from the Lord God among the trees of the garden. But the Lord God called to the man, 'Where are you?'

He answered, 'I heard you in the garden, and I was afraid because I was naked; so I hid.'

And he said, 'Who told you that you were naked? Have you eaten from the tree that I commanded you not to eat from?'

The man said, 'The woman you put here with me – she gave me some fruit from the tree, and I ate it.'

(Christian Bible (NIV version), Book of Genesis 3)

In the above passage from the Christian Bible, the reader is told the story of how humanity 'lost' the 'paradise' that God created for them. It is made clear that it is Eve who was the first to be tempted by, and then to give into, the desire to eat the fruit from the tree and to gain more 'knowledge'. It was then Eve who tempted Adam into also eating the fruit and then into acquiring clothes, directly against the instruction of God. At the end of the passage, the blame for the entire incident is place firmly on Eve, as Adam explains to God, 'The woman you put here with me – she gave me some fruit from the tree, and I ate it (line 17).' It is also important to note that when God first enters the Garden, searching for Adam and Eve who have hidden from God knowing that they have 'sinned', it is Adam who responds to his call and ceases to hide from him.

GLOBAL ISSUES *Field of inquiry:* **Beliefs, Values and Education**

STEREOTYPES OF WOMEN

Versions of this story can be found in the religious canons of many of the world's major religions. Many people around the world construct their values and attitudes around those that are taught to them through the belief systems of the religion that they follow. When reading the above Bible passage, and how Eve is presented within it, can you see any familiar stereotypes about women present within the story? For example, the archetype of women being 'femme fatales' or temptresses who have the ability to tempt men and lead them to their own destruction. Or, the stereotype of women being weak willed and needing a man to guide them morally. Or even, the idea that knowledge is dangerous for women and that through the acquisition of knowledge women can cause disruption and disorder.

The story of Adam and Eve has informed the construction of many archetypes in the representation of women that you will have been exposed to in the texts and works that you read. It has also informed societal attitudes towards women throughout time. However, as time has passed and societal values have changed, readers are now questioning this reductive and archetypal construction and representation of women in the works and texts that they read, and challenging the belief system that underpins this.

This next extract is from *Of Mice and Men* by John Steinbeck (1937). The novel tells the story of two migrant ranch workers, George and Lennie, in 1930s Depression-era California. The two ranch workers are forced to frequently move from farm to farm in search of work due to the economic conditions of the time. This is exacerbated by Lennie's mental disability (something little understood at the time) which often leads him into trouble as he lacks awareness of social boundaries and his own strength as a very large and physically capable man. Even though they are not related, their bond is akin to that of brothers and George occupies the role of Lennie's protector. In the extract, George and Lennie have just arrived at a new ranch and the daughter-in-law of the Boss, Curley's Wife, introduces herself to them both.

SENSITIVE CONTENT

Caution: the following extract includes expletives. We have chosen to allow you to view the words of this extract as they originally appear, so you can consider for yourself the effects of how these words are used. This is central to understanding the themes of identity and human behaviour at the heart of this book. Furthermore, the IB recommends that your studies in Language A: Language & Literature should challenge you intellectually, personally and culturally, andexpose you to sensitive and mature topics. We invite you to reflect critically on the various perspectives offered while bearing in mind the IB's commitment to international-mindedness and intercultural respect.

Both men glanced up, for the rectangle of sunshine in the doorway was cut off. A girl was standing there looking in. She had full, rouged lips and wide-spaced eyes, heavily made up. Her fingernails were red. Her hair hung in little rolled clusters, like sausages. She wore a cotton house dress and red mules, on the insteps of which were little bouquets of red ostrich feathers.

'I'm lookin' for Curley,' she said. Her voice had a nasal, brittle quality.

George looked away from her and then back. 'He was in here a minute ago, but he went.'

'Oh!' She put her hands behind her back and leaned against the door frame so that her body was thrown forward. 'You're the new fellas that just come, ain't ya?'

'Yeah.'

Lennie's eyes moved down over her body, and though she did not seem to be looking at Lennie she bridled a little. She looked at her fingernails. 'Sometimes Curley's in here,' she explained.

George said brusquely. 'Well he ain't now.'

'If he ain't, I guess I better look some place else,' she said playfully.

Lennie watched her, fascinated. George said, 'If I see him, I'll pass the word you was looking for him.'

She smiled archly and twitched her body. 'Nobody can't blame a person for lookin',' she said. There were footsteps behind her, going by. She turned her head. 'Hi, Slim,' she said.

Slim's voice came through the door. 'Hi, Good-lookin'.'

'I'm tryin' to find Curley, Slim.'

'Well, you ain't tryin' very hard. I seen him goin' in your house.' She was suddenly apprehensive. ''Bye, boys,' she called into the bunkhouse, and she hurried away.

George looked around at Lennie. 'Jesus, what a tramp,' he said. 'So that's what Curley picks for a wife.'

'She's purty,' said Lennie defensively.

'Yeah, and she's sure hidin' it. Curley got his work ahead of him. Bet she'd clear out for twenty bucks.'

Lennie still stared at the doorway where she had been. 'Gosh, she was purty.' He smiled admiringly. George looked quickly down at him and then he took him by an ear and shook him.

'Listen to me, you crazy bastard,' he said fiercely. 'Don't you even take a look at that bitch. I don't care what she says and what she does. I seen 'em poison before, but I never seen no piece of jail bait worse than her. You leave her be.'

(John Steinbeck 32–33)

John Steinbeck

John Steinbeck was an American author born in 1902. Most of his novels are set in California and mostly feature the stories of 'everyman' protagonists such as migrant ranchers, subsistence farmers and factory workers. He won the Pulitzer Prize for his work *The Grapes of Wrath* which tells the story of an impoverished sharecropper family who are forced to migrate due to environmental, social and economic conditions.

ACTIVITY 2

Read the questions below and write down your thoughts in response to them. There is a full commentary of the work provided below these questions.

1 Review the notes you made in Chapter 3.5 about the use of allusions within texts and works. How has Steinbeck used a biblical allusion in his construction of the character of Curley's Wife? What does that add to your understanding of her character?

2 Refresh your memory on archetypal reader-response theory as delineated in Chapter 3.4. Apply an archetypal reader-response to the work. How, with the passage of time, would the archetypes present in the work be potentially problematic for a contemporary reader?

Curley's Wife's character is clearly alluded to the biblical figure of Eve. She is, from the beginning of the extract, presented to be a danger and threat to the men on the ranch – 'for the rectangle of sunshine in the doorway was cut off. A girl was standing there looking in. She had full, rouged lips and wide-spaced eyes, heavily made up. Her fingernails were red (lines 1–2).' She is deliberately placed in the full frame of the bunkhouse door cutting off the light from entering the bunkhouse and casting the men into darkness – this placement metaphorically represents her potential to block the men's escape from the ranch and her potential to cut them off from life. Like Eve, she is the personification of the darkness that can befall a man if they are led into temptation. This idea is further extended in the repetitive use of colour imagery that is attributed to her in the form of her 'rouged' lips and 'red' fingernails. Red symbolically alludes to danger and again, like Eve, the writer is clearly connoting her role as a potential threat to the men on the ranch. When Lennie reveals that he finds Curley's Wife attractive, George's response is emphatic in its warning against her. He uses a series of **misogynistic** and derogatory examples of language to refer to her such as 'tramp' (line 21), 'bitch' (line 26) and 'jail bait' (line 27), all connoting to the ability of women to use their sexuality to lure men into sin – similar to the way Eve was able to tempt Adam into betraying God through her own femininity.

CONCEPT CONNECTION

TRANSFORMATION AND REPRESENTATION

Through the biblical allusion as delineated in the above paragraph, Curley's Wife is clearly constructed in the work as an archetypal 'femme fatale' – a female character who has the potential (and who does by the end of the novel) to lead men to their own destruction. The use of this archetype may have been acceptable at the time that Steinbeck wrote his novel, but for a contemporary reader this may not be as acceptable any longer. As the voices of female writers become more prominent and numerous in works and texts, the representation of female characters through such a reductive and damaging archetype is being challenged more and more. Through challenging this archetype, many female writers are transforming the representation of women in literature and are creating female characters that subvert stereotypes. Female readers are also questioning the use of archetypes such as these and through this questioning are also aiding the transformation in the way that women are represented in the works that they read. You will be able to see an example of how writers are doing this in a later example.

To read more about contemporary criticism of the use of the 'Eve' biblical allusion in works and texts, scan the QR codes on the right:

Interestingly, John Steinbeck never intended Curley's Wife to be interpreted as a negative character, and hoped that his readers would sympathize with her plight as a marginalized member of society within the patriarchal power structure of the time that limited her opportunities in life. He, perhaps, underestimated the power of deeply ingrained belief systems about women in part created by texts such as the Book of Genesis. To read Steinbeck's explanation of the character of Curley's Wife, scan the QR code opposite to read a letter that he sent to an actress who was playing the character in a play adaptation of the novel.

In the first part of the chapter we have explored how **interpreting** and **comparing** texts and works can **transform** the **perception** of a reader towards an issue, topic or theme. In the next part of this chapter we will explore how texts and works can be transformative in their ability to **provoke discussion or action** within a mass audience, and how a writer can alter the content and conventions of a text or work for a new **purpose**.

How can a writer's choices provoke or cause transformation?

The **transformative** power of a text or work can be caused or provoked not just by reader-response but by the choices that a writer makes in the creation and production of a text or work. The next set of texts will explore this process.

The next source we will explore is an advert for the company *Protein World* which sells supplements that claim to help you become healthier and to lose weight. Scan the adjacent QR code to read this text.

The print advert, created by the company *Protein World* in 2015, was intended to promote its range of 'health' supplements. The writer used a prominent image of a thin, toned woman in a revealing bikini against a bright yellow background, to communicate to the reader the potential benefits to one's physical appearance as a result of taking the *Protein World* supplements. The advert essentially suggests that you, too, can look like the model depicted in the advert if you take *Protein World's* supplements, which are called 'The Weight Loss Collection'. The advertisement also queries the reader, 'Are you beach body ready?' The advert was released in April when many people in the UK, where the advert was published, are planning their summer time beach vacations. This was an intentional choice by the company as the rhetorical question is designed to communicate to the reader a question about whether they have enough time in between planning their beach vacation and actually being on the beach to feel confident in a swimsuit while there.

CONCEPT CONNECTION

COMMUNICATION AND TRANSFORMATION

However, the communication that was intended by the writer was not the one that was received by many readers of this text. There was a huge backlash against the advert with many people criticizing it for perpetuating a depiction of beauty standards in the mass media that are not reflective of most within society. It was also noted that the advert seemed to be directly aimed at women, suggesting that they were the market that *Protein World* seemed to think would be most susceptible to the meaning communicated through the advert. How much of this transformation in communication from what was intended by the writer to what was received by many readers was due to the structural and stylistic choices made by the writer?

If the writer had chosen to use both a man and a woman on the advert, would it have been so controversial? The fact that the writer chose to only include a female model on the advert communicates to the reader that it is only women who need to worry about being 'beach body ready' which isn't a message that is entirely acceptable to a contemporary society. The decision of the writer to structure the advertisement so that the rhetorical question 'are you beach body ready?' is placed directly next to 'the weight loss collection' of supplements also communicates to the reader that the solution to not feeling confident about your body is to lose weight, which is a reductive and harmful message to convey to the mass public. It seems to also be a deliberate choice by the writer to have the model as the most dominating aspect of the advert and to place this image of the model in the middle of the advert, in the middle of the rhetorical question. This decision could be interpreted as a communication to the reader that unless you look like the model, the answer to whether you are 'beach body ready' is probably 'no' and as the vast majority of people don't look like the model, then the implication is that they need to buy the supplements in order to look more like her.

The above interpretation is evidence that the choices made by a writer are not static in their communication – a reader, by interpreting their choices in a specific way can transform the meaning that they intended to convey.

ACTIVITY 3

Read the question below and write down your thoughts in response to it. You will need to review the notes that you made in Chapter 3.2 about the deviation of conventions over time in order to help you answer. You will also need to refresh your memory about feminist reader-response theory as delineated in Chapter 3.4 and could also use the information given about allusion, parody and pastiche in Chapter 3.5 to help you answer the question.

Apply a feminist reader-response to the *Protein World* advert. What kind of criticism would a feminist reader apply to the text? Use this criticism to think about how the conventions of the advert could be transformed to ensure that it is more appropriate for a contemporary society that does not expect women to be represented in a misogynistic and stereotypical way in the mass media.

Read the following commentary in response to this task.

The next source we will explore is an advert by the British online clothing brand *Navabi* that sells clothes for plus-size women. They created this advert in 2018 as a response *Protein World's* 2015 advert. Scan the QR code to read it.

Navabi created an advert that is clearly a parody of *Protein World's* 'Are you beach body ready?' advert and may even look a little like what you may have envisaged in your response to the previous activity. The writer of the advert has interpreted the meaning and has transformed the conventions to create an original text that represents women in a completely different way. The writer replicated the decision to use a bright yellow background and female models in swimwear to promote their product, but they have subverted the traditional use of a 'swimwear' model by using models that are atypical. The three women are perhaps more representative of the variety of beauty that exists across society and have been deliberately chosen to depict a range of sizes, ethnicity, height and aesthetic style; using a body covered in tattoos is also further breaking down taboos from some societies and celebrating them as commonplace. The use of these models subverts the message that women need to look a certain standardized way in order to feel comfortable when wearing swimwear at the beach, and instead the writer transforms this into a suggestion to the reader that women should feel confident at the beach no matter what they look like. The writer has also deliberately modified the 'Are you beach body ready?' slogan. Instead, the writer has transformed this from an interrogative and demeaning rhetorical question into a positive, declarative of 'We're beach body ready'. This subverts the idea originally conveyed in the *Protein World* advert that women need to take health supplements in order to deemed 'ready' to be seen at the beach, and instead conveys the message that as long as a woman has a body and swimsuit then she should feel 'ready' to go to the beach.

A feminist reader of the *Protein World* advert would have criticized the depiction of unattainable (and standardized) beauty standards for women in the advert, as well as the exploitation of a woman's insecurities about her body to sell a product. They would also have taken exception to the suggestion that it is the role of a woman, and a woman only, to look a certain way when going to the beach and that this standard of beauty is not applicable to a man. The transformation in the use of conventions in the *Navabi* advert also transforms the meaning communicated in the advert making its representation of women far more suitable for a contemporary and socially aware reader.

If you would like to read more about the various reader-responses generated by these adverts, then scan the QR codes on the right.

TOK Links

In response to the controversy generated by *Protein World's* 'beach body ready' advert, the mayor of London at the time, Sadiq Khan, made a decision to ban all forms of 'body shaming' adverts from public transport in London. To read more about this, scan the QR code.

DISCUSSION

This prompts the question, to what extent does society have a duty to ensure that everyone in society is represented equally and fairly in the mass media? To what extent should politicians and lawmakers be involved in regulating adverts?

So far in this chapter we have explored how the **perspective** of a reader towards an issue, theme or topic can be **transformed** when **interpreting** and **comparing** texts and works. We have also inquired into how the choices made by a writer and the meaning that they intended to convey through a text or work can be **transformed** in the act of **interpretation**. We then discussed how a reader can use their response to the meaning communicated in a text or work to transform the text itself and use it to convey a completely different message to the reader. In the next part of this chapter we will explore the act of **translating** a text or work and analyse how this act of translation can **transform** the text or work itself and its meaning.

How can a writer deliberately transform a text or work through the act of translation, and how can that transform its meaning?

The Vegetarian by South Korean writer Han Kang is a novel told from the perspective of the husband, brother-in-law and sister of a woman who decides to become a vegetarian as a result of a recurring violent nightmare that she experiences. The consequences of this decision are substantial, leading to alienation from her parents, the breakdown of her marriage, the breakdown of her sister's marriage and a violent decline in her mental health.

The novel was first published in South Korea in 2007 and was then translated into English by Deborah Smith in 2015. Upon its translation, the novel received much critical acclaim and the novel won the Booker International Prize (the version of the Booker Prize given to works in translation) in 2016.

The source below is an extract from the novel. The narrator is the husband of the female protagonist, Yeong-hye, and he is describing her character to the reader. It would be useful for you to scan the QR code opposite in order to read this opinion article about gender equality in South Korea before reading the source.

She was a woman of few words. It was rare for her to demand anything of me, and however late I was in getting home she never took it upon herself to kick up a fuss. Even when our days off happened to coincide, it wouldn't occur to her to suggest we go out somewhere together. While I idled the afternoon away, TV remote in hand, she would shut herself up in her room. More than likely she would spend time reading, which was practically her only hobby. For some unfathomable reason, reading was something she was able to really immerse herself in – reading books that looked so dull I couldn't even bring myself to so much as take a look inside the covers. Only at mealtimes would she open the door and silently emerge to prepare the food. To be sure, that kind of wife, that kind of lifestyle, did mean that I was unlikely to find my days particularly stimulating. On the other hand, if I'd had one of those wives whose phones ring on and off all day long with calls from friends or co-workers, or whose nagging periodically leads to screaming rows with their husbands, I would have been grateful when she finally wore herself out.

(Han Kang 12–13)

Han Kang

Han Kang is a South Korean writer and teacher who was born in 1970. She is best known for her novel *The Vegetarian* which won the International Booker Prize in 2016. She is also known for her other works that have been translated into English, *Human Acts* and *The White Book*.

The writer has been praised by critics for her exploration of the role of women within the institutions of marriage and family in contemporary South Korean society and culture. The protagonist of the novel, Yeong-hye, is silenced throughout the novel. She does not have her own part through which she can provide her own perspective on the events that occur in the novel, but instead she is spoken about to the reader by other people. The only time we, as a reader, are given access to her voice is when she is recounting the terror of her recurring nightmare, passages that are placed within the parts belonging to other characters. This could be symbolic of patriarchal cultural norms in South Korea that are seen by some to silence the voices of women in society.

The way that she is described by her husband is as a person almost devoid of character and agency – 'It was rare for her to demand anything of me, and however late I was in getting home she never took it upon herself to kick up a fuss. Even when our days off happened to coincide, it wouldn't occur to her to suggest we go out somewhere together. While I idled the afternoon away, TV remote in hand, she would shut herself up in her room (lines 1–4).' However, it seems as though her husband regards this as a positive characteristic and sees the only other alternative as 'one of those wives whose phones ring on and off all day long with calls from friends or co-workers, or whose nagging periodically leads to screaming rows with their husbands (lines 9–11).' This reductive way of categorizing the behaviour of women could be, yet again, mirroring misogynistic attitudes towards women within some parts of South Korean culture. It is also important to note that we at no point hear Yeong-hye's husband refer to her by name, instead she is referred to using the pronouns 'she' and 'her'. In fact, we as a reader do not find out Yeong-hye's name until near the end of the first part of the novel. This again, could be seen as mirroring the purported lack of visibility of women in some parts of South Korean culture, especially their role within a marriage, where they are expected to be subservient to the husband.

CONCEPT CONNECTION

CULTURE AND TRANSFORMATION

This perspective of South Korean culture, as told by Kang, is only accessible to us as English speakers because of the transformation that the original Korean language of the novel has undergone in the process of translation. It could be argued that without this act of transformation it would be difficult for a reader from outside of South Korea to be able to hear an authentic and subversive voice like Kang's and be able to understand her perspective about her own South Korean culture.

However, the transformation of language in the act of translation can sometimes be a contentious one. Read the source below and then scan on the QR code opposite. Both discuss the issues involved in translating works from their original language.

The voice of the story, the unpleasant husband's, is stiff and formal, in line with this traditional and conventional mindset that his wife experiences as a straitjacket (along with her vegetarianism she also refuses to wear a bra, because she finds it constricting). So we have phrases like 'Ultimately, I settled for a job where I would be provided with a decent monthly salary in return for diligently carrying out my allotted tasks.' There is a rather nineteenth-century ring to it, as if we were reading an old translation of a Chekhov short story. Combining this stiffness with a determination to keep the prose 'spoken' and idiomatic leads to some uneasy formulations. 'However late I was in getting home,' the husband tells us 'she never took it upon herself to kick up a fuss.'

'To take something upon oneself,' the Cambridge dictionary tells us, is 'to accept responsibility for something without being asked to do so.' Does this make sense next to the idea of 'kicking up a fuss' about a husband's later return? Is this Han Kang indicating the husband's limited grasp of idiom, or a translation issue? There is always a danger, when translating a spoken voice, of opting for the idiomatic at the expense of precision. During the unpleasant dinner with the husband's business associates, for example, we are told that 'awkward silences … were now peppering the conversation.' One can imagine a conversation peppered with obscenities perhaps, but aren't silences just too long to be peppery? Earlier, complaining of his wife's reading habits, the narrator talks of her 'reading books that looked so dull I couldn't even bring myself to so much as take a look inside the covers.' Is that 'looked'/'look' repetition in the original? And the overkill of 'even bring myself to so much as look at'?

Sometimes this mix of the uptight and the colloquial creates an awkwardness at the limits of comprehensibility.

(Tim Parks)

CHECK FOR UNDERSTANDING

In Chapter 3.6 of this section you analysed some examples of opinion articles. The two texts above are also examples of photojournalism. Check your understanding of this text type by re-reading the information in Chapter 3.3 and filling in the table below which uses step 1 (genre, audience and purpose) and step 4 (other features of text type) of the non-literary analysis strategy that you were introduced to in Chapter 1.1. You can fill in the table for one or both of the opinion articles. You should focus on how the article(s) convey(s) the opinion of the writer towards the issue of transformation via translation.

Once you have done this, read the end of book commentaries for an example of a table that has been filled out for you which analyses the second opinion article.

Genre	
Audience	
Purpose	
Other features of text type	

CONCEPT CONNECTION

TRANSFORMATION AND CREATIVITY

The writers of these articles convey differing opinions towards the act of transforming language through translation. The writer of the first extract conveys the confusion that he felt when reading parts of *The Vegetarian*. He wasn't certain if some of the awkward and peculiar phrasing in parts of the novel were intentional or a casualty of the translation process – 'Is this Han Kang indicating the husband's limited grasp of idiom, or a translation issue?' He also expresses his misgivings about how precise the translation of language, especially spoken language, can be, 'There is always a danger, when translating a spoken voice, of opting for the idiomatic at the expense of precision.' The writer essentially conveys to the reader his opinion about what is lost in the process of transforming language through translation – security in interpretation for the reader and precision in authorial intention.

However, even though the writer of the second extract agrees that some precision has been lost through the process of translation, the key area of concern for her is Smith's 'stylistic alteration of the text' which shows that Smith 'took significant liberties with the text'. However, the writer of the first extract also concedes that any 'losses' in precision or authenticity the act of translation has led to was 'worth the "gains" of Smith's effort' as 'Readers and critics have enjoyed the work immensely, South Korea has been placed on the world's literary map, sales of both the original and the English version have exploded, and interest in Korean literary translation has soared. Most important, Smith successfully introduced Han, a highly respected South Korean writer, to much-deserved recognition abroad.'

It could be argued that an entirely accurate and precise transformation of one language into another is impossible and that something will always be lost in the process of this transformation. It could also be argued that the act of translation has to be a creative one on the part of the translator because of this. How far a translator goes in the amount of creativity they apply to their transformation of the language could be entirely contextual. For example, a transformation of language in a translation of a set of instructions should be as accurate as possible. However, the transformation of one language to another in a creative and artistic pursuit can probably be more liberal.

Ultimately, the interpretation of the original text or work by the writer will always be transformed through the translation process, but most readers will be unaware of the degree of transformation unless they have the linguistic capabilities to compare both texts or work.

GLOBAL ISSUES *Field of inquiry:* **Culture, Identity and Community**

LANGUAGE AND IDENTITY

Put yourself into the position of Han Kang – if you wrote a novel in a language that needed to be translated into English how would you instruct the translator to proceed? Would you want the translation of your novel to be entirely accurate and precise, a literal interpretation that perhaps reflects your identity as an author or the culture to which you identify? Or would you be willing to compromise this cultural and individual authenticity for the sake of clarity and commercial gain? Or, would you just be intrigued to see how a writer could transform your novel into a wholly original novel that is a fusion of both of your cultures?

TOK Links

To what extent can a text or work in translation ever be seen as comparable to its original form? Are all works in translation simply just adaptations?

Works cited

'William Leonard Laurence of *The New York Times*.' *The Pulitzer Prizes*. Web. 9 March 2019. **www.pulitzer.org/winners/william-leonard-laurence**.

Barr, S. 'Plus-size fashion brand transforms Protein World's "Beach Body Ready" advert into body positivity campaign.' *Independent*, 3 May 2018. Web. 9 March 2019. **www.independent.co.uk/life-style/fashion/beach-body-ready-plus-size-campaign-bodypositivity-protein-world-navabi-a8334516.html**.

'Bombing of Hiroshima and Nagasaki.' *History Online*, 18 Nov. 2009. Web. 9 March 2019. **www.history.com/topics/world-war-ii/bombing-of-hiroshima-and-nagasaki**.

Burton, J. 'Viewpoint: My Twitter battle with the people behind the beach body ad.' *BBC News*, BBC, 28 April 2015. Web. 9 March 2019. **www.bbc.com/news/blogs-ouch-32497580**.

Christian Bible (NIV version), Book of Genesis 3, Old Testament. *Bible Gateway*. Web. 10 March 2019. **www.biblegateway.com/passage/?search=Genesis+3&version=NIV**.

Calderwood, I. 'Remember That "Beach Body Ready" Ad? It Just Relaunched in the Best Way.' *Global Citizen*, 4 May 2018. Web. 13 Oct. 2019. **www.globalcitizen.org/en/content/beach-body-ready-protein-world-advert-plus-size**.

Coats, JR. 'Adam and Eve and the Gender Divide.' *Huffington Post*, 25 May 2011. Web. 10 March 2019. **www.huffingtonpost.com/john-r-coats/adam-and-eve-and-the-gend_b_624831.html**.

Conn, D. 'Hillsborough inquest: police admit Sun report of fans looting corpses was false.' *The Guardian*, 10 Oct. 2014. Web. 10 March 2019. **https://www.theguardian.com/uk-news/2014/oct/10/hillsborough-inquest-police-admit-sun-report-fans-looted-corpses-false**.

Conn, D. 'How the Sun's "truth" about Hillsborough unravelled.' *The Guardian*, 26 April 2016. Web. 10 March 2019. **https://www.theguardian.com/football/2016/apr/26/how-the-suns-truth-about-hillsborough-unravelled**.

Feller, G. 'The Disturbing Truth About Trying To Ban The Beach Body Ready Ads.' *Forbes*, 13 June 2016. Web. 9 March 2019. **www.forbes.com/sites/grantfeller/2016/06/13/the-disturbing-truth-about-trying-to-ban-the-beach-body-ready-ads/#328e9fd02a01**.

Goodman, A, Goodman, D. 'The Hiroshima Cover-Up.' *The Baltimore Sun*. Web. 9 March 2019. **www.baltimoresun.com/news/bs-xpm-2005-08-05-0508050019-story.html**.

Hackman, R. 'Are you beach body ready? Controversial weight loss ad sparks varied reactions.' *The Guardian*, 27 June 2015. Web. 9 March 2019. **www.theguardian.com/us-news/2015/jun/27/beach-body-ready-america-weight-loss-ad-instagram**.

Hersey, J. *A Bell for Adano*. Vintage, 1988.

Hersey, J. *Hiroshima*. Penguin Books, 2002.

'Hiroshima and Nagasaki Bombings.' *ican*. Web. 19 March 2019. **www.icanw.org/the-facts/catastrophic-harm/hiroshima-and-nagasaki-bombings**.

'Hiroshima Cover-up: Stripping the War Department's Timesman of His Pulitzer.' *Democracy Now*, 5 Aug. 2005. Web. 13 Oct. 2019. **www.democracynow.org/2005/8/5/hiroshima_cover_up_stripping_the_war**.

Kang, H. *Human Acts*. Translated by Deborah Smith, Hogarth, 2017.

Kang, H. *The Vegetarian*. Translated by Deborah Smith, Hogarth Press, 2016.

Kang, H. *The White Book*. Translated by Deborah Smith, Hogarth Press, 2019.

Koo, SW. 'South Korea's Misogyny.' *The New York Times*, 13 June 2016. Web. 9 March 2019. **www.nytimes.com/2016/06/13/opinion/south-koreas-misogyny.html**.

Parks, T. 'Raw and Cooked.' *The New York Review of Books*, 20 June 2016. Web. 9 March 2019. **www.nybooks.com/daily/2016/06/20/raw-and-cooked-translation-why-the-vegetarian-wins**.

Sanghani, R. 'London mayor Sadiq Khan bans body-shaming ads from public transport.' *The Telegraph*, 13 June 2016. Web. 9 March 2019. **www.telegraph.co.uk/women/life/london-mayor-sadiq-khan-bans-body-shaming-ads-from-public-transp**.

Scott-Marshall, K. 'The Enduring Legacy of the Original Dangerous Woman.' *The Dangerous Woman Project*, 9 Oct. 2016. Web. 10 March 2019. **http://dangerouswomenproject.org/2016/10/09/eve-dangerous-woman**.

Steinbeck, J. *Grapes of Wrath*. Penguin Classics, 2006.

Steinbeck, J. *Of Mice and Men*. Penguin Books, 2000.

Steinbeck, J. 'To Claire Luce.' Web. 10 March 2019. **www.hellesdon.org/documents/missluce.pdf**.

Yun, C. 'How the bestseller *The Vegetarian*, translated from Han Kang's original, caused an uproar in South Korea.' *Los Angeles Times*, 22 Sept. 2017. Web. 9 March 2019. **www.latimes.com/books/jacketcopy/la-ca-jc-korean-translation-20170922-story.html**.

Glossary

abstract – something that is not physical or tangible.

abstract noun – a noun (or name) that is given to something that is not physical or tangible, e.g. love, innocence, greed, anger.

accent – the pronunciation of words by an individual– usually denotes which geographical part of the country someone comes from.

acronym – taking the first letters of each word in a phrase and using these letters as a shorthand, e.g. TOK is an acronym for Theory of Knowledge; EE is an acronym for Extended Essay.

adjective – a word that describes a noun, e.g. beautiful, innocent, angry, soft, fragile.

aesthetic – the study of art (and literature is an artform) and beauty (beauty does not necessarily mean something attractive or appealing – but we can appreciate the beauty or skill behind the creation of the artform even if something terrifying is being depicted).

African American Vernacular English (AAVE) – the formal term for the African American particular way of speaking.

allegory – when a writer uses one thing to represent something else – Arthur Miller's *The Crucible* uses the 1692 Salem witch-hunt trials to represent the anti-communist McCarthy trials in America in the 1950s.

alliteration – when a number of words close to one another start with the same consonant.

allusion – when a writer refers to someone or something without mentioning the person or idea explicitly.

American Dream – American ideal that states any individual can achieve their goals and aspirations through hard work.

anaphora – a literary feature when the first few words of a sentence are repeated, e.g. Martin Luther King's 'I have a dream' is a good example of anaphora.

anecdote – a story that is personal to the speaker.

Anglophilia – the international allure of British culture and history.

anthropomorphism – using animals to denote humans. George Orwell's *Animal Farm* and Art Spiegelman's *Maus* both use this device.

anti-Semitic – being prejudiced against the Jewish ethno-religious group.

antithesis – words or phrases that are near to one another but have the direct opposite meaning.

archaic – an old-fashioned word that is either never or rarely used today, e.g. thou, thee, oft, cometh.

archetype – a character, idea or situation that represents the universal or the human condition.

ars poetica – translates as the 'art of poetry' and is a term that is used to describe literature that reflects on the artform of poetry, through the artform of poetry (see Chapter 1.6).

assonance – when several words use the same vowel sounds – it can create an internal rhyme, e.g. the cat sat on the mat.

asyndetic – see **listing**.

atmosphere – the feeling, emotion or mood of a text.

auditory imagery – imagery that appeals to our sense of hearing. Rhyme, alliteration, assonance and sibilance are types of auditory imagery.

bias – one-sided, prejudiced towards one side of the argument or the other.

binary opposition – two things that are polar opposites, e.g. devils and angels; black and white.

blank verse – a dramatic term. The use of verse without rhyme, often used with iambic pentameter in Shakespeare's plays.

brand activism – an advertising term – when a brand integrates a social movement into its advertising.

buzzwords – used on a magazine front cover – loaded words that promise there is even more inside the magazine, e.g. 'plus ...', 'exclusive ...'

caesura – a poetic term that describes the use of punctuation in the middle of a line – can have a jarring or a fragmented effect.

canon of literature – the collection of texts, narratives and writers considered to be influential and important to a particular culture.

captions – a graphic novel term. The text in a panel that explains what is going on. It is not display lettering and it is not dialogue.

catharsis – a term associated with tragedy. The feelings of pity and fear the audience is supposed to be cleansed of following the downfall of the tragic hero.

character – a fictional person within a narrative.

chronological – this is a type of structure. It describes a step-by-step linear structure. It is often used in instructional texts such as recipes.

circular structure – when the ending of a text parallels the beginning – Samuel Beckett used this structure in his play, *Waiting for Godot*.

cliffhanger – a plot device that ends with a character in a difficult or dangerous situation; can create suspense. Often used in gothic fiction texts.

climax – usually refers to drama but can be applied to other forms of literature. The crescendo that denotes the turning point for the protagonist.

code switching – the switching between two or more languages or varieties of language in conversation – this is something that we see in Junot Díaz' novel, *The Brief Wondrous Life of Oscar Wao*.

colloquial – informal language.

colour – the use of colour in visual images are often used because of their connotations, e.g. pink has connotations of romance, red has connotations of passion, anger or violence, white has connotations of innocence and purity.

commonality – when two or more things share something in common.

compound adjective – two adjectives that are joined together (usually by a hyphen) to make a new word, e.g. sad-coloured, bitter-sweet.

concrete poetry – a form of poetry that uses typographical and presentational features to determine the shape of the poem. Lewis Carroll's 'A Long Tale' is a well-known concrete poem – it is printed in the shape of a mouse's tail.

conditional verbs – verbs used to describe a hypothetical situation (one that might happen if a particular condition is met)

connotation – the associations a particular word had – this may change depending on the reader, e.g. white has connotations of innocence in Western countries and death in Eastern countries; red has connotations of lust and desire in Western countries and good luck in Eastern countries.

content – what is in the text, rather than external influences.

context – the weaving together of influences that affect the creation of a text and the interpretation of a text.

context clues – clues within the text (in terms of language, visuals or attitudes) that guide the reader into understanding the context within which the text was produced.

context of production – the historical time and the geographical and cultural space a text is written in influences the content of a text.

context of reception – the historical time, and the geographical and cultural space a reader reads a text in affects how a reader may respond to the text.

contraction – the process of shortening a word by elision and/or combining two words.

contrast – when two things are shown to be different in some way. There are many different devices that create contrast including antithesis, juxtaposition, oxymoron.

conventions – defining features of a genre of literature or a non-literary text type.

co-ordinating conjunction – a conjunction that joins two phrases, giving them equal weight. There are seven coordinating conjunctions. Remember this acronym – FANBOYS – for, and, nor, but, or, yet, so.

cover lines – text that reveals the other stories in the magazine – used on a magazine front cover.

cultural context (space) – what the inherent values, beliefs and attitudes of the time and place actually are when a text was written.

declarative – a sentence that makes a statement.

decode – the unpicking and interpretation of the language and visuals that a writer uses to make meaning.

defamiliarization – a technique that transforms something that is over-familiar and ordinary into something that is strange and unfamiliar.

demographic – a section of the population.

denotation – the dictionary definition of what a word means. This may evolve over time but it is more fixed than connotation.

dénouement – usually refers to drama but can be applied to other forms of literature. Follows the resolution. How the text ends – either harmoniously or tragically, depending on the genre.

deus ex machina – a dramatic term. Translates as 'god from the machine'. When a problem that appears unsolvable is suddenly solved in an unlikely way, e.g. Euripides uses this in *Medea* when the Sun God sends a chariot so that Medea can fly away and thus escape being punished for multiple murders.

dialect – a form of English that is specific to a particular region or social group.

dialogue – communication between two or more people.

diction – the words and phrases used.

direct speech – the words that are actually spoken in contrast to reported speech.

display lettering – a graphic novel term – the use of lettering in panels such as signs, banners, number plates. They are not spoken by characters and they are not captions that tell the story.

dominant reading – a reader who interprets and accepts the ideas as the writer intended.

elision – the omission of a sound or syllable when speaking, sometimes combined with contraction.

ellipsis – when a word or words are omitted from a sentence for expediency, creating an informal and casual tone.

emojis – pictorial images that denote feelings and emotions.

emoticons – using the symbols on the keyboard to denote emotions, e.g. :-) denotes happiness.

emotive language – usually adjectives that are loaded and describe how someone feels about something, e.g. atrocious, outrageous, fabulous.

encoded – the transformation of ideas and experience into the written form.

end focus – the way a text ends.

enjambment – a poetic term that describes a run-on line. A line that does not end with any punctuation but runs-on into the next line. Can also be used to run-on one stanza to the next stanza.

esoterica – language that is only understood by the few.

ethos – a term used by Aristotle. A key ingredient of a persuasive speech. Has an ethical appeal by alluding to universally accepted premise or a universally respected individual. The speaker will also attempt to build his/her own status of credibility with the audience to appeal to ethos.

exoticising – describing other cultures in romantic terms, falling back on stereotypes and simplifying them to fit an outsider's narrative.

explicit – this is the opposite of implicit. Meaning that is explicit is stated outright.

exposition – usually refers to drama but can be applied to other forms of literature. The beginning when the characters, place and time are introduced.

extended metaphor – a metaphor or symbol that is repeated more than once in a text to connote the same thing.

falling action – usually refers to drama but can be applied to other forms of literature. The opposite of rising action. The events that will lead to the unravelling relationship between the protagonist and antagonist. The series of events that will lead to either a harmonious resolution or a tragic resolution.

false starts – used in spoken language. When the grammatical construction of the sentence is not completed and another grammatical construction replaces it. David Mamet is a playwright famous for using this in the dialogue he writes.

fiction – something that is not true.

figurative language – language that is not literal. Devices such as similes, metaphors and personification are examples of figurative language.

filled pauses – used in spoken language. When uncomfortable pauses are filled in using sounds such as 'Mmmmm'.

flashback – when the narrative present is broken by a shift in time to the past.

foregrounded – the way key events are emphasized.

form – there are three forms of literary works – prose fiction, drama and poetry. There are multiple forms of non-literary text types, e.g. advertisements, advisory texts, letters, memoirs, infographics.

formalism – literary criticism that focuses on the form of a text rather than taking into account the context within which it was written or any external influences.

fricative alliteration – words that have longer sounding letters repeated, e.g. 'f', 'l', 'm', usually to create a gentle mood.

genre – a category within a literary form. For example, science fiction, gothic fiction and fantasy are all genres of prose fiction.

graphology – the visual aspects of how a text appears on the page.

gutter – a graphic novel term – the white space between each panel.

headline – the main heading in a newspaper or magazine, usually in a larger font.

hexameter verse – a line of verse that has six feet.

historical context (time) – the historical time at which the text is produced or received.

homophones – words that have the same pronunciation but different meanings, e.g. son and sun; carat and carrot. Newspaper headlines often exploit this for humour.

hyperbole – language that is used to exaggerate.

hyperlinks – used in online texts. A word or phrase that the reader can click on and then is taken to another article that explores the word/phrase in more detail.

hypophora – when a writer raises a question and then immediately provides an answer to that question.

iamb – a metrical foot. An iamb consists of one or two unstressed syllables followed by a stressed syllable. Iambic tetrameter consists of 4 feet of unstressed stressed iambs; pentameter consists of 5 feet of unstressed stressed iambs.

iambic pentameter – a line of poetry that consists of 5 iambs (10 syllables) that follows an unstressed stressed meter.

iambic tetrameter – a line of poetry that consists of 4 iambs (8 syllables) that follows an unstressed stressed meter.

icon – usually a pictorial graphic that represents an idea.

ideology – a collection of beliefs and values that form the basis of how someone views the world. These can be specific to an individual or can be shared widely across a society.

idiolect – the individual and unique voice everyone has – shown through the unique words and phrases that each individual uses.

imagery – literary devices (such as simile and metaphor) employed by an author in a written text.

imagism – an Anglo-American form of literature in the early-twentieth century that used sharply focused images and precise language.

immanent – the study of a text focusing on the text itself, rather than focusing on its context or its relationship to other texts.

imperative – verbs used to give commands

implicit – meaning that is suggested or inferred rather than stated outright. The opposite of explicit.

implied reader – the ideal or hypothetical reader the writer is addressing. The implied reader is often different to the actual reader.

implied writer – the imagined writer the reader constructs after having read the text in its entirety. The implied writer is usually different from both the narrator and the actual writer.

in medias res – this is a type of structure. It describes a text that starts in the middle of the action. The *Odyssey* by Homer is a well-known text that uses this structure.

inclusivity – language that is used that everyone can understand.

inference – understanding a writer's implied meaning.

intersectionality – an individual's interconnected social groupings, e.g. class, gender, age, ethnicity.

intertextuality – the ways in which a text is connected to other texts. Intertextuality also includes an exploration of how the reader, bringing with them their life experience and exposure to various works and texts, can shape the meaning of a text and as a result interpret a text in a variety of ways.

intrusive narrator – a narrator who stops the story to give the reader his/her own opinion – Charles Dickens used an intrusive narrator in some of his novels and Nathaniel Hawthorne did likewise in *The Scarlet Letter*.

irony – type of humour that mocks an individual, institution or ideology usually by saying the opposite of what is meant.

jargon – specialized words used by a group of people connected to a particular field which not everyone understands.

juxtaposition – two ideas that are placed close to one another but have opposite meanings.

layout – how a text is physically structured.

lingua franca – a global language that is the standard common language used between speakers whose native languages are different.

listing – a list of qualities or attributes that are similar. Can be asyndetic listing (commas are used to separate each item in the list rather than conjunctions – he loved football, basketball, netball, swimming and tennis) or syndetic listing (conjuctions such as 'and' or 'or' separate each thing in the list – he loved football and basketball and netball and swimming and tennis) or polysyndetic listing (when the quality is repeated – he ran and ran and ran). Dickens uses both asyndetic and syndetic listing in his novels, novellas and short stories.

literary tradition – those works that are handed down to the next generation as they have been deemed important.

loaded language – similar to emotive language. Words that are used for effect and encourage the reader to feel a particular emotion.

logos – a term used by Aristotle. A key ingredient of a persuasive speech. Has an intellectual appeal by constructing a clear, logical and rational argument often through the use of facts and statistics.

lyrical ballad – a genre of poetry. Traditional verse that includes a harmonious rhythm, meter and rhyme scheme.

masthead – the name of a magazine or newspaper which is featured on the magazine/newspaper front cover.

meme – a social media term. An element of a culture that is shared with others through manipulating an image with text – usually for humorous effect.

metaphor – a device that compares one thing to something else without using the words 'like' or 'as … as', e.g. the classroom is a furnace.

meter – the beat of (usually) a poem, created through the use of stressed/unstressed syllables.

misogyny – dislike or prejudice against women.

modernism – a European and North American literary genre of the late-nineteenth and early-twentieth centuries. Writers broke from the traditional forms of literature which often depicted reality in a recognizable way, by using unreliable narrators, stream of consciousness and multiple perspectives.

monosyllabic words – words that only have one syllable. May be used to speed the pace up.

mother tongue – generally understood to mean the language of your parents, and that you are exposed to from birth.

motif – an idea or symbol that is reoccurring in a text.

multimodal – a text that communicates meaning using at least two different modes of communication, e.g. the written word and visual images.

multivocal – many perspectives – either within or outside the text.

narrative – a discourse that tells a story. A narrative has a narrative voice and the narratee is the reader.

narrative persona; narrative voice – the persona the writer has created to tell the story. Even if the text is written in the first person, this does not necessarily mean that the narrative persona is the writer.

narrative present – this is the time the text takes place. The narrative present denotes that the time is in the present for the characters.

negotiated reading – a reader who partly interprets and accepts the ideas as the writer intended.

neutral language – language that is not loaded or emotive. It is objective language and does not expect an emotional response.

newsworthy – a topic that is current and relevant, in the news when the text is published.

non-fiction – something that is rooted in the real-world and describes reality as it is.

non-linear – this is a type of structure. It describes a non-chronological structure that may shift in time.

non-verbal language – communicating without using words (e.g. through photographs and other visual illustrations/pictures; symbols such as arrows, bullet-points, numbers; graphs and charts etc).

onomatopoeia – when the sound of a word imitates the word's meaning, e.g. 'boom!', 'shhhh', 'thump'.

oppositional reading – a reader who rejects the intended interpretation and ideas the writer intended.

orthographical features – use of spelling, capitalization and punctuation for effect.

oxymoron – two words that are next to one another but have opposite meanings, e.g. bitter-sweet.

panel – a graphic novel term – an individual frame, often denoted by a black border, within which there is usually a visual image and written text of some kind. Panels can be different sizes and different shapes.

paralinguistic – the elements of communication that does not rely on spoken language, e.g. body language, facial expression, tone of voice.

parody – an imitation of something for humorous effect.

pastiche – something that consciously imitates something else – usually for humorous effect.

pathetic fallacy – using the weather to foreshadow or imitate the mood, e.g. thunder and lightning foreshadows something unsettling is about to happen.

pathos – a term used by Aristotle. A key ingredient of a persuasive speech. Has an emotional appeal, encourages audience to identify with speaker's own pain or suffering experienced by others.

patriarchal – a social system in which men are the dominant empowered gender and women hold less power.

perfect tense – A tense used to describe things that have already been completed, using 'have' or 'had' followed by a past participle.

personal pronoun – a word that denotes the person, gender, number – I = first person singular; you = 2nd person singular; he/she/it = 3rd person singular. We = 1st person plural; you = 2nd person plural; they = 3rd person plural.

personification – a feature that gives human qualities to a non-human object. Wordsworth does this a lot in his nature poems to elevate nature.

perspective – a particular point of view.

phonetics – when words are spelt the way they are sounded.

phonology – the sounds of words.

photojournalism – a non-literary text type that relies on the photographic image rather than the written word to inform the reader of something happening in the world.

plastic theatre – a term usually applied to American playwright, Tennessee Williams. The use of non-realist elements in his drama to represent abstract ideas such as characters' states of mind, emotions, memories, mood and atmosphere.

plosive alliteration – words that have harsh sounding letters repeated, e.g. 'b', 'd', 'p', usually to create an unsettling mood.

plot – the main events of a narrative.

polemicist – someone who enjoys debating controversial subjects – George Bernard Shaw was a well-known polemicist.

polysyllabic – words that have multiple (four or more) syllables. May be used to slow the pace down.

polysyndetic listing – see **listing**.

preposition – a word that states the position of something, e.g. over, under, next to.

presentational features – this refers to the layout and organization of a text, often applied to an advertisement.

prose – this is the opposite of verse or poetry – realist drama uses prose for speech rather than blank verse. Prose fiction can include novels, novellas and short stories.

provenance – the origin of something.

proxemics – a term associated with drama or films. Where characters are positioned on stage.

puff – a magazine term – an incentive to buy the magazine, usually put in a different shaped 'balloon' to stand out.

pull quote – used on a magazine front cover – a quotation from the main article.

pun – a word that has more than one meaning – often used for humorous effect in newspaper headlines.

received pronunciation – the standard accent of English based on how it is spoken by educated people in southern England.

register – formal or informal language. May also be linked to use of accent, dialect, slang.

relevance – when what is written or said relates to the reader or the listener.

repetition – when a word, phrase, idea or sentence construction is repeated three or more times. It is usually used for emphasis.

rhetoric – the art of writing or speaking effectively for the purpose of influencing people.

rhythm – the tempo or pace of a piece of text (e.g. poem, song or prose).

rising action – usually refers to drama but can be applied to other forms of literature. The series of events that follows an inciting incident, builds to a crescendo or a climax.

sans-serif – font that uses letters that have no additional strokes at the top or bottom of the lines that make up each letter (i.e. Ariel typeface).

sarcasm – type of humour that mocks or ridicules an individual, ideology or idea.

satire – type of humour that mocks an individual, institution or ideology usually by exaggerating a vice or characteristic.

semantic field – words that are linked by a shared field, e.g. the shared field of medicine, gardening, art.

sensationalism – melodramatic style – wildly exaggerates something through emotive and exaggerated language. Often used in tabloid reporting.

sensory language – language that appeals to at least one of our five senses (visual – sight; auditory – hearing; gustatory – taste; olfactory – smell; tactile – touch).

serif – font that uses lettering with extra strokes at the top or bottom of the lines that make up the letter (i.e. Times New Roman typeface).

sestina – a poetic term – a poem with 6 stanzas of 6 lines each and a final seventh stanza of 3 lines (known as an 'envoi').

setting – the place in which a text is set – could be historical, physical or geographical location.

shape – this can be used when analysing visual texts. The illustrator or photographer may, for example, contrast the shape of images for effect.

shared line – associated with drama, usually iambic pentameter. When one line is shared between two characters – usually denotes their close relationship.

sibilance – words that have a repeated 's' or 'sh' sound – can create either a sinister mood or a soft and relaxing mood. Context is important here!

simile – using the words 'like' or 'as … as' to compare one thing to another thing, e.g. the classroom was as hot as a furnace.

slang – words and phrases regarded as very informal and often used in place of Standard English words.

slogan – a memorable phrase used in advertising that we associate with a particular product.

social satire – when satire is used to mock or ridicule a particular society or social convention. Jane Austen is well-known for being a social satirist.

soliloquy – a dramatic term. When a character is (usually) on stage alone and speaks out loud his or her thoughts. Only the audience can hear what he or she is saying.

spatial mechanics – a graphic novel term – the way in which space is used within each panel.

splash page – a graphic novel term – when the whole page is taken up with one image.

stagecraft – a dramatic term. Applies to the non-verbal features of a play – the stage setting, props, lighting, sound effects, entrances and exits, make-up and costumes.

standard English – the standard spelling, punctuation, grammar and vocabulary that is considered acceptable wherever English is spoken or understood.

stative verb – a verb that expresses a state, rather than an action, e.g. feel, like, believe, think.

strapline – the narrow strip of text at the bottom of a magazine front cover.

stream of consciousness – a type of writing that transports the reader inside an individual's head. It attempts to imitate the flow of thoughts or state of mind a character is experiencing.

structure – the organization of a text – it can follow a chronological structure (step-by-step and linear) or a non-linear structure (shifts in time).

style – dependent upon diction, sentence construction and devices a writer uses; how formal a text is.

subject-specific language – language that is related by subject matter, e.g. whisking, stirring, folding are all subject specific language relating to cooking.

subtext – the deeper meaning below the surface of a text.

subtitle – text in large font that summarizes main points of an article or other main stories in a magazine.

subvert – to overturn the conventions of something.

symbol – something that represents something else in a work of literature, e.g. in Golding's *Lord of the Flies*, the conch (a shell) is a symbol for democracy.

synecdoche – when a part is used to represent the whole – Dickens uses this when he uses Scrooge's 'tight-fisted hand' to represent Scrooge's miserly character as a whole.

synonym – a word that means the same as another word.

tagline – memorable phrase that is printed on the magazine front cover that readers may associate with the publication.

target audience – an advertising term meaning the particular audience the advertisement is targeting.

temporal mechanics – a graphic novel term – the way in which time is stopped, slowed down or speeded up within a sequence of panels.

tercet – a poetic term – a three line rhyming stanza.

text type – the way we classify non-literary texts. There are multiple text types (advertisements, letters, newspaper articles, infographics, etc.). Each text type has its own set of key conventions.

textspeak – the language used for SMS/text messaging – defined by its brevity, shorthand slang of abbreviations, emoticons and emojis.

tone – the tone can be bitter, romantic, critical, light-hearted, etc. The use of language affects the tone of the text; the tone conveys the attitudes of the narrator.

tripling – when a word or a phrase is repeated three times for added impact or emphasis.

trochaic tetrameter – a poetic meter. Contains 4 iambs (8 syllables) but, unlike iambic tetrameter that uses an unstressed stressed rhythm, trochaic tetrameter uses a stressed unstressed beat (Blake's 'The Tyger' uses this meter).

trope – a theme that is repeated; see **motif**.

typographical features – this is usually associated with non-literary texts. The type of text used – its font, size and colour.

univocal – having one meaning; unambiguous.

verbs – a word that denotes an action.

visual imagery – an image that appeals to our sense of sight.

voice – see **narrative persona; narrative voice**.

Western – originally a geographical term, this now more commonly refers to the countries of western Europe, North America, Australia and New Zealand. Put 'Western culture' into a search engine to gain a more detailed understanding of the term.

white space – an advertising term – the white space in an advertisement where there is neither text nor a visual image.

word balloons – a graphic novel/cartoon term – the shaped 'balloon' or dialogue box that surrounds the words spoken by a character in a panel.

Notes on the activities

Introduction

Activity 2

Text type	Purpose	1 = extremely objective 6 = extremely subjective
Newspaper article	to report	2 – attempts to be objective and impartial; however, in reality most newspaper articles include bias in line with newspaper's political stance.
Restaurant review	to review	4 – this should be based on the food and be objective but well-known restaurant reviewers often use hyperbolic and emotive language to engage their readers (see Jay Rayner's restaurant reviews in British newspaper *The Guardian*). Also our likes and dislikes of food is subjective, depending upon our taste buds so it is not always easy to be objective when reviewing restaurants.
Letter of application to university or for a job	to demonstrate your interest in and suitability for the course or job	5 – you should be selling yourself in a letter of application but in reality many people feel embarrassed to say how amazing they are(!), thinking they will come across as arrogant or egotistical. However, a successful letter of application does need to focus on your strengths and put a positive spin on your weaknesses so it should be fairly subjective.
Propaganda poster	to persuade	6 – one-sided, overtly biased. The purpose of a propaganda poster is to persuade large groups of society to support whatever cause is being advertised in the propaganda poster (usually, support one's country during wartime).
Set of safety regulations on an aeroplane	to inform	1 – totally objective. This should be a step-by-step list of instructions with neutral language. Often visuals are included along with written instructions and the visuals may be stylized rather than photographic to make the instructions all the more informative and objective.
Advice column in a magazine	to advise	3 – the writer will attempt to be reasonable and objective, using his/her experience and expertise to offer good advice. However, usually it is quite obvious what the advice columnist's perspective is and the purpose of the advice is to persuade the reader to act in a particular way.

Chapter 1.1

Activity 1

Different world views

1 Trump: internal world view. Focusing on America rather than the world.

Ardern: external more global world view.

2 Each reader will have his/her own point of view

3 Perhaps because Trump's election campaign was 'Make America Great Again', which was predominantly an inward-thinking philosophy. Focusing on domestic policies rather than international policies. Ardern however fostered a trusting relationship with the Maori population of New Zealand as well as the non-Maori population which was perhaps more in line with working with all people, rather than focusing on one group of people.

Differences

The transcripts are language based texts, rather than multimodal texts.

The language is extended, the vocabulary is wide – ideas can be developed through language. The cartoon is dependent upon the visual image reinforcing the message of the written text.

A range of traditional persuasive features are employed in these transcripts (tripling, anaphora, parallelism, first person plural pronouns, superlatives) whereas visual features, unique to multimodal or image-based texts, are employed in the satirical cartoon (spatial mechanics, colour, word balloon, display lettering).

The speeches are serious in tone; the cartoon is satirical which is a form of humour.

Similarities

Both texts convey a particular perspective about the subject being addressed.

Both texts attempt to engage the reader/listener through a range of devices typical of the genre.

Activity 2

Commentary on final paragraph of extract.

As the writer takes us inside the teahouses, we get a further glimpse of this traditional culture and lifestyle. From the description of teamaking itself, 'burning husks in the stove give off a greenish flame and the water in the pots on top is bubbling'; to the countryside women selling 'baskets or trays of sunflower seeds or fried food'; to the 'quack doctor' trying to sell 'sham tiger bones' we get a vivid picture of this particular Chinese culture. The archaic verb, 'reck', also highlights the age-old customs and lifestyle described here. However, even in these traditional teahouses, modern life is evident. The girls from the cultural centre 'with their faces rouged red as strawberries' symbolize the changing face of this traditional community. Just as they have changed their identity through their rouged faces, so is the traditional lifestyle changing. Their 'slide show on changes in the countryside' which as well as their reliance on technology being shown, is a visual reminder to these traditional 'tea addicts' that change is coming. The silence in the room is ominous and the description of 'the moaning of a fly entangled in a spider's web can be heard' perhaps symbolizes inevitable death and entrapment.

Activity 3

Step 2 commentary

The second paragraph focuses on how other people view Scrooge. Negative lexis is used in the first half of the extract with the repetition of 'nobody' and the negative quantifier 'no' which highlights how isolated and alone Scrooge is as everyone avoids him. Using so much negative language suggests that this is not a desired way to live one's life, however, rather than feeling sorry for Scrooge, the reader is encouraged to feel he is responsible for how others avoid him due to the way Dickens has structured the text. This paragraph follows the paragraph describing Scrooge's mean and selfish character which encourages readers to blame Scrooge for how he is treated by other people. This second paragraph lists a wide range of people of different ages, gender and from different backgrounds, all of whom avoid Scrooge: beggars, children, men and women. This suggests how Scrooge is ostracised by absolutely everyone. It is particularly shocking to the reader that beggars, who are desperate in their poverty, and children, who represent innocence and usually trust anyone, should avoid him – it suggests he has a well-known reputation for being mean and heartless. The fact that even the 'blindmen's dogs' avoid Scrooge is also shocking as dogs are supposed to be man's best friend – particularly a blindman's dog whose job it is to show compassion by helping the physically vulnerable.

Dickens' use of tripling of verbs connected to speech – 'implored…asked…inquired' – also highlights the lack of communication society has with Scrooge as it is made clear that these communicative words are never exchanged with him. The extract closes with the dog's imagined words to his blind master. The dog's words suggest that even though Scrooge can physically see – a quality a blindman may crave – it is better to be blind (like the dog's master) than have 'an evil eye' (like Scrooge). The adjective 'evil' links Scrooge to the devil – something that generates fear in many. This is hyperbolic, exaggerating Scrooge's unpleasant character. However, there is an element of humour – the words are spoken by a dog and the speech ends with an exclamative – readers wonder whether Scrooge really is as 'evil' as he appears or whether, as alluded to in the first paragraph's 'solitary as an oyster' simile, he may have a pearl hidden deep inside which will be revealed as the novella continues.

Step 3: Reader response to ideas and message

The first paragraph begins by describing Scrooge as a miserly and cold-hearted man and the second paragraph describes a wide range of people including children, men, women – and even beggars and blindmen's dogs! – ignoring him. Because of the way Dickens has structured this information – describing Scrooge's character first and then describing how others react to him – suggests that people are avoiding contact with Scrooge because of his miserly character. Therefore, we are encouraged to connect Scrooge's quality of selfishness with how he is isolated and alienated from the rest of society. Rather than feeling sorry for Scrooge's isolation, we blame him and feel he is responsible for the way others treat him. Dickens' underlying message seems to be that an individual is responsible for his own behaviour, and if he decides to reject his fellow man, then man (and dog!) will reject the individual. We could interpret this as being a warning to us, the reader. If we do not show compassion to others, others will reject us. This should, then, encourage us to look within ourselves – gain an understanding of the self – and realize that our own behavior has a consequence for how others view and treat us.

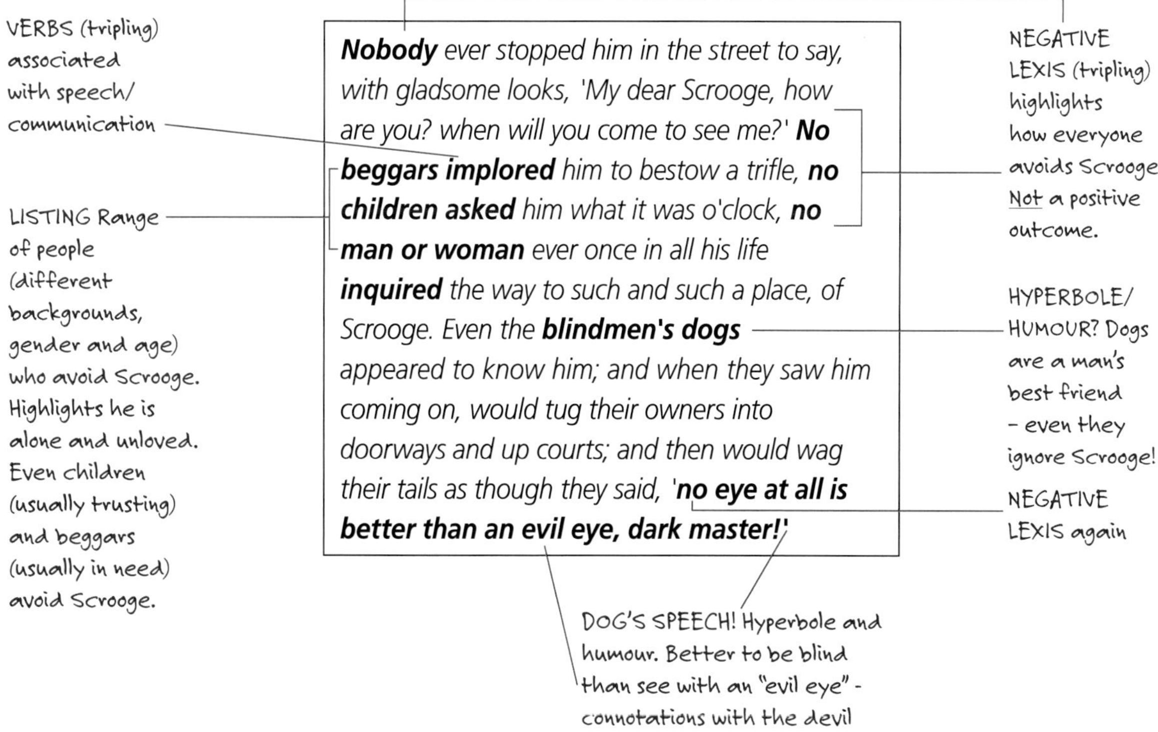

Activity 4

Analysis of 'Terror of War' (better known as 'Napalm Girl', see page 65).

Genre	Photograph published in newspapers around the world.
Audience	Millions of people globally who presumably are aware of current affairs if they read a newspaper.
Purpose	To inform readers of what is happening around the world; to elicit an emotional response.

Step 2: Structure and style

Because this text is a photograph, there is no written language; only a photographic image. In the foreground, it shows five young children running towards the camera; behind and to their sides are at least seven soldiers in uniform who appear to be herding the children away from the black cloud in the background, without helping them in any way. Because of the number of soldiers in the photograph, we assume this is a war photograph. The title, 'The Terror of War', also, makes explicit reference to this fact. The background consists of ominous dark smoke – a result of the country being at war, perhaps – which is what, we assume, the soldiers are herding the children away from. The children and soldiers take up the entire horizontal frame with the children in the foreground and the soldiers in mid frame. Although there are a number of children and soldiers, the reader's gaze is focused on the naked girl to the centre left. She is the only one not clothed and she is in obvious abject pain due to her arms akimbo and screaming facial features. The children are running down a wide road which is empty of traffic and to both sides of the road is the countryside. It is a hyper-realistic image (a photograph) which makes a powerful impact on the reader as we are aware this event actually happened as it is depicted in the photograph.

Step 3: Typographical and graphological features

The only typographical features are the display lettering on the noticeboard in the background of the image. The display lettering is difficult to decipher because it is in the far distance but we would assume, if we could read the lettering clearly, it would place the image in a particular country or even town.

The text is wholly taken up with a photograph and we will analyse the layout of the visual image in Step 5.

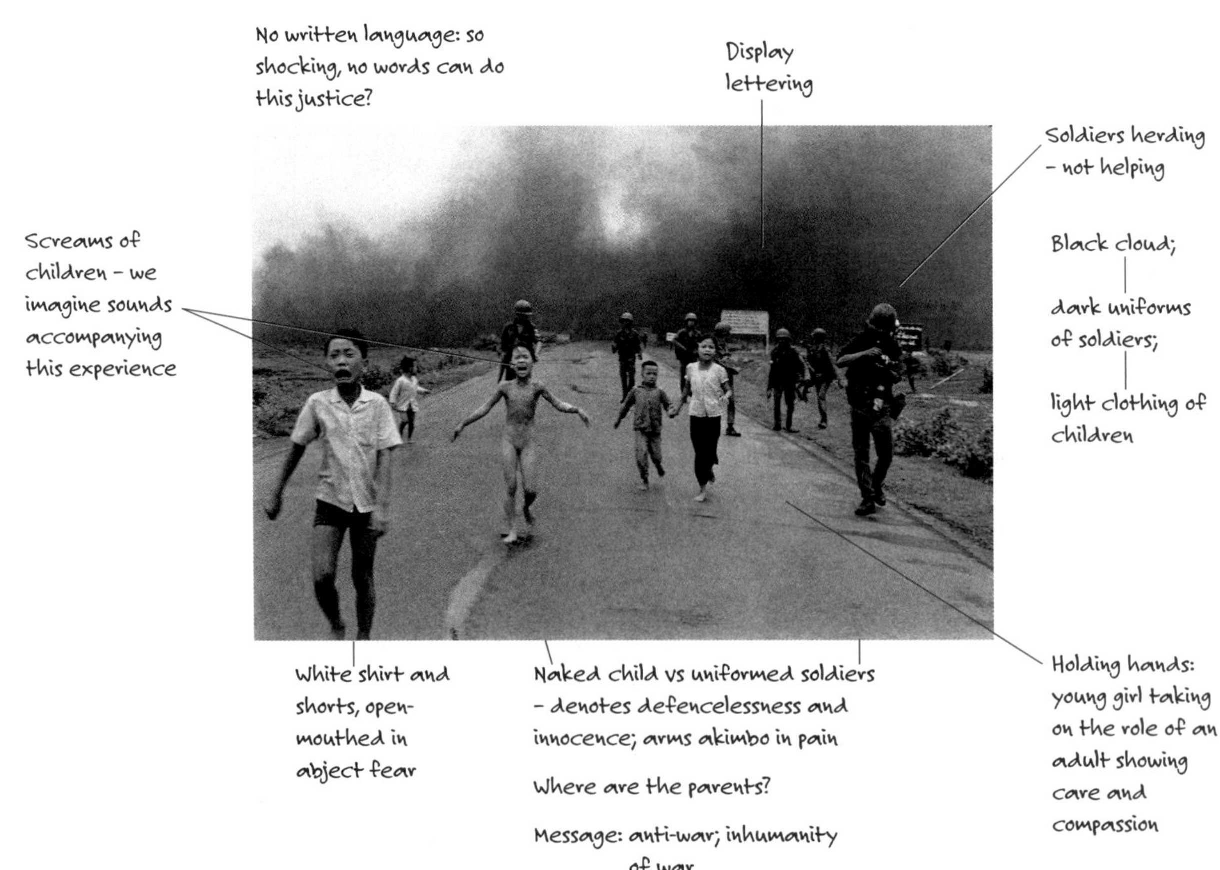

Step 4: Other features of text type

The only written language in this photograph is the display lettering on the noticeboard in the background. However, it is too far away to be legible and has no significance to the subjects of the image who have all passed it without giving it a glance. Other than that, there is no written language in this photograph. Sound is implied through the facial features of the two children in the foreground to the left. Both children – a boy and a girl – have their mouths wide open as if they are screaming in terror or in pain. Their screams are juxtaposed with the silence of the soldiers who follow/accompany/herd the children. It does not appear that any of the soldiers are attempting to comfort the children - the children are on their own with their pain and fear. This creates pathos for the children. Although we associate wars with the sound of guns and bombs, this image does not offer any war sound imagery other than the cries of the children. No guns are being fired, no aeroplanes or tanks are in the image and no bombs are falling. However, the background is taken up with a huge black smoke cloud which we assume is connected to the war and has destroyed whatever it is covering up (village, town, city?). Although we are aware the black cloud is a danger, it is a silent danger which creates a particularly eerie atmosphere.

Step 5: Visual image and layout

The image is in black and white – this makes it all the more stark and oppressive. The smoke cloud in the background is black, the soldiers' uniforms mid-frame are also dark and the children in the foreground are lighter with the boy in the front left wearing a white short-sleeved shirt. There is a gradient of colour imagery and the white associated with the children seems to connote their innocence in the face of war. There are a number of juxtapositions in the photograph. The soldiers are in full protective uniforms and are carrying guns whereas the children are either wearing thin civilian clothes or no clothes at all. They have no possessions and are completely defenseless. The naked girl in particular represents their defenselessness. The soldiers are walking as single units, neither speaking to one another nor attempting to comfort the children. The children, however, are running towards the camera and two of them are holding hands. The young girl has taken on the role of an adult, to offer comfort and companionship to the young boy (her brother, family member, friend?) It is as if the adult and child's roles have been subverted: the young girl offers comfort while the adult soldiers appear unperturbed and carry on regardless. The soldiers do not appear injured whereas the children are screaming with pain and terror. Apart from the soldiers, there are no other adults in the photograph and the reader is likely to wonder where the children's parents are. We feel these are orphaned children and their parents perhaps have died as a result of whatever caused the black smoke.

Step 6: Reader response to ideas, message and/or purpose.

Taking an imminent approach, we do not need to know the precise context resulting in this photograph, to recognise that this is an image that conveys the horrors of war. Rather than soldiers fighting and dying in war, the image makes it quite clear that often the victims of war are innocent children. Not only do children suffer during the war itself, but it would appear these children will suffer long after the war has finished, from the burns they have experienced and even becoming orphaned. Many readers would feel shame viewing this image, not just because of the pain and terror etched on the children's faces, but because of the lack of compassion and the inhumanity shown to the children by the soldiers. It therefore forces the reader to question the validity of war. The overriding message of this photograph would appear to be anti-war – the photograph's title, 'The Terror of War', is an explicit reference to this message and the image itself is a visual representation of this, too.

A secondary idea associated with this image is the role of the photographer. It may be that some readers would question whether the photographer, after he took his shot, offered any help to the children who were so alone, in so much pain and so frightened, and what role he should play as a war photographer.

Chapter 1.2

Activity 1

Step 2: LIFs in stanzas 2 and 3

- **Lexis** throughout this stanza connected to infinite number – 'continuous' (line 7), 'Milky Way' (line 8), 'stretched' (line 9), 'never-ending' (line 9), 'ten thousand' (line 11). This concept of the infinite suggests the daffodils cannot be understood using reason alone – reason is, therefore, flawed. Sense perception through actual experience is needed for acquisition of certain knowledge. The concept of the infinite fills us with awe and wonder because it is so beyond our rational thinking.
- This use of **hyperbole** emphasizes the daffodils' numeracy and thus fills the observer with awe.
- **Simile** 'Continuous as the stars … the Milky Way' (lines 7–8). The daffodils are being compared to something of another realm – not of this world; something infinite, 'never-ending' – again, these are concepts that cannot be understood using reason (bearing in mind the context of the poem, pub. 1807) and as well as showing how flawed our reason is, it also fills us with wonder at this natural phenomenon that can be compared with something so heavenly as the stars.
- **Verbs** used, 'shine' and 'twinkle' (lines 7 and 8): visual images – appeal to our senses. Not only are we seduced by the gentle rhythm of the lines and regular rhyme, but visually the daffodils are appealing, too.
- **Personification** of last line, 'tossing their heads in sprightly dance' (line 12): Wordsworth is fusing two worlds together – the natural world and the human world. He elevates the daffodils and so heightens their importance which fills us with wonder at the natural world.
- 'Sprightly dance' (line 12): **adverb** sprightly has mischievous or magical connotations attached to it – brings childlike joy to scene. Dance has sense of movement attached to it but there is a joy and musicality, an affirmation of life attached to this **verb/noun**. Fact that 'dance' can be either verb or noun symbolizes perhaps the fact that the daffodils are all things to the narrator and have utmost importance to his Romantic philosophy.
- **Repetition** of 'danced' (line 12, end of stanza 2 and line 13, beginning of stanza 3): highlights this sense of harmonious and joyful movement which appeals to our **visual sense**. Great sense of fun and life with **noun** 'glee' (line 14). Language used here has connotations of positivity – joy, fun, celebration.
- Middle 2 lines in this stanza directly refer to Wordsworth, the poet. 'A poet could not … / In such a jocund company!' (lines 15 and 16) by bringing himself so explicitly into the poem, it makes it more **direct and personal**; **more persuasive and convincing**. Idea he has no control over how he responds – his response is intuitive, not reasoned or logically thought out. (Idea of transcendentalism – responding instantaneously, spontaneously.) The **exclamative sentence** (line 16) reinforces this idea, too. The power of the daffodils on the poet fills us with awe and wonder.
- **Repetition** of 'gazed' (line 17) – **visual sense** highlighted. Sense that the observer cannot tear his eyes away from the sight. He is stopped in his tracks. The daffodils are like a magnet which hold him. Emphasizes their power over the individual which fills us with awe and wonder.

- 'But little thought' (line 17): **verbal phrase** shows insignificance of *thought* – of reason, of intellect, of mental faculty. Cannot rely on *thought* processes to bring truth or understanding. Effect daffodils have on him cannot be rationally explained; the effect is instantaneous and intuitive. Importance of sense perception over and above intellect.
- Final line **noun** 'wealth' (line 18): not material wealth, but spiritual wealth (links in to image of 'golden' in stanza 1, line 4). Elevates significance of daffodils which fills us with awe and wonder.
- **Metaphor** of 'the show' (line 18): daffodils compared to actors on stage, putting on a show for us the audience. They are actively attempting to affect us, just as actors actively attempt to create feelings and emotions within us; just as Wordsworth is actively attempting to fill us with wonder and awe at the daffodils! Again, this elevates the daffodils – makes them an active force and the individual merely a passive observer.

Activity 2

Having described the tramps in general and honed in on two or three individual tramps, Orwell then moves on to describe the inspection by the doctor. Initially, we would feel having a doctor inspect the tramps is a good thing – perhaps now they will be offered treatment for their many physical illnesses. However, it is quite clear that the inspection 'was designed merely to detect smallpox, and took no notice of our general condition.' Smallpox, being a contagious disease, was feared by many people in the 1920s and 1930s and we are led to believe that the purpose of the inspection is not to look after the tramps, but to ensure society as a whole is protected. It is clear that although the tramps may not have smallpox, they do have a number of shocking physical ailments that affect them individually but, being non-contagious, the doctor is not concerned. The doctor himself is described as being 'a young medical student, smoking a cigarette'. This description should have an effect on the reader – we should be feeling mortified that it is a 'young medical student' who is sent to the spike, rather than a qualified doctor. This suggests how little the tramps are valued and how badly they are treated. The fact that the student is 'smoking' also shows his lack of compassion or understanding – firstly, the tramps are unlikely to be able to afford cigarettes so the student smoking shows his lack of consideration for this basic fact; today we are also likely to feel his smoking is unwarranted and shows a lack of awareness, knowing the detrimental effects of both active and passive smoking. The language Orwell uses to describe how the doctor does his job also suggests a lack of compassion. He walks 'rapidly along the line glancing us up and down' – the adverb 'rapidly' and verb 'glancing' both suggest he is in a hurry, not concerned about doing his job properly or offering any kind words of support to any of the tramps. Orwell describes his room-mate as a 'cell companion' which furthers the idea alluded to at the beginning of the extract of the tramps being convicts, punished for a crime, and the spike is closer to a prison that punishes them than a place that offers solace or refuge for a night. The final image in this extract is the doctor examining the red rash of his 'cell companion' and saying how there is nothing to worry about as it is 'merely due to under-nourishment.' The extract ends on this note of irony: under-nourishment is something severe that, unless treated, leads to other diseases or death. However, because it is not smallpox and therefore not contagious, the doctor does not see it as a concern.

Activity 3

Step 4: Other features of text type

Feature/Device	Evidence	Effect
1 Embeds plants' **proper names** rather than their more commonly used names.	**C** *Monocotyledons, Cyperaceae, Coniferae.*	**iii** Assumes the reader has a certain knowledge base which appeals to readers. Even if reader is unfamiliar with these terms, the understanding is still clear.
2 **Typographical features:** such as italics for the Latin or Ancient Greek etymological names of the species.	**D** *Narcissus, Richardia aethiopica, Typha, Pothos, Plantago*, etc.	**i** This is a visual learning tool that identifies new vocabulary and encourages the reader to learn it.
3 **Statistics** that can be verified.	**A** 'In some palms it is 20 ft. long, and encloses 200,000 flowers.'	**vi** This information can be substantiated and therefore gives the text credibility and authenticity.
4 **Diction**: subject specialist language (jargon) is used	**G** *spathe, phyllody, staminody*	**iv** The first time it is used it is italicised. This is a visual learning tool to encourage readers to (a) identify the word and (b) learn it before it is used again not italicised.
5 **Typographical features**: use of parenthesis for additional information	**F** '(fig. 4)', '(fig. 5, gl)', '(*staminody* of bracts)'	**ii** Allows additional information to be added, aimed at developing readers' knowledge base and understanding even more.
6 **Other features**: includes listing	**E** '*Plantago major, P. lanceolata, Ajuga reptans,* dandelion, daisy, dahlia and in umbelliferous plants'	**vii** Implies the writer has a wide knowledge base which encourages the reader to trust the information.
7 **Tone:** uses neutral language	**B** 'A sheathing bract enclosing one or several flowers is called a *spathe*.'	**v** To create objectivity with the intention of informing and educating the reader rather than eliciting an emotional response.

Activity 4

Genre (text type)	Online opinion piece, published in a newspaper
Audience	Primarily American readers who would be familiar with Kaepernick's recent protest as well as historical American protests
Purpose	To persuade

Activity 5

Structure and style of text

The infographic is a non-chronological text. Readers do not have to start at the beginning of the text and move their way down; they can make sense of each piece of information irrespective of the order they read each box of text. It opens with a credible source, the UN Women Executive Director, Phumzile Mlambo-Ngcuka. The South African's words are directly quoted which gives them an added edge of authority and force. The fact that this is an infographic about women and armed conflict makes Mlambo-Ngcuka an appropriate choice to foreground the text. The end focus of the text is similar to the opening: there is a direct quotation, this time spoken by Ban Ki-Moon, the UN Secretary-General when the infographic was released. He is a recognisable figure and by having his photograph, name and position reproduced here, adds gravitas to the text. The text is, therefore, grounded in credible sources, both at the beginning and at the end, suggesting the topic is of utmost importance. The text is chunked into small boxes of information – some boxes are a mixture of photographic images and direct quotations; some are simple red bands with white text; and some are a combination of universal pictorial images, statistics and colour coded language. The infographic includes at the end the UN Women's logo and web address together with Ban Ki-Moon standing in front of the UN logo and wearing a blue tie to match his organisation's symbol. He is, therefore, visually connected to the UN as well as being its physical Secretary-General.

The style of the text is at times informative, particularly through the use of various statistics to illustrate points, and at times emotive, particularly through the use of emotive language which is highlighted in red. Apart from the two quotations which open and end the infographic, there is no extended text - any text is written in small chunks or used as headings or labels to reinforce the many pictorial images included. The language is predominantly neutral, although the facts included are shocking. The text is visually appealing due to its use of colour, symbols, pictorial and photographic images as well as different typographical and graphological features.

Typographical and graphological features

The text's headline, 'Women & Armed Conflict', is in a large font and is capitalised to draw attention to the subject of the infographic. The red typeface has connotations of a warning and immediately draws the reader's attention to this grave subject matter. The two quotations that open and end the text are written in smaller font, however, they are both foregrounded by large quotation marks to highlight that each piece of text is the direct words spoken by the UN Women Executive Director and the UN Secretary-General. Both individuals are credible and respected figures at the UN and including quotations from both of these figures grounds the text in credibility, authority and authenticity. Although some of the more extended text is in a smaller typeface, key words are highlighted in red so that they stand out. The words that are highlighted are emotive, including 'harmful', 'violence', 'conflict' and 'inequalities'. Many of these words and phrases are of a semantic field of harm which is accentuated by the red font used, with its connotations of warning and danger. There are four examples given of the consequences of armed violence and each different consequence is capitalised in a sans-serif font. The font chosen is simple, modern and minimalistic which accentuates how the information being conveyed is contemporary and emphasises the gravity of the subject.

One of the final boxes includes information about possible solutions to achieving sustainable peace. There is a long list of what women must be full participants in if this goal is to be achieved, and each item in the list is foregrounded with the tick symbol. The tick symbol denotes something positive and in this instance is used to suggest that each item in the list is an accurate representation of the areas in which women need to be involved if sustainable peace is to become a reality. Underneath this list are pictorial images which visually reinforce these suggestions - for example, the symbolic representation of two people holding hands denotes the need for collaboration, the scales denote the need for justice and the two people sitting at a table denote the need for communication. This is an example of how visuals can be used to complement and reinforce the meaning of the written text.

At the top of the text, the UN Women logo is included which reminds the reader of the organisation and again grounds the text with credibility. Because this is quite clearly a UN infographic, shown through the two quotations of UN personnel, the blocks of colour that match the UN logo and the UN logo itself, readers are likely to feel the information is factual rather than sensational as the UN is a diplomatic and intergovernmental global organisation which works with all countries to maintain peace and security.

Other features of infographic text type

The infographic uses colour effectively to break up each piece of information and guide the reader. Each piece of information is clearly presented in a different coloured box that makes the reading experience straight forward. As well as the written word and colour imagery, statistics are included that can be verifiable and substantiated. In each of the 'harmful consequences' examples, figures and percentages are used that shock the readers. For example, in the Maternal Mortality consequence box, we are informed that 531 deaths per 100,000 live births occurred in conflict and post-conflict areas in 2013 as opposed to the global rate of 210 deaths. This is over double, and the scale of this difference is depicted visually by two different-sized pictorial symbols of women. In the Land Rights section, we are informed that the percentage of women with legal titles to land in conflict and post-conflict areas in 2014 was 9% in contrast to the global rate of 19%. This is another statistic intended to shock, stating that over half of women lose their land rights during conflict. Similarly shocking statistics are given in the Education and the Child Marriage boxes. Collectively, the boxes convey to readers how women suffer dire consequences in many areas of their daily lives when experiencing conflict.

Alliteration and repetition are also used in the infographic to make certain phrases more memorable. In particular, the phrase 'Powerful women, powerful peace' uses these two devices to the effect that the phrase becomes almost slogan-like.

Visual image and layout

This is a multimodal text and images and text are used throughout to reinforce each other. A range of visual images are used including photographs which make the text credible and rooted in real life, pictorial symbols of females which reinforce the subject matter of the text: women and armed conflict, and other symbolic visual illustrations including books and an apple to denote school, round circles to present the Child Marriage statistics, a dove and open hand symbol to denote peace and freedom and the range of symbols described above that reinforce the ways in which women can become participants in achieving sustainable peace. These visuals are universal and are not tied to any cultural, ethnic or social group, thus a wide range of readers throughout the world will be able to recognise the significance of each of these visual symbols. Each block of text includes at least one visual image whether it is a photograph or a pictorial symbol and each of these visuals reinforces the written word. The layout is well organised and easy to follow. We are encouraged to start at the top and work our way through each different coloured box systematically, however, it is not essential that we follow this order. Each block of text makes sense as a stand alone chunk of information so readers can hone in on the section they are most interested in.

Reader response to ideas, message and/or purpose

Through a combination of written language, photographic images, symbolic pictorial images and other symbols, the reader is informed about the detrimental effects of conflict and armed violence on women and girls, and the steps that can be taken, by women, to create a sustainable future. It is not simply suggesting that women are weak and vulnerable; rather it is suggesting that women are powerful and can make a difference to the world in which we live.

Chapter 1.3

Activity 3

How is meaning **constructed, negotiated, expressed** and **interpreted** in second half of *A Streetcar Named Desire* extract?

So far Williams has **constructed** this scene to take place inside the flat and the meaning that is **expressed** appears to be that as long as Blanche remains inside the flat, presumably with Stanley, she is in a vulnerable and unsafe position. But now Williams shifts the reader/audience and we are forced to view the outside world. Although the scene itself does not change – Blanche is still standing inside the flat – the back walls of the rooms 'become transparent' and we can now see the sidewalk outside the flat. This is obviously an example of non-realist stagecraft – or plastic theatre – and we have to wonder what meaning is Williams attempting to **construct** by this piece of magic. Many readers may **interpret** this as representing how both inside the flat and outside the flat are nightmarish for Blanche. We have already heard the jungle-like cries of the night, now Williams transports us outside the flat into this jungle.

His stage directions describe a street scene with a prostitute, drunkard, policeman and Negro woman. With the exception of the policeman, the other three New Orleans residents are conveyed in a negative light: the prostitute robs a drunkard, the drunkard chases and fights the prostitute, the Negro woman has found the prostitute's bag and is 'rooting' through it. The policeman is shown to be ineffectual, he blows the whistle to break it up but does not actually do anything active to help any of these people.

So how do we **interpret** this scene? We are actually never quite sure whether this street-scene is actually taking place outside Stanley's flat, or whether it is all in Blanche's head. Certainly we understand the lurid reflections, grotesque shadows and cries like a jungle are being used symbolically here rather than literally, so this makes us **negotiate** a meaning that perhaps the street-scene, also, is being used in a similar manner – that is, that it is not literally happening, but is symbolic of Blanche's vulnerability and impending doom. Audiences may **interpret** this scene differently. Some audiences may feel the scene represents how the street is a jungle in the respect that it is survival of the strongest – or at least survival of the luckiest. Others may **interpret** it as how anything goes – the law is unable to protect those who need protecting perhaps because there are so many people who do need protecting – the prostitute, the drunkard, the Negro woman in 1940s America – as well as Blanche. Others may **interpret** it as showing how you cannot trust anyone, everyone is out for themselves. Others may **interpret** the scene as representing Blanche's internal turmoil and impending menace. The way we **negotiate** meaning and **interpret** this scene is also likely to be affected by how it is performed on stage – so how the director and actors have **negotiated** meaning will have an impact on our own **interpretation**.

Ironically, it is with Stanley's re-entry into the scene and his words 'You left th' phone off th' hook' that we are returned to reality – but now Williams has **constructed** a reality that appears just as nightmarish as the non-reality we have just experienced. Stanley's dialogue, deliberate hanging up the phone and thus severing Blanche's connection to an escape route, and his facial expression of 'his mouth slowly curving into a grin' all seem to suggest that Blanche does indeed have a lot to fear from Stanley and that she is in the middle of a living nightmare. Although none of this is explicitly stated, it is likely most readers would **construct** a similar meaning to this scene through a **negotiation** of what we are seeing and hearing on stage.

Activity 4

Translation of textspeak essay into Standard English.

My summer holidays were a complete waste of time. Before, we used to go to New York to see my brother, his girlfriend and their three screaming kids face to face. I love New York, it's a great place. But my parents were so nervous because of the terrorism attack on September 11 that they decided we would stay in Scotland and spend two weeks up North, what you see is what you get – nothing. I was extremely bored in the middle of nowhere. Nothing but sheep and mountains.

At any rate, my parents were happy. They said that it could be worse, and that they were happy with the peace and quiet. I don't think so! I wanted to go home as soon as possible, to see my mates again. Today I came back to school. I feel very saintly because I have done all my homework. Now it's business as usual …

Activity 5

In what ways is meaning ...	Write at least one paragraph for each keyword
Constructed?	Tan has *constructed* the panel to defamiliarize the reader by using an illustration of a serpent's tail as a visual metaphor to represent why the protagonist has to leave his homeland. We have to construct our own meaning regarding what the serpent's tail represents. Spatial mechanics are also used by Tan to heighten a sense of powerlessness: the family are in the foreground but are tiny, hidden in the shadows. They are juxtaposed with the vast serpent that is writhing around the houses, completely dominating the scene. This unsettles us.
Negotiated?	Through this panel, Tan is *negotiating* a way through for us – immigration is a complex problem and the serpent's tail that could represent so many things that force a family to leave, is used to *negotiate* this idea perhaps. Tan also attempts to raise an awareness that immigrants have no choice but to leave; they are powerless and blameless. Tan has opened up a discussion about immigration here and perhaps he wants us now to *negotiate* with him or with other people about this real-life global problem so that we work together to resolve this problem or at the very least show empathy to immigrants where we live. We have to *negotiate* an understanding of this panel. Being aware of how Tan has constructed it, we focus on the serpent's tail and try to make sense of it (each reader may *negotiate* a different meaning – poverty, war, famine). Once we have *negotiated* this, we can then start to *construct* our own interpretation of the panel.
Expressed?	The meaning Tan appears to be *expressing* is a sense of vulnerability experienced by the protagonist and his family. Because we are able to interpret the serpent's tail in a number of different ways, perhaps Tan is suggesting that there are multiple reasons why people are forced to leave their homeland (poverty, war, famine, natural disaster, intolerance).
Interpreted?	We may *interpret* the panel differently – it will depend on how we *interpret* the visual metaphor of the serpent's tail. A common *interpretation,* however, is likely to be that we show empathy towards the protagonist and his family. The serpent is an archetypal symbol of evil and it is likely to unsettle the reader so we can understand the protagonist's fear and loathing. Younger readers also are likely to feel unsettled – a serpent is a nightmare image for many young people. Even if young people do not understand the 'immigration' theme, it is likely they will understand that this family has to leave their hometown to be safe and to avoid being destroyed by this serpent.

Activity 6

Questioning hierarchy and/or class inequality:

Velázquez has constructed this artwork by focusing on a group of figures in the centre foreground. Apart from the wealthy girl in her splendid ivory dress, we see the meninas (the girl's ladies-in-waiting), two dwarves and the painter. Our eyes are drawn to them because of where Velázquez has positioned them. In contrast, as already discussed, the powerful couple who are the subject of the (fictional) painting are reduced to small objects in the mirror. Velázquez has, therefore, given prominence to the lower members of the social hierarchy and our eye is drawn to them rather than their masters. Moreover, the title of this artwork is *Las Meninas* – additional significance is given through the title to the ladies-in-waiting. Perhaps Velázquez, by including someone who represents himself (the painter) and the ladies-in-waiting, is challenging class inequality and is expressing, through the conscious construction of his art, that they too are worthy of having their lives documented and being the subject of art.

Questioning our own interpretation of and involvement with art:

Another way in which we might interpret *Las Meninas* is that Velázquez is playing with us as an interpreter of a text. The artwork may be suggesting that we can never arrive at a complete and perfect interpretation or understanding of a text. We look for clues in the way that we feel an artist or author may have constructed a text and we attempt to negotiate meaning in order to interpret the text's message/ideas. This overall understanding, however, is marred by uncertainties, gaps in our knowledge and assumptions. When we view the painter peering around his easel, how can we be sure that he is painting the image of the wealthy couple seen in the mirror's reflection? Perhaps the painter is painting us. Velázquez could be reaching out through time and space to suggest that we are a part of the painting. Just as we are viewing the artwork, the painter is viewing us; just as we are attempting to interpret the artwork, the painter is attempting to interpret us! This interpretation means we become active participants in the artwork, even though we are off-frame.

Chapter 1.4

Activity 1

These are possible examples you could have used. They are not however definitive answers and you may have come up with some of your own examples. This is the power of Martin Luther King's speech: he does not simply use a technique once, but his speech is full of techniques used multiple times that are seamlessly integrated into the text. This then is why it is such a persuasive text type.

Technique	Quotation from the extract	Effect
Alliteration	'a **state sweltering** with the heat of **injustice**, a **state sweltering** with the heat of **oppression**'	This use of sibilance – the repeated 's' and 'sh' (oppre**ss**ion) sounds – creates a sinister and harsh atmosphere, imitating the meaning of the words.
Anecdote	'I have a dream that my four little children will one day live in a nation where they will not be judged by the color of their skin but by the content of their character'	By referring to his own children, this makes the speech deeply personal to MLK and closes the gap between him and his audience; his own family are experiencing the same injustice that his speakers are experiencing.
Antithesis	'The **rough** places will be made **plain**, and the **crooked** places will be made **straight**'	This has the effect of suggesting how nothing is too much to be achieved. There is a great sense of faith in MLK's words – he genuinely believes that nothing is impossible. It also reminds the audience of how much is wrong, but there is a great sense of faith that all the wrong can be put right.
Emotive language	'one day in Alabama, with its vicious racists, with its governor having his lips dripping with the words of interposition and nullification'	The emotive language that is used here to describe the white supremacists in Alabama and its governor, clearly emphasize Martin Luther King's anger and disgust at their actions.
Inclusivity	'one day ... sons of former slaves and the sons of former slave-owners will be able to sit down together at the table of brotherhood'	The effect of bringing the sons of former slaves and the sons of former slave-owners together would have been shocking at the time but make it clear how important inclusivity is in creating an environment of equality and forgiveness. The abstract noun 'brotherhood' heightens this idea and attempts to bring the two traditional enemies, the victim and the aggressor, together, reminding them that they are both part of the brotherhood of all men.
Metaphor	'With this faith we will be able to hew out of the mountain of despair a stone of hope'	This is a visual image that helps his audience understand the monumental task ahead. It helps his audience feel that change *is* possible as well as making it clear that it will be hard and take a lot of effort from everyone.
Onomatopoeia	'the **jangling** discords of our nation'	This is an auditory image which encourages his audience to actually *hear* the misery that they are experiencing. It reminds his listeners of the jangling sounds of chains, perhaps, that he mentioned earlier in the speech – a reminder of their history of slavery.
Personal pronouns	'With this faith we will be able to ...'	This phrase is repeated three times at the end of the extract and so the first person plural personal pronoun 'we' is repeated a number of times. This has the effect of *uniting* the speaker with the audience; he is one of the audience and *together* they will work to achieve equality. It forms a bond between the speaker and the audience and closes the gap between the famous civil rights activist and the ordinary man and woman listening to him.

Technique	Quotation from the extract	Effect
Relevance	'I have a dream that one day on the red hills of Georgia'	By naming an actual place that many of his audience would have come from and by describing a geographical feature of that place encourages the audience to feel that MLK understands who he is speaking to, their background and their experiences.
Repetition (anaphora)	'I have a dream …'	This is repeated four times to introduce a new idea which makes it an example of anaphora. It is like a refrain. Its power comes through its simplicity. Each word is monosyllabic which makes it memorable. It is also a positive message – dreams are positive and the meaning of the phrase when MLK uses it is that the future he dreams of will also be positive. So it becomes uplifting and is inspiring.

Activity 3

Sun Tzu's *The Art of War*

The language of the front cover and title of text

Sun Tzu on The Art of War. The Oldest Military Treatise in the World; Translated From the Chinese With Introduction, and Critical Notes

- *Sun Tzu on The Art of War* – gives Sun Tzu authority. This is his treatise and we should read it because it is by Sun Tzu.
- 'The Oldest Military Treatise in the World' – it has withstood testament of time. The superlative gives the text authority.
- The text's title 'The Art of War' – Sun Tzu's *The Art of War* is an advisory guide on military strategy and tactics. The title of the book is significant in terms of Sun Tzu's purpose and the kind of readers who will be encouraged to read this text. *The Art of War* appears to be paradoxical: 'art' has connotations of beauty and creativity whereas 'war' has connotations of violence and aggression. However, by suggesting there is an art to war encourages readers to reflect on their prior attitudes and immediately implies that by reading this guide readers may discover a new way of understanding both art and war. This widens the potential readership – it will not just be readers with an interest in the military or warfare who will read the book, but readers who are interested in learning how something connected with violence and brute force can be transformed into something that is creative and connected to beauty. 'Art' also has the meaning of an occupation that requires great skill, expertise and creative thinking, thus, by using this abstract noun with 'war' Sun Tzu is implying that these qualities are essential in being successful in war, rather than simply the numbers or physical strength of an army. This also widens the readership to those who may now feel that any advice offered to military leaders regarding expertise through creative thinking may also be relevant to other fields where success is based on overcoming the competition – fields such as business, entertainment or sports.

Language that gives the writer authority

- *Sun Tzu on The Art of War* – front cover: gives Sun Tzu authority. This is his treatise and we should read it because it is by Sun Tzu.
- Extract is foregrounded with: 'Sun Tzu said'. Sun Tzu himself is important in giving the text its gravitas and sense of authenticity. He was a military leader and tactician. His background gives him authority.

Language that is repeated to emphasize a point

- Language of war (for example, 'battle', 'enemy') is repeated throughout – this is appropriate because of the text's title: 'The Art of War'.
- Military language is repeated throughout (for example, 'army', 'regiment', 'company', 'general') – appropriate because this is a 'military treatise'.

Language that is used to disguise opinion as fact

- 'Thus the highest form of generalship is to balk the enemy's plans; the next best is to prevent the junction of the enemy's forces; the next in order is to attack the enemy's army in the field; and the worst policy of all is to besiege walled cities.' No scientific proof is quoted; no actual battles are quoted where this has been the case. This is just on Sun Tzu's word.
- 'The preparation of mantlets, movable shelters, and various implements of war, will take up three whole months; and the piling up of mounds over against the walls will take three months more.' Given definitive time periods but no real-life examples to substantiate this.

Language that is used to warn if advice is not followed

- 'The general, unable to control his irritation, will launch his men to the assault like swarming ants, with the result that one-third of his men are slain, while the town still remains untaken. Such are the disastrous effects of a siege.' Figurative language – 'like swarming ants' – dehumanizes the men, suggesting they are insects. Sense that Sun Tzu has contempt for the general who does not take his advice. Hyperbolic and emotive language is used here: 'one-third of his men are slain' – suggests if his advice is not taken there will be huge negative consequences.

Other ways language is shaped by the text type

- Use of second person pronoun 'you' makes this a direct address to his audience. Forces reader to listen, thinking Sun Tzu is speaking directly to the reader.
- Use of present tense that suggests this is current advice that is timeless and universal. Not advice that is shaped by a time period, but advice that transcends time.

Activity 4

These are just ideas – you may have other quotations to illustrate each language feature.

Use of language	Quotation	Effect
Onomatopoeia	'crack'; 'rumble'; 'spit'	A number of words sound like the word they mean and this also helps the audience to hear the storm on stage.
Personification	'you'; 'your'; 'thou'; 'thy' 'Rumble thy bellyful!'	Lear addresses the storm as if it were a person through his use of personal pronouns. This elevates the storm to the human level and suggests it is wilfully and consciously attacking Lear and the country. 'Rumble thy bellyful' suggests the storm is some kind of hungry monster who is unleashing its fury in order to feed its hunger.
Plosive sounds	'Blow, winds, and crack your cheeks! rage! blow!'	Lots of harsh sounds in the language used – plosive 'b', 'd', 'c' and 'g'. Build up of sounds that imitate the sounds of the relentless storm. The combination of plosives and monosyllables suggest a single-mindedness behind the storm – how determined it is to destroy. The exclamatives emphasize this idea, too.
Violent verbs	'crack'; 'rage'; 'smite'; 'spit'	There is a preponderance of verbs with violent and aggressive connotations which also suggests how ruthless and destructive the storm is.

Chapter 1.5

Activity 2

May 2015 edition: 'Paul'	September 2015 edition: 'Florence'
'From writing Yesterday … … to collaborating with Kanye At Home With A Pop Genius'	'Florence wants to reach out and touch you …'

May 2015 edition: 'Paul'	September 2015 edition: 'Florence'
The image of Paul McCartney is very ordinary in that he is wearing a plain blue T-shirt and jacket. He is looking directly at the camera, appearing comfortable and relaxed. This is how we imagine he may look 'at home' – he is not in 'stage' clothes and is not posing for the camera. However, he is holding his guitar – the tool of his trade. The image, therefore, makes it clear that he is a musician (in case we didn't recognize him!) and this links in with the reference in the additional text to his most famous song from the past – 'Yesterday' which he composed when in The Beatles – and his most recent collaboration with the rapper, Kanye. Having the musical flexibility to compose a ballad like 'Yesterday' and also to collaborate with a contemporary rapper like Kanye is evidence of his 'pop genius'. The positioning of the additional text also makes the link between McCartney's past and present – the last word of the first two lines of the additional text (Yesterday / Kanye) rhyme which subtly connects Paul's past (represented by Yesterday) and present (represented by Kanye). The ellipsis that separates the first two lines of the additional text could perhaps represent the 50 years between the release of 'Yesterday' (1965) and the Kanye collaboration (2015) – suggesting that Paul's longevity is also evidence of his 'pop genius'. The positioning of the additional image at the top of the page and the word PRODIGY which is placed immediately above Paul's head is also a playful way to structure this text. Although Prodigy refers to the band whose image is displayed, the noun prodigy means someone with exceptional abilities – a 'genius' – which could also refer to Paul.	The photographic image is a clear representation of these words. She is looking directly at the camera and reaching out her hand as if trying to touch the reader. The look on her face is a look of contentment, linking in with how she 'wants' to do this. Because her hand is reaching out towards the camera, it is in the foreground and is larger than the rest of Florence and makes us feel it is very close to us on the other side of the camera lens. This now explains why the headline and additional text is on the bottom left of the image and not centrally positioned. If the text was centrally positioned, the impact of the hand reaching out would be lost. The text is immediately below the hand which accentuates the meaning all the more.

Activity 4

Before this ugly edifice, and between it and the wheel-track of the street, was a grass plot, much overgrown with burdock, pigweed, apple-Peru, and such unsightly vegetation, which evidently found something congenial in the soil that had so early borne the black flower of civilized society, a prison.

Society at the time	'Ugly edifice' and 'overgrown' grass plot – suggests a lack of care and pride. Perhaps this is their attempt to separate the prison from what they consider to be civilized – the 'wheel-track of the street'. Suggests once you are inside the prison, you are forgotten about and ostracized from society. The prison has been there for a long time 'the soil that had so early borne the black flower of civilized society, a prison' which suggests punishing people is of utmost importance to them. Does this suggest there is an inherent lack of trust in people – or that there are so many rigid rules and regulations that it is easy to commit a sin? Sense that this is a strict society, breaking a rule is punished and forgiveness is lacking.
Setting	The narrator suggests the setting is 'unsightly' – it is overgrown with 'burdock, pigweed, apple-Peru'. These are all plants and part of nature but considered weeds to this society. Suggests that people at the time are rigid in how they view things – certain things are good, everything else is 'unsightly'. Perhaps it suggests that only unappealing plants are able to grow here because of the construction of the prison – the prison is polluting and destroys goodness and beauty. The metaphor of a 'black flower' to describe the prison is powerful – black flowers do not exist in nature so this is suggesting that the prison is unnatural. Black has connotations of evil and darkness so it also suggests the prison is likewise evil, a dark place.
Suspense	Foregrounds with 'ugly edifice' – but it is not until the end of this long complex sentence that we are told exactly what the edifice is. End focus is 'prison' – delays explaining exactly what is being described in such a negative way.

Activity 5

Written language:

Slogan:

There's A Man In There

Being in the bottom centre (structure) our eyes are drawn to the slogan. It is in classic white capitals. It plays with the stereotype of there being 'a man' but that that stereotype is difficult to achieve for the everyday male. Initially we feel the slogan applies to the visual image of the male in two halves, suggesting that underneath the ordinary student there is a rock star waiting to burst out – the rock star being the 'man'. However, when we look closely at the product that is being advertised we note that the product's name is 'After Hours' so perhaps the slogan applies to the product – you can become 'a man' after hours when you use this product.

Additional text:

The additional text is much smaller. Above the slogan are the words 'Somewhere in there' suggesting that although it may be hidden, every male has 'a man' inside them. Likewise, if we apply this to the product itself, the exterior of the product appears very ordinary and it does not stand out. However, the additional text is suggesting that hidden behind an ordinary exterior, you will find a product worthy of 'a man'. The additional text at the bottom states 'Smell Better Than / Yourself'. By explicitly referencing 'smell' this refers to the product – shaving foam, aftershave and deodorant. These products are not only cleansing and beauty products, but they also have a distinct smell to them. We interpret the additional text, then, as suggesting that if you use this product, it will make you smell 'better' than who you are – presumably, make you smell like 'a man' (which in this advertisement is visually depicted as a rock star). The additional text is also in white classic font – it is simple and gets its message across clearly. The image is more complicated. In contrast, the text is simple so we understand the message immediately.

Written language:

Brand:

In contrast to the simple classic font used for the slogan and additional text, the brand name *Old Spice* is in its well-known curly font which makes it stand out. The font is immediately recognizable as being the *Old Spice* font and because it is such an established brand, we sub-consciously think it must be good because of its longevity. Being in this curly font also gives it an element of the exotic and the personal both of which are appealing to most readers. It may also allude to the idea that being 'a man' is also exotic and using this product will bring out this quality in you.

All of the text, including the brand, is inside a shield-like box. The shield suggests that the slogan and text should be viewed as a motto. A motto is usually a maxim that gives someone or something its identity that is lasting and transcends time. It has a long tradition and is a phrase that is motivating and something of which to be proud. Conveying that 'There's A Man In There' is a motto suggests that this is an undisputable fact and should be something every male is motivated to find. It is supposed to be inspiring – and it is of course a clever way to give the slogan extra significance.

Visual image:

The visual image stands out! It is humorous and is supposed to reinforce the slogan and additional text. The image is of one individual cut in half. The left-hand half is the individual in his day-clothes. In this particular advert, the male appears to be a student. He is wearing a T-shirt, a satchel and ordinary beige trousers. He is wearing glasses (often a symbol of intelligence and study) and has a sensible haircut. It appears he is in a library with a long history. There is a globe in the front right. It is the student who is holding the product, 'After Hours'. The right-hand half is presumably the student after he has used the product! He has been transformed into a rock star. He is no longer wearing a T-shirt – he is bare-chested and covered in lipstick kisses! His satchel has transformed into heavy metal guitars and a saxophone and his sensible trousers have changed into what we can only assume will be black leather trousers with a studded belt. He is no longer wearing glasses but has a black star-like drawing surrounding his eye and his sensible haircut has been transformed into long black hair billowing behind him. His face is also covered in lipstick kisses and he is sticking his tongue out. He reminds the reader of a rockstar in the vein of Gene Simmons from the 1970s American rock band Kiss. This then is the 'man' that every student is concealing and which may be revealed 'after hours' when the library is closed and after he has used the *Old Spice* product! It is a clever advertisement which works on the understanding of stereotypes but does so in a playful manner. The image is a high resolution photograph and the two halves of the individual have been Photoshopped together skilfully. This suggests that the 'man' hidden under the student garb is really there, just waiting to be released in the 'after hours'! The globe perhaps can now be viewed in a different light: perhaps this connotes all the places the rockstar 'man' is going to visit on his next world tour. Rather than finding out about the world through books and globes, the 'man' is going to experience the world first-hand.

This particular advertisement is part of a campaign – if the consumer has no yearnings to be a rockstar, then there is a similar advertisement that suggests 'a man' is an action hero. The advertisements are aimed at young male adults who may have dreams of being either a rockstar or an action hero even though in reality they are a stereotypical student or an everyday regular boy-next-door type!

Chapter 1.6

Activity 2

How does Hughes' 'The Thought Fox' offer us insights and challenges?
Step 1: Structure and form The enjambment used mirrors the idea of the process of creating a poem as being wild, free and uncontrolled. It suggests the idea that creativity is a fluid process. The four lines per stanza, however, suggests that there is some sense of order. The process of creating poetry is not a completely random arrangement of words on a page. It may be suggesting symbolically that the imagination has to run free but that somewhere there is a unifying pattern that gives the poem sense and cohesion. **Insights**: gives us insights into the creative process. Use of structure in this way is creative in itself so reinforces that this is a poem about creativity and the imagination. Insight into the idea that creating a work of art (like this poem) is not random. It takes a long time of quiet and patient waiting, reflecting perhaps. It cannot be rushed. An idea is hazy to begin with but once it becomes clear in the mind's eye, the creative process is rapid. **Challenges:** This poem suggests creativity is both wild and free whilst at the same time being disciplined. Is this possible? It also suggests the creator is not responsible for what he creates; that he is not responsible for his imagination - almost as if he is just a vessel for the imagination. Some readers will find this challenging - readers who are in awe of Hughes and think he is ultimately responsible for what he creates, rather than a 'thought fox'.
Step 2: LIFs **Language** Hughes makes incredible use of figurative language. The fox's nose touches the twig and leaf which could be a reference to a pencil (twig) and paper (leaf) - the tools of a writer (before digital literacy!) The neat prints the fox makes on the snow could be the writing on the paper, and the stumps and hollows the shapes of the letters on the page. Hughes also uses puns (clearings and eye) to show how the poem/idea almost has a life and identity of its own and comes into focus and thus becomes clearer! **Insights**: Insightful way to depict the imagination. Clever way to embed tools of writer and give them a central position within the poem. Just as fox is leaving prints in the snow, the fox is leaving its prints (its presence, identity) on the page we are reading. The creative use of language and puns is evidence that the imagination is working; that the fox has perhaps entered the hole in his head and allowed him to access his imagination. **Challenges**: Some readers may interpret this fox as a literal fox and not realise it is a symbolic fox until final stanza. If this is how we interpret the poem then it is likely the other playful uses of language will not be fully appreciated until the very end. **Images** The poem is likened to a wild fox. A fox is considered wily - it comes in its own time and cannot be tamed. It is furtive and slowly comes into vision. First its nose, then its eyes - it resembles the idea of an idea slowly taking shape. Finally, the fox at the end of the poem is fully visible like the poem itself and enters the hole in the writer's head. The poem and the writer become one.

Insights: Insightful way to describe something intangible like the imagination as something tangible like a fox. Allows the reader to understand better the abstract idea of creativity or the imagination through this physical and concrete entity of the fox. Using an extended metaphor is creative and imaginative in itself, so this is evidence that creativity exists.

Challenges: Initially we may think Hughes is simply describing an actual fox. It is not until the final stanza that we are aware this fox is not a literal fox, but is a symbolic fox.

Other features: The poem is written in the first person which gives the poem a sense of intimacy which perhaps represents the uniqueness and individuality of the creative process. The language is figurative and full of natural imagery, perhaps suggesting that the process of creating art is something elemental and that the natural world speaks to us and inspires us to create. He also uses fairly formal language which elevates the thought fox, making it seem all the more significant.

Insights: The use of language tends to heighten the importance of the imagination, suggesting its significance. The figurative language is evidence that this artwork has been consciously created and again is evidence of creativity and imagination.

Challenges: It would appear this is a carefully and consciously constructed poem - some readers would find it challenging to believe that Hughes had written it suddenly once inspiration came to him.

Step 3: Reader's response to ideas and message

The poem is perhaps about the process of creation. The poet seems almost passive in the process. At the end of the poem he states "The page is printed."

Insights: we are offered an insight into Hughes's creative process and how he viewed the imagination.

Challenges: We are challenged by the passivity of the creator; the powerlessness of the creator - just has to wait patiently for creativity to appear, cannot hurry it.

Activity 3

The first two lines of text are in a large blocked font which is capitalised. This is a similar font to the one used for Jess at the beginning of the video. It stands out and viewers cannot miss it. This gives us an **insight** into one of the underlying purposes of the video: to persuade viewers to sponsor a child. It is also a clear **challenge** to the viewer to support other children in a similar situation to Jess.

The next line of text gives the viewer the charity's website address so that viewers are enabled to donate immediately, rather than having to search up the charity's details. The website address is followed by The Smith Family's logo – this is the second time we have seen this logo and we should now recognise the red hands on the blue background as the charity's brand. These lines are also **insightful** as we are given information about the charity which we can use now (to donate) but which we will also recognise in the future. By giving us this information, it also **challenges** the viewer to do something practical with it – to donate or sponsor a child.

The final line of text is 'everyone's family'. It is in small typeface but is inclusive, suggesting no child is too small or disadvantaged to be part of the family, just as no sponsor will be turned away. It is a positive message and gives us an **insight** into the charity's ideology which, it is hoped, will be inspirational to those viewing. It also **challenges** the viewer to become part of this family by sponsoring a child.

Activity 4

Time of shift	Shift in mood, situation, perspective and/or time	Explanation
0:19	Shift in mood	Trouble-free and happy mood to troubled and sad mood
0:34	Shift in situation	Jess has to spend more time working because of her mother's debilitating illness
1:25	Shift in mood, situation and perspective	Shift in mood from depressing and overwhelming to relieved and joyful Shift in situation from living in a car to having money for Jess' education Brief shift in perspective – it is Jess' mother who discovers The Smith Family charity
2:12	Shift in time	From Jess' past to Jess' present and future

Activity 6

Genre	Online science magazine article
Audience	Audiences interested in science, but not necessarily experts in the field
Purpose	To explain to audiences what de-extinction is; to offer a personal opinion about the ethics of de-extinction

Chapter 2.1

Activity 1

Identifying context clues in adverts for similar products from different eras.

Typographical and graphological features: The font used is old fashioned and the prominent use of a the heraldic badge of the Prince of Wales is not something you would expect from a modern advert. **Visual image and layout:** ■ Models: The black child has the qualities of a racist caricature, and his blackness being 'cleaned' off reveals this to be from the past, when such racist ideas were more common and accepted. They are now unacceptable and would not be tolerated in a modern-day advert. ■ Clothing: The style of clothing is relatively formal and certainly archaic. ■ Props: The tin bath and lack of running water suggest this advert is from the past. ■ Layout and graphic design: the design is quite 'busy' and it makes use of an illustration rather than a photo, suggesting it is an older advert. The circular images mimic the circular shape of the soap. **Structure and style:** The use of formal language and advanced vocabulary such as 'complexion' suggests this is an advert from the past as modern adverts tend to use simple and straightforward language. **Context:** As you should have gathered, this text is from the past and a white-majority society – the UK in 1899.	**Typographical and graphological features:** The font is clear and defined and in a modern style. **Visual image and layout:** ■ Models: The women here have a range of skin tones, suggesting this is a representation of a multicultural society. As globalism has developed, representation of varieties of races in adverts has become common to reflect the multicultural demographics of many places. ■ Clothing: The women are in their underwear, suggesting a relaxed attitude to semi-nudity and a focus on the body. ■ Layout and graphic design: The use of high quality photography suggests this is a modern text, as does the minimalistic design and extensive use of white space. **Structure and style:** The advert uses simple, straightforward language in simple sentences that get across the information concisely. **Context:** As you should have gathered, this text is modern and from a Western multicultural society – the UK in 2005.

These adverts demonstrate how time can affect cultural attitudes and values: this same country has gone from racist caricatures to showing a range of races as equals – quite the cultural shift.

Activity 2

British English/slang	Standard English
mate	friend
skiving	avoiding going somewhere
pants	not very good
well	very
dodgy	suspicious
pillock	idiot

British English/slang	Standard English
lost the plot	does not know what one is doing
footy	football/soccer
telly	television
plastered	drunk
nicked	steal
bloke	gentleman
peng	good-looking
trainers	sneakers
give me a bell	phone me

Activity 3

1 Unlike the original ending, Nora is shown to be more emotionally fraught and doubtful. This can be seen in the stage direction 'trembling' (line 17), conveying a physical sense of fear and doubt on stage through the actor's performance. She also speaks in exclamative fragments such as 'I cannot!' (line 11) and 'Motherless …!' (line 17). In facing up to the reality and guilt of leaving her children 'motherless' her determination fades and she decides to not break away from her role as a mother, implying her innate sense of maternal care for her children overrides her need for independence and self-discovery. This reassertion of traditional gender roles and expectations reinforces the audience's belief that women are emotional by nature and defined by their motherhood.

2 Nora is shown to waver as Torvald takes the initiative and controls his wife. This is most clear in the stage directions 'seizes her arm' (line 9) and 'draws her over to the door' (line 12). The dynamic verbs 'seize' and 'draw' show Torvald as a man of action and dominance, forcing his wife to look at their children to remind her of her role as a mother. This represents the traditional power dynamic in a marriage: the man is in charge and a woman is his inferior. This is reinforced as he 'opens the door' (line 13). The original ending has Nora actively opening a door herself, symbolic of her transgressing boundaries. In the alternative ending, it is once again men who are in control of these symbolic doorways, and Torvald uses the now revealed sight of their children to control Nora. This reassertion of the patriarchy will have placated German audiences, and suggested a continuation of the status quo.

3 Ultimately, Nora fails to leave Torvald and their children and it is implied they will work through their problems and reconcile. Helmer, 'joyfully, but softly' exclaims 'Nora!' (line 23). The adverb 'joyfully' conveys Torvald's relief at Nora's submission to her maternal role. Nora, who decries not leaving as a 'sin against myself' (lines 20–21), gives Torvald a second chance. In describing it as a sin, Ibsen clearly implies there would have to be changes for the reconciliation to be successful, but the ultimate outcome is that they remain together. This is a much more conservative ending when compared to the revolutionary act of rejecting motherhood and marriage outright in the original ending, and lessens the impact and consequent debate about Nora's roles.

Activity 4

2 Vuong takes the lyrics of an iconic American song with close ties to Christmas and positivity, and then juxtaposes them with images of suffering. One prominent example is the lyric 'hear sleigh bells in the snow' followed closely by 'In the square below: a nun, on fire' (line 52). The jarring shift from 'sleigh bells' and their association with Christmas, Santa, and childhood excitement to someone burning, probably about to die, prompts the reader to reflect on the human capacity for beauty, in Christmas, and violence, in war. The religious

connotations of Christmas are also undercut by the image of the Buddhist nun suffering a violent end, and the contrast between 'snow' and 'fire' is a further reference to the extremes that coexist and conflict in the world.

3 Vuong shows how close the rescued were to being caught in the violent aftermath of the evacuation. When he writes 'a helicopter lifting the living just / out of reach' (lines 37–38) his use of enjambment puts 'out of reach' on a new line, as if the line itself is just out of reach of danger. The use of 'helicopter' is a reference to Operation Frequent Wind, adding historical detail to create authenticity to the poem. Just prior to the lines about rescue, he writes of 'snow scraping' and 'snow shredded' (line 34). The use of the violent verbs 'scraping' and 'shredded' emphasize the danger those who were rescued were in, and reminds the reader that many of those left behind suffered a violent end.

Activity 5

Models and clothing: This advert features only boys, suggesting a cultural attitude that guns are boys' toys. One is dressed as a hunter, one as a soldier, and one as a cowboy – these are stereotypically games boys play. They also suggest an open cultural attitude to guns and simulated violence.	**Model and clothing:** The design of this packaging is intended to appeal to shoppers from the toy store shelf. The product is a bow and arrow and the model used is a teenage girl dressed in casual clothes, suggesting the product is aimed primarily at girls. The model and her look is not unlike Katniss Everdeen in 'The Hunger Games' movies, perhaps as an attempt to appeal to this target market. She has long hair, partly braided with colours that complement the box art. In embracing the typically feminine trait of long hair, the product is showing that toy weapons can also be sold to conventionally feminine girls, an audience rarely targeted by toy weapons makers in the past.
Body language: The boys are in authentic-looking shooting stances, suggesting they are enjoying role-playing and that the toys are engaging products.	**Body language:** The girl is in an authentic shooting pose and has a determined facial expression, with a hint of a smile. This suggests the toy is an engaging product and, by showing the toy in action, it allows prospective buyers to imagine using it themselves.
Props: The toy guns look authentic. This reinforces the open attitude towards weaponry and suggests a culture that is accepting of simulated violence.	**Props:** The main prop is the toy itself. The bow does not look like a real weapon through its bright colours and unusual design. This perhaps suggests an aversion to accurately simulated weaponry and a mixed attitude to violence in its target market. The darts have individual patterns and designs as a way of accessorising the product, and use complementary pink, purple and white colours to appeal to girls.
Language: Here we have our most obvious historical and cultural clues – a date and a location. This advert is from 1965 and the USA. The adjective 'real-looking', once again, emphasizes the open attitude to guns in US culture.	**Language:** The name 'Rebelle' means 'rebel' in French, appealing to confident girls who wish to stand up for themselves and challenge convention. The use of French imbues a sense of class and beauty due to the French language's typical connotations, and the open vowels of 'Rebelle' make the name gentler and appealing to a female target audience. The imperative 'step up, stand out' reads as a challenge to the prospective buyer, implying a sense of 'girl power' and non-conformity in buying the product. Brief exclamatives such as 'Real bow action!' convey product information in an engaging and succinct way. The name 'Heartbreaker Bow' links the product with relationships and assertiveness, reinforcing its 'girl power' message to appeal to teen girls.
Layout and graphic design: The illustrative style and heavy use of text suggests this is an old advert – modern adverts tend to be more minimalist.	**Layout and graphic design:** The colour scheme here is traditionally more 'feminine'. In making such liberal use of pink and purple, the product aligns itself with other accessories of this colour designed for girls, and makes its target audience more obvious. The font is bold, curved and stylish, yet with sharp edges that reflect the aggressiveness of a toy weapon. The background contains other girls with different products from the same Nerf range, highlighting the social aspect of playing with the toy and encouraging further purchases. The subtle curlicues in the background create an appealing background pattern that would typically be less apparent in advertising targeted at boys.
Conclusion: USA, 1965	**Conclusion:** USA, 2013

Chapter 2.2

Activity 2

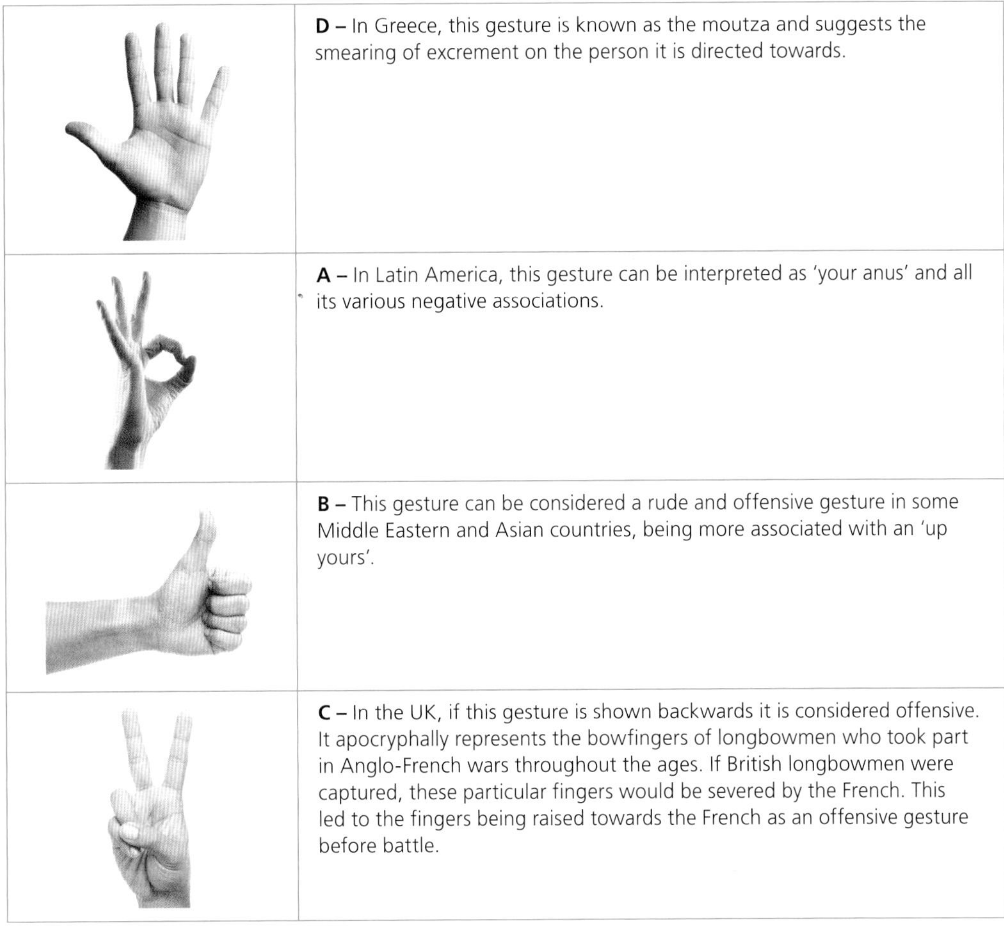

	D – In Greece, this gesture is known as the moutza and suggests the smearing of excrement on the person it is directed towards.
	A – In Latin America, this gesture can be interpreted as 'your anus' and all its various negative associations.
	B – This gesture can be considered a rude and offensive gesture in some Middle Eastern and Asian countries, being more associated with an 'up yours'.
	C – In the UK, if this gesture is shown backwards it is considered offensive. It apocryphally represents the bowfingers of longbowmen who took part in Anglo-French wars throughout the ages. If British longbowmen were captured, these particular fingers would be severed by the French. This led to the fingers being raised towards the French as an offensive gesture before battle.

As this demonstrates, approaching texts from other cultures, even if they are simply gestures, opens up the possibility of miscommunication. Without growing up with this cultural background and its shared frame of reference, you cannot always accurately interpret the gesture – that Greek fellow on holiday may not have been giving you a friendly wave!

Activity 3

1. 'Tsurezuregusa', Essays in Idleness Yoshida Kenkō, 1330–1332
2. *Memoirs of the Bloomsgrove Family*, Reverend Enos Hitchcock, 1790
3. *Rhetoric*, Aristotle, fourth century BCE
4. *The Psychology of Adolescence*, Granville Stanley Hall, 1904
5. 'A Generation with a Huge Sense of Entitlement', *Daily Mail*, 2017

Activity 6

1. Universal text features:
   - salutation and signing off – these are necessary to clarify who the letter is for and who it is from, but are often embellished to add personal detail, for example our letter uses the superlative 'Dearest' to emphasize the strength of feeling the writer has for the recipient.

- emotive language – in letters of a personal nature, there is a clear focus on the emotions to help maintain a close relationship with the recipient. This is particularly important to the example letter, as this was the only method of communication between the two lovers.
- loving pronouns – terms like 'darling' are known as terms of endearment, and again emphasize the feeling of love and attachment the writer feels for the recipient.

2 Universal themes:

- expressions of missing a loved one – unsurprisingly, the writer misses her husband-to-be, and her sense of longing permeates the entire letter.
- calling on 'God' to look after someone – this text is from a time when religion was more central to lives of the majority of Britons, and divine intervention to protect a loved one during wartime was a common feature of these kinds of letters.
- Arthur rebelling against his parents – as we have seen earlier in the chapter, younger generations rebelling against the wishes of the older generations is something anyone throughout history can relate to.

Activity 8

CGAP: 1950s UK / print advert / housewives / inform and persuade	**CGAP:** 2000s UK / print advert / general / inform and persuade
Though there are universal text features present, the way they are used reveals the texts to be from different time periods. The modern Persil advert is minimalistic, using white space to draw the reader's attention to the product. Digital manipulation has been used to show a fluid flying through the air about to create a stain, and the copy is simple: 'for whatever life throws'. This suits the modern reader and their short attention spans, and the product is not gendered showing both men and women may use the product. The old advert, by contrast, has a busy design with lots of copy. This requires time to be invested by the reader, reflecting the slower pace of life in the past. The product is gendered with references to 'women' throughout. The model in the advert is a woman next to a washing machine with her daughter holding the Persil box. This implies that wives perform domestic chores, and girls may help in the process. The copy is more detailed and features more rhetorical devices such as comparatives and exclamatives ('whiter whites', 'best in it!') and repetition of the adjective 'best' to create excitement for the product. Both these adverts together show not only a change in attitudes and values, but also a change in advertising styles over time.	

Activity 9

2 That the Abiku are born but then inevitably return to the spirit world creates grief for their worldly parents. The most obvious reference is 'the grief I had caused' (line 24). From this, the reader can infer that the parents suffer terrible hardship in losing their children so young. The listing of 'sacrifices', 'offerings', and 'blandishments' (line 23) show traditional attempts by people in the human realm to please the spirits, and is a sign of their desperation caused by suffering at the hands of the Abiku.

3 The duality of Yoruba belief is evident throughout the extract. The threshold between is referred to as a 'gateway' (line 19), a metaphor for the point of transition between the spirit and the material worlds. Binary opposition such as 'coming' and 'going' (line 11) is used to show this boundary is frequently crossed, and that Abiku exist in both realms. This is reinforced with the description of Abiku as having 'half our beings in the spirit world' (line 18) – they are a bridge between the two realms, passing through the 'interspace' (line 21) of the material and the spiritual.

Chapter 2.3

Activity 1

The next stanza centres around the narrator's child. Paralleling the livestock in the first stanza, the child is also revealed to have ended up 'dyin'' (line 26). Like the slow withering of the crops, the child had a 'cruel week in dyin'' (line 26). This painful loss of children symbolizes the uncertainty of Australia's future – if new life is so vulnerable, it will be a battle to build a flourishing future nation. There are also hints at the psychological damage caused by living in the bush and losing children at an early age with adjectives such as 'wild' and 'despairin'' (line 30). However, determination and grit is shown in having 'pulled' (line 35) through children, making clear the constant struggle against death in the bush can be overcome. The preposition 'since' before the usual refrain of being 'past carin'' (line 36) shows that this loss of children was a defining moment in the narrator's life, and it was from this point she was hardened against the suffering she encounters.

The penultimate stanza contains the adjective 'dusty' in 'dusty clearin'' (line 38) to reference the years of drought that would often wipe out crops and livestock. The reality and scale of Australia is shown in her man having gone away 'shearin'' (line 40). This refers to shearing sheep, as men would often spend long periods away from their homes herding and dealing with livestock over the vast expanse of Australia, in this case the 'great North-west' (line 41). She describes that she 'loved him best' (line 43), using the past tense to reiterate how her emotions even towards her husband have now hardened in response to life in the bush.

The final stanza ends on a poignant note, with the narrator's 'dry' (line 49) eyes symbolizing her lack of emotional response to the loss she is now inured to. Even her youngest child has run away from home, leaving her with a 'dull and empty achin'' (line 52). That she still aches, and her 'wish to be / Beyond all signs of carin'' (lines 55–56) shows that, despite her hardened shell, she still has some humanity left. This kernel of humanity perhaps shows the resilience of the human spirit, but it also evokes pathos for the woman's plight.

Activity 2

3 We can see the narrator's struggle with identity as the Aboriginal sites and land is described using the second person possessive 'your', as if the narrator does not yet feel she has a full claim over them. In showing separation both from the white people and the Aboriginal, she inhabits a transitional space in between the two, showing her mixed upbringing as an Aboriginal child in a white family's care. She makes clear that, for her, these traditions and this culture was replaced by a 'mission', a reference to the Christian religion she was brought up in after being stolen from her mother. The reference to a 'Brolga in flight' alludes to Aboriginal tales and represents her reconnection with Aboriginal culture and its oral tales which, we imagine, were denied her in the mission.

4 The symbolic importance of name is made apparent at the end of the poem. In being brought up in a different culture, the narrator was given a new name and her original Aboriginal name was never revealed to her. The moment of being given back her true name signifies her reclaiming her lost cultural heritage, and easing the 'burden' of having been away from her roots for so much of her life.

Activity 3

- **Expresses an opinion:** Sum up the opinion of the writer and explain how it may be considered surprising.

  In celebrating slums and speaking about them using language usually more associated with business, the writer offers a fresh and positive perspective on slums. Due to the writer's cultural knowledge, they are able to put the conditions in slums into context, and explain that, relative to rural Indian villages, they are good places to live.
- **Solid foundation:** Look for examples of statistical and factual evidence used to back up the writer's opinions.

The writer uses statistics such as '70% of slum households have TVs' to give more authority to their arguments by showing they are grounded in research. The statistics put slum conditions in perspective, and make the reader realize slums offer much better conditions than rural villages.

- **Clear structure:** Explain how the points the writer makes are ordered to keep the ideas clear and effective for the reader.

  The writer succinctly sums up their argument in the opening paragraph, has short and easy to follow paragraphs with clear topics and discourse markers. Sentences are straightforward and easy to follow. Includes a clear and powerful end paragraph.

- **Rhetoric:** Look for persuasive techniques in the article.

  Tripling in the headline of positive abstract nouns 'hope, progress and dignity' – statistics to appeal to logos – metaphor of 'climbing the ladder' to illustrate progress – parallel structure to convey points 'They should be objects of envy, not objects of pity' – anaphora in 'more slums, more hubs of opportunity' and 'see them as … see them as …' – use of experts in paraphrasing writers.

- **Strong ending:** Explain how the article ends with a call to arms and a clear sense of how things need to change.

  Use of imperatives through modal verb 'need' in the final paragraph, use of first person plural pronoun 'we' to encourage community action.

Activity 5

CGAP: UK 2007 / Film poster aimed at a general audience to inform and entertain.	**CGAP:** Japan 2007 / Film poster / general / inform and entertain
Models: We get a close-up of Nick Frost and Simon Pegg, two actors with a cult following in the UK, thus grabbing the attention of fans of their work. Neither particularly fits the typical, square-jawed action hero convention of the assumed genre.	**Models:** As the actors are less well-known in the Japanese market, they are instead shown in action to show how action-packed the film is. Unlike the UK poster, the film appears to be more of an action film than a comedy in this poster.
Graphic design and layout: Humour is generated through juxtaposition of action movie tropes (such as the smoking gun, the serious facial expressions, the mirrored sunglasses and the chewing of toothpicks) and images of English rural life (the bunting, the fields and the reflection of a village church in their sunglasses). This clash of American action movie culture and British rural life is reinforced with the tagline 'they are going to bust your arse' – the addition of the Britishism 'arse' subverts the typical 'bust your ass' slang of cool, slick American action heroes. Through this contrast, humour is generated and the receivers of the text understand that the film is a parody of the action movie genre. The poster is also reasonably simple and focused, typical of modern advertising in the West.	**Graphic design and layout:** The poster uses the Union Flag as well as Big Ben in the background to show how British the film is, something which may appeal to a Japanese audience. As the actors are not well-known, they are shown with guns in various states of action, reinforced by an explosion in the background. The heavy use of text reflects the more dense information often included in Japanese advertising.

Chapter 2.4

Activity 2

(a) The song follows a question – answer pattern, with a father asking his son about what he has seen out in the world. This inter-generational aspect of the poem immediately gets the listener considering ideas of legacy and the future – the image of the next generation heading out into the world whilst the older generation sits back represents the world left by the old being discovered by the young. This, of course, is an example of a universal theme, and in this context, many young people see pollution and climate change as a consequence of the previous generation's lack of care for the planet and their wasteful lifestyles, with the younger generation being left to deal with the consequences. The personification of 'sad forests' and 'dead oceans' suggest the ecological damage caused by rising sea temperatures and a shifting climate.

(b) The image of a 'newborn baby' surrounded by 'wolves' is a clear symbol of the weak and innocent being preyed on by the corrupt and powerful. The baby could represent the children of places like Bangladesh that will be badly affected by climate change, or the younger generations that are being left defenceless to the future ravages of climate. The image of men with 'hammers a-bleedin' represents industry and the damage it is doing to the planet. This is reinforced by 'black branch with blood', with the plosive alliteration creating an aggressive tone that suggests the violence being done to branches, symbols of nature. The white ladder 'covered with water' creates an image of flooding, and the 'guns' in the hands of small children relate to the predictions of conflict as natural resources become increasingly scarce.

(c) The final verse has images of a world once climate change has caused further damage to the planet. The 'hard rain' refers to the acid rain caused by pollution. The many people with 'empty' hands shows the humanitarian disaster that would follow as millions starve to death due to the effects of flooding and drought. References to 'black' and 'poison' reference the pollution spreading throughout the planet, with the 'well-hidden' executioner's face reflecting the difficulty of dealing with climate change – it is not one 'executioner' but a collective failing of people living environmentally damaging lives. The ultimate ending of the poem, with the son sinking in the ocean, shows the rising seas wiping out humanity.

Activity 4

The writer is clearly thankful for the existence of the guide. His use of the adjective 'ernest [sic]' when describing the writer's 'efforts' shows his belief in the good intentions of the writer and imply that the guide is a worthy cause. He goes as far as saying its production is a 'credit to the Negro race', showing that such endeavours are a point of pride for the African-American community as their people increasingly enter the middle class and become entrepreneurs and writers.

The letter writer reflects the divisions in 1930s America in a few different ways. He makes clear that *The Negro Motorist Green Book* exists in contrast to the AAA (the American Automobile Association, which also produced a guide book) which is aimed at the 'white race'. The idea that each race needs its own guide makes clear that race plays a fundamental part in how travel is experienced, and implies that the AAA guide is unsuitable for African-Americans due to the prevalence of racist attitudes throughout the country. The writer also makes use of collective plural pronouns such as 'us' and 'our' to convey a sense of community and camaraderie between African-Americans, and makes clear the readership's shared experience in travel and needing of the book. This also implies that they exist separately from the 'other' of white America.

Chapter 2.5

Activity 1

In one of these panels we can more clearly see her guides in India. They both have symbolic significance: an elephant is a creature that is important to Indian culture, in particular as one of their Gods, Ganesh; her other guide is the Indian national bird, an Indian peacock. Both are anthropomorphized. They take her on a tour of Rajasthan and introduce her to its cultural practices. She is introduced to the food and festivals of this culture that have been lost to her, and each is named using Indian words such as 'dosa', 'sitafal', 'jamun', 'pichu' and the 'Holi' festival. Some of these terms demand research, but many of them used are included in a glossary found at the end of the graphic novel. In doing so, Chanani is making clear that the text is there to educate audiences about Indian culture in much the same way as Pri is being educated by her guides. When she experiences the Holi festival, she beams with joy as she says it is better when 'everyone plays', suggesting she feels a sense of belonging as cultural practices are now shared, unlike in

America where few others understood. When asked whether she has tried the Indian food before, she repeatedly says 'no', showing that yet another aspect of the culture she is descended from is opening up to her.

Activity 2

(c) This poem begins with a series of binary oppositions, emphasizing the traditional dichotomies we expect as human beings. The arrows, also both opposing each other, meet in the middle and cease to exist as they slice the void – this brings to mind a sense of oneness, of the oppositions earlier in the poem merging and cancelling each other out, illustrating the sense of moving beyond our material existence and understandings and instead going back to 'source'. Death is an opportunity to return from whence we came, not a final ending.

(d) This poem shows the struggle and ephemerality of life by describing it as 'frost' on a summer's day, something destined to disappear quickly. This ending of life changes frost to 'water' – something that can re-enter the earth in a different form to what it was before, much as his spirit moves into another realm in another form. The washing of the brush perhaps demonstrates the purity of death, wiping out all the struggles of life and leaving things cleansed.

(e) Again, our oppositional understanding of the world is expressed in this poem. The 'coming' and 'going' symbolizing life and death are shown to be one and the same, things that became entangled in life cease to be tangled in death. The adjective 'simple' in 'simple happenings' expresses an understanding and clear perspective of life, demystifying his release from it. All the stress and complication of life is now something he can move beyond. In entering life 'empty-handed' and leaving 'barefoot' we once again have a sense of purity and lack of adornment that shows a peace with death, and a cyclical pattern to the process. His nakedness also conveys the meaninglessness of material objects.

Chapter 2.6

Activity 1

'Now then, Freddy: look where you're going, dear.'

'There's manners for you! Two bunches of violets trodden into the mud.'

'Oh, he's your son is he? Well, if you had done your duty by him as a mother should, he'd know better than to spoil a poor girl's flowers than to run away without paying. Will you pay me for them?'

Activity 3

(c) The English use of 'gracious living' (line 26) and the reference to the American 'Great Society' (line 28) (a set of domestic programs enacted in the USA by President Lyndon B. Johnson in the 1960s) are both examples of American wealth being used to create better lives, and an implication that Canadians need to embrace the English language and the American way of doing things to have similar benefits. Subsequently, the English speakers are characterized as the 'foremen' (line 30), the people symbolically in charge of the work sites. Contrastingly, the Francophones are hard of hearing from living 'too close to the machines' (line 32). This is the master-servant dynamic between the two languages and cultures in microcosm. Due to the lower socioeconomic status of French Canada, where the economy was not as strong as English-speaking areas like Ontario, many people had tough, working-class jobs. This inferior position creates resentment as they are told what to do by the foremen in English, not French, and their suffering seems to go unrecognized.

(d) English words then start to assert themselves over the French as we get a series of lines in English. American slang such as 'big shot' (line 44) is used to show American culture being forced on French Canadians, and the language of business with jargon such as 'production profits' (line 47) makes clear that, in order to have American-style economic success, they are expected to adopt the American English language of business. The pun of English being a 'rich' (line 49) language references both culture but also capitalism, but this is characterized as negative with the anaphoric 'but for' preceding the 'selling your soul' and 'selling out' (lines 51–53). For this economic success, the deal is that they give up their culture and their identity, they let English take over and English-language companies enact a kind of economic colonialism in Québec.

Chapter 3.1

Activity 1

3 In *Wuthering Heights* by Emily Brontë, the writer utilizes elements of the gothic fiction literary tradition in order to evoke specific emotive responses from the reader. For example, when the novel's narrator, Lockwood, is spending his first night at 'Thrushcross Grange', he has a nightmare wherein he hallucinates the ghostly apparition of the Grange's former owner, Catherine, trying to enter his bedroom via the window. Lockwood describes how, 'Terror made me cruel; and, finding it useless to attempt shaking the creature off, I pulled its wrist on to the broken pane, and rubbed it to and fro till the blood ran down and soaked the bedclothes.' Here, the writer uses conventions commonly found in gothic works to shock and horrify the reader. For example, the violence here is graphic and sensory language is used to add clarity to the brutality of the narrator's actions, for example, through the usage of descriptive verbs such as 'pulled', 'rubbed' and 'soaked'. The polysyndetic listing used in the description builds the image gradually in the reader's imagination, gradually increasing their feeling of horror. Gothic fiction often harnesses the power of the horror and fear of a reader to create impact, and the writer here does this effectively to ensure a lingering atmosphere of unease as the reader continues with the novel.

'Porphyria's Lover' by Robert Browning also utilizes graphic and sensory language to evoke an emotive response from the reader. At the end of the first half of the poem, the speaker describes murdering his lover 'Porphyria' in the quote,

'In one long yellow string I wound

Three times her little throat around,

And strangled her.'

Like in *Wuthering Heights*, the writer of the poem also uses the sensory language of the colour 'yellow' (which perhaps links to traditional aesthetics associated with Christian angels connoting the innocence and naivety of Porphyria) and the active verbs of 'wound' and 'strangled' to effectively bring the reader uncomfortably close to the violent murder of Porphyria. The premodifying adjective of 'little' before 'throat' also symbolizes the child-like nature of Porphyria thus heightening the horror the reader feels while reading the description of her murder. Like in *Wuthering Heights* the use of these techniques are designed for impact upon the reader, and the reader after reading this part of the poem will alter their perspective of the speaker of the poem which may previously have been more positive. In both of the works, these violent actions are committed by powerful men against vulnerable women and this is representative of patriarchal values prevalent at the time when the works were written, reflecting perhaps a desire of men to fully control women they perceive as threatening their power.

Chapter 3.2

Activity 6

1 The plot of the work tells the story of Ayoola, sister of Korede, who has killed many of her past boyfriends. After she commits the murders, she enlists her sister to help her avoid being caught and charged for the crimes. In this extract there are clear elements of gothic fiction used, for example, the reference to blood (belonging to Ayoola's most recent victim, Femi) through the image of the 'bloody napkin down the back of the sofa'. The appearance of the napkin, evidence from their clean-up of Femi's body, is symbolic of the guilt that follows Korede in the aftermath of helping her sister. Coupled with the pathetic fallacy of the 'hot day', there is a tension that pervades the extract, making the reader wonder not if, but when the sisters will be exposed for their crime. The blood motif and the utilization of tension are both conventions that would be associated with the gothic fiction genre. However, there are some conventions that Braithwaite has modified that evolves the usual genre conventions of gothic fiction. For example, in works belonging to this genre, women are usually presented as the victims of acts of violence committed by men and are often depicted as being wholly reliant on male authoritarian figures to save them from these acts of violence. However, Braithwaite has created a female character who is actually the perpetrator of the violence and the person who she relies on to help her avoid the consequences of her crimes is another woman, her sister. This atypical representation of female characters as uncontrollably violent (Ayoola) and calculated (Korede) could be a response to the one-dimensional way in which women are often presented in earlier examples of gothic fiction, a representation that is no longer acceptable to many women today. Similarly, the tone of usual works of gothic fiction are usually serious and earnest in tone whereas Ayoola's nonchalance towards her crimes can be ironically humorous, 'Defending myself; the judge will understand that, right?' This blasé response to the potential consequence of her acts of murder could be seen to parody the attitudes of violent and abusive men in earlier examples of gothic/horror fiction who display a similar callous attitude towards their female victims. By parodying this attitude, it is clear that there is a hypocrisy inherent in some literature that while abuse and violence towards women is normalized and therefore not as shocking to the reader, violence and abuse towards men is unusual and therefore more shocking. This could be a response to a societal shift towards what is sometimes seen as the overly gratuitous depiction of violence against women within books, films, music and other sources of entertainment – a depiction that women are increasingly beginning to question.

2 In Adichie's TED talk 'The Danger of a Single Story', she describes how when she went to university in America, 'My American roommate was shocked by me. She asked where I had learned to speak English so well, and was confused when I said that Nigeria happened to have English as its official language. She asked if she could listen to what she called my 'tribal music', and was consequently very disappointed when I produced my tape of Mariah Carey. She assumed that I did not know how to use a stove. What struck me was this: She had felt sorry for me even before she saw me. Her default position toward me, as an African, was a kind of patronizing, well-meaning pity. My roommate had a single story of Africa: a single story of catastrophe.' In this extract we can see that Braithwaite has subverted stereotypical representations of Nigeria as described by Adichie. For example, she clearly conveys that the characters belong to an urban, middle-class demographic that is wholly familiar to those living in similar circumstances in the West. She refers to the luxuries of such a lifestyle in the form of access to smartphones and social media, 'it's all there on Snapchat', staff that help with domestic chores, 'Femi's family sent a cleaner to his home' and a home which is big enough

for the sisters to have separate bedrooms which are also big enough to contain a 'dressing table'. It is clear that Korede has a professional occupation working in a hospital (the rest of the novel reveals that she is a nurse) which also subverts stereotypes about the 'single story' of Africa described by Adichie where her American roommate presumed that all Africans lived a pastoral, tribal existence.

3 Braithwaite includes many examples of non-Standard English in the extract. She uses colloquial, conversational English in some parts of the extract – 'the judge will understand that, right?' which helps to authentically replicate the style of speech that would most likely be used between two, young, urban sisters. Also, Braithwaite includes the use of the Yoruba language in the middle of the English being spoken between Korede and her 'ma' – 'Jésù ṣàánú fún wa o' which translates as 'Jesus loves you'. Again, this lends authenticity to the characters as it is likely that a middle-class family in Lagos, Nigeria would code-switch between English and another language native to Nigeria naturally in the course of conversation. If Standard English was used throughout this extract, the two pieces of dialogue would seem unrealistic and wouldn't effectively convey the culture and identity of the characters.

As previously stated, Adichie's TED lecture 'The Danger of a Single Story' is one of the top-ten most viewed TED talks of all time. What is it that makes this lecture so effective?

Adichie uses many language and structural techniques in order to convey ideas and messages about the danger of narrow representations of people and groups to the reader persuasively and powerfully. She begins by creating pathos, using a humorous, ironic anecdote about her childhood in order to emotionally connect with her audience- 'All my characters were white and blue-eyed, they played in the snow, they ate apples, and they talked a lot about the weather, how lovely it was that the sun had come out. Now, this despite the fact that I lived in Nigeria.' Adichie makes the point here that despite living in Nigeria where the vast majority of people are not 'white and blue-eyed', this was the most common way in which she represented the characters in her writing as this was the representation of characters that she was most commonly exposed to in her own reading. Adichie also repeatedly uses the first person pronoun 'I' to convey to the reader how personal this story is, thus making it more emotional and more powerful for the reader- important when considering that Adichie is making a serious point about how the lack of diversity in her reading impacted the construction of her own identity.

Adichie also establishes ethos throughout her lecture. Her opening line uses the declarative, 'I'm a storyteller.' The short-sentence is simultaneously authoritative in tone and self-deprecating considering that Adichie is an incredibly successful novelist. This establishes her credibility with the audience as the impression is given that Adichie does not need to elaborate upon her credentials as a 'storyteller'. Adichie also reveals to the reader that she, herself, is guilty of placing people within a 'single story' representation (which she is speaking out against), 'All I had heard about them was how poor they were, so that it had become impossible for me to see them as anything else but poor. Their poverty was my single story of them.' This encourages the audience to believe that since Adichie herself knows how easy it is use stereotypes when constructing the identity of a person or place she is perhaps well-placed to speak about the ills of this.

Adichie's lecture also has intellectual appeal (logos) through her use of a clear, logical and easy-to-follow argument- she uses clear topic sentences for every section of her lecture, alongside conjunctions and connectives that add fluency and cogency to her arguments. She also clearly focuses upon a few key themes in her lecture (stereotypes and the power of literature/storytelling in representation and identity) and uses them as the foundation on which to build the rest of her speech, ensuring ultimate clarity when conveying her ideas about these themes to the reader.

Chapter 3.4

Activity 4

1 As the novel was written in the Victorian era, there could not be any graphic or explicit description of the act of sexual violence perpetrated by Alec against Tess. The language used to describe the actual act is figurative and ambiguous, 'Why it was that upon this beautiful feminine tissue, sensitive as gossamer, and practically blank as snow as yet, there should have been traced such a coarse pattern as it was doomed to receive.' By metaphorically referring to Tess as 'beautiful feminine tissue' and to Alec's act of sexual violence as 'a coarse pattern', Hardy is able to implicitly describes the rape as an act of violation without offending Victorian sensibilities (though it is worth mentioning that the book was still censored and considered immoral in its Victorian context). The ambiguity in the description of the act also suggests that maybe Tess was not raped at all but was seduced by Alec. This could provide potentially two interpretations – one that in the writer's view, the seduction of a character as innocent and naive as Tess is an act of violation that cannot be separated from rape. It could also, or alternatively, suggest that Tess consented to this sexual liaison with Alec which would have been shocking to a Victorian era reader who would be likely to see a sexual relationship outside of marriage as immoral, but also may have been made uneasy at the suggestion of a woman having sexual agency.

2 The witnessing of Elizabeth Martha Brown's execution is a significant event to consider when interpreting the extract. In the extract Tess is depicted as innocent. She is referred to metaphorically as a 'jaded animal' which portrays as prey, at the mercy of Alec the predator. White colour imagery is often used in conjunction with her character, she is described as 'moonlit' and 'blank as snow', for example, and this colour traditionally connotes to purity. Thomas Hardy was haunted by the execution of Elizabeth Martha Brown and may have felt that her sentence was unjust considering the exacerbating factors in the murder of her violent and abusive husband. This may have contributed to his construction of Tess as an innocent figure within the novel and the extract.

3 A feminist reading of the extract may focus on the presentation of Tess as being wholly vulnerable to the sexual advances of Alec. Feminists may balk at the presentation of Tess as frail, weak and utterly helpless in the attack. By metaphorically referring to Tess as 'beautiful feminine tissue' she is objectified and connoted as easily broken. The use of sexual violence against a woman as a literary tool through which to explore a man's perspective about society may also be of concern to a feminist reader who may see this as a trivialization of the very serious issue of rape. They may also be concerned by the ambiguity in the description of the act of sexual violence as it plays into harmful stereotypes about consent.

A Marxist reading of the extract may focus on the class power dynamics presented in the extract through the relationship between Alec and Tess. Throughout the extract, Alec is described as being in control, 'D'Urberville stooped; and heard a gentle regular breathing. He knelt and bent lower, till her breath warmed his face, and in a moment his cheek was in contact with hers. She was sleeping soundly, and upon her eyelashes there lingered tears.' The semantic field of action being committed by Alec towards the insentient Tess suggests his power over her – power he derives wholly from his status as a member of the upper classes. Alec's ability to subsume Tess in the act of sexual violence is a microcosm of class hierarchy in

Victorian era England where the upper classes in society had the power to wholly control and subjugate the lower classes through financial and social capital.

A psychoanalytical reading of the work would focus on Alec's Freudian desire to control Tess completely – the intimidating natural imagery used in the extract symbolizes the power that he yearns to exert over her, 'Darkness and silence ruled everywhere around. Above them rose the primeval yews and oaks of The Chase'. This culminates in the ultimate assertion of power through his act of rape. The ambiguity in the description of the act of sexual violence, which may suggest that Tess actually consented to the sexual liaison with Alec, also links to ideas about the subconscious; that the repression of female sexual desires in the Victorian era led to women pushing their sexual desire to their subconscious which Tess acts out in this extract.

Chapter 3.5

Activity 1

	Similarity between *If This is a Man* by Primo Levi and *The Diary of a Young Girl* by Anne Frank
Perspective	Both of the writers are Jewish and are being persecuted under the Nazi regime. Even though they are of a different nationality, age and gender their writings are bound by their joint, first-hand experience of what it was like to live, and to try and continue living, under a political system and ideology that wanted to eradicate them and anyone else belonging to their race and/or religion.
Context	Both of the writers experienced the events of the Holocaust first-hand during the time when they occurred. Even though Levi wrote his account of the Holocaust many years after it ended, the events detailed within the work occurred roughly around the same time of those detailed in Frank's. They are unified in having this shared context of experience that is, as years pass by, becoming rarer and harder to find.
Structure	Even though *If This is a Man* is prose and *The Diary of a Young Girl* is a diary, they are both personal, first-hand forms of writing. *If This is a Man* is autobiographical in nature and even though it is literary in its style, it still recounts actual events that happened to the writer in a first-person narration. Both of the sources are, as a result, intensely personal and allow the reader to also experience the events described more fully as they are told through the eyes of someone who actually experienced them and who can convey the full range of thoughts and feelings connected with them.
Stylistic features	Both of the writings, even if not intended in *The Diary of a Young Girl*, are highly emotive and thought-provoking. Levi intentionally crafted his writing for emotional impact by using figurative language to help convey his thoughts and feelings with clarity to the reader and to make them as relatable as possible. The simple vocabulary and expression used by Frank helps to remind the reader of Frank's youth – she was only 13 years old when she wrote *The Diary of a Young Girl*. Her innocence and vulnerability is obvious when reading the extract, making the writing a poignant read when the reader considers the fear and pressure she must have been experiencing when she was writing the diary. This similarity in both sources' emotive style of writing helps to convey how the terrible consequences of extreme ideologies can touch everyone in society regardless of age.

Activity 2

1 *Burmese Days* by George Orwell and 'Sixteen Dead Men' by W.B Yeats could be seen as diverse in a number of ways. For example, the two sources are written in two different forms – *Burmese Days* is prose and 'Sixteen Dead Men' is poetry. They also deviate from each other in the way in which they convey their criticism of British colonialism. The writer of *Burmese Days* implicitly symbolizes this criticism through the characterization of Flory, for example, through his desperate decision to kill himself rather than face continuing to live in the isolating and dehumanizing system of the British colonial administration of Burma – 'Flory pulled the trigger with his thumb'. Whereas, the writer of 'Sixteen Dead Men' directly challenges those who suggest ceasing revolutionary activities calling for the end of British rule in Ireland – 'You say that we should still the land Till Germany's overcome; But who is there to argue that Now Pearse is deaf and dumb?' The story of *Burmese Days* is narrated in a third person perspective where the reader is positioned outside of the action, a deliberate decision by Orwell to encourage the reader to critique the British system of colonial power rationally as an outsider.

'Sixteen Dead Men', instead, is written directly to the reader, questioning their perspective and directly appealing for them to take action as part of the Irish Nationalist cause. It is also worth noting that the two works were written in different contexts and from different perspectives, *Burmese Days* was written by a Briton about Burma in 1934 and 'Sixteen Dead Men' was written by an Irishman about Ireland in 1916 (though the poem wasn't published until 1920).

2 However, the two works are similar in the way that they both explore the brutality and the violent consequences of the British system of colonial power. For example, in *Burmese Days* Flory also kills his dog, Flo, rather than leave him to live not only without Flory but within the colonial administration in Burma – 'She crawled very slowly towards his feet, flat on her belly, whining, her head down as though afraid to look at him. When she was a yard away he fired, blowing her skull to fragments.' The graphic violence enacted against the innocent animal here is a symbolic microcosm of the violence that is enacted against innocent people in the process of colonial systems of power. The fact that Flory is able to kill the dog at all is symbolic of how living within a colonial society has inured him to violence and destruction of life. A similar sentiment is conveyed in 'Sixteen Dead Men' through its naming of the sixteen men executed in the aftermath of the Easter Uprising in Ireland and other Irish revolutionaries executed by the British – 'Pearse', 'MacDonagh', 'Lord Edward' and 'Wolfe Tone'. The deaths of these men, and the violence meted out to them by the British, act as metaphors for the wider brutality of British rule in Ireland – brutality that Yeats utilizes as a reason for not scaling down revolutionary activities even in war time and for not engaging in dialogue with the British. An understanding of these similarities is important in constructing a reader response towards the issue of British colonial rule in the early part of the twentieth century. Despite the differences in context and perspective, the writers of both works are unified in their presentation of British colonial rule as brutal and violent. This helps to support a contemporary and alternative interpretation of the ills of European colonization around the world, in opposition to the positive way it was largely depicted in works and texts at the time.

Activity 3

1 The *Stranger Things* advert has been constructed deliberately as a pastiche of the *Firestarter* advert. The writer of the *Stranger Things* advert replicates elements of the *Firestarter* advert, for example its use of symbols, characterization and graphology. In the *Stranger Things* advert, the character of Eleven is depicted by the writer using the same symbols as in the *Firestarter* advert, for example, she has an aura of light glowing around her and she is surrounded by the debris of the parallel 'world' that she is able to access because of her powers in psychokinesis. The graphology used in the *Stranger Things* advert is also similar in style to that used in the *Firestarter* advert – especially in terms of typography and layout. However, the writer of the *Stranger Things* advert has also changed and modernized elements that are used in the *Firestarter* advert in order to make the poster appropriate for its contemporary audience. For example, in the *Stranger Things* advert the colour imagery is more muted and the background image is less sensational than that of the *Firestarter* advert. Also, there is far less written text in the *Stranger Things* advert when compared to the *Firestarter* advert. By utilizing a pastiche of the *Firestarter* advert, the writer of the *Stranger Things* advert is able to celebrate the stylistic aspects of 1980s popular culture which audiences enjoy while also being able to change aspects to create a unique and contextually appropriate original text.

2 The *Firestarter* print advert could be seen as an allusion to Painting of 'Elijah Taken up in a Chariot of Fire'. For example, the depiction of Charlie as she walks away from the fire that she has created to burn down the Government facility mirrors the depiction of Elijah riding his chariot of fire into Heaven. Fire is used symbolically in both sources to connote strength and to act as a defence against 'evil'. Elijah in the painting and Charlie in the advert are both depicted to have an aura of light surrounding them which connotes to the purity of their action to use fire as a show of power against sinister forces. Elijah in the painting is sat on a chariot of fire that is ascending to Heaven and Charlie is depicted in the advert as walking away from a fire that she has created with her mind. These are both inexplicable events that connote to the ethereal nature of both Elijah and Charlie, suggesting that their actions and abilities have been allowed or created by a higher power. The biblical allusion adds depth to the characterization of Charlie in the advert. By linking her character and actions to that of a biblical figure, it suggests that her story has a wider meaning and significance than what may be superficially assumed.

Chapter 3.6

Check for understanding

Genre	Photojournalism – the photograph has been taken to report on the devastation caused by the atomic bombing of Hiroshima in 1945.
Audience	Once of the benefits of photojournalism is its capacity to transcend language barriers (as there is no written text) and so the photograph could be easily distributed to a worldwide, international audience.
Purpose	The photograph could have a variety of purposes. Perhaps the photograph could be used simply to inform its reader of the huge devastation caused by the atomic bomb. It could also be used more politically as a warning to enemies of the USA (the country who used the bomb) about the consequences that can befall a nation who is at war with the USA. It could also, be used to generate pathos for Japan and its people – the photograph clearly depicts the scope of the devastation wrought upon the landscape of Japan and this would perhaps make some readers feel pity for the nation and people who had to experience this devastation first hand.
Other features of text type	The photograph is shot in a black and white colour. Though colour photography was still only burgeoning at the time that the photograph was taken, it may have been a deliberate choice by the photographer to use black and white colouring to take this photo. Certainly, the decision to develop the photograph so that the nature that should be surrounding the building is a dark, black colour is deliberate. This ironic depiction of nature which should be vibrant and which is now blackened and dead is a clear depiction of the unnatural consequences of the atomic bomb. The photograph is almost panoramic, taking in a wide angled shot of the building and the landscape that surrounds it. It is stark in its simplicity. All that can be seen by the reader is the ground, the remains of the building and the sky. The layout feels empty and barren, almost lifeless. The absence of any human or animal form within the photograph also contributes to this feeling of lifelessness – connoting to the reader that the bomb has destroyed all life that has come into its vicinity. The central focus of the photo, to which the reader's gaze is drawn, is the destroyed building. This is seemingly the only building that has survived the devastation of the bomb and even this is in complete ruins. It would, perhaps, be unbelievable to a reader that a once thriving city has been reduced to this one building. The building, therefore, could act as a metaphor for the fragility of the physical societies that we build around us and is a powerful reminder of how easily the things that we, as humans, build and create over time can be destroyed so easily.

Check for understanding

Genre	Opinion article – the article has been written to convey the writer's opinion regarding the perceived flaws in the Korean to English translation of Han Kang's novel 'The Vegetarian'.
Audience	The opinion article is published in an American-based news website and so you could surmise that the intended audience is primarily America-based. However, the online news platform gives readers all over the world the opportunity to access the article. As the article focuses on the issue of translation in literature, it may be of particular interest to people who are also interested in the literary arts. Similarly, the focus specifically on Korean to English translation could be of interest to those who are proficient in both languages.
Purpose	The purpose of the opinion article is primarily to convey the opinion of the writer to the reader – that though the Korean to English translation is imperfect in places, it shouldn't detract from a reader's enjoyment of the novel and that the benefits gained from the translation far outweigh any of the negatives. However, the article also aims to persuade the reader to agree with their opinion while entertaining them.

Other features of text type	The writer of the opinion article utilizes a conversational tone- for example by using examples of internal dialogue '"Fantasic!" I thought' and idioms 'Smith's mistranslations are something of a red herring.' This helps to keep the discussion of the topic, which is quite complex and sophisticated, lively and engaging which encourages readers to fully engage with the writer's opinion regarding the issue. The writer also includes examples of linguistic terminology 'Smith amplifies Han's spare, quiet style and embellishes it with adverbs, superlatives and other emphatic word choices that are nowhere in the original' and refers to other works in translation '*The Vegetarian* may not be a masterpiece like *Cathay* but like *Cathay* it has morphed into a "new creation"'. This helps to lend credibility to her argument that the benefits of the translation outweigh the negatives – as someone who is proficient and has good knowledge of Korean, English, linguistics and works in translation then the reader will feel like her opinion on this topic is one that they can trust.
	The writer also skilfully uses figurative language throughout the opinion article to synthesise the complex issues involved in transformation via translation – 'imagine the plain, contemporary style of Raymond Carver being garnished with the elaborate diction of Charles Dickens'. But utilizing an analogy that many readers of the article will recognise, the writer of the article is able to convey clearly what she sees as the pitfalls of translation in literature – that often the translation, while conveying the correct vocabulary to a reader, can completely change the style and essence of the work. By synthesising this complex idea into an easy to understand analogy, the writer ensures maximum clarity for their reader in the comprehension of this idea. The article is structured clearly and logically and the writer methodically counters the arguments that various scholars and literary critics have made regarding their perceived inaccuracies within the translation. By introducing the criticism and then countering it with their own argument, the writer makes clear to the reader, and perhaps convinces the audience, that this act of transformation via translation, though imperfect, is still better than the work not being translated at all, limiting its readership.

Acknowledgements

The Publishers would like to thank Ebony Burnside for her valuable comments and review of the manuscript.

From Lindsay Tandy: Thank you to my fellow co-writers, Alice and Joseph, who have helped make this such a memorable experience! Thanks to Carrie for her guidance and advice. Thanks to the Hodder crew whose patience is limitless: So-Shan, Rachel, Aileen and Rong. Thank you to Paul Hoang who started the ball rolling. Thanks to Gill who provided a room, shelves full of books and lots of sustenance that Christmas I was sourcing material. And finally a huge thank you to Carlos, Inez and Benjamin whose unending support, encouragement and oodles of love made this journey possible.

From Alice Gibbons: I would like to thank my friends Janice Carmichael, Alice Gould, Lawrence Thompson, Kate Turbo, Sarah Gez and Snowy Baker in Hong Kong for the food, drink and their endless patience (while listening to what must have been incredibly tedious monologues) throughout the process of writing this book. Without Aaron Morris' charitable and unwavering dedication to 'the cause' during my time at Wright Robinson College then I would never have been in a position to write this book in the first place. I also need to thank Sha Tin College's English department – their gallows humour is always balanced with an unbelievable level of professionalism and expertise, and no group of people both challenge and make me laugh more.

I especially thank my fellow Hodder Hunniez and co-authors, Lindsay and Joe, for helping me reach the finish line even when it seemed like they might have to drag me there, I couldn't have done it without you both. Thank you also to the team at Hodder, our overall editor and our proof-readers (namely So-Shan, Rachel, Carrie, Aileen and Rong) for all of your invaluable support over the past year.

I dedicate my section of this book to my parents (Marguerite and Robert) and my sisters (Sarah and Helen) who have loved, supported and gave me everything they could for over thirty years. As one of my dad's favourite sayings would go, there are many crimes for which they would have received a lesser sentence. Finally, I also dedicate my section to James Legge – in the words of Alex Turner, 'with the exception of you I dislike everyone in the room'.

From Joseph Koszary: With particular thanks to Lindsay, without whom this opportunity may not have come my way, and a special thanks to Carolyn for her unwavering guidance and support. Thanks to Alice for her friendship and support, and thanks to everyone behind the scenes, including So-Shan, Rachel, Aileen and Rong. I'd also like to thank the long suffering Frankie for her patience.

Photo credits

The Publishers would like to thank the following for permission to reproduce copyright material. Every effort has been made to trace all copyright holders, but if any have been inadvertently overlooked, the Publishers will be pleased to make the necessary arrangements at the first opportunity.

p.5 © Pixabay; **p.7** © https://commons.wikimedia.org/wiki/File:A_true_report_of_certaine_wonderfull_ouerflowings_of_waters,1607.jpg, https://creativecommons.org/publicdomain/zero/1.0/; **p.11** © tech_studio/stock.adobe.com; **p.12** © Rudie/stock.adobe.com; **p.16** © 02irina/stock.adobe.com; **p.19** © https://commons.wikimedia.org/wiki/File:Bibleplacedkkk.jpg/https://creativecommons.org/publicdomain/zero/1.0/; **p.21** © Bazmark Films/Warner Bros/Kobal/Shutterstock; **p.35** © Adrienne/stock.adobe.com; **p.40** © J. Vespa/WireImage/Getty Images; **p.41** Cartoon by Steve Nease, neasecartoons.com. Used by permission; **p.50** © Jiti Chadha/Alamy Stock Photo; **p.62** © Nilufer Demir/AFP/Getty Images; **p.63** © Nilufer Demir/AFP/Getty Images; **p.65** © Nick Ut/AP/Shutterstock; **p.76** © Sutton Hibbert/Shutterstock; **p.86** *t* © Encyclopaedia Britannica, *b* © Encyclopaedia Britannica; **p.95** © UN Women. Produced in 2015; **p.104** Copyright of The University of Manchester; **p.116** © Jeremy sutton-hibbert/Alamy Stock Photo; **p.117** © Alvaroc/stock.adobe.com; **p.120** Images reprinted with permission from *The Arrival* by Shaun Tan, Hachette Australia, 2006; **p.123** © Duncan Bryceland/Shutterstock; **p.124** Images reprinted with permission from *The Arrival* by Shaun Tan, Hachette Australia, 2006; **p.126** © INTERFOTO/Fine Arts/Alamy Stock Photo; **p.135** © Warren K. Leffler/Granger Historical Picture Archive/Alamy Stock Photo; **p.143**

Graphic Novel Excerpt from *Cook Korean!: A Comic Book with Recipes: A Cookbook* by Robin Ha, copyright © 2016 by Robin Ha. Illustrations copyright © 2016 by Robin Ha. Used by permission of Ten Speed Press, an imprint of Random House, a division of Penguin Random House LLC. All rights reserved; **p.146** © Beeton, Mrs. (Isabella Mary), 1836–1865; **p.164** © Schemev/stock.adobe.com; **p.165** *t Eomji Dick*. Courtesy of the Amazon Turk workers, *b* Xu, Bing, *Book from the Ground: Windows OLE object*, figure: first three chapters as listed in the Table of Contents, © 2014 Xu Bing, by permission of The MIT Press.; **p.172** © Agf/Shutterstock; **p.176** © Azoor Photo Collection/Alamy Stock Photo; **p.178** © Photo Researchers/ Science History Images/Alamy Stock Photo; **p.185** *(all photos)* Q Magazine/ H Bauer Publishing'. Photography: N/A; **p.197** Photographer: Jeff Minton; **p.199** Photographer: Jean-Yves Lemoigne; **p.226** https://commons.wikimedia.org/wiki/ File:Daddy,_what_did_You_do_in_the_Great_War%3F.jpg, https://creativecommons.org/publicdomain/zero/1.0/; **p.233** © PiyawatNandeenoparit/stock.adobe.com; **p.237** *l* © Old Paper Studios/Alamy Stock Photo, *r* Model: Jislain Duval / PMA Models, Germany for Nivea Men Campaign; **p.238** © Chronicle/Alamy Stock Photo; **p.246** © AF archive/Alamy Stock Photo; **p.250** © Paul Grover/Shutterstock.com; **p.259** © Georgios Kollidas/stock.adobe.com; **p.264** *t* © Aaron Amat/stock.adobe.com, *b* © Bravissimos/stock.adobe.com; **p.265** *t* © Thawornnurak/stock.adobe.com, *b* © Thongchai/ stock.adobe.com; **p.270** © DC Stock/Alamy Stock Photo; **p.278** *l* Techtronic Cordless GP, *r* Techtronic Cordless GP; **p.279** *l* Reproduced with kind permission of Unilever from an original in Unilever Archives, *r* Reproduced with kind permission of Unilever from an original in Unilever Archives; **p.280** © GARY DOAK/Alamy Stock Photo; **p.306** *l* © Entertainment Pictures/Alamy Stock Photo, *r* © *Hot Fuzz* 2017/Reproduced with Permission from NBC Universal; **p.310** *l* © Robbie jack/Corbis Entertainment/Getty Images, *m* © Bettina Strenske/Vibrant Pictures/Alamy Stock Photo, *r The Merchant of Venice* (2018 touring production) © Shakespeare's Globe; **p.315** © Keystone Pictures USA/ZUMA Press, Inc./ Alamy Stock Photo; **p.328** © BFA/Alamy Stock Photo; **p.329** *l* © Natalieburrows/stock.adobe.com, *m* © Lkeskinen/stock. adobe.com, *r* © Mybaitshop/stock.adobe.com; **p.330** *l* © The National Archives/SSPL/Getty Images, *r* © Pictorial Press Ltd/Alamy Stock Photo; **p.336** © Jehsomwang/stock.adobe.com; **p.339** *l* 'Shake A Leg' page 22. Text copyright © Boori Monty Pryor 2010. Illustrations copyright © Jan Ormerod 2010, *r* 'Shake A Leg' page 23. Text copyright © Boori Monty Pryor 2010. Illustrations copyright © Jan Ormerod 2010; **p.341** © CSU Archives/ Everett Collection Historical/Alamy Stock Photo; **p.352** *t* © Dach_0418/stock.adobe.com, *m* © Pixabay, *b* © Dach_0418/stock.adobe.com; **p.356** © Lebrecht Music & Arts/Alamy Stock Photo; **p.368** © https://en.wikipedia.org/wiki/Sestina#/media/File:Sestina_system_alt.svg/ https://creativecommons.org/publicdomain/zero/1.0/deed.en; **p.371** © IanDagnall Computing/Alamy Stock Photo; **p.376** © Peshkova/stock.adobe.com; **p.388** © Classic Image/Alamy Stock Photo; **p.393** *t* Daily Mail, *b* Daily Mail; **p.409** © Jeff Morgan 03/Alamy Stock Photo; **p.412** © Roger parkes/Alamy Stock Photo; **p.420** © Nils Jorgensen/Shutterstock.com; **p.431** © Pictorial Press Ltd/Alamy Stock Photo; **p.433** © Beowulf Sheehan/ ZUMA Press, Inc./Alamy Stock Photo; **p.450** © North Wind Picture Archives/Alamy Stock Photo; **p.454** © United Archives/IFTN Cinema Collection/Alamy Stock Photo; **p.460** *l* © IanDagnall Computing/Alamy Stock Photo, *r* © Library of Congress Prints and Photographs Division Washington [LC-DIG-ppmsc-03521]; **p.462** Committee to unsell the war; **p.464** *l* © Universal Pictures/Everett Collection, Inc./Alamy Stock Photo, *r* © Netflix/Kobal/Shutterstock.com; **p.465** © Gibon Art/Alamy Stock Photo; **p.469** © Pictorial Press Ltd/Alamy Stock Photo; **p.480** © GARY DOAK/Alamy Stock Photo; **p.494** © Nick Ut/AP/Shutterstock; **p.513** *(from the top)* © Aaron Amat/stock.adobe.com, © Bravissimos/stock.adobe.com, © Thawornnurak/stock.adobe.com, © Thongchai/stock.adobe.com.

Text credits

p.3 'Nothing Gold Can Stay' by Robert Frost from the book *The Poetry of Robert Frost* edited by Edward Connery Lathem. Copyright © 1923, 1947, 1969 by Henry Holt and Company, copyright © 1951 by Robert Frost. Used by permission of Henry Holt and Company. All Rights Reserved.; **p.4** 'Sonnet 44' by William Shakespeare; **p.14** Sophocles, 'Oedipus the King', Translated by F Storr, The Internet Classics Archive | *On Airs, Waters, and Places* by Hippocrates, Massachusetts Institute of Technology; **p.24** George Eliot, *Middlemarch*, Project Gutenberg, 14 May 2008, Web, a www.gutenberg.org/ files/145/145-h/145-h.htm; **pp.24–5** 'Hymn to Demeter' *The Homeric Hymns and Homerica with an English Translation* by Hugh G. Evelyn-White. Homeric Hymns. Cambridge, MA., Harvard University Press; London, William Heinemann Ltd. 1914; **p.25** Excerpt(s) from *In A Sunburned Country* by Bill Bryson, copyright © 2000 by Bill Bryson. Used by permission of Broadway Books, an imprint of Random House, a division of Penguin Random House LLC. All rights reserved (US, Philippines and Open market (excl. European Union) rights); Bill Bryson, *In a Sunburned Country*, New York, N.Y: Broadway Books, 2001 (UK, Commonwealth and European Union rights) Bill Bryson, *In a Sunburned Country*, New York, N.Y:

Broadway Books, 2001 (Canadian rights); **p.30** Chimombo, Moira and Roseberry, Robert L., *The Power of Discourse: An Introduction to Discourse Analysis*, Routledge, 1998, page ix.; **pp.38–9** 'Perhaps the World Ends Here' from *The Woman Who Fell From the Sky* by Joy Harjo. Copyright © 1994 by Joy Harjo. Used by permission of W.W. Norton & Company, Inc., www.wwnorton.com; **p.43** 'Contrasting styles: Trump and Ardern speak at the UN - video.' UN Web TV (2018, September 28); **pp.44–5** Zhao, Pei. 'Water Town', translated by Song Shouquan. *Yangtze River: The Wildest, Wickedest River on Earth* selected and edited by Madeleine Lynn. Oxford University Press. 1997; **p.46** The Younger Pliny, "The Letters of the Younger Pliny", Penguin UK 1969; **p.49** Excerpt(s) from *The God of Small Things* by Arundhati Roy, copyright © 1997 by Arundhati Roy; **p.53** Dickens, Charles, *A Christmas Carol*, Penguin English Library, 2012 (print); **p.54** Dickens, Charles, *A Christmas Carol*, Penguin English Library, 2012 (print); **p.70** Wordsworth, William. 'I Wandered Lonely as a Cloud', Poetry Foundation, Poetry Foundation, Web, accessed 5 February 2019; **pp.75–6** Clarke, Gillian. 'Miracle of St David's Day'. Retrieved from http://www.gillianclarke.co.uk/gc2017/miracle-on-st-davids-day/ Date retrieved: 5 February 2019 10.33 UTC; **p.79** Orwell, George. *Down and Out in Paris and London*. Penguin Modern Classics. 1986; **p.82** Excerpt from *Kitchen*, copyright © 1988 by Banana Yoshimoto. Translation copyright © 1993 by Megan Backus. Used by permission of Grove/Atlantic, Inc. Any third party use of this material, outside of this publication, is prohibited; Excerpt(s) from *Kitchen* by Banana Yoshimoto, Faber and Faber 2001. Reproduced with permission by Faber and Faber Ltd; **p.86** *The Encyclopaedia Britannica: A Dictionary of Arts, Sciences, Literature and General Information*, Volume X Slice V, 'Fleury, Claude' to 'Foraker' Release Date: April 1, 2011 [EBook #35747] p554-5:) Retrieved: https://www.gutenberg.org/files/35747/35747-h/35747-h.htm#ar55, first published 1910-1911; **pp.90–1** From 'Colin Kaepernick's national anthem protest is fundamentally American' by Ijeoma Oluo. Published on 29 Aug 2016. https://www.theguardian.com/commentisfree/2016/aug/29/colin-kaepernick-national-anthem-protest-fundamentally-american. Copyright Guardian News & Media Ltd 2019; **p.98** 'The Red Wheelbarrow' by William Carlos Williams, from *The Collected Poems: Volume I, 1909-1939*, copyright ©1938 by Directions Publishing Corp. Reprinted by permission of New Directions Publishing Corp. (World e-book and world print incl. Canada, excl. British Commonwealth); 'The Red Wheelbarrow' by William Carlos Williams, from *The Collected Poems: Volume I, 1909-1939* reprinted with permission of Carcanet Press Limited (British Commonwealth rights); **p.100** *t* Rizzo, Sergio, (2005) 'Remembering Race: Extra-poetical Contexts and the Racial Other in "The Red Wheelbarrow"', Journal of Modern Literature, 29 (1): 35. Web, accessed 9 March 2019, https://muse.jhu.edu/article/192243, *b Concise Oxford English Dictionary Twelfth Edition,* Edited by Angus Stevenson & Maurice White © Oxford University Press 1964, 1976, 1982. 1990, 1995, 1999, 2001, 2004, 2006, 2008, 2011. Oxford Publishing Limited 2011. Reproduced with permission of the Licensor through PLSclear; **p.105** Herbert, George, 'Easter Wings', Poetry Foundation, Poetry Foundation, Web, accessed 9 February 2019, https://www.poetryfoundation.org/poems/44361/easter-wings; **p.108–12** Extract from *A Streetcar Named Desire* by Tennessee Williams, published by Penguin Group © Tennessee Williams 1947. Reproduced by permission of Sheil Land Associates Ltd working in conjunction with Georges Borchardt Inc.(UK & Commonwealth rights), Extract from *A Streetcar Named Desire* by Tennessee Williams. Reprinted by permission of New Directions Publishing; **p.114** Morrison, Toni. *Beloved.* Pan Books 1988. (Picador); New Ed edition (1988); **p.117** Cramb, Auslan, 'Girl writes English essay in phone text shorthand' (2003, March 03), The Daily Telegraph, https://www.telegraph.co.uk/news/uknews/1423572/Girl-writes-English-essay-in-phone-text-shorthand.html; **p.136** Reprinted by arrangement with The Heirs to the Estate of Martin Luther King Jr., c/o Writers House as agent for the proprietor New York, NY. Copyright: © 1963 Dr. Martin Luther King, Jr. © renewed 1991 Coretta Scott King; **p.137** Lee, Harper, *To Kill A Mockingbird*, Arrow; The 50th Anniversary edition (2010); **p.140** Reprinted by arrangement with The Heirs to the Estate of Martin Luther King Jr., c/o Writers House as agent for the proprietor New York, NY. Copyright: © 1963 Dr. Martin Luther King, Jr. © renewed 1991 Coretta Scott King; **pp.146–7** Beeton, Isabella Mrs. *The Book of Household Management* (1861); **p.151** From *Sun Tzu on the Art of War*; **p.154–5** Shakespeare, William, *King Lear*, Edited by Prof. Cedric Watts & Dr Keith Carabine, Wordsworth Editions; New Ed edition (5 Mar. 1994), [Act III, scene ii].; **p.161** Mamet, David. *Oleanna.* Methuen Drama; First Edition (24 Jun. 1993); **p.164** Oxford University Press, https://en.oxforddictionaries.com/word-of-the-year/word-of-the-year-2018; **p.169** Homer, *The Odyssey*, Translated by Emily Wilson, W. W. Norton & Company; First edition (6 Nov. 2018); **p.170** Márquez, Gabriel García, *Chronicle of a Death Foretold*, Translated from the Spanish by Gregory Rabassa, Penguin; Re-issue edition (6 Mar. 2014); **pp.173–4** Euripides, *Medea*, Translated by John Harrison, Cambridge University Press, 2016; **pp.176–7** Beckett, Samuel. *Waiting for Godot: A Tragicomedy in Two Acts.* Grove Press / Atlantic Monthly Press (5 May 2011); **p.188** Hawthorne, Nathaniel, *The Scarlet Letter*, Alma Classics; First edition (15 Jun. 2015); **p.190–1** Hawthorne, Nathaniel,

The Scarlet Letter, Alma Classics; First edition (15 Jun. 2015); **p.192** Esquivel, Laura. *Like Water for Chocolate.* Translated by Carol Christensen and Thomas Christensen. Black Swan. (1993); **p.194** *t* Joyce, James. *Finnegans Wake.* Wordsworth Editions; Wordsworth Classics edition (7 Jan. 2012), *b* 117 words from *The Brief Wonderous Life of Oscar Wao* by Junot Diaz. Printed with permission of Faber and Faber Ltd; **p.204** Tolstoy, Leo, 'Kholstomeer: The Story of a Horse by Leo Tolstoy', The Long Riders Guild Academic Foundation The world's first global hippological study, Web, accessed 2 March 2019, http://www.lrgaf.org/training/kholstomer.htm; **pp.206–7** 'Monologue for an Onion' from *The Divided Country* by Suji Kwock Kim. Copyright © 2003 by Suji Kwock Kim. Reproduced with permission of Louisiana State University Press; **p.211** 'The Thought Fox' by Ted Hughes from *New Selected Poems* 1957- 1994 (Faber, 1995), by permission of the publisher, Faber & Faber Ltd (World excluding US rights), From 'New Selected Poems' by Ted Hughes, copyright © 1995 reproduced with the permission of Farrar, Straus and Giroux (US print rights); **pp.213–4** From *'Master Harold' … and the Boys* by Athol Fugard, published by S. French, 1982; **pp.227–8** Fleischfresser, Stephen, 'What is de-extinction and how do you do it?' 08 March 2017, Cosmos The Science of Everything, Web, https://cosmosmagazine.com/biology/what-is-de-extinction-and-how-do-you-do-it; **pp.241–3** Samuel Pepys, *The Diary of Samuel Pepys* Volume 2, Random House, 1665; **p.247** Ibsen, Henrik. *Four Major Plays (Doll's House; Ghosts; Hedda Gabler; and The Master Builder)*, Oxford University Press, 1998, p86 & p89. Reproduced with permission of the Licensor through PLSclear; **pp.250–1** From *Night Sky with Exit Wounds* by Ocean Vuong. Published by Jonathan Cape. Reprinted by permission of The Random House Group Limited. © 2017 (world excl. US, Philippines and Canada); Ocean Vuong, 'Aubade With Burning City' from *Night Sky with Exit Wounds.* Copyright © 2016 by Ocean Vuong. Reprinted with the permission of The Permissions Company, LLC on behalf of Copper Canyon Press, www.coppercanyonpress.org (US, Canada, Open Market rights); **pp. 259–60** Jane Austen, *Pride and Prejudice* published by Thomas Egerton, 23 December 1815; **p.268** Dickens, Charles, *A Christmas Carol*, Penguin Classics, 2012; **pp.271–2** Mandela, Nelson. *The Prison Letters of Nelson Mandela*. Liveright Publishing, 2018; **p.273** Emily Chitticks, World War I letter; **pp.274–5** Defoe, Daniel, *The Life and Strange Surprising Adventures of Robinson Crusoe, of York, Mariner : Who Lived Eight and Twenty Years Alone in an Uninhabited Island on the Coast of America, Near the Mouth of the Great River Oronoko*, Palala Press, 2015.; **pp.280–1** *The Famished Road* by Ben Okri, Vintage Publishing 1992; **pp.282–3** 'The stress of a night during wartime' by Sivaramani and N Kalyan Raman, Indian Literature Vol. 53, No. 6 (254) 2009, pp. 63-64. Published by: Sahitya Akademi. Retrieved from https://www.jstor.org/stable/23348111; **p.285** 'Coronation of Queen Victoria', Web, accessed 12 March 2019, https://www.saturdayeveningpost.com/2017/01/coronation-queen-victoria/; **pp.289–91** Henry Lawson 'Past Carin" https://www.poetrylibrary.edu.au/poets/lawson-henry/past-carin-0002014 Date retrieved 13.03.19 UTC 1545; **pp.293–5** 'A Letter to My Mother' by Eva Johnson, 1983 poetry; **p.297** Gregory Davis Roberts. *Shantaram.* Hachette UK, 2012; **pp.300–1** 'Slums are hubs of hope, progress and dignity' in *Times of India* March 31, 2013; **pp.303–4** Federico Lorca, Lorca Plays: 1: *Blood Wedding; Yerma; Dona Rosita the Spinster.* Methuen Drama, 2008; **p.311** William Shakespeare, *The Merchant of Venice*. Wordsworth Editions, 2000; **p.316** Miller, Arthur. *The Crucible.* Penguin Books Ltd, 2000, Excerpt(s) from *The Crucible* by Arthur Miller, copyright 1952, 1953, 1954, renewed © 1980, 1981, 1982 by Arthur Miller. Used by permission of Viking Books, an imprint of Penguin Publishing Group, a division of Penguin Random House LLC. All rights reserved; **p.318** *t* Arthur Miller, *Life and Letters Why I Wrote 'The Crucible' An artist's answer to politics* https://www.newyorker.com/magazine/1996/10/21/why-i-wrote-the-crucible retrieved 15.03.19 1618; *b* 'Timeless Crucible themes familiar in China' by Raymond Zhou, *China Daily* 2015; **p.322** 'Swing Low, Sweet Chariot'; **p.341** Márquez, Gabriel García. *Chronicle of a Death Foretold*. Penguin; Re-issue edition (6 Mar. 2014); **pp.343–4** Soyinka, Wole. *Death and the King's Horseman*. Methuen Drama (2 July 1998); **pp.346–7** Hoffmann, Yoel. *Japanese Death Poems: Written by Zen Monks and Haiku Poets on the Verge of Death*. Tuttle Publishing; Reprint edition; **p.350** From *Notes from a Small Island* by Bill Bryson Published by Black Swan. Reprinted by permission of The Random House Group Limited. © 2015; **p.352** Walford, Ros. 474 words from 'A Rough Guide to: the Japanese Tea Ceremony'. 15 May 2017; **p.357** Shaw, George Bernard. *Pygmalion*. Reprinted with permission from The Society of Authors, on behalf of the Bernard Shaw Estate; **p.359** Shaw, George Bernard. *Pygmalion*. Reprinted with permission from The Society of Authors, on behalf of the Bernard Shaw Estate; **p.361** Johnson. 'Black voices, white voices: the cost of accents'. The Economist. August 2 2018; **pp.362–3** Wright, Laura Dr. 'There needs to be a more diverse range of voices reading the news'. *Radio Times*. Tuesday, 9th January 2018 at 12:15 pm; **pp.365–6** Lalonde, Michèle. 'Speak White'. Translated by Albert Herring; **pp.368–9** Alvarez, Julia. 'Bilingual Sestina'; **pp.371–2** 'Mother to Son' from *The Collected Poems of Langston Hughes* by Langston Hughes, edited by Arnold Rampersad with David

Roessel, Associate Editor, copyright © 1994 by the Estate of Langston Hughes. Used by permission of Alfred A. Knopf, an imprint of the Knopf Doubleday Publishing Group, a division of Penguin Random House LLC. All rights reserved (US, Philippines, Canada, Open market (incl. European Union) rights), Langston Hughes, 'Mother to Son' from *Collected Poems*. Copyright © 1994 by Langston Hughes Estate. Reprinted by permission of Harold Ober Associates (worldwide electronic rights, print rights in the UK and open market), **p.373** Boylorn, Robin. 'Now that white people have declared 'bae' over, black people can use it in peace'. Copyright Guardian News & Media Ltd 2019. Wed 14 Jan 2015; **p.378** 'Thibaw, King of Myanmar' Reprinted with permission from Encyclopædia Britannica, © 2019 by Encyclopædia Britannica, Inc; **pp.378–9** Ghosh, Amitav. *The Glass Palace*. Ravi Dayal, Penguin India, 1997; **pp.382–3** Shakespeare, William, *Macbeth*, Oxford School Shakespeare, edited by Roma Gill, Oxford University Press, 2009. Act I scene vii; **p.386** Brontë, Emily, *Wuthering Heights*, Wordsworth Editions Ltd, 1997; **pp.387–8** Browning, Robert, *Porphyria's Lover*, New Oxford Student Texts, Oxford University Press, 2011; **pp.405–6** Shelley, Mary, *Frankenstein*, Norton Critical Editions, W. W. Norton & Company; Second edition, 2012; **p.407** McCarthy, Cormac. *The Road*. Picador, Pan MacMillan, 2009; **p.409** Adichie, Chimamanda Ngozie. 'The Danger of a Single Story', TED. Retrieved from https://ngl.cengage.com/21centuryreading/resources/sites/default/files/B3_TG_AT7_0.pdf; **pp.411–2** Nagra, Daljit. 'Parade's End' in *Look We Have Coming to Dover!* Faber and Faber, 2007; **pp.418–9** 'Cleaner' from *My Sister, The Serial Killer: A Novel* by Oyinkan Braithwaite, copyright © 2017, 2018 by Oyinkan Braithwaite. Used by permission of Doubleday, an imprint of the Knopf Doubleday Publishing Group, a division of Penguin Random House LLC. All rights reserved (US, Philippines, Canada, Open market (incl. EU) rights); **p.424** *t* 'The Man Booker Effect', Leah, *The Man Booker Prize Online*; **pp.424–5** Barnes, Julian. 'Diary', *London Review of Books*, Vol. 9: No. 20 , 12 November 1987, page 21; **pp.426–7** 'Anna Burns's Man Booker prize is more than a fairytale – it's a lesson', Rhiannon Lucy Cosslett, *The Guardian Online*; **p.428** 'It's time to diversify and decolonise our schools' reading lists', Anjali Enjeti, *Al Jazeera Online*; **p.429** 'The Canon Is Sexist, Racist, Colonialist, and Totally Gross. Yes, You Have to Read It Anyway', Katy Waldmen, *Slate Online*; **p.431** Conrad, Joseph, *Heart of Darkness*, Dover Publications; 1st edition, 1990; **p.432** Achebe, Chinua. 'An Image of Africa: Racism in Conrad's Heart of Darkness' Massachusetts Review. 18. 1977. Rpt. in Heart of Darkness, An Authoritative Text, background and Sources Criticism. 1961. 3rd ed. Ed. Robert Kimbrough, London: W.W. Norton and Co., 1988, pp.251-261; **p.434** Achebe, Chinua. *Things Fall Apart*. Penguin Books, 1994; **p.449** Hardy, Thomas, *Tess of the d'Urbervilles*, Penguin Classics; 1st edition, 2003; **p.453** *t* Levi, Primo. *If This is a Man/The Truce*. Little Brown Book Group, Abacus, 2003; *b The Diary of a Young Girl*, Anne Frank, Alpha History; **p.457** Orwell, George. *Burmese Days*. Penguin Modern Classics, 2010; **p.458** 'Sixteen Dead Men', WB Yeats, Poetry Foundation; **p.470** Hersey, John. *Hiroshima*. Penguin Books Ltd, 2002; **p.473** Christian Bible (NIV version), Book of Genesis 3, Old Testament; **p.475** Steinbeck, John. *Of Mice and Men*. Penguin Books Ltd, 2000; **p.480** *The Vegetarian* by Han Kang, translated into English by Deborah Smith. Hogarth Press, 2016; **p.481** 'Raw and Cooked', Tim Parks, From *The New York Review of Books Daily* Copyright © 2016 by Tim Parks; **p.503** Reprinted by arrangement with The Heirs to the Estate of Martin Luther King Jr., c/o Writers House as agent for the proprietor New York, NY. Copyright: © 1963 Dr. Martin Luther King, Jr. © renewed 1991 Coretta Scott King.

Index

W

Y

Z